The Manuscripts Club

The Manuscripts Club

The People Behind a Thousand Years of Medieval Manuscripts

CHRISTOPHER DE HAMEL

PENGUIN PRESS
NEW YORK
2023

PENGUIN PRESS
An imprint of Penguin Random House LLC
penguinrandomhouse.com

First published in Great Britain as *The Posthumous Papers of the Manuscripts Club* by Allen Lane, an imprint of Penguin Random House UK, 2022.

Illustration credits appear on pages 586–92.

ISBN 9780525559412 (hardcover)
ISBN 9780525559429 (ebook)

Printed in China
3 5 7 9 10 8 6 4 2

FRONTISPIECE: Two patrons, a monk and an illuminator: dedication miniature in the *Bible moralisée*, France, *c.*1230, bought by J. Pierpont Morgan in the time of Belle Greene.

‘We never had printed books here!’

Mrs Yates Thompson

Contents

TENES LE VRAYE

Introduction

At a dinner of the Medieval Manuscript Society meeting in 2016 in Cambridge, Massachusetts, I tried to explain the initial concept of this book to my neighbour at the table. I said that it would be about men and women throughout history who were obsessed with medieval manuscripts or devoted their lives to them. As I outlined all the many kinds of people I hoped to bring into the narrative, I realized that there could hardly be a better illustration than in the room where we were then all sitting and talking. The Society, established by Professor James Marrow and Dr Emily Rose Marrow of Princeton, aims to bring together in conviviality and fellowship all people fascinated by manuscripts, irrespective of occupation or age. It includes well-known academics and curators, but also dealers and private collectors, students just beginning or finishing, publishers, art historians, freelance enthusiasts, calligraphers and others. I was one of several who had come from Europe. A delight in manuscripts is the only qualification for belonging and there is no hierarchy or subscription. We looked around the room with a real sense of being among like-minded friends.

I found myself recounting and comparing occasions when I worked for Sotheby's and might be invited home by a manuscript collector, who could perhaps be an Asian industrialist (to invent an example at random), someone infinitely different from my own domestic world or childhood. After possibly slow conversation over dinner with his wife about children or British weather, we would finally go through to the collector's library to see his medieval manuscripts. From that moment onwards, all those inequalities of background fall away, and we would both enjoy

LEFT: The bookplates pasted inside the front cover of *Histoire de Thèbes* (1469), bought by the Abbé Rive and owned by John Towneley, Lord Ashburnham, Dyson Perrins, and others.

ourselves uninhibitedly, pulling out books, asking, showing, comparing styles, making discoveries and observations, telling stories of acquisitions and losses, joyously learning from one another, until long after midnight. A shared passion can bring very different people together.

That same crossing of boundaries can be experienced in international conferences in almost any specialized field, which might be medieval manuscripts. Interests in common unite all the participants: a collector from one country can sit down at breakfast with a student from another, for instance, and a retired professor from a third, talking animatedly and immediately understanding each other's interests and encounters with manuscripts. Email addresses and invitations to visit might be proffered and correspondences sometimes extended over lifetimes, probably on first-name terms from the outset.

This book takes those same excited conversations and exchanges back through a thousand years of history. It tries to imagine what it would be like to meet the widest range of enthusiasts in Europe and America who spent their lives among illuminated manuscripts, not as an outsider looking into a different world but as a fellow member of the same club. The title, which echoes the convivial adventures of Pickwick, suggests not only comradeship and good company but also sharing of experiences. Whether we are visiting a monk or an autocrat or even a forger, we already have much in common. We ask, as one would, how they too became involved and what it meant to them, and we will look at manuscripts together and see them through the eyes of others.

The word 'manuscript' means written by hand. Direct human involvement has been part of the existence of every medieval illuminated manuscript from its very beginning. The illuminator and the patron were often in dialogue before the work even began. Each page was touched many hundreds of times and usually by several people long before it was finished. More than almost any other works of art, manuscripts then need to be handled to have ongoing life at all: they talk with words but only when people turn their pages to read them, and their illuminations can only be understood by moving back and forth throughout the cycles of decoration. At any one moment, most of the book is invisible. Manuscripts are not at their best when motionless in glass cases or in photographs. A medieval manuscript is three-dimensional and tactile, usually made of skin, as we are, and any specialist in manuscripts will tell you of the delight in cradling a precious volume in their hands, feeling its weight and experiencing the distinctive smell and the soft sound of opening it up and turning its medieval leaves. Light falling on burnished gold from different angles seems to make the pictures move. In the Middle Ages books were always read aloud, or at least murmured quietly as the words were articulated, borrowing the reader's voice. Using a manuscript has always been a very intimate and personal experience. It is also one we can share with everyone else who has encountered or owned the manuscript in the past.

Manuscripts survive, if they do, because of the men and women who preserved and valued them. With rare exceptions, they are not archaeological items, excavated from the ground directly into the museums of our world. They have come down through human history in libraries and personal collections; they may have been bought and sold, neglected or treasured, used, copied, taken apart and not always reassembled, rediscovered, loved, read, ignored, identified, and very often in the end they have been gathered up through different routes into the public collections where most of us now know them.

This, then, is an inquiry into the relationship between people and manuscripts, and why they mattered and still do in human lives. It encompasses book production and patronage, but also the history of scholarship and rediscovery, and the evolution of taste and of the economics of the art market. Manuscripts have journeyed through time in a real and human world, with all its complexities of political instability and religious intolerance, as well as carelessness and fallibility. They reflect an ever-changing understanding of beauty and sensitivity to craftmanship, and the fascination of transmitting knowledge through the centuries. They reveal different ways of looking at and using the past, whether these are texts which were already many centuries old when they were copied or manuscripts which are themselves now of great age. They have ancestors and descendants, and are tangible links to antiquity. They are also objects of desire: a yearning for possession can be among the most powerful of emotions. We will consider what it means to be born as a collector or a scholar, or an obsessive, sometimes bordering on madness and certainly on villainy, and we will share the uplift of the heart which many people experience on meeting a beautiful manuscript.

We have twelve visits to make, from the eleventh century to the twentieth, to castles and libraries and private houses. In theory, we could have started in the ancient world, when people were first inspired to make and pass on written records of thought and experience, or in the monastic libraries of the very early Middle Ages, when scholars undoubtedly took pleasure in the manuscripts they gathered. However, there is too little sustained historical documentation from so long ago, and much is speculative or frankly unknowable. There are no archives of the manuscript acquisitors at Qumran or the librarians of Alexandria. The genius of a great manuscript illuminator such as the Master of the Registrum Gregorii in the tenth century or the Rohan Master in the fifteenth could stand with that of Simon Bening, subject of Chapter 4, but we do not even know their names. All people chosen here left some particular historical sources – the 'papers' of the book's title – which allow aspects of their lives to be illuminated.

Anselm (*c.*1033–1109) was a Benedictine monk and teacher but also a canonized saint, which ensured the early preservation of many of his letters and reported conversations as well as a detailed life by his hagiographer and pupil Eadmer (who was himself a manuscript scribe). All these include references to book production and the monastic traditions of copying and publishing. Anselm will therefore speak for countless monks of the Middle Ages who rejoiced in manuscripts, and he certainly does speak, often in his own words from eleventh-century Normandy.

The Duc de Berry (1340–1416) was the son of the king of France, and his life is documented at a national level. There are immensely detailed domestic inventories of his vast private collections of manuscripts, both antiquarian and newly commissioned, together with extraordinary jewellery, relics and other works of art. We can experience the Duc's insatiable lust for acquisition and possession, and his delight in beauty and originality. We see too his sense of royal duty to be well-read and to possess knowledge. Admission to his library brings us into the company of marvellous illuminators, often introduced by name, and medieval authors, such as his friend Christine de Pizan.

Few people can talk to us about Italian Renaissance book production better than Vespasiano da Bisticci (*c.*1422–98), bookseller and agent for making a new style of manuscripts for the fashionable humanists. He was a gossip and chatterer in the streets of Florence, and we have

RIGHT: The *Grandes Heures* of the Duc de Berry, illuminated by Jacquemart de Hesdin and others, completed in 1409.

Deus in adiuto
rium meum i
tende.
Domine ad adiuuan
dum me festina.
Gloria patri et filio: et spi
ritui sancto.
Sicut erat in principio
et nunc et semper et in secula
seculorum amen alla. ant.
Benedicta tu in mul. psalmus
Dominus regnauit
decorem indutus e
dominus indutus est: et
fortitudinem precinxit se.

Etenim firmauit orbem
terre: qui non commouebi
tur.
Parata sedes tua deus ex
tunc a seculo tu es.
Eleuauerunt flumina
domine: eleuauerunt flumina
uocem suam.
Eleuauerunt flumina
fluctus suos: a uocibus aqua
rum multarum.
Mirabiles elationes ma
ris: mirabilis in altis do
minus.
Testimonia tua credibi
lia facta sunt nimis: domũ
tuam decet sanctitudo dñe i
longitudinem dierum.
Gloria patri et filio: et spi
ritui sancto.
Sicut erat in principio
et nunc et semper: et in secu
la seculorum amen. ps.

many letters he wrote and hundreds of manuscripts he sold, often signed by scribes whose lives we know too, as well as numerous short biographies which Vespasiano wrote of his clients in the courts and libraries of Europe. Through him, we meet patrons and merchants and students with money. Vespasiano was aware of the encroachment of printing but rejected it as tasteless and uncalled for.

Simon Bening (*c.*1484–1561) was not even born until well after the invention of printing, and manuscripts by then had already become luxuries, not necessities. Bening realized and exploited this, becoming so famous as an illuminator in Bruges that his work was sought across Europe and his name was known even to Vasari in Italy and probably to most kings and emperors of his day. We can trace his life through the guild records of Flanders and some of the most exquisite of all illuminated manuscripts, as Bening defiantly continued catering to Catholics through the turbulent Reformation, skilfully blurring the distinction between book illustration and the high art of the early Netherlands.

The triple and almost simultaneous arrival of printing, the Renaissance and the Reformation had devastating consequences for many medieval manuscripts, especially in England after the closure of the monasteries under Henry VIII and the dispersal of their libraries. Sir Robert Cotton (1571–1631) was the most voracious of the early antiquaries, gathering up thousands of discarded manuscripts to form a political and intellectual arsenal for the nascent British nation, located at the heart of government in Westminster. His library gave him intimacy with the great men of his time, poets and philosophers as well as statesmen. Although damaged in 1731, his manuscripts mostly survive in what is now the British Library, telling their story of Cotton's tragically lonely and unwavering obsession.

A very different obsession is represented by David Oppenheim (1664–1736), rabbi in Germany and Chief Rabbi of Moravia and then Bohemia. He sought out Hebrew manuscripts across the whole diaspora of international Judaism, contending with intrinsic rarity and wilful destruction; and then he read and mastered his manuscripts, using them as living texts and evidence of Jewish practice. After tribulations of almost a century, his vast collection and its associated records were acquired in 1828 by the Bodleian Library in Oxford, where we too can see them.

Back in France, a fascination with manuscripts remained a largely clerical pursuit until the Revolution. The Abbé Jean-Joseph Rive (1730–91) was immensely difficult and quarrelsome, but was the first bibliographer and writer to interpret illuminated manuscripts as monuments with defined places in the history of art. He followed auctions and understood bibliomania, urging connoisseurship and judgement on librarians and collectors of manuscripts. His immense knowledge and dogmatic opinions are crammed into numerous pamphlets and publications often never quite finished, overweighted with footnotes where his real learning and insights are revealed.

On Sir Frederic Madden (1801–73), keeper of manuscripts in the British Museum, there is no lack of personal material, for he maintained an uninhibited and extensive journal every day for fifty-four years, documenting a lifetime's encounters with manuscripts, both in private hands and as they were selected and gathered by him into the public custody of the national collection. He was a high-profile figure of the British establishment and in the promotion of knowledge in Victorian London. He knew everyone important in the manuscripts world of his time, including the notorious hoarder Sir Thomas Phillipps (1792–1872), the most obsessive of them all, who enters this and all subsequent chapters.

Not all these people are conventional heroes. Rogues and thieves may be caught up in a passion for manuscripts too with no less enthusiasm and dedication, sometimes more so. Constantine Simonides (*c.*1824–*c.*1890) was a forger, a confidence trickster and a fantasist. He was also a marvellous magician with a quill pen, a beguiling Mephistopheles, conjuring up whatever Greek manuscripts people most desired, so convincingly that even now no one can be quite sure of the boundaries between illusion and reality. We know of him mainly through lawsuits, contemporary scandal and conspiracy theories which still endure.

Professor Theodor Mommsen (1817–1903) is the only manuscripts scholar to have won a Nobel Prize. He was a Germanic polymath and promoter of *Altertumswissenschaft* and university learning. He was the colossus of the editing of classical texts from their surviving sources, pursuing manuscripts and Latin inscriptions with the passion of an explorer and the certainty of a zealot, tireless, unrelenting, opinionated, self-righteous and ultimately strangely vulnerable. He sometimes kept journals and always wrote letters, and he published as prolifically as almost anyone since Martin Luther.

Sir Sydney Cockerell (1867–1962) first experienced manuscript collecting with John Ruskin and William Morris. Although he is primarily remembered for his dynamic directorship of the Fitzwilliam Museum in Cambridge, medieval manuscripts were always what animated his long life, recorded by a scrupulous diary kept daily from his teens until his nineties, thousands of letters in his elegant and tiny handwriting, and the private collection of manuscripts he gathered and cherished at home. His taste and way of looking – really looking – at manuscripts changed how they are still understood by institutions as well as collectors.

We finally reach the manuscripts vault of the Morgan Library and Museum in New York in the beguiling and exhilarating company of Belle da Costa Greene (1879–1950). She emerged from an unexpected background in Washington to become private librarian and acquisitor to two generations of the richest banking dynasty in America, in a new society of almost limitless money. Even her library ledgers and love letters shine forth her joy in manuscripts. Almost single-handedly, Belle Greene created the fashion for millionaire manuscript libraries and she eventually became director of the finest public collection of medieval illuminated manuscripts outside Europe.

They are a very diverse group, these people, men and women from a very wide range of the social scale. They are not all professionals or academics. Only two had university qualifications – Cotton in his early teens and Mommsen – or possibly three, if Simonides was telling the truth. They include both a Christian saint and a rabbi; as many were atheists or indifferent to religion. Some were rich; others, like Rive, had no money at all. Several were concerned almost exclusively with texts and others principally with illumination, but all loved manuscripts. Members of the club bring guests of their own into the circle, and we meet Eadmer, the Limbourg brothers, Federico da Montefeltro, Antonius van Damme, John Donne and Ben Jonson, the Duc de La Vallière, Francis Douce, Sir Thomas Phillipps, Henry Yates Thompson, Junius Morgan and many others, all welcome as participants in our meetings.

Manuscripts themselves are crucial for this experiment in metaphorical time travel because so many survive and we can still share the same books with those who knew them long ago. I have handled numerous manuscripts known and touched by people in every chapter in this book. Some were seen by many of them in succession, weaving their way in and out of the narrative. The Duc de Berry would have closely watched the creation of his *Très Riches Heures*. Simon Bening almost certainly turned those same pages when the manuscript was owned by Margaret of Austria and, much later, so did Frederic Madden and Sydney Cockerell (with Bernard Shaw), as I have too. Cotton owned books once held in the hands of Anselm and the Duc de Berry. Mommsen used libraries assembled by Vespasiano. The Abbé Rive knew of the collections of the Duc de Berry, Cotton and Oppenheim. Madden, Cockerell and Belle Greene all acquired for their museums manuscripts illuminated by Bening. These books are all important participants in meetings of the club, and our understanding of them and their significance is enriched by knowing the company they have kept. Their story is not yet over, for most medieval manuscripts, like baby tortoises and oak trees, will still outlive us all by a very long time.

The first idea for this book, like that for my earlier *Meetings with Remarkable Manuscripts*, arose out of a conversation with Caroline Dawnay. As before, I am grateful to have been guided through all stages by Stuart Proffitt, of Allen Lane in London and his team including Richard Duguid, Mark Handsley and Alice Skinner. Cecilia Mackay, as for so many authors, made contributions far beyond the gathering of pictures. Virginia Smith has sent welcome help from Penguin Books in New York. Maria Cardona Saenz made me soup every Friday. Individual chapters have benefited from advice and information from numerous people, as acknowledged in the notes. Chapter 6 especially would have been unimaginable without Brian Deutsch. People who have read and commented on drafts of more than one chapter include Scott Schwartz, as always, Richard Linenthal, Lieve De Kesel, Nicolas Barker, Laura Cleaver and the late Claire Donovan, all members of the manuscripts fraternity. These are among my friends, as are Anselm, the Duc de Berry, Vespasiano, Bening, Cotton, Rabbi Oppenheim, the Abbé Rive, Madden, Simonides (even Simonides), Mommsen, Cockerell and Belle Greene, and all their medieval manuscripts. Come to dinner. Let us meet them.

n

u

ur

n

ce uelociter.

tatione. Nec deb

tam plegat: sed

CHAPTER ONE

The Monk: Saint Anselm

I could never have been a monk. Everything about monasticism is alien to my world, including the obvious, and yet any time I have ever spent as a guest in a monastery, sharing for a few days an idealism and a rhythm of life that is thousands of years old, I have found myself wondering why anyone would choose to live in any other way. In addition to this, there are manuscripts, often hundreds of them.

Christianity has used written texts since the very beginning. European monasticism evolved in the fourth and fifth centuries and always required books, which were necessary at the very least for the daily recitation of the liturgy. Moreover, the Scriptures and the recorded experiences and wisdom of Christian witnesses were important guides to the piety of monks. Chapter 38 of the Rule of Saint Benedict (written in the sixth century) directs that books are to be read aloud during meals, and Chapter 48 ordains particular hours each day, varying with the seasons, for private study, using texts from the monastery's library. Most surviving European manuscripts from before about 1100 originated in monastic settings, and almost all, like the communities' prayers, were still in Latin. Copying a book was itself a devotional exercise for a monk and brought its own spiritual rewards. Monasteries worked in collaboration with each other: they were the earliest publishing houses, making books and distributing them to other abbeys and communities, who, in turn, transcribed texts and passed them on. From time to time, there were monks in the Middle Ages with exceptional reputations in the creation and use of libraries and in the promotion of monastic learning. One such figure was Saint Anselm (*c.*1033–1109), theologian, Benedictine monk, prior and then abbot of

LEFT: Saint Anselm (*c.*1033–1109), portrait in a manuscript of his *Prayers and Meditations*, England, mid-twelfth century.

Bec Abbey in Normandy, south-west of Rouen, before becoming archbishop of Canterbury following the Norman Conquest of England.

Actual letters sent in the eleventh century generally do not survive, but people sometimes assembled anthologies of instructive correspondences. A collection of letters written by Anselm to different recipients was put together by his fellow monks at Bec Abbey, based on copies retained by the author. The earliest surviving manuscript of these is now in the British Library in London, and we will begin by examining it, sitting at one of those long tables in the manuscripts reading room. It is a small chunky volume on parchment, hardly bigger than a thick modern paperback but quite heavy. Anselm is described in the manuscript's opening heading as being 'the lord abbot', which reasonably dates it to the period between 1078 and 1093, when he still held this office in Bec, where the book was very possibly made. Across the foot of the first page is the flourished signature of Sir Robert Cotton (here already is a meeting of the manuscripts fraternity, for Cotton will be the subject of Chapter 5). Several of Anselm's letters in the volume touch on manuscript production in a detail which is almost unique for Romanesque Europe. People consulted him about obtaining manuscripts, and he brought together people who were able to make them. Books and book production were an important part of his life. We will therefore eavesdrop on a few of Anselm's exchanges, as Cotton probably did when he acquired the volume, to listen to fragments of conversations with his friends.

Just for a moment, consider the position of Normandy at that time. Most monasteries were largely cut off from the daily world and, in establishing a community in the deep countryside of western France in the 1030s, the monks of Bec had probably expected a life of rural isolation very far removed from international politics. All that changed in 1066, when the Normans conquered England, and a French province suddenly became the hub of an empire. Some of Anselm's letters are addressed to Lanfranc (*c.*1010–89), his former teacher and earlier prior of Bec. In 1070, Lanfranc had been appointed by William the Conqueror as his archbishop of Canterbury, part of an invasion force of Normans tasked with securing England and transforming it to continental standards. Lanfranc found the ancient Anglo-Saxon library in Canterbury to be impoverished and ill-equipped. Perhaps hardly yet knowing where else to turn, he had written home to his old colleagues in Normandy for help with obtaining manuscripts of some of the most necessary monastic texts, which he knew were available there. Anselm's reply to Lanfranc in England, written probably in the earlier 1070s, is preserved in the anthology of letters. 'As regards the *Moralia in Job* which you requested from me', Anselm tells him in Latin, 'Brother Abbot William of Caen and Brother Hernost, your faithful friends, have in fact found a scribe, and, since he already has our book, I think he has started on yours.'

The *Moralia* is the commentary on the Old Testament book of Job by Gregory the Great (*c.*540–604), relating the patience and faithful submission of Job to the daily life of monasteries in his own times. Gregory was the first monk to become pope, and he was initiator of the evangelization of Britain. The *Moralia* is a wise and humane text with much practical advice for times of tribulation, very suitable for monastic reading at mealtimes. It was one of the fundamental texts for Benedictine libraries of the Middle Ages, and it is shameful that there was apparently no copy in Canterbury, unless it had been destroyed in the fire there in

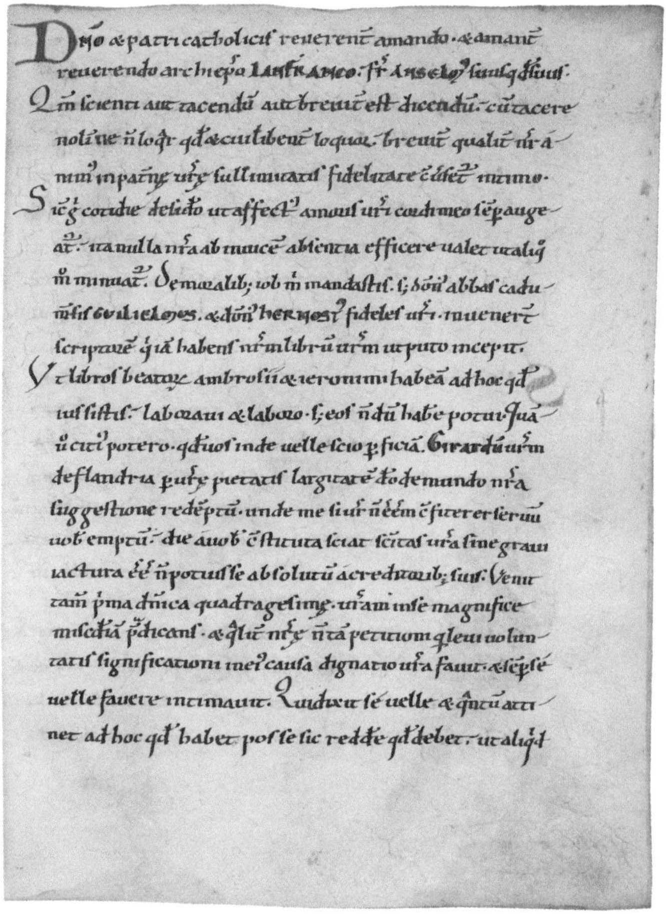

The letter collection of Anselm, perhaps Bec, late eleventh century, with the opening of his reply to Lanfranc about copying manuscripts.

1067. Lanfranc knows that Bec possesses one and so he has asked to have it copied and sent to him in England. It is actually a huge text. The library catalogue of Bec Abbey in the twelfth century, the earliest extant, lists the monks' copy of the *Moralia* as being in two volumes, with sixteen books in the first part and eighteen in the second. Copying this quickly for Lanfranc in England was clearly too large a task for the monks within Bec itself, and Anselm had consulted two former colleagues, friends of Lanfranc too from the old days. In the British Library manuscript, the names of William and Hernost are written in small capitals touched in red, and the scribe who copied out Anselm's letter here probably knew them personally. Brother Abbot William was the son of the bishop of Séez in Normandy and he had by this time been appointed to the abbacy of Saint-Étienne in Caen, a post which Lanfranc held on leaving Bec and had then vacated again on his transfer to England. William was later archbishop of Rouen and died in 1110. Brother Hernost was then the prior at Saint-Étienne. He had himself been a scribe at Bec and was afterwards (briefly) bishop of Rochester in England before an early death in 1076. Here we first see the networks of contacts and connections which were so important in the transmission of manuscripts and, indeed, in the intellectual subjugation of England. These people were all old colleagues, acquainted with one another. Under Anselm's direction, William and Hernost have found a scribe for Lanfranc, probably a professional copyist rather than a monk, doubtless working in the cathedral city of Caen, about fifty-five miles west of Bec, and the scribe has been lent the master copy of the *Moralia* from the library of Bec Abbey to use as his exemplar. It all seems to be in hand.

The *Moralia* was not the only text Lanfranc was trying to obtain for Canterbury. Anselm's letter to Lanfranc continues further, 'To accomplish what you commanded, I have worked and am working to obtain the books of Saints Ambrose and Jerome, but I have not been able to get them yet. As quickly as I can, I shall complete what I know you want from them.' This time these are texts – unnamed but possibly their Epistles – which were evidently not available for loan from the resources of Bec, and so Anselm is asking around. Like Gregory, these were authors represented in all self-respecting Norman monasteries: Ambrose (*c*.339–97), bishop of Milan, and his contemporary Jerome (*c*.342–420); both were prolific writers and commentators on the Bible and on Christian life.

Acquiring the books you need is never as simple as it seems. In the event, all was not well with the order for Gregory's *Moralia* and the texts of Ambrose and Jerome. There is a subsequent letter from Anselm copied in our manuscript a few pages later, now writing again to Lanfranc to report a problem: 'Regarding the *Moralia in Job*, it was not executed as I told you. There is disagreement (I do not know what about) between the scribe and those with whom he came here.' It seems that the transcription has not even been started. 'For this reason', Anselm continues, 'Brother Helgot and Brother Hernost came and spoke with the scribe of Brionne as you ordered, in the presence of Brother Abbot, but we did not achieve anything.' Helgot and Hernost were both then at Saint-Étienne in Caen: Hernost, as we have seen, was the prior, and Helgot was later to succeed him there in 1075. Lanfranc has suggested a local scribe he remembered from Brionne, the nearby town just to the south of Bec. The scribe does not seem to have been a monk. He was interviewed at Bec in the presence of the abbot, the very elderly Herluin (*c.*995–1078), himself also from Brionne, the founder and first abbot of Bec. Anselm's use of the 'we' suggests that he was present at the meeting too. Anselm had been concerned only with what really mattered, which was whether the scribe suggested by Lanfranc was competent for the task. It seems that he was not. Anselm explains:

> I also asked our aforementioned brothers, your faithful servants from among the scribes of the monastery, to examine his writing and ability, but there was not one among them who did not either disapprove of his handwriting or condemn his unexpected slowness. And so they are returning to Caen, taking with them our book, which they had brought in the hope of finding a scribe.

The candidate from Brionne has failed his interview, and they are starting all over again.

It is that phrase about the brothers being among the abbey's scribes which gives a clue as to why Helgot and Hernost were involved now. They had experience in the scriptorium. Having been unable to secure local help, they came back again to Caen, still with Bec's copy of the *Moralia* as a would-be exemplar, to begin looking for a new scribe once more. Speed as well as competence were qualifications they required. There is one further letter many pages later to another correspondent, which seems to suggest that it all worked out eventually. This time Anselm was writing to an unidentified Abbot 'O', who had evidently also asked to borrow the Bec manuscript of the *Moralia* to have his own

A scribe, probably the author, writing a manuscript of Eadmer's *Vita Anselmi*, mid-twelfth century.

copy made. He explains that they would gladly have lent it, but that it is already in use:

> The lord abbot of Caen has it, and another copy is being made there for him, besides the copy being made for the lord Archbishop Lanfranc. Therefore, do not think that we do *not* want to lend it to you . . . I write our excuses to you to let you know our good intentions, that as soon as we receive the book, we will gladly hand it to your lordship's messenger, according to your wish.

These exchanges reveal what was doubtless a common problem in the eleventh century, so obvious that it is easy to overlook. You cannot write out a manuscript without having already located and arranged the use of an exemplar to copy it from. Having done so, you must assign a scribe capable of undertaking the labour. If your own monastery cannot do it, you must look elsewhere. It is apparent that in the 1070s there were already scribes in Normandy available for hire, and these letters furnish very early allusions to a trade which by the later Middle Ages had taken over most medieval book production. It must have been an inconvenience for the monks of Bec if their only copy of the *Moralia* was forever absent on loan to scribes elsewhere, but that was a penalty of being neighbourly to other monasteries or obedient to authority. Two copies were evidently being made from it in Caen. The one for Lanfranc was doubtless finally finished and sent off to England. The early fourteenth-century library catalogue of the cathedral priory of Canterbury in England does indeed record a copy of the *Moralia in Job*, presumably the one made at Lanfranc's request. Like its probable exemplar in Bec, it was in two volumes. It lasted until the fifteenth century, when what seems to have been the flyleaf of its second volume was cut into strips and reused to strengthen the binding of a manuscript then being newly made in Canterbury. It preserves part of its original title, *Secunda par M[oralium]* (most of this last word being now concealed in the spine), and is on parchment of good quality, just over 14 inches in height. It is as close as we can get to the enterprise orchestrated with such difficulty for Lanfranc in England by his friend Anselm in Normandy.

Let us now take a trip to Bec itself, to see something of the setting where Anselm was a monk and teacher and where their library was kept. These days you drive down the A28 south of Rouen in the direction of Le Mans, turning right at junction 13, through Malleville-sur-le-Bec, descending through the dense forest into the little town of Le Bec-Hellouin in the valley. It is probably not much bigger now than it was in the eleventh century, when a large monastery required a supporting community of workers and suppliers. 'Le Bec' is the name of the tiny stream which still trickles through this peaceful pastoral landscape. It is a Viking word for a little river, *bekkr* in Old Norse, reminding us that Normandy had been occupied and named from Scandinavia. 'Hellouin' is derived from Herluin, that local landowner and first abbot who established his monastery here in 1035 in Anselm's lifetime. There is easy parking by the trees in the gently sloping Place Guillaume le Conquérant near the Rue de Canterbury. They have not forgotten their history in Bec-Hellouin. Outside the abbey gateway is the Place de l'Abbé Herluin, a small and neat municipal precinct bounded along one side by a row of ancient half-timbered houses in the style so characteristic of the architecture of Normandy, in which chocolate brown beams criss-cross over mellow cream plasterwork, unlike the strident panda black and white of medieval and Tudor buildings in England. Roofs are the soft grey of slate. There are window boxes and flowers everywhere. The fifteenth-century abbey gateway is in the far corner of the square, opening between two rectangular towers topped by conical steeples, like the fantasy turrets of Disney castles or the tall head-dresses of fashionable princesses in the late Middle Ages.

You enter by the gateway crunching across the gravel of a kind of forecourt before passing under another arch through an eighteenth-century block, emerging into the abbey grounds themselves. A sense of the medieval layout is made clearer by a large reproduction on the wall of an engraving of the monastery dated 1677. No visible construction now survives above ground from the time of Lanfranc and Anselm, and there is not even a great deal from the medieval period at all, apart from a very fine free-standing bell tower on the left begun in 1467 and still in daily use. The monastery was extensively rebuilt in the seventeenth and eighteenth centuries. It was suppressed at the French Revolution and large parts were demolished around 1810, including the entire medieval gothic chapel which once dominated the view, connected at one time to the bell tower by a low covered walkway. Unusually for France, the old abbey buildings were then reoccupied by the Benedictines, who returned in 1948, monks of the reformed congregation of Olivetans. Once again the bells of Bec sound out the hours of the monastic offices and monks in medieval white habits and sandals walk the premises in companionable silence, sometimes with books, much as Lanfranc and Anselm did almost a thousand years earlier. A sense of timelessness and eternity was characteristic of medieval monastic life and there is something of that here still. I sat in at Vespers on my first night and, except that it was in French, it might have been in the Middle Ages.

The present chapel of the monastery is round the far right-hand side of the main complex of buildings, entered by a garden door into the end of what had formerly been the long narrow refectory of the monks before the Revolution. Visitors are encouraged, at least as far as a low rope barrier which separates off the monks' area with their pews on either side at the east end. The air is agreeably cool, after the sultry heat and dust of the French summer outside, and the chapel smells of masonry and oak. It is austere, with little decoration. There is a small tablet dated 1968 commemorating the historical links between Bec and the cathedral of Canterbury. The modern altar is of green marble, a gift from Aosta in the

Italian Alps, where Anselm was born. In the centre of the nave in front of the altar, just beyond the rope, is a glass-topped crypt into which one can look down onto the huge stone sarcophagus of Herluin, restored to his abbey from interim exile in the parish church between the French Revolution and the time of the monks' return. Near the entrance are four large fifteenth-century statues, also reinstated from the medieval chapel, representing the great patristic authors Saints Ambrose, Augustine, Jerome and Gregory. By coincidence, three of these four were the writers whose texts Lanfranc had asked Anselm to have copied and sent to England. In all four statues, the authors are represented with manuscripts, Ambrose writing, Augustine with an open book, Jerome reading, and Gregory holding a volume closed in its medieval binding. There is also a fourteenth-century sculpture of the Virgin and Child – the abbey is dedicated to Notre Dame – and the Child too is holding a book. Manuscript culture was always a very visible part of the Benedictine life.

Contemporary religious art is represented in the chapel by a recent brightly painted icon on a stand under the first window on the right of the entrance, showing Saint Anselm himself as an archbishop with small panels down either side depicting events from his life. The scene at the lower left illustrates the saint when prior of Bec writing the manuscript of his *Monologion* on the existence of God. He did that here in 1071. In the icon Anselm is dressed as a monk hunched up in an architectural chair before a sloping lectern draped with cloth. The manuscript is open and Anselm is writing with quill pen and knife, the essential tools of any medieval scribe. An inkhorn is slotted into a hole in the lectern. Two junior novices are seated on a stool at the saint's feet, one with a book, representing Anselm's role as teacher. It is set beside a stylized view of the Romanesque church of Bec, although presumably in reality this activity would have happened in the abbey cloisters, the usual location of scribal enterprise in a medieval monastery.

To see this cloister, we are obliged to buy tickets in the shop for a guided tour. Our little group was led in through a barely noticeable door on the left-hand side of the chapel, which leads directly into the corner of the monks' cloister, rebuilt in the mid-seventeenth century but incorporating parts of its thirteenth-century predecessor. It is quite small – half a dozen arches on each side – but the walkway is broad and uncluttered. In the Middle Ages the Bec scriptorium was most probably on this site, and the abbey's manuscripts were doubtless once kept in wooden furniture almost exactly here. The cloister has not been refurbished much by the modern monks, and the old lime wash is peeling away from the pitted white stonework. There is a sleepy fountain in the centre among pebbles and a purple dusting of wild cranesbill flowers. Some columns of the cloister are scratched with names from the late nineteenth century, manuscript words of a sort, when these buildings were being occupied as military barracks. Pigeons coo from the upper galleries. There is a locked fourteenth-century door in the corner furthest from where we entered, below a weather-beaten tympanum showing the Virgin and Child with angels, which would once have led up a few steps into the south transept of the medieval chapel. Outside here there is only grass now, and a few stones piled where the sanctuary had once been.

Imagine coming to see Anselm at Bec Abbey in the eleventh century. On my own visit I might have brought (but did not) a letter of introduction from the archbishop of Canterbury, for the present incumbent, my near neighbour in Lambeth in London, is the eighty-fourth in succession to Lanfranc of Bec. Inquiries would be made at the gatehouse. Chapter 53 of the Rule of Saint Benedict enjoins the welcoming of guests, who would first pray with the monks in the chapel: 'After the guests have been received and taken to prayer, let the Superior or someone appointed by him sit with them.' The earliest pictures of Anselm in manuscripts show him as a solemn man with arched eyebrows and long nose, features commonly ascribed to clerics of the period, with short, curly brown hair cut into a monastic tonsure. As abbot, he might have agreed to meet us after the service and could then have taken us through that door in the transept (if it then existed), down the low steps into what was in his time a Romanesque cloister on this site. We would doubtless sit, as the Rule directs. It is recorded by Anselm's biographer Eadmer that he was a fluent conversationalist. He might note that de Hamel is reputedly a Norman name (very dubious). There would be courteous inquiries as to where I was staying. I tell him that I am booked into a nearby hotel in the centre of the village.

'We were surprised and grieved that you passed close to us instead of staying with us', Anselm remarks solicitously. There is indeed an abbey guesthouse, even today.

(It is at this point that I must explain that every sentence ascribed to Anselm here is a direct quotation from his own words, in translation, in this case from what his modern editors call Letter 24, written in reality in the 1070s to one Henry, a monk from Canterbury.)

Anselm, guided by the hand of God, in conversation with his pupil Boso at Bec, perhaps France, first half of the twelfth century.

He would ask where I come from and we might speak a little about England and Anselm's own first visits there in 1079 and again 1086, in connection with the Domesday survey and the English properties owned by Bec. I tell him what a pleasure it is to be here in this peaceful place.

'Turn aside now from heavy cares, and set aside your wearisome tasks', Anselm says kindly (this is from Chapter 1 of his *Proslogion*). I say how grateful I am. As any visitor might, I ask him about his career and how he came to be a monk at all.

'My life terrifies me, when I carefully examine it', says Anselm, at the opening of his *Meditations*, quoted back to him in a letter to Anselm by the abbot of La Chaise-Dieu in the mid-1070s. In old age, however, he recounted the story of his life to his secretary and confidant, Eadmer of Canterbury, who in turn wrote it up as the *Vita Anselmi*. The earlier part is more vivid than the later years, and probably elements of the tale had been recited many times to colleagues and to abbey guests who asked. Eadmer, writing after Anselm's death, buttresses anecdotes with phrases like "ut fatebatur", 'as he used to say'. Anselm might perhaps tell me too. He was born around 1033 in Aosta into a good family. His father was a fickle spendthrift called Gundulf, but his mother, Ermenberga, was a pious woman whom he adored. As a boy, Anselm showed an aptitude for learning. After a falling out with the father, he wandered vagabonding up through France and Burgundy for almost three years, searching for his destiny. Eadmer reports that, as Anselm was already wearing himself out in studying manuscripts, he resolved that he might as well become a monk so that he would at least receive some reward for his labour. He considered Cluny, but was attracted by the international scholarly reputation of Lanfranc, a fellow Italian (born in Pavia), who had himself joined Bec Abbey in 1042, becoming its prior around 1045. It had then been a poor and newly founded house, with negligible facilities for learning. Within a few years Lanfranc began building up a library and an extraordinary school for the teaching of theology as well as grammar and logic. In 1059, Anselm reached Bec, introducing himself to Lanfranc and asking his advice. Lanfranc suggested consulting the archbishop of Rouen. The *Vita Anselmi* reports a touching description of the two of them setting out on this mission together through the great woods which lie above Bec – they are still there on the Rouen road – and Lanfranc saying, 'Stay in this wood, and see that you never come out as long as you live.' The archbishop agreed. At the age of twenty-six, Anselm joined the community.

In 1063, four years later, Lanfranc left Bec to take up the appointment as abbot of Saint-Étienne in Caen (hence the connection with Helgot and Hernost), and Anselm, still young, unexpectedly succeeded him as prior of Bec, giving him responsibility for the library and for teaching. Herluin was abbot, as he had been since the foundation, living into considerable old age and finally dying in 1078. At that moment, Anselm was elected to the abbacy in his place.

Everything we know of Anselm at Bec tells of his commitment to monasticism and his ability to inspire the vocation in others. It is an often-quoted statistic that, in the nineteen years between Anselm's arrival as a novice and his election as abbot, sixty-nine new monks were recruited to Bec, but during his fourteen years as abbot there were no fewer than 160. The pattern of peace and security and shared purpose of a monastery must have been very appealing during the capricious and dangerous eleventh century. I might have said something like this to Anselm. He nods. 'I could tell you much, dearest friend' – this from Anselm's Letter 121 – 'about the sublimity and moral certainty, the tranquillity and the joy of monastic life.' He speaks with the directness and unwavering confidence of a committed Christian. Where his own father had perhaps failed him in childhood, Anselm turned with trust to Saint Benedict. His own prayer to the founder of his Order beseeches, 'And you, my good leader, my gentle master, my dear father, blessed Benedict . . . I beg you to be my protector.'

During our imagined conversation in the cloister, the library of Bec was probably stored within sight. This is why I have come to France. I might or might not see eye to eye with Anselm's joy in the Benedictine life, but we would certainly share the delight of looking at manuscripts together. I would give almost anything to be able to rummage through the book chests in the cloister with Anselm beside me, opening volumes and asking about their origins and usefulness, exclaiming at rarities and admiring the qualities of script and decoration. Without doubt, Anselm would know every manuscript. His writings show an intimacy with a huge range of literary sources, and many of them were here.

There are two extant medieval catalogues of books at Bec Abbey, both from the twelfth century, after Anselm's death. They survive together on leaves at the end of a manuscript now in the town library of Avranches in southern Normandy. The first is a long list of books given to Bec by Philip of Harcourt, bishop of Bayeux 1142–64, who just might, as a child, have met Anselm personally, for the village of Harcourt, where he had been born, is only about eight miles from Bec. Philip came to England as dean of Lincoln and later as chancellor to King Stephen, but he quarrelled with the king's brother Henry of Blois and was sent back to Normandy. This was more than half a century after Anselm's departure, but it may say something about the enduring reputation Bec still had for the custody of books that Philip bequeathed his personal collection to a local monastery rather than to his own cathedral.

The leaves in Avranches also preserve an inventory of the general library of the monks at Bec from the second half of the twelfth century, almost a hundred years after Anselm's time. This itemizes the contents of 165 volumes then stored in the "almarium" of the abbey, the large book cupboard or possibly group of chests. By crossing off titles from the list of Philip of Harcourt's bequest (and they cannot all be accounted for there) and by eliminating books by twelfth-century authors, such as Saint Bernard and Peter Lombard towards the end of the inventory, we are left with a core of texts which could very plausibly have already been at Bec in the time of Lanfranc and Anselm. Many of them are conventional monastic texts, which might be sought by any well-stocked abbey. The inventory opens with nearly three dozen manuscripts of works of Saint Augustine, beginning with his sermons on the Gospel of John and the monumental *City of God*. Then there are books by Saints Gregory (eight volumes, including the much-lent *Moralia in Job*), Ambrose (six volumes) and Jerome (thirteen volumes). It is no surprise that Lanfranc turned to Bec for works of these three authors. There are also good runs of Origen in Latin translation, Cassiodorus, Isidore of Seville and Bede.

Of all these, almost the only surviving manuscript which was at Bec in Anselm's time is a volume of seven short homiletic works by Augustine now in the Bibliothèque nationale de France in Paris. The book is tall and narrow, about 11 inches by 7½, and its various texts correspond precisely with the contents of the manuscript listed as the sixth item in the twelfth-century catalogue of the abbey. It opens with the *De pastoribus*, 'On shepherds', a sermon based on Ezekiel 34, where the Scriptures exhort the faithful to behave like shepherds, gathering up and tending their sheep rather than caring for themselves, a text with obvious resonance for monks in a farming community in a valley in Normandy. The titles of the various texts in the manuscript are listed on the front flyleaf (a formula found in later Bec manuscripts); its lower half, where there may also have been some ownership inscription of the abbey, is now cut away. It is a handsome but not showy book, made of thick soft parchment, probably calf skin, with the characteristic monastic indifference to natural flaws and arcs in the margins caused by the shape of an animal's neck or leg joints. It is elegantly written and easy to read. The script is quite distinctive, with a rather prickly effect, like holly leaves, made with a sharply cut pen held at an angle, and the tops of ascenders of letters like 'l' and 'd' split in two directions, the longer stroke leaning forwards. The manuscript's opening initial is drawn in a design of leafy tendrils outlined and veined in red ink, partly filled with washes of pale green and blue. There is no gold. Other initials in the manuscript are

RIGHT: Manuscript of Augustine, *De pastoribus*, from Bec Abbey in the time of Anselm, second half of the eleventh century.

AVRELII AVGVSTINI DOCTORIS DE PASTORIB; SERMO INCIPIT.

SPES TOTA NRA QVIA IN XPO EST. ET QVIA OMNIS VERA
& salubris gla nra ipse est. non nunc primu didicit ca
ritas ura. Estis enim in ei grege. qui pascit isrl. Sed qm
sunt pastores qui pastoru nomina audire uolunt.
pastoru officiu implere nolunt. quid ad eos per p
pham dicit sicut lectu audiuim recenseamus.
Audite uos cu intentione. audiam nos cu tremore.
& factu est uerbu dni ad me dicens. fili hominis.
ppha ad pastores isrl. & dic ad pastores isrl. Hanc lectionem
modo cu legeretur audiuimus. hinc cu ura sanctitate aliquid
loqui decreuimus. Adiuuabit ipse ut uera dicamus. si n nra
dicamus. Nam si nra dixerimus. pastores erimus pascentes
nos non oues. Si autē illius sunt que dicimus. per quemlibet
ipse uos pascit. Haec dicit dominus deus ad pastores isrl.
qui pascunt se solos. Numquid non oues pascunt pastores.
Id est non se pascunt pastores. sed oues. Hec prima causa
est quare arguantur isti pastores. quia se ipsos pascunt non
oues. Qui sunt qui se ipsos pascunt. De quib; apls dicit.
Omnes enim sua querunt. non que iesu xpi. Nos enim
quos in loco isto de quo periculosa ratio redditur. dominus
secundum dignationem suam non secundum meritum
nostrum constituit. habemus duo quaedam.
Vnum quod xpiani sumus. alteru quod prepositi sum. Illud
quod xpiani sum. ppt nos est. Qd prepositi sum. ppter uos est.
In eo quod xpiani sum. attendat utilitas nra. In eo quod prepo
siti. non nisi ura. Et sunt multi. qui xpiani & non prepositi per
ueniunt ad dm faciliore fortasse itinere. & tanto forte expe
ditius ambulantes. quanto minorem sarcinam portant.
Nos autē excepto quod xpiani sum. unde rationē reddem do
de uita nra. sumus etiā prepositi. unde rationē reddem do
de dispensatione nra. Ad hoc istam difficultatē ppono. ut
compatientes nobis. oretis p nobis. Veniet enī dies. quo cuncta
adducantur in iudiciu. Et ille dies si sclo longe est. unicuiq;

modest in blue or green. Headings are in red. Words at the opening of texts and sometimes elsewhere are written in small capitals heightened with splashes of red or green, rather as in the British Library manuscript of Anselm's letters. It is very graceful, and the evident elegance of the book would have added to the appeal (and hence the use) of the manuscript to the monks in the abbey.

The *De pastoribus* survives in its original binding, doubtless made at the monastery too. The gatherings were sewn on two broad leather thongs pegged into wooden boards pared flush with the edges of the pages, in typical Romanesque style (most modern covers slightly overlap the text block), covered with what looks like white leather, although it is technically alum-tawed skin, not tanned as in leather-making. The whole resembles a neat white brick. Unlike paper, sheets of parchment can cockle and flex considerably with changes of temperature and humidity, a common hazard in cloisters open to the air, and so manuscripts in the Middle Ages were usually stored tightly closed under pressure. There are traces of a pair of straps extending from the edge of the manuscript's upper cover to be secured with metal finials which fitted over pins once nailed in the centre of the lower board. Opening such a book in the Middle Ages would have been a process of revelation, squeezing the volume slightly to release the clasps before lifting the cover. This manuscript was evidently stored in Bec with its spine outwards or upwards in the *almarium*, for it is inscribed with a title along its length in large faded capital letters contemporary with the manuscript, "DE PASTORIBUS". No author's name is given there. In the Bec catalogue the book is listed in a section of works by Augustine, but the absence of his name on the spine may mean that it was kept in a box or shelf exclusively dedicated to him or even labelled on the furniture as all being by Augustine. A title, however, was a practical necessity if all the volumes were bound the same. The upper cover is inscribed in a hand probably of the seventeenth century, "Le Bec".

One of the things which always surprises and pleases me about good cooks is how willingly they seem to share recipes. (If I had devised some special signature dish for dinner parties, I might be inclined to keep the secret to myself.) The same applies to monks in their libraries. I expect that if I had complimented Anselm on the Bec manuscript of the *De pastoribus*, he would have graciously invited me to borrow it to have my own copy made. It seems that the monks of the abbey were happy for their precious manuscripts to be used as exemplars, like the *Moralia* with which we began. A letter from Anselm to an unidentified Prior Ralph of another monastery in Normandy assures him they will always lend manuscripts, with the abbot's permission. The Bec copy of the *De pastoribus* is of an unusual textual family designated by its modern editor by the *siglum* 'α', of which this is the earliest example. Its same distinctive variants of wording, together with every one of the supplementary texts in precisely the same order, are all found in a late eleventh-century manuscript now also in the British Library, which belonged in the Middle Ages to Bath Abbey in Somerset. That copy was presumably acquired through John of Tours (d. 1122), who had been William the Conqueror's physician and was present at the king's death in 1087. In 1088 he was appointed to the bishopric of Wells, which in 1090 he merged with a new cathedral in Bath Abbey, to which he gave many books. He was consecrated by Lanfranc. In seeking texts for his new foundation, he probably consulted his archbishop and obtained a copy of the Augustine, or a copy of a copy, descended from the master manuscript then in Anselm's custody in Bec.

The preservation of the library catalogue of Bec, mentioned above, is not due to the abbey itself, where it was hardly needed (a few hundred books, not as many as most of us have at home today, would all be findable without a catalogue). Instead, it is recorded on the flyleaves of the chronicle of Robert of Torigni, which belonged to Robert's own island monastery of Mont Saint-Michel at the south-western tip of Normandy. He had previously been prior of Bec from 1149, and he probably ordered this record of its library after he become abbot of Mont Saint-Michel in 1154. It is even possible that he reconstructed it from memory. The monks of his new abbey could thus use the Bec catalogue as their working checklist of texts which might be available for copying. Sure enough, the library of Mont Saint-Michel soon had its own slightly later but otherwise textually identical copy of Augustine's *De pastoribus* from the same family as the manuscript from Bec, doubtless another of its descendants.

In turn, Bec's copy had ancestors. When Lanfranc had become prior there around 1045, the abbey was quite new and probably owned very few books at all, except for those essential for its daily liturgy. The acquisition of every single item for the monks' use in the cloisters represented serious logistical effort and labour. To seek a manuscript required first of all knowledge that such a text existed at all. The Bec inventory includes a manuscript of Jerome's *De viris illustribus* with its supplement by Gennadius, a catalogue of famous authors with specimen titles of the books they had written. This is a text which was used as a wants list by many medieval librarians. Lanfranc cited it in a letter he wrote to the abbey of Saint-Cyprien in Poitiers in the 1070s, and so we know it was available at that time. It includes Augustine in the supplement (Chapter 39). We also see Anselm sourcing books for Bec when he too became prior. In one letter he asks the former Bec monks Maurice and Gundulf, who had gone to Canterbury with Lanfranc, to try to locate for him anywhere in England an exemplar for the text of the Rule of Saint Dunstan, sought for the Bec library. If the catalogue is a guide, none was found.

The common image of monks in their scriptorium peacefully copying books belies the fact that a great deal of travelling was required in equipping a monastic library. These journeys moving valuable books around were often dangerous. Anselm writes from Bec to his cousin Folcard in the 1070s reporting his reluctance to send him a manuscript since their monk Ralph has been robbed on the road in the diocese of Reims, and his horse was stolen and his clothes were torn apart as the thieves searched for anything of value. A later extraordinary story recounted by Eadmer tells of a journey in England by a monk Robert, servant of the bishop of Rochester, whose horse was being led across London Bridge, when – imagine this – it fell through a hole in the bridge into the Thames, together with one of Anselm's books in the saddle bag. (Anyone anxious may be reassured: the horse swam ashore, the manuscript was undamaged, and London Bridge is in better repair today.) Logically, a monk sent from Bec to borrow a book which was copied in the abbey scriptorium and then returned required four journeys, there and back twice, two of them with someone else's property, but if the monk were also a scribe he could instead go to the cooperating library, transcribe a book *in situ* and return with the new copy ready-made, involving only two trips and less inconvenience. This must have happened much more often than historians recognize, and to attribute a manuscript to the style of a particular monastery or even to a known scribe does not necessarily mean that it was actually copied in the home scriptorium.

RIGHT: The library catalogue of Bec Abbey, copied for the monks of Mont-Saint-Michel, mid-twelfth century.

TITULI LIBRORUM BECCENSIS ALMARII;

Libri beati aug. epi. In uno uol. sr Johe serm. xxii. In al. de ciuitate dei. l. xxii. In al. Enchiridion. l. i. de doctrina xpiana. l. iiii. Simbolu ab eod dictatu. disputacio q felic [illegible] contra [illegible] de ciuitate. de pfectione iustic. l. i. de natura et gra l. i. Epla eid ad ualentinu. de gra et lib arbitrio. l. i. de correptione et gra. l. i. Epla psperi ad eu. Epla hilarii arelatensis ad eu. de pdestinatione scor. l. i. de bono pseuerantie. l. i. In al. q faustu manicheu. l. ii. de mendacio. l. i. q mendaciu. l. i. de cura p mortuis gerenda. l. i. de uera religione. l. i. de natura et origine aie ad renatu. l. i. Ad petr [illegible] de ead re. l. i. Ad uincentiu uictore de ead re. l. ii. Sermo arrianor. Confl eid simone. l. i. de utilitate credendi l. i. q aduersariu legis et pphar. l. ii. et lib q appellat pronosticon. In al. de trinit. l. xv. In al. sermo de pastorib; Sermo de ouib; de baptismo adus donatistas. l. vii. de baptismo paruulor. l. ii. Epla aug. ad marcellinu. de unico baptismo. l. i. de spu et litta. l. i. In al. sup genesi ad littam. l. xii. In al. de consensu euglistar. l. iiii. de sermone dni in monte. l. ii. Sermo d' uerbis dni q dixerit blasphemia q spm scm n remittet ei. Sermo de x plagis egypti. et de x pceptis dei. In al. Sermo de x cordis. Sermo de disciplina xpiana. de penitentia l. i. de patientia l. i. de cathecizandis rudib; l. i. Soliloquior. l. ii. de lib arbitrio uoluntatis. l. iii. Sup genesi q manicheos l. ii. Adus manicheos q eplam fundamenti. l. i. de [illegible]. l. i. [illegible] sr t'ciam partem psalmor. In al. sr sedam. In al. sr iii. In al. q iulianu heretic. l. vi. q [illegible] l. i. de agone xpiano. l. i. Epla ysidori epi de x. hebreis nobis; Saluatoris. Smo cipriani epi de ope et elemos. Smo eid d' orde dnica. lib [illegible]. Exemplu eple ieronimi. In al. qfessionu libri. xiii. In al. de quantitate aie. l. i. Sr epla Johis tctat. decem. In al. retractation. iiii. l. ii. de morib; ecclesie. et de morib; manicheor. l. ii. Expo eide sr canticum salom. de muliere forti. et vii. alii eide. Semi [illegible] et alior decem et vii. In al. q pelagianos. Ad papa bonifaciu. l. iiii. In al. eide semi. de simbolo iiii. et de resurrectione. xi. et alii alii. In al. eple eide. et in eod. d'. vi. qstionib; l. i. Itm ad bonifaciu. l. i. Itm ad paulina de uidendo deo. l. i. Itm d' psentia dei ad dardanu. l. i. In al. d' uerbis dni. et d' uerbis aptl. et de psalmis semi. lxxxv. In al. sr eplam ad romanos. et sr prima ad chorinthios. In al. sr ceteras eplas aptl. In al. de bono coniugali. l. i. de nuptiis et concupiscentia. l. ii. q parmenianu. l. iii. q petilianu. l. iii. In al. q achademicos. l. iii. de uita beata. l. i. de ordine. l. i. d' ii. aiab; l. i. de regula fidei uerit. l. i. Sermones. iiii. lib d' conflictu uitior et uirtutu. Omelie [illegible]. Regula cleric. In al. d' nuptiis et concupiscentia. l. i. Semi. iii. de pdestinatione diuina. l. i. de utilitate. l. i. de [illegible]. l. i. Eple ad [illegible]. Questionu orosii. l. i. Confl parte donati p gesta. l. i. Annotationes in iob. l. i. de fide et opib; l. i. de regula uere fidei. l. i. de fide et simbolo l. i. Ad ianuariu. l. ii. In eod sermones plures aug. Iohis et alior [illegible]. In al. q cresconiu. l. iiii. Itm in eod gesta altercationis beati aug. q maximinu arrianor epm. Itm q eunde maximinu. l. ii. In al. de lxxxiii qstion.

l. i. Sententie ab eod dictate; xxi. sermo eide de epicureis et stoicis. Itm alii sermo de eo qd dictu e a dno ad moysen. Ego sum q sum. de natura boni. l. i. q manicheos. l. i. Expositio quarundam ppositionu ex epla pauli ad roma. l. i. In al. de magistro l. i. de diuinatione demonu. l. i. de penitentia. l. i. de sermone dni. l. i. de inmortalitate aie. l. i. de patientia. l. i. de heresib; l. i. Electio et ordinatio eraclii pbri successoris sci aug. ab eod aug. facta. et gestis ecclasticis qfirmata. Omelie eid. xviii. in apocalypsi Johis. Lib de testimoniis diuinar scripturar q appellat speculu. q n e beati aug. In al. de gra noui testamenti ad honoratu. l. i. de uita xpiana. l. i. Ad simplicianu. l. ii. Ad casulanu pbrm de ieiunio sabbati l. i. de qstionib; euglior. l. ii. de viii. dulcitii qstionib; l. i. In al. speculu. In al. locutionu sr eptatic. l. vii. In al. qstionu l. vii. In al. de musica. l. vi. In eod cassiodori de orthographia In al. enchi. l. i. de disciplina xpiana l. i. in eod tctat beati cipriani de oratione dnica. In al. de ope monachor. l. i. Itm de expone eple ad galathas. l. i. Itm de orig. aie. l. i. Itm de sententia iac. aptl. l. i.

LIBRI [illegible] GREGORII

In uno uolum. Registri libri. xiiii. In al. sup ezechiele l. ii. xl. omeliar. l. ii. pastoralis cure. l. ii. Regula sci benedicti. In al. sr ezechielem. l. ii. In al. dialogor. l. iiii. pastoralis cure. l. ii. In al. lib. iob. et moraliu i prime partes. l. xvi. In al. ultima pars [illegible] moral. i. extreme partes. l. xviii. In al. paterii ex dictis beati gg [illegible] test. In al. [illegible]

LIBRI ORIGENIS. In uno uolum. sr eplam ad roma. l. x. [illegible] In al. sr leuitic omel. numero xvi. In al. sr uet testamentu.

LIBRI SCI AMBROSII.

In uno uol. de fide ad gratianu impatore. l. v. de misteriis. l. i. de sacram. semi. vi. In al. de ysaac et aia. l. i. de bono mortis. l. i. de uirginib. l. iii. de uiduis. l. i. de uirginib; l. i. Exhortatio uirginitatis. Smo eid de ppetua uirginitate sce marie. de fuga seli. l. i. de media nocte surgend. l. i. q nouatianos de penitentia. l. ii. de iac [illegible]. l. ii. de ioseph. l. i. de bndictionib; patriarchar l. i. de ieiunio. l. i. de obseruantia epor. l. i. de paradiso l. i. Epla ad uercellenses. In al. de obseruantia epor. In eod eple eide. In al. sr luce euglm. l. x. In al. de officiis ministror. l. iii. Exameron eide in eode. In al. de qsolatione ualentiniani impatoris. l. i. Itm de excessu frs sui. l. ii. Itm. l. i. de xii. abusiuis seli. Itm. l. i. de abraha. Itm. l. i. de eo qd salomo ait. tria sr impossibilia m. et qrtu qd n ualeo agnosce. Itm l. i. de penitentia dauid regis.

LIBRI SCI IERONIMI. In uno uol. q iouinianu l. ii. Apologetic. l. i. q heluidiu. l. i. ad eustochiu uirgine. l. i. de uirginitate. Sup ecclastem expositio. l. i. In al. eple eide. In eode qtinent libri ipsi de [illegible] et [illegible]. l. i. Ad amandu pbrm de diuisis qstionib; l. i. Ad palmachiu de optimo genere interpretandi. l. i. Apologetic ad eude. q heluidiu de ppetua uirginitate sce marie. l. i. q uigilantiu. l. i. de xii. qstionib; ad hedibia. l. i. de xi. qstionib; ad algasiam. l. i. disputatio de rone aie p dialogu sumpta ex dictis beati aug. et ieron. Itm. lib. i. beati aug. de origine aie ad ieron. Itm alii lib. beati aug. ad eude de eo qd scriptu e q tota lege seruauit. Itm eple eide aug. ad eunde ieron. In al. sr psalteriu. et qdam eple eide aug. ad eude ieron. In al. sup ieremia. l. vi. In al. sr ezechiele. l. xiiii. In al. sup [illegible]

In another letter to Maurice still on his visit to Canterbury, Anselm asks for the text of the *Aphorisms* of Hippocrates to be copied out for Bec. Brother Maurice was evidently expected to do the work himself while in England. If there is time, Anselm says, he would like the commentary too. If the manuscript is not ready by the time Maurice returns home, he wonders whether Gundulf could find another scribe to finish it, or (better still) whether Gundulf could have his own copy made, which he could then lend to Bec. There is perhaps an implication here that Anselm would prefer a manuscript properly executed under his own supervision at Bec than too hastily in England. There were at least five manuscripts of the *Aphorisms* in the medieval library of Canterbury Cathedral, and Maurice was probably using one or several of them. In a further letter on the Hippocrates, Anselm exhorts Maurice to take care when making his copy and not to leave out words in Greek or any he does not understand (this is quite a common habit in medieval manuscripts); he tells Maurice that they would rather have only part of an obscure and rare text faithfully copied than the entirety corrupted by careless mistakes.

This seemingly casual remark may conceal the old monastic method of reading books. In the modern age we tend to expect books to run consecutively from beginning to end. In the early Middle Ages, manuscripts (principally religious texts) were often opened almost at random. A monk would mutter a few words aloud to himself, and would then pause, meditating on what he had read, looking for divine enlightenment or multiple layers of meaning which God might have concealed in the author's words. This process continued after the book had been closed up and put back into its cupboard. It was known as *lectio divina*, or spiritual reading, and it was itself an act of devotion, like prayer. This is one reason why many books had distinctive and coloured ornament, for this helped impress a page visually in the reader's memory. Because texts were studied in such short passages, an incomplete book, exactly copied, might be more precious to a monk than a faulty but entire text.

In a curious way, some aspects of *lectio divina* still survive when modern manuscript historians look at monastic books of the Middle Ages. We mostly examine them in the reading-rooms of institutional libraries, with limited opening hours. Manuscripts cannot be taken away; consultation is a communal experience, as in a cloister. We usually look at the decoration and perhaps read a page or two of the text, enough to identify it or to extract short pieces of information, and there is value in being in the presence of the original. Then the closing bell sounds and the manuscript is collected up by the librarians and is returned overnight to its modern *almarium*, while we continue to think about what we have seen, recalling it in the mind and benefitting long after the manuscript is no longer present. Perhaps I am unusually slow, but sometimes the best ideas and connections occur later during tranquil recollection and reverie.

The spiritual life of medieval Christian monks would have been unimaginable without manuscripts. Not all religious faiths depend on written texts: the Roman and Greek religions, for example, had been mostly bookless, and the Celtic and northern mythologies were transmitted only by oral tradition. European medieval monasticism, however, was very literate. There was an often-quoted medieval aphorism that 'a monastery without books is like a fortress without armaments' (or 'a city without wealth', as cited in the *Name of the Rose*, or sometimes 'a table without food'). Even in the time of Anselm, literacy was still almost a monastic monopoly. This centrality of libraries to the life of monasteries had two effects. One is that bookish people, like the young Anselm, frequently became monks, which meant that any inheritable inclination to intellectualism was often eliminated from families by monastic celibacy. The other is that the use of books became associated with virtue. On the face of it, this need not necessarily have been self-evident, but the expense and difficulty of making manuscripts in the Middle Ages rendered books precious. This was transmitted through the Reformation and it remains true today. Despite our consumerist and throwaway society, it is still difficult to discard or destroy a book, even one of negligible cost. Our sense of the moral value of possessing books and the duty of care we owe to them can be traced back to monastic libraries.

On Anselm's first visit to Canterbury in 1079, he was introduced to his future disciple the young Eadmer, who was mesmerized by Anselm's discussion of manuscripts, 'both sacred and secular', as he recalled. Secular books usually meant classical or pre-Christian texts. These might seem unexpected for monastic use, but they too were part of medieval learning, which respected the perceived wisdom of the ancient world. Classical Rome was closer to them in time than the foundation of Bec is to us. In his theological writing, Anselm cited or showed familiarity with the works of Horace, Virgil, Lucan, Persius and probably Terence. We have seen him sourcing the *Aphorisms* of Hippocrates. The twelfth-century library catalogue at Bec included a volume of most of the works of Ovid, "omnes libri ovidii, excepto magno et de fastis" (they not only had the text, but they knew what was missing). Bits of Ovid's poems on the art of love are seriously racy, but this was not necessarily a problem for monks: Christian relevance could always be found concealed even in pagan literature. Virgil's *Eclogues*, for example, were interpreted by many, including Saint Augustine, as containing cryptic prophecies of the birth of Christ. Anselm's letters urge Brother Maurice to study Virgil, and there must have been a manuscript of his works at Bec, although it was gone or stored elsewhere by the time of the twelfth-century catalogue. The library owned the works of Fulgentius, a writer of the fifth to sixth centuries, who explained even the *Aeneid* as a covertly Christian allegory.

Although a monk, Anselm was also a teacher, trained in the classical organization of knowledge. When he visited Rome in 1098, Pope Urban II in his speech of welcome (recorded by Eadmer, who was present) praised him as 'a master steeped in all branches of the liberal arts'. These seven divisions of learning formed the curriculum of medieval secular teaching, divided by tradition into the *trivium* (grammar, dialectic and rhetoric) and the *quadrivium* (arithmetic, geometry, music and astronomy). Two multiple volumes listed in the library at Bec wonderfully sum up the range of these subjects as they are likely to have been known in the classrooms of Lanfranc and Anselm. The books' contents are itemized in the catalogue. The first begins with the 'Marriage of Mercury and Philology' by the fifth-century North African writer Martianus Capella, a complex allegory in prose and verse in which the gods of intellect and learning are married by Apollo, followed in the manuscript at Bec Abbey with the commentary on this strange pagan text by the Carolingian monk Remigius of Auxerre. The volume continues with the standard textbook on Latin grammar by Priscian (also from North Africa around AD 500), copied with texts on rhetoric and dialectic and commentaries by Boethius on Porphyry's *Isagoge*, itself an introduction (which is what 'isagoge' means) to the *Categories* of Aristotle, the principal ancient text on pure logic and language, and further commentaries on Aristotle and on Cicero's *Topica*, on how intellectual arguments are presented.

If we were actually being shown these manuscripts by Anselm in the library of Bec, we might be forgiven for remarking that these subjects sound rather complex and irrelevant for the simple life of Benedictine monks. On the contrary, Anselm would tell us, with the delight of a true teacher, they are fascinating. In reading manuscripts, probably very slowly and under guidance, the pupils of Lanfranc and Anselm in the little cloister here in the remote countryside had the chance of knowing as much as anyone in northern Europe about the nature and capacity of human intellect. There must have been a thrill of discovery and revelation through manuscripts which was utterly exhilarating.

The second composite volume for the classroom, immediately following the first in the Bec catalogue, included the fifth-century commentary by Macrobius on the *Dream of Scipio* by Cicero, the fictional vision of the spheres of the universe which is almost all that now survives from Cicero's lost *De re publica* (and is itself the classic statement of Neoplatonism). This was bound up with many other late-classical texts on music, arithmetic and philosophy, including the commentary on the *Timaeus* of Plato by Calcidius, the translator of Plato in the fourth century. In a time when all books were copied by hand, each of these texts would have connected the book cupboard of Bec through unbroken but unknowable chains of transmission back to lost exemplars in classical antiquity. The local guide, who escorted our little group of modern tourists through the cloisters at Bec, proudly told us that the medieval schools here had been a veritable Sorbonne.

These texts lead us to the final class of book in the library at Bec, although Anselm might have been reluctant to talk about them. The abbey owned an almost complete set of works by Anselm himself, in two large volumes. Some of them may even have been autograph or at least emended and approved by the hand of the author. Among other texts, the first volume of the set included the *Meditations*, composed around 1070, Anselm's most widely read work today among spiritual Christians and historians (and still available as a Penguin Classic). The second volume had Anselm's *Cur deus homo*, 'Why God [became] man', written in 1098, on the necessity of atonement, one of the great philosophical texts of the Middle Ages. Most of the treatises in these two manuscripts involve the application of philosophical reasoning to theology. For example, Anselm argues that we may obey God for the merit we might accrue from doing so, whereas when Christ obeyed God even to death, he himself, being already divine, had no need of personal merit and could apply it instead towards paying off the accumulated debt owed by mankind to God because of sin. Anselm's use of logical deduction in matters so profound as the existence of God, salvation and the nature of free will is often seen as the beginning of medieval scholasticism. Many of his arguments are constructed as dialogues, rather as I have done in parts of this chapter, in which he envisages a pupil asking him questions, to which he gives replies. It is a philosophical technique which goes back to Plato and Socrates. Dialogues can convey an extraordinarily personal vividness, as if the reader were sitting in the cloister beside the author. In his book *On Truth*, for example, the text which opens the second of the two volumes we are looking at, Anselm picks up one of the many pebbles in the garden in the centre of the cloister, and lets it fall. He observes that it did not act by free will in clattering to the ground, but it behaved correctly according to nature. The pupil asks:

'Why, then, is a man any more righteous than a stone, if both behave correctly?'

'Don't you think that the activity of a man differs in some respect from the activity of a stone?' says Anselm.

'I know that a man acts freely but that a stone acts by nature and not freely.'

'That is why we do not call the stone righteous; for if a thing which does what it ought does not do what it does by choice, then it is not righteous.'

The student has an idea: 'Shall we say, then, that a horse is righteous when it chooses to eat, because it willingly does what it ought?'

'I did not say that something is righteous which willingly does what it ought; rather, I said that whatever does *not* willingly do what it ought is *not* righteous.'

The atmosphere of the tutorial leaps from the pages of the manuscripts, centuries after Anselm's death. Sometimes the fictional pupil catches him out. There is laughter and good humour. 'What you are asking of me exceeds my capabilities', Anselm replies to one question in the *Cur deus homo*.

The philosophical texts are what ensured Anselm's lasting reputation as probably the greatest intellectual author in Western Christendom between Saint Augustine in the early fifth century and Thomas Aquinas in the thirteenth. He writes with elegant reasoning on the very fundamental questions of human existence and their inseparability from Christianity. At a different level, Anselm's *Meditations* reached and still speak to an audience of private piety, like the later *Imitation of Christ* of Thomas à Kempis and Bunyan's *Pilgrim's Progress*, and for centuries Anselm's name was wishfully attached to popular prayers of every kind.

It is very rare for writers to command enduring respect among such different readers.

The copying and dissemination of Anselm's own works give us our clearest evidence of manuscript production within Bec Abbey itself. Eadmer supplies an image of the composition in the late 1070s of Anselm's *Proslogion* ('Discourse') on the existence of God. He presumably heard the story from the author, or from someone who was there. Eadmer describes how Anselm jotted down sudden ideas on wax tablets during Matins before dawn one day and entrusted these to a monk for safekeeping. A few days later, when he asked for them, the tablets had mysteriously been lost. Anselm rewrote his draft on a new set and he gave them to the same monk, who hid them securely beside his bed. In the morning, the tablets were found shattered into fragments on the floor. The Devil is not named but was obviously the principal suspect. Anselm pieced the bits together and ordered the text to be copied onto parchment.

Wax tablets were used in Roman antiquity but they also survived far into the Middle Ages and beyond, for notes and drafts and taking texts by dictation. Pictures of tablets sometimes appear in manuscript illustrations, showing wooden panels, some with handles resembling table tennis paddles or laced together in pairs like adjacent round-topped windows. Their centres were carved into shallow rectangular troughs filled with coloured beeswax mixed with resin or oil. One can scratch text on the smooth surface with a metal stylus. The added colour, usually black or sometimes green, makes words clear to read. Tablets can be easily erased or corrected, rendering them ideal for making ever-changing drafts, a luxury not enjoyed by authors again until the advent of word-processing. Unlike laptops or manuscripts, wax tablets can be used anywhere, even outside in the rain. Once very familiar to medieval scribes, wax tablets are a class of manuscript almost entirely lost to us.

In the case of his *Monologion*, on the attributes of God, Anselm had a first draft transferred onto parchment and sent it around 1077 to Lanfranc in England, begging him for criticism. Like most authors making such requests, he was clearly hoping only for praise and was then offended when Lanfranc did indeed write back with corrections. The correspondence suddenly bristles with the author's indignant self-justification. Lanfranc's suggestions were not incorporated, and final versions were distributed to friends with slightly more circumspection. One went probably in 1078 to Rainold, abbot of Saint-Cyprien in Poitiers, with a covering letter from Anselm inviting him to show it only to people who are sensible and discreet, not to prattlers and critics. Manuscripts of both the *Monologion* and the *Proslogion* were sent a year or so later by Anselm to Hugh, archbishop of Lyons. There was no method of professional publication in the eleventh century, texts being given as gifts and then copied (or not) entirely as readers deemed them to be useful. The circulation of musical scores today is sometimes like that, transcribed or photocopied and passed on in accordance with demand, rather than through an edition produced speculatively by a publisher.

Given the close connections between Bec and Canterbury, it is probable that manuscripts of Anselm's early works first arrived there either as gifts from Bec or as direct copies commissioned from the exemplars in the cloister in Normandy. The medieval library catalogue of the cathedral priory in Canterbury includes one composite manuscript of multiple works by Anselm exactly corresponding in their sequence to the first of the two volumes of his collected texts in the catalogue at Bec. Their copying for Canterbury was probably due to friendship with Lanfranc, archbishop until 1089, or with former monks of Bec in the cathedral priory. The Canterbury library catalogue also listed yet another manuscript of Augustine's *De pastoribus*, with precisely the same six accompanying texts as the Bec copy in Paris. It surely descended also from that fruitful exemplar.

The text of the London manuscript of Anselm's letters must have derived from Bec too. That is where the selection of letters was assembled, and there was a copy in the library catalogue at Bec, probably the ultimate progenitor of all its descendants. As the volume exists today in the British Library, it is bound also with the collected correspondence of Lanfranc in Normandy. (His letters are not as intimate as Anselm's and mostly comprise records of administration.) These two parts must have travelled together out of Bec, and the manuscript was certainly already in England in the Middle Ages, to judge from the marginal notes. A possible recipient might have been Gundulf, former monk of Bec, pupil and friend of Lanfranc, who brought him to Canterbury, from where he became bishop of Rochester from 1077 to 1108. A manuscript of these two texts bound together like this is listed in the library catalogues of

RIGHT: Anselm presenting a luxury copy of his *Meditations* to Matilda of Canossa (*c.*1046–1115), countess of Tuscany, Austria, mid-twelfth century.

Rochester Cathedral in 1122–3 and 1202: it may be this very book. Since nothing else by Anselm is listed at Rochester, this might even have been the volume ('one of the books of Father Anselm of blessed memory') which the servant of the bishop of Rochester was taking up to London when his horse fell through the bridge, plunging the book unharmed into the Thames.

If nothing else, there would undoubtedly have been trained personnel at Bec occupied in making these various presentation copies, under Anselm's direction. His letter to Lanfranc, which we read at the beginning of this chapter, referred to two monks 'among the scribes of the monastery'. If there was a significant publishing programme, which kept the scriptorium occupied, this might explain why outside help was needed when Canterbury suddenly sought a copy of the huge *Moralia* on Job. One of the earliest of Anselm's letters, written from Bec probably around 1071–2, accompanied a manuscript which he had had written out for a woman called Adelida. She is addressed as a venerable lady of royal nobility. In all probability, this was Adelaide, unmarried daughter of William the Conqueror, who became a kind of domestic nun under the patronage of Baron Roger of Beaumont, near Bec. She had asked for a selection of psalms for her private use, 'Flowers of the Psalms', as Anselm calls it, similar to a Book of Hours in later times, to which he added a few prayers of his own composition, including one to Saint Stephen (which may reflect the dedication of the ducal abbey of Saint-Étienne in Caen, founded by William the Conqueror, who was later buried there). Anselm begs Adelida to accept the manuscript, even though (he says) it is not decorated with gold and gems, which probably refers to the manuscript's binding rather than to any internal illumination. That is a manuscript I would very much like to find one day. (Note, incidentally, that Anselm's earliest known reader was a woman, and that she was capable of reading Latin.) About a year later, Anselm sent another collection of prayers to Gundulf in England, adding that he had divided the texts into paragraphs to make them easier to read, an indication of his own close supervision of the scribes.

There are also two references to Anselm himself working as a corrector in the library of Bec, something considered so remarkable that this is cited by Eadmer as noteworthy evidence of his hero's saintliness. In one, which is part of a miracle story, Anselm was once urgently sought in the night to help a dying monk and was found in the cloister correcting books. In another, Anselm underwent privations during the day and even so spent his nights correcting ancient texts, 'which in all countries before this time were disfigured by mistakes'. It is not quite clear how he did this, if there was only a single copy of a text available; presumably he relied on excellent Latin and perhaps divine intuition.

Examples of contemporary corrections occur on many pages of the Bec manuscript of Augustine's *De pastoribus* in Paris. Medieval pictures of scribes, as well as the modern icon of Saint Anselm in the chapel, show a knife being held in the left hand. This was for steadying the parchment during work and for sharpening the pen and especially for scratching out mistakes, so that the text could be corrected. The surface of parchment can easily be scraped back and re-inscribed, although not as easily as wax. Alternative readings or omissions which could not be fitted into the line were added in the margins. I noted down numerous examples of textual emendations made in the Paris manuscript and afterwards compared them with the printed text; all corrections on my list correspond with what are accepted today as authentic readings across a range of manuscripts from a far wider orbit than the cloister of Bec Abbey. These cannot all have been inspired conjectures, therefore, but the result of checking against another exemplar. In some instances, a book would be borrowed for copying by one scribe and would be proofread by another before the original was sent back to its owner. That may be why Anselm was working into the night, if they were under pressure of time. In one letter sent to Canterbury in the 1070s, Anselm asks his correspondent to look out for an accurate manuscript of Bede's *De temporibus*, which was as likely to be found in Britain as anywhere. He proposes to borrow it for use in correcting the Bec copy, and promises to return it when this has been done. The *De temporibus* is indeed listed as a large manuscript at Bec in the twelfth-century catalogue, presumably now rendered as accurate as human skill could make it. This obsession with accuracy is a characteristic of Anselm's life among books and was rare enough for it to be noticed. The reputation of Bec as a reliable source of exemplars may even stem from it.

Curiously, there are almost no texts by Lanfranc recognizable in the Bec library catalogue, and only as minor components of composite miscellanies of unrelated texts. They might have been kept elsewhere, such as in the prior's lodgings. One of Lanfranc's great enterprises at Bec had been a commentary on the New Testament letters of Saint Paul, and he

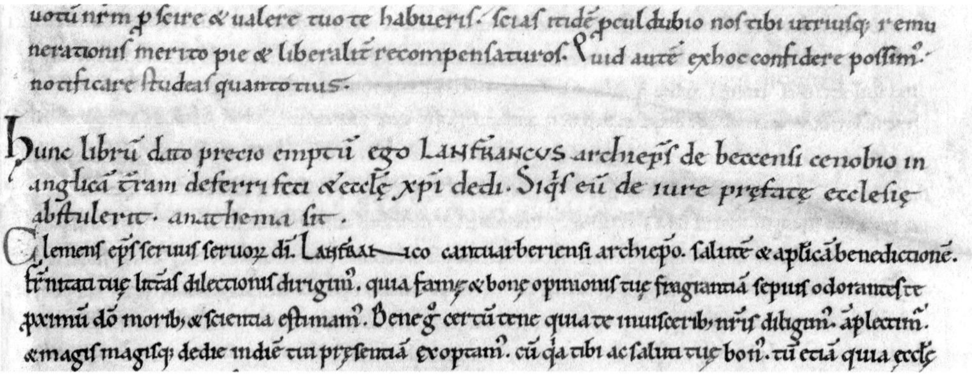

Inscription in a manuscript of papal decrees recording that Lanfranc had it sent from Bec Abbey to Canterbury, with a curse on anyone who steals it, *c.*1080.

had evidently left his own manuscript behind in Bec. In the mid-1070s he wrote to ask for it to be sent to Canterbury. Anselm's reply forwards the manuscript to him graciously but reluctantly, for they had no other copy of the text, and he begs Lanfranc for a transcript. That was probably never made, and no complete version is now known. What is presumably that original in three volumes is listed in the medieval library catalogue of Canterbury among the eventual bequests of Lanfranc himself. A similar story lies behind an eleventh-century manuscript of papal decretals now in the library of Trinity College, Cambridge. It was formerly at the cathedral priory in Canterbury and it ends with an added inscription in the name of Lanfranc recording that he had paid to have it sent to England from the monastery of Bec and that he then gave it to Canterbury. The loss to Bec is a bonus for us, for it is now another of very few surviving manuscripts which were provably at Bec Abbey in the eleventh century. Anselm must have been interested to see it again when he too reached Canterbury. It is a noble and graceful volume written on soft parchment in long lines of small and legible script, with headings in red capitals and with simple initials in red and green, like the Augustine in Paris. Here is the very satisfying coincidence. Close comparison of the handwriting shows that this manuscript of papal decrees was copied by the same scribe as the *De pastoribus* of Augustine from Bec. In this moment we find ourselves within touching distance of the abbey scriptorium, and it gives us a second manuscript which overlapped with Anselm's time there.

By now, our imaginary visit to the cloister in the company of Anselm is over. Chapter 48 of the Rule of Saint Benedict allows the monks quiet time after lunch for resting or reading, and we take our leave. 'Farewell, dearest friend, farewell', said Anselm, pressing my hand (this is from Letter 133, actually addressed to one Lambert, who was considering becoming a monk); 'always recall to mind how insecure and short is human life and how infinite are the good or the evil which follow.'

I emerged into sunshine from the end of the modern chapel. Directly ahead is a double avenue of beech trees so old and tall that their uppermost branches touch together, like a natural extension of a gothic nave. Rooks and chaffinches call from their leafy vaulting, as timeless as the alternating antiphons of monks. The avenue leads out towards the boundary of the Bec property between green meadows on either side, all once part of the monastic farms. These are now inhabited by lethargic white cows and their calves, moving slowly about their endless business. They seem to be Charolais, the colour of the Caen stone of the monastery and of the cathedrals built by the eleventh-century Normans in England. Their ancestors, or something like them, would have supplied the parchment for manuscript pages. The ink was made from gall nuts, gathered from oak trees, found all across Normandy. The red and green initials of the Bec manuscripts were probably from red lead and copper, locally sourced. There is almost no gold in eleventh-century monastic books, and Anselm had apologized to Duchess Adelida for failing to use it. Bindings were wood, usually oak or beech, probably culled from the woods you can still see across the fields. The creamy whiteness of the covering leather on the binding of the Saint Augustine manuscript in Paris is exactly the colour of Charolais cattle.

Beyond the end of the avenue on the far side of the valley against the edge of the forest on the facing hillside is now a picturesque cross-country bicycle track, called *La voie verte d'Évreux à la vallée du Bec*, following the path of a former railway line. It runs today from Évreux in the south-east northwards to Pont-Authou. In the Middle Ages this route would probably have continued right up to Vieux-Port on the Seine, downstream of Rouen, connecting Bec to the Channel and to England. This really very small rural abbey, transformed by the Norman Conquest, sprouted arteries far into the new land. It came to possess property as distant as Tooting Bec in south London and it supplied a network of former pupils who ruled the churches of England following 1066. On the side of the abbey bell tower is a large mosaic plaque erected in 1930 recording how only two generations of monks of Bec from the late eleventh century

ANNO DOMINI 1930
DEO GRATIAS
GLORIAE MAJORUM
CETTE PLAQUE A ETE POSEE PAR DES ANGLAIS POUR COMMEMORER LES RAPPORTS ETROITS QUI UNISSAIENT L'ANCIENNE ABBAYE DU BEC-HERLUIN ET L'EGLISE D'ANGLETERRE AUX ONZIEME ET DOUZIEME SIECLES. LORSQUE TROIS DES FILS DE CETTE ABBAYE OCCUPAIENT LE SIEGE PRIMATIAL DE CANTORBERY. TROIS DEVENAIENT EVEQUES DE ROCHESTER, ET PLUSIEURS AUTRES, EN QUALITE D'ABBES, GOUVERNAIENT D'IMPORTANTES MAISONS RELIGIEUSES.
ILS TRAVAILLERENT TOUS EGALEMENT A FIXER LE CARACTERE DES INSTITUTIONS DE LEUR PAYS D'ADOPTION ET PAR LEURS DOCTES LEÇONS ET LEUR HABILETE DE CONSTRUCTEURS ILS CONTRIBUERENT GRANDEMENT A LA SPLENDEUR DES EGLISES CATHEDRALES ET DES ETABLISSEMENTS MONASTIQUES DE LEUR JURIDICTION.
EN TEMOIGNAGE DE LA RECONNAISSANCE QUE LEUR GARDE L'ANGLETERRE CE MEMORIAL RAPPELLERA LEURS NOMS A LA POSTERITE.
ARCHEVEQUES DE CANTORBERY:
LANFRANC: 1070-1089.
PRIEUR DU BEC, 1045; ABBE DE ST ETIENNE DE CAEN, 1063.
ANSELM, ST: 1093-1109. ABBE DU BEC, 1078.
THEOBALD: 1138-1161. ABBE DU BEC, 1137.
EVEQUES DE ROCHESTER:
HERNOST: 1076.
GUNDULF: 1077-1108:
SECRETAIRE DE LANFRANC A CAEN ET A CANTERBURY:
ARCHITECTE DE LA TOUR DE LONDRES.
ERNULF: 1114-1124:
PRIEUR DE CHRIST CHURCH, CANTERBURY, 1096;
ABBE DE BURGH, PETERBOROUGH, 1107.
ABBES:
GILBERT CRISPIN: WESTMINSTER, 1085-1117.
RICHARD: ST WERBURGH, CHESTER, 1093-1117.
HENRY: BATTLE ABBEY, 1096-1102.
RICHARD: ELY, 1100-1108.
GILBERT: COLCHESTER, 1104-1119.
HUGH FLORY: ST AUGUSTINE, CANTERBURY, 1108-1124.
ALBOLD: ST EDMUND, BURY, 1114-1119.

Tablet at Bec Abbey, erected in 1930, recording the many appointments of monks to positions in England following the Norman conquest.

onwards included three Norman archbishops of Canterbury (the third was Theobald of Bec, 1139–61), three bishops of Rochester (including Hernost and Gundulf – we have encountered them both), and abbots of Westminster, Chester, Battle, Ely, Colchester, St Augustine's in Canterbury, and Bury St Edmunds. To this list we might add also bishops in France at Rouen, Bayeux, Chartres and Beauvais.

Although it is not unexpected that the Norman conquerors imported administrative personnel from their own homelands, that tablet on the bell tower reminds us what a high number of key positions in the new realm were recruited from this single abbey. Stand in the Roman forum today or on Westminster Bridge and you can sense the majesty of empire, but the meadows of the Bec valley do not resonate with temporal power. Bec, however, was probably the most intellectual and highly literate monastery in Normandy, known for its library and scriptorium, and each of those new appointees came to England from a place with an exceptional culture of manuscripts. Whole new forms of literacy entered government with the Conquest. Norman civil administration began to operate with script, hitherto largely restricted to the business of monasteries. Transactions increasingly came to be conducted by charter – manuscript authority – rather than by oath swearing, as often in the old regime, and record-keeping moved into Latin, the language of the continental churches and the papacy. It would be a gross over-simplification to credit this revolution to the Norman monks of one abbey alone, for cause and effect are always more complex, but the members of the diaspora from Bec were certainly in force in England to witness and participate in the change. The English national administration and its civil service have been based on the written word ever since.

Archbishop Lanfranc died in May 1089. William Rufus, petulant son of the Conqueror, delayed and prevaricated over what many people regarded as an obvious replacement to the archiepiscopacy of Canterbury. Finally, on 6 March 1093, during an illness when he was afraid he might die, King William summoned Anselm to his presence and ordered him to take up the archbishopric and primacy of all England. Anselm had to be forcefully carried weeping into a church to accept the position.

Our story of Anselm and manuscripts could have ended here, because the remaining sixteen years of his life were occupied with obligatory administration and difficult Anglo-Norman politics, at which he did not excel. Anselm was not as effective an archbishop as he had been an abbot and supervisor of the literary tradition of Bec. His reluctance to move to Canterbury was probably far more than conventional modesty. Canterbury is a fine walled city, but it lacks the wooded hillsides and contemplative peace of Bec. The appointment was to what was known as the Cathedral Priory of Christ Church, Canterbury, one of the uniquely English cathedrals which were structured and run as Benedictine communities. In that sense, Anselm was still in a monastic setting with which he was familiar. As archbishop, he was effectively the abbot, delegating downwards to a prior, who handled the routine business of the cathedral and the community, much as a non-monastic bishop would delegate to a dean. However, Anselm had little opportunity to participate in the daily life of the Canterbury monks or in teaching philosophy to students. He was dragged into the bitter controversies of those centuries over the respective rights of church and state, and he spent two periods of his unsettled archiepiscopacy in voluntary exile abroad. Anselm's archiepiscopal seal shows him holding a book, but in reality he no longer had much time to teach or to engage with the practicalities of manuscript production. His lack of skill as a statesman seems to reflect a man suddenly adrift from the reassuring and enduring certainties of the scriptorium and the library.

The tasks of manuscripts were taken up on Anselm's behalf by Eadmer (*c.*1060–*c.*1126). He has flickered in and out of this chapter, as indeed he did in the life of Anselm, who had originally met him in 1079 on his first trip to Canterbury, when Eadmer had joined in a learned discussion about books with the visiting abbot of Bec. He was then a young monk and, as his name suggests, was of Anglo-Saxon descent, born shortly before the Conquest. One can imagine that when rumours of Anselm's nomination reached the cathedral priory of Canterbury in 1093, Eadmer, older now, would have recounted proudly to his colleagues that he was already acquainted with the new appointee. At a time when many traditional English-speaking monks resented continental masters imposed on them highhandedly from Normandy (a big problem at the neighbouring abbey of St Augustine's), Eadmer seems to have made himself indispensable to Anselm from the start. They formed a close working relationship: Eadmer was clearly very efficient and organized, and he became (in effect) secretary and diary keeper to the new archbishop. He accompanied Anselm on his long exile into Italy for the three years following 1097 and was in charge of arrangements. The almost contemporary historian William of Malmesbury tells an anecdote from Anselm's conversation with Pope Urban II in Rome. The former monk of Bec, accustomed to living under a rule of obedience, remarked that as archbishop he now had no one to obey. The pope pointed to the obviously bossy Eadmer and quipped, 'How about him?' (Eadmer does not record this.)

Although he no longer had students, Anselm was able to resume writing books while in exile. He finished the *Cur deus homo* in 1098 while they were still in Italy, and he dedicated it to Urban II. In the preface, Anselm says that unofficial copies seemed to have got into circulation before it was properly ready, and (if this is true) it is most likely that Eadmer was the culprit. In a world of manuscript culture, there is no absolute moment of publication as there is with printed books. Probably in 1099, Anselm wrote to Bec, promising to send them the new text, which, he says, 'Brother Eadmer, my dearest son and prop of my old age . . . will gladly copy for the church of Bec.' Note those words: Eadmer was to copy it.

Now let us go back to the cathedral priory in Canterbury on the eve of Anselm's arrival as archbishop. There were still some monks there brought over earlier by Lanfranc from Bec, including Henry, who was the prior of Christ Church from about 1079 until 1096 (well into Anselm's time), when, as the plaque on the bell tower told us, he became abbot of Battle, the monastery founded by the Normans on the site of their victory at Hastings. Canterbury also by then owned a number of manuscripts from Bec. Among these was that book of papal decrees, and Lanfranc's three-volume text on the Epistles of Saint Paul, and (presumably) the copies of Gregory, Ambrose and Jerome discussed and ordered by Lanfranc from Anselm in the 1070s.

Remember that distinctive style of crisp Norman script used at Bec for writing the *De pastoribus*, made with a very angular pen. By 1086 one of the monks of Canterbury had begun imitating the style, and there is every reason to believe that this scribe was Eadmer himself. He copied not only documents for Canterbury (which is where the date comes from) but also whole texts for the library of Christ Church, including surviving manuscripts of works by Ambrose, Augustine and Jerome, three of those four church fathers later commemorated in the chapel of Bec.

By the time Anselm arrived, Canterbury had an invigorated scriptorium producing books in an English version of this Bec script. The distinctive handwriting was first noted by M. R. James (1862–1936), palaeographer and writer of ghost stories, who named it the 'prickly' hand of Christ Church. It is more or less unique to Canterbury and to Rochester nearby, where two successive bishops had also been monks at Bec. Rather like the faux accents of pretended Russian aristocrats, native born to Britain or America, it became almost an exaggerated imitation of its continental original. The 'prickly' script of Christ Church manuscripts is immediately recognizable. Eadmer would have liked his cathedral priory to be a kind of Bec-in-exile. The letter sent from Italy offering a manuscript of the *Cur deus homo* to Bec actually describes him as a monk of Bec. This might be an error of textual transmission, or it may have been Eadmer's wishful thinking, or a sense that they were all now part of the world of Bec. The fireside conversations between Anselm and Eadmer travelling together through Europe cannot fail to have touched nostalgically on the fine library of Bec and on Anselm's passion for it. Eadmer must have longed to have been there then.

Requests for copies of texts by Anselm continued to arrive in Canterbury, as they had in Bec. Malchus, bishop of Waterford in southern Ireland, wrote asking for copies of Anselm's writings on the Holy Trinity, endorsed (Malchus had heard) by the pope himself. A manuscript of Anselm's *De processione spiritus sancti* was probably sent from Canterbury to Lambert, bishop of Arras. Another of the same text went out to Walram, bishop of Naumburg in Saxony, south-west of Leipzig. Towards the end of 1104, Anselm, abroad once more, wrote home to Canterbury asking the prior to arrange for a scribe with a clear hand (an interesting detail) to copy out two texts for Pope Urban's successor, Pascal II. Demand was becoming very international. Probably also in 1104, Anselm wrote from Lyons to Matilda of Canossa (*c.*1046–1115), countess of Tuscany, sending her a copy of his *Meditations*, which, in turn, became the ancestor of a whole textual family found later in Austria and southern Germany with the letter to Matilda still used as its preface. The dedication copy was probably an impressive book, fitting for presentation to a ruler's consort from an archbishop. Anselm's much earlier gift of a volume of 'Flowers of the Psalms' to Duchess Adelida had been a plain monastic manuscript and Anselm had apologized then that it had no noble jewelled binding. To judge from what is probably a direct copy of Countess Matilda's volume more than thirty years later, her book had pictures, including a scene of Anselm presenting the manuscript in a binding obviously decorated with gemstones. Since Eadmer was with Anselm in Lyons in 1104, it is quite possible that he was the scribe and possibly the illustrator of the copy destined for the countess.

In 1993, I bought a small item in the Sotheby's sale of the private library of my very old friend Alan G. Thomas (1911–92). It is a rather stained half-leaf of an early twelfth-century manuscript of the *Meditations* of Anselm, recovered from reuse during the Reformation as a flyleaf at the beginning or end of an English bookbinding. It is written in the Canterbury/Bec 'prickly' script, and it must have been made in the

RIGHT: Manuscript of Ambrose, *Hexameron*, on the six days of Creation, Canterbury, late eleventh or early twelfth century, copied by Eadmer in the prickly script learned from Bec.

Sc̄ty Ambrosius sic Hexameron illius compilauit, ut magis Hyppolitij sententias Basiliiq́ sequeretur. Hieron. ad Sanctum Oceano Epist. 42.

INCIPIT LIBER EXAMERON IDEST SEX DIERUM SANCTI AMBROSII MEDIOLANENSIS EPI.

DE PRIMO DIE IN QUO DIXIT DEUS. FIAT LUX ET FACTA EST LUX. APPELLAUITQ; LUCEM DIE. ET TENEBRAS NOCTEM.

ANTUM NE OPINIONIS ASSUMPSISSE HOMINES PRAESUMPSERUNT. ut aliqui eorū tria principia constituerent omniū. dm̄ & exemplar & materiā. sicut plato discipuliq; eı̄. & ea incorrupta & increata ac sine initio esse asseuerarent. dm̄q; non tanquā creatorem materię sed tanquā artificē ad exemplar hoc est ideam intendentē fecisse mundū de materia quā uocant ylen. quę gignendi causas rebus omib; dedisse asserāt. ipsū quoq; mundū incorruptū nec creatū aut factū estimarent aliqui. alii q̄q; ut aristoteles cū suis disputandū putauit. duo principia ponerent. materiā & speciē. & tertiū cū his qd̄ operatoriū dicit̄. cui suppeteret cōpetenter efficere qd̄ adoriundū putasset. Quid ḡ tam inueniens. quā ut eternitatē opis cū dı̄ omipotentis coniungerent eternitate. uel ipsū opus dm̄ esse dicerent. ut caelū & terrā & mare diuinis psequerent̄ honoribus. Ex quo factū est. ut partes mundi deos esse crederent. quāuis de ipso mundo n̄ mediocris int̄ eos questio sit. Nam pytagoras unū mundū asserit. Alii innumerabiles dicunt esse mundos. ut scripsit democritus. cui plurimū de physicis auctoritatis uetustas detulit. Ipsū quoq; mundū semp fuisse & fore. aristoteles usurpat dicere. Contra aut̄ plato non semp fuisse & semp fore psumit astruere. Plurimi ū nec fuisse semp nec semp fore. scriptis suis testificant̄.

Int̄ has dissensiones eoꝝ quę potest esse ueri estimatio. cū alii mundū ipsū dm̄ esse dicant quod ei mens diuina ut putant inesse uideat̄. alii partes eı̄. alii utrunq;. in quo neq; figura sit deorū. neq; numerus neq; locus aut uita possit aut cura cōprehendi. siquidem mundi estimatione. uolubilē. rotundū. ardentē. quibusdā incitatū motibus. sine sensu dm̄ conueniat intelligi. q̄ alieno n̄ suo motu feratur. Unde diuino spū preuidens scs̄ moyses hos hominū errores fore. & iam forte coepisse. in exordio sermonis sui sic ait.

In principio fecit ds̄ celū & terrā. initiū rerū. auctorem mundi. creationē materię cōprehendens. ut dm̄ cognosceres ante initiū mundi esse. uel ipsū esse initiū uniuersoꝝ. sicut in euangelio dı̄ filius dicentibus. tu quis es.

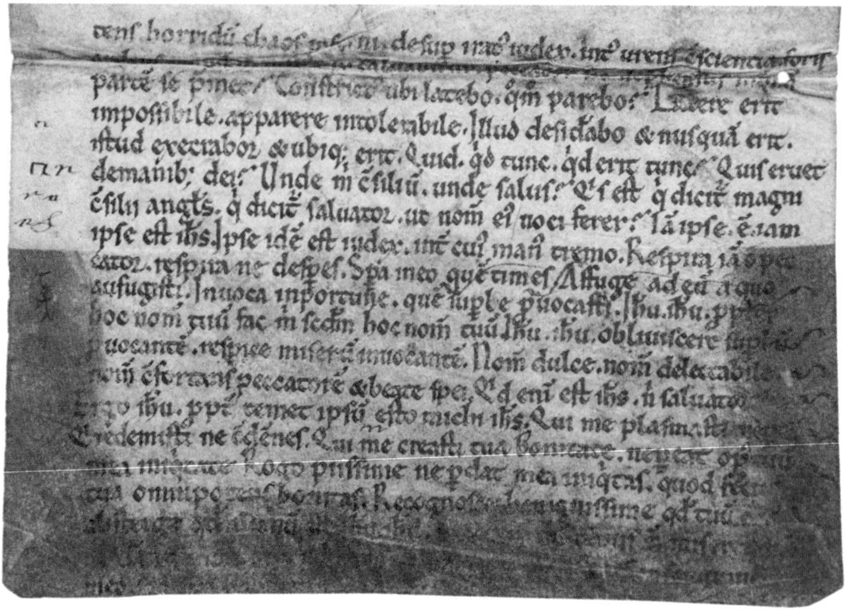

Fragment of a manuscript of the *Meditations* of Anselm, Canterbury, early twelfth century, recovered from reuse in a bookbinding after the Reformation.

cathedral priory. It would have been a moderately small book, probably around 8 inches by 6, well-spaced and easy to read, like the manuscripts from Bec. The fragment was once the upper half of the second leaf of the volume: the sixteenth-century binder probably began tearing it up from the front. Manuscripts are triggers to the imagination, and it was initially because of this chance acquisition that Anselm came into my household. The piece is from a manuscript probably made for use by local monks who had known Anselm in his lifetime, although it might be from a copy written in Canterbury for a recipient elsewhere. Let us hear Anselm speak for the last time. Here he is contemplating death and judgement, translated from the verso of my scrap:

> How can I show myself? It will be impossible to hide; it will be intolerable to appear. I shall desire to hide and there will be nowhere to go; I shall curse being seen, and I will be exposed everywhere. What will happen then? Who will deliver me out of the hands of God? Where shall I find counsel, where safety? Who is he who is called Angel of mighty counsel, who is called Saviour, that I may call upon his name? But it is he himself, he himself is Jesus. The same is my judge, between whose hands I tremble. Take heart, sinner, and do not despair.

Anselm's final involvement with book production, at least as reported by Eadmer, concerns his biography on which Eadmer had been working for some years. It was first drafted, like the *Proslogion*, on wax tablets. (This is the second reference in the *Vita Anselmi* to the use of tablets, hard to envisage with a text in two books and a total of 107 chapters.) Eadmer gradually transcribed the tablets onto parchment and showed the unbound sheets to Anselm, by then in his mid-seventies and in declining health. Anselm made some corrections (an old habit from his time at Bec) and, a few days later, decided that he did not merit a biography at all and ordered Eadmer to destroy the manuscript. Obediently, Eadmer did so; but, ever the efficient secretary with an eye to the future, he had secretly kept a second copy.

After a long illness, Anselm died on 21 April 1109 and was buried in Canterbury. Eadmer outlived him by almost twenty years, tirelessly (and probably sometimes tiresomely) promoting and distributing the texts of his late master and copies of his own evolving biography of him, supplementing it with accounts of miracles which took place after Anselm's death, including that story of the horse and London Bridge. Thomas Becket, astute politician, formally requested Anselm's canonization as a saint in 1163. It is strange, given the importance and fame of Anselm, that we do not know precisely when this was done. In 1720, Pope Clement XI declared Saint Anselm to be a 'doctor of the Church', elevating the monk of Bec to the rank of Saints Ambrose, Augustine, Jerome and Gregory, those four patristic giants standing as sculptures holding manuscripts in the chapel of Anselm's own abbey in Normandy.

CHAPTER TWO

The Prince: The Duc de Berry

Probably the best-known illuminated manuscript of the late Middle Ages is the *Très Riches Heures*, a sumptuous prayerbook made around 1415 for the private use of Jean, Duc de Berry (1340–1416), son, brother and then uncle of successive kings of France. He is generally considered to be the most important royal patron of manuscripts in medieval Europe. The Duc's *Très Riches Heures* is now in the museum of the château of Chantilly, north of Paris, presented in the nineteenth century by the Duc d'Aumale, son of King Louis-Philippe. I am quite proud to have examined the manuscript twice, for the original is not easily made available. It opens, like many Books of Hours, with a calendar of the Church year, illustrated with scenes of the characteristic secular occupations appropriate for each month. January is frequently represented in medieval art by a man eating at a table indoors during the cold winter. In the *Très Riches Heures* this familiar imagery is transformed for the Duc's delight into a banquet of wondrous luxury. It is set before a huge fireplace in a medieval gothic hall in one of the palaces or castles of the Duc himself. The narrow beams on the ceiling are emblazoned with his arms. The far wall beside the fireplace and along to the corner at the left is hung with a large and costly medieval tapestry depicting chivalric knights in battle, apparently a scene from a Trojan romance. Parallel to the fireplace is a refectory table laid for a very great feast. The position of a long table across the width of the far end of the room would be normal for the high table in a medieval great hall, a custom which survives in the dining rooms of the old colleges in Oxford and Cambridge, while the lesser guests would be seated below at trestles laid at right angles

RIGHT: The Duc de Berry (1340–1416) at his New Year feast in the January miniature of the *Très Riches Heures* illuminated by the Limbourg brothers, *c.*1415.

aproche aproche

along the length of the room. The angle of the view from above, looking down from at least the height of the top of the chimney breast, suggests that the artists may have sketched it from a minstrels' gallery at the far end, perhaps surrounded by musicians. This must be New Year's Day or possibly Twelfth Night, 6 January. It is a scene evoking noise and smell and bustling activity.

On the table and sideboard are pieces from the Duc de Berry's private collection of domestic treasure, including dishes of silver and gold and a magnificent salt cellar shaped like a gothic ship with the Duc's emblems of a bear and a swan on its pinnacles. This was an actual artefact described in the inventory of the ducal household in 1413, when it was known as the "Sallière du pavillon". It was made of gilded chalcedony (similar to quartz), set with rubies, sapphires and pearls. The bear and the swan were formed of jewelled enamel and bore the Duc's arms around their necks. There was a cover, not shown here, in the form of a tent (*pavillon*) of white enamel with its knob shaped like a fleur-de-lys, set with jewels. After the Duc's death this salt dish alone was valued at a thousand gold *livres* in the currency of Tours, twice the figure assigned to the *Très Riches Heures* itself.

Around the table in the illustration are the Duc's arriving guests and his many servants, bringing flagons of wine and carving game birds for dinner. Everyone is wearing festive costumes of great expense, generally trimmed with gold. A boy in the foreground is giving titbits of meat to a dog. Dominating the scene is the Duc de Berry himself, son of King Jean II and by this date the uncle of the current king, Charles VI. He was duke of Berry and Auvergne, count of Poitou, governor of Languedoc and beneficiary of vast estates in central and southern France. He is seated in profile directly in front of the fireplace, sheltered from its rising sparks by a circular wickerwork fire screen, like a huge halo behind his head. There is no sign of his wife, Jeanne de Boulogne, whose lands had greatly increased his wealth, or of any other women. The Duc is crowned with a fur hat, for it is midwinter, even indoors. He wears a long rich robe of ultramarine and gold, the heraldic colours of France. Round his neck is a golden collar with a hanging jewel, perhaps the so-called collar of the Ruby of David given to him by his brother the duke of Burgundy in 1401. He turns to his principal guest, a deferential bishop, and in gold lettering floating in the air either the Duc or his chamberlain is declaiming hospitably, "aproche, aproche", 'come in, come in!'

In reality, it would probably have been as difficult to approach the Duc de Berry as it is to get close to his *Très Riches Heures* today. He was imperious and autocratic, even despotic, and gaining an audience with him would certainly have been tortuous for anyone without the highest connections of nobility and wealth, which would have excluded me. In our world I came down by car from Paris past Orléans to Bourges, the former capital of the dukedom of Berry in central France. It is an enchanting medieval town of old houses with a fine early gothic cathedral and some remnants of its ancient fortified walls. It seems to have almost no traffic. Walking in from my hotel towards the city centre I passed a little antiquarian bookshop, of the kind which still exist only in France. Of course, I looked in, rapidly skimming spines of leather and vellum, and I inquired of the proprietor, as always (hope over experience), whether he had any medieval manuscripts. This led to mention of the Duc – 'Duc Jean', they call him in Bourges – and I asked him to mark on my map the exact location of the ducal palace, which he did. Such a conversation in almost identical words could have happened exactly here over 600 years ago, and every bookseller in the region would have known the Duc's address.

The street plan of Bourges has probably not changed much since the time of the Duc de Berry but the old names have, for the French like to keep up to date. From the south-west corner of the cathedral you follow the Rue Victor Hugo into the Rue Henri Ducrot and down to the triangular Place de la Préfecture which opens onto a half-paved square signposted as "Place Marcel Plaisant, sénateur du Cher, membre de l'Institut 1887–1958". Rising up along one side is the medieval wall of the Duc's palace.

The Duc de Berry was a great patron of architecture and built or substantially renovated for himself more than a dozen great castles and palaces across France, some of which appear recognizably in the backgrounds of illustrations in his *Très Riches Heures*. The dukedoms of Berry and Auvergne had been given to him as compensation in 1360, since his earlier dominion of Poitou had been lost to England following the disastrous Battle of Poitiers (1356), during the early stages of the Hundred Years' War. The Duc built palaces for administration in Bourges (Berry), Riom (Auvergne) and elsewhere, and in Paris he later secured and extended the vast Hôtel de Nesle, acquired from the king in 1381 on the left bank of the Seine, where the Institut de France now stands. He mostly divided his time between Paris and Bourges. The ducal residence here was a long and high construction of several connected halls running approximately north to south, with the Duc's private apartments at its southern or left-hand end as you stand looking at it from the street. Old engravings and drawings show tall gothic windows between substantial buttresses, under a very steeply pitched roof with dormer windows and chimneys. What survives today is only a small part of the central hall. From the Place Marcel Plaisant you can see a white stone wall with three lofty mullioned medieval windows, one alone, two as a pair. There are four attic windows above and a single remaining chimney. This was the palace's eastern facade. On the right is a concave recess almost the height of the building. It was formerly the inside wall of a round tower once projecting outwards from the north-east corner of that central hall, rather like the indented impression left by a fossil of some long-vanished creature. There is now a stone stairway up to a small doorway in what would have been the tower's inner wall.

Apart from the wear of time and reuse, there were fires here in 1693 and 1986. Like many medieval castles in European cities, the site is still used for government administration, and this is now part of the Conseil départemental du Cher. It flies the flags of France and the European Union. The demolished ends of the Duc's palace are replaced by office buildings. The surviving fragment must have been the setting for many January feasts like that in the *Très Riches Heures*. Photographs from before 1986 show a medieval fireplace at the end of the hall and a ceiling of narrow roof beams.

Blue and white signs beside the entrance up that stairway state the current public opening hours of the office and give a recommended telephone number for appointments. There is also a bell and an intercom for visitors from the street and so I rang it, mentally preparing a little speech in French about why I wanted to see inside. A two-tone chime sounded in the interior. No one responded and the door would not open. That, I suspect, is much as it would have been if I had arrived in the early fifteenth century, when the Duc de Berry was in residence.

One way into the complex of the ducal palace of Bourges in the Middle Ages would have been through its Sainte-Chapelle. This once projected out at right-angles from the north-east corner. A visitor approaching the palace from its north end would have mounted a series of wide steps up to the main entrance, for even now the site is on noticeably higher ground. There was a kind of stone porch. On the right was the Galerie

The Duc's palace and Sainte-Chapelle in Bourges, where he intended his art collections to be kept after his death, in a drawing of *c.*1615.

du Cerf, a free-standing treasury with a statue of a deer outside. To the left was the principal entry into the end of the chapel. Descriptions and detailed early drawings give a good idea of what was undoubtedly once one of the masterpieces of late French gothic architecture, with a thin spire soaring upwards from the centre of its high-pitched roof.

The Sainte-Chapelle in Bourges was reputedly built as a result of a falling-out with the cathedral of Bourges, where the Duc had initially hoped to be buried. When the canons proved reluctant to sacrifice their beautiful thirteenth-century choir for an incongruous tomb, the Duc resolved to erect his own church instead, to outshine the cathedral. Papal permission was granted in 1392 for a new building on the model of the earlier and better-known Sainte-Chapelle in Paris. The document still survives. The epithet 'Sainte' was accorded to the proposed construction because it was to house a relic of Christ himself, a piece of the True Cross which the Duc's brother Charles V had presented to him in 1372. The fragment had been cut at the time by the king from the original sacred relic conferred on his own Sainte-Chapelle by Saint Louis (the royal brothers' great-great-great grandfather). The chapel in Bourges resembled its 150-year-old Parisian prototype in its exaggeratedly tall and narrow shape, but it was to be bigger and to eclipse Bourges Cathedral in beauty. The Duc employed the finest architects, sculptors, painters and makers of stained glass. Construction work was complete by 1405. The *Très Riches Heures* includes two miniatures of a prince supervising the building of the Temple in Jerusalem with winches and scaffolding, and the Duc probably envisaged himself as a modern Solomon. He continued to pour money and treasures into his Sainte-Chapelle year after year. Among these were many illuminated manuscripts, even secular texts which would have no obvious relevance to the life of a chapel, such as luxury copies of Seneca and Virgil (which both survive), as if he could not bear to be separated from his art collections even in death and would be surrounded by them for ever. The Duc was indeed eventually buried here in a fine marble tomb by the sculptor Jean de Cambrai, but he left no male heirs and his vision of a dynastic mausoleum in Bourges was ultimately unfulfilled. The Sainte-Chapelle fell slowly into neglect. The fire of 1693, which destroyed much of the palace, seriously damaged the chapel. A great winter storm in February 1756 sent pieces of stonework crashing to the ground, reducing the building into terminal dilapidation. The cathedral chapter, which had never recovered from the insult of 1392, authorized its demolition in 1757. Stand in the Place de la Préfecture and not a single trace of it can be seen. Ozymandias at least left trunkless feet in the sand: of the Duc de Berry's Sainte-Chapelle in Bourges there is now absolutely nothing.

However, there was salvage. The cathedral acquired and reused several panels of stained glass and some sculpture; it even accepted the Duc's tomb (agreeable irony here) but put it into the crypt, out of sight. There are fragments from its carved pedestal in the Musée du Berry and elsewhere. Above all, there are many of the Duc's illuminated manuscripts, scattered across the world; he owned about 300, of which about a quarter still survive. The Duc himself would probably have thought that his massive stone castles and chapels were indestructible, but his delicate books have mostly outlasted them all.

The old municipal library or Bibliothèque patrimoniale de Bourges is on the edge of the Place des Quatre Piliers, about five minutes' walk north of the site of the Sainte-Chapelle. It is not to be confused (as I did at first) with the city's fine new Médiathèque out on the ring road. The 'Quatre Piliers', as it is known locally, occupies most of an eighteenth-century townhouse. It is open on Wednesdays, Thursdays and Fridays from three to six in the afternoon only (very civilized). I had asked about its manuscript Lectionary acquired from the demolition of the Sainte-Chapelle. When I was taken through to an office near the front of the building, four truly enormous volumes in boxes were waiting on a trolley and we heaved the first onto the table. It is about 23 inches high and about 14 across. The binding is original, of stout medieval wood sewn onto nine thongs pegged into the thickness of the board. The outside is covered with soft off-white leather, perhaps originally red, nailed in place with very small metal pins, some of which are shaped like tiny fleurs-de-lys. There are big metal bosses on each cover and a long dangling strap (of two originally) which once fitted over pins on the lower cover. Even before opening it, it is a gorgeous artefact. Lift the heavy cover and the manuscript becomes a revelation. There on page 1 are all the colour and the sparkle and splendour of the Duc de Berry's benefaction, and there is no question of this being anything but a princely book.

The Lectionary opens with the biblical readings from the beginning of Advent onwards. There is a miniature of four Old Testament prophets holding scrolls. A glittering illuminated border surrounds the page and the columns of text. At the top and bottom centre are the arms of the Duc de Berry: *France ancien* (a semé of gold fleurs-de-lys on a blue ground) within an indented red border. In the lower corners are monograms of the letters 'E' and 'V', found in other books made for the Duc de Berry and (among other places) on fragments of stained glass from the Sainte-Chapelle now in the museum in Bourges. They may represent the motto 'En Vous'. In the upper corners are the Duc's two famous emblems of a muzzled bear hunched up with its head in its paws and a swan wounded on its breast, which is spattered with blood, creatures we also saw on the tips of the salt cellar displayed on the Duc's New Year table in the *Très Riches Heures*. There has been much speculation as to their meaning. As early as 1457 the romantic royal poet René d'Anjou was interpreting the wounded swan as a symbol of the Duc's undying love for an English maiden whom he had met when he was a hostage in London in the 1360s, following the Battle of Poitiers. With a little imagination, the bear and swan, *ours* and *cygne* in French, became a rebus for the girl's supposed name, Oursine. There is no historical evidence or real likelihood of this, and it may allude instead to Saint Ursin, first bishop of Bourges and its patron saint. The Duc honoured him and gave to the Sainte-Chapelle a silver-gilt reliquary of the head of Saint Ursin, decorated in sapphires, garnets, emeralds, rubies and pearls. A bear lies at the Duc's feet on his tomb.

In volume III of the Lectionary we finally encounter the Duc de Berry in person, in the miniature for the feast of Saint Andrew, about a quarter of the way through the book. He has a pale thick-set face, seen in profile, as later at dinner in the *Très Riches Heures*. If the figure on his tomb in Bourges Cathedral is accurate, the Duc was just under 5 foot 10 inches in height. In the manuscript he is dressed in a pale-red robe with a high collar held at the neck by what seems to be a jewelled brooch. He is kneeling under a canopy of textile woven with his own arms at a prayer-desk draped in green cloth, using an open book with two clasps on straps, rather like volume I of the Lectionary. In front of him is a little seated dog, wearing a collar apparently ornamented with bells. It is an old chat-up technique that if you want to strike up a conversation with someone you do not know, admire their dog. This is something we may need to do. The Duc had many dogs – up to 1,500 hounds at one time for hunting but also tiny lapdogs like this at home. One domestic favourite was called 'Lion'. Two of the same breed as the animal shown here can be seen snuffling about up on the table itself in that January feast scene. Standing in front of the Duc is Saint Andrew, holding his cross and cradling another book, in a jewelled cover. The artist, who knew his employer, shows him gazing more towards the book than at the apostle's face. That would be an enviable acquisition for all three of the Duc de Berry's collections: relics, gemstones and illuminated manuscripts.

The occasion was the Duc's birthday, for he was born in 1340 on Saint Andrew's Day, 30 November, in his father's castle of Vincennes to the east of Paris, seen towering over the royal forests in the December miniature of the *Très Riches Heures*. He was exposed to literary culture from an early age. The musicians and poets Guillaume de Machaut and Philippe de Vitry had both been intimates of his father's court. Petrarch came as a house guest. The Duc eventually owned illuminated manuscripts which had belonged to both of his parents, including the Book of Hours from which his father, Jean II, king of France 1350–64, had learned to read as a child, and another Book of Hours once owned by his mother, Bonne of Luxembourg. Either or both may have been the manuscripts from which

RIGHT: The Duc de Berry with Saint Andrew, miniature in the Lectionary made for presentation to the Duc's Sainte-Chapelle, early fifteenth century.

Passionem
sancti andre
e apostoli.
quam corã
oculis nr̃is vidimus om̃
presbiteri et diaconi eccle
siarum achaie scripsimus:
universis ecclesiis que sunt
in oriente et occidente. et in
meridiano et in septentrione

Prince Jean had himself been taught to read. Years later, in 1377, the Duc bought a Book of Hours to give to his former royal nursemaid, Dame Gille de Caumont, perhaps in memory of his earliest education. A Jean de Breuil, 'chaplain and tutor of the king's young children', was recorded in 1352, when the future Duc was twelve. Princes were expected to be literate and widely knowledgeable.

Running right through the childhood of the Duc and beyond was the recurrent spectre of the Hundred Years' War with England. It was a period of knightly chivalry, romanticized by his friend Jean Froissart, but also of terrible privation and sudden and deadly changes of fortune. In his late teens, the Duc (as I am calling him, although he was then only a count) had been present at the Battle of Poitiers, in which his father was taken prisoner. In the king's tent was a fine manuscript *Bible historiale* with ninety-three miniatures. Both the captured king and his manuscript were brought to England (the book was never returned and is still in London). In 1362 the Duc and his brother Louis of Anjou were exchanged as hostages in place of the king during continued fund-raising to pay the royal ransom. The Duc's custody in London seems to have been no more rigorous than the life of a nobleman at university in the eighteenth century and he was allowed unexpectedly frequent leave for trips home to France. Louis, however, simply escaped. King Jean II therefore considered the terms of his freedom to have been breached and, following a code of honour against all sensible advice, he voluntarily surrendered himself as a prisoner of the English once again and in 1364 was back in London, where he fell ill and died at the Savoy Palace in the Strand on 8 April. The Duc de Berry was now free to return to France. By January 1365 he was in the court of his elder brother, the new King Charles V, who secured for him what would have seemed to most people an almost limitless income.

The Duc's acquisitions of art can be documented from a wonderful series of detailed inventories, probably unparalleled for any private collections of the Middle Ages, at least outside fifteenth-century Italy. They all include manuscripts, as well as pictures, works of art, silver and gold, jewels and tapestries. The first was begun in November 1401 by the keeper of the Duc's treasure, Guillaume de Ruilly, soon succeeded by Robinet d'Étampes. The cataloguers began listing items of every kind in the ducal castle of Dourdan near Paris in December and worked their way south to Mehun-sur-Yèvre by the middle of May 1402, and into nearby Bourges itself at the end of that month. An even more comprehensive inventory was completed by Robinet d'Étampes on 31 January 1413 and then supplemented year by year as further acquisitions were made, up until the time of the Duc's death in June 1416. It overlaps with the list of 1401–2, with the benefit that we can see additions made in the intervening years. Robinet d'Étampes is a second hero of this chapter, for he clearly knew his employer's collections with intimacy, sometimes adding precious details of provenance, acquisition date, artistic style, cost of purchase and subsequent history. There are also two documents listing works of art and manuscripts given or promised by the Duc to the Sainte-Chapelle in Bourges, and an eventual posthumous inventory drawn up by Jean Lebourne, the Duc's last secretary, recording valuations and the eventual dispersal of possessions after the death of the Duc.

Most great collectors can trace the genesis of their obsession to childhood. Since the Duc's earliest inventory dates from 1401, by which time he was over sixty, we can only guess at how his addiction began. The playfulness of some of his natural history specimens listed might suggest acquisitions of boyhood. There is a section in the Duc's first inventory of items described as being of no or little value, such as two boar's tusks, a bird's egg, and the tooth of a giant in a leather box. They sound like childhood treasures. The Duc owned a ring with an image of his father. It could have been a gift from the king, who died when his son was twenty-three. He owned a manuscript called the 'Chronicles of England', "escript en mauvais françois", doubtless Anglo-Norman, barbaric to the French ('after the scole of Stratford atte Bowe'), which may well have been acquired during his imprisonment in London in 1362–4. Within weeks of his return to France he seems to have commissioned an illuminated chronicle of ancient history in proper French, copied by a scribe from Poitiers, his own county, who began in October 1364 and completed the manuscript in Paris the following April. By 1364 the Duc was employing his own goldsmith, and he had artists on the payroll by 1369. He was still only in his late twenties.

An aspect of having unlimited income is that there is no need for the ordinary or mediocre. A recurrent theme in the Duc's artistic taste is his delight in the quite exceptionally large and the astonishingly small, and an evident pleasure in the contrast. From the later 1360s onwards, he was commissioning stone castles on the most enormous scale, rising tower upon tower, dominating the skylines and contrasting with peasant lives in the *Très Riches Heures*. He was also collecting items which were absolutely minute, such as single jewels, as small as crumbs, and manuscript decoration which can really only be appreciated with a magnifying glass. The quantities of little gemstones described are extraordinary, often loose and unmounted. Keeping track of them must have been an ordeal for the Duc's curators. Some single jewels were so famous that they even had names, like celebrated diamonds today. The inventories several times mention a Venetian dealer in Paris called Ludovico Gradenigo, who sold the Duc rubies such as the *Grain d'orge* and the *Ruby de la fossete*, 'the barley grain' and 'the dimple ruby'. The Duc acquired gems with a frenzy and urgency which show a real passion. There is a tale, reported in 1394 by Thomas de Saluces, of the Duc attending a major council at court to discuss the regency of Languedoc when he heard whisper of the arrival of two dealers from Venice who were waiting outside to show him rubies and other precious stones: his fellow delegates were shocked that the Duc left the meeting at once to see them. That is a glimpse of a true collector.

Gemstones and semi-precious crystals not only had rarity and beauty: they were also understood in the Middle Ages to have spiritual and therapeutic properties. In 1404 the Maréchal de Boucicaut, another manuscript patron, sent the Duc a gold pendant with a gem described as being

Merchants offering precious gemstones to a prince, very probably the Duc de Berry, *c.*1405.

efficacious against poison. The Duc's library had multiple copies of the thirteenth-century treatise on the natural world by Bartholomaeus Anglicus, which includes accounts of different kinds of stones and jewels: sapphires, for example, were said to be most appropriate for the fingers of kings, and to aid reconciliation and peacemaking, and, if suspended over the heart, to cool temperatures and fevers. The Bible lists different gemstones integral to the New Jerusalem and the throne of God, and their close presence to divinity endowed them with preternatural virtues. They were not so different in this from relics of saints, also prized for their metaphysical properties, and which the Duc gathered passionately too. He owned hundreds of them.

As with book collecting, the thrill of possessing a relic is enhanced by a good provenance and a knowledge of its place in history. The Duc must have trembled to acquire the engagement ring of the Virgin Mary given to her by Joseph, or a stone which Jesus had changed in the wilderness into the shape of a loaf of bread, which the Duc had set in gold, or the body of one of the Holy Innocents of Matthew 2:16, delivered to the Duc by the dealer Constantin de Nicolas from the doge of Venice, all documented in the inventories. (To be fair, Robinet d'Étampes privately doubted the engagement ring.) Relics require trustworthy sources, but most relics in the collection were plausible, at least from the perspective and knowledge of the time. The Duc's piece of the True Cross, which was to be the principal treasure of his Sainte-Chapelle, can genuinely be traced back many centuries to the ancient imperial treasury in Byzantium, from which Saint Louis had bought it. The Duc's fragments of the nails used at the Crucifixion were presented to him in 1389 by Pope Clement VII, on the face of it as reputable a source as Christendom could command. The Duc owned various relics of Saint Ursula's Eleven Thousand Virgins. One group was acquired in 1404–5 from Cologne, where their shrine was in the cathedral. Another head of one of the virgins was described as accompanied by a certificate of authenticity. It came wrapped in green silk in a wooden box, and the Duc had it enclosed in a silver reliquary shaped like a head and then gave it to his Sainte-Chapelle. It is a debatable point whether a true relic has to be identifiable to be efficacious: the inventory has an entry 'Item, certain relics in a paper package with no inscription', which the Duc nevertheless passed on to his chapel, just in case.

To understand the Duc's manuscripts, we can watch the way he treated his gemstones and relics. He liked them with a known history, as collectors do. He enjoyed doing things with them, forever having them remounted and rearranged into different settings. The Duc's most precious ruby was bought by him in 1408 from Janus de Grimault, a dealer from Genoa, for the sum of 16,000 gold francs, and he afterwards had it mounted with diamonds acquired from the dealers Antoine Manchin and François de Passan and a pearl which had been given to him by the king of Navarre. He often commissioned gold and jewelled displays for relics, having them set into ever more splendid confections of the goldsmith's art, as conscientiously and sometimes as frequently as a philatelist today rearranging his stamps. It is ongoing patronage as well as collecting, and involvement continues after acquisition. The Duc was impatient but also probably exciting to work for. Like many very rich people, he never had to consider any wish but his own. His jewellers must sometimes have despaired when fine pieces were sent back to the workshops again and again to be taken apart to provide components for yet further new ideas. One wonders about the domestic reaction when he ordered the sapphire in his wife's coronet to be removed for reuse elsewhere.

Among the Duc's most valuable relics were several long thorns extracted from the reputed Crown of Thorns, another of the supreme possessions of the original Sainte-Chapelle in Paris. Four of these thorns were described in the inventory of 1402 as being set in a gold crown among 20 rubies, 17 sapphires, 8 emeralds and 66 pearls. A note added to the inventory records that the Duc subsequently had this crown dismantled in order to give three of the thorns and some of the gemstones to his own Sainte-Chapelle in Bourges. The fourth sacred thorn and the rest of the gems and gold were assigned to the goldsmith Renequinus de Hallen to fashion into a jewelled work of art, which is very possibly the artefact now called the 'Holy Thorn Reliquary', one of the iconic treasures of the British Museum.

The reliquary is about 12 inches high. It is like the most astonishing toy model imaginable. It resembles an arch-topped frame rising up out of a miniature castle or walled city, with turrets and battlements, all in solid gold. In panels on the city walls are the Duc's arms, as in his Lectionary in Bourges. Here again we see the delight of the Duc de Berry in rendering huge architecture into tiny scale. There are fairy steps up to the front door, microcosms of those formerly leading to the entrance of his Sainte-Chapelle or still by the west front of Bourges Cathedral. Herman and Jean de Limbourg, two of the three brothers who painted the *Très Riches Heures* and other manuscripts of the Duc, had themselves been apprenticed to a goldsmith in Paris around 1398, and the extraordinarily detailed gothic buildings depicted in their illuminations may have had their genesis in designing miniature architecture like this in goldwork. It was perhaps how the Duc first met them. Emerging out of the castle in the reliquary is a hill with the resurrection of the dead from their graves at the end of the world, and then in the aperture above is a diorama of the Last Judgement, with Christ on a rainbow attended by the Virgin and Saint John the Baptist and with a single holy thorn itself held between his knees and supported on a very large sapphire. Above again is God the Father in a starburst. Encircling the perimeter of the central compartment are the twelve Apostles. It is all in gold and white enamel, studded with rubies and pearls and another sapphire. Whenever I have gazed at it in its display case in the British Museum, I have been constantly jostled by insistent tourists holding cameras, not unlike the ring of white enamel Apostles circling round the thorn with their own symbols in gold. The flashing of photography illuminates the reliquary in its modern gallery in sudden sparkles of light.

It is now time to seek permission to visit the library of the Duc de Berry at home. My introduction to him could have been effected in a number of ways. Maybe the Duc would simply have heard that I had been looking at his Sainte-Chapelle Lectionary in Bourges, and I might have been peremptorily summoned, especially if he thought I had access to manuscripts for possible purchase. We learn from the inventory of 1402 that most of the Duc's books were kept in his gothic castle at Mehun-sur-Yèvre, some eight miles north-west of Bourges. It is now about a twenty-minute drive from the city. I would certainly wear a good suit to meet the Duc. There is a car park for the 'Jardins du Duc Jean de Berry', where the Yèvre river and its tributary the Annain wind through a pleasant municipal woodland of trees and walkways leading towards a high castle mound visible through the leaves in the far left-hand corner of the park. You can scramble up a steep crumbling bank to find yourself in a medieval ruin with most of two substantial remaining towers of pale stone among large chunks of masonry overgrown with ivy and tufts of grass. There are signs warning not to climb on the ruins but it is all freely open to the public. There are surviving steps down into a dark underground chamber, its entry barred from over-curious visitors. From one side the high site looks out steeply over a deep valley adjoining the park. On the other it backs right up against the town of Mehun at the top of the hill. This was said by Jean Froissart to have been the Duc de Berry's favourite castle. It is depicted in remarkable detail in the Duc's *Très Riches Heures*, where it illustrates the psalm for the first Sunday in Lent. In the manuscript the castle becomes the setting for the Temptation of Christ. In that day's Gospel narrative (Matthew 4:8–9, etc.), the Devil takes Jesus to a high mountain and shows him all the kingdoms and riches of the world which he may enjoy if he will worship Mammon instead of God. For the Duc, no secular luxury could have been more tempting than his castle of Mehun-sur-Yèvre and all its treasures. I crossed a walkway where the medieval drawbridge once stood and came round into the side of a town square called the Place Général Leclerc, and then along the edge of the former moat opposite the ruin until I could sit with my back to what I think is a school, at almost exactly the vantage point where the Limbourgs must have taken their drawing.

The central tower is still there, with its three windows, at least up to the first row of battlements. It now contains a small museum reached by a spiral staircase. The tower on the right is partly standing, broken open on its inner side to reveal the fireplaces of the different floors of the wing which once connected the towers. The matching turret by the gateway survives only in its foundations, but the general outline of the buildings in between can still be seen. Where the Duc's swans are shown swimming in the moat in the foreground is today a deep empty ravine of newly mown grass, but the waterway on the right which once fed it still exists. Notices now forbid bathing and canoeing. I had crossed it from the park over a little arched bridge about where the small boat is depicted. The Duc probably travelled by river between here and Bourges, doubtless the idealized city in the far background of the miniature, with the spire of the Sainte-Chapelle rising from a blue roof. The lion at the lower right looking up at the Duc's bear in a tree is the artists' nod to the biblical scene being set in a wilderness, but it also marks the Duc's menagerie, which was kept here at Mehun-sur-Yèvre, presumably in the park. In addition to lions and bears, the Duc owned a leopard, a monkey, a wolf, a camel and an ostrich, a great rarity at the time, each with its own keeper. Once more, he may have relished the contrast between the largest birds and wild animals and the harmless little lapdogs scampering around his feet. 'Lion' (its name another conceit on size) might

The Duc's favourite castle at Mehun-sur-Yèvre, illustrated by the Limbourg brothers in the *Très Riches Heures*, *c.*1415. Two of the same towers survive today.

accompany us as the Duc finally takes me up to see his library. I imagine the walk through the castle with the Duc would be silent and in an atmosphere of overwhelming condescension. I might bring him a present of a modern facsimile of one of his own manuscripts (there are many), and I have no doubt it would intrigue him. He would fetch out the original for comparison, and an enjoyable afternoon together would begin well.

The inventories give no indication of how the manuscripts were stored. One small image in the *Très Riches Heures* shows people seated in rows of carved wooden benches reading books propped open on sloping shelves in front of them, very like those still extant in the library of Malatesta Novella, lord of Cesena, built in 1447–52. It is possible that the Duc de Berry had similar furniture. Other manuscripts might be kept in chests or cupboards. The Duc might perhaps initially have brought out liturgical texts and prayerbooks to show me, knowing that I had admired his Lectionary. For a layman, he had very many of these, but some were destined for his various chapels or kept simply for the quality of their illumination. One of his finest manuscripts was a family heirloom, the famous two-volume Belleville Breviary, which now survives (rather damaged) in the Bibliothèque nationale de France, inventoried by the Duc as "très bien et richement historiez, enluminez", with gold clasps enamelled

with the arms of France. The word *historié* – historiated – means decorated with pictures. The Breviary had been made in Paris around 1330 and had later belonged to Charles V, whose son, Charles VI, gave it to Richard II, king of England, whose own successor, Henry IV, in turn presented it to the Duc de Berry. The progress of the Hundred Years' War seems scarcely to have interfered with friendly relations between the royal families.

Since it was not possible to take a manuscript apart to use its components in different creations, as with relics and jewels, the Duc reused the calendar pictures of his Belleville Breviary by having them carefully copied into a new manuscript known today as the *Grandes Heures* (now also in the Bibliothèque nationale), completed in 1409. It is about 15½ inches high by nearly a foot in width, showing again the Duc's delight in extraordinary and unexpected size. As in the Lectionary, the shimmering borders of the *Grandes Heures* are emblazoned with the Duc's arms, the devices of a bear and a swan, the letters 'E. V.', and portraits of the Duc himself, inhabiting his own book. In the inventory it was valued at 4000 gold *livres*, eight times more than the *Très Riches Heures*. It was described as "très notablement enluminées et historiées de grans histoires de la main Jaquemart de Hodin et autres ouvriers de Monseigneur", that is, 'very notably illuminated and illustrated with big pictures by the hand of Jacquemart de Hesdin and others of his highness's artists'.

Archival information like this is extraordinarily unusual. Identifying a manuscript by the name of its artist is almost unknown before the Renaissance. It would have been inconceivable that the catalogue of Bec Abbey would have recorded an illuminator or that anyone would have known or cared who had painted a book. Jacquemart de Hesdin is documented as an artist in the Duc's employment by 1384. It is known that he and his brother-in-law were pardoned for their part in the murder of another painter in Poitiers in 1398. By 1399 he was living in Bourges. There is a second manuscript attributed to Jacquemart in the inventory, described as "Unes très belles Heures". That manuscript still exists too and is in Brussels, with the residue of the collection of the Duc's nephew, the duke of Burgundy. It is indeed by the same artist, and it includes another portrait of the Duc kneeling before his patron saints,

LEFT: The *Très Belles Heures* of the Duc de Berry, now in Brussels, illuminated by Jacquemart de Hesdin and assistants, *c.*1402.

Saint Andrew (as in the Lectionary) and Saint John the Baptist, after whom he had been named.

If I had mentioned artists, the Duc might then have shown me his late fourteenth-century Psalter listed in the first inventory as being "de la main feu maistre André Beaunepveu", which also survives. It begins with a series of elegant portraits of prophets and apostles seated on elaborate gothic thrones, all painted in delicate tones of grey, like soft stonework reduced into miniature format. The late master André Beauneveu, as we usually spell him, who had previously worked for Charles V, entered the service of the Duc de Berry around 1385 here at Mehun-sur-Yèvre, where he was in charge of painting and large sculpture. Froissart, who knew him (they were both natives of Valenciennes), says that his work was famous in France, the Netherlands and England. By stylistic comparison with the Psalter, surviving fragments of delicate stone carving from the Sainte-Chapelle in Bourges are now sometimes also ascribed to him. He died at the end of 1402, and that word 'feu' (deceased) in the inventory suggests that his death was recent.

I expect that the Duc would have brought out the exquisite little Hours of Jeanne d'Évreux, which I have actually held a number of times, for it is now in the Cloisters collection in the Metropolitan Museum of Art in New York. It was made in Paris in the 1320s for Jeanne d'Évreux, queen of France, who bequeathed it in 1371 to Charles V. It is extremely small, fractionally over 3½ by 2½ inches, delicate and almost weightless. You can just about enclose it in the palm of your hand. The Duc was doubtless captivated by the extreme contrast of size between this minuscule Book of Hours and his exaggeratedly large *Grandes Heures*. If I had commented on this, he would probably have been amused to show me an even more miniature manuscript in his collection. It is described in the inventory as a tiny Gospel of Saint John no larger than the size of a *blanc*, a common base silver coin of the period about an inch across. Miniature books are well-known bibliophilic collectibles today, but it is remarkable to learn of one from the Middle Ages. It had probably no purpose except to amaze and beguile. The Hours of Jeanne d'Évreux is listed in the Duc's inventory as (I am translating) 'a very small Hours of Our Lady called the 'Hours of Pucelle', illuminated in black and white, of the Use of the Dominicans'. 'Pucelle' is the name of the illuminator, Jean Pucelle (d. 1334), about whom we now know a good deal, including the fact that he and his wife, Pernelle, lived in the Rue Erembourg

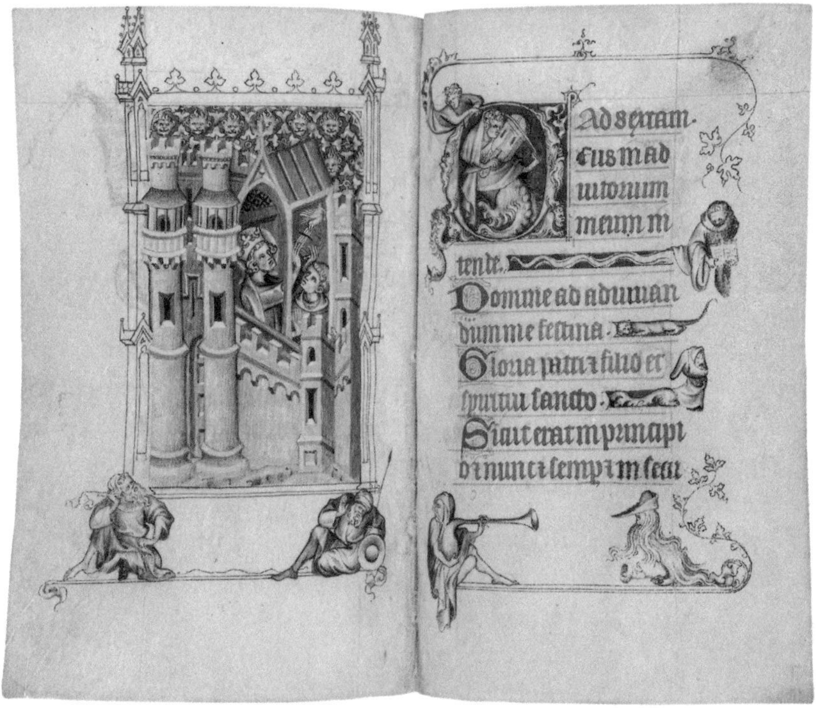

The Hours of Jeanne d'Évreux, identified in the Duc de Berry's inventory as having been illuminated by Jean Pucelle *c.* 1324–7.

de Brie on the left bank in Paris, near the Dominican convent of Saint-Jacques. The book was already eighty years old when the Duc owned it, and its artist had died before the future Duc was born, and yet Pucelle's name was still attached to it. There is no signature in the manuscript itself, and the attribution had been preserved entirely by memory. The Duc might not have known (and I can imagine him delighted to be told) that the Belleville Breviary, still out on the table, is today partly ascribed to the hand of Jean Pucelle too. I expect he would have had an opinion on whether this is right.

The *Très Riches Heures* was never in the library at Mehun-sur-Yèvre. It was still unfinished and in loose sheets when the Duc died in 1416 and is recorded only in the inventory of his posthumous estate. In translation again: 'Item, in a box a number of gatherings of a very rich Hours, which Paul and his brothers were making, very richly illustrated and illuminated – value 500 *livres*.' That single name is the unique documentary evidence for identifying the hands of the Limbourg brothers. The *Belles Heures* (now also in the Metropolitan Museum in New York) is listed in his inventory as having been ordered by the Duc from 'his artists', without actually naming them, and the style is identical. The three Limbourg brothers – Paul, Jean and Herman – appear regularly in the Duc's accounts from 1404, following the death of the duke of Burgundy, who had previously employed them to illuminate a Bible. They became members of his household, exchanging gifts as well as receiving salaries. Several items of jewellery are listed in the Duc's inventories as having been given to one or more of the brothers, including an emerald ring with the Duc's emblem of a bear which was presented to Paul de Limbourg in 1408, about the date of the completion of the *Belles Heures*. As fellow members of the manuscripts club, the fearsome prince and the hired painters met almost as equals. In 1411 the brothers gave the Duc a fake book formed of a solid block of wood painted to resemble a manuscript in a velvet binding with silver-gilt clasps. It was presumably a shared joke, attesting to friendship with a bibliophilic patron who would have grappled in vain to open it, perhaps with much hilarity.

We do not know where the Limbourgs illuminated the Duc's manuscripts, but Paul was given a large house in Bourges, previously occupied by the Duc's treasurer. As you walk around the modern block in Bourges where the ducal palace once was, you pass the famous Portail Saint-Ursin of *c.*1100, a stone gateway on the street frontage inscribed by its sculptor, Giraldus. Its columns are carved with bears and it has panels of the Occupations of the Months beneath round arches, which must have been seen almost daily by the Limbourg brothers. The subjects are standard throughout medieval art, but they might have been an inspiration. Giraldus's carving of a man in a tunic killing a pig in November, for example, is more or less identical in composition to that painted for the December page of the *Belles Heures*. This may be coincidence, but not necessarily.

There is no reason to doubt the Duc's Christian piety, but the number of Books of Hours and Psalters in his possession was far more than any person could possibly need for use. Until about this date, Books of Hours had mostly been women's texts, hardly owned by men at all. The Duc was a collector, clearly enjoying engagement with artists and their ideas. One commission followed another, often running ahead in his impatience. Before the *Belles Heures* was quite finished (and it never was entirely), the Duc was probably already discussing the *Très Riches Heures* (never finished either). That desire to do something new with Books of Hours is comparable to the Duc's practice of forever sending his reliquaries back

The *Belles Heures* of the Duc de Berry, illuminated by the Limbourg brothers, completed around 1408–9.

to the goldsmiths for refashioning. Sometimes there was overlap between manuscripts and jewellery. His liturgical books were often bound with clasps and fittings in silver gilt and enamels, usually with his arms and sometimes with little images and gemstones. The *Grandes Heures* was described as being in a binding of purple velvet with gold clasps each set with a ruby, a sapphire and six big pearls, all wrapped in damask and kept in a leather box. The heavy treasure value of the outside of a grand medieval Book of Hours is easy to forget, when most surviving manuscripts are rebound in the simpler and sober taste of later times. Even the pigments used in illuminating manuscripts had a symbolic value, as gemstones did, adding a further spiritual dimension to the pages. Listed among the jewels and precious stones in the first inventory were two leather bags of lapis lazuli, described as being for use by the Duc's artists. Precious lapis, or ultramarine (literally from 'beyond the sea'), was probably the 'sapphire' of the Bible. Profuse use of blue and gold, not least in the Duc's own arms and those of France, as he must have noticed, were the twin minerals of God and royalty. The intense and matching lapis blue of the Duc's robes and of the celestial firmament is the most immediately striking feature on opening the *Très Riches Heures*.

The artists Jacquemart de Hesdin, André Beauneveu and the three Limbourg brothers were full-time employees in the ducal household, exclusively available to the Duc. They mostly made ever finer copies of texts which he already owned, such as Psalters and Books of Hours. As far as I can judge, the *Belles Heures* and the *Très Riches Heures* were both written by the same scribe, and the work was doubtless entirely executed on the premises. For many other books, however, the Duc needed to send out commissions to professional artisans. In his time, Paris was by far the principal centre of the book trade in northern Europe, infinitely eclipsing anything available in Bourges. From the period from about 1390 until the Duc's death in 1416, we know the names of some fifty *libraires* in the capital, or people describing themselves as such, and nearly as many in the associated trades of scribe, illuminator or bookbinder. A *libraire* was a bookseller, but also the project manager who coordinated commissions for manuscripts and subcontracted the various craftsmen. Many had premises in the Rue Neuve Notre-Dame, the street which ran from the west front of the cathedral up towards the royal palace on the Ile de la Cité (now an open pedestrian area with the outlines of the medieval street marked in the paving stones). Others had shops on the bridges spanning the Seine, or on the south bank. The Duc owned manuscripts executed in the commercial workshops of several prolific Parisian illuminators such as those known to us as the Virgil and Boucicaut Masters, and it is simplest to suppose that such books were ordered from a *libraire*, as any other customer might do.

It would not always have been possible to walk into a Paris bookshop and commission an unusual text. In all manuscript production, as we saw in Bec, a scribe cannot make a book without access to an exemplar to copy it from. Major booksellers probably retained some exemplars of their own for popular titles, and there were doubtless also friendly loans from neighbours in the Rue Neuve Notre-Dame and elsewhere in the trade. If the customer wanted something unusual, however, as the Duc de Berry generally did, he probably had to supply the *libraire* with the exemplars himself. Sometimes the Duc borrowed texts which he wanted copying. A convenient source for him was the royal library, as in the case of the originals of new French translations of Aristotle and Livy, which were clearly used as exemplars of the Duc's copies. Like many book collectors, he was not always scrupulous about returning volumes he had borrowed. The king lent him the famous illustrated *Bible historiale* which Jean de Vaudetar had given to Charles V in 1372, and the royal library was obliged to claim it back from the Duc's executors in 1416.

A text which clearly appealed greatly to the Duc de Berry and which he had professionally copied several times both for himself and for presentation to others as diplomatic gifts was the *Grandes Chroniques de France* or *Chronicle of Saint-Denis*, a trumpet fanfare to the French monarchy. The Latin original appears in the Duc's inventory of 1413:

> A book of the *Chronicles of France*, in Latin, in gothic script, which his highness of Berry borrowed from the church of Saint-Denis to show to the emperor and also to have copied, and he wishes that at the end of his life it should be restored to the said church.

The 'emperor' was presumably Charles of Luxembourg, the Duc's maternal uncle, Holy Roman emperor 1355–78, whom the Duc entertained in Paris in January 1378. The royal abbey of Saint-Denis, north of Paris, would not have dared refuse if the Duc demanded to borrow a book. It seems that he then kept their chronicle for nearly forty years, even if the wording of the inventory attests to a lingering twinge of guilt that it should eventually be returned.

The *Grandes Chroniques* was a supreme symbol of the glory of medieval France. There was no other country comparable in Europe: England was still a cultural backwater, which made its occasional successes in the Hundred Years' War all the more distressing, and Germany, Italy and the Netherlands were confederations of little principalities. Spain had not yet become wealthy from American gold. France, however, was a great nation, and Paris was the largest and richest city in Europe. It held the seat of royal administration and the greatest of all medieval universities, and it was the unchallenged destination for the art of goldsmiths, painters and illuminators. Wordplay between *Paris* and *Paradis* was invoked by Jean de Jandun in 1323. Manuscripts of the *Grandes Chroniques* are emblazoned with pictures of French coronations and victorious battles, and their borders are sometimes formed of cascades of half *fleurs-de-lys* in azure and gold, the royal emblem which an angel brought from Heaven to Clovis, king of the Franks, in the early sixth century. The Duc de Berry, patron and accumulator, was conscious of his own family's destiny in this paradise on earth.

The Duc is most famous now for commissioning manuscripts, and it is that aspect of his collection which has attracted most attention from art historians. However, he was also a buyer of ready-made books, some of which were of considerable age. Many of the *libraires* of Paris would also have kept small stocks of used books available for immediate purchase. Sometimes the Duc was probably attracted by the oddity of their size. His oldest manuscript known to me was an eleventh-century English Psalter. I first saw it in the Anglo-Saxon exhibition in the British Library in 2018 and was astounded by its shape: it is nearly 21 inches high, by only 7 wide, a narrow format so peculiar that it must have been irresistible to the Duc for that reason alone. The Duc's inventory calls it "un très ancien Psautier long" (note that word *long*, which is what distinguished it; 'long' not 'tall' suggests it was kept lying down). In the library in Bourges I looked at a twelfth-century manuscript of Peter Lombard's *Sentences* which the Duc had given to his Sainte-Chapelle. It is an extremely common and by then old-fashioned scholastic text of no use to the Duc or his chapel. However, it is 20½ inches by 14½, almost twice as big as any normal copy. I have never seen one on such a scale, as unexpected and irresistible to the Duc's taste as a little Gospel the size of *un blanc* or an Anglo-Saxon Psalter three times taller than it was wide.

Names of notable earlier owners are sometimes listed in the inventories, and these must have appealed to him too. The Duc had a Psalter which was said to have belonged to Saint Thomas Becket, martyred in 1170. He promised it to his Sainte-Chapelle but possibly never gave it. It was listed as "bien ancien" (in contrast to the eleventh-century Psalter, which was "très ancien") and was richly illustrated. The Duc had a thirteenth-century Bible inscribed by his secretary, Jean Flamel, as having been owned by Saint Louis, who died in 1270. Books did not usually qualify as relics, but any association with saints such as Thomas Becket or Louis doubtless gave them value to the Duc. Their antiquarian nature probably appealed too. In 1405 the Duc bought a book on the Crusades described as being in old script, "de vieille lettre", romantically dating from long ago, like memories of the Crusades themselves. He paid the huge sum of 2,025 *livres*, and so it was greatly valued. These are very

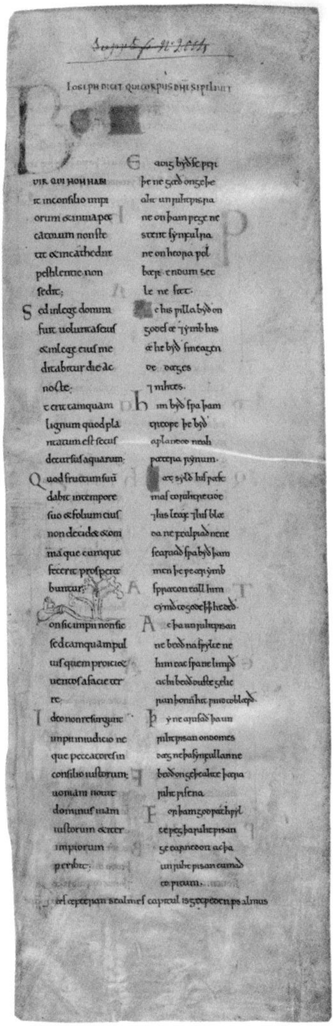

The Duc de Berry's oldest surviving manuscript, an unusually shaped Psalter in Latin and Old English, England (perhaps Canterbury), mid-eleventh century.

early uses of the adjective 'old' as a mark of approbation. In most inventories of medieval libraries the word means obsolete or worthless. A century before the Renaissance reached France, the Duc de Berry was already appreciating antiquity.

The manuscript once owned by Saint Louis was not the Duc's only Bible with an illustrious provenance. As well as one inscribed by Flamel as having been the property of Philippe le Bel, king of France 1285–1314, the Duc owned another from the library of the Avignon antipope Clement VII (d. 1394), probably a gift, since Clement had also given him the fragments of the Holy Nails. Although the Duc's arms were duly added, those of the Pope were carefully left intact, preserving the record of the book's earlier history. The Duc later gave it to his nephew Louis d'Orléans, perhaps in August 1407 in exchange for an even finer Bible, which had once been owned by Robert of Anjou, king of Naples (d. 1343). Two months later, Louis was assassinated in Paris and the Duc de Berry successfully retrieved the papal Bible back into his own library.

This trading and recovery of manuscripts, usually to his advantage, is characteristic of the Duc. Many collectors have similar stories of quick opportunism. The Duc once gave a copy of the *Miroir historial* of Vincent of Beauvais to Jean de Montaigu, master of the household of Charles VI. Later, Montaigu was charged with treason by the duke of Burgundy and was beheaded in Paris on 17 October 1409. On 25 October, only eight days later (we learn the date from the inventory), the Duc de Berry made inquiries from Fremin de Revelle, a dealer with a shop on the Pont Notre-Dame, about acquiring Montaigu's collection. The deft and timely intervention paid off, for he not only recovered the *Miroir historial* but also secured a fine Psalter and prayerbook, a two-volume illustrated Breviary, and a *pater noster* (or string of jewels) which he then took apart to enhance the binding of his *Grandes Heures*. Jean de Montaigu's family regarded this quick footwork as unethical and they were still contesting the transaction as late as 1418, after the Duc de Berry's death, when the Breviary was eventually ceded back to Montaigu's brother Gérard, by then bishop of Paris.

A miniature from the *Miroir historial* of Vincent of Beauvais given by the Duc de Berry to Jean de Montaigu and deftly reacquired after Montaigu's execution in 1409. It shows the death of Saint Eustace and his family, martyred in a brazen bull over a fire.

Some buyers of rare books slow down as they get older. Committed collectors (I have known many) often increase their frenzy of acquisition as time seems to be running out. On the death of Charles V in 1380 and the accession of his eleven-year-old son, the Duc de Berry had become joint regent of France with his brothers, an uneasy alliance which eventually evolved into a deadly and ongoing struggle for power between successive dukes of Burgundy and Orléans and their heirs. The young Charles VI was frequently ill and ineffectual. By 1404, however, the Duc de Berry, generally sympathetic to the Orléans faction, had outlived his brothers and gradually found himself little more than a secondary participant in a country descending into anarchy, buffeted by changes of political fortune beyond his control. He had no dynastic succession. His last surviving son by his first wife, Jeanne d'Armagnac, had died without issue in 1397. The Duc's second marriage in 1389, to the callow Jeanne de Boulogne, was financially advantageous but childless. As can happen in times of chaos and loneliness, he seems to have returned to collecting with a dedication and delight which are exhilarating to watch. The commissioning of an inventory in 1401 was perhaps the first stage in a decision to upgrade his collection, which he then continued with unprecedented vigour for the rest of his life.

A major Parisian bookseller patronized by the Duc over many years was Renaut de Montet (*c.*1375–*c.*1424). He had a shop called the sign of the Étoile on the corner of the Rue de la Parcheminerie and the Ruelle Saint-Séverin. It is about five minutes on foot across the river at the Petit Pont and up the Rue Saint-Jacques, third street on the right. More relevantly, it was near what must have been the rear entrance of the Duc's Hôtel de Nesle in Paris. The Duc perhaps looked in regularly as he walked past. In January 1404 he bought from Renaut a manuscript of sayings of the philosophers in French, a Book of Hours, and an account of the exotic travels of John de Mandeville; in May that year he paid him 200 gold shillings for "un gros volume", which must indeed have been immensely thick, for it is reported as containing the histories of Thebes and Troy, Orosius, Lucan, the *Roman de la Rose*, the *Consolation* of Boethius and much else; in January 1405 he bought from Renaut an illustrated romance of Lancelot; in February 1410 the *Livre de l'information des rois et des princes*; in March 1410 a lives of the Church fathers, "bien ancien", another manuscript evidently precious for its antiquity; in October 1412 a book on the marvels of the Orient, and a Missal; in January

1413 a little Book of Hours; the following month, a volume of saints' lives by Saint Gregory, and, in a different transaction, a manuscript of the moralized tales known as *Cy nous dit*. Finally, on 2 March 1416, Renaut de Montet was at last invited to see the ailing Duc at home in the Hôtel de Nesle, and even on that occasion he sold him three more books. These were Corbechon's *Livre de la propriété des choses*, a chronicle and an illustrated *Pèlerinage de la vie humaine*. The Duc died at home in June, and Renaut was then one of four booksellers called in two months later to value the library in the Duc's estate.

It is one thing to commission a manuscript, which might take months or even years to complete. It is another to buy a second-hand book, back on the market. There is always a third possibility. It would be fascinating to know whether *libraires* like Renaut de Montet ever took the risk and cost of preparing ready-made books in advance, in the hope of selling them profitably to impulse customers such as the Duc de Berry. A lavish manuscript would be very expensive to make, and it is generally assumed that such investment was not normal practice for booksellers until the invention of printing in the mid-fifteenth century. It is possible that every purchase from Renaut, for example, was either already second-hand or had been commissioned and funded by the Duc from the outset. However, consider the instincts of an addicted collector. Most art obsessives in my experience are regularly overwhelmed by the need for acquisition, requiring instant gratification. The Duc was buying precious gemstones and relics at exactly the same rate as he was buying manuscripts, with the difference that a ruby or a sacred relic can be taken home at once. A commissioned manuscript cannot. Booksellers must surely sometimes have risked having manuscripts prepared in advance in order to tempt him. I have looked in the British Library at a world chronicle, bought by the Duc de Berry on 29 October 1407 for 160 gold shillings, as its entry in the inventory records. It is a luxury book by a commercial workshop in Paris and is not obviously earlier than the date of purchase. The Duc's arms are not in the original illumination. Flip idly through the miniatures and you come upon a striking image of Charlemagne receiving the relic of the True Cross and the Crown of Thorns from the

RIGHT: The Duc de Berry's romance of Lancelot, early fifteenth century, probably the manuscript bought by him from Renaut de Montet in Paris in 1405.

Cest le livre de mess. lancelot du lac ou quel livre sont contenus tous les fais et les chevaleries du dit mess. lancelot et la queste du s. graal faicte par le dit mess. lancelot le compaignon galaor le bon chevalier et les compaignons de la table ronde.

Cil qui se tient et iuge au plus petit et au plus pecheur de tous mande salut au commencement de ceste histoire a tous ceulx qui le cuer ont et leur creance en la saincte trinite cest ou pere et ou filz et ou saint esperit. Ou pere par qui toutes choses sont establiez et recoiuent commencement de vie. Ou filz par qui toutes choses sont delivrez des paines denfer et ramenees a la ioye pardurable. Ou saint esperit par qui toutes choses sont mises hors des mains au maligne esperit et raemplie de ioie par lenluminement de lui est vray enlumineur et vray confort. le nom de cellui qui ceste histoire fist nest mie nomme au commencement mais par les paroles qui cy apres seront dittes pourres bien apparcevoir le nom de lui et le pays dont il fu ne et une grant partie de son lignaige. mais au commencement ne se voult pas descouvrir. Et si y a trois raisons pour quoy. la premiere est pour ce que sil se nommast et il deist que dieu lui eust descouverte si haulte histoire les felons et les envieux le tenroient en vieulte. la seconde raison si est pour ce que se on savoit son nom tel le pourroit ou nommer qui le cognistroit si en priseroit moins listoire pour ce que par tant petite personne eust este mise en escript. la tierce raison si est que sil eust mis son nom en listoire et on trouvast aucune chose desavenant par mauvais escrivain qui apres le translatast dun livre en autre tout le blasme en fust sur moy Car on dist plus voulentiers le mal que le bien. Et plus est un homme blasme dun seul mal sil le fait quil ne seroit de cent biens Et pour ces .iij. choses que vous aves oyez ne veult il mie que son nom soit du tout descouvert ia soit ce quil se vueille couvrir le sen il plus congneu quil ne vouldroit mais il dira

emperor Constantine IV. I had thought (and so surely did the Duc) that these treasures reached France with Saint Louis, and so I stopped to read the text. It describes how Charlemagne acquired parts of the Cross and the Crown and a Holy Nail and the chemise of the Virgin, and gave all these to Chartres. The Duc de Berry owned pieces of all of them, including a bit of the cathedral's True Cross presented to him in Bourges by the chapter of Chartres on 3 December 1406, hardly eleven months earlier. It is easily imaginable that the Duc riffled through the pages of this ready-made manuscript in a bookshop and that he too paused at that miniature, read it exactly as I did, and bought it on an irresistible impulse.

On acquisition, the Duc personalized his books. Sometimes his secretary, Jean Flamel, who had beautiful handwriting, added flamboyant title-pages, proclaiming the Duc's ownership. Very often the Duc wrote in his own hand at the end of a book, "Ce livre est au duc de Berry & auvergne . . ." with other titles and his flourished signature, "Jehan". This was no bureaucratic library assembled by other people in the Duc's name; he was handling and labelling the manuscripts himself. Acquisitions were often embellished with his arms on the first leaf or anywhere that space could be found. That eleventh-century Anglo-Saxon Psalter has the Duc's arms painted on the outside edges of the pages. Possession and ownership mattered to him, and he took a continued interest in his books after they had been gathered in.

The Duc's inventories are fascinating reading today and give a sense of the pleasure we might have had together in poking along the shelves at Mehun-sur-Yèvre. As a palaeographer, I would be interested to observe the variety of scripts among his books. Most of the manuscripts at Bec, by contrast, would have been uniform in the handwriting of the time and place. The Duc's inventories sometimes describe script, such as "de lettre boulonnoise", which generally means Italian (for the book trade of Bologna was the best-known in France); and "de lettre de court", which is a regular Parisian book hand; and "de lettre courant", cursive; and "de lettre de forme", which is formal gothic, sometimes qualified here further as unusually good or large or small. One manuscript is "de lettre gascoigne", perhaps written in the *langue d'oc* dialect of Gascony in the far south-west, which the cataloguer probably could not read, since the text is unidentified. They are aware too of different styles of illumination. The Anglo-Saxon Psalter was "historié d'ouvrage romain" – Romanesque – and any Italian art was called "de l'ouvrage de Lombardie". Today we

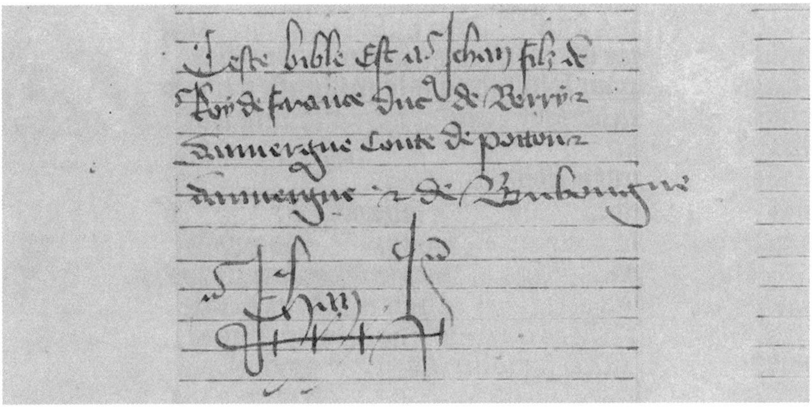

The Duc de Berry's signed inscription of ownership in a *Bible historiale*, with the added title of count of Boulogne, acquired on his second marriage in 1389.

generally attribute medieval manuscripts to a region by localizing their script and decoration. The inventories of the Duc de Berry are very probably the first time such judgements were ever attempted.

The cataloguers also make comments on the quality or extent of the illumination, extremely unusual for the period. We can practically hear them gasp as they open some manuscripts: "richement historié", "très bien historié et enluminé", "historié en plusiers lieux très richement", "très notablement historié et enluminé au commencement et en plusieurs lieux", and so on, as they turned the glittering pages. The titles used now for the Duc's extant Books of Hours such as the *Belles Heures* or *Très Riches Heures* are in fact simply words taken from opinions expressed in the inventories. Such connoisseurship is hardly seen again until the eighteenth century.

The Duc's library was not as large or as wide-ranging as the royal collection in the Louvre, but it was undoubtedly of consistently finer quality. Books in French and Latin were mixed up together. The Duc did not know any other languages. Many books contained religious texts in some way or another. The Duc was clearly devout, probably beyond the convention of the time. Maybe he half hoped for canonization, like his forebears Louis IX and Charlemagne. There were many saints' lives, consistent with the taste of a man who collected relics. Some of these read like heroic romances and lent themselves to illustration. I am glad to see two texts by Saint Anselm. One, a copy of his *Meditations*, was given to the Duc in 1410 by Gérard du Puy, bishop of Saint-Flour 1404–13.

The other, with the *Cur deus homo*, was listed in 1404 as having previously belonged to the artist André Beauneveu – it is interesting that an illuminator owned a quite complex philosophical treatise – but there is an awkward note in the margin of the inventory that it had apparently disappeared. I am not in the habit of stealing other people's manuscripts, but if my executors find it hidden among my books at home, they will know that even I can be tempted.

There were illustrated encyclopaedias and dictionaries, often of simple theology. There were also teaching texts on good government, and the wisdom of ancient philosophers, actual and attributed, and works of Aristotle in translation. There were not many Latin classical texts, fewer than in a princely library of Italy. One was a Seneca sent to the Duc in 1403 by his sister's son, Giovanni Maria Visconti, duke of Milan. The library was especially rich in works of history, which were valued both as narratives and as guides to noble or Christian conduct. Universal histories usually opened with the Creation and the Old Testament. There were also Josephus, and Livy in at least four copies (generally "très richement historié"), and Valerius Maximus, who wrote anecdotal history often hardly more credible than saints' lives. There were several narratives of the heroes of Troy, from whom the royal families of Europe claimed descent. The tapestry hanging behind the Duc in the January feast in the *Très Riches Heures* shows a scene from a Trojan romance. There was some astrology and magic, one of them in Spanish; some medicine; and a profusely illustrated Pliny on natural history, given to his Sainte-Chapelle, where it can have been of little use. Exotic travel was well represented, including Mandeville, already mentioned, two manuscripts of Marco Polo (both survive) and books on the wonders of the world. These parallel the Duc's fascination with gemstones from the distant Orient and unimaginable rarities such as two coconuts brought from Constantinople, which were acquired in 1402 and valued at eight *livres*. The Duc had three copies of a *Mappa Mundi* on rolls of parchment, two kept in special boxes, one of wood, one of leather, and other maps which were laid down on wooden panels hinged together like books. They doubtless had pictures of monsters and hybrids from the fringes of the world. Literature as such is not extensive but included Ovid (in French), some Lancelot and Arthurian romances, Petrarch and Boccaccio in translation, the *Roman de la Rose*, Machaut, Christine de Pizan, and several manuscripts of music and song. Christine, who knew the Duc personally, characterized him as a 'great lover of beautiful books of moral philosophy and history, notably on Roman conduct and exemplary teachings'.

Here perhaps is another clue to understanding the manuscripts of the Duc de Berry. Beauty was important to him, but a library offered more than that. We should not see the Duc as simply a busy book collector, like some modern free-spending bibliophile who loves reading. There was a moral purpose to his books, and a sense of duty and even destiny. Most substantial book collections in the Duc's time were still the prerogative of churches and monasteries, like Bec, or had religious contexts, such as the comprehensive libraries of the popes in Avignon or of the Sorbonne, still very ecclesiastical, or were gathered by clerics or scholars who mostly intended them as bequests to institutions. The *Philobiblon* (*c.*1345), attributed to Richard de Bury, no relation, is often heralded as the first text on the joys of book collecting, but it is really a treatise on the merits of libraries for religious use, and its presumed author was a bishop.

In a very unusual way, the French royal family, the *rois très chrétiens* and descendants of Saint Louis, regarded themselves as being practically of the status of priests, with the privileges and responsibilities of such rank. The French kings were all anointed with the sacred oil first used at the baptism of Clovis in 508, lifting them above the level of laity, as emphasized in the *Grandes Chroniques de France* distributed by the Duc de Berry. Other royal houses of Europe and even the Holy Roman emperors did not quite share that sense of religious entitlement. As we saw among the treasures of the Duc's library at Mehun-sur-Yèvre, his family all owned and used many Missals and Breviaries, texts which one would usually think of as being exclusive to clerical use. The Duc's numerous Books of Hours were generally written in two columns, a very unusual format characteristic of Breviaries, which were priestly texts. We cannot really separate his manuscripts from his relics and other sacred ornaments of piety. The Duc de Berry's book collection resembled a private ecclesiastical library or storehouse of knowledge, upgraded for royal use. As Aristotle was believed to have tutored Alexander the Great, so in the new age Christian teachers such as Augustine and Gregory enlightened the Duc de Berry and his family with wisdom, often deferentially in their language of French. History illuminated the heritage of the dynasty of France, and it taught right conduct and courtesy. The Duc himself eventually owned four copies of the *Livre du gouvernement des rois et des*

Je qui estoie pensif et en esmai.
et par desdaing courroucie cõ
tre les hommes gloutons: ie tour
noie mon visaige et ma pensee
devers la charoigne du gloutõ
empereur aulus vitellius qui
dedans les undes du tybre flotto
it puis ca. puis la. Et ainsi que
tournoie mon visaige et ma pẽ
see contre la charoigne de vitel
lius. ie vi si grant nombre de hõ
mes malleureux qui par trou
peaulx accouroient vers moy q̃ ie
ne cuydoie pas que nature mere
de toutes choses en eust tant en
gendre. Tous ces hommes accou
rens devers moy disoient quilz
descendirent iadiz du noble et
sainct patriarche iacob le pere
du peuple israel; ilz gemissoiẽt
tous. ilz estoient couvers de mise
rables et douloureuses robes. Ilz
huloient ainsi comme len brait
a lenterrement des mors. Et aus
si ilz racomptoient les diverses
mes miseres quilz souffrirent a
vant la mort. cestassavoir leur
plaies. leffusion de leur sang.
la faim. et la pestilence quilz en
durerent. les chaines dont ilz fu
rent loiez. les prisons ou ilz fu
rent enclous. les servitutes en
quoy ilz furent vendus. et les
nouvelles manieres de leurs
mors. et des mors de leurs parẽs
et amis. Et si tost que ie res
gardai les iuifs enfans de iacob
gemissens pour leurs males for
tunes. Je congneu que entreulx
tous estoient plusieurs nobles

hõmes et

princes, a textbook on royal erudition dedicated to Philippe le Bel, his great-uncle. Universal knowledge was an attribute of a perfect Christian prince. All the Duc's brothers formed libraries – Charles V, the largest collection of all, Louis, duke of Anjou, and Philippe le Hardi, duke of Burgundy, with superb books – while their sister Isabelle de France married Gian Galeazzo Visconti, progenitor of one of the great Italian families of book collectors. In turn, the Duc's nephews acquired manuscripts, especially Jean sans Peur, duke of Burgundy. Within a generation, this new royal fashion for domestic libraries (and Books of Hours) was trickling down the social scale into the aristocratic and aspirational households of France and Burgundy, and in fifteenth-century Italy into the courts of the Italian renaissance princes, who now sought to reconnect themselves with classical learning, eventually bypassing the Christian purpose of book collecting altogether.

Not everything owned by the Duc de Berry was bought or commissioned. In so far as the inventories make note of where manuscripts were obtained, approximately seventy had been gifts to the Duc, nearly a quarter of the total. Diplomatic presents were listed from the king and the royal dukes and from members of his household, and from visiting heads of state, and from the pope and various bishops and from the patriarch of Alexandria and the grand master of Rhodes. His reputation as a manuscript collector was known internationally. There are also formal presentations of texts from authors, hoping to gain royal patronage and to inspire other people to commission copies in turn. The donor would make the manuscript as luxurious and eye-catching as possible. The dedication copy of the French translation of Boccaccio's *De casibus* was there, for example, delivered in 1411 by Martin Gouge, the Duc's treasurer and the bishop of Chartres, on behalf of the translator, Laurent de Premierfait, a secretary in the ducal household. The title means approximately 'book of falls', rendered into French as *De cas des nobles hommes*, telling how famous and noble people throughout history generally came to bad ends. It was perhaps brave to dedicate such a text to one of the most high-riding princes of Europe, which is possibly why the translator gave it through the uncontroversial intermediary

LEFT: The *Cas des nobles hommes et femmes*, the dedication copy of the French translation of the *De casibus* of Boccaccio, presented to the Duc de Berry at New Year, 1411.

hands of a bishop. However, the Duc de Berry loved it and, as Premierfait must have hoped, he showed it around. The duke of Burgundy soon ordered a copy, probably taken directly from this one. Today more than fifty other manuscripts are recorded, spreading out in a proliferating family of descendants from the Duc's own manuscript, all still with the endorsement of his name in the preface.

A famous donor of her own works with a view to their propagation was Christine de Pizan (1364–*c.*1430), writer and exponent of the role of women. When her husband died in 1389, Christine had turned to supporting herself and her family by writing, regarded now as the first professional woman author in European history. Her unusual personality clearly appealed to the Duc. She presented him with copies of her *Épistre de Othéa à Hector*, written 1399–1400, *Le Chemin de long estude*, given in March 1403 "en son hostel de Neelle" (she had clearly got into the house), the *Livre de la mutation de fortune* in 1404, and others, through to the *Livre de paix* in 1413. The Duc in turn bought from her a copy of her *Ballades et dits*, "bien historié et enluminé", composed in 1402. In some of Christine's books, he may have found references to himself, such as in the *Livre de paix*, in which the Duc's young nephew, Louis of Guyenne, is described as hearing the Gospel reading for the feast of Saint John the Baptist in 1412 and exclaiming his wish for peace between the Johns of his own time, the dukes of Berry and Burgundy.

The Duc also gave books away, although not as many as he received. Some surviving manuscripts which seem quite conclusively to have been made for him cannot be matched in his inventories, and probably they were presented to other people before being inventoried. The Duc had a practice of reacquiring former gifts when their recipients died. He clearly regretted deaccessions or never felt he had truly relinquished ownership. Even his donations to his Sainte-Chapelle were not as extensive as promised, and in any case he probably continued to regard items as his own property (a problem familiar to modern museum directors in relation to donors). The Duc gave a Missal to the Sainte-Chapelle in 1404, for example, but took it back in 1412, which the custodians would not have liked to refuse.

Gift giving was a big part of formal medieval life. The biggest annual occasion for the exchange of presents in late-medieval France was New Year's Day, 1 January, when items of enormous value, known as *étrennes*, were given and received. Our custom of Christmas presents is a poor

Christine de Pizan shown in the manuscript of her *Mutation de fortune*, given by her to the Duc de Berry in March 1404.

and diluted survival of a tradition on which medieval society based its obligations, duties and political allegiances. Some of the Duc's finest manuscripts were acquired as *étrennes*. We should not regard these as unwanted intrusions. On the contrary, no one paid good money for a fine manuscript in the early fifteenth century without knowing in advance that it was precisely what the Duc wanted, probably more like a modern wedding present wish-list than a surprise from beneath the Christmas tree. A manuscript, unlike a piece of goldwork, had to be rightly judged because it could not be refashioned and adapted to taste. A well-judged gift could establish a relationship with the Duc de Berry for life, and everyone knew that nothing touched his soul as much as jewels and manuscripts.

Cy commence le livre de lestat du grant Caan

Cy commence de lestat et de la gouvernance du grant kaan de cathay souverain empereur des tartres. et de la disposicion de son empire. et de ses autres princes. Interprete par un arcevesque que on dist larcevesque saltensis. au commant du pappe iehan. xxij.e de ce nom. Translate de latin en francois par frere iehan le lonc dyppre moisne de s. btin en s. aumer.

Le grant kaan de cathay est tres puissans entre tous les roys du monde. A luy sont subget et font hommaige tous les grans seigneurs de ce pays. Especialment trois grans empereurs. cest assavoir lempereur de cambaleth. lempereur de boncsay. et lempereur bolboch. Ces trois empereurs envoient tous les ans lieppars tous vifs camelz gerfaulx et tres grant

We can end where we began, in the New Year banquet of the Duc's *Très Riches Heures*. The manuscript is assumed to have been commissioned in 1413. Let us suppose that it shows 1 January of that year. It was a Sunday. The Duc had spent it at the Hôtel de Nesle in Paris. The *étrennes* acquired that day, as extracted from his inventories, included a diamond in a gold ring, given to him by the king; a gold goblet enamelled with scenes from the life of Saint George, given by the duke of Burgundy; the book of Marco Polo and the marvels of Asia, with some 300 miniatures by the Boucicaut Master and his collaborators, also given by the duke of Burgundy (it survives, in the Bibliothèque nationale), and a great ruby on a gold ring, given by his son, the teenage Philippe le Bon, later duke of Burgundy himself; a gold ewer, with an inscription saying that it had once belonged to Saint Louis, given by the bishop of Chartres (Martin Gouge again, bishop 1406–15, doubtless the bishop shown seated beside the Duc in the Limbourgs' miniature with his right hand raised in greeting); a gold cup; a multiple gold reliquary with an image of Christ as the Man of Sorrows (later passed on to the Duc's great-niece, a nun at Poissy); an enamel pax with a relic compartment (transferred to the Duc's Sainte-Chapelle); a carbuncle ruby, given by Ludovico Gradenigo, that gem dealer from Venice; a gold ring with a cameo cut with the Duc's portrait; a gold ring with a sapphire bear on an emerald ground; an agate salt cellar with the knob on its gold lid enamelled in blue; another salt cellar of Venetian work on four wheels like a chariot; yet another salt cellar in enamelled gold in the shape of a little dog on a gold ground decorated with rubies and pearls, given to the Duc by his wife, a charming choice for a man inseparable from his lapdogs; a silver-gilt goblet enamelled with a design of three bears, again a ducal emblem; an illustrated manuscript of medical texts, on the virtues of plants and animals, given by the Duc's doctor, Simon Alligret (d. 1415); and the manuscript of Christine de Pizan's *Livre des fais d'armes et de chevalerie*, with a miniature at the beginning and in a binding of stamped red leather with clasps, given by Christine herself. 1 January was a red-letter day both in the calendar of the *Très Riches Heures* and in the life of a real collector. It is no surprise that the Duc is telling his guests to approach.

LEFT: The manuscript of Marco Polo, *Livre des merveilles du monde*, illuminated by the Boucicaut Master and given to the Duc de Berry by the duke of Burgundy for New Year, 1413.

CHAPTER THREE

The Bookseller: Vespasiano da Bisticci

William Gray was an English postgraduate student on an extended research trip, drifting around the big cities of Europe at his family's expense. He had been in Cologne with a friend from Balliol College in Oxford, where they were both junior Fellows, and he and his party decided to include a tour of Italy, perhaps hoping to escape the German winter. They stopped first in Florence in late 1444 or the very early months of 1445. On arrival, Gray introduced himself to Vespasiano da Bisticci (*c.*1422–98), then in his early twenties – younger than Gray – who was employed in a bookshop in what is now called the Via del Proconsolo. This is the shopping street which runs down from the south-eastern corner of the Piazza del Duomo, with its stupendous pink-domed cathedral newly dedicated by the pope in 1436. At the second intersection you cross the narrow Via de' Pandolfini and continue walking south towards the Piazza di San Firenze. Between those two points this part of the street was formerly called the Via dei Librai, 'the street of the booksellers', and it was here that Vespasiano worked. Since at least 1434 he had been apprentice and then assistant to Michele Guarducci, *cartolaio* at this address. A *cartolaio* was a stationer, selling materials for all aspects of writing and literary culture, including parchment and quills, and usually offering a service of bookbinding. The shop doubtless had a seductive smell of fresh leather, still characteristic of the markets in Florence. The Via dei Librai was conveniently placed for the premises of the notaries, further back up the same street. Some *cartolai* dealt also in manuscripts, either bought and sold second-hand or newly ordered on commission, like the *libraires* of medieval Paris who had supplied books to the Duc de Berry, and the young Vespasiano was responsible for this side of the business.

LEFT: Vespasiano da Bisticci (*c.*1422–98), author portrait in a manuscript of 1506, painted by the illuminator Attavante, who knew him.

The location of the shop can be guessed with reasonable certainty. Vespasiano later described it as being 'on the corner opposite the palace'. This refers to the Bargello, formerly the medieval palace of the *podesta*, still there on the left-hand side at the southern end of the Via del Proconsolo, beyond the junction with the Via Ghibellina, facing the Badia (abbey) of Florence across the road. The street frontage a few shops up preserves a stately and apparently fifteenth-century marble doorway with an arched top surmounted by a carved cornice showing swags of classical foliage around an open manuscript, and it is often supposed this motif would be appropriate for Vespasiano, eventually the most successful bookseller in Europe. It is now the entrance into a fashion shop called Bramada, at Via del Proconsolo no. 12. However, it is not strictly opposite the palace, and there were other booksellers too in the Via dei Librai. Vespasiano's description fits better for the site at no. 10, quite literally on the only corner opposite the palace, across the Via Ghibellina. It is now the Trattoria-Pizzeria Gusto Leo, and I have eaten both lunch and dinner there on different occasions.

You can sit today either indoors or on the edge of the street at tables under white umbrellas, shielded from traffic by a row of shrubs in plastic pots. Inside there are beams on the high ceiling and traces of blocked-up arches around the walls. The outlook has not changed much in almost 600 years, and there are still more pedestrians than vehicles (and even a few of those are horse-drawn), in the colours and costumes of many nationalities, as they were in the *quattrocento*, jostling and chatting and looking into shop windows as they idle past. It is not difficult to tell the well-dressed big spenders from the casual tourists. Vespasiano clearly knew who was visiting Florence at any moment and he picked up the gossip and news of likely business, much probably espied from the shop front. We do not know his first words to William Gray, but we do have his meeting with János Pannonius, Hungarian poet, who first came to Italy in 1447. Vespasiano describes the encounter among the brief biographies he wrote of his famous friends, the *Vite di uomini illustri*:

> After his arrival at Florence with horses and servants, the first person he wished to address was myself, because through me he could have introductions to the learned men of the city. He wore a purple mantle and was a distinguished figure, and as soon as I saw him I said, 'Are you indeed the Hungarian? This is a most welcome moment. I feel that you must be,

> because of what I have heard of you, and I seem to know you already.' He then embraced me, and addressed me in the most gracious and apt words I have ever heard, saying that I had guessed rightly.

William Gray too appears among Vespasiano's short biographies. On their first meeting they made conversation about the journey down from Cologne. Gray had worried that his wealthy appearance would make him the target for robbers on the road, and so he had pretended to be ill and summoned a doctor to visit his lodgings on several successive days; during this charade Gray and his companion slipped away disguised as Irish pilgrims. 'He told me about this adventure', Vespasiano reported. His Englishness and evident manner led to a misunderstanding, for Vespasiano was convinced that William Gray was closely related to King Henry VI. It can happen. Many times abroad I have encountered variants of the familiar refrain, especially in republics, as Florence then was, 'So you are from England: do you know the Queen?' and the mistaken assumption that all Englishmen are intimates in Buckingham Palace.

William Gray (*c.*1414–78) was undeniably well-connected, however, and he had money. Despite his own account, he probably travelled like Pannonius with a household of servants. He was the third and last son of Sir Thomas Gray, of Heaton Castle in Northumberland, beheaded for plotting against Henry V in 1415, and his mother was one of the twenty-three children of Ralph Neville, first Earl of Westmorland, and his successive wives. Gray was therefore a nephew of Cecily Neville, his mother's half-sister, who eventually married Richard of York and became the mother of Edward IV and Richard III; but their reigns were still long into the future when William Gray arrived in Italy.

The 1440s were an exciting time for books in Florence, as Gray would have known before his visit. The beginnings of the passion for manuscripts in the Italian Renaissance can be traced to Florentine writers there in the fourteenth century, such as Petrarch and Boccaccio, and to their convert Coluccio Salutati (1331–1406), chancellor of Florence and a zealous collector, and through him to his younger circle of enthusiasts, including Niccolò Niccoli (*c.*1364–1437) and Poggio Bracciolini (1380–1459). Vespasiano knew both these men, and his biographies of them are a valuable source of personal information. He says admiringly of Niccoli that he collected a library without regard to cost and once sold several farms to spend the proceeds on books; and that Poggio had

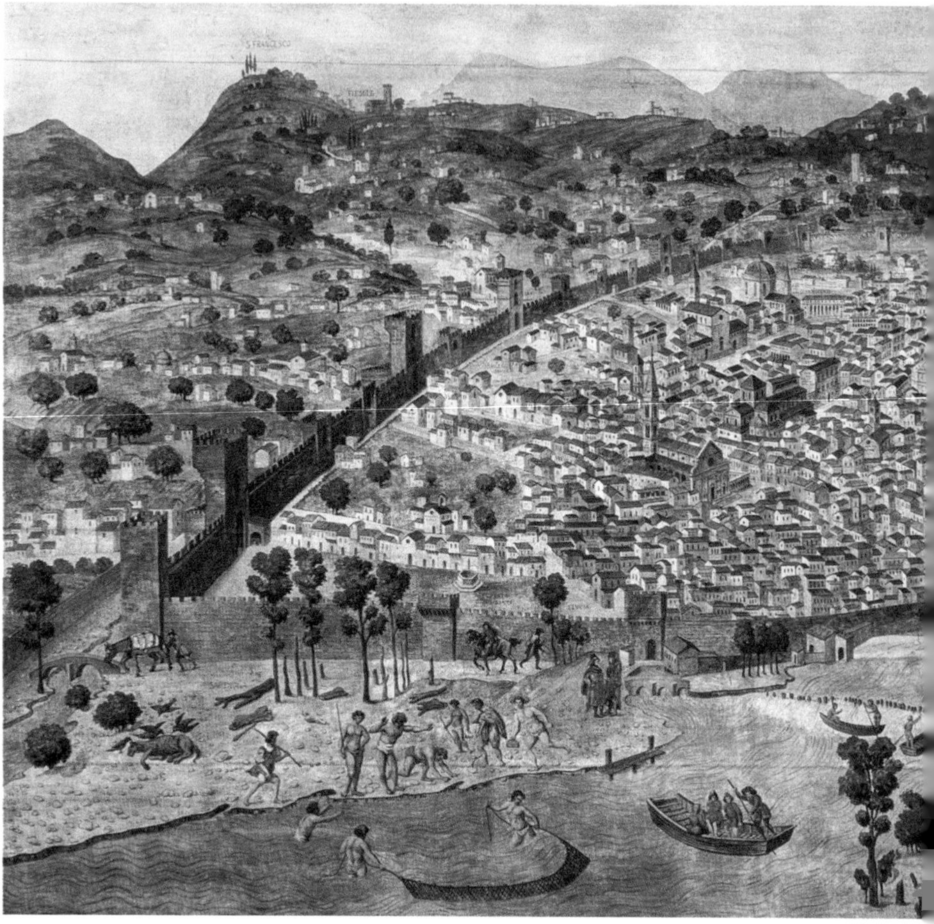

copied manuscripts 'in ancient script' to finance his own purchases. The fraternity of Florentine humanists sought out and carried home lost classical texts from overlooked libraries across Europe, and they re-created what they thought was a suitably antique style of rounded humanistic minuscule script, which we still call 'roman' type when it is used in print, decorated with initials entwined with white vine stems, like the foliage of ancient marble carving. Their enthusiasm was limitless and infectious. Here was a manuscripts club, if ever one existed, dizzy with the joy of finding, collecting and creating books. Vespasiano had the acumen to capture the thrill of the moment and to turn it into a business.

ABOVE: The 'Carta della Catena' in the Palazzo Vecchio in Florence, *c.*1471, showing the city as known to Vespasiano.

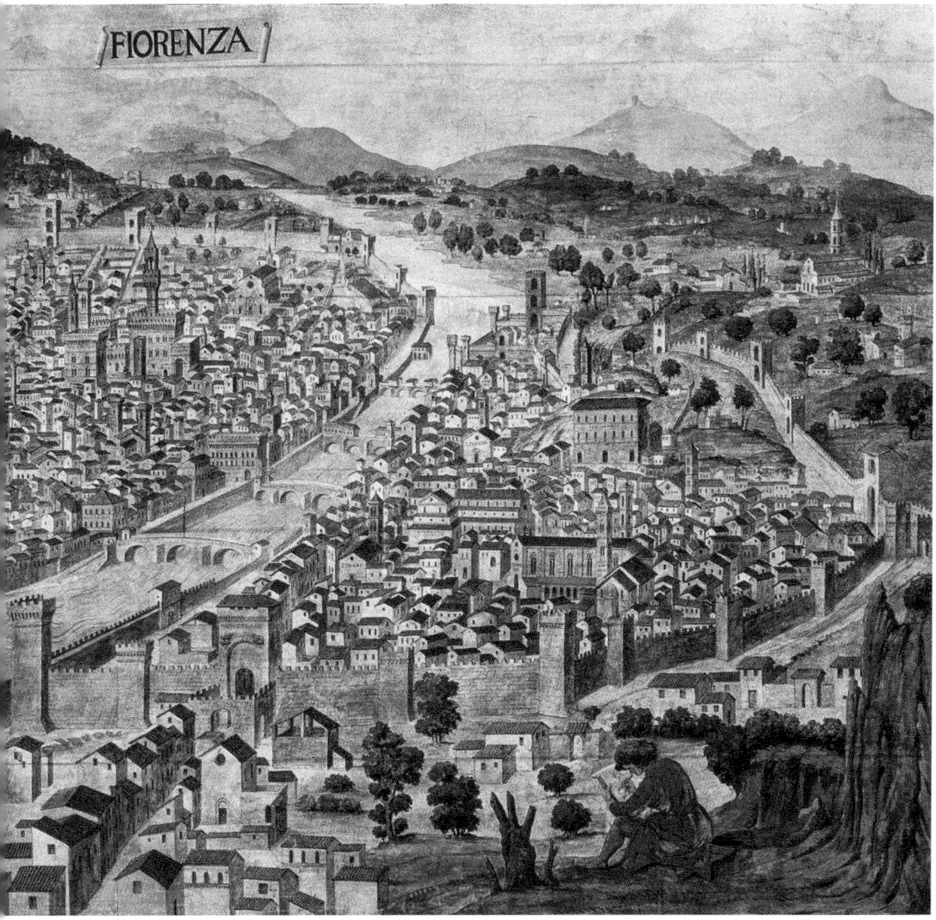

Gray was already a book buyer and he had commissioned manuscripts in Oxford and Germany. He eventually bequeathed his collection to Balliol College, where much of it survives. It includes several volumes dated 1444, when Gray had still been in Cologne, mostly theological, such as commentaries on texts of the New Testament and on the *Sentences* of Peter Lombard, written on paper in Germanic gothic hands with initials coloured with wash in green and violet. They were mostly traditional and rather dull. Vespasiano must have charmed his visitor to Florence with visions of something entirely different and more fashionable, and he probably showed him sample manuscripts too. The account of the reception of János Pannonius, quoted above, continues by saying that Vespasiano gave him lunch and that afterwards Pannonius took a volume of Plotinus from the shelves, retired into the bookshop's study and read quietly for three hours without raising his eyes, before evidently leaving a commission for a copy.

Vespasiano did not make books himself or employ scribes on the premises. He was simply the agent. He would locate suitable manuscripts of texts to be copied and would introduce clients to approved freelance scribes, who then worked at home or in whatever library owned the exemplar. He probably supplied the parchment and other materials needed. He would keep watch on the progress, check the unbound pages as they came back and arrange for the insertion of any last-minute additions and illuminated initials where appropriate. He probably had the finished books bound in the shop and would convey them to the client or have them sent, together with his invoice. Vespasiano belonged to the commercial world of Renaissance Florence, a city dominated by the banking and brokerage of the Medici family. Like them, he made money as an intermediary and a facilitator.

Vespasiano says of William Gray, 'He ordered many books, which were transcribed for him, and then left for Padua to carry out his studies in the humanities.' One of the first of these commissions must have been his five-volume set of the works of Cicero, which I have looked at in Oxford, where they are all part of Balliol College MS 248. The manuscripts and archives of the college have now been moved out of the main site of Balliol into the former parish church of St Cross, closed for religious use in 2008, about ten minutes' walk away. You go in through a little iron gate off the street and ring the buzzer to the right of an ancient gothic door. It opens directly into the former nave, now shelved as a reading-room. The building is mostly medieval although considerably restored in the nineteenth century. It is very far removed from Florence and the Via dei Librai, but there is a certain fulfilment of the Renaissance to find oneself studying humanistic manuscripts of a classical author in a setting which represents the overtaking of medieval gothic religion by secular learning from Antiquity.

The first striking thing about Gray's Cicero manuscripts is that they are of very great size, even by the standards of the late Duc de Berry, up to 16 by 11 inches by about 5 inches thick, comprising altogether more than 3000 handwritten parchment pages. These are massive and weighty, and this can have been no quick commission. Out of curiosity, I had brought my kitchen scales. The first volume of the Cicero weighs 6.8 kg, or 15 lb; the other volumes are slightly smaller, averaging about 4.4 kg each, around 9½ lb. The whole set would therefore weigh about the same as (for example) a boy of seven or eight. These are not manuscripts to be read easily on the lap, like the Plotinus of Pannonius, and they presuppose eventual study at a substantial reading desk. That itself says something about Gray's plan for his collection and Vespasiano's eye to an institutional market.

Two of the five volumes of Gray's Cicero were dated on completion by their scribes. Before the fifteenth century it was relatively unusual for scribes to sign manuscripts: with the Renaissance and the rediscovery of the individuality of people, it became much more common. Gray's manuscript containing Cicero's rhetorical texts is signed by its scribe, Antonio di Mario, describing himself as 'citizen and notary of Florence' (the notaries were neighbours of the booksellers, in the same street), dated 12 November 1445, ending with a cheery "Valeas", 'go well' or 'goodbye', with a great upwards flourish. He was a prolific scribe, who often worked for Vespasiano. He was writing manuscripts by 1417, was still active in 1456 and probably died in December 1461. Volume II of the Cicero set is signed and dated at the end by the scribe Gherardo del Ciriagio on 30 September 1447. He finishes with the common but charming Renaissance wish "lege feliciter", 'read happily'. Note the date. A check against the calendar for 1447 reveals that this was a Sunday. It is almost inconceivable that a monastic scribe would be working on a Sunday, but Gherardo was also a Florentine notary in his day job, and he was using his weekend to moonlight for Vespasiano. His documented manuscripts extend from earlier in 1447 until shortly before his death in 1472. In two manuscripts he actually states that he worked for Vespasiano, and his name appears as a witness to a land transaction for Vespasiano's brother Jacopo drawn up in the bookshop in 1470. The third volume of Gray's set of Cicero, containing the Epistles, is unsigned, but the script is clearly recognizable as the work of Domenico Cassio of *Narnia* (Narni in Umbria, no transwardrobe kingdom). He, too, often made books for Vespasiano, including several which explicitly record the fact. One manuscript attributable to him is now in Auckland in New Zealand, the gift of Sir George Grey, no relation, and I have known it most of my life.

One might think that worthy Cicero was an unexciting author for a bestseller, but he was an idol to the first generation of Italian Renaissance book collectors. His numerous texts were avidly sought by Boccaccio and other early humanists. He represented the Florentine ideal of a statesman

inani gloria. fluxisque uite presentis commodis. Hec audiens xpianus
& uera esse constanter tenens: que a iudeo dicebantur: imperatori quidem
piissimo iustiniano huiusmodi rem non indicauit: ne zelo fidei maxi
mus imperator incitatus: effusionem sanguinis frustra moliretur: abso
effectu eius operis quod intendebat. Plurimis tamen amicis & cognitis
negotium istud manifestauit. quod nos ex his qui a predicto philippo argentario id
se percepisse asserebant: audientes: curam non minimam adhibuimus
nosse cupientes: an ueram iudeus ille rationem huiusmodi inscriptioni
attulisset. Inuenimus autem iosephum historicum uetem hebreorum
cuius meminit eusebius pamphili in historia eclesiastica: in suis libris
quos de captiuitate iudaica conscripsit: aperte asserentem quod iesus cum
sacerdotibus in templo sacrificabat. Hoc igitur inuenientes dixisse io
sephum: uirum apostolorum temporibus proximum: etiam ex diuinis li
teris auctoritatem huius rei inquirere studuimus: inuenimusque in
euangelio secundum lucam. quod ingressus est iesus in synagogam iudeorum
datusque est illi liber ut legeret. & legit isaiam prophetam dicentem.
Spiritus domini super me: ideo unxit me: euangelizare pauperibus
misit me. Reputans igitur: quod nisi ordinem aliquem sacerdotalem
habuisset apud iudeos: xps iesus: nunquam illi traditus fuisset in syna
goga liber ad legendum in aures populi: neque rursus apud nos xpianos
cuiquam licet in eclesia legere libros scripture sacre: nisi ex clero
sit. & ex his que a iosepho conscripta sunt: & ex eis que ab euangelista
luca tradita sunt agnouimus: theodorum iudeum huiusmodi hi
storiam memorato philippo non abs se confictam enarrasse: sed uerissi
me ueluti amico fideli & carissimo: mysterium quod apud iudeos
occultum seruabatur: aperuisse.

A M E N.

ANTONIVS MARII FILIVS FLORENTINVS CIVIS ATQ NOTARIVS TRASCRIPSI FLORENTIAE AB ORIGINALIBVS EXEMPLARIBVS III IDVS IVNII M CCCC XLVIII. QVO TEMPORE NOSTRA R. PVBLICA INIQVITER ET INIVSTE AB INMANISSIMO REGE ARAGONVM UEXABATVR.

VALEAS MI SUAVISSIME GHVIGLELME FELICITER.

and articulate scholar of Greek philosophy, who devoted his life to public service. Cicero's collected works are exactly the kind of acquisition Vespasiano might have recommended as a first classical purchase for a buyer newly arrived in Florence from northern Europe. Some components of the corpus were quite recent rediscoveries. The long-lost personal letters of Cicero, the *Epistolae ad familiares*, had been lately found in an early ninth-century manuscript in Vercelli recovered on an expedition instigated by Coluccio Salutati, and all Florentine copies derive from it, including this. Of course, these are transcripts, as all manuscripts are, but reading private letters in handwriting brings an intimacy to Cicero's correspondence which seeing them in print does not.

Gray's set too includes Cicero's *De oratore* and *Brutus* among the rhetorical works. These were texts which had been located in Lodi, between Milan and Piacenza, as recently as 1421. Vespasiano describes the discovery in his life of Niccolò Niccoli, who probably told him about it first hand: 'The book was found in a chest in a very old church; this chest had not been opened for a long time, and they found the book, a very ancient example, while searching for evidence concerning certain ancient rights.' The original had gone missing by 1428 but early transcripts survive, including one in Niccoli's own hand, now in the Vatican Library. The excitement of the humanists is easy to imagine.

Volume I of Gray's set comprises Cicero's speeches, including the *Pro Murena* (his defence of a consul charged with electoral bribery), which descends from a manuscript perhaps of the eighth century or earlier found at Cluny Abbey and brought back to Florence by Poggio in 1415. It was quickly duplicated by the manuscripts club (during the course of which the original also vanished). Gray's copy allows spaces for passages of the text which had been missing in that precious exemplar, such as one where the scribe explains in a marginal note, 'In the oldest manuscript there was nothing further, except the words given here', which is indeed still true, for the text of the *Pro Murena* is defective at this point (it is 43:72), even today. The fact that the scribe left a gap, so that the lost words of text could be supplied as soon as they might be rediscovered, conveys vividly that this is a manuscript from a moment when ancient

LEFT: Colophon by the scribe Antonio di Mario, 'citizen and notary of Florence', recording that he finished copying this text in Florence from early exemplars for 'my dear William' (William Gray) on 12 June 1448.

copies were indeed coming to light. William Gray or other early readers of these volumes would receive a sense of textual transmission which was new and still ongoing. Bliss was it in that dawn to be alive. This thrill of rediscovery and publication of lost texts would have been unimaginable to the Duc de Berry, and it is almost as exhilarating to experience it at a library table in the former church of St Cross as it must have been to Gray stopping for the first time in the Via del Librai in the 1440s.

It would have been Vespasiano's task to arrange requisite exemplars. In the instance of the set of Cicero, they may have been several different manuscripts, if only because at least three scribes needed access to them at once. Some marginal notes, especially in volume I, offer variant readings from different manuscripts, preceded by the letters 'Al.', for *Aliter*, or 'alternatively'. A letter from Vespasiano to a French client, Jean Jouffroy, in 1461 says that obtaining sufficient exemplars for a full set of Jerome's biblical commentaries had been achieved only with great difficulty. Vespasiano had a reputation for being able to locate and borrow suitable texts. In 1446 an abbot in Arezzo seeking an exemplar for the transcription of the text of Pliny decided to consult Vespasiano, 'who is the best finder of such things'. In 1454 a friend in Rome needed exemplars for manuscripts of Orosius and Euclid, and so he wrote to Vespasiano in Florence. It was a matter of his experience but also his charm and persuasion with manuscripts' owners.

Once the texts had been copied, the fresh pages would be brought to Vespasiano in the bookshop to be checked, and any final additions could be inserted. For example, the scribe Domenico Cassio could not write Greek. When he encountered Greek words as he was copying Gray's manuscript of Cicero's letters, he left spaces blank with a key letter 'g' in the margin, a coded signal to Vespasiano, who then had the words inserted by a known scribe in Florence who may have been Greek himself, since he also did work for Cardinal Bessarion (who came to Florence from Greece in 1439). Even more personal involvement occurs in the first volume of the speeches in the set of Cicero at Balliol. The scribe there had omitted the headings at the start of each text (perhaps they were not in the exemplar) and the manuscript now has the proofreader's tiny guidewords in the margins to indicate what these should be. Such marks would usually be erased when the headings were inserted, but somehow they survived. Comparison with known autographs in the Archivio di Stato in Florence and elsewhere shows that these minute guidewords are in Vespasiano da Bisticci's own handwriting. Almost a thousand miles from Florence and nearly six centuries later, we are suddenly very close to the man himself.

Finally, the manuscripts had to be decorated. This was not the task of the scribes, who might indicate a required initial by use of a tiny and erasable guide letter, but of professional manuscript artists in Florence, subcontracted in by Vespasiano. He commonly employed Filippo di Matteo Torelli (*c.*1408–68), whom he calls 'Pipo' in his correspondence (an endearing intimacy from the *quattrocento*), and, to judge from the style, Torelli was the artist used for Gray's manuscripts. Illumination might take a few extra weeks. Classical texts would require elegant initials but not large pictures. There are two letters from Vespasiano to Piero de' Medici in 1458: one on 19 April reports that the copying of a manuscript of Livy was complete, and the other on 19 May says that its illumination was now finished exactly a month later, "molto bene e richamente". Gray's set of Cicero has very fine illuminated initials in sparkling gold entwined with white vine stems on grounds filled with bright colour and dotted in white. Unfortunately, their graceful beauty was an irresistible temptation to scrapbook collectors in later times of barbarism in Oxford, and many have now been crudely snipped out.

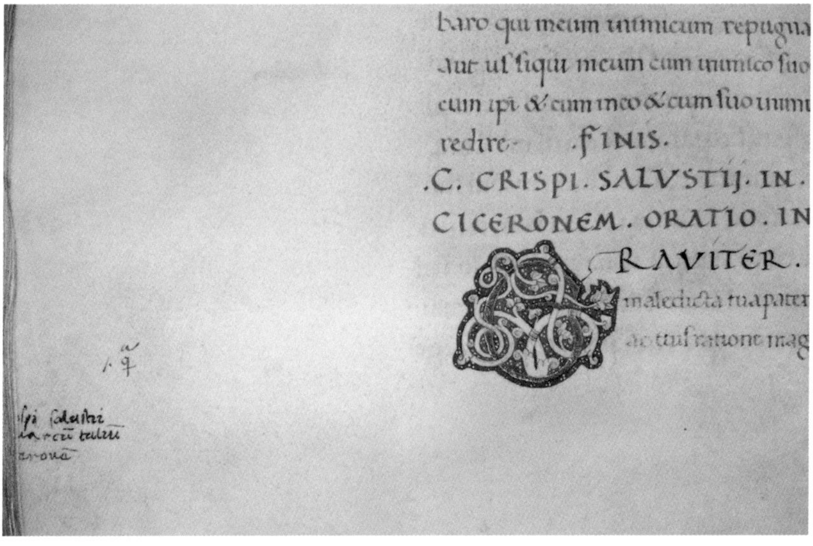

Guidewords in the handwriting of Vespasiano (lower left) in William Gray's manuscript of the Orations of Cicero, Florence, late 1440s.

Only the volume dated 1445 retains any substantial part of its original elaborate border by Torelli on the opening page. It includes exotic birds in the foliage and two chubby putti blowing golden trumpets. They may allude to the epigram quoted here in capitals in black and red at the end of the *De inventione*, the first text, to the effect that Cicero's works resemble battle trumpets sounded to the people of Latium. If so, it was probably Vespasiano's idea. Nothing was too good for a client related to the king of England.

Cicero was not the only author ordered by Gray from Vespasiano. Others included Sallust, Quintilian, Virgil and Pliny, all now mostly in the possession of Balliol College. The Pliny was copied partly by Domenico Cassio again, together with another scribe, Piero Strozzi (1416–*c.*1492), who was a parish priest in Ripoli, just to the south-east of Florence. Vespasiano knew his father, Benedetto Strozzi, and wrote his biography, mentioning the son as 'the most beautiful scribe of his day and the most accurate'. The work on Cicero must have brought the scribe, Antonio di Mario, into a personal relationship with William Gray. He was afterwards employed to write two further volumes for him, including theological works of Saint John Chrysostom, the archbishop of Constantinople who died in 407, a Greek contemporary of Saints Ambrose and Augustine. Vespasiano recommended him to clients, and several times quoted Thomas Aquinas as saying he would rather have a book by John Chrysostom than the city of Paris. (This was probably his standard line in the bookshop.) The Latin translation used was that of Ambrogio Traversari (1386–1439), abbot of Santa Maria degli Angeli in Florence. One volume for Gray was finished by Antonio di Mario in mid-August 1447, with the happy wish, 'Go well, o reader', but the other, on 12 June 1448, is addressed personally, "Valeas mi suavissime Ghuiglelme feliciter", 'Goodbye and good luck, my dearest William.' The scribe and the client are now on first-name terms, and the unofficial manuscripts club of Florence has opened up to include William Gray.

All this copying would have taken some time, and before the whole commission was completed Gray had long left Florence – moving on to Padua and then Ferrara and finally to Rome. These books were too heavy to slip into hand luggage. There survive two letters written in Latin on behalf of Vespasiano by the humanist and author Donato Acciaiuoli (1428–78) addressed to Gray in Rome. Acciaiuoli was a good friend of and a better classicist than Vespasiano, who expressed embarrassment at his limited skill in writing Latin. Gray probably did not speak much Italian and Vespasiano certainly no English (hence perhaps the confusion over Henry VI). Latin would have been the common language for many European humanists. The first letter is dated from Florence on 30 December 1448. It says that they have been working unstintingly on various commissions for Gray, including copying works of Tertullian, Athanasius and Gregory of Nazianzus, that only the finishing touches are needed for a manuscript of Diogenes Laertius, and that they now await instructions on copying Plutarch's *Lives* and other books. A year later Acciaiuoli writes to Nicholas Saxton (one of Gray's travelling companions, also from Balliol), reporting on behalf of Vespasiano that Gray's order is now ready to be sent to Rome and asking how Gray would like the manuscripts to be delivered, whether through the Medici bank or by other means. It is striking to witness an apparent mere tradesman of the Via dei Librai in such comfortable partnership with the noble families of Florence, the Acciaiuoli and the Medici, and on terms of friendship with many of the literary figures of the Renaissance.

Vespasiano da Bisticci was born in late 1422 or possibly in the early months of 1423. His father was Filippo da Bisticci (d. 1426), a wool merchant, son of Leonardo di Francesco. Filippo married Mattea di Piero Balducci (*c.*1394–1467), and Vespasiano was the fourth of their six children. His eldest brother, Jacopo, worked initially for a goldsmith before becoming a successful medical doctor. As a boy, Vespasiano considered the priesthood, a detail he mentions in his biography of Cardinal Cesarini, but rejected it after two weeks' careful thought. He never married, and quite often in the lives of his contemporaries he writes admiringly of the blessings of a chaste life. We know what he looked like in maturity from the author portrait in a manuscript of his life of Gianozzo Manetti, illuminated in 1506 by the artist Attavante degli Attavanti (1452–1520/25), who had worked for Vespasiano in the 1470s. It shows a curly-headed man with a straight but large nose and an underslung mouth and receding chin, and he has a wrinkled forehead as if listening attentively, gazing forwards. By February 1434, when hardly into his teens, Vespasiano was already employed in the shop of the stationer Michele di Giovanni Guarducci. In all likelihood, the papal councils in Florence in 1434–6 and 1439–43 opened Vespasiano's eyes to an untapped market among visiting courtiers, clergy and politicians with both time and money on their hands. (The shopkeepers in the Via del Proconsolo today still know how to sell luxury goods to tourists in holiday mood.) Guarducci was probably more interested in bookbinding and stationery than in supplying new manuscripts, and he wisely left this speculative part of the business entirely to his precocious assistant.

Vespasiano's first recorded sale of a manuscript was in 1442, when he was about twenty. His attention to detail, seen in his handwritten corrections to Gray's manuscripts at Balliol, doubtless endeared him to customers. He was also, quite clearly, a thoroughly likeable young man, with an inquiring mind, a love of an interesting story, and a good memory. He would have been easy to meet. His short biographies of his contemporaries, the *Vite di uomini illustri*, include countless snippets of conversational exchanges when Vespasiano had asked questions and elicited confidences. The narratives sparkle with the chatter of the street and the wine bar. Even quite grand dignitaries must have been flattered by Vespasiano's attentiveness and they enjoyed his company. He was probably also rather a gossip. The aristocratic Acciaiuoli brothers, Donato and Piero, knew him well and often invited him to their country villa in the Val di Pesa. A letter addressed to Vespasiano in 1449 tells of a conversation they once held there, when Vespasiano and others of the house party had engagingly discussed whether Moses had lived before Homer or the other way round.

Early in his life, Vespasiano had come to the notice of Cosimo de' Medici (1389–1464), 'the elder', progenitor of the dynasty of Medici bankers and princes who dominated Florentine politics for centuries. Patronage by the Medici became a major factor in Vespasiano's career. His biography of Cosimo is among the longest and most intimate he wrote. It opens by describing the banker's credentials as a scholar, 'well versed in Latin letters, both sacred and secular'. Vespasiano tells that, for all his vast wealth and social status, Cosimo de' Medici was never happier than in the company of the manuscript enthusiasts and men of letters, such as Niccolò Niccoli and Poggio Bracciolini, and how he sought their society and companionship. He bankrolled their researches and they delighted in including him in their fellowship. One of them must

RIGHT: Manuscript of Pliny, doubtless the copy made through the agency of Vespasiano for Pietro de' Medici in 1458, with the Medici arms, illuminated by Francesco d'Antonio del Chierico.

INCIPIT PREFATIO PLINII VERONENSIS AD TITUM AUGUSTUM IMPERATOREM I LIBROS NATURALIS HISTORIE

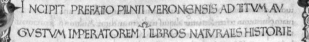

LIBROS NATURALIS HYSTORIE NOVI CUM
CAMENIS QUIRITIUM TUORUM OPUS NATU
apud me proxima fetura licentiore epistola nar
rare constitui tibi iocundissime imperator Sit
enim hec tui prefatio uerissima dum maxime co
senescit in patre. Namq. tu solebas putare aliquid
esse meas nugas. ut obicere molliam catullum
conterraneum meum agnoscis & hoc castrense uer
bum. Ille enim ut scis permutatis prioribus sylla
bis duriusculum se fecit q̄ uolebat existimari a uer
niolis tuis & famulis simul. ut hac mea petulantia
fiat quod proxime non fieri questus es in alia pro
caci epistola nostra ut in quedam acta exeant.
Sciant q. omnes q̄ ex equo tecum uiuat imperii
triumphalis & censorius tu sexies q. consul ac tri
bunitie potestatis particeps & qd̄ his nobilius fe
cisti dum illud patri pariter & equestri ordini
prestas prefectus pretorij eius. Omnia q. hec
rei p. & nobis quidem qualis in castrensi cōtu
bernio nequicq̄ inte mutauit fortune ampli
tudo in his nisi ut prodesse tantundem posses
ut uelles. Itaq. cum ceteris in uenerationem tui pateant omnia illa nobis ad colendū te
familiarius audacia sola superest. hanc igitur tibi inputabis & in nostra culpa tibi igno
sces. Perfricui faciem nec tamen profeci. quoniam alia uia occurris ingens & longius et
sūmoues ingentibus facibus fulgorat in nullo unq̄ uerius dicta uis eloquentie tribunitie
potestatis facundie. quanto tu ore patris laudes tonas. quanto fratris amas. quantus in poe
tica es. O magna fecunditas animi quemadmodum fratrem quoq. imitareris excogitasti.
Sed hec quis possit intrepidus extimare subiturus ingenij tui iudicium presertim laces
situm. Neq. enim similis est conditio publicantium & nominatim tibi dicantium. Tu
possim dicere quid ista legis imperator humili uulgo scripta sunt agricolarum opificum
turbe deniq. studiorum ociosis quid te iudicem facis. Cum hanc operam condicerem
non eras in hoc albo. Maiorem te sciebam q̄ ut descensurum huc putare. Preterea est quedā
publica etiam eruditorum reiectio. Utitur illa & M. Tullius extra omnem ingenij aliā
positus & qd̄ miremur per aduocatum defenditur nec indoctissimis manium persium hec
legere nolo iunium congium uolo. Qd̄ si hoc lucilius qui primus condidit stili nasum
quasi abusionem & uituperationem reputabit. Primus enim satyricum carmen conscripsit
in quo utiq. uituperatio uniuscuiusq. continetur. Nasum autem dixit qd̄ uituperatio
nis signum uel maxime naso declarandū dicendum q. est. Si aduocatum sibi putauit
cicero mutuandum. presertim cum de re p. scriberet quanto nos excusatius ab aliquo

have introduced him to the young Vespasiano. In a letter written in 1476 to Lorenzo the Magnificent, Cosimo's grandson, Vespasiano recalled that he had worked for the Medici family for thirty-five years. If precisely true, this would take it back to 1441, when Vespasiano was in his late teens. In the 1440s, Cosimo was sponsoring the new library of the Dominican convent of San Marco, still one of the marvels of Florence, north of the cathedral. As executor, Cosimo had acquired a large part of the private library of Niccolò Niccoli, following the collector's death in 1437. Vespasiano says that it had been Niccoli's own wish that his manuscripts should be available in a public collection, and many were made over to San Marco. Cosimo de' Medici sent Vespasiano on two trips with Fra Giuliano Lapaccini, prior of San Marco, to buy additional books, first to Siena and then to Lucca, where the Franciscan convent was disposing of its library. The name of Vespasiano appears in the abbey accounts as often as seventy-four times between 1446 and 1454 in connection with re-binding and often chaining books on the library shelves, all paid for by Cosimo. His access to the manuscripts at San Marco would have given Vespasiano invaluable information when he later sought exemplars for texts ordered by other clients.

Especially in the 1450s, both Cosimo's sons Piero (1416–69) and Giovanni (1421–63) were ordering many manuscripts for their own collections from Vespasiano. There are three letters from Vespasiano to Piero de' Medici in 1458, reporting progress on copying works of Livy, Pliny, Plutarch, Statius and others. The Livy and the Plutarch are probably identifiable with manuscripts now in the Biblioteca Laurenziana in Florence, both copied by Piero Strozzi, the scribe who had also been contracted by Vespasiano on the Cicero project for William Gray.

The greatest Medici commission of all came about in the early 1460s. Cosimo de' Medici was nearing the end of his life and around 1456 he had decided on a final benefaction to restore the ancient Badia at Fiesole, today effectively a suburb of Florence in the hills to the north-east of the city centre, transferred into the custody of Augustinian canons in 1439. From the Badia you can look down on the domes and towers of Florence far off to the left. Vespasiano says that Cosimo spent 7000 florins on new construction work (for comparison, the annual rent of Vespasiano's shop in the Via dei Librai was 15 florins a year), and then he worried that, if the Badia was to attract novices of sufficient merit, it would need a good library too. A special room was prepared with gilded beams and silver bars on the windows. Here is the story in Vespasiano's biography of Cosimo:

> One day when I was with him, he said, 'What plan can you suggest for the formation of this library?' I replied that if the books were to be bought [i. e. acquired second-hand], it would be impossible, for the reason that they could not be found. Then he went on, 'Then tell me what you would do in the matter.' I said it would be necessary to have the books transcribed, whereupon he wanted to know whether I would undertake the task. I said that I would, whereupon he replied that I might begin when I liked, that he left everything to me, and that, as for the money for daily costs, he would order Don Archangelo, the prior, to present the invoices at the bank, where they would be duly paid. He was anxious I should use all possible dispatch, and, after the library was begun, as there was no lack of money, I engaged forty-five scribes and completed 200 volumes in twenty-two months, taking as a model the library of Pope Nicholas, and following directions written by his own hand, which Pope Nicholas had given to Cosimo.
>
> First came the Bibles and concordances with commentaries ancient and modern. The first of the commentators was Origen, who showed the way to all his followers. He wrote in Greek, and a portion of his work *On the five books of Moses* was translated by Saint Jerome. There were the works of Saint Ignatius the martyr, who also wrote in Greek, and was a pupil of Saint John the Evangelist, most zealous for Christianity as a writer and as a preacher; those of Saint Basil of Cappadocia, a Greek; those of Saint Gregory of Nazianzus, of Gregory of Nyssa his brother, of Saint John Chrysostom, of Saint Athanasius of Alexandria, of Saint Ephraem the monk, of Giovanni Climaco, a Greek, and of all the Greek doctors which are translated into Latin; and after these came all the sacred works of the Latin doctors, beginning with Lactantius.

This is the happiest memory of Vespasiano's life: forty-five scribes, 200 manuscripts and an unlimited budget! The wish list of texts prepared by Pope Nicholas was the so-called *Canone bibliografico* drawn up under his pre-papal name of Tommaso Parentucelli (1398–1455) for Cosimo de' Medici when he had secured Niccolò Niccoli's manuscripts for San Marco and had wanted to broaden the scope to make the library there more suitable for religious use. In the 1430s Parentucelli

sit per se et proprie illa libertas que denominat arbitri
um. a qua dicitur arbitrium esse liberum non in ipsius arbitri
i. quoniam prior in natura libertas quam sit arbitrium quia ante
quam aliquis arbitratur in eo est libertas. Siquis dicat
quod arbitrium sumitur ibi pro potestate arbitrandi: pa
tet quod est verum non esse verum. probatur quia ipsa potestas arbitrandi est in ro
nalis et arbitrium aliquando in processu et illa non est in rationa
li. quoniam arbitrium non est in effectu si libertas hominis sit per
se et proprie. patet hoc esse falsum. probatur quod non essentialiter libertas ar
bitrii est in deo et in angelis. non sic ipsius domus. Et ideo est for
ma. libertas est forma. ergo libertas per se et proprie non est in ratione.
Sed dicatur ei in esse hoc erit per accidens. et non secundum eius propri
am interdici ab hoc dicendum: est quod denominat essentie per se et propri
e et libertas arbitrii et ius subiectum non excedit libertatem ar
bitrii. nec alia excedit quoniam libertas arbitrii est in omni
in quo est ratio. et convertitur. sed tamen libertas quando impedita est
a suo effectu ita quod non potest exequi suum effectum. ut in demo
ne. Est enim in eo libertas arbitrii sed nichil eius quoniam in
ipso est potestas conservandi rectitudinem voluntatis. tamen recti
tudinem iam non conservat. per hoc sine illuminationis pote
ns apertura est sicut oculus ceteris in tenebris potestate
[illegible] videndi. non tamen videt per lucis absentiam. Per premissa la
bem potest quod in brutis animalibus non est liberum arbitrium cum
ipsa rationis examinatione careant. est tamen in eis vis con
cupiscibilis et vis irascibilis qua expetunt eis expedienti
a vel que apparent esse expedientia vis irascibilis in eis
est qua respuunt ea que eis nociva vel que apparent sunt
nociva et per hoc vis appetitiva. qui est cum electione vel prie
spirituum nocivam que est cum fuga. videtur in eis esse
discretio inter expediens et nocivum. ita in eis libe
videtur esse arbitrium cum eis relinquatur unum
vel aliud eligere. ¶ Est experimento videtur idem lucet per
se pluribus ovis eligit suum agnum inter alios agnos
et prout quod discernere non unum ab alio consimile pater inter
iuvenes et apibus apes enim eligunt flores sibi competenti
ores et quos nocivos respuunt. ¶ Solo harum obiecti
onum patet plus quod superius dictum est in tractatu de viribus
anime sensibilis. autem enim estimativa est huiusmodi electio
in brutis animalibus autem ancillarum. bruta enim distinguunt
autem rem per accidentia rerum et non ordinemur aliquis tu
m laqueis in proprio diem animal brutum discernere unum
ab alio ut canes et simias. ¶ Est notabile autem quod liber
tas arbitrii est inter tres vires divisa. scilicet vis ira. vis
im. vis rationalis. vel quod liberum arbitrium sit in anima
secundum illas tres ita quod non tamen secundum aliquam illarum obiecto
concupiscibilis est appetitus boni vel apparentis boni. autem irascibilis
mali detestatio. autem rationalis. discretio vel iudicium. ¶ Ideo
hoc dictum est quod ad esse liberi arbitrii non exigitur vis concupi
scibilis. vel vis irascibilis. sed dicimus quod sufficit vis rationa
lis quoniam rationatur: cum in intellectu apprehendit ratione in
tellectus intellectum discernit et arbitratur. In homine au
tem est inchoatio tendens ad discretionem autem concupiscibilis. sit
quoniam aliquis homo appetit aliquid. vel autem irascibilis.
secundum quod homo aliquid respuit. sic aliquis homo aliquid
appetit non tamen illud eligere. Similiter autem aliquis aliquid
respuat velim irascibiliter non tenetur illud fugere nisi p
ius quanto ratione suam adhuc quod ipse appetit. et adhuc quod
ipse respuit. et sic arbitrium rationis. eligunt tunc ap
petendum vel fugiendum. quoniam ideo ut dicitur ars minus
proprius inpreit in concupiscibili. et in irascibili. nisi prius a

fuerit anima hominis. si enim secundum viam concupiscibilem vel
irascibilem tenetur homo aliquid exequi non ratione ar
bitrium suum venerit ad cognitionem: utrius quod illarum vir
Explicit iste liber. Sit scriptor crimine liber:
¶ Augustinus in vi. musice. Ea mentem et amare manu
festum est quorum fetamine sensus eius afficitur.
¶ Ab augustino. in vi. libro. musice. quod prudentia est affectio
anime vel motus quo intelligit eterna quibus inferiora
esse temporalia. et in se ipsa. et ab appetenda potius que superio
ra sunt. quoniam illa que inferiora sunt novit. ¶ In eodem
augustinus. temperantia est effectio qua sese anima opitu
lante deo et domino nostro ab amore inferioris pulchritu
dinis extrahit et debellas atque interficies adversus se mili
tantes consuetudines: suam ea victoria triumphaturam in se
met ipsa de passibus actus huius quibus in iuventibus et speculati
capientibus evolat ad suam stabilem ritem et firmamentum
domini si ne amisso rerum temporalium aut morte ullo eam
deterreat subsequitur tertia virtus que fortitudo dicitur:
¶ Augustinus in eodem fortitudo est affectio que nullas
ad necessitates mortem ne formidat. ¶ Augustinus
in eodem. iustitia est ordinatio anime qua nulli fuit
nisi soli deo. nulli coequari nisi purissimus animus. et
nulli dominari appetit natura bestialem atque corporis.
¶ Ab augustino post libertatem in eodem libro quod quoniam est in
in patria habemus. istas. iiii. feliciores virtutes. et eam
nulla sunt ibi adversa alios habebunt ibi usus. quam hec
dum sumus in via. ¶ Post augustino. hic eo
dem libro. quod prudentia est virtus iudicii unum boni auc et
sciendi. et in ipso. et summe tuo. in. lu. s. in. t. sci. te.
in lumine. scilicet in ipso accipiendo. qui sapientia dei est et lumine
totiens appellatur. hoc ergo dicimus et scientibus te
negari non potest ibi prudentia futura ibi non est. ¶ Augu
stinus in eodem. prudentia subiungit. et iustitiam. huius
qui. r. s. [illegible] colligitur quod iustitia est rectitudo cor
dis. ¶ Ab augustino. in eodem temperantia est virtu
stabilis et impassibilis. ut molestie pati potens erit et in celi
contemplatio. quod est prudentie et satisfacte quod est temperantie.
et impassibilitas. quod est fortitudinis et ordinatio anime quod
est iustitie. ¶ Augustinus in vi. libro. de musica. delectatio quasi pon
dus est anime. delectatio ergo ordinat animam. Ubi enim
erit thesaurus tuus ibi erit et cor tuum. Ubi delectatio.
ibi et thesaurus. ubi autem cor ibi beatitudo vel contra fideliumque
intelligere que non sunt in caritate:

himself had been one of the group of manuscript enthusiasts, including Poggio, who used to meet up for conversation every morning and evening at the bookshop 'on the corner opposite the palace' (that is how we know the address). These would have been the coolest times of day, for by midday the hot sun fills the Via del Proconsolo from the south. Vespasiano recalled that Parentucelli often arrived wearing a blue cloak. He became pope as Nicholas V in 1447 and later founded the Vatican Library. One of his own books which he gave the library still has a note that he had bought it from Vespasiano.

The prominence given to the Greek writers of the early Church reminds us that the Italian Renaissance was not entirely secular. Byzantine Christendom was as fascinating and as fresh to many of the humanists as the classical civilization of Roman Italy, and as worthy of recovery. Ecumenical reunion with the Orthodox Church was a principal aim of the Council of Florence from the late 1430s, and the fall of Constantinople in 1453 brought many Greek refugees and their manuscripts into Renaissance Italy. Contemporary translations of early Greek texts into Latin were as much revelations to Vespasiano's customers as the works of Cicero. The study of the Greek language was new and exciting to many. Some texts of Saint John Chrysostom were rendered into Latin by Ambrogio Traversari, as above, and many of those of Saints Basil and Gregory of Nyssa by George of Trebizond (1395–1486), a Greek who had come to Florence for the Council and stayed on as secretary to Nicholas V. Vespasiano includes both Traversari and George of Trebizond among his biographies. In addition to classical texts, William Gray had also bought Latin versions of many works by these early Greek theologians.

Most of the manuscripts made for the Badia still survive together, never having travelled more than a few miles. They were transferred down the hill to the Biblioteca Laurenziana in central Florence in 1778. We can envisage their original location from a library catalogue made soon after April 1465, which does indeed list almost precisely 200 volumes, some with multiple texts, a number tallying so closely to Vespasiano's recollection that presumably he knew the catalogue and may even have

LEFT: Manuscript from the library of Coluccio Salutati bought in Florence from his heirs through the agency of Vespasiano by Tommaso Parentucelli of Sarzana (later Pope Nicholas V), who gave it to the Vatican Library.

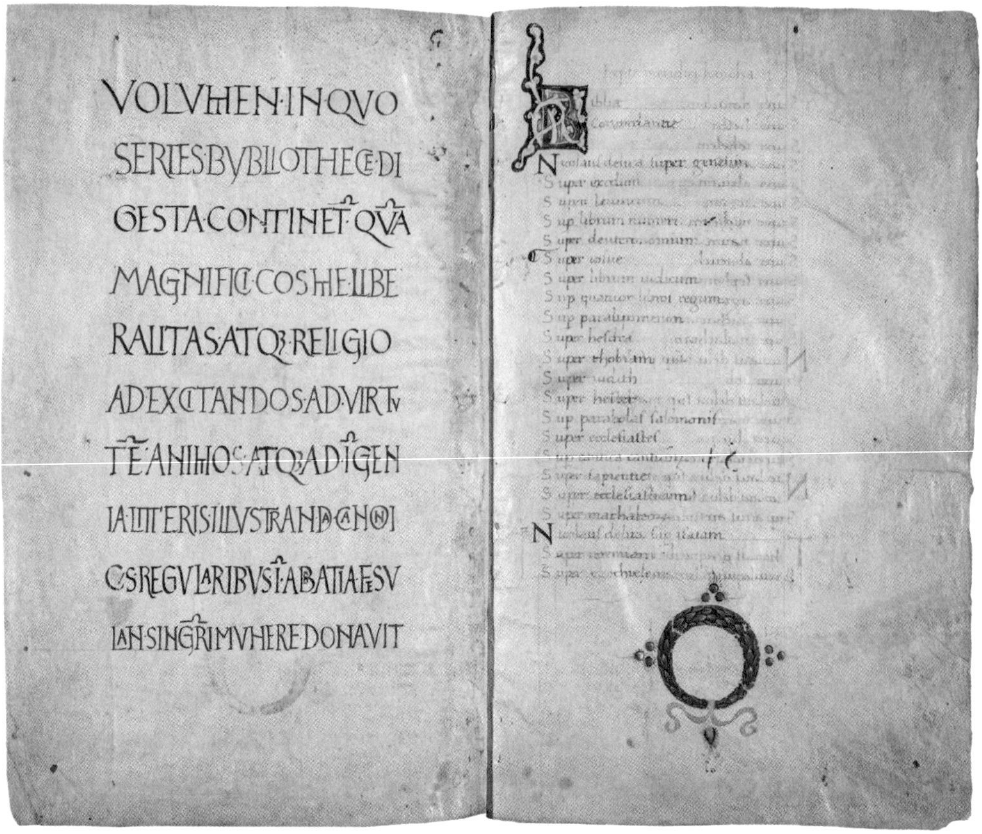

Catalogue of the library of the Badia in Fiesole endowed by Cosimo de' Medici, *c.*1465.

had a hand in making it. It is a very grand volume, no archival ledger, illuminated on parchment with white-vine initials and a blue and red title page rightly praising the liberality and piety of Cosimo de' Medici. It lists the books in two aisles of ten benches each, to which the volumes were attached by chains. The library probably looked something like the fifteenth-century Biblioteca Malatestiana still intact in Cesena, resembling the pews in a modern church. In the first row on the south side at the Badia were a Bible and commentaries by Nicholas de Lyra and others. In the second and third rows were the writers of the early Greek Church, as in Vespasiano's account, and a few other texts, including five by Saint Anselm, never forgotten. Rows 4–6 comprised the Church fathers of the Latin West, such as Ambrose, Jerome and Augustine, and then a series of miscellaneous theological texts of all periods in rows 7–8. The final two rows on that side comprised classical authors, beginning with Livy and Plutarch but especially comprehensive in Cicero and Seneca. The first three rows on the other side of the library were canon law. Most of the shelves behind were medieval scholastic theology, but the back row was different, principally grammar, dictionaries and a complete set of Virgil. Perhaps that was where schoolboys were to sit for instruction.

There are also archival accounts from the Badia for much of this period, including records of payment for manuscripts. In reality, not all of the 200 volumes on the benches were new books, and many must indeed have been acquired second-hand, some (but not necessarily all) bought through Vespasiano. Towards the end of the sixth bench on the south side, for example, were a twelfth-century manuscript of Augustine's *City of God* with annotations by Niccolò Niccoli, and an eleventh-century copy of Augustine on the Psalms once owned by Coluccio Salutati. They were perhaps overlooked remnants from those libraries brought out and dusted off from the back shelves in Vespasiano's bookshop, or were books back in circulation in Florence from the next generation of collectors. Nonetheless, there are almost a hundred newly made manuscripts from the Badia at Fiesole which can be matched exactly with dated entries in the abbey's accounts listing payment for books which Vespasiano "fece scrivere", 'caused to be written'. Prices vary but about 30 florins a volume is a reasonable average. There is a letter from Vespasiano to Cosimo de' Medici from late 1463 or early 1464 asking for his help in persuading the friars of San Marco to lend books for use as exemplars.

So far, the hands of some thirty-eight different scribes have been distinguished among the manuscripts made for the Badia, and so it sounds as though Vespasiano's memory of employing forty-five may be about right. The necessary speed was a logistical challenge. All the old stalwarts were brought in, including Gherardo del Ciriagio, Domenico Cassio of *Narnia*, Piero Strozzi and many others. An unexpected participant, who copied four extant manuscripts for the project, was a hermit, who lived in a cave in Fiesole, Fra Girolamo da Matelica. Vespasiano included him among his lives of authors, since Fra Girolamo had also written a book of his own on the solitary life. He describes him as a fine and educated scribe who had previously supported himself as a student in Paris by copying manuscripts. Fra Girolamo did not make formal contracts for employment, Vespasiano says, implying that other scribes did. By the marshalling of scribes even as unlikely as this, the deadline was met. Cosimo de' Medici settled the bookseller's invoices and died on 1 August 1464.

By now Vespasiano da Bisticci was at the height of his career and reputation. The *De politia literaria* of Angelo Decembrio (1415–*c.*1467) reports from Ferrara that in his time the finest books in Italy were obtainable from Florence: 'They say that there is one Vespasiano there', he wrote, 'an excellent bookseller, with expert knowledge of both books and scribes, to whom all of Italy and foreigners as well resort when they want to find elegant books for sale.' A letter sent from what is now Slovenia in 1469 ordering various classical texts described Vespasiano as 'the bookseller king of the world'. Real kings were now among his clients, not mere putative relatives of Henry VI, and the business had become very international. Vespasiano supplied manuscripts for Alfonso the Magnanimous (1396–1458), king of Naples and Aragon; Alfonso II (1448–95), duke of Calabria and briefly king of Naples; Louis XI (1423–83), king of France; probably Matthias Corvinus (1443–90), king of Hungary; Pope Pius II (Enea Silvio Piccolomini, 1405–64); Alessandro Sforza (1404–66), lord of Pesaro and brother of the duke of Milan; Cardinal Bessarion (1403–72), Greek patriarch and benefactor of Venice; János Vitéz (*c.*1402–72), archbishop of Esztergom in Hungary; Jean Jouffroy (*c.*1412–73), cardinal and abbot of Arras and then of Saint-Denis near Paris; Iñigo Lopez de Mendoza (1398–1458), marquis of Santillana in Spain; John Tiptoft (1427–70), Earl of Worcester, Lord High Constable of England; and many others. There is even a tenuous and entirely accidental link with the New World, through the three Vespucci brothers, scribes and collectors, one of whom (Nastagio) was the father of Amerigo Vespucci (1454–1512), who gave his name to America.

Vespasiano often knew his clients socially as well as professionally. His letters to Lorenzo the Magnificent are refreshingly informal, addressing him by his first name and signing himself simply 'Vespasiano'. Many of the more notable customers for manuscripts appear in Vespasiano's biographies, often with his own memories of their tastes and a shared passion for books. He recollected of Pope Nicholas V, 'He used to say that there were two things he would do, if he had money to spend, that is to say, buy books and build houses.' Archbishop Vitéz ordered manuscripts 'regardless of cost, provided they were fine and carefully revised'. Cardinal Giuliano Cesarini (1398–1444) did not like to make notes in other people's books and so bought his own. Vespasiano had even met Cardinal Branda da Castiglione (1350–1443), who was widely travelled and could have known the Duc de Berry: 'I remember how one evening . . . ', he began, recalling an occasion of half a century earlier when he brought a book to the aged cardinal propped up in bed, who had peered at the manuscript by candlelight, asking for the spectacles which he kept in a case in his bedroom. When Alfonso the Magnanimous thought he was dying, Vespasiano tells us, he lay reading a manuscript of the *Meditations* of Saint Anselm.

Books for the bedside had a market. So did books which could be taken on travels. Not everything was as massive and institutional as Gray's five-volume Cicero. My own publisher in London, Allen Lane, is said to have founded Penguin Books as a result of standing on Exeter railway station in 1934 without a decent book for the journey. That letter from Slovenia calling Vespasiano the 'bookseller king', cited above, was actually an order commissioning a Virgil and a Juvenal and Martial in one volume (all texts, incidentally, available in Penguin), in cursive script, really small, pocket-shaped, so that the book would be portable, "solacium itineris jocundumque vehicolum", 'a comfort for the journey and a pleasure in the carriage'. They might almost be Sir Allen's own words.

The length of time which manuscripts took to make is a recurrent refrain of these chapters. Vespasiano tells of Poggio that, when he had discovered a complete copy of Quintilian in Switzerland in 1416, he spent thirty-two days transcribing it: 'this I saw in the fairest manuscript'. The professional scribe Giovanmarco Cinico records in a large-format Pliny copied in 1465 that it took him 120 days. It has 635 leaves, which would be just over five leaves a day. If several scribes were involved simultaneously, as often happened, the overall time could be reduced. Some clients were impatient. The humanist Niccolò Perotti wrote from Bologna in 1454 about a manuscript of Homer ordered for Pope Nicholas V, urging and beseeching Vespasiano to get it finished and bound in the next eight days, when it was needed. A more patient client was John Tiptoft, Earl of Worcester. Vespasiano says of him:

> While certain books which his lordship desired were being transcribed, he tarried in Florence several days, and was minded to visit the whole city, alone and unattended. He would turn to the left hand, then to the right, and next to the left again and in this fashion he went into every part of it.

He was evidently the first recorded English tourist.

If a buyer did not have the leisure to wait in Florence until an order had been completed, the manuscripts would have to be sent. We have seen how William Gray's purchases were to be dispatched to Rome, perhaps through the messenger service of the Medici bank. Gray's compatriot Andrew Holes (or Hollis) had bought so many books from Vespasiano that they could not be sent by land and had to wait until a ship was sailing to England. A further difficulty might be extracting payment from a client who had already returned home. There is a rather delicate letter from Vespasiano on 19 January 1461 to Jean Jouffroy, by then back in Arras in northern France. Jouffroy had ordered more manuscripts, and Vespasiano was obliged to remind him that there were still two finished volumes which he had commissioned earlier and had not yet paid for, 'for which I implore your grace to settle the debt to me, so that I may continue to praise your grace as I have until now'.

One solution to the problem of delay was to have some copies of popular texts pre-prepared in advance for sale to customers visiting the shop. As suggested in the previous chapter, the Parisian *libraires* patronized by the Duc de Berry may sometimes have made manuscripts on speculation in the hope of tempting their client. Like all *cartolai*, Vespasiano would have had a shelf or two of second-hand books. These doubtless included some remnants of the libraries of Coluccio Salutati and Niccolò Niccoli, or items returned from San Marco or elsewhere as duplicates. By the later part of his working life, Vespasiano seems also to have had a small selection of new manuscripts for sale, responding to competition from printing (introduced into Italy probably in 1464), in which editions were available for immediate purchase. A feature of such manuscripts is that they often contain inscriptions attesting that they had been made for Vespasiano, rather like printers' colophons or labels on designer clothing, alerting customers as to where they could be bought. Some have illuminated borders with spaces originally left blank for the insertion of a buyer's arms. (If the purchaser had no arms, he could be flattered by the implication that he might.) About twenty such manuscripts are recorded, usually with notes on the flyleaf in some variant of "Vespasianus librarius librum hunc Florentie transcribendum curavit", 'Vespasiano the bookseller had this book transcribed in Florence.' The scribes involved in such undertakings include our old acquaintances Domenico Cassio and Gherardo del Ciriagio. The texts were the usual safe choices, especially Cicero but also Sallust, Saint John Chrysostom and others. Buyers or early owners of such pre-prepared manuscripts generally came from outside Florence, including John Tiptoft and Jean

Jouffroy (twice, on behalf of Louis XI). Perhaps for Jouffroy, Vespasiano had now learned to prefer cash up front.

There is even a hint, hard to document, that Vespasiano sometimes had volumes made ready in advance to be sent out on consignment to other places in Italy where there might be customers. There is a manuscript in Brescia containing an erased note that Vespasiano had had it made in Florence; it has the inserted arms of Juan Margarit y Pau (*c.* 1424–84), bishop of Girona and cardinal, with the information that he bought it in Venice 'from a certain bookseller' for four Venetian gold ducats. There is also a manuscript now in Valencia with a note dated in Mantua on 11 October 1459 saying that it was purchased from Vespasiano, bookseller of Florence, for 7 papal ducats. It could have been sent for possible sale in Mantua during the residence of the papal court there between 27 May 1459 and 20 January 1460, attending the Congress of Mantua. Possibly Vespasiano sometimes travelled himself, rather as someone from the workshop of Gutenberg had attended the book fair in Frankfurt in 1455 to solicit buyers for their printed Bible. In about 1457 Vespasiano sent some books on consignment to an agent in Naples, including four manuscripts of Cicero, as we know from a lawsuit of 1471 in which he was still trying to get paid fourteen years later.

The old *cartolaio* Michele Guarducci had died in February 1452 and Vespasiano had become proprietor of the bookshop in the Via dei Librai, technically still co-owned with Guarducci's heirs. In February 1458 he bought his own house. We even have a picture of it, by an illuminator who had probably visited him there. There is in Paris a princely manuscript of the *Cosmography* of Ptolemy in the Latin translation of Jacopo Angeli da Scarperia made around 1470 for Vespasiano's client Alfonso II, then duke of Calabria. It includes a spectacular full-page illustrated map of Florence, viewed from the north facing south. All the principal public buildings are shown as little coloured vignettes with their names. Just across the Arno about two thirds of the way up the map is a long house with a gently sloping red tiled roof and three tall round-arched windows looking out directly over the river. It is captioned in red, "Domus vespasiani", 'Vespasiano's house'. Additionally, up in the far left-hand corner of the map is an area behind some houses between the church of San Giorgio and the medieval city wall, similarly marked in red "Orti vespasiani", 'the gardens of Vespasiano'. The house is in the Via de' Bardi, which you reach by crossing the Ponte Vecchio and turning immediately

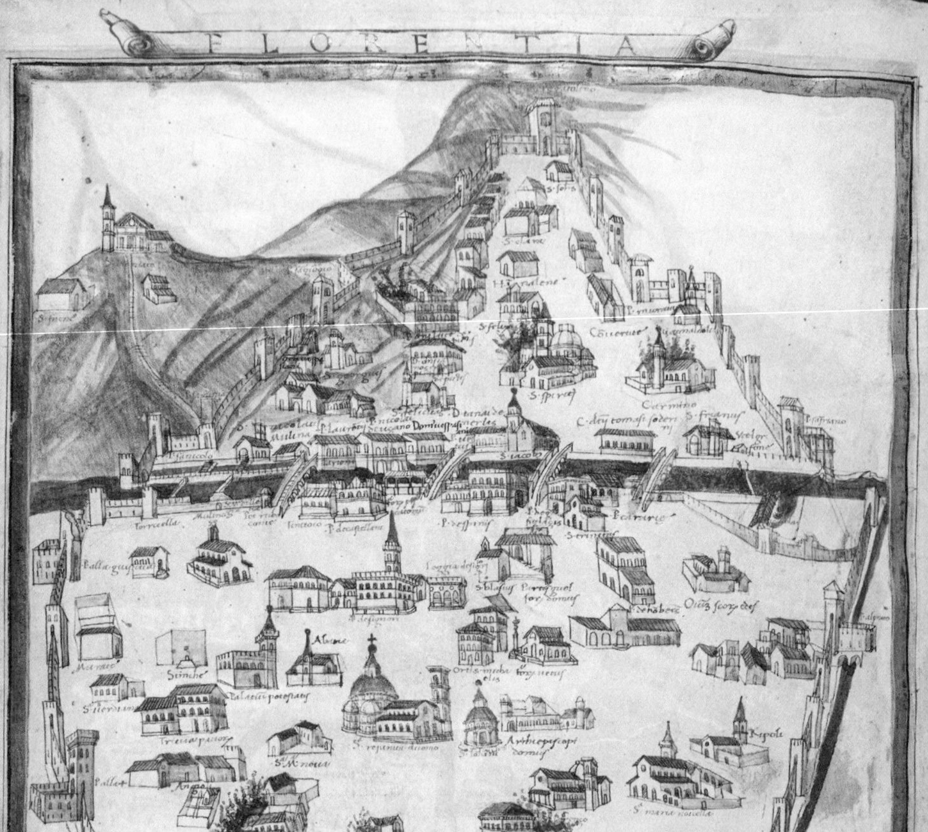
FLORENTIA
Carmino
Stinche
S. Antonius

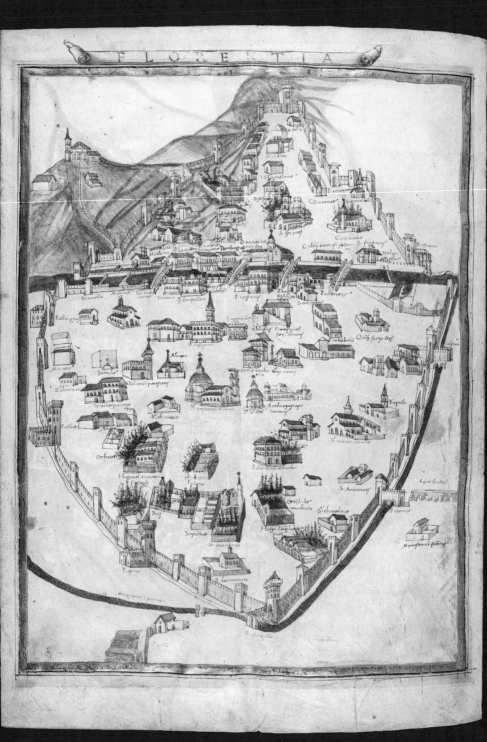

left. The street now begins with modern buildings which block off the river, but Vespasiano's outlook must have been about what you see now from the Golden View Ristorante. He bought the house for 500 florins from Lorenzo d'Illarione de' Bardi, described as being in the parish of Santa Maria sopr'Arno. It is likely that he lived there with his mother, who died in 1467. In 1478 he is recorded as occupying it with his brother Leonardo and with his sister-in-law, Andrea Gotteschi, widow of his late brother Jacopo, who died in 1468. Jacopo, the doctor, had owned several properties nearby and one in the parish of San Giorgio – that sounds like Vespasiano's garden. If it was known to the artist of the map, it must have featured in some way in Vespasiano's life or conversation. It is a very steep climb from the far end of the Via de' Bardi up to the church of San Giorgio alla Costa, and the area between there and the medieval wall is still mostly cultivated parkland, with a vista across Florence and a fresh breeze which must have been welcome in the high summer. The smell of a medieval city is something we forget in our age of hygiene and drains. In his biography, Vespasiano recalls that Cosimo de' Medici had himself enjoyed gardening and pruning his own vines. William Gray also became a gardener, and his house in London later became famous for its home-grown strawberries. From the site of Vespasiano's garden back to the Via de' Bardi is about a ten-minute walk downhill, and from there less than ten minutes across the river and past the Palazzo Vecchio to the shop in the Via dei Librai.

Vespasiano was by no means the only bookseller in Florence. The best-known among the others was Zanobi di Mariano (1415–95), who also supplied some books to the Badia in Fiesole, but there were several in his street. Each probably had specialities. Vespasiano largely cornered the upper end of the market for humanistic books, classical and Renaissance, and the standard texts of medieval intellectual history. He did not generally deal in liturgy, which was a huge business in *quattrocento* Italy. Churches and religious houses, not least in Florence, spent enormous sums on great manuscript choir books, usually with illumination by the finest artists, and they commissioned lavish Missals, Breviaries and Psalters, but not from Vespasiano. He did not handle Books of Hours. These had a late start in Italy, compared with the southern Netherlands

LEFT: Map of Florence in a manuscript of Ptolemy made for Alfonso of Calabria, *c.*1470, showing (centre, just across the river) Vespasiano's house and (upper left) his garden.

or France in the generation of the Duc de Berry, and they did not really reach their peak of popularity in Florence until the third or even fourth quarter of the fifteenth century, too late for Vespasiano. Even more unexpectedly for a bookseller not entirely confident in his own knowledge of Latin, Vespasiano hardly dealt at all in vernacular texts, not even in popular Italian translations of classical texts. There is a notable absence in his repertoire of copies of Dante's *Divina Commedia*, probably the greatest work of medieval literature and certainly the most popular text by any Florentine author. We look in vain for Boccaccio's *Decameron* and the love poems of Petrarch. Vespasiano's shop did not sell them. The penultimate entry in his biographies is an account of Nuño de Guzmán, whose library is disdainfully dismissed as unserious, no more than a gathering of texts in the Tuscan vernacular (the language in which the biographies themselves are written).

Vespasiano's last supreme client was Federico da Montefeltro (1422–82), duke of Urbino, soldier, statesman and patron of art. He was married to Battista, daughter of Vespasiano's old customer Alessandro Sforza. Montefeltro's palace in Urbino, about sixty-five miles east of Florence, is one of the finest private buildings in the world. The ducal library there was incomparable. It was eventually bought by Pope Alexander VII in 1657, and the manuscripts are now in the Vatican. Vespasiano says of it: 'In this library all the books are superlatively good, and written with the pen, and *had there been one printed volume it would have been ashamed to be in such company*. They were beautifully illuminated and written on parchment.' That phrase about no printed book ever being admitted to Montefeltro's library (my italics) is probably now the most famous written by Vespasiano. It could be the mantra of his whole life. It also marks his downfall, for he never adapted to the black art of the printing press, then sweeping across Europe. (Nor is it strictly true of Montefeltro. There is, for example, a copy of Origen printed in Rome in 1481, now at Bryn Mawr College in Pennsylvania, illuminated with Montefeltro's arms.)

The enterprise was on an even greater scale than those of Cosimo de' Medici for San Marco and the Badia at Fiesole. Vespasiano writes of Montefeltro:

> He alone had a mind to do what no one had done for a thousand years or more: that is, to create the finest library since ancient times. He spared neither cost nor labour, and when he knew of a fine book, whether in

Italy or not, he would send for it. It is now fourteen or more years since he began the library, and he always employed, in Urbino, in Florence, and in other places, thirty or forty scribes in his service. He took the only way to make a fine library like this: by beginning with the Latin poets, with any commentaries on the same which might seem merited; next the orators, with the works of Cicero and all Latin writers and grammarians of merit, so that not one of the leading writers in this faculty should be lacking. He sought also all the known works on history in Latin, and not only those, but likewise the histories by Greek writers done into Latin, and the orators as well. The duke also desired to have every work on moral and natural philosophy in Latin, or in Latin translations from Greek.

Vespasiano had begun supplying books for Montefeltro by at least 1467–77, and the fourteen years which he mentions for his continuing involvement were no exaggeration. Although it was eventually an even bigger library than for the Badia, there was much less pressure of time. Vespasiano's contract was not exclusive, as he makes clear, but the scribes employed in Florence were under his supervision. More than fifty different hands can be distinguished among them. An unusual scribe was Aaron, son of the rabbi Gabriel, who was hired to copy the Hebrew text for what Vespasiano described as 'a wonderful Psalter in Hebrew, Greek and Latin, verse by verse', made for Montefeltro in 1473. More familiar is Gherardo del Ciriagio, still busy. He was employed for a manuscript of the dialogues of Plato, in the Latin version of Leonardo Bruni. Gherardo's career as a scribe was almost entirely centred round work for Vespasiano. He is first recorded copying manuscripts in 1447, when he wrote the Cicero for William Gray. Here he is twenty-five years later, writing what was probably his last manuscript shortly before his death. The informal style of youth, inviting William to read happily, has long gone: he ends the manuscript of Plato (in translation), 'Gherardo del Ciriagio of Florence wrote [this] in the year 1472, for the magnificent lord, Federigo lord of Urbino and lord of Montefeltro, by the intervention of Vespasiano son of Filippo, prince of all the booksellers of Florence, Thanks be to God.' He is working for two undeniable aristocrats; as many people do as they grow into old age, he remembers God too.

Like the collections at San Marco and Fiesole, Montefeltro's wish list of texts was probably based on the *Canone bibliografico* of Parentucelli,

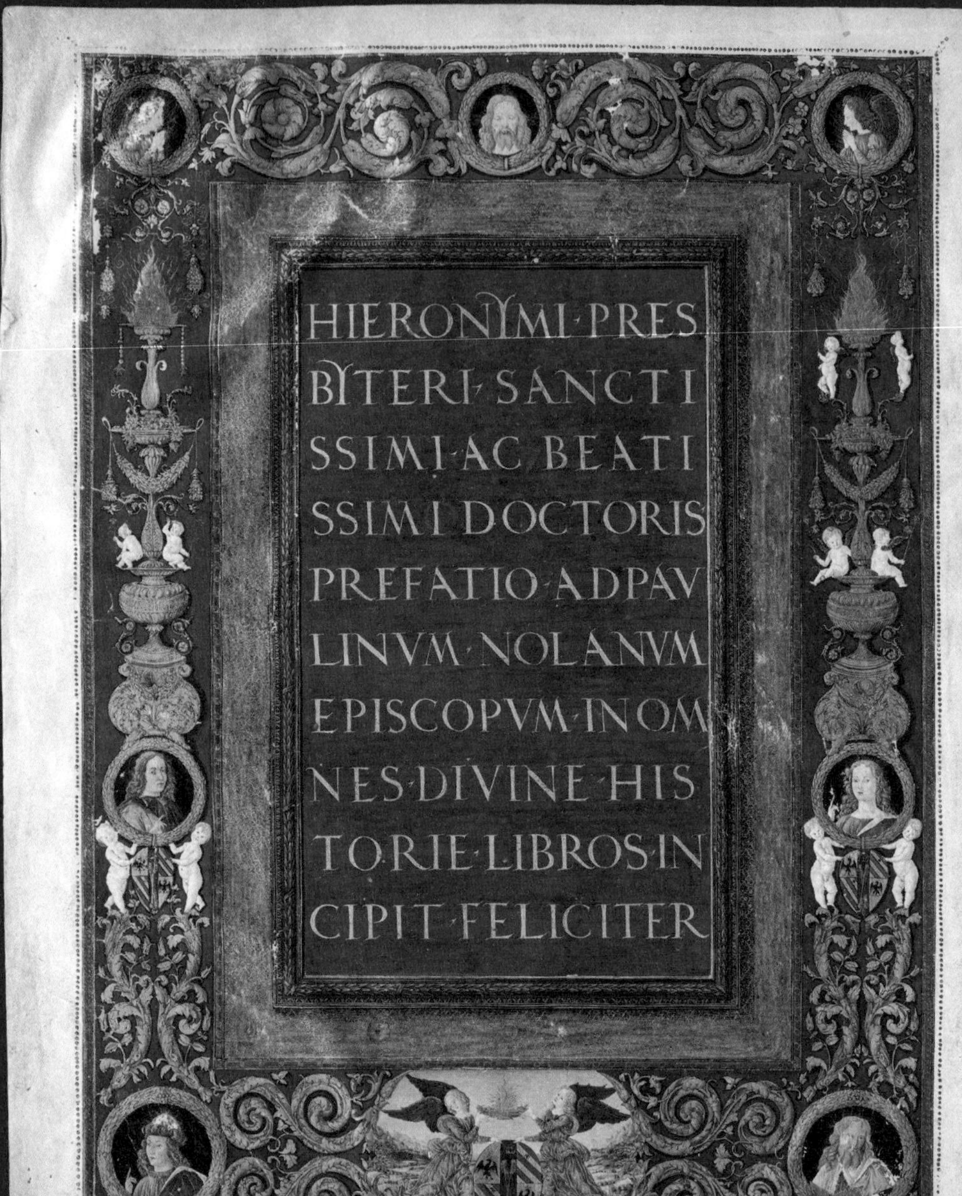
HIERONYMI·PRES
BYTERI·SANCTI
SSIMI·AC BEATI
SSIMI·DOCTORIS
PREFATIO·AD PAV
LINVM·NOLANVM
EPISCOPVM·IN OM
NES·DIVINE·HIS
TORIE·LIBROS·IN
CIPIT·FELICITER

but it went much further. Vespasiano recounts a visit to Urbino when he took with him the library catalogues of San Marco, the Vatican, the Sforza library in Pavia, 'and even that of the University of Oxford, which I had procured from England' (perhaps through Gray or Tiptoft). Montefeltro's collection, he reports, was found to be more comprehensive than any of them. The duke's little *studiolo* in Urbino, where Vespasiano was doubtless received and which he describes, was (and still is) an extraordinary room, the high point of any visit to the palace today. Around at eye level are cupboards, inset with wooden marquetry in *trompe l'oeil* designs showing a deceptively naturalistic abundance of manuscripts deliciously piled and propped up, with the occasional candlestick and musical instrument. A little door leads out onto a terrace with a view across Urbino. Around the walls at a higher level in the *studiolo* were formerly paintings of the duke's twenty-eight favourite authors, mostly holding manuscripts, from Plato (the author copied by Gherardo), Aristotle, Cicero and others, on to the Middle Ages, including Saint Thomas Aquinas and Duns Scotus, and to heroes of the Renaissance, some of whom Vespasiano had met, such as Pius II and Cardinal Bessarion. Aquinas was well-represented in the duke's library, but Duns Scotus is unexpected. Vespasiano perhaps pointed this out. Montefeltro told him that he had read the works of both of them, but 'he rated Saint Thomas as clearer than Scotus though less subtle'. This may be an actual conversation they had, standing here together in the *studiolo* gazing up.

The greatest manuscript made for Montefeltro and by far the most luxurious manuscript ever orchestrated by Vespasiano was an astonishing two-volume Latin Bible. The fact that it is now in the Vatican Library, a collection overwhelmed with early Bibles, has almost eclipsed its quite exceptional Renaissance grandeur. In any other national collection, it would stand out as a monument of the highest fame. It is absolutely vast, some 23½ by 17½ inches, about as large as the dimensions of animal skin will allow any manuscript to be, and over a thousand pages thick. Reproductions can hardly adequately convey the scale of the volumes or their impact when they are heaved open onto a table in front of you. In general, fifteenth-century Italian manuscripts are not richly illustrated, except for choir books, and most books arranged by Vespasiano have

LEFT: Title-page of the manuscript Bible of Federico da Montefeltro, duke of Urbino, commissioned through Vespasiano and illuminated here by Francesco Roselli, *c.*1477.

hardly more decoration than a few illuminated initials and perhaps borders on their opening pages. The Bible of Federico da Montefeltro has two huge title-pages, nearly a hundred smaller miniatures and historiated initials, and thirty-five breathtaking large illustrations the width of the pages, as big and as complex as panel paintings. The entire narrative of the Scriptures is transported into the sunlit landscapes and stately palaces of Tuscany. 'It was given this rich form', wrote Vespasiano in his life of the duke, 'as the chief of all writings.' He describes the original binding as having been of gold brocade with silver fittings. The main artist of the manuscript was Francesco d'Antonio del Chierico (1433–84), with several others, including Attavante, who later painted the portrait we have of Vespasiano. The manuscript is written in perfect humanistic script, like a classical text. It is as if in its appearance the familiar medieval Bible was being newly presented as a Latin translation of a Greek source from the ancient world, which it essentially is. The scribe was a Frenchman living in Florence, Ugo de Comminelli (or Hughes Commineau), originally from Mézières and a graduate of the university in Paris. He specialized in writing books on a grand scale, including five copies of Ptolemy's *Cosmography*, among them the manuscript with the map showing Vespasiano's house. Ugo records that the first volume of the Bible was finished in Florence on 25 February 1477 and the second on 12 June 1478, trumpeting, as probably directed, that 'Vespasiano son of Filippo, bookseller of Florence, procured the making of this most ornate Bible.' This date must have included the illumination, because there is a letter from Federico da Montefeltro to Lorenzo the Magnificent in Florence, written from Urbino on 21 June that year, asking for his help in having it sent. As when the manuscripts for William Gray were forwarded to Rome long ago, the Medici bank was willing to facilitate deliveries. Lorenzo replied on 25 June, agreeing.

In all probability, this was Vespasiano's final manuscript of any importance, perhaps the very last of all. By that summer of 1478 he was fifty-five and rapidly becoming disillusioned with the relentless modern world. Printing had been invented some twenty-five years earlier and was now firmly established across most of Europe, including Italy. From Gutenberg onwards there had been at least thirty-five printed editions

RIGHT: The exodus from Egypt in the Bible of Federico da Montefeltro, illuminated by Francesco d'Antonio del Chierico, *c.*1477, Vespasiano's last great manuscript.

HAEC SVNT NOMINA

filioꝝ isrl' qui ingressi sunt in ægyptũ cum Iacob
singuli cũ domib⁹ suis introierunt. Ruben: Syme
on: Leui: Iudas: ysachar: zabulon: et Beniamin.
Dan: et Neptalim. Gad: et Aser: Erant igitur
om̃es animæ eoꝝ q egressi sũt de femore Iacob.
septuagĩta. Ioseph autẽ in ægypto erat. Quo
mortuo et uniuersis frib⁹ eius: omĩ q cognatio
ne sua: filii isrl' creuerũt et quasi germinantes
multiplicati sũt. ac roborati nimis impleuerũt
terrã. Surrexit interea rex nouus super ægyptũ
qui ignorabat Ioseph. Et ait ad pplm suum. Ec
ce populus filioꝝ israel mltus: et fortior nobis ẽ.
Venite sapienter opprimamus eũ: ne forte mul
tiplicetur: et si ingruerit contra nos bellũ: ad
datur nris inimicis: expugnatis q nobis egredi
atur de terra. Preposuit itaq magistros operũ:
ut affligerẽt eos oneribus: Ædificauerũt q urbes
tabernaculoꝝ Pharaoni Phiton: et Ramesses.
quãto q opprimebant eos: tanto magis multi
plicabantur: et crescebãt. Oderant q filios isrl
ægyptii: et affligebãt illudentes eis: atq ad a
maritudinẽ perducebant uitã eoꝝ operibus
duris luti: et lateris: omni q famulatu quo in
terræ opibus premebãtur. Dixit autẽ rex æ
gypti obstetricibus hebræoꝝ: quaꝝ una uoca
batur Sephora: altera Phua: precipiẽs eis. Qñ
obstetricabitis hebreas: et partus tẽpus aduene
rit: si masculus fuerit interficite eũ: si femina
reseruate. Timuerunt obstetrices deum: et nõ
fecerunt iuxta preceptũ regis ægypti: sed con
seruabãt mares. Quib⁹ ad se accersitis rex ait.
Quid nã est hoc quod facere uoluistis ut pueros
seruaretis: Quæ rñderũt. Non sũt hebrææ si
cut ægyptiæ mulieres. Ipsæ enim obstetricãdi
hñt scientiã: et priusq̃ ueniamus ad eas pa
riũt. Bene ergo fecit deus obstetricib⁹. Et cre
uit pplus cõfortatus q est nimis. Et qa timue
rũt obstetrices deũ: ædificauit illis domos. Pre
cepit autẽ Pharao omni pplo suo dicẽs. Quicqd
masculini sexus natũ fuerit: in flumẽ proicite;
quicqd feminini reseruate:

· C · I I ·

Gressus est post hæc uir de domo Leui accepta
uxore stirpis suæ: q̃ cõcepit et peperit filium.
Et uidẽs eum elegantẽ: abscõdit mensib⁹ trib⁹.
cũ q iam celare non posset: sumpsit fiscelam
scirpeã: et liniuit eã bitumĩe ac picæ: posu
it q intus infantulũ: et exposuit eũ in carep
to fluminis stãte procul sorore eius: et cõsi
derãte euentũ rei: Ecce autẽ descẽdebat fi
lia Pharaonis ut lauaretur in flumine: et pu
ellæ eius gradiebãtur p crepidinẽ alueí. Quæ
cũ uidisset fiscellã in papirione misit unã de

of the Latin Bible, including those published in Rome (1471), Piacenza, Venice (both 1475), Vicenza and Naples (both 1476). A manuscript Bible was by now completely unnecessary as a text, and no doubt many people told him so. It might even be copied from a printed exemplar and would probably be more accurate if it was. Many scribes and booksellers welcomed printing, allowing them to speed up book production while (in theory) eliminating scribal error. Vespasiano was not among them. His self-delusional assertion that Montefeltro would never admit a printed book to his library tells us as much about himself as his client. There are those of an older generation in our own times who defiantly blocked their minds to digital technology and found themselves becoming unexpectedly lonely. Montefeltro and Vespasiano were exactly the same age, and they perhaps muttered together that a proper book ought to have been handwritten, words transmitted through human intellect rather than a machine, but they were outnumbered. There were high-profile presses in Rome and Venice by the late 1460s, supplying a market with exactly the kind of classical and early Christian texts with which Vespasiano had dominated the world. Bernardo Cennini printed an edition of the commentary of Servius on Virgil in Florence itself in 1471. This was a flagrant encroachment into Vespasiano's territory. It might be that his disapprobation deterred other attempts for several years afterwards, but printing returned modestly to Florence in 1476 and never left. By then many other *cartolai* in the Via dei Librai were already selling imported printed books for a fraction of the cost of manuscripts. Vespasiano's principal competitor, Zanobi di Mariano, had them in stock by 1473. Bernardo Machiavelli, father of the writer, bought a copy of Livy in Florence in 1475; it was a printed book, and it was sold to him by Zanobi di Mariano. Vespasiano's monopoly was being cut from under his feet.

1478, the year of the completion of the Montefeltro Bible, was also the darkest in the history of Renaissance Florence. In late April, a band of well-connected plotters, known as the Pazzi conspiracy, assassinated Giuliano de' Medici in the cathedral and wounded his brother Lorenzo, resulting in many months of bitter reprisals and public terror. The whole city was placed under papal interdict for the hanging of Francesco Salviati, archbishop of Pisa and the pope's protégé, implicated as a conspirator. The Sienese were up in arms, advancing across Tuscany. Savonarola arrived that year in Florence, bearing the apocalyptic wrath of God against a city deemed to be in terminal decadence. In addition to all this, plague broke out in the city, the worst in a generation, and the Arno flooded in December. The Florentine apothecary Luca Landucci (1436–1516) recorded in his diary in 1478, 'At this Christmas-time, what with the terror of the war, the plague and the papal excommunication, the citizens were in a sorry plight: they lived in dread, and no one had any heart to work.' Vespasiano sensibly gave up: towards the end of 1478 he made over his shop in the Via dei Librai to the *cartolaio* Andrea di Lorenzo and retired from business. On 19 January 1479 he presented a small group of manuscripts to the library of San Marco in Florence, including a Seneca which had once been owned by Coluccio Salutati. He was presumably clearing the shelves of the shop.

Vespasiano rented out the house in the Via de' Bardi and from 1479 moved principally to a villa in the countryside in Antella, about five miles south-east of Florence. I have been to find the house, with Mara Hofmann and Patricio Molina. It is credibly identified with what is now called the Casa Il Monte, a substantial pale cream-coloured building on a commanding site carved into the steep Belmonte hillside, terraced with very old dry-stone walls. We came up a private drive lined with cypress trees, and I was both shocked and impressed that Mara simply rang the doorbell and asked the owner if we could be taken round. From the back, where we parked, the house has two storeys, but the front rises three storeys high, each with three small round-topped windows with shutters, looking out over a lawn into a forest of olive trees which extend almost down to the E35 motorway in the distant valley far below, part of the very ancient Via Francigena which connected northern Europe to Rome. The house was divided in the 1990s into two, but its Renaissance structure is substantially intact.

In or soon after 1480 Vespasiano wrote an enchanting letter from here to Pierfilippo Pandolfini (1437–97), hoping to persuade him to come to stay. He urged his friend:

> to leave Florence and come to this pleasant and charming place, where the woods, fine hillsides, springs and clear streams and cascades invite you, and press you to wait no longer as time rushes by; the trees say that they will keep their leaves and pray you to come before they lose them [the letter is dated 22 September, in the early autumn]. A room here awaits you . . . it has many worthy qualities: the first is that it has never held any thought that may hinder you, not even for a minute, let

> alone an hour; and there is another, that it has never hosted a woman, the cause of the sorrow of all our lives. There is another quality: there are no animals here to disturb your sleep, no mosquito or similar, and the air is such that the body, however weak and sick it may be, immediately recovers its original strength.

Vespasiano never married: his allusion to the sorrow caused by a woman refers not to his own experience but to paradise undisturbed by Eve in a new garden of Eden, with its wholesome air offering relief from the plague in the city. There is a breeze up on the hillside; we were there in October and the leaves had just begun turning colour. The woodlands in Vespasiano's time sound even prettier than they are now, giving joy to a man who had maintained a garden in Florence even during his rigorous working life.

Initially he continued advising Federico da Montefeltro, who caught the plague and died in 1482, and he stayed in touch with several former clients, including the duke of Calabria. It was here in Antella that Vespasiano wrote his *Vite di uomini illustri*, the collection of over a hundred brief biographies of people he had once known, which has provided much material for this chapter. Perhaps he saw himself as a modern Plutarch, an author he had often had copied. He looked back on an extraordinary life of intimacy with major figures of his time, into whose acquaintance and often close friendship he had been thrown, not as a result of birth or any public life, but because of a love of manuscripts. He took much credit for several great collections still intact today, although now transferred into national libraries. He also recorded some disasters. He says that the library of Nicholas V was squandered and given away by his successor, Calixtus III, pope 1455–8 (an exaggeration); that the collection of Mateu Malfrit was lost in a shipwreck on the way to Majorca; and that the frivolous books of Nuño de Guzmán 'came to grief' (no details). He describes the execution in the Tower of London of his client John Tiptoft in 1470, for which Vespasiano's account is the most detailed surviving record, derived from an Italian Dominican who spoke to Tiptoft on the scaffold and overheard the earl asking for his head to be cut off in three strokes, in honour of the Trinity. About forty of Tiptoft's manuscripts are now known, widely scattered. Vespasiano brings us up to date on William Gray, telling how he went on to become bishop of Ely (1454, enthroned in March 1459 during a snowstorm) and that he left his books to the cathedral on his death in 1478. This last information was fortunately not true, since most of the library of Ely was lost at the Reformation and the rest through subsequent indifference, whereas Balliol College, which did receive Gray's bequest, still preserves the manuscripts safely.

Vespasiano died on 27 July 1498 and was buried in the vast church of Santa Croce in Florence, joined there later by Machiavelli, Michelangelo and Galileo, all *uomini illustri*. His small memorial tablet is low on the south wall, just to the right of the floor tomb of Leonardo Bruni. Several of Vespasiano's longer lives, including those of Gianozzo Manetti, Palla Strozzi and Alessandra di Bardo de' Bardi, found their way into circulation and exist as slight but pretty manuscripts, illuminated for discreet presentation perhaps by Vespasiano's heirs. Most of the *Vite* remained more or less unseen until a manuscript of 103 lives was rediscovered in the Vatican by the librarian, Cardinal Angelo Mai (1782–1854), who, with great difficulty and some creative imagination, published an edition in 1839–43. There was an interesting consequence. A copy was lent in 1847 to the young Swiss historian Jacob Burckhardt (1818–97). He claimed in old age that it had been the astounding revelation of reading Vespasiano's intimate and gossipy narratives which so caught his imagination that he decided to write what became *Die Kultur der Renaissance in Italien*, or *The Civilization of the Renaissance in Italy*, 1860, the foundation text for the modern rediscovery of the Italian *quattrocento*. A book (by now a printed book) by Vespasiano da Bisticci, bookseller and determinedly unreformed member of the manuscripts fraternity in the Via dei Librai, inspired a latter-day renaissance all of its own.

SIMO·BINNIK·ALEXADRI·F·
SEIPSU·PIGEBAT·ANO·ÆTATI
1558

CHAPTER FOUR

The Illuminator: Simon Bening

We have arranged to meet Simon Bening at the Victoria and Albert Museum in London. You come in by the main entrance in the Cromwell Road and are now obliged to walk through the full length of an insistent shopping mall, as inescapable in museums these days as in airports. Then you turn right at the far end by the central courtyard and along the sculpture corridor, up the nineteenth-century staircase, through sacred art and stained glass (some of it from the southern Netherlands from Bening's own time), and into several little exhibition galleries for prints and drawings. On the right is Room 90a, displaying portrait miniatures. Simon Bening is in the first case on the left. It is a self-portrait in old age, one of very few examples by a known manuscript illuminator, wonderfully painted on parchment pasted to card and now elaborately framed. It is unexpectedly small, a little under 3½ inches by 2¼. Bening sits half-length in front of his steeply sloped desk and turns wearily to face the viewer, wearing a black cap over tufts of grey hair. In his left hand he holds a pair of spectacles or lenses, necessary for all of us as we get older but also showing that Bening doubtless worked under magnification. He is a miniaturist. The fingers of his right hand just touch the lower edge of an image of the Virgin and Child which he is painting. To the left of the desk is a rack for brushes and pigments. It is not easy to see details as the portrait is displayed, since the museum lighting in the glass case is low for conservation reasons and it constantly strengthens and fades in intensity as you watch. Bening gave himself better light, for he is seated up against a gothic lattice window in a wooden casement. Glass was still relatively expensive in the sixteenth century and this was a prosperous room. The window is over his left shoulder, as recommended

LEFT: Simon Bening (*c.*1484–1561), self-portrait, 1558, in the Victoria and Albert Museum.

in medieval craftsmen's manuals, because it means that the shadow of the artist's hand will not fall across his work. Through the coarse glass we can see hazily outside onto trees in leaf (therefore in summer) and a brick house with a tall chimney, like many medieval buildings in Bruges, where this picture was doubtless painted. Below the portrait is a caption in gold capitals on a deep red ground, the colours of ancient imperial manuscripts, "SIMO[N] BINNIK. ALEXANDRI F[ILIUS] SE IPSU[M] PI[N]GEBAT. AN[N]O. ÆTATIS. 75. 1558", 'Simon Binnink, son of Alexander, painted himself in the 75th year of his age, 1558.'

Considering how little we know of the lives of most medieval manuscript painters, there is precious information even here. He gives the name of his father, also an illuminator, Alexander (or Sanders) Bening, independently recorded in Ghent in what is now Belgium in the later fifteenth century. It is always supposed that Simon was seventy-five in the portrait, but he actually says that he was in his seventy-fifth year, which presumably means he painted this when seventy-four. He was therefore born in about 1484. This was already thirty years after the invention of printing in Europe, and even about a decade after printing presses had been introduced into the southern Netherlands. Simon Bening then spent his entire life making and illuminating manuscripts at a time when they were frankly quite unnecessary. This may or may not qualify him as an obsessive, but it is certainly evidence of relentless dedication against the trend, and his career reveals a great deal about the continuing and evolving market for luxury illumination even as the Middle Ages ebbed away.

There are two contemporary records of manuscripts commissioned from Simon Bening which allow us to recognize his distinctive hand in numerous surviving books. The municipal archives of Diksmuide, near the coast south-west of Bruges, recorded the itemized expenses of a manuscript Missal made for the town hall there in 1530–31, including 10 *livres* paid to "meestre Symon de verlichtere te Brugghe" ('Master Simon the illuminator of Bruges') for a full-page miniature of the Crucifixion. That Missal survived until the almost total destruction of Diksmuide and all its manuscripts during repeated bombardments in the First World War. Fortunately, the miniature is known to us from old photographs. It shows Christ on the Cross between the Virgin Mary and Saint John. The figures are not of great delicacy, for this was a Missal, mostly to be seen at some distance, but the landscape in the background is beautiful, with a tall tree and a party of horsemen following a road back to the hilltop city of Jerusalem against a great range of mountains. This was an artist familiar with foreign paintings or travel, for there are no mountains in Flanders.

The second commission is documented in successive letters of Damião de Góis (1501–73), Portuguese diplomat in Antwerp. He reported in 1530 that Dom Fernando, duke of Guarda and brother of the king of Portugal, had asked him to arrange the illumination of a costly manuscript of the genealogy of the Portuguese royal family from the time of Noah onwards, and that this was entrusted to 'the principal master of this art in all of Europe, by the name of Simon of Bruges in Flanders'. The designs had been sketched out in advance by the Portuguese artist and royal herald António de Holanda, and they were then sent singly or in batches to the southern Netherlands to be painted by Simon. The ongoing correspondence tells of the frustration of the artist in Bruges who had set aside two years for this project, but was constantly being held up by delays in delivery of the sheets from Portugal. Dom Fernando died in 1534, and the commission was abandoned. António de Holanda was still asking for payment for his own work as late as 1539.

By happy chance, thirteen of the sheets survive, out of perhaps thirty originally, and are now in the British Library in London. (How they came to be there will be part of Chapter 8.) They are kept in three massive dark-blue cloth boxes, so big that they had to be carried sideways on the library trolley used to deliver them to my table in the manuscripts reading-room. The separate sheets are now sealed within modern thick card mounts, which conceal the edges of the pages and their versos, but they are truly huge, each about 23 by 17 inches, about as large as the immense Bible orchestrated by Vespasiano for Federico da Montefeltro. Only in Spain and Portugal were manuscripts commonly made on such a scale, in giant choirbooks for use by many choristers at once. Parchment makers there knew more about preparing enormous sheets than anywhere else in Europe, even Italy. The leaves of the Portuguese genealogy would not possibly have fitted on Simon Bening's work desk as it is shown in the self-portrait. They are in various stages of completion. All have been drawn out carefully in outline by the designer (António de Holanda) and twelve of the thirteen are more or less fully illuminated. Spaces remain for small panels of text to be supplied back in Portugal, and most of the many coats of arms are still left blank, for these too were presumably to be filled in by Portuguese heralds with their

TAVOA PRYMEIRA
RA DONA SANCHA
ELREY DOM YNHEGO ARISTA
REYS DARAGAM

specialized knowledge on the completion of the project. The colouring and illumination are by two very different hands. A useful measure for distinguishing them happened to come my way in 1989, when a similar but very much smaller illustrated genealogy of the Portuguese counts of Pereira was brought for sale at Sotheby's (it is now in the national archives in Lisbon). It includes an attestation dated February 1534 stating that the manuscript had been illuminated for its patron by "António d'Olanda", officer of the nobility of the king and a name now familiar to us. Comparison with the sheets in the British Library shows clearly that seven were painted in Portugal by António de Holanda himself, and, taking account of the one never coloured at all, the remaining five are therefore documented works by Simon Bening of Bruges. Their quality is breathtaking. The figures of the many kings and queens are in precisely the style of Bening's self-portrait, delicately built up from microscopic dabs of pure colour. For almost the first time in manuscript art, they look like actual people one might know in Belgium today. Flemish panel painters in the later fifteenth century had brought the art of portraiture to extraordinary levels of realism. Faces in the manuscript genealogy are often shown close up and in sharp focus. Male complexions are sometimes ruddy as if after a few beers or having been in the sun; women are pale and pretty but also solemn, with little lips and modest downcast eyes. Rich velvet textiles and jewels are wonderfully evoked, as finely as by any panel painter. Animals abound. The marginal vignettes, probably executed by Bening without underdrawing by Holanda, include (for example) the coronation of King Garcia Íñiguez in Pamplona in the mid-ninth century but anachronistically transferred here into a characteristic late-medieval Bruges street with stepped gable Flemish houses and tall Renaissance chimneys. Others are in beautiful atmospheric and hazy northern landscapes. Francesco de Holanda (the son of António) wrote a book about famous painters in 1548, mentioning the Flemish illuminator Master Simon as quite simply 'the finest painter of trees and distances' of the time.

These characteristics of Bening's style can be seen in photographs of the Diksmuide Crucifixion, and what is today a considerable body of surviving manuscripts and single miniatures now attributed to him. Some

LEFT: The genealogy of the royal house of Portugal, documented as illuminated by Simon Bening, *c.*1530–34.

are precisely dated, allowing us to plot a basic chronology of Bening's work. These fixed dates extend from a tiny prayerbook of 1511 to four single miniatures in the Brooklyn Museum inscribed in 1521, parts of a Book of Hours in Lisbon apparently dated 1526, a Book of Hours now in the Morgan Library in New York, written by the scribe Antonius van Damme in Bruges in 1531, and a Rosarium (devotional prayers to the Virgin Mary), signed by the same scribe in 1545. A bit of caution is still needed in accepting every modern attribution to Simon Bening. When the artists of most late Netherlandish manuscripts are still anonymous and can be designated today only by stylistic comparison, often with tongue-tying modern names such as the 'Master of the David Scenes in the Grimani Breviary', there is a natural temptation to seize upon one of the very few real names of the period and to attach it breezily to almost any reasonably competent miniature of the right date. Some of the manuscripts now optimistically ascribed to Bening must surely fall within a wider orbit than the exclusive hand of the master himself, or they might be collaborative works, so characteristic of Netherlandish art in later generations.

The Prayerbook of Joanna de Ghistelles, illuminated by Simon Bening, probably *c.*1516.

Fresh from examining the Portuguese Genealogy, I asked that same afternoon to see the Prayerbook of Joanna de Ghistelles, also in the British Library. It has twenty-two beautiful miniatures credibly attributed to Simon Bening by their distinctive style. The manuscript was made for Joanna, noble abbess of the Benedictine convent of Messines from 1516 until her death in 1561, and it probably belongs towards the beginning of that period. It may actually have been written by the nuns there and then sent on to Bening in Bruges to be illuminated and bound. Messines (Mesen in Flemish) is between Ypres and Lille, near the Belgian border about thirty miles south-west of Bruges. This is an enchanting and personal little manuscript, about 6 by 4¼ inches, agreeable to handle and much more characteristic of Bening's famously intimate books than the oversized and almost unusable genealogy. It is still in its original binding, with the edges of the pages ornately gilded and decorated and leather covers stamped with repeated impressions of a rectangle comprising animals in foliage with the legend in Latin around its margin, "OB. LAUDEM / XPRISTI LIBRUM HUNC / RECTE LIGAVI / LUDOVICUS BLOC", 'For the praise of Christ, I truly bound this book – Ludwig [or Lowys] Bloc.' The same stamp also occurs on a Benedictional now in Cambridge University Library, illuminated by Simon Bening for Robert de Clercq, abbot of the Cistercian monastery of Ter Duinen near Bruges from 1519 until 1557.

The first identification of Simon Bening (and indeed of Antonius van Damme and Ludwig Bloc) goes back to the mid-nineteenth century. Like the self-portrait, the story is at least partly set in the Victoria and Albert Museum. The figure of W. H. James Weale (1832–1917) has never been entirely forgotten in the oral lore of the Museum. He was the first proper keeper of the Art Library in 1890–97 in what was then called the South Kensington Museum, and he was famous for his huge white beard, exceptionally wide-brimmed black felt hat, shuffling gait and terrible temper. He had been a childhood convert to Roman Catholicism and refused to attend Oxford University because of its Anglicanism. After an unfortunate incident as a young schoolmaster when Weale was accused of inappropriate chastisement of a boy, he quickly married (his new wife was only sixteen) and moved to Bruges, then as unshakably Catholic as it had been in Simon Bening's time. Here for two decades he set about scouring the local archives for references to artists and craftsmen. More than 200 fragile exercise books and folders of his notes are in the city library in Bruges. There are thousands of pages of careful extracts in Weale's neat and gently sloping hand. Some discoveries are fascinating and little known, such as the existence of an Agnes Zegaerts *illuminatrix*, a woman illuminator in Bruges in 1481–2. Others are slight sightings, such as one Jacquemijne d'Havre, widow of Olivier Loonis, who transferred certain unspecified rights to Meester Sijmon Bennyck in April 1551, a negligible but unpublished reference to our illuminator. Weale founded a local antiquarian journal called *Le Beffroi* in 1863, named after the famous medieval tower in Bruges, and he quarried his own notes for several issues devoted to the records of the medieval book trade, including an account of Bening. He published the first descriptions of the Diksmuide Missal and of the Prayerbook of Joanna de Ghistelles (both in 1872–3), a critical account of the Portuguese genealogy (1903), and the earliest specialized article devoted to Simon Bening (1906).

It was Weale who initially disentangled the family relationships of the Benings. As in much art history of the late Middle Ages, there is a good deal of dynastic legacy. Simon's father, Alexander, had been a manuscript illuminator in Ghent, where he was a paid-up member of the painters' guild by at least 1469. He married Kathelijn van der Goes, perhaps a niece or even a sister of the celebrated panel painter Hugo van der Goes (d. 1482), and Alexander's own sister married Goswijn van der Weyden, similarly presumed to have been a relative of the painter Rogier van der Weyden (d. 1464). In 1481, Alexander sponsored the nomination of another kinsman, Cornelis van der Goes, to the guild in Ghent. The close connection between the major artistic families of the time is important for understanding the world of Simon Bening's childhood. Manuscript illumination was as closely related to the business of panel painting as it was to book production. Alexander Bening rented a house in Ghent in 1476–7, and it is likely that Simon was born there around 1484. In one place Weale asserts him to have been born in Antwerp and in another in Ghent, but he supplies no source for either statement. Ghent is probable. Presumably Simon was trained in his own father's workshop, as was common practice, perhaps from about the mid-1490s.

No surviving miniatures can be definitively ascribed to Alexander Bening, the father, but everything recorded of his documented life is consistent with the work of an anonymous illuminator known today as the 'Master of the First Prayerbook of Maximilian', named after a manuscript in Vienna, made probably in Ghent in 1486 for Maximilian of Burgundy, later Holy Roman emperor. It is very striking to see how miniatures by this anonymous illuminator resemble the style of panel paintings by Hugo van der Goes, Alexander Bening's likely relative by marriage. Many compositions used in manuscripts by the Master of the First Prayerbook were then repeated over and over again in the subsequent work of Simon Bening, all suggesting (as would be likely anyway) that the son inherited his family's pattern books.

Art historians have commonly referred to a general style of late Flemish manuscript illumination as the 'Ghent–Bruges' school, as if this were a single place. The art is characterized by miniatures made like tiny panel paintings resembling windows seemingly opening through a manuscript page into a parallel world beyond. The artists are struggling with the problem of conveying a three-dimensional effect on a flat surface. The borders surrounding the pages are commonly decorated with plucked flowers and plants painted with astonishing realism, looking as though they had been randomly scattered across yellow or pale-gold backgrounds, casting shadows on the manuscript pages. This illusion is sometimes compounded by naturalistic insects which appear to have alighted on the painted flowers, as if they were real, and when we try to brush them away we realize that they too are painted. It is certainly true that artists in both towns and elsewhere in western Flanders all produced manuscripts in this fashionable style.

In fact, Ghent and Bruges are rather different cities. In simple terms, imagine a line from Brussels to the sea. Half an hour on the train today brings you to Ghent, another half hour to Bruges, and the final third (or a bit less) to the coast. Until the early sixteenth century, Bruges was accessible to the open sea up the Zwin channel, a tidal inlet which gradually silted up and is now entirely closed. Medieval Bruges looked westwards. Its wealth derived from export, trading easily by ship with England and down to southern Europe, where Spain and Portugal were closer than Italy. Ghent, by contrast, was bigger and further inland, the regional capital and, with Mechelen (Malines) and Brussels, an important administrative centre of the new Burgundian empire. Despite the art historians' catchphrase, relatively few manuscript illuminators moved between the two cities. The Benings, father and son, were among the few exceptions.

Simon's father was first recorded in Bruges from 1486 and was still there when he eventually died in 1519. Simon Bening and several of his siblings also settled in Bruges, although not necessarily at the same moment. In time, Simon married Katherine Scroo, and they had five daughters, Levina, Alexandrine (named after her grandfather), Anne, Claire and Barbara. Katherine Scroo died in 1542, and Simon later married Jane Tancre, who predeceased him too, dying in 1555. Her name sounds as though she may have been English. In addition, Simon Bening had a relationship with one Jozyne Dullaerts, and they had an illegitimate daughter, Lauwereinekin, little Laura, who died in 1561, the same year as Simon Bening himself at the age of about seventy-seven. All this was discovered and published by James Weale.

Personally, I have a fondness for Bruges which dates back to childhood. It was the first (and for many years the only) European city I had visited, for we had a family holiday there in the late 1950s; my rather lopsided painting of the medieval belfry won second prize in the children's art section of our church fete back in England. Because access to the sea was gradually cut off in the sixteenth century, Bruges was slowly eclipsed as a trading centre by the port of Antwerp to the north-east, and it fell gently into a fortuitous neglect which has preserved for us many of the old merchants' houses from the time of Simon Bening. The town centre is still encircled and connected by a web of medieval canals, crossed by hump-backed bridges and lined by tall gabled brick buildings, like those depicted in many Bening miniatures. Some are now hotels and hostelries. Idle swans drift gently past, as they do in pictures in the manuscripts. Because of the water, Bruges can be very cold in winter. The principal squares are the large marketplace with the belfry, and the nearby Burg, which was the old administrative centre with the town hall. Surviving medieval churches include Sint-Salvator, Onze-Lieve-Vrouwekerk, dedicated to the Virgin Mary, and the basilica of the Holy Blood. Narrow streets are mostly cobbled. Traffic is minimal, although there are buses and bicycles, and rather expensive (but recommended) horse-drawn carriages clip-clopping around the tourist circuit. Shops supply both local delicacies – fresh-smelling bread and pastries, good beer – and eye-catching goods for visitors, including lace, leatherwork, metalwork, amusing toys and little commemorative pictures. Most of these were available here in the Middle Ages too, with other luxuries of that time, such as oranges, figs, pepper, quicksilver, furs, carpets, monkeys and parrots.

Illuminators in Bruges had been making manuscripts for foreigners and the export market since the late thirteenth century. Their well-established

The Beatty Rosarium, a manuscript made for the Spanish market, quite possibly for the emperor Charles V, in which biblical scenes are set in the streets of Bruges, *c.*1540–45.

trade in relatively affordable personal Psalters reached private buyers in France and England. By the fifteenth century probably even the majority of Books of Hours for English use were made in Bruges, prepared in advance for sale across the Channel. A provable example which was certainly in England very soon after completion is a Book of Hours now in the library of Ushaw College in Durham, signed by its scribe, John Heineman, who attests that it was written and finished in Bruges on 21 January 1409. Countless other Books of Hours for overseas customers in the middle third of the fifteenth century were painted by the Bruges artists known as the Masters of the Beady Eyes, the Masters of the Gold Scrolls, or in the prolific style of the illuminator Willem Vrelant, who is documented in Bruges by 1454 and died there in 1481. The printer William Caxton, shrewdly tapping into an already existing network of distribution and sale of books to his native country, set up his first press in 1473 not in England but in Bruges, where the book trade was the most securely established north of Paris. In all likelihood, that is also why Alexander Bening had originally moved there from Ghent in

1486, sensing a declining market in Flanders and Brabant and a necessity to look to a city still trading westwards beyond the boundaries of his native country. Eventually his son's business would become almost entirely one of export, catering to clients in Portugal and Spain and in Germany and Italy, and hardly at all to domestic buyers. This diaspora of Flemish manuscript art has its legacy even today, for Simon Bening's illuminations have always been and still are very widely scattered. Of all the dozens of manuscripts attributed to him, almost the only example now in modern Belgium is the Hennessy Hours in Brussels, which was purchased back from Portugal in 1874. There is not a single miniature by Bening in Bruges.

This was also the time of the famous early Netherlandish panel painters, admired across Europe. Jan Van Eyck (d. 1441), Petrus Christus (d. 1476), Hans Memling (d. 1494), Gerard David (d. 1523), Jan Provoost (d. 1529) and Adriaan Isenbrandt (d. 1551) all worked and died in Bruges. The Benings, related to both Hugo van der Goes and Rogier van der Weyden, were as much at home among the Flemish artists as they were in the book trade.

Much of the documentary evidence for Bruges illuminators and painters is derived from the archives of two of the city guilds, and we are going to look at original documents from both of them. The first is the painters' guild, or *ambacht van de beeldenmakers* in Flemish, dedicated to Saint Luke, who had in folklore been an artist himself. The guild admitted citizens of Bruges who had duly qualified by apprenticeship. Not all artists were obliged to belong, and exceptions included clerics (who might also be painters) and anyone employed directly by the Burgundian ducal household, both loopholes which excluded from the records some of the names of most interest to art historians today. The guild of Saint Luke brought together painterly artisans of many kinds, such as panel painters and artists working on fabric and glass and illuminators on parchment, which by extension came also to include workers on leather and thus also makers of saddles and harnesses, which were often painted and gilded too. Its principal purpose was to preserve professional standards of the trade and to protect members' rights against undercutting from unqualified and foreign competitors. (Any London black-cab taxi driver has a great deal to say on that general subject today.)

The second and even more relevant guild for us in Bruges was the confraternity of Saint John the Evangelist (and later also of Saint Luke), which was a fellowship of book trade professionals, including scribes, illuminators, binders, and eventually printers and booksellers and finally even schoolteachers, considered to belong to a bookish occupation. It was founded in 1454 and formalized in 1457. This was less like a modern trade union than the earlier painters' guild and it had no restrictive prescription on membership. It gave greater emphasis to civic festivals and feasts and to religious duties. In an age of uncertain life expectancy and minimal health care, a confraternity would provide for widows and those in sudden need, and it would hold religious services to commemorate the dead and to try to relieve deceased members from excessive ordeals in purgatory.

We will begin in the Stadsarchief of Bruges, the town archive. This is entered through a narrow entrance in the extreme south-east corner of the Burg, beside the old municipal registry building, which dates from Bening's time. The admission desk and coat rack are at the back of a former court room and the reading-room is straight ahead, a long narrow chamber with a high ceiling, resembling an old chapel, lit by windows down one side. It has the atmosphere of an old-fashioned schoolroom, and a display at the far end, like a class project, includes a wooden model of the medieval mechanical crane as depicted in the Grimani Breviary, a manuscript in which Bening was involved. Several boxes of papers and books from the painters' guild of Saint Luke had been ordered in advance and were already laid out waiting for me. The first I picked up was a calligraphic late fifteenth-century manuscript bound in contemporary blind-stamped leather, comprising the texts used at memorial services for deceased members of the guild, asking for divine mercy on brothers, associate brothers, sisters, parents, friends and benefactors of this congregation. The manuscript provides a constantly updated roll call of departed members, to be intoned at the services. There is an undeniable thrill in turning pages and recognizing legendary names in the history of early Netherlandish art, like sitting in a restaurant in Hollywood and spotting celebrities at neighbouring tables. Here is Petrus Christus, *scilder* (painter), the illuminator Jan le Tavernier, *scilder*, and a bit later Gerard David, *scilder* and also illuminator, and many hundreds of others, extended in various declining levels of handwriting right through to 1801. However, the names of Simon Bening and his father are not among them. It is not clear from this, at least, that they were ever members of this guild at all.

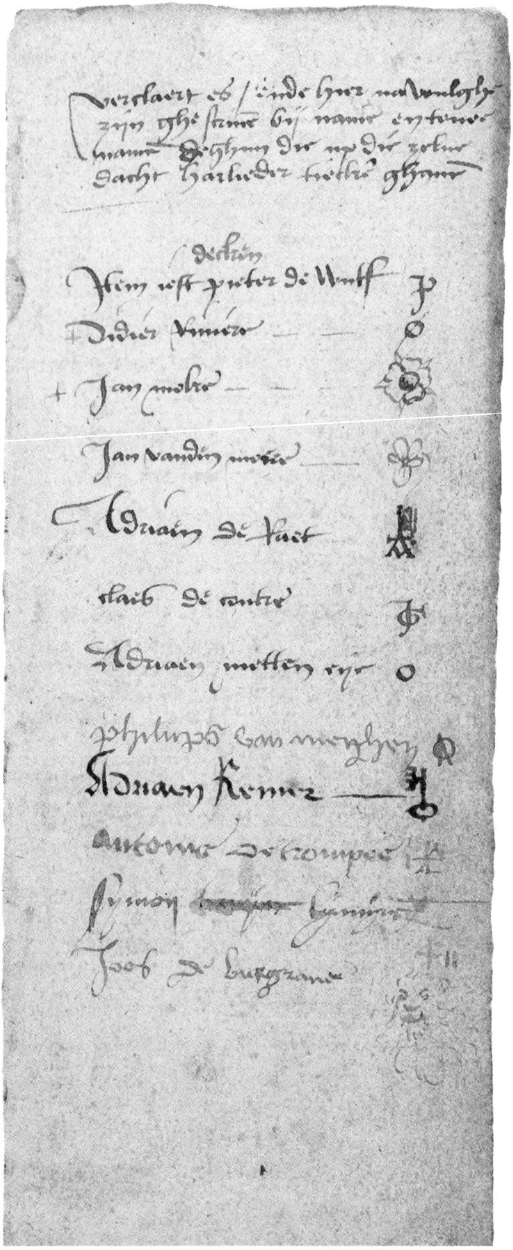

Register of the Painters' Guild in Bruges, signed by illuminators from outside the city with their distinctive marks, including the young Simon Bening (second last entry), 1501.

A second important volume from the same guild of Saint Luke is its register from 1450 to 1578. This is a tall narrow ledger about 11¼ by slightly over 4 inches, bound in original limp parchment with a fold-over flap secured by a dangling string tie. This book does indeed involve Simon Bening, who has signed his name in the manuscript in a puzzling and fascinating entry on folio 113r. It is not exactly a record of admission to the guild, as sometimes suggested, but is rather different. It is in Flemish and is dated 21 March 1501. The preamble states that the dean and the officers of the guild have decreed that certain illuminators should come before the dean to inscribe their names and the distinctive marks which they use to sign their work, for registration by the guild. It explains that all those who practise the art of illumination by hand and who are not citizens of Bruges are required to obtain the consent of the guild in advance, as those inscribed here have duly done. Then follows a list of twelve names, all in different hands and inks, doubtless autographs. It is interesting that there were so many practising professionals at a time when one might have imagined that book illumination was almost extinct. Each name is accompanied by a unique symbol or mark, which might be a flower, a key, a lion's head, a monogram or some other device. The second-to-last entry is Simon Bening. He wrote his surname "bennync" and then crossed it out and rewrote it as "bynnync". He was seventeen or eighteen years of age, and any teenager under pressure can panic over a signature. Then he gives his personal mark, which is a cross followed by two vertical strokes.

There are enigmas here which are not yet solved. Many people have searched in vain for any of these marks used in manuscript illuminations of the early sixteenth century. These twelve names – Pieter de Wulf, Didier Rivier, Jan Moke and so on – quite possibly conceal the actual identities of anonymous Flemish illuminators familiar to us now only by modern sobriquets as the Master of this-or-that named from characteristic manuscripts. Any PhD student could make his or her reputation by finding even one of these marks signing an actual surviving miniature, but this has never happened. Weale traced most of the names in the archives of Bruges: de Wulf died in 1518/19, Rivier in 1509, Moke in 1504, and others, but we cannot yet match these names with any known works of art, except in the case of Bening.

There is a related piece of evidence from much earlier, which is probably relevant to this archaic piece of formal business in 1501. It is a particular feature of Netherlandish illumination, from both north and south, that miniatures were very commonly painted on single sheets of parchment, rather than directly onto the page of a book, as was usual in most of Europe. Simon Bening too often produced his miniatures separately. These sheets would then be trimmed to shape before being bound or even pasted into a manuscript. There is record of a municipal law in Bruges in 1427, brought about at the insistence of the painters' guild and referring to a previous incident of 1402 (details of which are lost). The legislation noted that foreign illuminators, especially from Utrecht in the north, were making and selling cheap single miniatures to be bound into manuscripts in Bruges, and that this was damaging the trade of the local craftsmen. The culprits were said to be operating anonymously in the streets around the church of Saint Donatien (now destroyed but formerly in the Burg, a few yards from where the city archives now are). Such miniatures therefore were required from 1427 to be signed by the artists with their distinctive marks, which were to be registered with the guild. This document was published by Weale in 1872–3, but no one had ever explained it until 1980, when the American art historian Douglas Farquhar first noted tiny stamped symbols impressed usually in pink into the margins of miniatures by the northern Dutch illuminators known as the Masters of Otto van Moerdrecht, working in Bruges in the 1420s–50s. About thirty manuscripts are now known in which such marks occur. Here is the crucial point. The marks are found only in the work of foreign illuminators living in Bruges, who were thereby given licence to operate there. Suddenly, that may explain why Simon Bening was required to register a mark in 1501. He had arrived from Ghent; he was an outsider, an alien. He and those eleven others summoned were not actually members of the guild, because they were not citizens of Bruges. Bening took citizenship in 1519, and after that he would no longer have needed to use the mark. The only manuscript by Bening which seems to have any kind of personal symbol is the Prayerbook of Albrecht of Brandenburg, which he painted in the late 1520s. An illuminated margin at the end incorporates a kind of monogram formed of a cross entwined with an 'S' closed on its right-hand edge so that with the stem of the cross it could possibly, perhaps with wishful thinking, be read as 'S. B'.

However, both Alexander Bening and his son were soon very visibly members of the other Bruges confraternity, the book trade's guild of Saint John the Evangelist, and two volumes of the account books of this more informal company are by far the most consistent record we have of Simon Bening's life. The first volume, covering the years 1454–1523, is in the town archives, where we have been looking at the records of the painters' guild. It was given to the municipality in 1813, when it was inscribed inside the upper cover, "Monument très précieux pour l'histoire de la typographie", because the early printers were members too. It continues into a second volume for 1524–55, still in its original (but crudely repaired) limp leather cover, stamped with the names "ihesus" and "maria". This later part is now in the state archives, or Rijksarchief, a huge modern building in the Predikherenrei on the far side of the canal which follows the line of the medieval boundary of Bruges.

An important component of both these volumes is the meticulous recording of annual subscriptions from members of the confraternity. We see Simon Bening's father paying his due in 1486 and 1487 and then, after a gap (perhaps back in Ghent), again each year from 1495 to 1499. The annual fee was usually 12 *groschen* (one shilling), a figure which remained generally consistent through the sixteenth century. There on folio 156v we first encounter Simon Bening himself, simply called 'symeon' (but it must be him), paying his own subscription as one of the 'new guild brothers' in 1507. The next year he is called 'Master Symon', perhaps acknowledgement of having finished some level of apprenticeship; in 1512 he is 'Simon the illuminator', and in 1517 'Simon Bening, Sanders' son'. From 1519, the year of his father's death, he is generally called 'Master Simon Bening', by now head of the family.

In the early part of his career, Simon Bening was sometimes absent from Bruges. In 1508 the confraternity's treasurer, Cristiaen de Cock, noted that 8 *groschen* remained unpaid by Simon because he had gone away ("met dat hy wech ghinc": this is in the second column of folio 160v). He was not mentioned again in Bruges until 1512. We can perhaps guess where he was. The earliest surviving dated work by Simon is a tiny prayerbook which ends with an inscription by the scribe telling that it was written and finished in Antwerp in 1511. The 'and finished' would usually mean that the illumination and binding were done there too. Simon's sister Cornelia lived in Antwerp, and he may have stayed with her. This was the same year as the completion in Antwerp of the altarpiece of the Joiners' Guild by Quentin Matsys, and it is almost inconceivable that Bening would not have met him. The manuscript has ten full-page miniatures by Bening and numerous illustrated borders and smaller pictures. This book has particular resonance for me. I brought it back for sale in London from its elderly owners in suburban Amsterdam a few days before Christmas in 1987 and my flight to Stansted Airport, where I had left the car, was cancelled because of the weather. I recall the harrowing experience of trying to get back from a

The Imhof Prayerbook, the earliest dated manuscript by Simon Bening, completed in Antwerp in 1511.

diversion through Heathrow in the freezing early hours of a midwinter morning with the oldest manuscript by Simon Bening in a shopping bag. By chance, another book waiting for sale at Sotheby's at that time was an early seventeenth-century armorial from Nuremberg. This allowed me to identify the prayerbook's original erased coat of arms as that of Imhof, and the strong probability is that it was made for Hans Imhof (1461–1522), of Nuremberg, friend of Albrecht Dürer and Willibald Pirckheimer, whose family traded spices extensively through Antwerp. He was the first of several important German clients of Bening and it marks the launch of the artist's international reputation.

In 1512, Bening was back in Bruges. The account books record that he came in on Saint Luke's Day (18 October) and paid 6 *groschen* but promised a further *livre*, as was witnessed by several members of the confraternity, including Ludwig Bloc. That was the bookbinder, mentioned above, who later bound the Prayerbook of Joanna de Ghistelles and the Benedictional of Robert de Clercq, both illuminated by Bening. Bloc occurs frequently throughout the accounts until his death in 1529. In the same entry of 1512, 16 *groschen* were paid by Antonius van Damme. We have encountered him earlier too – the scribe who afterwards collaborated with Bening on several manuscripts, including those dated 1531 and 1545. Damme is the closest town north-east of Bruges. Antonius must have been an almost exact contemporary and was possibly something of a personal friend, because in 1516 he paid Bening's subscription on his behalf. His name also appears time after time. We even know his address in Bruges, for in 1545 he described himself in Spanish as living in the street of the *sombreros* ('hats', or *hoeden* in Flemish), behind the Augustinian abbey. If the lists of payments represent the order in which members lined up at the desk, then Simon Bening was standing beside him in the queue in 1538, and Antonius van Damme was still included in the final entry mentioning Bening's name many years later in 1555.

We must remember that these were people who all knew and worked with each other over many years, and that making a manuscript involves parchment sellers, scribes and bookbinders, as well as a community of illuminators. That sense of a medieval fraternity of professionals is unlike the popular image of modern artists often living in isolation. Members of a close community would be more likely to collaborate within manuscripts or even single miniatures than solitary geniuses. Many of the great Flemish manuscripts of the early sixteenth century include the work of multiple artists and illuminators, sometimes working together even on the same pages. The magnificent Book of Hours made in the 1520s for Cardinal Albrecht of Brandenburg includes refined and beautiful miniatures by Simon Bening enclosed within illuminated borders which are crudely executed, many of them by a painter tellingly known now as the 'Master of the Garish Features'. To modern eyes, their coarseness detracts from the manuscript's overall quality. Presumably neither Bening nor his client really cared, or pressures of time or money necessitated compromises considered acceptable. In the Portuguese genealogy Bening was collaborating within single pictures with a lesser artist who lived over a thousand miles away. It was the nature of business. That sense of the uncontaminated hand of a great master, so important to the Italian renaissance and to Vasari, was always less evident in the Netherlands. Artists such as Pieter Bruegel, father and son, Rubens and even Rembrandt collaborated with colleagues and pupils without inhibition. It was one reason why guilds and fraternities were so important.

A regular shared activity of the brotherhood of the book trade in Bruges was attendance at church services, both on feast days and in commemoration of the dead. The records of annual expenses often list

Villagers on their way to church, single miniature attributed to Simon Bening, *c.*1550.

the festivals – Candlemas, the Sundays in Lent, Ascension Day, the feasts of Saint John the Evangelist, Saint John the Baptist, Saints Peter and Paul, Saint James, Saint Christopher, Saint Bartholomew and so on. The rhythm of the church year, in which members were active participants, is reflected in the very many calendars in manuscripts illustrated by Simon Bening over the years, in which major festivals are singled out in red, still very Catholic. There is a mid-sixteenth-century calendar miniature in the style of Bening in the Getty Museum, showing villagers with their children and dogs all lining up outside to attend Mass. Inside the door of the church itself priests and clerics can be seen waiting for the congregation holding lighted candles. Sometimes Bening himself paid for candles (as in 1508), and the cost of wax was a frequent expense.

Attendance at funerals and Masses for the dead was probably obligatory for members of the confraternity. This is how we know that Bening's father died in 1519, because the costs of his funeral are listed, as are those for Simon's two wives in 1542 and 1555. There were also Masses for those who had died earlier. In 1508, for example, there was still a Mass in memory of the famous Bruges illuminator Willem Vrelant, who had died in 1481. There are many pictures of funeral Masses in the manuscripts by Simon Bening, for it was a standard subject in illustrations

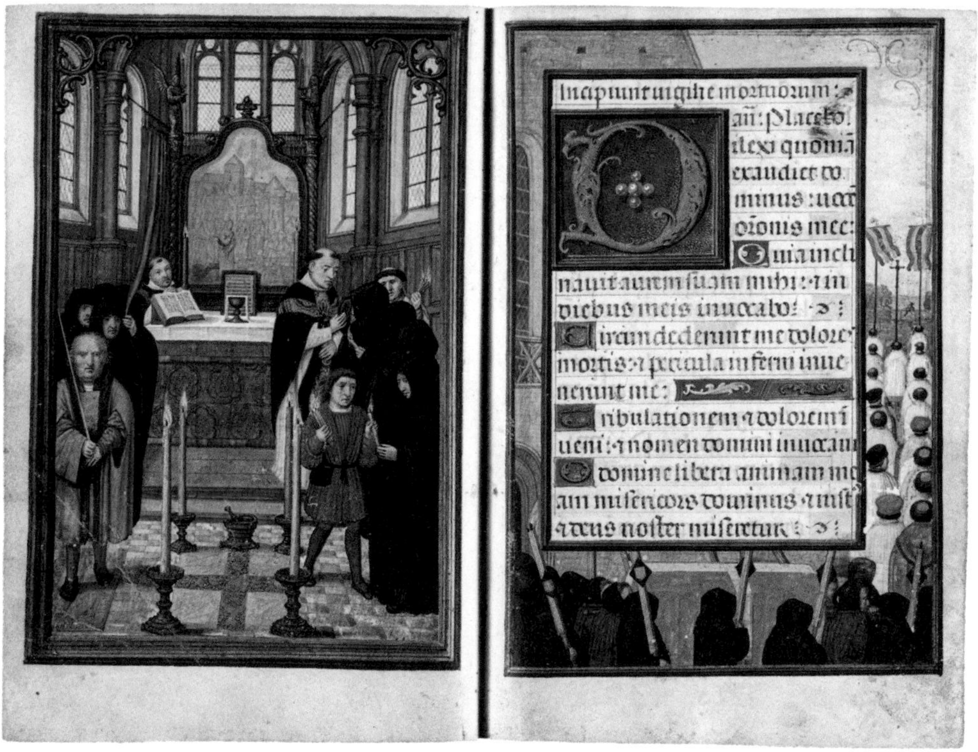

Funeral rites, part of a Book of Hours or prayerbook illuminated by Simon Bening, *c.*1520–30.

for the Office of the Dead in Flemish Books of Hours. One in the Victoria and Albert Museum, exhibited in the same case as his self-portrait, shows priests and hooded mourners carrying a bier through the street and then in a gothic church with the deceased's family holding flickering candles and receiving holy communion.

The confraternity held its regular services in the chapel of Saint Nicasius in the twelfth-century Augustinian abbey of Eekhout in central Bruges, where it had its own altar dedicated to Saint John the Evangelist and Saint Luke. In 1477–8, Hans Memling had painted an altarpiece for this chapel in Eekhout, commissioned by the same Willem Vrelant and his wife, who were shown on the panels. Members of the confraternity, including Bening, must have seen these portraits almost daily. The altarpiece is lost, and Eekhout Abbey has entirely vanished too. It was on the site of what is now the Groeningemuseum, the city gallery for Flemish art, in the avenue called the Dijver, facing the canal along from the

Gruuthuse house and the Onze-Lieve-Vrouwekerk. In 1522 members presented their altar with a new Missal. Bening gave (and presumably painted) its Crucifixion miniature, in exchange for being released from his dues towards the cost of candles that year. Ludwig Bloc supplied its blue initials and musical notes. He was therefore more than simply a binder but was responsible for all finishing details. In 1529, Bening contributed 22 *groschen* for altar cloths and 8 *groschen* in 1538 for restoring the embroidery of the chapel seats.

Most of the official meetings of the book trade took place in Eekhout Abbey. Several, however, are recorded as being held "in de colve". They were probably convivial transactions made over drinks, perhaps with dinner. The Colve – the name means 'the (sign of) the hammer' – was a tavern in Hoogstraat, literally 'high street', which runs north-eastwards from the Burg, beginning from the former site of Saint Donatien's church, around which the illuminators had been working in 1427, and the Colve was already there in 1377. A house on what is now the site of no. 9 Hoogstraat was still being described in 1618 as adjacent to it. Early histories of sport are as notoriously fanciful as those of ancient schools, but there is one legend that the name of 'golf' is a corruption of the word 'Colve', a supposed inn somewhere in the Netherlands where the game was first played. One of Simon Bening's fragmentary Books of Hours, now in the British Library, is famously known as the 'Golf Book' because its calendar for September shows four men holding clubs to knock balls into holes in the outside yard of what might well be a tavern, equally dubiously but commonly claimed to be the earliest depiction of the sport.

The 'Golf Book' illuminated by Simon Bening, with the calendar scene for September showing a supposed early game of golf, *c.*1540–45.

We know from volume I of the confraternity's account book that Simon Bening was in the Colve with Ludwig Bloc and other members on 9 January 1518, and I went to find it. Its former neighbour no. 9 is part of a modern hotel, but no. 5, nearly adjacent on the corner of Hoogstraat and Mallebergplaats, is still an old tavern, now called the Restaurant Diligence. I pushed into the bright light, out of the January cold. I ordered for 19 euros the *Vlaamse stoverij met trappiest en verse appelmoes*, Flemish beef stew with Trappist beer and apple, doubtless not so different from a menu of 500 years ago, and several glasses of the 'winter edition' of Dubbel, or brown ale. I sat looking around. There are beams on the ceiling and two ancient arched fireplaces. The walls are very old, to judge from their thickness in the window apertures. I have no idea whether this could actually have been the Colve, but the food and the setting were entirely imaginable for a supper with Simon Bening and his colleagues from the confraternity in 1518, reminding me of his evocative full-page calendar miniature for the month of January in the Da Costa Book of Hours in the Morgan Library, where people are being served at table by candlelight near the roaring fire, while the shutters keep out the winter weather.

In 1524, when he was about forty, Bening was elected dean of the confraternity of the book trade. His autograph signature, much more confident than in his late teens, is towards the end of the first volume of the account book. The second volume opens with a reckoning of the state of the guild during his year of office. It then had forty members, mostly paying 12 *groschen* each, together with sisters and other associates, including widows, usually contributing 2 *groschen*. Further income came from bequests. The entire budget for the year under Bening's administration was 7 *livres*, 17 shillings and four *groschen*.

By this time, Bening was probably already the best-known manuscript illuminator in Flanders. He had worked extensively on the lovely Da Costa Hours, now in New York, apparently intended for a member of the Portuguese family of Sá but soon afterwards in the possession of Don Alvaro da Costa (*c.*1470–1540), chamberlain to Manuel I, king of Portugal 1495–1521. It was Bening's first Book of Hours to have full-page illustrations of the months in the calendar, a model doubtless learned

OVERLEAF: The Prayerbook of Cardinal Albrecht of Brandenburg, illuminated by Simon Bening, *c.*1525–30.

from seeing or hearing of the hundred-year-old *Très Riches Heures* of the Duc de Berry, then much admired in Flanders in the library of Margaret of Austria. The different seasons depicted in Calendar pictures became a famous feature of Simon Bening's later art. He had already established connections with clients in Spain, to judge from fragments of a Rosary Psalter of the mid-1520s, of which leaves are in the Boston Public Library, the Fitzwilliam Museum and elsewhere, with texts in the Spanish language. Above all, he had become the favourite illuminator of Cardinal Albrecht of Brandenburg (1490–1545), archbishop and elector of Mainz and a principal opponent of Martin Luther. For him Bening contributed perhaps originally as many as eighty half- or full-page miniatures to a large two-volume manuscript Book of Hours, which can be dated to 1522–3 because of its inclusion of the arms of the short-lived pope Adrian VI. Even more refined and creative is the smaller manuscript Passion Prayerbook made by Bening for Cardinal Albrecht, probably around 1525–30, mentioned earlier. It comprises sixty-two devotional prayers in German and has forty-one full-page miniatures. Some of the night scenes are especially extraordinary, such as three for the betrayal and arrest of Christ and the escape of the apostles from Gethsemane, in which burning torches of the soldiers sizzle and scatter sparks into the midnight sky, or the denial of Peter around a glowing coal fire in the centre of the courtyard of the house of the high priest, lighting the drama in the encircling darkness. Others in the Brandenburg manuscript transpose biblical narratives into the cityscape of Bruges. Joseph of Arimathea speaking to Pontius Pilate is set before a building almost indistinguishable from the town hall in the square of the Burg. David entering Jerusalem in triumph bearing the head of Goliath passes through a medieval city gateway over a moat or canal. Bening cannot have failed to make the comparison with the celebrated pageant of the Entry of Charles V into Bruges in 1515, which he had most probably witnessed.

One might have thought that by the second quarter of the sixteenth century the market for illuminated manuscripts in Europe would have long died out. Vespasiano had struggled with competition from cheap printing even in the 1470s. When Bening was at the height of his fame, printing had been already universal for almost all European book production for seventy years. Printed Books of Hours were easily available in almost limitless quantities from Paris, often with very sophisticated cycles of engraved illustrations. However, human nature does not change as fast as technology. In our own time we heard in the 1990s that books as physical artefacts were finished: the volume in your hands is evidence that the report of their death was premature. For several generations after the invention of printing, the old and new crafts fed from one another, especially in northern Europe. Raphael de Mercatellis (1437–1508), illegitimate son of Philippe le Bon and abbot of Saint Bavo in Ghent, formed a fine library of illuminated manuscripts even at the end of his life, which scribes mostly copied out from printed editions, reversing the revolution in an unexpected way. The texts of at least two of the manuscripts illuminated by Bening were taken from printed books. The prayers of his Da Costa Book of Hours were copied from the edition of the *Hortulus animae* published in Strassburg in 1498, and those of the Brandenburg Prayerbook were taken directly from an edition of German prayers printed in Cologne in 1521. The fact is that there were still people who preferred manuscripts.

Bening's niche business survived and even flourished well into the sixteenth century for three reasons. First of all, he traded in religious nostalgia. Prayerbooks are almost always retrospective in appearance, even now, looking back to beliefs that most people learn as children. An old format seems somehow more dignified for prayer, even more efficacious. There is every reason to suppose that Simon Bening was personally devout. He did not sell in Lutheran countries. His clients were in Spain and Portugal, Italy up to a point, and in southern Germany, all Catholic. The few in Flanders were religious institutions. There were none in the northern Netherlands or in England, despite its historic connections with Bruges and the fact that his daughter moved there (as we will come to). Bening was the master of traditional and even reactionary Catholicism – saints, martyrdoms, confession and Mass, with a dash of sentimental piety. As Protestantism began to split loyalties in Europe from the 1520s, Simon Bening astutely became the visual spokesman for the old religion and by extension for proper handmade prayerbooks as they used to be.

Secondly, he was technically a superb painter and colourist in the tradition from Jan Van Eyck and Hugo van der Goes, able to create dramatic and emotional atmospheres on the smallest scale, with a dexterity and freshness which is utterly beguiling. Vasari's lives of the artists (1568) mentions "Simone Benich da Bruggia", including him in the company of panel painters. No printed woodcut or engraving could ever match the skilful gradations of colour and light and darkness evoked by Bening in such tiny spaces, or his dreamy distances. There had been other great manuscript painters in Flanders, but by about 1530 he was the finest left in business. As he got older, the detail of his miniatures became even smaller, probably consciously exploiting something which he knew could not be matched by the printing press.

Finally, he was expensive. He learned, as companies specializing in luxury goods do now, that the more you charge, the more highly valued is the commodity. There was huge private money in Europe as the sixteenth century advanced, especially in Iberia with new access to American gold. Isabella of Portugal, patron of a Book of Hours with miniatures by Bening in the Huntington Library in California, was the wife of the emperor Charles V, sometimes claimed as the richest man there has ever been. The Beatty Rosarium in Dublin, painted by Bening, was probably made for Charles V himself, and certainly belonged to his son Philip II of Spain. The crowned heads of Catholic Europe and their socially ambitious courtiers increasingly competed for manuscripts by Simon Bening.

Although his craft was old, Bening was an artist of the newly arrived Renaissance, when individual painters first became revered and sought after as celebrities, not merely as ancillary functionaries infilling the spaces in manuscripts left by the scribes. There is no evidence of booksellers or *libraires* in sixteenth-century Bruges, handling commissions and sub-contracting craftsmen, as Vespasiano had done in Florence. If you wanted a manuscript by Bening, you almost certainly went to the artist himself. He probably arranged the contracts and employed the scribes. The ultimate irony is that when, after a thousand years, the illuminator had finally become the principal virtuoso in the production of manuscripts, the market was almost over.

Bening adapted to the inevitable changes. We encountered earlier the characteristic Netherlandish tradition that miniatures were often executed on single sheets of parchment, which could then be traded and bound up to illustrate books. Bening too had often followed this practice, sending out miniatures, such as those that went to Toledo to be bound into the Hours of Isabella of Portugal. Sometimes his miniatures were so admired that they were not included in manuscripts at all. There is a folding quadriptych in the Walters Art Museum in Baltimore with rows

RIGHT: The Stein Quadriptych, panels of small miniatures attributed to Simon Bening, *c.*1530–40.

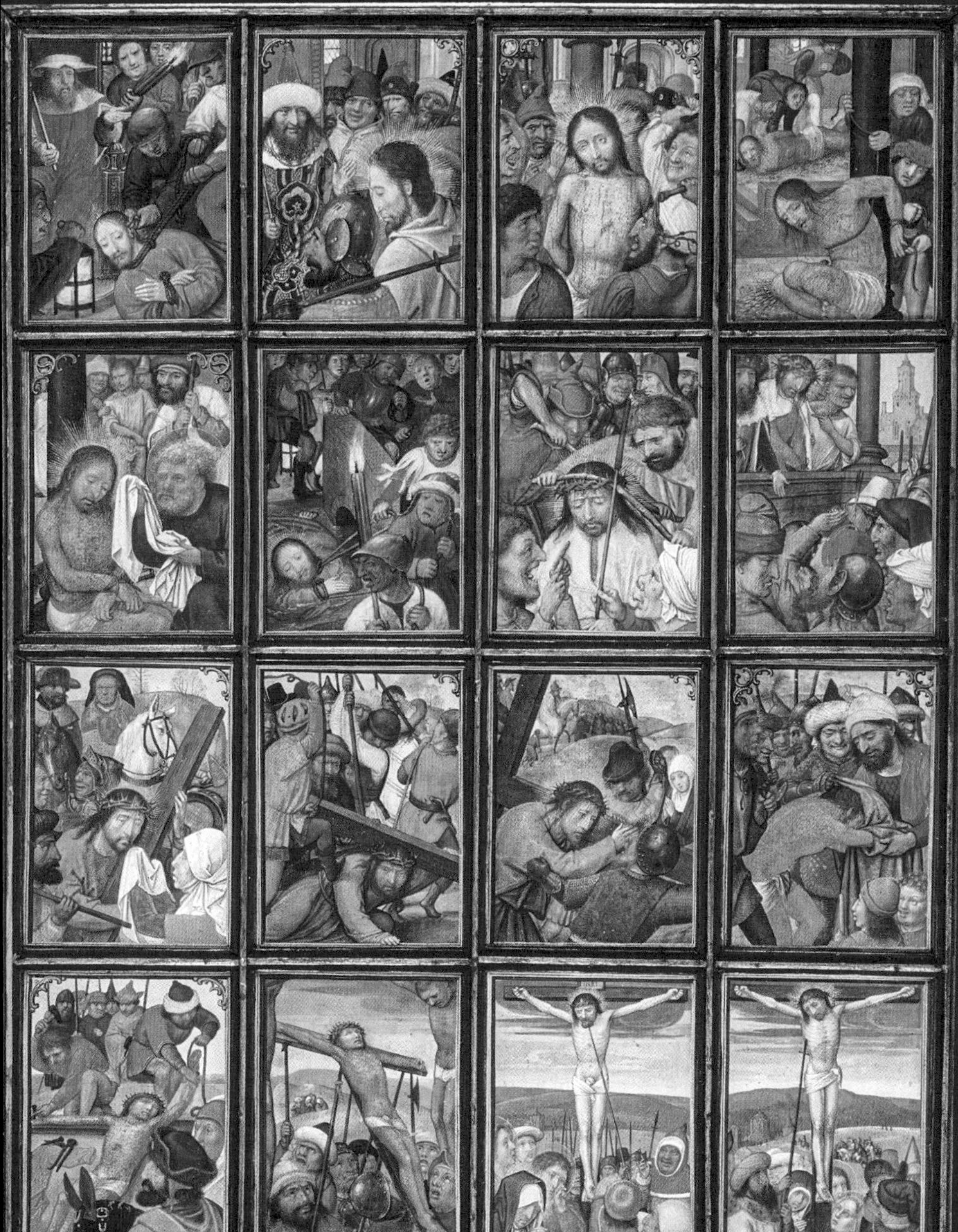

of sixty-four little pictures painted by Bening and his workshop, resembling those narrative icons in Ethiopian art. It is not clear whether the separate miniatures in Baltimore were intended for a book (or removed from one), or whether they were planned from the outset to be mounted and displayed as works of art by Bening in their own right.

The market for single-sheet miniatures increased as the demand for whole books declined. In parallel with manuscripts, framed illuminated texts and miniatures sometimes hung in houses and churches. There is one from around 1500 still in the church of Sint-Salvator in Bruges, in praise of the Holy Sacrament. They can often be seen on walls or church pillars in the backgrounds of early Netherlandish panel paintings, and indeed in some of Bening's own miniatures of domestic or church interiors. One is shown quite incongruously in his scene of the Last Supper in the Prayerbook of Johanna de Ghistelles, where there is a tiny triptych on top of a dresser depicting the Virgin and Child apparently between two standing saints (see p. 136). Its central image resembles the one Bening was working on in his self-portrait, which too was probably not for a manuscript at all. Two more framed pictures appear on the panelled walls in the background of another miniature by Bening of the Last Supper, sold by Christie's in 2019. A number of late miniatures by Bening were clearly designed to be mounted on boards as tiny altar panels or as separately framed devotional pictures. A truly beautiful example re-emerged at Sotheby's in 2020, showing the Virgin and Child in a landscape surrounded by female saints. Its sale price catapulted Simon Bening into the commercial category of major Old Master panel painters. There are even a few portrait miniatures attributed to Bening, and several calendar scenes from the end of his career are so self-contained that they must surely always have been intended as individual *kunstkammer* objects for admiration and display. Bening's latest datable manuscript in codex format is probably the Rosarium of 1545, written by van Damme and illustrated by Bening, effectively the last book of the Middle Ages. Other work made by him after that date was probably all separate pictures.

Simon Bening twice again served as dean of the book trade confraternity of Saint John the Evangelist in Bruges. Volume II of the account book shows his familiar signatures once more on taking office in 1535 and again in 1545. By then he was in his early sixties. A few pages later there is a list of members of the confraternity in 1548 arranged by occupations.

They include five scribes, still with "M[eeste]r Anthonis van damme" among their number, but now only three illuminators (Bening together with Thomas de Raet and Pieter Claeys), but as many as five printers.

We do not know (or at least I do not know) exactly where Simon Bening lived. Both his wives were buried in the churchyard of Sint-Kruis, which was presumably their parish church, and their house was doubtless nearby. The church has gone, but it was just outside the north-east perimeter of the city wall, not far from where the Rijksarchief is now. It would have been about ten minutes' walk to the Colve and another five to Eekhout Abbey.

To get some flavour of what it might have been like to visit Simon Bening at home, I arranged to go to see Brody Neuenschwander, scribe and illuminator in Bruges. Brody is an American by birth, genial and articulate, and it was he who first taught me how to lay gold leaf on parchment at a course in Minnesota more than thirty years ago. He is a professional maker of illuminated manuscripts, about the age Bening was at the height of his fame, and his own clients are even more international. Brody Neuenschwander is in no sense a creator of spurious medieval pastiches, but a modern artist working in startlingly original styles. He does, however, use traditional manuscript makers' techniques and tools, and his house and workshop might not be so different from Bening's in the 1540s. Brody and his Belgian wife, Nadine, live in a tall medieval Flemish brick house in the Spinolarei. Its principal original room up a little staircase to the left on entering has two walls of astounding late fourteenth-century wall paintings, which are quite likely to have been seen by Jan Van Eyck, who lived nearby, and not impossibly by Bening. The Neuenschwanders also have a dog, called Orlando. This is not mere extraneous detail, for Simon Bening almost certainly had one too. Orlando is a Kooikerhondje, an ancient breed of Dutch hunting dog, with brown and white markings, floppy brown ears and a fluffy tail. It was noticed by Beth Morrison at the Getty Museum that for about a dozen years a dog looking exactly like this appears consistently in miniatures by Simon Bening. He is a puppy snuffling in the street outside Herod's palace in the Brandenburg Prayerbook in the late 1520s; he bounds along on the falcon hunt in the July miniature of the Hennessy Hours in Brussels; he lies loyally on the floor with his head on his paws in the study of Jacques de Lalaing's biographer as his master begins to write his reminiscences (also in the Getty Museum); and by about 1540 he is distinctly old with drooping eyes and shuffling feet in the autumnal October scene of the calendar of the Golf Book in London.

Brody took me out across to see his studio. As in many old Belgian town houses, there is an enclosed courtyard behind and then a two-storey outhouse at the back, which he has converted. The Neuenschwanders' garden is formal with little parterres, a bit like that shown for March in the Golf Hours, where the gardener tips his hat deferentially to the lady of the house. Most late-medieval craftsmen worked at home, and Bening's window in the self-portrait shows an outlook which was probably upstairs, to judge from the angle of the view. The tree shown in the foreground and a house behind might even have been the view back across his own courtyard. Brody led me up the steep steps into his studio. Orlando was made to wait downstairs on the ground floor.

Like Bening, Brody works at a sloping desk, although it is not at such a high angle. The window is behind him, but he does also have the additional advantage of electric light. Parchment and pigments and works in various stages of completion lie on tables around the room. We spoke a bit about materials. Parchment, which he mostly uses, is still a major expense. In the Middle Ages, Brody told me, it was brought in from Torhout, south-west of Bruges, and sufficient for a substantial manuscript was said to cost about as much as a house. For an important miniature, only the central part of a parchment sheet is fine enough to be usable.

All Brody's pens are quills. He picks up all he needs, he said, discarded from the swans along the canals in Bruges. Bening's picture of the chronicler of Jacques de Lalaing writing shows the barbs of the feathers all peeled away, as does his image of Saint Luke holding his pen aloft in the Hennessy Hours. Brody, however, likes to leave a few vanes of the feather in place, partly to help distinguish one pen from another in the rack. He put on magnifying lenses even more powerful than Bening's and cut the nib of a quill to show me how quickly and sharply it was done. He wrote a few lines as I watched, transported back to the Renaissance. As far as we know, Bening never wrote his own manuscripts, but his elegant gold capitals below his self-portrait show considerable calligraphic dexterity. Most medieval ink was iron gall ink, made from copperas (ferrous sulphate) and crushed-up oak apples infused in water. It is easier to use than

RIGHT: Single devotional miniature of the Virgin and other saints, by Simon Bening, *c.*1530–40.

carbon ink, Brody explained, because it is much thinner and has unusually high surface tension, and he demonstrated how it holds on the page as it dries and becomes dramatically darker as it does so. It is very acidic, which etches it slightly into parchment. I asked whether writing in different languages was a problem, for Bening's scribes produced books in Latin, Flemish, French, German, Spanish and Portuguese. Not at all, he replied, for a scribe can easily copy without understanding, as long as it is in a Roman alphabet and even that is not wholly necessary. Antonius van Damme wrote in a multitude of languages which he need not have known. For commission work, the client supplied the textual exemplar and sometimes a manuscript already written.

We looked at photographs of Bening's self-portrait and I commented that it seemed odd for a right-handed man to have his rack for brushes and pigments on the left. On the contrary, it would be quite normal, said Brody: when you are working you prefer to keep hold of the brush and to reach with your left hand for paint. Pigments were usually mixed with raw egg and dispensed from shells. Mussels and oysters are still staple foods in Belgium, especially this close to the sea, and shells of both were used by artists for holding paint, for they have smooth and washable interiors. Brody told me that he himself prefers oyster shells, because their rough outside can prevent them wobbling. Their small capacity tells us how little paint was mixed up at one time. A small white package visible on Bening's shelf, which I had supposed to be a folded-up letter, is how artists' pigments were sold. Brody said that during the restoration of the medieval part of their house, they found a packet of just this size hidden between the brickwork and a beam, containing powdered gold.

The fact that Bening in his self-portrait is sitting with the window over his left shoulder led me to mention that in every one of Simon Bening's miniatures and borders of daylight scenes, without exception throughout his career, the shadows are painted to the right. This was so standard for Bening that he probably never thought about it. Brody was not particularly impressed by the observation.

At this point I revealed that I had benefited from an unusual resource. Through the kindness of Sandra Hindman and Les Enluminures, I had previously borrowed a miniature by Simon Bening from the remarkable illustrated prayerbook which he made probably in the late 1520s, evidently for Fadrique Enríquez de Ribera (1476–1539), marquis of Tarifa. I had then brought it to Andrew Beeby and Richard Gameson, of Durham

University, who, in a rare collaboration between science and manuscript history, have been analysing the pigments of medieval illuminations by the non-destructive techniques of fibre-optic reflectance spectroscopy and Raman spectroscopy, both in Durham and at the Bodleian Library in Oxford. By bouncing laser light off colours and by measuring different vibrations of molecules as the light is refracted, it allows precise chemical analysis of the pigments. Much of our knowledge of medieval art is formed from a cumulation of probabilities and judgements; with spectroscopy we are dealing with absolute fact. By this method, we now know exactly what materials Bening was using in his paint shells that day. In some ways, the result was to me slightly disappointing. I had hoped that Bening's dazzling colour effects might reveal the use of new pigments, perhaps from America or the Far East, unknown to his medieval predecessors. On the contrary, his palette was revealed by spectroscopy to be finite and traditional, and the skill was all in the application. Most blue in the miniature is azurite; there is no lapis, not even in the robe of the Virgin Mary. There is some dark indigo. Reds are all vermilion, with different shades achieved by varying its intensity and occasionally by adding organic ochre. There are white lead, and carbon black, some lead tin yellow, probably vergaut for green (formed from mixing indigo and orpiment), a little ground-up silver and gold, and that is about all.

Brody looked through these tabulated results without great surprise, noting the absence of cool lakes and dyes. There is no crimson, madder or turnsole. He observed that bluey-green verdigris, not apparently used, is tiresome to manipulate as its granules require constant stirring. The colours would all be applied with tiny brushes, some soft, others stiff, usually in tiny quick dabs, one over another. The trick, he said, is not to let the surface get too damp. Wetness is especially a problem with parchment, which is extraordinarily responsive to changes in humidity, expanding and curling when in contact with liquids and contracting rapidly as it dries. Many of the late Bening miniatures were apparently attached onto card or wood: that can be catastrophic if the sheet is too big, for it will tear as the pigment or paste dries and the parchment shrinks. That must be why large parchment compositions, such as the quadriptych in Baltimore, were assembled from multiple tiny pieces.

I wondered about daily life in an illuminator's shop. Would Bening undertake other jobs too? Of course, said Brody; any artist is constantly consulted on everything from wall painting to decorated cakes. Bening's book trade colleagues in the Colve must sometimes have sought his advice on many subjects. There is doubtless more research to be done on the design of engravings in printed books from Bruges, in which he might easily have been involved, at least in informal conversation with his colleagues at guild meetings. In both Paris and Venice early sixteenth-century manuscript painters certainly designed woodcuts. Jean Bourdichon (*c.*1457–1521), court illuminator in France, was called upon to paint the banners for the Field of Cloth of Gold in 1520. Brody drew the labels for Brugse Zot beer bottles. Would Simon Bening, I asked, have worked in his studio alone? Absolutely not, Brody told me, with unexpected conviction. At the very least, he explained, an illuminator in the midst of a tense and difficult manoeuvre under magnification needs to be able to shout for more blue paint or for blotting paper. The two other illuminators remaining in Bruges in 1548, Thomas de Raet and Pieter Claeys, may both have been assistants in the workshop, or he might have been helped by his wife or one of the daughters. It is not easy being a manuscript maker in the wrong period of history. It requires persistence and constant imagination. "I have to do something that the people with computers cannot do", said Brody Neuenschwander; "that has been the basis of my career." Bening probably said exactly the same about printing. Later, during lunch in their little dining room overlooking the street along the canal, a man with a face like a portrait by Rogier van der Weyden walked past the window. Nadine waved to him and then explained, "He is the man who rings the bells in the belfry." Simon and Jane Bening would doubtless have known his predecessor in the 1540s.

The last entries mentioning Bening in the accounts of the booksellers' confraternity concern the death and funeral of his wife on 9 May 1555. Simon attended, in the company of Simon van der Muelen, bookseller, Raphael Roost, scribe, Pauwel van Vaerdebeke, bookseller, Pieter Claeys, illuminator, and Jan van Buene, bookseller; a few lines below is Antonius van Damme, "reste inn ho" (does that mean his old friend the scribe too is dead?).

Simon Bening and his first wife, Katherine, had had five daughters. He might have preferred a son, to carry on the manuscript business, except that by the middle of the century there was hardly a trade to inherit. One daughter died in 1544. Of the others, we know only of the two eldest. As James Weale first discovered, Bening's second daughter, Alexandine, married Clement Claeiszuene, and became a dealer in works

The author portrait illuminated by Simon Bening in a manuscript life of Jacques de Lalaing, *c.*1530.

of art, parchment, silk and other luxury goods. She may have supplied materials or sold miniatures for her father. The eldest daughter, Levina, is the best-known. She became a portrait miniaturist in her own right, the newly fashionable development from manuscript illumination into which even Simon was edging by his old age. He doubtless taught her, probably a pleasurable activity for both of them. Levina may well have collaborated in some of her father's paintings, at least until her marriage to George Teerlinc, citizen of Blankenberge, in 1545. She had moved to England within two years and by the summer of 1547 "Maistris Levyn Teerling paintrix" was on the royal payroll in London. She is recorded successively as a painter of miniatures in the households of Henry VIII, Edward VI, Queen Mary and Queen Elizabeth. Vasari mentions her too in his lives of the artists, "Levina figlia di maestro Simone da Bruggia". To have lived securely in England she probably had to abandon her father's Catholicism, which may have been disappointing for him, or even the reason for her emigration. A number of tiny Tudor portraits are sometimes ascribed to Levina, especially of women, mainly as she is almost the only documented miniaturist at the English court between Hans Holbein the younger and Nicholas Hilliard in the 1570s, but none can be attributed with certainty. She died in Stepney in East London in 1576.

The word 'miniature' as applied to manuscript decoration has nothing to do with size. It derives from the Latin *minium*, meaning red lead or vermilion, with the corresponding verb *miniare*, to colour in red. An ancient Roman manuscript with decoration was said to be coloured, *miniatus*. In time, it came to mean any book illustration. An Italian geography of the

Simon Bening, a second version of his self-portrait, 1558, now in New York.

Netherlands by Lodovico Guicciardini (1567) mentions Simon Bening as "grandissimo maestro nel miniare", a great master of illumination, but perhaps he was also thinking of the word in a new sense in contrast to *grandissimo*, as a very big master of the very small. By then, the old art of manuscript painting had passed out of currency. A portrait miniature, the art which Bening bequeathed to his daughter, is so called because it is minute. The techniques are almost the same, but the words have quite different derivations.

Curiously, some of Bening's artistic legacy may be in something unexpectedly large. It has often been noted how compositional details of Bening's late calendar miniatures resemble the vast masterpieces of Pieter Bruegel the elder. The famous paintings of the Seasons commissioned from Bruegel in Antwerp in 1565, now in Vienna, were originally planned as six (or twelve) for the whole cycle of the year, like an outsized calendar from a Bening Book of Hours. They are each more than 5 feet across. The artist and printer Hubert Goltzius (1526–83), a kinsman of Pieter Bruegel's wife, was working in Bruges when Bening died there as a widower in 1561 and the workshop was closed. It is very likely that they knew each other from the confraternity or the Colve. Simon Bening had inherited pattern sheets from the Master of the First Prayerbook, probably in 1519. It is not impossible that his own were eventually acquired or at least seen by Bruegel.

This brings us back at the end to Simon Bening's miniature of himself dated 1558, three years after he had ceased attending meetings of the confraternity and not long before his death. There is, in fact, a second self-portrait, almost identical to that in the Victoria and Albert Museum, now in the Robert Lehman Collection in the Metropolitan Museum of Art in New York. Curators at each institution have long compared the two, back and forth, trying to decide that their own is the original and the other a copy. Sandra Hindman suggests to me that they are both originals by Simon Bening, made exactly the same, one for each of his surviving daughters; if their sisters Anne and Barbara were still alive, he might have made more than two. The elderly miniaturist knows the end is near. He looks back to his family and the vanished business as it used to be in the fifteenth century, and for the first time in fifty years Simon calls himself 'son of Alexander'.

16 29
Sir Robert Cotton
1571 1631

CHAPTER FIVE

The Antiquary: Sir Robert Cotton

The many hundreds of manuscripts which once belonged to Sir Robert Cotton (1571–1631) have very quaint classification numbers, still used by the British Library in London, where most of his huge collection is now kept. They are catalogued under the names of the twelve early Caesars from Julius and Augustus, founders of the Roman empire, to their successors Tiberius, Caligula, Claudius, Nero, Galba, Otho, Vitellius, Vespasian, Titus and Domitian, in that order, emperors once familiar to our classically trained ancestors, if no longer always to us, supplemented by two women, Cleopatra, never forgotten, and the less recognizable Faustina, probably the wife of Antoninus Pius. These were the names given to the fourteen bookcases or cupboards around the walls of the original library in Cotton House, part of the complex of medieval and later buildings which once made up the old Palace of Westminster. Sir Robert Cotton had bought the house in 1622, making many alterations and renaming it after himself. It was conveniently situated for his work as a former and future Member of Parliament, between Westminster Hall and the House of Lords. The house was on the river and had a garden down to the water's edge. Cotton's manuscripts were kept in a long narrow library upstairs on the south side of the building, with a window at the end looking out over the Thames. That room had originally been a private chapel built for Henry III, which would have appealed to Cotton as an antiquary, if he knew. The bookcases were in gothic apertures around the walls, each ornamented by a classical bust which gave it its name. A visitor in 1692 described these figures as "heads in brass'" on the top of each bookcase, presumably bronze or possibly gilded plaster. They were probably installed only in the last years of Cotton's life,

LEFT: Portrait of Sir Robert Cotton, attributed to Cornelius Janssens (Cornelius Johnson), 1629.

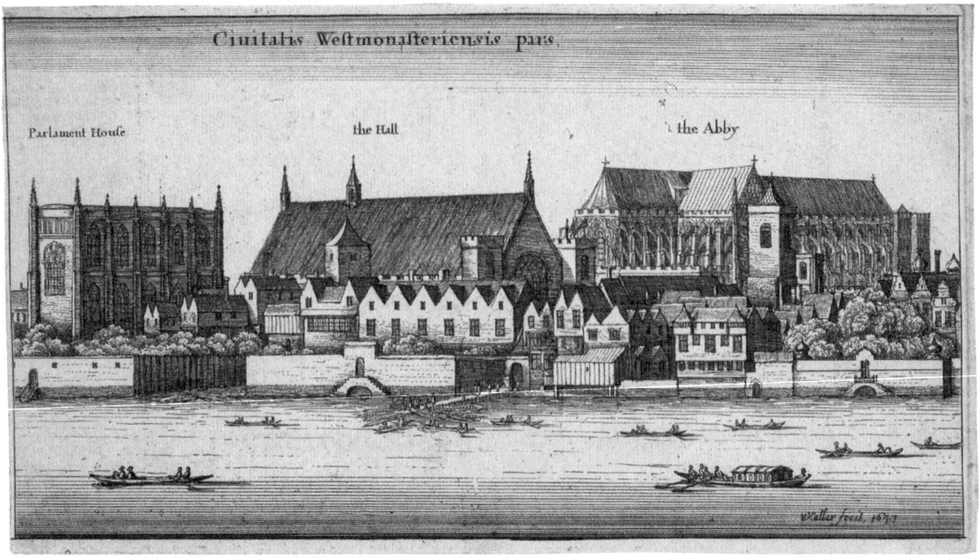

The houses on the river at Westminster, engraved by Wenceslas Hollar in 1647: Cotton House is probably the low building just visible at the far left.

for the emperors' names were hardly used (if at all) until shortly after his death, and indeed Cleopatra and Faustina may have been additions to the set on the north side when the collection was rearranged slightly by Cotton's family. Already in the use of imperial figureheads we have a sense of authority and antiquity in a collection which was stored and classified near the heart of national government. Cotton's was a new kind of manuscript library, not for the piety of monks or the domestic delight of princes, but for the preservation of history and the service of state at a time when English nationhood was being reshaped and defined.

Within the bookcases of the emperors, the manuscripts were ordered and numbered by approximate size from the upper shelves downwards. Like most books at that time, volumes stood upright with their fore-edges facing outwards. They might have looked rather dull to us, without the gilt spines and titles which enhance the appearance of a modern library. Subjects were generally mixed up in no obvious combinations. To choose an example not quite at random, let us walk down to the cupboard named 'Nero', probably at the far right-hand end nearest to the river. Up at 'A', its top shelf, were eighteen small volumes, including the chunky little manuscript of the letters of Anselm and Lanfranc described in Chapter 1, which sat beside items as diverse as an eleventh-century copy of the laws of King Alfred and others in Old English, a little twelfth-century Bestiary, or book of animals, from the abbey of Holme Cultram in Cumbria, the unique manuscript of the *Pearl* poem and *Sir Gawain and the Green Knight*, one of three copies of the *Ancrene Riwle* in the Cotton library (the earliest generally recognized text in Middle English), and the Beaulieu Abbey cartulary. The smallest volume on that uppermost shelf was about 4¾ by 3½ inches, a fifteenth-century chronicle of Ely bound up with an unrelated late twelfth-century life of the would-be saint Hamo of Savigny, who died in 1173. On the next shelf down, lettered 'B' in the Nero cupboard, were major state papers especially relating to England and Europe, mostly Elizabethan. Shelf 'C' below had, among eight other books, the illustrated twelfth-century Winchester Psalter perhaps made for the bishop, Henry of Blois, brother of King Stephen, and the autograph diary of King Edward VI. These are astounding treasures by any standard. The fourth shelf began with Matthew Paris's own thirteenth-century manuscript of his lives of the abbots of St Albans, where he was a monk. Four books along was the early eighth-century Lindisfarne Gospels, no less, probably even now the most precious illuminated manuscript in Britain, still known formally as Nero D. IV. Finally, the cupboard's biggest books of all were on Nero's fifth and lowest shelf, 'E', near the floor. Among them were a text on cosmography illuminated for Henry VIII and Katherine of Aragon 16½ inches high; the thirteenth-century Walsingham Cartulary, nearly 18 inches tall; and an even vaster copy of the *Grandes Chroniques de France* in two volumes (the text promoted by the Duc de Berry), illuminated in Paris in the early fifteenth century, with ninety miniatures, mostly by the Boucicaut Master. The original Emperor Nero has a reputation of presiding indifferently over the burning of Rome, a theme with sinister recurrence in the story which follows, but that single five-shelf bookcase under Nero's titular patronage in Cotton House in the seventeenth century was almost certainly the most valuable there has ever been in English history.

On other nearby shelves in the same room were the famous illustrated Cotton Genesis of the fifth or sixth century, five of the seven known Old English manuscripts of the Anglo-Saxon Chronicle, the unique text of Asser's life of King Alfred, the illustrated Gospels of King Æthelstan, two of the four surviving original copies of the Magna Carta, and the only extant manuscript of any Anglo-Saxon epic, the incomparable *Beowulf* itself. There were no mere printed books in the room at all.

LII INFINEMPRO PROAMALECHIN TELLEGENTIAEDD

DIXITINSIPIENSIN
CORDESUO NONESTDS;
CORRUPTISUNT ETABOMINA
BILESFACTIST INIQUITATI
B; NONESTQUIFACIATBONU;
DSDECAELOPROSPEXITSUPER
FILIOSHOMINU UTUIDEAT
SIESTINTELLEGENSAUTRE
QUIRENSDM;

OMSDECLINAUERUNTSIMULIN
UTILESFACTISUNT ~NESTQUI
FACIATBONU ~NESTUSQ; ADUNU;
NONNESCIENTOMSQUIOPE
RANTURINIQUITATE
QUIDEUORANTPLEBEMME
AMUTCIBUMPANIS;
DMNONINUOCAUERUNT
ILLICTREPIDAUERUNTTI

MOREUBINONFUITTIMOR;
QMDSDISSIPAUITOSSAEORU
QUIHOMINIB;PLACENTCFU
SISTQMDSSPREUITEOS;
QUISDABITEXSIONSALUTARE
ISRAHEL CUMCONUERTERIT
DSCAPTIUITATEPLEBISSUAE
EXSULTABITIACOBETLAE
TABITURISRAHEL

On Cotton's death in Westminster on 6 May 1631, the collection and house were bequeathed to his son, Sir Thomas Cotton (1594–1662), with the stipulation that they would pass in turn to Thomas's own son Sir John Cotton (1621–1702). The heirs maintained the legacy as a national reference resource with varying degrees of diligence and family piety. From time to time, modest additions were made. Researchers and antiquaries were generally allowed to consult manuscripts in Cotton House, although the library was still reached by going through the family's drawing room. Sometimes it was less trouble to allow outsiders to borrow material than to have them working in the house. However, it is in the nature of books to wander, as it is of animals, and not everything came back. Cotton himself, for example, had lent a number of manuscripts to Thomas Howard, earl of Arundel, who failed to return several of the best. Like the Duc de Berry, Arundel was also a collector who could interpret loans somewhat open-endedly. Among other items, he borrowed the Utrecht Psalter, the great illustrated ninth-century manuscript from Reims which had been in Canterbury in the Middle Ages and is now in the Netherlands (hence its name), and the Cotton Genesis, which had to be bought back from the Arundel descendants for almost £40 in about 1690. It was duly returned to be reshelved in the emperor Otho's bookcase, where it belonged, second shelf down, sixth book from the left.

A catalogue of the collection by the Reverend Thomas Smith was published in 1696, listing some 950 volumes then safely on the shelves, mostly with multiple components, giving a combined total of about 6200 different texts, all of them manuscripts. That number alone is sufficient to place Sir Robert Cotton in the highest rank among manuscript obsessives. No library of such size existed in the Middle Ages. The eighteenth-century poet Thomas Fitzgerald exclaimed, "See what a glorious Trophy Cotton rears – The learned Spoils of twice a thousand Years!" The catalogue may have been a preparation for the Cotton family's decision in 1701 to transfer the entire library to the nation "for Publick Use and Advantage" with effect from the death of Sir John, which, as it happened, took place a year later, in 1702. Cotton House was inspected in 1703 by Sir Christopher Wren, who reported dolefully on necessary repairs. The building was purchased by the government in 1707. The old

LEFT: The ninth-century Utrecht Psalter, made in France but formerly at Canterbury, borrowed by Lord Arundel from the Cotton library and never returned.

Royal Library was moved in there too in 1714 from its previous home in St James's Palace. Conditions were cramped and insecure, however, and a more appropriate location was sought for the joint collections. Initially, a seven-year lease was taken in 1722 on Essex House on the north side of the Strand, but in December 1729 the officers of the Board of Works reported to the Treasury that they had identified a more suitable location for both libraries, "much more safe from fire & more commodious in all other respects". This was a vacant property on the south side of Westminster Abbey. It had been acquired in 1662 by the family of Lord Ashburnham, who, the report noted, was prepared to sell his lease to the Crown. It was consequently fitted out with shelves in February 1730, and the Cotton and the Royal Libraries were both moved into what was by then known as Ashburnham House.

Nothing now exists of Cotton House on the river. Any remaining structure was lost in the devastating fire which eventually destroyed Westminster Palace in October 1834. This is a third allusion to fire in this chapter and an ironical one, since that conflagration was caused by an ill-judged bonfire beneath the House of Lords to dispose of obsolete tally sticks from the archives of the Exchequer, manuscripts of a kind. The compensating result was the construction of the noble Houses of Parliament by Charles Barry with Augustus Pugin entirely covering the eight acres of land where the many medieval and later buildings had once clustered untidily along the Thames.

Ashburnham House not merely exists: it is still (or is once again) a library, now part of Westminster School. The principal entrance to the school site is adjacent to the west front of Westminster Abbey, always thronged with people. There is a gothic gateway with a raiseable barrier and sentry boxes for security. Inside is Dean's Yard, a large green square enclosed by tall old buildings of different periods. Over at the far left-hand side, almost diagonally opposite, is no. 18, with a medieval doorway beneath the gilded arms of the Abbey. There is a small low-ceilinged vestibule with a reception desk on the left, where I waited for the archivist and school historian, Elizabeth Wells, who had very kindly agreed to show me round. She escorted me out through a passageway in the direction of the river and the towering Houses of Parliament, an inspiring sight for any schoolboy, into another smaller paved quadrangle called Little Dean's Yard. In the early eighteenth century, as Elizabeth explained, this area had been a cluttered mass of buildings with a narrow

Ashburnham House (on the left) with the projecting east wing, where the fire occurred in 1731, shown in a lithograph of 1845.

passage between them, now marked by different paving stones along a route we followed. On our left, between the School and the Abbey, is Ashburnham House, still called that.

It had once been the late fourteenth-century house of the prior of Westminster Abbey. The foundations might be much older. The stone wall on the Abbey side is medieval, and access when it was in monastic use would usually have been through the cloister. The house was mostly rebuilt in brick by the Fortescue family and their successors after 1595. It became a two-storey Jacobean hall parallel to the Abbey with a projecting wing at right angles, like a sideways 'T', on the eastern end (on the right as viewed from Little Dean's Yard). We stood looking at it for a bit. Elizabeth showed me old plans and pictures of the building as it was when Cotton's library was here. In the eighteenth century there was a little walled enclosure at the front, now cleared away except for a low stone parapet, and the wing on the left (famous to generations of boys as the location of the school tuck shop) had not yet been added. A top floor has been built on too, where once there was a sloping roof with dormer windows. However, the building as known in 1730 is basically intact. The central hall, which we now entered, is used today for meetings and functions. There is a spectacular seventeenth-century staircase at the left-hand end, commonly but probably wrongly attributed to Inigo

Jones. Elizabeth led me upstairs and into an unexpectedly modern school library. We walked back through the length of the building. That far wing at right angles was apparently originally constructed as a gallery running from the front of the building to the back, and it was precisely here at the east end of the first floor of Ashburnham House that the Cotton and Royal manuscripts were duly installed in 1730. It is now broken by the insertion of a nineteenth-century central stairwell for use by the pupils. The front (School) end has tables and chairs; the back (towards the Abbey) has a mezzanine gallery with bookshelves and beanbag chairs at floor level for snuggly reading.

The first resident keeper of the Cotton library was the young Richard Bentley (1708–82), giddy-headed son of the famously curmudgeonly classicist of the same name (1662–1742), former librarian of the royal collection and by then Master of Trinity College, Cambridge. The junior Bentley doubtless installed himself in some comfort in the principal rooms of Ashburnham House. One day his parents came to stay. The date was Saturday, 23 October 1731. They were apparently assigned guest apartments on the ground floor immediately beneath the library. This space is now part of the school library entrance with glass-fronted noticeboards for societies and careers advice, but the old stone floor is probably original and at the back is a little kitchen. Somewhere in here was once a fireplace. Old pictures show a high chimney stack approximately above where the modern staircase descends in the centre. It is a cold building. Like the Bentleys, I was there in late October and I kept my overcoat on during my visit. On that evening in 1731 a good fire was lit for the warmth of the guests. It was not properly checked and during the night a wooden jamb in the chimney caught alight. Dr Bentley is said to have been woken in the early hours of the morning by his wife's coughing, to find the room filled with woodsmoke and the library above on fire.

In later accounts of the ensuing catastrophe, Dr Bentley's escape was embellished with a probably fictitiously heroic role for himself rushing out in his nightgown and wig with the Codex Alexandrinus under his arm. If only he could have taken the Cotton Genesis under the other! Once the alarm was raised, helpers working rapidly throughout the dawn managed to get most of the books out to safety. Volumes were thrown from the windows, probably the two at the south end now overlooking Little Dean's Yard. The manuscripts of the Royal Library were unharmed. Perhaps they were stored at that end with easier access to windows, or even in another room altogether, while the Cotton collection on the Abbey side of the building suffered the worst of the terrible inferno. That entire wing, which was restored afterwards, has lost all its original plaster mouldings, which still ornament the other ceilings of Ashburnham House, and doubtless it was all very badly damaged in the flames.

The next day charred fragments from Cotton manuscripts were being gathered up from all about the ground outside, and some of the cindered scraps were probably spirited away by Westminster schoolboys as dreadful souvenirs. Tragic relics were brought out from the smouldering shelves. The busts of the Caesars, if they were there at all, were never heard of again. A first report in 1732 suggested that 114 volumes of manuscripts were entirely destroyed (a considerable exaggeration) and that another ninety-eight were severely damaged (certainly an underestimate). Parchment does not burn easily. Extreme heat will cause the pages to crumple and contract dramatically, like frying bacon. There is also a sickly smell, like burning flesh. Firemen's water is almost as dangerous to books as fire and it glues the pages together. Some Cotton manuscripts were found to have shrunk into black and shapeless lumps. Many more were so baked and singed that their extremities became brittle and the slightest jarring would scatter crumbling flakes of text from their perimeters. The Anglo-Saxon manuscripts of Asser's life of King Alfred and the Old English poem on the Battle of Maldon, bound in the same volume and both unique witnesses, were lost in their entirety. Their texts are known now only because of fortuitous transcripts made in the sixteenth and early eighteenth centuries respectively. *Beowulf* was badly burned on its edges and many words vanished for ever. (Coincidentally, the poem itself ends with a great funeral pyre, "swógende lég, wópe bewunden", 'roaring flame, woven with weeping'.) One of Cotton's copies of the 1215 Magna Carta and the original papal bull of 1521 naming Henry VIII as 'Defender of the Faith' were reduced to ruin. Half an eighth-century insular Gospel Book was melted and crunched into tiny misshapen deformities from the centres of its pages, made more poignant by the survival intact of another portion of the same manuscript in Matthew Parker's library in Cambridge. The beautiful illustrated Gospel Book given in the tenth century by King Æthelstan to the community of Saint Cuthbert in Northumbria was shrunk to twelve darkened scraps.

It was not all destruction. The stately Lindisfarne Gospels, which legend tells was washed out to sea in the ninth century and recovered unharmed, now sailed through its second cataclysm in perfect serenity. Many Cotton manuscripts show no more damage than any books of their age might have suffered through time. To their credit, the authorities reacted immediately and every item recoverable from Ashburnham House was removed at once to storage in the adjacent school dormitory, under the supervision of Arthur Onslow, Speaker of the House of Commons. Pages were cut out and dried one by one. Manuscripts stuck together by damp were prised open. Stained paper leaves were washed in a solution of alum (still an arguably acceptable conservation practice) and hung up on washing lines to dry. Even charred blocks of congealed parchment were wrapped and kept carefully in drawers. Repair and reconstruction began within a few days of the disaster and the work is still continuing, almost 300 years later.

One result of the fire (although at a terrible price) was that it focused the minds of Hanoverian England on the pressing necessity of securing the safety and future of the national collections. When Sir Hans Sloane died in 1753, he left his own vast accumulation of books and curiosities to the king on the condition that they be properly housed and made available to the public. A new state museum was consequently established by Act of Parliament. Its august trustees inspected the salvage of the Cotton library in Westminster School in February 1754. Soon afterwards, they purchased Montagu House in Great Russell Street, and in 1757 the Cotton manuscripts were brought across, together with the old Royal Collection, the Sloane library and the newly acquired manuscripts from Robert Harley's collection, to form the nucleus of the British Museum. It opened to the public two years later. Until the present Museum building was begun in 1823, there were still open fireplaces in the reading-room.

Under the care of Sir Frederic Madden in the nineteenth century (Chapter 8), lengthy efforts were made to render the burned Cotton manuscripts usable. Parchment pages which had crumpled up in the heat, like poppadoms in a frying pan, were flattened by cutting radiating slits around their edges, so that they could be forced outwards like splayed hides and mounted into apertures of new paper leaves. Frames were ruled in ink around the approximate dimensions of what the pages would once have been before the fire. Examples include Cotton's tenth-century

RIGHT: The Lindisfarne Gospels, early eighth century, glossed in Old English, undamaged by the Cotton fire.

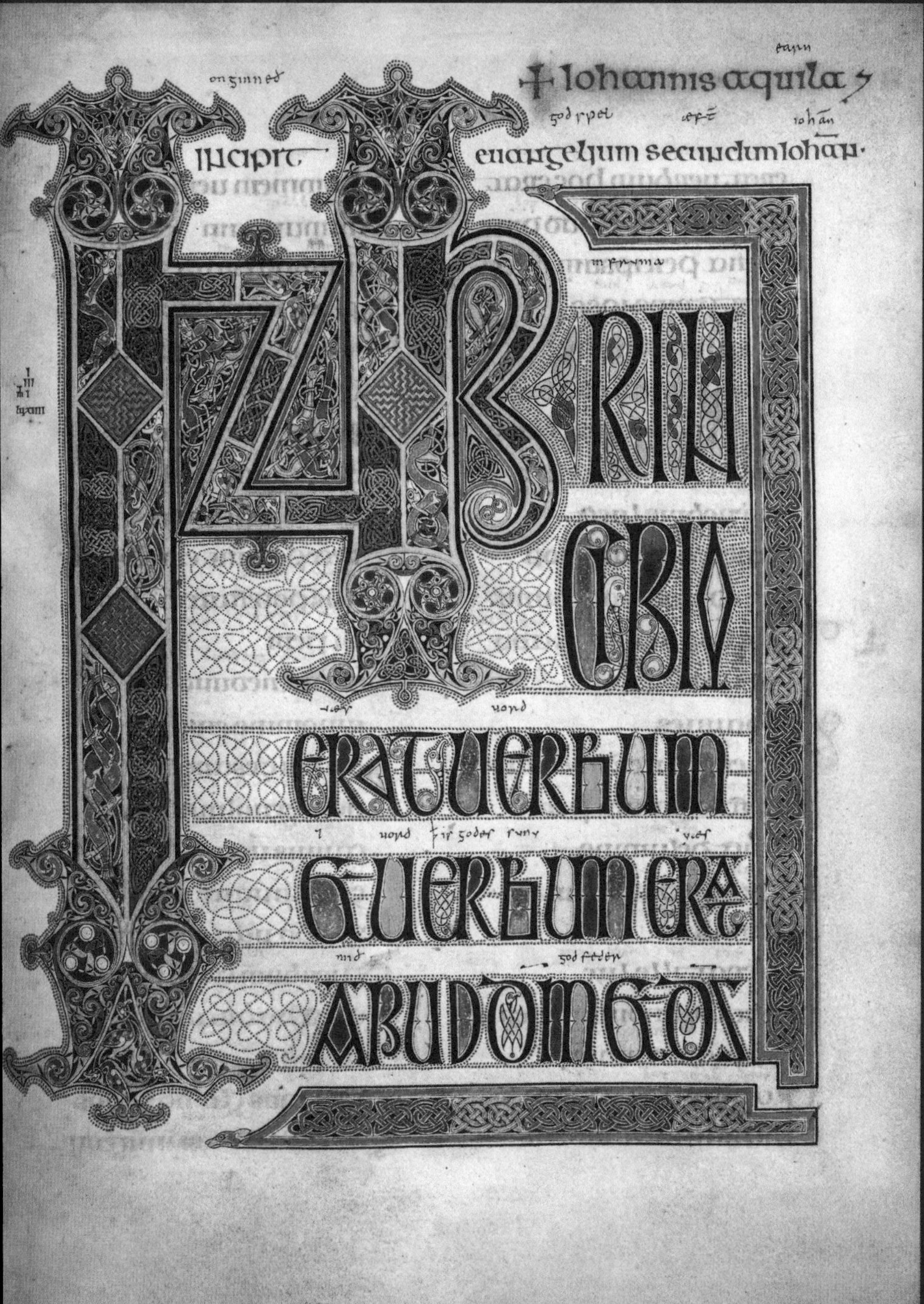

+ Iohannis aquila
INCIPIT
euangelium secundum Iohan·
ERAT UERBUM
ET UERBUM ERAT
APUD DEUM

manuscript of Gildas on the ruin of Britain (not a new subject), the Gospels in Old English from Malmesbury Abbey and the translation of Boethius ascribed to King Alfred. In many others, such as *Beowulf* and an Anglo-Saxon illustrated herbal, the leaves were simply cut out and set within paper margins, rebound like albums. In the case of *Beowulf* this was only just in time, for the transcript made of the manuscript in the 1780s by the Icelandic antiquary Grímur Jónsson Thorkelin preserves numerous ends of words subsequently lost as the charred margins continued to crumble whenever pages were turned; the edges are now safely sealed with paper. Folios were numbered and bound up. The results are certainly usable, but as books they are sad relics to see. There was a further truly dreadful event in 1865: yet another fire broke out, this time in the bindery of the British Museum itself, where various Cotton manuscripts were awaiting attention. The late ninth-century copy of Alfred's translation of Gregory's *Pastoral Care* was almost entirely destroyed, and others were badly damaged. The whole library of the Museum was split away to form a separate national institution in 1973 and was moved up to near St Pancras Station, where the most magnificent brick fortress was built for the new British Library, opened by the Queen in 1998. The Cotton Library is now as safe as it could ever be.

We are going to inspect the charred remains of what Sir Robert Cotton's generation regarded with good reason as the greatest book in Christendom, more precious to them than *Beowulf*, more sacred and older than Lindisfarne. When Cotton's portrait was painted in 1626, he was shown with the fingers of his left hand spread proprietorially across an illuminated page of his famous Greek manuscript of the book of Genesis. The volume was made somewhere in the eastern Mediterranean (possibly Egypt) in the late fifth or early sixth century. It is hard to emphasize the unimaginable rarity of any surviving book of such antiquity, especially one preserved above ground since it was made. The portrait shows the edges of the book's red binding, described in 1616 as being "red Turkey lether" with clasps and Cotton's arms on the cover in gold. The volume was then about 13¾ by 11¾ inches, with 166 leaves (of an original total of perhaps 221), and it once had some 360 illuminated illustrations, one of the richest and most astonishing sources of late-classical art. It had unprecedented status in the seventeenth century, when knowledge of Greek and appreciation of the Scriptures were both at a height.

(The opening of Genesis was the subject of Milton's *Paradise Lost.*) The antiquary Humfrey Wanley was shown the manuscript by Thomas Smith, the Cotton cataloguer, in 1695. He described it in a letter to Thomas Tanner:

> I saw too, the most antie[nt] & incomparable Copy of Genesis, which the Dr said, he thought was older than the Alexandrian MS, it is a large folio, well written, with [a] Picture in almost every page; it is in Capitals without accents & in mo[st] places without any distinction of words, I remembered the Letters of Dr Bernards Greek Alphabets, so I could read it, after my fashion.

Apart from a fifth-century fragment in Berlin, it is still the earliest illustrated manuscript of any part of the Bible. The manuscript's only remotely comparable younger cousin is the extremely fragmentary sixth-century Greek Genesis in Vienna, with forty-eight surviving pictures, about a quarter of its original total. The Cotton Genesis remains one of about half a dozen supreme national treasures in the British Library designated by the most exclusive category of access known as "Keeper's Permission".

To reach the Manuscripts reading-room of the Library you cross a courtyard off the Euston Road and enter a vast lobby before proceeding up a few steps and then by a narrow escalator to the first landing, where you confront a glittering glassed-in tower filled with the King's Library, presided over by a marble bust of George III dressed as a Roman emperor, in an unconscious but fitting contrast to the doomed Caesars of Cotton House. You double back up another staircase, turn right at the portrait of Hilary Mantel and left after that of Robert Harley, into the reading-room. I had arranged to meet Scot McKendrick, Head of Western Heritage Collections (or 'Keeper of Manuscripts' in its old designation), in the enclosed study room around the corner from the issue desk. Several boxes with all that remains of the Cotton Genesis had been laid out for me on the long table and Scot was sitting ready.

The principal manuscript is kept in a big blue cloth box, lettered simply in gilt "British Library Cotton MS Otho B. VI". The book itself is in a rather ecclesiastical-looking dark-brown stamped-leather binding of the mid-nineteenth century, about 11 inches high, a bit like a Victorian family Bible, with gilded edges. The spine title is in gilt, in Latin, "LIBRI GENESEOS LITT. UNCIALIB. GRÆCE EXARAT. RELIQUIAE", that is, 'The remains of the Book of Genesis written in Greek uncials', with the Cotton number again and, at the foot of the spine, "OLIM R. HEN. VIII". The fact that it was once (briefly) in the library of Henry VIII was regarded as important enough to emblazon the spine. We know that the manuscript had been in Venice at the beginning of the sixteenth century, and it was almost certainly there much earlier, since several pictures were apparently copied into a thirteenth-century mosaic in the cathedral of San Marco. It was probably brought to England in the 1520s. It was owned by Thomas Wakefield (d. 1575), appointed in 1540 as first Regius Professor of Hebrew in Cambridge University, who doubtless gave it to Henry VIII. His daughter, Queen Elizabeth, presented it to Sir John Fortescue, her remote cousin and Greek tutor (and occupant of what later became Ashburnham House). He died in 1607, and by 1611 the manuscript was in Cotton's possession.

Open it up. Cotton's arms are emblazoned in gilt at each end. Then look inside. It is an album of paper pages into which tiny shrunken blackened shreds of burned parchment have been pasted in painstaking sequence, with both sides visible. The largest are several inches high.

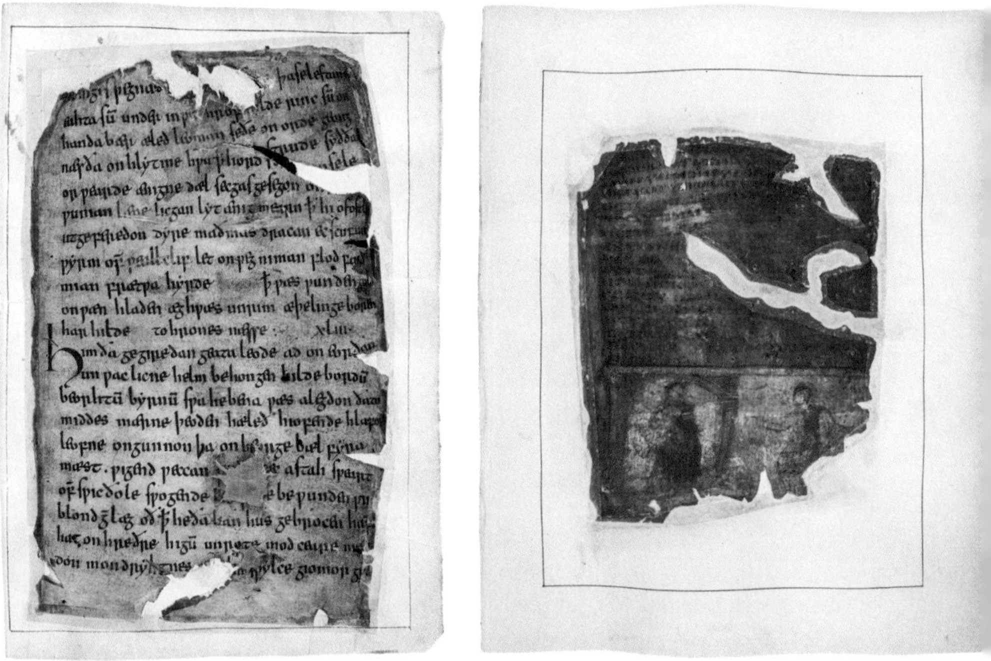

The fire-damaged manuscript of Beowulf, late tenth or early eleventh century, repaired and flattened in the nineteenth century (left) and one of the charred and defective fragments of the Cotton Genesis, late fifth or early sixth century (right).

Some towards the ends are no bigger than bits of cornflake. There exist 129 fragments, out of the 166 whole leaves the volume had before the fire. The parchment has actually shrunk dramatically as well as having melted out of shape. The edges are ragged and many pieces are perforated. In some the acidity of the ink has eaten right through, causing the uncial writing to fall out, leaving holes almost like stencils, or paper doilies. The pieces are quite flat (however that was done in the nineteenth century, it was successful) but the glue used to attach them to their paper pages has turned pale brown, forming ghostly haloes around their perimeters, like the outlines of sea coast in hand-coloured maps. The nineteenth-century paper pages are often more undulating and foxed than the 1500-year-old parchment. Some parts of the ancient pictures survive with unexpected clarity, in soft colours like shadowy frescoes from Pompeii, and enough is visible to convey details of vigorous movement and drama. Some of the gold is quite bright. Curiously, the chalky blue and bright orange pigments are the clearest. Chalk is an alkali and vermilion is prepared by heating mercury and sulphur from which excess sulphur is removed with a strong alkali solution. When the book's remains were wet, they probably became very acidic from tannin in both the ink and the wooden binding, but the intensity of alkali in two of the colours counteracted and preserved them. Overall, although what we see is devastating, there are at least substantial visible portions. Many Dead Sea Scrolls are in much worse condition and no less precious.

At the front of the volume is a long pencil note initialled by Sir Frederic Madden. He records how George Vertue made watercolour copies of some of the least damaged miniatures of the Genesis as they survived the fire. These were exhibited at the Society of Antiquaries in 1743 and engravings were soon afterwards published in the Society's *Vetusta Monumenta*. However, the fragments removed for copying did not all find their way back into the set. Several came into the hands of the Bible collector Andrew Gifford, an assistant librarian in the Museum, who by oversight bequeathed them in 1784 with the rest of his private collection to the Bristol Baptist College ("where I saw them in 1845", Madden notes). The four that survived were purchased back from Bristol in 1962. Scot McKendrick showed me the little lidded red lacquer floral box in which Gifford had originally kept them, about 4¾ by 2½ inches, hardly big enough for the fragments, which must have been folded or rolled up. They were initially thought by Gifford's legatees to be Roman relics from Herculaneum. Two of the four pieces recovered from Bristol are sandwiched between glass, and two are now mounted for exhibition. Five further fragments copied by Vertue have never been seen again and might even still exist unrecognized somewhere.

I came back downstairs in the British Library in sombre and reflective mood. High on the right-hand wall of the half landing at the foot of the escalator are busts of four great benefactors of the national collection, Robert Cotton, Joseph Banks, Thomas Grenville and Hans Sloane. The figure of Cotton is one of several made more than a century after his death by Louis-François Roubiliac (1702–62); another is in the library at Trinity College, Cambridge. It shows a confident Jacobean courtier in a pleated ruff and with a hint of a smile on his face, but it is not an intimate portrait or made by anyone who knew him. We need to look at the man himself.

Robert Cotton was born on 22 January 1571 in Huntingdonshire near his grandfather's house at Conington, about seventy miles directly north of London. It was a well-connected family with reasonable financial means. His mother died when Robert was small and his father remarried in 1579 and produced a second family, never easy for a solitary child of the earlier marriage. He was sent to Westminster School, the very place where his library was to return with tragic consequences in the eighteenth century. It had been newly refounded by Queen Elizabeth, and the choice proved to be hugely significant in Cotton's life. The school was still very small, with forty boys and only two masters (there are now about 750 pupils and more than 100 members of staff). The 'under master', as he was called, responsible for the junior boys, was William Camden (1551–1623), antiquary and herald, with whom Cotton may have boarded. He was clearly one of those teachers with an ability to inspire his pupils with his own enthusiasms. The school was housed in the former monastic buildings of the Abbey, closed in 1540 and briefly reoccupied during the reign of Queen Mary: the Middle Ages were within touching distance. Camden, who later succeeded to the headmastership, was at that time working on the first edition of his *Britannia* (1586), a survey of the surviving antiquities of the British Isles, begun in 1577 at the suggestion of his friend the Dutch cartographer Abraham Ortelius. Because of his fascination for Roman Britain, a period of little interest to many sixteenth-century antiquaries, Camden may have justified any digression from the school syllabus under the general heading of classical studies. I would guess (there is no real evidence from this period of his life) that Robert Cotton was probably a clever but shy little boy who was entranced by Camden's exuberant and innovative excitement for the past, which seemed to offer fellowship that was perhaps not to be found with his half-siblings at home.

In those days when the precocious or well-connected passed on to university at ages which seem unimaginable to us, Cotton matriculated at Jesus College, Cambridge, in November 1581, two months before his eleventh birthday. This too was in ancient monastic buildings, previously (and still within living memory) occupied by the Benedictine nunnery of Saint Radegund. By February 1588, Cotton, already with a BA degree, was admitted to the Middle Temple in London to train as a lawyer.

The siren call of William Camden's passion for historical inquiry was still reverberating from Westminster School. Cotton was soon beguiled into joining the original Society of Antiquaries, founded by Camden and others in London in 1586. Members gathered once a fortnight to discuss topics which had been circulated in advance of each meeting, allowing time for preparation. Everyone present was obliged to speak. It is quite likely that the need to impress his elders without saying too much led its youngest member into buying his first medieval manuscripts, which were still plentiful on the market and easily affordable, even for a student. An early acquisition was a Penitential Manual, possibly from Exeter, written around the middle of the tenth century, a sophisticated purchase for a boy. He may not have known its age precisely, but it includes texts in Old English, perhaps the first he had encountered, and the language alone would have dated the manuscript to before the Norman Conquest. Cotton signed a blank page at the end in a consciously gothic-looking hand among calligraphic flourishes, with the date 1588 and his own age as seventeen. Two other manuscripts were similarly inscribed by him in 1588 but giving his age as eighteen. Since the archaic method of counting years still began from 25 March and Cotton did not reach eighteen until 22 January in what would now be called 1589, these second and third purchases must have been made between late January and March of that latter year.

One of these books is a fifteenth-century copy of the *Polychronicon* of Ranulph Higden, not a rare text or a historically innovative one, but Cotton (apparently) has mistakenly inscribed it as being the twelfth-century *Topographia Wallie* of Giraldus Cambrensis, and he has decorated the opening margin with naïve drawings of sprigs of oak and chestnut trees. His name and the book's erroneous title are now partly erased, perhaps by the collector himself in wiser years. (I myself bought my first antiquarian book when I was thirteen and disfigured it by an inscription in black ink in a faux-gothic hand, which makes me cringe every time I see it.) Cotton's second acquisition of early 1589 is a late-medieval manuscript of the *De regimine principum* by Giles of Rome, a popular European textbook on statecraft. It is quite irrelevant to the theme of Cotton's later collection and he eventually gave it to Sir Thomas Bodley for his new library in Oxford, where it still is. Its last leaf, however, is embellished with charming sixteenth-century coloured drawings. One shows a monk selling indulgences and another (especially delightful) two grinning devils teaching monks how to mix up gunpowder in a cauldron. A note in a contrived calligraphic hand below explains, "Neare aboute An° 1378 was browght to passe ye full makeng of gonnepouder as Reporth ye swisers Cronicle Be[ing] sertayne of ye Religius[.] No name sertainely knowen of ye inventor". I suspect that this may even be in Cotton's hand, deliberately inventing quaint-looking spelling obsolete by his time. It is just the kind of quirky information which might have been opportune for any teenager hoping to contribute to discussion at an antiquarian meeting. Because every manuscript is unique, even the humblest example can offer something no one else knows, a useful lesson. The history of gunpowder was a subject of interest to Camden, who wrote about it at some length in the 1605 edition of his *Britannia*, the year of Guy Fawkes.

In 1595, Cotton's father died and the family estates at Conington passed to Robert, who returned home to manage them. He also married, not very faithfully in the long term. The manor house at Conington has now been demolished, but the parkland exists and the former entrance gate is still there up against the A1, the former Great North Road, or (to give its even earlier name) Ermine Street, the Roman route connecting London to York. Cotton would have known and relished that fact. He was back in London in 1598, coinciding with the revival of meetings of the Society of Antiquaries, which had gone into temporary abeyance for a period while London was troubled by plague. By this time Cotton was already lending manuscripts to other members for use in discussions at meetings. The antiquary Arthur Agarde (1540–1615), for example, acknowledged one of Cotton's manuscripts on the history of Ely in a paper he gave to the Society in 1599. It must have given satisfaction to a collector in his twenties to be credited by a published historian twice his age who, as deputy chamberlain of the Exchequer of Receipt, already had professional custody of incomparable treasures such as Domesday Book. In time, Agarde bequeathed his own notes to Cotton, including his researches on Ely Cathedral.

Cotton was never remotely as rich as the Duc de Berry or Cosimo de' Medici, but he probably had significantly more money than many of his fellow antiquaries, famously shabby in all periods. His income is known to have been about £1000 a year in 1610. One might compare the moment in the 1420s when Cosimo de' Medici joined the fellowship of Niccolò Niccoli and Poggio Bracciolini in the search for classical manuscripts; or when Baron James de Rothschild was captivated to be enrolled in the Société des Anciens Textes Français in 1874. For a relatively small outlay, a possibly lonely rich man was swept welcomingly into an antiquarian circle which provided camaraderie and a shared interest without regard to age or social inequality. Cotton was spellbound and longed for inclusion.

In 1599–1600, leaving his now estranged wife at home, he joined his former schoolmaster Camden on an antiquarian tour of many months in northern England, fossicking together around Hadrian's Wall and elsewhere for Roman inscriptions, coins and archaeological remains, all to be incorporated into subsequent editions of Camden's *Britannia*. Cotton probably paid their expenses, and he made drawings. He also acquired fourteen Roman monumental inscriptions on dedication slabs and tombstones, especially from the site of the Roman fort at Risingham in Northumberland and along the Wall itself. Connections between classical inscriptions and manuscript studies had first been made by the antiquaries of Padua and Mantua in the fifteenth century. Much later, Theodor Mommsen (Chapter 10) would regard Roman inscriptions as legitimate manuscripts of the highest testimony. Nine of Cotton's inscribed stones were cited in the 1607 edition of *Britannia*. He eventually installed them in a walkway connecting two summerhouses in the garden at Conington. In the eighteenth century those that survived were given to Trinity College, Cambridge, and they are now on loan to the university's Museum of Archaeology and Anthropology. When I asked where to see them, the woman on the information desk there assured me that no such items were in their custody. One, however, is indeed on exhibition, an altar to Fortune gathered by Cotton and Camden from Bowes, the site of a Roman fort and a medieval castle in County Durham.

By 1603, when Queen Elizabeth died, Cotton was in London pursuing a political and diplomatic career, at first through the patronage of his remote kinsman by marriage George Carey, Lord Hunsdon (1547–1603), grandson of Mary Boleyn, sister of Anne, and therefore first cousin once removed of the queen. Cotton always exploited connections and contacts, a characteristic necessary in manuscript collecting too. Doubtless through Hunsdon's governorship of the Isle of Wight, Cotton had first become Member of Parliament for Newton, a constituency on the island. When Hunsdon died, Cotton moved in with his widow, Elizabeth ("possibly as her lover", as the *Dictionary of National Biography* reports), and transferred his loyalty to another nobleman of distant affinity, Henry Howard (1540–1614), soon to become earl of Northampton. On the succession of James VI of Scotland as James I of England, Cotton, antiquarian and genealogist, suddenly remembered that the Bruce family of Conington, his presumed forebears, were surely descendants of Robert the Bruce and that he, Robert Cotton, was doubtless therefore also of ancient Scottish royal lineage, like the new king. He expediently added 'Bruce' to his surname and to his flourished signature on the opening pages of manuscripts

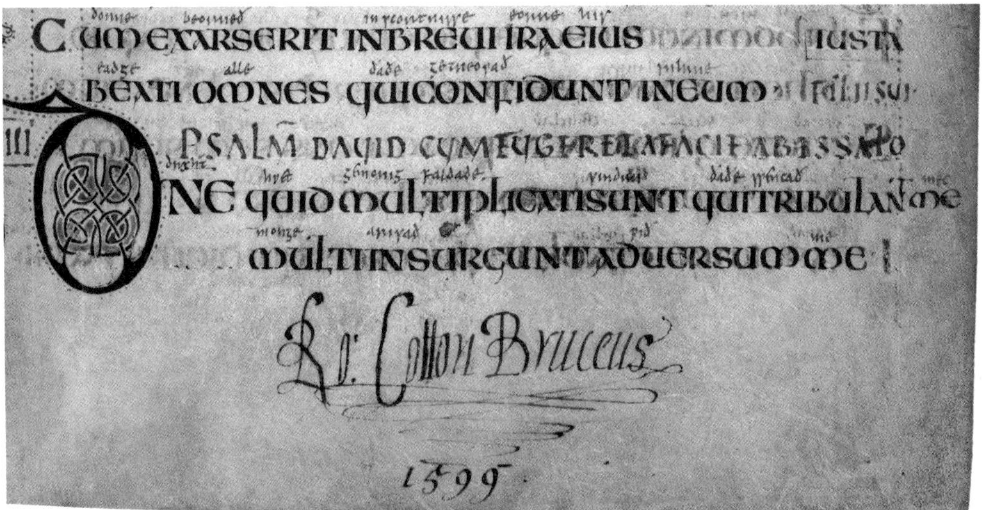

Signature of Robert Cotton with his added name 'Bruce' (in Latin), on the eighth-century Vespasian Psalter, with the probable acquisition date of 1599.

in his growing collection. He promptly used his library to document the descent of James I from the Anglo-Saxons too, thereby strengthening the Stuart claim to the throne on both sides of the border.

It was a politically well-timed move. Perhaps as a result, Cotton secured a knighthood from the king in 1603 and was later consulted on James's fund-raising innovation of baronetcies, buying one himself in 1611. He became a member of the Committee of Privileges, which was (and still is) concerned with overseeing the conduct of Parliament, in accordance with precedent. He was there during discussions relating to the Gunpowder Plot of 1605 and the king's projected union with Scotland (abandoned on parliamentary advice). Cotton's professional life in government is one of perpetual presence and near invisibility, advising and listening, reporting on precedent, gathering up documents, contributing to pamphlets and speeches for others and never quite in his own name, attending committees and eventually representing Old Sarum in Parliament, the most notoriously non-existent constituency in England. He was never a primary participant. Cotton was a facilitator, an arranger of the lives of important people, and a supplier of useful information. This gave him sufficient prestige and satisfaction, and admission into the labyrinths of Westminster which he had first eyed longingly from his school across the road. It is absolutely typical of Cotton that he would eventually aspire to owning a house within the parliamentary compound itself.

This aspect of Cotton's character is probably the key to his manuscript collection. To understand it, we need to look back to the vigorousness of the English Reformation. Between the mid-1530s and 1540, some 800 or so monasteries and religious houses in Britain had been unilaterally suppressed. Say they had owned 200 manuscripts each (many did not, but some had thousands): that would be upwards of 160,000 manuscripts thrown into the public domain in a period of less than a decade. Unguessable quantities of discarded monastic and church books were burned and destroyed or cut up for use as waste material. This frenzy of politically motivated destruction coincided almost precisely with the arrival of the Renaissance in England, bringing a new fascination for literature and historical culture. The first generation of antiquaries confronting the avalanche of exiled manuscripts is represented by John Leland (*c.*1503–52), who was primarily concerned with saving the nation's learning from total annihilation. Leland was among those who advised the king on a vast salvage operation which stocked the original Royal Library of Henry VIII, later to be stored with Cotton's collection. Almost 500 of its manuscripts are from known monastic libraries. The transferred books were safe but largely unavailable, especially after the death of Henry in 1547. Leland himself lost his mind and died insane.

Elizabethan antiquarianism found a champion in Matthew Parker (1504–75), who wanted manuscripts as evidence of the antiquity and purity of the reformed Church, of which he became archbishop in 1559. Parker and his contemporaries convinced themselves that the Anglo-Saxons had lived in a golden age of national independence before it was lost to Europe and the papacy after 1066. Parker commandeered manuscripts especially from the cathedral libraries, which had mostly weathered the 1540s by submission to reform. He wrote his own history of the Church in England and facilitated publication of medieval texts which furthered his cause of demonstrating that England had a religion and a cultural identity all of its own, often in the English language, older and superior to the corrupted Roman Catholicism of late-medieval Europe. Manuscripts were his tangible evidence. He transferred most of his collection of some 400 manuscript volumes and several thousand printed books to Corpus Christi College in Cambridge, where he had previously been Master, in the expectation that they would be a scholarly and evidential resource for ever. In reality, the college locked the library and admitted almost no one until the twenty-first century. When I myself first applied to see Parker's manuscripts in the 1970s, I was refused access.

Both Leland and Parker had been born before the Reformation hit England and both had originally been ordained as priests of the old Catholic faith. At first, no one quite knew whether the religious revolution would blow over, or even whether an excessive concern for the former monastic culture might be considered treasonable. Some early manuscript hoarders were undoubtedly clandestine Catholics waiting for better times. A king and an archbishop, however, would both be uncontroversial custodians. By Cotton's time, it had become clear that the English Reformation was to be permanent and irreversible. Manuscripts were already beginning to acquire an antiquarian and even nostalgic value. In fact, Cotton, although a sound Protestant, was openly fascinated by former monasteries, 'bare ruin'd choirs where late the sweet birds sang', and he visited many sites with Camden on their tour of the

North. Some 360 manuscripts in his collection today were formerly owned by identifiable English monasteries. He was also interested in the administrative records of religious houses and came to own about fifty monastic cartularies, or transcripts of charters, now often the unique sources for the business affairs of medieval abbeys (a subject of negligible interest to Parker).

Cotton's manuscripts are all primarily concerned with Britain and Ireland or had come into national life during some notable period of British history. This was the time when a new sense of national identity was entering society, with a realization that the country's own history mattered and that this was the dawn of a new and glorious age. The famous speech "This royal throne of kings, this sceptred isle" would have meant much more when Shakespeare wrote it in the mid-1590s than in the fourteenth century, when John of Gaunt was supposed to have spoken it.

Unlike Henry VIII or even Parker, who still had access to undisturbed medieval cathedral libraries, Cotton was gathering up medieval books which were already in private hands. It is an important distinction. The panic of Cotton's generation was not so much that the manuscripts of national history were being destroyed, but that they had already disappeared into the wilderness of private families and had become inaccessible. Liberated manuscripts existed in Elizabethan and Jacobean England in quantities which would have seemed unimaginable to Anselm or the Duc de Berry in the Middle Ages, but no one now necessarily knew where they were or what was in them.

Robert Cotton, facilitator of Westminster and supplier of information to antiquaries and statesmen, dreamed of a national resource with himself as its controller. In 1602, he had signed a petition to Elizabeth I for the establishment of an 'Academy for the study of Antiquity and History'. To an extraordinary degree, documented genealogy and ancestry determined personal status in Tudor and Stuart England. Possession of land depended on knowing who had owned it or been granted it in previous generations: this was why cartularies mattered. The execution of law and custom relied on verifiable precedent. This is still true to some extent, but it was paramount in Cotton's lifetime. Knowledge of history no longer rested on a few monks in religious houses but on the written evidence of whatever manuscripts could be located and gathered in. Whoever owned the sources of the past could therefore be of immense service to the present. Cotton did not publish texts himself or include

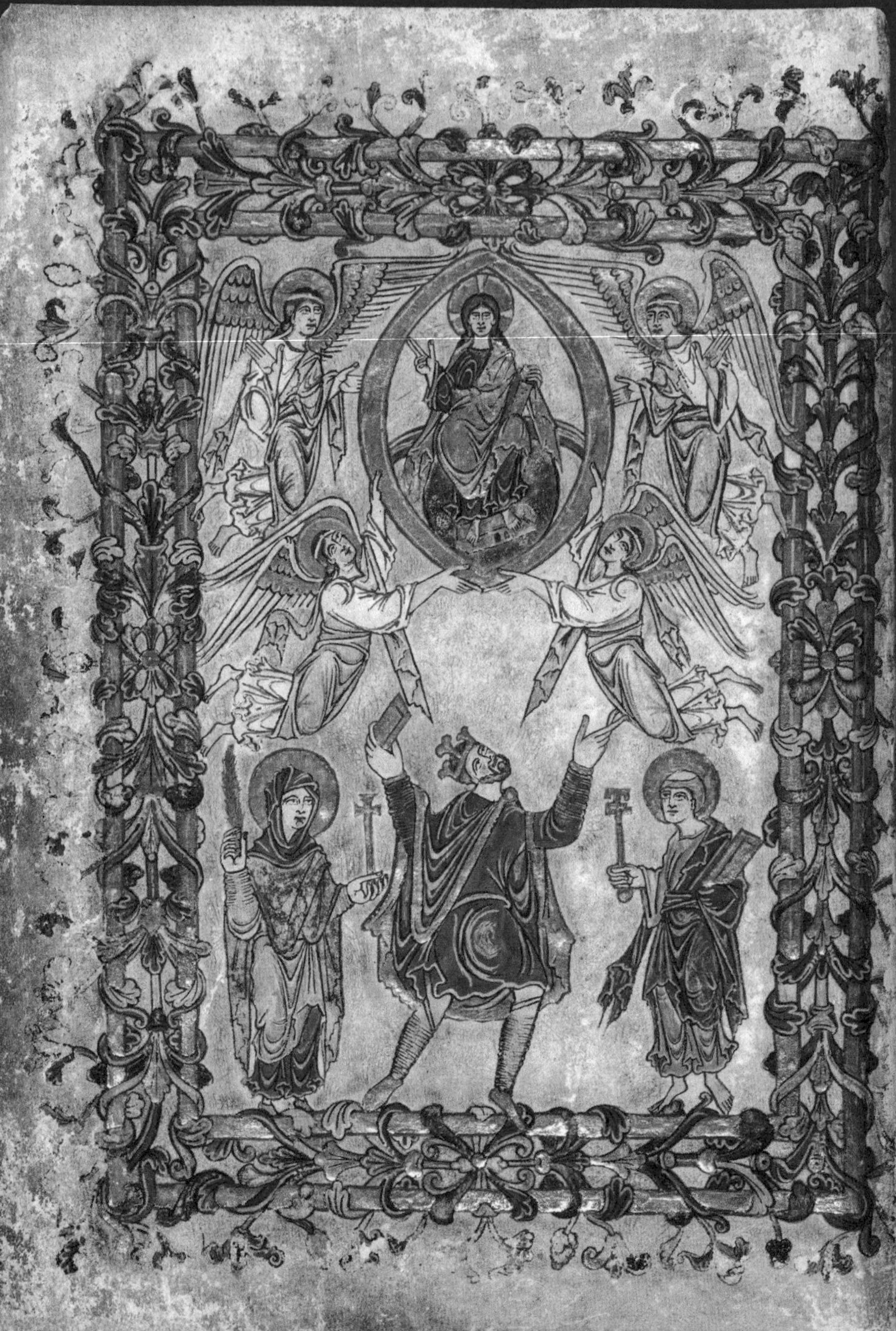

printed books in his chief library. He sought manuscripts only because every item is exclusive to its owner, and he relished that it was by definition a unique authority. He then made them strategically available for consultation by politicians, landowners, churchmen and antiquaries.

Although there was no full catalogue of the collection until 1692, there are quite good records of individual loans of manuscripts in Cotton's lifetime and during the custodianship of his son, Sir Thomas. The most comprehensive of these is a large album now in the Harleian Collection in the British Library recording names of borrowers and detailed titles of manuscripts, often crossed off as the volumes were returned. There are also several notebooks in Cotton's hand. They are evidence that some manuscripts were being used in his time perhaps even more than they are now. For 1621, for example, there were no fewer than 125 separate loans of manuscripts from the collection. It must have been the highest-quality lending library there has ever been. A few examples will give a flavour.

In 1604, following the accession of James I, Cotton lent to his patron, Henry Howard, then a Privy Counsellor, two volumes of papers on the relationship of England to Scotland in the 1560s and 1570s, especially on the delicate position of Mary, Queen of Scots, mother of the new king. James I himself seems to have borrowed King Edgar's illuminated charter for New Minster in Winchester dated 966, with one of the earliest of all portraits of any English king, dandily dressed between the Virgin Mary and Saint Peter (and bigger than either of them; King James was exceptionally conscious of his own appearance and attributes of royalty). Sir Clement Edmunds, Clerk of the Privy Council, borrowed two fifteenth-century volumes of the Acts of the Privy Council during the reign of Henry VI. Sir Francis Bacon, philosopher and later Lord Chancellor, was lent manuscripts of Anglo-Saxon laws and on the Greek islands; he was also a donor to the Cotton library. In 1611, Daniel Dunn, Master of the Court of Requests, consulted a manuscript of fifteenth-century Admiralty ordinances (and in 1694 Samuel Pepys borrowed it too). By 1617, Sir Fulke Greville, Chancellor of the Exchequer 1614–21, had Cotton's famous early thirteenth-century manuscript of the *Dialogue of the Exchequer* by Richard FitzNigel, the bishop of Ely, who died in 1198.

LEFT: King Edgar offering a document to Christ, frontispiece to the illuminated charter for the refoundation of New Minster, Winchester, dated 966, apparently borrowed from the Cotton library by King James I.

retorned the 7 August	A Arraignment of Tower records of Ed. 2. time and divers notes of forrayn bisnes out of record and of Hen. 8 and H. 7 time with Mr Henry's hand bound in volom and grene strings. Fol.	Mr Selden
+	Sprott and Thorne of Canterbury lent I had of my lord William	Doctor Barkham
+	Red book of Canterbury lent Fol. great	Cosen Borough
	Book of the Marshall office in 4 bound with my armes. Mr Thenes	Earl of Arrundell when he was in the tower
	My Collections of treatises of Marriages bound with my armes in Fol. thick.	Erl of Arrundell in the tower
	My great Book of collections of printed maps and plotts with many loose in it bound in whitt	Erl of Arrundell
	Benedictus Monachus vita Hen. 2. bound in parchment. 8	Mr Bourgcher
	Giraldi Cambrensis distinctiones et vita Arnulfi	Mr Bourghcher
	My discourse of peace and warr in Fol.	Mr Bourghcher
Mr Dene of Kent my cosen Borough's brother	Gesta et liber Cartarum monasterii Sti Augustini in 8	~~Mr Bradshaw~~
	Mr Agar's observation out of Domesday for hard words bound in loose and Mr Agar's name	Mr Selden
	A volume in whitt volom and past of treatises with France in H. 7. H. 8 and Ed. 6 time	Mr Selden
	Treaties with Burgundy in H. 6. H. 7. H. 8. Ed. 6. and Mary a great book in whitt	Mr Selden
Mr Selden	My great book of the Chancery lent to my Lord keper	Lord keper
	Divers paper of the Admiralty and the Navy.	Mr Selden
	My Great book of the Heraulds bound in lether having many Originall letters in it	Mr Selden
	Magnum Intercursum lether vellom	Mr Selden
	A discorse di Cambio in Italian. 8 lent	Sr Tho. Wilson
	Lyf of Henry the 3 by my self	Sr Tho. Wilson
	Mr Phillipps direction of letters 1620	Sr Th. Wilson
	Registrum Wharrowtoniensis Ecclesie old bound	Mr Montague
	Radulphus de Diceto and other in Fol.	Mr Selden
+	A Book of treaties with Russia and Turky and som loose paper of Dutchy's grants	Mr Selden
+	A letter of the kings 1604 to Sr Th. Parry about answering the pope's Hunkes in France the Originall	my lord William Howard and Sr Basill Brooke
	A roll of the state of Naples my lord Carew gave me	Sr Th. Wilson
	A Book of the kings gifts in Fol. larg in velom	Sr Th. Wilson
	A Book of Forrayne treatises at Bloys. Treaties and of marriages. Ed. 4 with Scotland. Charles with Mary. Ed. 6 with Eliz. of France. Q. Mary. and the kings daughter with the now palatine and many mor in Fol. thick bound in velom and past it was Sr Dan. Donne's book	Sr Tho. Wilson
	2 Books of Peppwell Abbey bound with my armes lent to Mr Henchman Chaplein to my Lord keper who cam in his name	Mr Henchman parson of Rusden
	Alfricus Grammar Saxon to Ben. Jonson	Beniam Jonson

(It is hard to envisage any modern Chancellor being able or interested to read thirteenth-century Latin handwriting in preparation for his job.) In 1621 the Lord Treasurer, Sir Henry Montagu, borrowed a manuscript on coinage, including a tantalizing account of a gold mine in Scotland. There are very numerous similar examples. It is not easy to document how far individual manuscripts necessarily determined points of national policy, but the fact that historical sources were being routinely examined at this level is relevant both in the study of Jacobean administration and for our own understanding of Sir Robert Cotton as the master of precedent.

Cotton's library was also open for literary research. One name which stands out is the dramatist Ben Jonson. He had been at school with Cotton and in 1603 came with their schoolmaster Camden to stay with him at Conington. There is an undated letter from Jonson to Cotton asking to borrow a book, which he promises to return that night, on the geography of Campana, almost certainly when gathering background for his Roman tragedy *Sejanus his Fall* (1603). In 1621 he borrowed a manuscript life of Henry V, conceivably reliving Shakespeare's play in preparation for the First Folio (1623), to which he contributed. He was back in 1624, borrowing a mid-eleventh-century manuscript of Ælfric's grammar and glossary. Jonson's own grammar of the English language was published among his posthumous works in 1640: it alludes to practices of "the *English-Saxons*" and now we know one of his sources.

The architect Inigo Jones also used the library. He was responsible for the staging and scenery of hundreds of royal masques in London, often in uneasy collaboration with Jonson. Towards the end of Cotton's life, Inigo Jones borrowed two manuscripts on royal festivities performed in Paris in the early sixteenth century, for even drama has precedent. One is an illuminated record of the pageants put on in 1514 following the short-lived marriage of Mary Tudor, sister of Henry VIII, to Louis XII of France, illustrated with seven miniatures showing the public entertainments staged on the route into Paris. The second, also richly illuminated, shows a similar triumphal entry of Claude de France in 1517.

Especially tantalizing is the use of the Cotton library made by the great metaphysical poet John Donne. In 1602, Donne returned some

LEFT: Autograph list by Cotton of "items lent out of my study", 23 April 1623, including loans of manuscripts to John Selden, the earl of Arundel, and (last entry) the poet Ben Jonson. Sir Francis Bacon left the post of Lord Keeper (centre right) that same year.

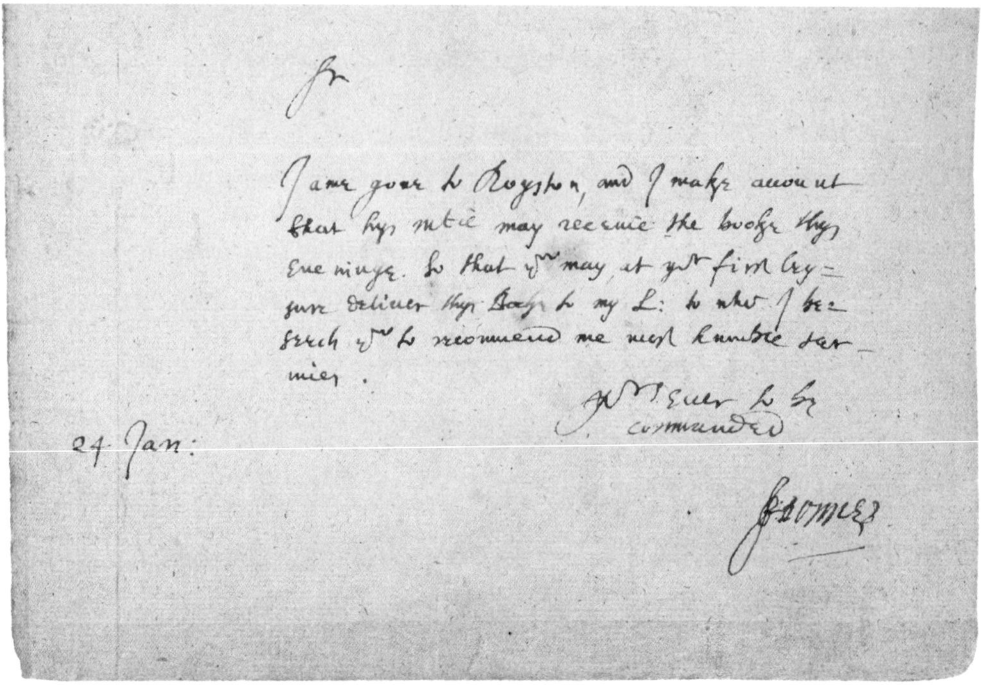
Sr

I am goen to Royston, and I make account that hys Mtie may receive the booke thys Evening. So that yow may, at yor first leysure deliver thys Booke to my L: to whom I beseech yow to recommend me most humble servies.

Yrs ever to be commanded

24 Jan:

J. Donne

Autograph letter from the poet John Donne, returning a book he had borrowed from Cotton's library, 24 January 1614 or 1615.

manuscripts lent to him by Cotton. His autograph letter of thanks is bound up in one of Cotton's volumes, dated on 20 February 1602 "fro[m] my prison in my Chamber" and addressed "To my very honest and very assured friend Robert Cotton Esq at his home in Blackfriars", which was where Cotton was soon living with Elizabeth Hunsdon. Donne also borrowed a volume which still survives among the Cotton books, Cleopatra F. VII, on the supposed precedency of Spain over other nations. He wrote a long critique of it to Cotton around 1602–4, ending, "Sir, I have both held your booke longer then I ment, and held you longer by thys letter, now I send it backe. But yow that are a reall and free doer of benefits, I presume are also an easy pardoner of unmalicious faults," although late return of loans was a fault of most of Cotton's borrowers. Donne's reply was carefully kept too and Cotton had it bound up into the manuscript itself.

There is a famous poetic image used by John Donne twice in his verses about a man's grave being excavated to find tresses of a woman's hair entangled around the bones. The source was almost certainly the *Speculum Ecclesiae* of Giraldus Cambrensis, of which the unique and then still-unpublished early thirteenth-century manuscript was in Cotton's library (Tiberius B. XIII), perhaps from the priory of Llanthony Secunda in Gloucestershire. Donne quite possibly read it or was conceivably told about it. Giraldus recounts how the bones of King Arthur were exhumed at Glastonbury in the twelfth century and were discovered to be entwined with female hair, presumably that of Guinevere. Here, then, is the opening of Donne's poem *The Relic*:

> When my grave is broke up again
> Some second guest to entertain
> (For graves have learn'd that woman-head,
> To be to more than one a bed)
> And he that digs it, spies
> A bracelet of bright hair about the bone,
> Will he not let us alone,
> And think that there a loving couple lies,
> Who thought that this device might be some way
> To make their souls, at the last busy day,
> Meet at this grave, and make a little stay?

Fate and fire are constant companions at this time and Donne's (solitary) tomb in St Paul's Cathedral was destroyed in the Great Fire of London in 1666; Jonson's notes on Old English grammar were lost during his lifetime in a conflagration in his chambers.

Above all, Cotton's library was a lending resource for antiquaries and historians and would have brought many together. Today, researchers in the British Library might meet up for conversation in the cafeterias over coffee or lunch. The equivalent community of readers in Cotton's time included many familiar names, such as William Camden the schoolmaster, who was borrowing manuscripts right up to the end of his life. He sometimes relied on Cotton to choose what he should look at. There is an undated letter from him explaining that he needs to avoid the deadly sin of sloth in his solitary life and so he asks Cotton to send any "booke or Papers wch you shall think fitting my studies or delighte". Others with more specific borrowings include James Ussher, later archbishop of Armagh; Richard Bancroft, archbishop of Canterbury; Baron Herbert of Cherbury; John Selden; the cartographer John Speed; Francis Junius (then librarian to Lord Arundel); Sir William Le Neve; Sir Edward Dering; Sir Symonds D'Ewes; Sir Christopher Hatton; Sir William

SCOCIA: VLTRA MARINA
hec et albania dicta est
Orkade insule
Sutherlande
Dunde
Dunbrinn
Cluid
Bancor ep
WALLIA
Karlin
karleolū
Dunelmu
Rokesburc
Kokec insula
Tinemue
Beverle
Eborac
Cest
Linc
London
Cantuar
Doura
Wincestre
Bristol
Dunstap
Norhamt
Bedef
Bachonia
Wellesia
Glastigb
DORSET
SVMSET
CORNUBIA
NORTH FOLK
SVFOLK
Tanet
Sephe
Lundi
Wict
Gen
Grencesio
AUSTER
ORIENS
OCCIDENS

Dugdale; and many others. The number of knighthoods among them is noticeable: not so many readers in the British Library seem to be baronets these days. Gentleman historians were mainly consulting chronicles, cartularies and monastic registers, and Anglo-Saxon books. For example, the original thirteenth-century manuscript of Matthew Paris's abridgement of the chronicles of England, with drawings by the author himself, was borrowed five times between 1608 and 1626. Cotton's spectacular eleventh-century illustrated Hexateuch in the Old English translation of Ælric of Eynsham and others was also lent out a similar number of times between 1611 and 1653. These are extraordinarily important manuscripts to be circulating freely around private houses of London. John Speed acknowledges Robert Cotton in his *History of Great Britaine* (1614), describing him in words which he knows will please him, as "that worthy Repairer of eating Time's Ruins . . . whose Cabinets were unlocked, and Library continually set open to my free access". Cotton, who never published anything on his own collection, had entered the company he most coveted by supplying them all with manuscripts.

Although Cotton signed his name in many manuscripts, he only rarely dated his acquisitions. Plotting the progressive growth of the collection is difficult, and sometimes identities of previous owners or records of loans are the only means of guessing when books must have entered Cotton's possession. The Vespasian Psalter had been previously owned by Sir William Cecil, Lord Burghley, Queen Elizabeth's chief minister. This is the famous manuscript of the eighth century, probably from Canterbury, written in uncial script and glossed in Old English; it is as marvellously and as intricately worked as the jewellery of Sutton Hoo. Cotton wrote the date 1599 beside his signature, a year after Cecil's death, which seems credible. The illustrated Coronation Book of Charles V of France, brought to England by the duke of Bedford, was signed in 1604 by Cotton, who may have enjoyed setting his own name and date next to that of Charles V, who inscribed it himself in 1365. The supreme early manuscript of Genesis, as we saw, had belonged to Sir John Fortescue, who died in 1607, and we know it was Cotton's by 1611, since he lent it that year to Sir Henry Savile of Eton (there was no 'Keeper's Permission' then).

LEFT: Map of Britain in the abridgement of the chronicles of England in the handwriting of the author, Matthew Paris, monk of St Albans, *c.*1255–9, frequently borrowed from the Cotton library.

A number of books had been in the library of John Dee, the astrologer and magician, who died in 1608, and we can assume they came after that date. They include a manuscript of the *Cosmographia* of Aethicus of Istria, made around 1000, and a Psalter of about 1060, probably from Winchester, glossed in Old English and with added charms and spells, some in secret writing.

Cotton knew who owned manuscripts and he waited for their deaths, like a cat patiently staking out a mousehole. One notable collector well known to him was John, Lord Lumley, owner at one time of Nonsuch Palace, which was filled with marvels. There is an undated memorandum among Cotton's library notes, headed "Books I want", listing twenty-two manuscripts which were clearly in Lumley's possession, mostly chronicles but ending with a Psalter of King Æthelstan and an "Evangelist old written in Saxon carecters". Lumley died in his mid-seventies on 11 April 1609, without issue, bequeathing his library to Henry, Prince of Wales and heir to James I; Prince Henry in turn died suddenly of typhoid in 1612, and his books were subsumed into the Royal Library. Some time between or around those years, 1609–12, however, Cotton managed to extract most of what he wanted from the Lumley collection, either legitimately or through discreet expropriation by his helpful friend Patrick Young, royal librarian. They included an illustrated manuscript of John Gower's Middle English *Vox clamantis* about the Peasants' Revolt of 1381, later damaged in the fire, and Asser's life of King Alfred, now lost altogether. In the Cotton library too, successfully gathered in, is the Æthelstan Psalter, which was on his Lumley wants list. It is a French manuscript of the ninth century. Full-page pictures were added in the tenth century for Æthelstan, first king of all England, who had given it to Winchester Cathedral. There too is the Gospel Book Cotton coveted in Lumley's library. It is now known as the Coronation Gospels, and it was apparently given first by Otto I, king of Germany, to the same Æthelstan, who then presented it to the cathedral priory in Canterbury.

It is not altogether clear to what extent Cotton was buying manuscripts on the open market from booksellers and dealers, or whether he relied primarily on persuading owners and executors of estates that items would be of better use to the nation in his own collection. There was probably a bit of each. As with the Duc de Berry, there were undoubtedly many invited gifts which were made advantageous to the giver. Cotton must have enticed would-be donors with a beguiling vision of a

Sir Robert Cotton with his hand on the Cotton Genesis, portrait attributed to Cornelius Janssens (Cornelius Johnson), 1626.

permanent public resource, and a good word at court for the benefactor. He traded manuscripts to other people as well, for they were currency in antiquarian commerce. He presented eleven volumes to Sir Thomas Bodley in 1602–3 for the new library in Oxford, including a twelfth-century Origen and the manuscript with the drawings of monks making gunpowder. He was ceding books to Patrick Young for the Royal Library but receiving more than he parted with. There are several manuscripts still in the library of the Cecil family at Hatfield House with inscriptions recording that they were New Year gifts from Cotton to Sir Robert Cecil, rather like the *étrennes* in the Duc de Berry's time; in turn, Cotton acquired for his own library important manuscript maps from Hatfield, presumably after Cecil's death in 1612.

Antiquaries to whom Cotton had lent books felt obliged or sufficiently indebted to bequeath or give their own collections to him when the time came. Robert Bowyer (*c.*1560–1621) was keeper of the Tower records and later Clerk of the Parliaments. He appears in the lists as a frequent borrower of Cotton manuscripts, including a Gospel Book in Old English and the cartulary of Westminster Abbey. It was a valuable relationship: Bowyer owned not only one of the manuscripts of the Anglo-Saxon Chronicle but also the unsurpassable Lindisfarne Gospels. In due time, perhaps on Bowyer's death, both these finally entered

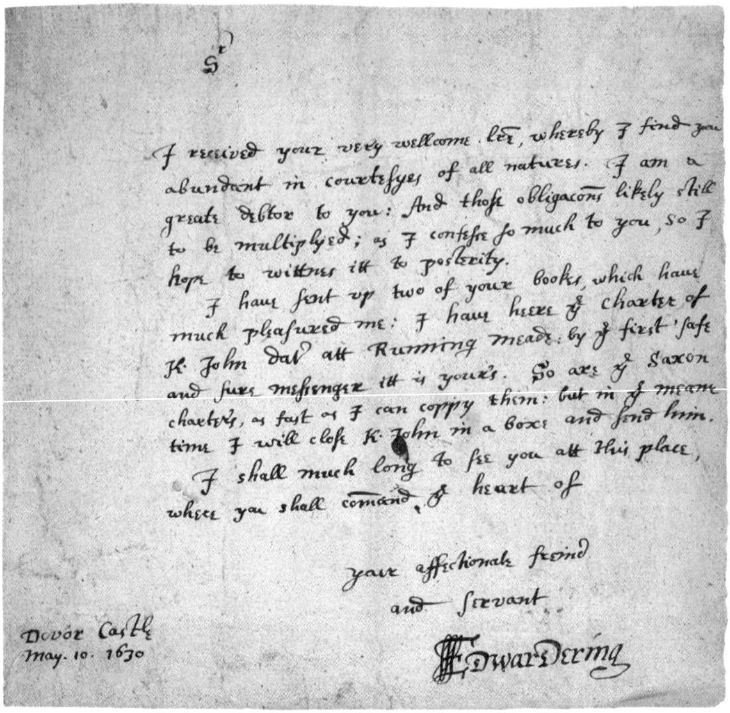
Sr

I received your very wellcome lre, whereby I find you abundant in courtesyes of all natures. I am a greate debtor to you: And those obligacons likely still to be multiplyed; as I confesse so much to you, so I hope to witness itt to posterity.

I have sent up two of your books, which have much pleasured me: I have heere ye charter of K. John dat[ed] att Running Meade: by ye first safe and sure messenger itt is your's. So are ye Saxon charters, as fast as I can coppy them: but in ye meane time I will close K. John in a boxe and send him.

I shall much long to see you att this place, where you shall comand ye heart of

your affectionate freind
and servant
Edward Dering

Dover Castle
May. 10. 1630

Letter from Sir Edward Dering sending a Magna Carta to Cotton, 10 May 1630.

Cotton's possession. The house in Westminster was bought a year after Bowyer died, and by then the aspiration of a permanent library seemed to be taking shape. Sir Francis Bacon gave the Golden Book of St Albans in 1623; it is a late fourteenth-century illustrated record of that abbey's benefactors. One of Cotton's two copies of the 1215 Magna Carta was reputedly found in a tailor's shop and was given to Cotton by Humphrey Wyems of the Inner Temple in 1629. The other was a gift to the library from Sir Edward Dering, antiquary, who was a frequent user of the collection. It was offered to Cotton in a charming letter written from Dover Castle on 10 May 1630 in which Dering was returning two manuscripts he had borrowed:

> I have sent up two of your books, which have much pleasured me: I have heere ye charter of K. John dat[ed] att Running Meade: by ye first safe and sure messenger itt is your's. So are ye Saxon charters, as fast as I can coppy them: but in the meane time I will close K. John in a boxe and send him.

It would be a fascinating experience to meet Sir Robert Cotton in his library. I suspect that he would not have said much. I have even wondered whether he had a stammer or other impediment to speech, which would make him self-conscious. It would explain a lifestyle with little conversation. He would tacitly watch me examining his shelves, pulling out and exclaiming about particular volumes. When I had left, he would quietly take out again the manuscripts I had looked at, wondering to himself what it was that had caught my interest, seeing his books newly through the eyes of his visitor, replaying and reliving in his mind the pleasure of approbation.

Inspection would show that Cotton was assembling manuscripts within certain areas. These were principally (1) manuscripts in the Anglo-Saxon language, (2) monastic records and cartularies, (3) early biblical texts and lives of saints, especially if English, (4) genealogy and heraldry of Britain, (5) histories and chronicles, and (6) state papers. Within these, he cornered the market for a generation and his comprehensiveness has never been equalled. Not everything was medieval, and especially in genealogy and political papers the collection extended right up to his own time. That he was obsessively committed to manuscripts and loved history is not in doubt. Whether he was a true bibliophile is a different question. Did he love his books, as the Duc de Berry and Federico da Montefeltro certainly did, or were manuscripts commodities in the business of politics and social network? He wrote his name in very many of them, often a sign of pleasure in ownership, but that also had a practical value, for it would help ensure the return of manuscripts from loan and remind borrowers of where credit was due, which Cotton longed for. With some spectacular exceptions, most Cotton manuscripts are not especially beautiful or necessarily in good condition, although this may be unfair, since we can only see them after their dreadful holocaust of 1731. When Anglo-Saxon books are exhibited at the British Library, it is very striking to see the difference of appearance between Cotton and Harleian manuscripts, for example. The former may be of extreme rarity and textual merit but can appear brown and mean in their display cases, often closely cropped and sometimes visibly defective. By contrast, manuscripts selected by Robert Harley, earl of Oxford (1661–1724), are usually fresh and wide-margined and often wonderfully illuminated. Harley had taste and a true book collector's discriminating eye for beauty. Cotton, I think, did not.

One aspect of Cotton's custodianship which has puzzled and exasperated modern historians is his persistent practice of disassembling manuscripts and of creating composite volumes from unrelated components. A single book in the Cotton collection might be made up now from some priceless Anglo-Saxon text bound up with something like a collection of papers on Tudor administration and a late-medieval monastic rental. This is also frustrating for anyone attempting to follow the history of his collection or of any individual text, for parts of a single volume as it is now might have easily been acquired in very different times and circumstances. The Cotton manuscript of Anselm's letters which opened Chapter 1 here, for instance, is bound with a surely unconnected romance of around 1200 about a monk descending into Purgatory, and a sixteenth-century collection of Irish laws. It is true that Cotton's habit has an established precedent from the late Middle Ages, when multiple components were often assembled into thick books, called *Sammelbände* in German, and Cotton is much nearer to the medieval past than to the nineteenth century, when collectors and librarians routinely broke up such anthologies to create as many slim volumes as possible for their shelves and catalogues. The difference is that the contents of a medieval *Sammelband* usually had some connecting theme, whereas Cotton's groupings often seem baffling. He discarded earlier bindings, which would have been precious to us now, and he sent his new assemblages of manuscripts to be re-bound, usually with his arms on the covers. A slip of paper survives in one of Cotton's collections of parliamentary transcripts from the time of Edward IV, addressed to his bookbinder: "Bind this Book as strong as you can. Cut it smoothe. Beat it and press it well . . . Let me have it on Thursday at the furdest." That instruction to cut smooth means to trim the edges of the pages tidily to the same size, which may explain why many Cotton manuscripts have negligible margins. He liked them neat and they had to fit his shelves.

Sometimes Cotton also cut leaves or sections out of manuscripts and had them inserted elsewhere. For example, he removed pages with documents which had been transcribed into King Æthelstan's Coronation Gospels. He bound seven of them into an anthology of fragments of Pontificals and other texts, and he relocated four into a volume which also included the chronicle of Croxden Abbey and the legend of Mediadoc, a knight in the court of King Arthur. There seems no sense in that. There are many instances of this activity. We cannot always be sure that all such transferrals were done by Cotton, for some might have been detached leaves carelessly reassigned to the wrong books by well-meaning restorers following the fire of 1731. There is certainty in the case of the ninth-century Utrecht Psalter, which had by that time been lost to the Cotton collection, but not before Cotton had already cut out one leaf with a document, still in his library, and had added into the Psalter unrelated fragments of an uncial Gospel Book, still there in Utrecht.

Cotton also occasionally embellished manuscripts with decorative cuttings removed from elsewhere. He cut the opening initial from a sparkly thirteenth-century gothic Psalter to make a most inappropriate replacement for the missing first page of his eighth-century Vespasian Psalter. Random miniatures removed from Books of Hours and Psalters occur pasted into a number of manuscripts for no apparent reason except decoration. Cotton owned or had access to a richly decorated breviary made in the southern Netherlands around 1475–80 for Margaret of York, duchess of Burgundy. Presumably before about 1618, when the manuscript was given by Sir Thomas Gardiner to St John's College in Cambridge (where it is now), Cotton used snippets from its illuminated borders and miniatures to decorate some of his best books, including as a tailpiece to the Vespasian Psalter and to ornament the Æthelstan Psalter and the Coronation Gospels. Cotton owned a clutch of leaves of the 'Codex Purpureus Petropolitanus', a sixth-century Byzantine purple Gospel Book probably looted by crusaders in the twelfth century. He enhanced their opening with a scrap of inscribed papyrus which he had

Fragments of a sixth- to seventh-century papyrus and a border from the Breviary of Margaret of York, *c.*1480, both cut out and pasted by Cotton as ornaments into his portion of a sixth-century Byzantine Gospel Book.

probably found in a bookbinding, pasting it into a frame cut from a border of the breviary of Margaret of York again. Only as recently as the 1990s was that papyrus piece finally identified as being from a sixth- to seventh-century copy of the Gospel homilies of Gregory the Great. It might have come from one of the books brought from Rome to Canterbury by its earliest missionaries. Cotton could never have known that and would probably not even recognize it as papyrus (no other examples were seen in England until the eighteenth century), but he had the antiquary's instinct to save it.

It is easy to laugh at Cotton's misguided efforts and to accuse him of vandalism or stupidity, but actually this is where we do finally encounter Cotton as a closet bibliophile. In a distant time with few fellow collectors to give advice and no art history as a guide, here is a solitary man instinctively trying to make some connection with his treasures. He delights in the process of arranging texts and assembling books. It is his most intimate engagement. He is looking for order and neatness in his troubled times. Cotton knows, truthfully, that some of the manuscripts are of rather dull appearance and he wishes they were prettier. In the long evenings, untutored and alone in his library, he tries to make up for this. There, at last, is his soul, and his love of the manuscripts.

By the 1620s, Cotton was reconciled with his wife at Conington and he had shifted his professional allegiance at court to Thomas Howard, earl of Arundel, great-nephew of his earlier patron Henry Howard, earl of Northampton. He too was a notable collector of art and antiquities such as the Arundel Marbles, and formed a fine library, including medieval manuscripts. It is easy to imagine how Cotton, fifteen years his senior, might have capitalized on their shared interests. However, loyalties are dangerous in politics. As Arundel's fortunes collapsed through his opposition to the duke of Buckingham, royal favourite, Cotton found himself dragged into controversy. There is a dreadfully sad story from 1626. He was convinced that his ninth-century Coronation Gospels had been used for taking the oath during the crowning of the Anglo-Saxon kings from Æthelstan onwards. This belief is itself evidence that he understood the charisma of manuscripts as physical objects. Through Arundel, who was Earl Marshal and thus responsible for state ceremonies, he had arranged (as he thought) that it would be used in the coronation vigil of Charles I in Westminster Abbey on 2 February that year. On that keenly anticipated Thursday morning on what should have been the proudest day

The Æthelstan or 'Coronation' Gospels, late ninth century, acquired by Cotton from the Lumley library and brought out in vain for the coronation of Charles I in 1626.

of his life, Cotton had dressed in his finest clothes and was waiting for the arrival of the king on the river steps outside Cotton House, holding the precious manuscript. Fine carpets had been laid on the landing stage and Cotton's guests were crowding the windows of his house. The royal barge came into view on the Thames, and, as Cotton held his breath disbelievingly, it sailed past on the orders of Buckingham, ignoring him completely. If you have tears, shed them now in sympathy for his heart-rending disappointment.

Worse was to come. In 1627 a little book by Cotton appeared in print, *A Short View of the Long Life and Raigne of Henry the Third*, which (Cotton protested) had been privately drafted in 1614 and was now suddenly published without his knowledge or consent. It was interpreted, not unreasonably, as an attack on Charles I and the duke of Buckingham, with thinly veiled judgements supposedly set in the thirteenth century, such as, "For nothing is more against the nature of the English, than to haue strangers rule over them." Cotton was interrogated for sedition. Historical precedent, like democracy, is only an excellent system as long as it delivers the right result. By 1629, as tensions between Crown and Parliament escalated, Cotton's library was suspected of owning material which could be used for treasonable propaganda, and Buckingham recommended its closure. In November of that year Cotton was briefly arrested and his library was locked on the king's orders. It was the end of Cotton's dream. He is said to have died of grief on 6 May 1631, exactly a hundred years before the fire.

Robert Cotton is buried in Conington Church. You drive from London up the A1 past the former entrance to Conington Manor, turning right along a winding lane into the village. The church of All Saints is out beyond the far end, beside what is clearly the residue of the park. It is now closed, having been declared redundant and placed in the care of the Churches Conservation Trust. The key can be obtained from a resident in Bruce's Close in the village (Cotton's added middle name is not forgotten). It is as big and heavy as the key held by Saint Peter in Cotton's illuminated charter for King Edgar's foundation of New Minster in 966. You approach up the private drive of a large modern house, and the venerable fourteenth-century church is on the right. It is high and wide but not especially long. The floor is damp as you enter and there are atmospheric old wooden box pews. There are monuments around the walls to all the Cotton dynasty and to the Heathcotes, their successors to the manor. Sir Robert's is in off-white marble on the wall in the right-hand corner of what was a chapel at the far end of the south aisle, which is fenced off by a wooden screen with a gate. There is a portrait bust in an oval. We meet him at last, face to face. Cotton has a slightly arched nose, big lips and a pointed beard, not unlike Charles I. His long hair, white as the marble, is blowing back. He looks thin and tired, with hollow eyes. He is wearing a big collar, like Shakespeare, and buttons down the front. Above him are coats of arms and below is a swag of classical leafage resting on a Latin inscription describing him as the descendant of a noble line and almost in passing as a preserver of the nation's history. There is nothing about his character, and perhaps there was little to say. His son, Sir Thomas (d. 1662), is nearby, in the left-hand

The monument of Sir Robert Cotton in Conington Church, *c.*1631.

corner. His Latin tablet proclaims in more detail his piety in maintaining his father's incomparable library at no small expense and dedicating it to the learning of posterity. Even this tribute is modest in comparison with the monument to Sir John Cotton (d. 1702) at the end of the north aisle, just accessible behind the wooden organ. For fourteen swaggering lines it praises the riches of his grandfather's library in Cotton House in Westminster, devoted to the history and antiquities of Britain, which John has now, out of charity and patriotism, transferred to public use for ever. John Cotton was also responsible for having an enigmatic four-word quotation from Lucan added to the foot of his grandfather's own monument. It says "Communis mundo superest rogus". A *communis rogus* is a public funeral pyre, an uncannily prophetic allusion, carved at least thirty years before the disaster of 1731. It means something like, 'His funeral pyre survives for the world.'

DAVID BEN ABRAHAM
OPPENHEIMER.

CHAPTER SIX

The Rabbi: David Oppenheim

Chapter 11 of Genesis, in the Jewish Torah as in the Christian Bible, describes God's deliberate confusion of languages and scattering of the descendants of Noah, who had been impiously building the Tower of Babel. The multiplicity of languages and diversity of cultures have always been a feature of the city of Prague in what is now the Czech Republic. For a thousand years the capital of Bohemia was the great meeting point of central Europe for international trade and for administration of the royal or Holy Roman imperial courts. On one side of the Vltava river are the castle of the kings of Bohemia and the towering cathedral of Saint Vitus. On the other is an old city where many nationalities lived, including a sizable population of Jews. Today the famous Charles Bridge between them is noisy and crowded, jostling with tourists babbling in seemingly every language of the world. It was probably no different when the bridge was first embellished with its baroque sculptures in the late seventeenth and early eighteenth centuries.

About five minutes' walk into the town from the eastern end of the bridge is the Old Jewish Cemetery, one of the well-known sights for visitors to Prague. You now dodge across a very fast road by the Rudolfinum concert hall and proceed up a cobbled street called Široká into the area which was once the Jewish ghetto. There is a security guard at a gate on the left. At a very low kiosk you stoop to buy a ticket for 500 crowns issued by the Jewish Museum in Prague, admitting you to several neighbouring synagogues and exhibitions as well as into the cemetery. Male visitors are given a little blue and white paper *yarmulke* to wear in sacred spaces, and the ticket (quite reasonably) prohibits smoking and bringing

LEFT: Rabbi David Oppenheim (1664–1736), engraving, Prague, 1773, based on a drawing by Johann Kleinhard.

firearms. You go down a few steps through a metal turnstile into a little courtyard. Straight ahead is the flag-stoned and red-tiled Pinkas Synagogue, originally sixteenth-century but reconfigured after the Second World War as a Holocaust memorial, desecrated during the Communist era of Czechoslovakia and now fittingly restored. As you walk round, it plays recordings of liturgical singing and prayers in Hebrew. At the east end of the courtyard, around several corners and past a bookstall, is a narrow entrance into the adjacent Jewish burial ground.

It is all very unlike the ordered lawns of most modern municipal cemeteries. The area is a wild garden in a strange and uneven shape now tightly hemmed in by high city offices and apartment blocks. There is a low central mound overgrown with trees – beech, I think – and you are made to follow a roped-off walkway around the perimeter of the ground and then back across the centre towards the exit at the far end. Everywhere you look are old tombstones, mostly sixteenth- to nineteenth-century, some 12,000 in all, piled up or planted or half buried in the unkempt grass of this secret wilderness, leaning like gossiping old men this way and that, many of them almost black with age and infirmity. Jewish law prohibits

The Jewish cemetery in Prague.

the moving of graves, and so each generation in the former ghetto of Prague simply heaped more and more burials into the limited space available, as earlier tombs were allowed to subside and totter. Within here, it is very monolingual. The stones are all inscribed in Hebrew. Here in this secluded refuge in a modern city is an outdoor library of one of the most ancient forms of writing, in its oldest format, which is cut into stone.

The script runs from right to left. The Hebrew alphabet evolved from the northern Semitic scripts of the Near East in the second millennium BC and is still largely unchanged since about the time of Ezra around 450 BC. Many of the tombs in Prague are inscribed under pictorial symbols, echoes of forms of graphic communication even older than writing. A good name, for example, may be symbolized by a crown or fertility by a bunch of grapes (an emblem from the Bible probably hardly known in reality by most masons of northern Bohemia). Animal pictograms represent the names of the twelve tribes of ancient Israel, such as a lion for Yehuda, a deer for Naphtali, a wolf for Benjamin, and so on, all derived from readings of Genesis 49. The very great antiquity of Judaism and its written legacy, and the unimaginably long journeys of the Jews across the world and through many millennia, are all vividly reflected on these stones.

There is living nature too. There are blackbirds and lazy pigeons, contentedly undisturbed. There are dandelions and nettle flowers, and a rampant little pink weed which I am told is probably cranesbill, a cousin of the larger flowers in the cloisters at Bec. I furtively picked one, to press into my notebook for later identification, and in an instant the security guard was beside me, afraid that I might be disturbing the pebbles left by pious pilgrims to the tombs. Talmudic law discourages the leaving of cut flowers at gravesides, since the practice was thought to be pagan, but depositing little stones is regarded as a less transitory sign of respect. I explained to the guard that I was interested in David Oppenheim, chief rabbi of Prague from 1703 until his death in 1736. "Come with me", he said, and lifted the rope and led me up a less trodden path to one of the largest graves in the whole Jewish cemetery, parallel to the north wall of the Pinkas Synagogue, under a tree. It is the shape of a sarcophagus with a steep roof, like a little house with a high gable at each end, inscribed in Hebrew in cartouches beneath a Star of David, an emblem of the first name of the deceased. Like so many of the tombs here, it is beginning to sag and give way and it is now protected from collapse by a rusty metal brace. However, on the small flat surfaces on either side of the gables visitors have deposited little pebbles. The memory of Rabbi Oppenheim is still revered in Prague.

As one emerges into the street from the far side of the cemetery, there are several synagogues to see on the same admission ticket. One of these, along the Maiselova, crossing Široká Street where we entered, is the Maisel Synagogue at the southern end of the ghetto area. It is behind a tiny precinct on the left. It had been founded in 1590 at the expense of the philanthropist Mordecai Maisel, but has been reconstructed several times and is now a museum of Jewish life in Prague. In the exhibition case along the right-hand wall is an engraved portrait of Rabbi Oppenheim himself, published in 1773. Hundreds of people now buried in the cemetery knew him in real life. Although posthumous, the engraving may be as near as we can get today to a plausible recollection of the man. It shows a half-length figure with an opulent white beard, like a Victorian image of Father Christmas, gazing solemnly out at us through a round-arched stone window. The beard is so straight that it looks almost as if it had been painted wetly and had then begun to run down the page before it dried. The rabbi's eyebrows are raised quizzically and his eyes are very large and his mouth small. He is expensively robed in decorative court dress and wears the Jewish fur hat known as a *shtreimel*. There is a lighted oil lamp above his right shoulder, signifying wisdom, but no books. The stone window itself is cracked and overgrown with plants, suggesting great antiquity, like the tombs in the cemetery now.

The name below the engraving is given in Latin script as 'David ben Abraham Oppenheimer'. His family surname is variously spelled Oppenheim and Oppenheimer: the latter version is German but the former is normal in Hebrew and Yiddish, and I will adopt it here.

The idea of including Rabbi Oppenheim in the manuscripts club was suggested to me by my old friend Brian Deutsch, who will recur prominently throughout this chapter; I owe much to his exhilarating and sometimes relentless conversations. Brian has a white beard, neater than Oppenheim's. He trained as a rabbi in Israel but instead entered business, including pioneering work in cable television and picture libraries. He is also an antiquary of great energy, whom I first knew more than forty years ago as a perceptive collector of manuscripts, mainly in Hebrew. With the name 'Christopher', I cannot pretend to be Jewish, but, like George Eliot's Daniel Deronda, I have often wished that I could have been. The sense of historical membership is something many of us lack in our muddled ancestries. Oppenheim presents a compelling reason for living among manuscripts entirely different from any other in this book, with the added advantage for me that his own vast collection was eventually bought in 1828 by the Bodleian Library and is available intact for study in Oxford. Talking to Brian Deutsch, sometimes with Oppenheim's own medieval volumes open on the table in front of us in the Bodleian, brings me as near as I can get to witnessing the unique fascination with manuscripts among the most intellectual and oldest of the Peoples of the Book.

David ben Abraham Oppenheim was born in 1664 in Worms in the Rhineland, a free city in the Holy Roman Empire. About a quarter of the city's population were Jewish. The eponymous ancestral town of Oppenheim is on the Rhine, about twenty miles to the north, between Worms and Mainz. David was one of the sons of Abraham Oppenheim (as his middle name tells us), wealthy city merchant and prominent member of the Jewish community, with a house in the Judengasse. David's uncle was Samuel Oppenheim (1630–1703), court Jew and *Oberfaktor* to the Holy Roman emperor, Leopold I, and principal financier of the defence of Vienna against the Turks in the 1680s. This was a family with substantial money and connections across Europe. They all spoke numerous languages. The easy internationalism of early modern Jews is conspicuous, especially in a period of history when Christian Europe was being fragmented by very local and newly assertive political identities. The Thirty Years' War had disrupted much of seventeenth-century Germany but also created a need for goods and finance. Jewish wealth was often in ready money, not tied up in land like that of Sir Robert Cotton or the Duc de Berry, and many Jewish families did well in Europe as traders and bankers during post-war reconstruction. Unlike their gentile counterparts, however, seventeenth-century Jews – even highly successful court Jews – led lives which were desperately insecure, and every single day they faced the possibility of persecution at a legislative whim, sudden forfeiture or total destruction of everything they had ever built up, and even national expulsion. Both these factors – money and precariousness – greatly affected Jewish book collecting.

As a small child David Oppenheim was taught by a private tutor, and was later sent round various *yeshivas*, houses of Jewish learning, to study under different religious masters in Metz, Friedberg and Landsberg.

ספר
עברונות לחשוב
מתוכו מולדות
ותקופות כמאמר
חז"ל מצוה לחשוב
תקופות ומזלות שנא'
כי היא חכמתכם
ובינתכם לעיני העמים

שייך להבחור יש"ן וחבי"ב יתקרי דוד בה[illegible] הנ"ל
פרנס ומנהיג כהר"ר אברהם [illegible]
היו' יו' ד' כ"ו בחדש [illegible] בשנת תל"ה לפ"ק

יוני דוד בן [illegible]
[illegible]
היו' יו' ד' [illegible]
[illegible] תל"ה לפ"ק
[illegible] דוד

יוני דוד בן [illegible]
[illegible]
[illegible] ד' כו [illegible] תל"ה לפ"ק
[illegible] דוד

1

It was a concentrated education, instilling the value of book learning together with an overwhelming sense of the inheritance and responsibility of Judaism. Even as a boy, David Oppenheim owned books himself. A very early acquisition, quite possibly his first manuscript, was a little sixty-year-old book of rules for the Jewish calendar, beginning in 1617, which was given to him by Zalman Kinstein. Its ostensible subject is astronomy, but in Judaism even science is studied for its religious application, for the solstices and lunar cycles determine the festivals. The manuscript's architectural title-page is inscribed in Hebrew that it now 'belongs to the clever youth called David, son of the chief warden and leader Abraham, man of Oppenheim, today Wednesday the 27th of Elul 5435', corresponding in the Christian calendar to 18 September 1675, when the recipient was about eleven. Ten years later, Oppenheim used the same volume to make a list of titles of some 480 books by then in his possession. He opens it with a heading, 'With good fortune' – *mazal tov* is a Hebrew term even I know – 'the books that I have bought with my wealth, to honour my God who formed and acquired me . . . ', continuing further down, 'and may God grant me to collect and accrue them so that God's Torah in Israel may spread far and wide, and to make books without end, and to sustain us and speedily bring the days of the end, Amen, Amen, Amen'. In the slightly pompous wording of a very young man, he already saw a divine purpose and urgency in cultivating a library. The making of books without end is an allusion to Ecclesiastes 12:12.

Hebrew books have never been numerous or safe. Latin manuscripts in Europe generally survived untroubled from the Middle Ages because of a custom of safekeeping and benign neglect, often in institutional ownership, and medieval Christian texts in general are quite common. It was different in Judaism. There were not so many books to start with. There were no equivalents of monastic libraries. Jews were a much smaller percentage of the population and Jewish manuscripts were forever subject to overuse by their owners, Christian censorship and anti-Semitic destruction – dangers still very current in the late seventeenth century.

Oppenheim's early catalogue of the 1680s does not record whether his purchases were printed or handwritten. One item identifiable on the list was a commentary on the Midrash on Genesis by Elijah ben Moses

LEFT: An early seventeenth-century manuscript on the Jewish calendar, acquired by Oppenheim in 1675, when he was about eleven years old.

Ashkenazi Loans (1555–1636), rabbi of Worms. This was certainly a manuscript, for it is still among the Oppenheim books in the Bodleian, a large volume, almost as thick as it is wide, containing nearly 2000 paper pages in the author's handwriting with many corrections and additions. It is occasionally embellished with modest headings in gold on coloured panel grounds, but its value lies entirely in its unpublished text. The author was local to Worms and at least two of his children lived into the 1670s; the Oppenheims doubtless knew the family,

One source for Oppenheim's early acquisition of manuscripts in Worms can be partly illustrated from his printed edition of Rashbam's commentary on the Pentateuch, published in Berlin in 1705. ('Rashbam' is the abbreviated name from the initials of the twelfth-century Rabbi Samuel Ben-Meïr, grandson of the more famous biblical and Talmudic scholar Rashi, of Troyes, contemporary of Saint Anselm.) In the preface to the edition, Oppenheim recounts that he had acquired what was then the unique manuscript of Rashbam's text some twenty years earlier from the synagogue of Worms, together with a prayerbook known as the Mahzor Vitry. This would date his acquisition to the mid-1680s, when Oppenheim was around twenty or twenty-one. He tells that a local dealer had reported to him thousands of manuscripts in the upstairs *genizah*, or storeroom, of the synagogue, 'fetid, dusty, mouldy, infested with vermin, and rotting from exposure to rain', and that 'the Lord brought this book into my hands'. His sense of godly destiny is explicit. The intermediary who reported the find may have been Sofer (the scribe) Zanwil ben Benjamin Wolf, a dealer who is recorded as selling other books to Oppenheim in 1686. The title-page of the 1705 edition of Rashbam alludes to Oppenheim's library as if it were endorsed by Providence: 'This is the book of Rashbam, discovered in the trove of holy books of our master and our rabbi of all the diaspora, David Oppenheim, may his creator protect him'.

Curiously, once the text was in print, the old manuscript of Rashbam from Worms was never seen again. Maybe it was sent to the typesetter in Berlin and not returned. This is a first sighting of a distinctively Jewish attitude to book collecting. The text mattered more than the manuscript: once it was safely and definitively rendered into print, the original was

RIGHT: Commentary on the midrash on Genesis by Elijah ben Moses Ashkenazi Loans, owned by Oppenheim in Worms by the time he was in his early twenties.

תולדות נח. נח איש צדיק תמים בדר'
בעבור שופה וכו' הוקשה לו למה ה
הזכיר כאן כשהתחיל על דור המבול שנח
היה צדיק תמים ולא הזכיר זה לעיל
כשהזכירו ועל זה אמר בבר' כלומר
סופה ורשעים אין וצדיק יסוד עולם. שבא ואמר הפסוק הקשה שאינו דבר זה שום
הבל ואין רשע וצדיק יחדיו אלא יהיה. על כן אמר שהפסוק מתחיל בדור ה
המבול. שהרשעים עברו ונעקרו מן הארץ. וצדיק יסוד עולם זה נח שממנו הולדת
העולם עוד כל ימי הארץ. ועכ"ז נתיישב שפה שהזכיר כאן נח איש צדיק תמים
בוא לפי שבא להזכיר עקירת דור המבול. ונח מצא נתייסד העולם. הפסוק ראיה
ונהם כל חפשו ראיון דדרש הפסוק רשעי' כרא' לא דריש בעבור שופה וכו'
על דור המבול ובב' הבית. ומונם ואפשר שבכר בזו החכם להורות בכבוד
חילו הדברים כדי שישמעו הבני אדם לכם על זה. ופת צדיק' יעמוד זה נח
אלה תולדות נח. שואת שהדרש הזה סבר שהפסוק אמר אלה תולדות נח והזכיר
נח איש צדיק תמים הוא להורות שאם התולדות היו צדיקי' כמוהו ולכן פתח ב
בתולדותיו. והדרי' ואפשר דמפרש נפי איש צדיק תמים היה בדורותיו
בדורותיו משמעות עם כל בית ונבחר בעולם מלידת אבי עם עולם
וו עם שלמותו שיש לו שלא אלמוד שלכן. ואפשר דגם הדור שדבריו כוון
ומוחל רשעי' ובריח דכל העי' והבית' המריך ברכה לפי דעתו והעלה בתנאי
ב' דבר אחר אלה וכו' כרשב"ל אמר וכו' המדרש הזה כמו אמר שמה שנח נעשה
הוא היה בעבור שהיתה מחשבתו לבסורות והרעות והעביר בני כמוו
ולא להשחית רדע ולכן קרא צדיק תמים שהאמר בוירא נקרא תמ' כמו שב
ונאל אברהם התהלך לפני והיה תמים ולפרש הבי הנזכרו נעדה על המבול ובפרש
נח שמעד שהוא בדורותיו כמו דר' נחן. ואמר עוד המבול כי הוא על פני
בראיה כמו שדריש ר' בהלך אמר שהיה נח מוכיחם ואמר עשו תשובה ואם
לאו הקב"ה מביא עליכם את המבול ואתם לזה הקב"ה ומכסה את גופתם על
הקודש. ואמר ויקם ויצא ועל כן אמר כהן כלל שנתפשו לעיל בדור המבול
במקום פ' לב' סי' ו' מפרש לה

הביא ברזי' שאין לו הוא
על פני המים והתוהו'
על רוב. על שפי טויב
שנה והשווה היו מוכחל

ואתם ואמרו לכם שעתיד המבול לבוא עליהם היו מוחל' לים ואם לשוב על פני המים ויש לו קצוות ורשעים שלים
ובשנות שבם חטאות ולשוב. שהרי הגוף לא דרשו כך ואם שדרשו זה על דור המבול לפי שבפסוק הקודם ואמר על

The Mahzor Vitry, an eleventh-century manuscript prayerbook bought by Oppenheim from the *genizah* of the synagogue in Worms in about 1685.

effectively exhausted. Conversely, even today, manuscripts are deemed especially precious while they remain unpublished. We used to see this in the catalogue descriptions of Hebrew manuscripts in Sotheby's sales, prepared by my then colleague Chimen Abramsky. If at all possible, Chimen would write of a manuscript that it was unprinted or had differences from the published text, a merit which rendered it more valuable to Jewish buyers. This was in contrast to entries for medieval Latin manuscripts catalogued for sale by me, where conformity to the received and known text was a mark of good copying, and excessive divergence was unsettling and suggested scribal carelessness.

The Mahzor Vitry, bought from the *genizah* with the Rashbam, still survives in the Oppenheim collection in Oxford. It comprises prayers with liturgical rules and poems by Rabbi Simcha ben Samuel of Vitry (d. 1105), a contemporary and disciple of Rashi. It is massive and heavy, in a late-medieval wooden binding with a spine of white leather. The manuscript is an assemblage by various scribes, without decoration. It is defective and rubbed at the front and elsewhere, and damp-stained, presumably from its neglect in the *genizah*. It had already been in Worms at an early date, for it has marginal notes in the hand of the scholar and mystic Eleazar ben Judah Rokeach (*c.*1176–1238), or Eleazar of Worms.

Like many orthodox Jews then and sometimes now, David Oppenheim married very young, doubtless arranged by the parents. His wife was Gnendel, daughter of the court Jew Leffman Behrens of Hanover, another well-connected family of considerable wealth from business in cloth and tobacco. Gnendel was several years older than her seventeen-year-old husband, and they eventually had seven children. David Oppenheim was ordained as a rabbi at the age of twenty. There was no conflict for a rabbi, as there might be for a Christian cleric, in engaging in personal business across Europe while simultaneously performing religious duties in the local community. On the contrary, there are Halachic imperatives that a rabbi should learn a trade, so that teaching the Torah should be free and not a profession. Even the great rabbinical scholar Rashi himself is reported as having been a wine merchant in his day job.

Oppenheim was also raising a family. Through financial brokerage and investment, he prospered prodigiously, but these were uneasy times. In 1689, Worms was among the cities of the Rhineland besieged and sacked by the French armies during the Nine Years' War. In one of his printed books Oppenheim added a note about the burning of both synagogues and other buildings in Worms during the hostilities, when the Jews were forced to flee, as he says, like birds from branch to branch. This might explain the charred edges of one of his manuscripts, a chunky little Ashkenazi Pentateuch made around 1400 with inscriptions of an owner in Worms in 1588. The ever-present threat of disasters added to the sense of urgency in keeping safe the written testimony of Judaism.

In 1690 or 1691, David Oppenheim was appointed rabbi of Nikolsburg and chief rabbi of Moravia. He was to remain there for nearly thirteen years. The town, now called Mikulov, is in the south-east corner of what is today the Czech Republic, not far from the northern border of Austria, just above Vienna. It must have seemed a safer place than Worms for his growing Hebrew library, which was transported to Moravia with him and his family. Nikolsburg had the largest Jewish population in the country. The striking feature of the town, then as now, is how it is entirely dominated by the vast castle of the Dietrichstein family, ennobled as princes of the Holy Roman Empire in 1624. Their pale-yellow fortress fills the hilltop above the fertile plains of Moravia, a ring of

The Jewish quarter in Nikolsburg, *c.*1890, with a view up to the old synagogue at the top of the lane.

fortified turrets connecting huge palace buildings and courtyards, tiled in bright orange and surmounted by a high tower capped with bulbs of gleaming green copper.

The old Jewish synagogue is on the north-western slope of the hill, just under the castle walls. Its square central hall is built beneath four cupolas. At the south-eastern end is the ark, or *aron ha-kodesh*, where Torah scrolls are kept, a great sparkling architectural fantasy in pink and green marble flanked by heraldic stone mantling in red and gilt. Eighteenth-century Hebrew title-pages sometimes look like that. Sunlight pours in from round-topped windows on either side, decorated with trefoils of coloured glass. In the centre of the synagogue is a tower with four marble columns supporting the roof, enclosing the pulpit, or *almemor*, on a dais. The chief rabbi would read and preach from here. I sat on one of the benches around the outer wall, reading the information sheets enclosed in plastic envelopes in a folder lent to me by the supervisor in the lobby. I learned that there were two synagogues in the town when Rabbi Oppenheim arrived. This was the 'upper' synagogue, known as the *Altschul*, built in 1550 and expanded in 1659 with the addition of a women's area to the south, which I looked at too. However, the whole synagogue was largely reconstructed following a fire in August 1719, in

Oppenheim's lifetime but not during his rabbinate here. He must have used a building very like this, but not exactly the fabric of this one. There was also a seventeenth-century 'lower' synagogue, the *Neuschul*, which was demolished in 1977–9 during the time of Communism.

I read too of the arrival of the Jews in Nikolsburg after 1421, when they had been expelled from Vienna and Lower Austria. By the eighteenth century there were some 620 Jewish households in the ghetto district here. They mostly lived in what is now Husova Street (formerly Přičná) and Zámecká, which both curve up the side of the hill near the synagogue and where one can still see traces of substantial late-medieval stone houses, some with modern plaques naming Jewish merchants who had once occupied them. The Oppenheim family probably had one of them. I do not know whether the rabbi's books were kept at home or in some more public space. Upstairs in the *Altschul* is an enormous gallery, certainly spacious enough to accommodate a library and facilities for study, as would have been traditional.

After leaving the synagogue, I walked round to its far end, up the steps there into the landscaped terraces which surround the castle, and sat for a moment looking out at the view. The old Jewish quarter fills the foreground, now a sea of red-tiled roofs. Beyond is the undulating Moravian countryside of fields of vivid yellow rape flowers and dark-brown earth enclosed by hedges, reaching to forests on the hazy and distant horizon, like an idyllic pastoral landscape by Claude Lorrain. Rabbi Oppenheim must sometimes have gazed out here too, over the house tops of his prosperous but very fragile community, completely enclosed by the mighty territories of Christendom.

I followed the circumference of the castle gardens and eventually came up through the steep approach into the complex itself. To my delight, I found that there was to be a guided tour of the palace library in twenty minutes' time and I signed up at once. There were formerly spectacular illuminated manuscripts here, mostly dispersed in a sale in Luzern in 1933 during the Depression, when many old European families needed cash. Survivals from the Dietrichstein auction have sometimes reappeared on the market in my lifetime, and I am familiar with the castle's bookplate in manuscripts. The library had been formed principally by Prince Ferdinand Joseph von Dietrichstein (1628–98), and was greatly enriched by his acquisition of the entire collection of Ferdinand Hoffman von Grünpühel und Strechau (1540–1607), marshal of Austria. It

Collection of medical texts, with the opening of a Hebrew translation of the surgical treatise of Rogerio dei Frugardi, Byzantine, fifteenth century.

was a traditional European aristocratic library, with the selection of early printed books and grand manuscripts found in most noble collectors' cabinets, including Books of Hours, classical poetry, illustrated chronicles (such as a *Weltchronik* dated 1449 with 238 miniatures), literary texts and many others. More unusually for the period, the Dietrichstein library in Nikolsburg also included an important clutch of Hebrew manuscripts. One of these was an Ashkenazi commentary on the *Halakhoth* of Isaac ben Jacob Alfasi, dated 1456, which had come with the Hoffman library. By a very different route, it is now in the Bodleian in Oxford and is a neighbour once again of the collection of David Oppenheim. Others at Nikolsburg were a group of Sephardi Hebrew medical texts from medieval Spain, such as a manuscript of book III of the *Canon* of Avicenna written in 1463, and a Hebrew translation of Bernard de Gordon's *Lilium medicinae* dated by the scribe Joshua ben David Hakohen in 1468. These are now in the Boston Medical Library in America.

To enter the castle library now you go up an open-air stair off the central courtyard. In the event, I was the only customer for the tour. There was a great rattling of keys and I was admitted along a corridor and round to the right. It is a fine long room with globes and a few moderately interesting books on display, left over from the sale of 1933, but what I had not anticipated is that I had unexpectedly reached the northwestern corner of the castle, and the library quite literally overlooks the synagogue just beneath it.

The chief rabbi of Moravia and the prince would surely have known each other in this small town, despite differences of religion. Ferdinand Joseph von Dietrichstein was imperial chamberlain and privy councillor in the court of Leopold I in Vienna, where Samuel Oppenheim, the rabbi's uncle, was principal financial officer. When in 1692 there was a dispute over whether David Oppenheim was indeed to be chief rabbi of Moravia (the position was contested by one Issachar Baer Frankfurter), it was Prince Ferdinand Joseph who stepped in on Oppenheim's behalf. It is almost unimaginable that these two great book men did not sometimes look at manuscripts together in the court library of Nikolsburg Castle. Like all collectors, they would discuss their aims and plans, although from very different perspectives. It seems strange that Oppenheim failed to beguile the prince into ceding to him his shelf of rare Hebrew books, which cannot have been in much demand by the library's users, unless the rabbi somehow felt (wrongly, as it turned out) that a stone-built castle of a Holy Roman prince was a safer location for their long-term survival than even the most obsessive private collection. It has never been suggested that Oppenheim might have given these Sephardi medical manuscripts to Prince Ferdinand Joseph, but that is possible too.

By this time, Rabbi Oppenheim had developed into a serious acquisitor of Hebrew manuscripts. Books were being sent to him from all over Europe and beyond. Some were certainly gifts, as many of Cotton's manuscripts were, for books were currency, traded for patronage, as we have seen in England and in the *étrennes* of the Duc de Berry. There is, for example, an undated manuscript of the Babylonian Talmud, or commentary on the Mishnah, inscribed as having been presented to Rabbi Oppenheim in Nikolsburg. Most acquisitions, however, were purchased, and payment was clearly no problem for him. Even that youthful inscription of the mid-1680s had unashamedly described his library as 'bought with my wealth'. Books were purchased from members of many Jewish communities who were glad of the money. Oppenheim still travelled a great deal on family business and in pursuit of manuscripts, back and forth across the Holy Roman Empire. There is an extant letter from a Rabbi Meir Katzenellenbogen, of Stampfen (now Stupava in western Slovakia), who was acting as intermediary in Oppenheim's purchase of a group of manuscripts from a member of his congregation. (His name, which literally means 'cat's elbow', is a German town.) The price was 50 Rhenish thalers. Rather than taking a commission, which was evidently normal, Rabbi Katzenellenbogen asked instead whether he might keep two of the books himself, one of which was a copy of the code of religious law *Sefer Yad ha-Hazaka* ('Book of the strong hand') by Maimonides.

Jerusalem was an especially fertile hunting ground for acquiring manuscripts brought to the eastern Mediterranean by Sephardi Jews who had been expelled from Spain and Portugal in the 1490s. These might often be texts not easily found in central or northern Europe. One travelling agent was Eleazer ha-Levi, of Holleschau (in Moravia, now Holešov, north-east of Mikulov). He bought books for Oppenheim in Palestine, Egypt and elsewhere, doubtless also on a commission. An example (of no great antiquity) is a commentary on Rashi's work on Genesis written in Spanish rabbinic script, which has a note that Eleazer ha-Levi acquired it for Oppenheim in Jerusalem in 1703. Such international reach would have been unimaginable to Sir Robert Cotton.

There is a good group of Byzantine Hebrew manuscripts in the Oppenheim library, a class of books then little known in Europe. There were many Sephardi Jews in Constantinople. Among Oppenheim's acquisitions are a fifteenth-century anthology including the expositions on the visions of Isaiah, Ezekiel and Zechariah by the fourteenth-century neoplatonist Rabbi Hanokh el-Constantini; a grammatical and allegorical commentary on the Pentateuch by Eliah ha-Qatan ('the small'), written in Greek rabbinic cursive in 1468–9, with precious additions and corrections in the hand of the author's grandson; and an extraordinarily rare Karaite commentary on the nature of priesthood as found in Leviticus, translated from Arabic into Hebrew, dated 1353. I saw this manuscript in Oxford with Brian Deutsch. It is not very beautiful, written on paper, freckled with spots and worn on its edges. I do not suppose that Ferdinand Joseph von Dietrichstein would have given it a second glance or a place on his shelves. Brian, however, could hardly emphasize to me

RIGHT: Rashi (Rabbi Shlomo Yitzchaki), Commentaries on the Bible, Ashkenazi, early thirteenth century.

וה כל לשון חרון אף שהיו׳ עחר בו ומעלה הב׳ וי׳
ואש מפני הוכל׳ א׳ אגירה רגרמו ח׳
א׳ הוכל רשעים יוש מרשעים ויט שו׳
שוי׳ להעקב ווויבן ג׳ ויעים ופרשה׳
וישה ח׳ חשך פניכותו ל׳ לפני כג׳
כענין ש׳ ויהי הענן והחשך ומפסיק בין
ויעים לישר׳ חשרה ויים עבי שחק׳
ויוון ג׳ ה׳ היה החשך עבי שחקים
היין ג׳ חושרין ויכע׳ הארץ חש׳ רת
לשו׳ טבה הוין ג׳ א׳ דבר הטפל דיק׳ יק׳
ו׳ וכן הוין מוגדות הרגע שחושרין אותו
כבדה ג׳ ויש לפ׳ לפטור חשרת לשון׳
ק׳ קשר שו׳ שוה קשרים השוו׳
מעלים על׳ א׳ ידי הויים כמו וח׳ שו׳
וחשורים האומר מוטב ה׳ המורכב׳
המכונה שהם זרו שה העץ חושרה׳
המהרק׳ ס׳ וקושרים עג׳ עגלה
יחד׳ ומעגה ער׳ רי׳ שלו הטור
א׳ מושך הוין ש׳ ר׳ שרוי יוון הע׳
הענג לפנים מן הזה הוחיקה וויוות
ענג יושר לפנו כשה גחלי אש שנשה
שנשהלחו ח׳ נים ע׳ ויג׳ ויעים׳ עלו וזוכר
ומפרות הבל׳ א׳ שנבקען ההוים משנבקש
ים פוו ו׳ ונבקש כל וייוה שבעולם׳
ק׳ וי׳ ומעשוות ג׳ ויכח טוכה רוח
ומפ׳ כי יוריע׳ כושר יקחיע׳ בער׳ א׳
בער קם שי׳ נוו יוחרין לוירבר ופוים לג׳
לג׳ לוורבר על׳ ומבטחו׳ עבר
חפיד׳ נבר׳ הויים׳ כער של׳ שלשה
ומכה שלש הקבה גמול ערק׳ ערקתם
לבנים׳ עש׳ עקש׳ טר׳ ט׳ ער׳
וה׳ הבל לשון עבל ועקש ונב׳ טר
הליס הבטל ג׳ א׳ ישלח וו׳ וו׳ וים
יקחני על׳ עמוו א׳ יוור שו׳ מטה ה׳
שחט ללכה ג׳ א׳ ומפ׳ שאול נג׳
נבלי המחלקה והורה קרוב להבט׳
וולד בא יל׳ שאול לוור מהרה
ל׳ ע׳ כי פשטו ט׳ ל׳ ט׳ עשותם׳
בערק׳ ג׳ ילו רה הרגביו עדרים׳
והנג׳ ה ג׳ לו רו וורהג׳ עופר׳
נחל׳ ומנייר׳ ושו ושורר ושוה׳
והר׳ ג׳ כי׳ רכי וירג׳ דרכי אל מכשול ואל הכות׳

ער כי היה שלג וכטנה ועוה קשה עושה זרוע
ורושה׳ ורכה ק׳ קשה עושה על׳
ו׳ ורעי שיש כמו לורה קשה א׳
וה קשוה היה לוין לו לרור כמה
והיו ולכ׳ המורות במין ו׳ וי׳ ורוון
יוור ואו זה לוה יוות פנר׳ שהוא
יטל לורם יוון זה כי יום ליראו ודור
שוועו ועטלו ורוכטו ל׳ לפני הכ׳
ודרכה קשה לשון חירה הוא וכן
חינך עוט ג׳ ו׳ ורור שו שוועו ועשוק
הר׳ הרבנו הגלה ל׳ ודה עטוהו וחך׳
ק׳ הרחיב עשרי׳ כשוויס ורבק
רגלין וו יגע וו הוון לו עח ליפול וכ׳
ווה כלטק לו ישר שעדך ר׳ קרמלי׳
עקימי ישע וזון ומושי׳ וג׳ הרן
א׳ וה מקרין ומורם׳ א׳ ישע יאל
א׳ ולא ענו ווון מוע מין שעה
הורס יול עשהו כמו יפנה׳ ויפנם
חבן עם וישע אל הכל א׳ ופקד בלשן
שמרה והלשון ט׳ טפל על היע
הוע׳ הר׳ וישנר ישחק וישע לו א׳
יוו׳ טון ישש א׳ וזון וישע ט׳ טפל
ע׳ הוהכל׳ וישע ט׳ טפל הלשון ק׳
על וי שוהם לפנן ווהרש יוגרה
ישע לש׳ של׳ ט׳ והם וזון בה יפלה
א׳ להושיע ווחר ך׳ ולא ולון עבו׳
וון ל׳ יורקשו ונים והרבה יט׳
במטר יחוקוו ורק׳ ע׳ במלך ו׳ ורקע׳
בעג׳ ג׳ וריב עם עשי ורווג ווחיהו
ושוו ו׳ והדיפים השורש לרוט ג׳
גוי׳ עטנו לך וירדש יקו׳ וו׳
דוד רכוט של׳ עלם העולמור
ודין של ישראל שוס יוטה
וו׳ ורדה ישר בעגוה וע שעש׳ א׳ ווון
לווש נוים השיוון א׳ ורס יע׳ יעבוש
ועליהם לו וע׳ ועשי׳ ג׳ יהבחשו לי
וחורה ל׳ ורוה יוורי ישוע לי טנים׳
לשויענון ישויע לו יוח׳ שלון מג׳
יגו׳ ומפ׳ ומשויע א׳ יוג׳ יוניהם׳
לקור יול ושו׳ ג׳ ר׳ בני נבר
יבלו ולון ג׳ א׳ לשון נבל עלר׳ ות׳
א׳ טעש בלש׳ ווהג׳ לשון רבויב ג׳

ומפני׳

strongly enough the absolute rarity of Karaite texts, and how impressive it was that Rabbi Oppenheim would want any manuscript from so far into the Jewish occult. Many words are underlined by an attentive later reader, perhaps Oppenheim himself. The Karaites were (and still are) a very ancient religious sect beyond the acceptable fringes of mainstream rabbinic Judaism, recognizing only the Torah as divine law and rejecting all subsequent traditions of the midrash and Talmud. Brian told me that, under the Nazis, the Karaites managed to save themselves from the Holocaust by arguing that they were not really Jews at all. Oppenheim's manuscript is signed by its scribe, Tobhiya, calling himself 'one of the mourners of Sion', alluding to the Jewish exile from their sacred places. He continues, 'and I wrote this manuscript from a treasured source, and it is on the order of priests and the words of our master David the prince' – presumably the Karaite Anan ben David (*c.*715–*c.*795) – 'and I added what I heard from those men of knowledge, and I translated this from Arabic into Hebrew'.

There is a tradition of memory in Judaism. They never forgot Ezra the scribe who in Babylon in the fifth century BC could reconstruct the entire Scriptures by heart. Brian Deutsch recounted to me tales told of Rav Judah (Judah bar Ezechiel), one of the Jewish scholars still in Babylon 600 years later (he died in AD 299): it is reported that he knew everything and allowed himself the leisure to pray only once every thirty days in order to have time in the meanwhile to rehearse all knowledge in his mind. Preserving knowledge comes first and is at the heart of Jewishness. Collective memory was (and is) extremely important. That dreadful sense that accumulated Jewish wisdom might be lost lies closely behind the library of Rabbi Oppenheim and other great collections of Hebrew books.

Look at what Oppenheim sought, and what he did not want. There are very few Hebrew Bibles or biblical texts, not even Psalters. There are only eleven altogether, out of almost 800 volumes. He did not need Bibles for their text: that was not in danger of disappearing and he probably knew most of it by heart anyway. There are certainly no Torah scrolls, which he would consider as belonging in synagogues, not in private possession at all. Compare that with no fewer than twenty-eight medieval Hebrew Bibles or part Bibles owned by the Jesuit priest and collector Matteo Luigi Canonici (1727–1805), now also in the Bodleian Library. The Duc de Berry had at least forty Latin or French Bibles or component texts from the Scriptures and would have regarded these as symbolic of his commitment to religion. Federico da Montefeltro's most expensive manuscript was a Bible. The early Genesis and the Lindisfarne Gospels were the most prized treasures of Sir Robert Cotton. The library of Prince Ferdinand Joseph in Nikolsburg had many Bibles and no objections to an illuminated church Missal from Salzburg. It was different with Oppenheim. Every one of his few biblical manuscripts has some additional feature beyond the scriptural text, providing records of Jewish use or scholarship. Many include Masoretic notes, especially with variant readings, or marginal commentaries or additional poems and prayers, and information about the scribes and owners and circumstances of their lives and devotion. That is why Rabbi Oppenheim wanted them.

I examined several of his Hebrew Bibles in the Bodleian with Brian Deutsch. There is a large Ashkenazi Pentateuch with the *targum* (or Jewish Aramaic translation) of Onkelos alternating verse by verse, with the five *megillot* (Song of Songs, Ruth, Lamentations, Ecclesiastes and Esther) and the *haftarot* (readings from the prophets). It is about 13 by 8 inches, and very heavy. "Such a beautiful copy!" Brian exclaimed, sighing with pleasure; "A fantastic thing! This is one in a million!" He read me the scribe's colophon: 'I am Isaac the son of Abraham; I wrote and finished this Pentateuch and targum in the year 5062 from the creation of the world' – that is, AD 1302 – 'on the twelfth day of Ab on the third day of the week – May He send messiah quickly in our days, Amen.' Then there is a note in the name of the manuscript's patron: 'A person should always sign his book in order that no one should come to claim it for his own – Meshullam the son of Baruch, I signed this for eternity.'

Another biblical lectionary, even larger, has abbreviated *targum* but includes commentaries by Rashi too. It has a poem by its scribe, Shlomoh, the son of Eleazar Hayyim, the priest for Rabbi Moshe ben Judah in 1340, and a long inscription of sale in 1486 with a note of the birth of the buyer's son the following year. Brian crossed his arms over his chest, like a Renaissance painting of Gabriel at the Annunciation, and declared, "Oh, this is gorgeous! Look!" It is a handsome book, undoubtedly, but its beauty is more in the text than in any decoration.

We asked for a third Bible too, a smaller thick and chunky Ashkenazi manuscript of about 1400. It includes not only biblical texts but also a calendar with instructions for calculating the months from the phases of the moon, and rules on the reading of the Pentateuch in synagogues on different festivals. Evidently this particular manuscript was used as an approved exemplar for making other copies. Near the end is a certificate of 1588 confirming that a scribe, Meshullam ben Eleazer, was qualified to make Torah scrolls, *tefillin* (boxes for phylacteries, little inscriptions worn on the body) and *mezuzot* (scrolls hung on doorways in houses). It also includes a detailed record of how the manuscript was then purchased in 1593 from Judah bar Levi ha-Kohen, grandson of the scribe of the additions to the volume, Nathaniel Katz, who had himself been a qualified scribe and writer of *tefillin* and *mezuzot*; it also says that this manuscript is marked up according to the guidelines of Maimonides for making Torah scrolls for public reading, with all the tiny and ancient embellishments to aid correct pronunciation, such as *tagin*, tiny marks inside or above letters. Brian found me examples in the text, and he explained the rarity of *tagin* in Bibles of codex format. The manuscript also has names of others who learned to write scrolls from this exemplar, including one calling himself 'scribe of the holy community of Prague'. A later owner, possibly Oppenheim himself, wrote in Hebrew, 'This is a Pentateuch which is very annotated and very old.' Brian read this and exclaimed, "He was as excited as I am." He gazed again dreamily at the book, as I hope Rabbi Oppenheim would have if I could have met him. "Now you understand why I love manuscripts!" Brian declared and slapped me on the back. The Bodleian staff watched in silence.

Texts among the Oppenheim manuscripts include interpretations of Jewish law, biblical commentaries sometimes with a second level of exposition on the first, known as 'super commentaries', guides to the practice of ritual and ethics, divorce, education, legal precedents, collections of *responsa* (the decisions and answers given by other rabbis on particular issues), homilies, books of medicine (often good, with access to Arabic sources not necessarily known in the West), cosmography, Hebrew grammar, poetry (primarily religious), astrology and the more esoteric extremes of Jewish mysticism and the occult – the kabbalah and its core text, the strange *Zohar*. Some texts are refreshingly unmystical. There is a late twelfth-century commentary on the Song of Songs which interprets this puzzling biblical book quite literally, as an actual description of a couple in love, something no medieval Christian commentator

RIGHT: Pentateuch in Hebrew, copied by the scribe Isaac son of Abraham in the Jewish year 5062 (AD 1302) for Meshullam son of Baruch, with decoration in micrography.

בראשית ג ריש פסו וסימנהון בראשית ברא אלהים · בראשית ממלכת · בראשית מלכות ·· תהו ובהו ב וס
והארץ היתה תהו ובהו · והנה תהו ובהו ·· וחשך ב וסימנהון וחשך על פני תהום · וחשך איזה מקומו ·

בראשית

בְּרֵאשִׁית

ברא אלהים את ה
השמים ואת הארץ
בקדמין ברא יי׳ ית
שמיא וית ארעא:
והארץ היתה תהו
ובהו וחשך על פני
תהום ורוח אלהים
מרחפת על פני המ
ים: וארעא הות
צדיא וריקניא וח
חשוכא פריס על
אפי תהומא ורוח
מן קדם יי׳ מנשב
מנשבא על אפי
מיא: ויאמר אלהים
יהי אור ויהי אור:
ואמר יי׳ יהא נהור

והוה נהורא: וירא
אלהים את האור
כי טוב ויבדל אלה
אלהים בין האור
ובין החשך: וחזא
יי׳ ית נהורא ארי
טב ואפריש יי׳ בין
נהורא ובין חשוכא:
ויקרא אלהים לא
לאור יום ולחשך
קרא לילה ויהי ע
ערב ויהי בקר יום
אחד: וקרא יי׳ לנ
לנהורא יממא ולח
ולחשוכא קרא ל
ליליא והוה רמש
והוה צפר יומא

חדא: ויאמר אלהים
יהי רקיע בתוך המ
המים ויהי מבדיל
בין מים למים: ואמר
יי׳ יהא רקיעא במ
במציעות מיא ויה
ויהא מפריש בין מ
מיא למיא: ויעש
אלהים את הרקיע
ויבדל בין המים א
אשר מתחת לרקיע
ובין המים אשר מ
מעל לרקיע ויהי כן:
ועבד יי׳ ית רקיעא
ואפריש בין מיא
דמלרע לרקיעא
ובין מיא דמעל לר

והארץ ה ריש פסוקים וסימניהון והארץ היתה תהו ובהו וחשך · והארץ אשר אתם עברים שמה ·
והארץ תעזב מהם ותרץ את שבתתיה · והארץ הגשמה · והארץ חנפה תחת יושביה · והארץ אשר
אתם עברים שמה · והארץ הגבלי וכל הלבנון · והארץ אשר אתם מגשאים ·· פני תהום ב וסימני

ever dared to imagine. Probably everything was at least partly religious or had application in the practice of Judaism. Among the manuscripts are probably thousands of named authors and signatures of many hundreds of scribes, all part of a shared Jewish experience forever on the move across Europe, the Near East and northern Africa, now meeting together in the custody of Rabbi Oppenheim.

There are a number of manuscripts associated with women, including texts in Yiddish: like the use of vernacular languages in medieval Christian manuscripts, this often indicates use by female readers, who were literate but not necessarily in classical languages. Generally, women had a higher and more central status in Judaism than in Christianity or Islam. Oppenheim owned a very curious manuscript made in 1544 for one Yutlin, daughter of Naphtali Levi and wife of Josvil. It is a translation of the Pentateuch into German and a paraphrase of Esther into rhyming Judaeo-German verse, but it is written in the Hebrew alphabet. Each verse opens with a word in the original Hebrew (recognizable because it uses markings for vowels, whereas Judaeo-German does not). This presupposes that the reader – Yutlin or whoever read it to her – knew

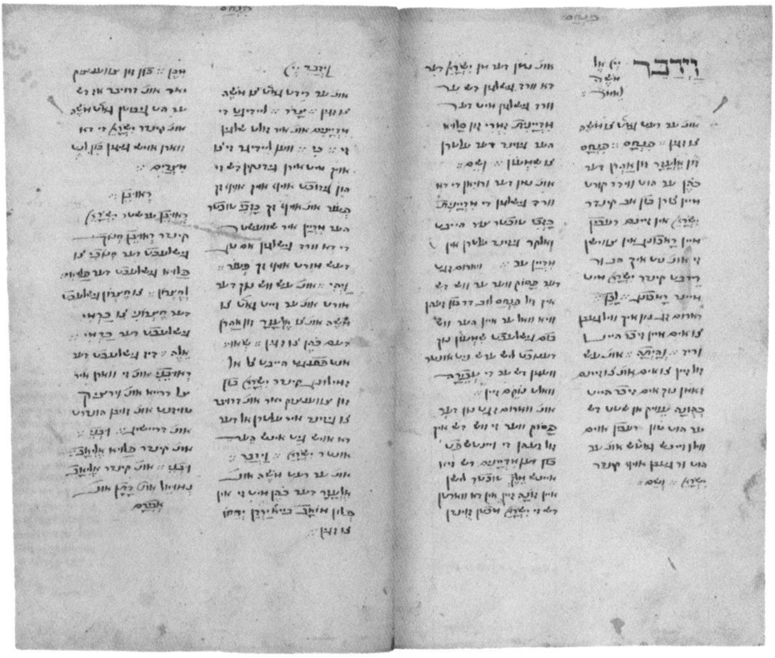

Translation of the Pentateuch and Esther into Judaeo-German, made for Yutlin, daughter of Naphtali Levi and wife of Josvil, 1544.

the opening of each sentence in the Hebrew, rather like the headings still printed in Latin in the Anglican *Book of Common Prayer*, because the old opening words from before the Reformation had become familiar as titles, such as the *Venite* or the *Jubilate*. It is unexpected that in the lifetime of Martin Luther (d. 1546), someone else, quite unheralded by history, was simultaneously translating the Bible from Hebrew into German. This is not Luther's version, which I checked against a printed copy as Brian Deutsch declaimed the words of the manuscript aloud. The colophon says that it was finished by Joseph ben Jakob, of Wetzlar (in Hesse, north of Frankfurt). This may mean he was the translator, since it also names the scribe, Isaac "der Schreiber".

The high number of signed and precisely dated Hebrew manuscripts is always striking to those of us more accustomed to books of the Latin Middle Ages. This is partly because of different circumstances of production. Most Hebrew books were not made in commercial or institutional workshops, but more slowly and with greater accolade at home, often for the personal use of the copyists or their families and friends. Medieval Judaism had no monastic or collegiate scriptoria; there was not even an equivalent of a Church as a corporate body, with a professional hierarchy and a need for books. Hebrew manuscripts often remained with their scribes and might be passed by descent through Jewish families for generations. There is an example of this in a copy of Rashi's commentary on the Pentateuch in the Oppenheim library. The scribe Isaac ben Judah finished writing it for his own use in 1408, adding a wish, 'may God give me the merit that my children may be able to inherit it'. They were, and the manuscript was duly inscribed in turn by his son and then by his grandson. There is a touching note in Oppenheim's copy of a seventeenth-century commentary on the Pentateuch by Shalom ben Leb Shalom, who says that he had composed this manuscript twenty-four years after his marriage, since, having had no children in all that time, he might at least leave a book as his posterity instead of descendants; and then, a year later, his wife, Breindel, daughter of a rabbi in Cracow, had a son after all, like Sarah and Abraham, late in life. He now had both a manuscript and a descendant to inherit it (although Breindel herself died). Insights into sudden moments of human life and aspiration are a part of the fascination of Hebrew manuscripts.

My experience of Hebrew libraries is that the curators are usually astonished and delighted when a gentile shows interest. I could imagine first meeting Rabbi Oppenheim in the Dietrichstein castle, where I might have contrived to be a guest. We would probably speak German, although he was doubtless fluent in many European languages. Since the Bible is our primary text in common, I would ask if we might begin by looking together at the Latin biblical manuscripts in the castle library. In his time, these included two characteristic small thirteenth-century French Bibles, with up to 120 illuminated initials each, and a larger Bolognese Bible of around 1300 with 145 illuminated and illustrated initials bursting into coloured borders filled with human figures in roundels with tumbling birds and monsters in the foliage. Its Genesis initial depicts God himself seven times in scenes of the Creation. In the Christian tradition, which goes back at least as far as the illustrated Cotton Genesis of the fifth to sixth centuries, illumination was seen as honouring the sacred text. Oppenheim would be courteous but appalled. It would be extremely rare to illustrate a Hebrew Bible. It is inconceivable that a Torah scroll could ever be decorated, and to depict God in art at all is unimaginable. Hebrew script does not even allow for initials, since all letters are usually written in the same size. In medieval biblical manuscripts in codex format, there might sometimes be pages of Hebrew text broken into geometrical shapes to achieve patterns of elegance but great restraint. Occasionally the rule on illustration might be circumvented by constructing simple marginal drawings formed entirely from lines of tiny micrographic script, which were technically writing, not illustration. Sometimes, plain text is laid out in decorative shapes, as in an early thirteenth-century manuscript of Rashi. Rabbi Oppenheim would shake his head in despair at the fifteenth-century Dietrichstein biblical Lectionary in German, which has 103 column-width miniatures, in which scriptural scenes are recast by the artist into jaunty domestic settings of fifteenth-century Germany. We would walk down the hill in Nikolsburg back to his house in Husova Street or Zámecká, and he would be convinced that Christian taste was profane and frivolous.

If I had found a few manuscripts in Oppenheim's library with illustrations, he might explain that these are mostly scientific and medical treatises, where pictures were necessary to understanding the text. I might have picked out his little Hebrew prayerbook, or *Siddur*, of Ashkenazi use, dated 1471, bound in bright green leather. It is calligraphically written, with headings in red and blue. It has numerous panels with titles in gold usually in gothic architectural surrounds, often including pictures of Jewish people singing and playing musical instruments, as well as dragons,

Siddur, prayerbook in Hebrew, with illustrations of Jewish people with manuscripts, Ashkenazi, 1471.

lions, rabbits, birds and wildmen, all utterly charming. It is rightly now one of the treasures of the Bodleian. Oppenheim was perhaps indifferent to its decoration. Adolf Neubauer (1831–1907), Reader in Rabbinic Literature at Oxford and author of the standard catalogue of Hebrew manuscripts in the Bodleian Library (1886), certainly disapproved of its ornament. He dismisses this lovely book in a couple of lines as having "common illuminations". To him, at least, it was a vulgar aberration.

Because I do not know, I would constantly have been asking Oppenheim the dates of manuscripts. Many collectors of Hebrew books, very probably including him, hardly cared how old they were. The identity and status of the author were important, but whether a particular manuscript copy was itself twelfth- or sixteenth-century was of negligible interest to many Jewish scholars, and this is true even now. Neubauer's catalogue, still the principal guide to all Hebrew manuscripts in the Bodleian, makes no attributions of age whatsoever unless the volumes are actually dated by their scribes, information included only because it was part of the text. He misread the date in the *Siddur* by two centuries, oblivious and indifferent to stylistic inconsistency.

If Prince Ferdinand Joseph had joined us on our visit to see his neighbour's library in lower Nikolsburg, he might have been baffled not only by the plainness of many of the manuscripts but also the poor condition.

A wealthy gentile bibliophile, such as David Oppenheim's almost exact contemporary in England Robert Harley, earl of Oxford (1661–1724), would care immensely about a manuscript's freshness and the quality and sparkle of the artwork. Hebrew books are generally judged differently. Many times at Sotheby's, I would feel embarrassed to bring out some worn and damaged Hebrew manuscript to show to a Jewish collector, who would then sigh ecstatically, because thumbing and wear seemed to him to be almost a virtue, or at least not a problem. Damage was evidence of past study, shared by others in a long tradition of the manuscript's usefulness. A flawless and untouched Hebrew manuscript, admired by mainstream collectors in my own world, would be deemed unloved, unused and somehow less desirable. It is difficult to deny the logic of this. There is a quotation from Sir Joshua Reynolds written over the main entrance of the Victoria and Albert Museum in London, "The excellence of every art must consist in the complete accomplishment of its purpose." The purpose of a Hebrew manuscript was to be used.

This is essential to understanding Rabbi Oppenheim's engagement with manuscripts, often gathered from great distances. There is a real sense of what is called the '*kehillah kedoshah*' in Hebrew, the 'holy community' which crosses the centuries, sharing a duty to know and to remain faithful to one another and to all accumulated Jewish tradition and learning. In an unachievable ideal, the person who could read all the Hebrew texts there had ever been would end up like semi-mythical Rav Judah in ancient Babylon, who knew everything there was to know. The fact that Jewish manuscripts were by the late seventeenth century already increasingly rare and desperately vulnerable added to Oppenheim's race against time to locate and master them before the end of the world. More than merely possessing them, he wanted to read and absorb their contents.

I see this characteristic in Brian Deutsch too. It is hard to restrain him when he picks up a manuscript: he begins rapidly reading out passages, one after another, delighting in direct encounter with a writer of long ago. It is doubtful whether Prince Ferdinand Joseph von Dietrichstein ever expected to read any of the early illuminated manuscripts in his castle library, or even whether he could necessarily decipher their abbreviated medieval scripts. Formal square Hebrew handwriting, however, is more or less unaltered since well before the Middle Ages. Even today an educated Hebrew speaker can often read a thousand-year-old manuscript or a Dead Sea Scroll twice as old with a fluency envied by those of us who can struggle with the ever-evolving Latin hands of the Middle Ages.

It is often said that one of the most unifying aspects of Judaism was (and remains) the conscious preservation of the Hebrew language after the exile of the Jews from Jerusalem in the first century. The ability to read Hebrew books gave a sense of membership, generally experienced only by fellow Jews. That retained exclusivity of Jews in their access to Hebrew books, however, also carried its risks for the manuscripts themselves. When these were lost, impounded or stolen, they were of no obvious intelligibility to gentiles at all, and the parchment pages were often cut up to be recycled in strengthening bookbindings or for other purposes; Hebrew fragments are generally as common now in Christian contexts as complete Hebrew manuscripts are rare.

Prince Ferdinand Joseph died in 1698 and was succeeded in the castle by his son (one of his twenty children) Prince Leopold Ignaz Joseph von Dietrichstein (1660–1708). In 1700 the new prince supported Oppenheim in a local dispute over Jewish law courts. In 1701, Oppenheim was offered the post of rabbi of the Ashkenazi community of Jerusalem, together with the title *Nasi Eretz Yisrael*, or 'Prince of the land of Israel', mainly in gratitude for his financial support there. He eventually refused the position but retained the title, which caused some ill-feeling: it was even challenged in a Bohemian law court in 1717–18 on the grounds that he was falsely pretending to royalty. Then, in 1702, Oppenheim was proposed as chief rabbi of Prague, about 130 miles north-west of Nikolsburg. This was the largest Jewish community in central Europe. This time he accepted. He finally left Nikolsburg after a happy and productive period for his library, and in 1703 he and his family settled in Prague. Later, he was also confirmed as sole national rabbi of all Bohemia.

We began in the Jewish cemetery in Prague. Let us now approach the former Jewish ghetto from the other direction. From the Old Town Square of Prague with its admired astronomical clock, follow the Pařížká avenue running north-west off the square. This is now a broad and expensive shopping street for fashion and international luxury goods. Although everything is different, these were both trades in which eighteenth-century

OVERLEAF: Biblical Lectionary for use in a synagogue, with the Targum Onkelos and commentaries by Rashi, copied by the scribe Shlomoh in 1340.

בימי אחשורוש הוא אחשורוש המלך מהדו ועד
כוש שבע ועשרים ומאה מדינה׃ בימים ההם כשבת
המלך אחשורוש על כסא מלכותו אשר בשושן הבי
הבירה׃ בשנת שלוש למלכו עשה משתה לכל שריו
ועבדיו חיל פרס ומדי הפרתמים ושרי המדינות לפניו׃

בהראתו את עשר כבוד
מלכותו ואת יקר תפארת
גדולתו ימים רבים שמני
שמונים ומאת יום׃ ובמלו
ובמלאת הימים האלה
עשה המלך לכל העם ה
הנמצאים בשושן הביר
הבירה למגדול ועד קטן
משתה שבעת ימים בחצ
בחצר גנת ביתן המלך׃

חור כרפס ותכלת אחוז ב
בחבלי בוץ וארגמן על
גלילי כסף ועמודי שש
מטות זהב וכסף על רצפת
בהט ושש ודר וסחרת׃
והשקות בכלי זהב וכלים
מכלים שונים ויין מלכות
רב כיד המלך׃ והשתיה
כדת אין אנס כי כן יסד ה
המלך על כל רב ביתו לע

[illegible]

שנה במתו לא כהתה עינו ולא נס לחה
ויבכו בני ישראל את משה בעׄ
בערבות מואב שלשים יום
ויתמו ימי בכי אבל משה
ויהושע בן נון מלא רוח
חכמה כי סמך משה
את ידיו עליו וישׄ
וישמעו אליו בנׄ
בני ישראל ויׄ
ויעשו כאׄ
כאשר
צוה
יהוה
את
משה
ולא קם
נביא עוד
בישראל כמׄ
כמשה אשר
ידעו יהוה פנים אל
פנים לכל האתת והמׄ
והמופתים אשר שלחו
יהוה לעשות בארץ מצרׄ
מצרים לפרעה ולכל עבדיו
ולכל ארצו ולכל היד החזקה
ולכל המורא הגדול אשר עשה

בר מאה ועסרין שנין משה כד מית לא כהאה עינוהי ולא
שנא זיו יקרא דאפוהי
ובכו בני ישראל ית משה
במישריא דמואב תלתין
יומין ושליםו יומי
בכיתא אבלא דמשה
ויהושע
בר נון אׄ
אתמלי רוח חׄ
חכמתא ארי סמך
משה ית ידוהי עׄ
עלוהי וקבילו מׄ
מיניה בני ישראל
ועבדו כמא
דפקיד יׄ
ית משה
ולא קם
נביא עׄ
עוד
בישראל
כמשה דׄ
דאתגלי לׄ
ליה יׄ אפין
כאפין
ולכל אתיא ומׄ
ומופתיא דשלחׄ
יׄ למעבד באׄ
בארעא דמצרים
לפרעה ולכל עבדוהי
ולכל ארעיה
ולכל ידא תקיפא ולמׄ
חזוו חיזונא רבא
דעבד משה לקדם
כל ישראל
חזק ותקת

ולא כהתה עינו אף משמת ולא נס לחה
לחלוחית שבו לא שלט בו רקבון
ולא נהפך תואר פניו בני ישר
הזכרים אבל כשמת אהרן שהיה
שהיה רודף שלום ונותן
שלום בין איש לאשתו
בין איש לרעהו נאמר
בו כל בית ישראל זכרים
זכרים ונקבות אשר
פנים אל פנים שהיה
לבו גס ומדבר
עמו כל שעה שהיה
שהיה רוצה כענ
כענין שנאמר
עתה אעלה אל
עמדו ואשׄ
ואשמעה
מה יצוה
לכם
ולכל היד
החזקה
שקבל
משה
הלוחות
בידיו
ולכל
המורא
הגדול
נסים
וגבורות
שבמדבר
הגדול והנורא
והנורא אשר
עשה משה
לעיני ישראל
לבו לשבר הלוחות
הלוחות לעיניהם
שנאמר ואשברם
לעיניכם והסכימה
דעת הקב"ה לדעתו
שנאמר אשר שברת
יישר כחך ששברת
חזק ונתחזק

חסלת ברכה

[illegible]

Jews had also excelled. About halfway along, turn left, steeply down ten stone steps into the narrow medieval lane of Červená. Almost immediately on the right is the Staronová Synagoga, which translates into the clumsy-sounding English name of 'Old-New Synagogue'. Many Jews know it by its Yiddish name of *Altneuschul*. It was built in the thirteenth century, when it was 'new', and in time it additionally became old as well. It is an extraordinary survival from the Middle Ages and it would have been known intimately to Rabbi Oppenheim during his period here. It is one of the earliest in Europe, after the destruction during Kristallnacht riots of 1938 of the twelfth-century synagogue in Worms (which he would have attended too).

The pale-yellow building is high and long with a steeply pitched gabled roof, a bit like the Duc de Berry's lost Sainte-Chapelle in Bourges, with tall deeply inset lancet windows at the western end. You enter by a low side door off the street, under a star of David, and you descend to a tiled vestibule and into the ancient double nave, with finely carved soaring gothic vaulting, resembling many medieval churches or castle halls. It is still a functioning synagogue with dark wooden prayer desks around the perimeter and the rabbi's seat and *almemor* all in place, where David Oppenheim would have read the Torah, lit as always by brass chandeliers hanging down from the high ceiling.

On the other side of the little lane is the old Jewish Town Hall, partly sixteenth century and so already there too when Rabbi Oppenheim arrived from Nikolsburg in 1703, but now refaced later that century, including the addition of its famous black and gilt Hebrew clock of 1764, which appears to run 'backwards', like Hebrew writing. Straight in front is the narrow cobbled street which leads towards the exit from the cemetery, lined with tiny shops and kiosks, some selling trinkets and jewellery and also the 'Golem Bakery', commemorating the mythical artificial man supposedly created and brought to life here by Judah Loew ben Bezalel (d. 1609), notable chief rabbi in Prague a century before Oppenheim. Most of these shops seem to be closed on Saturdays and presumably the proprietors are still Jewish.

It would have been in the Town Hall that David Oppenheim carried out many of his duties as chief rabbi. These included the interpretation and application of Jewish law throughout the region. We can gain a flavour of these from the many recorded *responsa*, or official answers, given by Oppenheim to particular problems brought to him. For example, a request was addressed to him by Meir Katzenellenbogen, that same rabbi of Stampfen who had been acting as agent in the purchase of manuscripts. His congregation had elected a man as *hazzan*, the cantor who would lead the synagogue in music, and as *shohet*, a ritual slaughterer. For the previous twelve years the appointee had held office as *shohet* in Kolín, near Prague. One day, after drinking too much at a wedding, he had boasted that he had never actually qualified as a *shohet* at all or bothered to learn the laws of unclean food. Rabbi Katzenellenbogen suspended him and now sought Oppenheim's consent to forbid the man to practise as a *shohet* or even as a *hazzan* ever again.

Some questions might require careful application of precedent. A strange situation occurred in 1709. A woman had been cutting up a chicken, watched attentively by her cat, which stood beside the table waiting as giblets were thrown down. No heart was found in the chicken and, as far as the woman could recall, she had not given it to the cat. Was it therefore possible that the chicken had never had a heart at all and so was unclean and unkosher? Anyone with experience of the deviousness of cats might guess what had happened, but the problem had escalated into a bitter controversy among local rabbis, not all of it to the credit of the testimony of women (or cats). One rabbi consulted an undated

The thirteenth-century *Altneuschul* or 'Old-New Synagogue' in Prague, with the Jewish Town Hall to the right, a photograph of *c.*1920.

book said to have belonged to Judah Loew ben Bezalel, the 'golem' rabbi, which asserted quite reasonably that life without a heart was impossible. David Oppenheim, however, found a provably older source in a manuscript by Rabbi Israel of Marburg copied in 1530, confirming the possibility that a chicken might indeed have no heart. It was the priority of rabbinical opinion that decided the case, not common sense, one reason why manuscripts mattered.

Oppenheim employed scribes. Two and a half centuries after Vespasiano had confronted possible extinction of the scribal craft, many manuscripts were still being written in Hebrew in the eighteenth century; Torah scrolls still are. Books for special occasions, such as Megillot and Haggadot for the festivals of Purim and Pesach (Passover), were very often handmade. Oppenheim's own daughter Sara, wife of Hayyim Yonah Teomin Fränkel, copied a Megillah. Several scribes worked for Oppenheim. Curiously, as an Ashkenazi, he seems not to have been comfortable with reading the Sephardi rabbinic cursive scripts of southern Europe. When he acquired such items, he had them copied out all over again into north European hands instead. It is possible that he was thinking more of future users than himself. An example among many is his manuscript of the Mishnah commentary by Asher ben Jehiel (d. 1327), made in Safed in Palestine by two Sephardi scribes in 1506; Oppenheim had it rewritten out by Samuel ben Shlomo in 1701 in a more familiar German cursive hand, no small task, for the new transcript fills 271 leaves. An unnamed copyist who transcribed texts for Oppenheim recorded in one of them in 1716, 'I was his scribe and faithful member of his household and I copied . . . books in Nikolsburg and in Prague and in Vienna and in Hanover,' evidently travelling with the rabbi on his journeys. A legible modern transcript was more precious to Oppenheim than an unusable old one. For him, reading and understanding were once again everything.

Oppenheim was accustomed to consulting the library in his daily work. In one response written when rabbi in Moravia, he had been in Austria when a question of law had arrived. He wrote back to Nikolsburg: 'I am here in Vienna, far from my home and library, and I have no *responsa* or other books to refer to in answering your question – I, who am a lover of books and like to examine every source as far as my small ability will allow, cannot do it now.'

The absence of his library was now about to become permanent. For Jews, Prague could be very different from the relatively peaceful life in

Nikolsburg, under the castle walls of the cultured Dietrichstein princes. Anti-Semitism was never far from the surface in the big capital. There were several tense situations in Prague in the 1690s involving deaths of Jews at the hands of Christians. The Jesuits, in particular, undertook campaigns to convert the Jews to Christianity, and they vigorously promoted the right to censor Hebrew books and to destroy them if they deemed it necessary (as indeed happened in 1714). The Jesuit college at the Clementinum was only a moment's walk from the ghetto in Prague. The size and increasing reputation of the Oppenheim collection placed it at risk in a volatile society. The censor noted that many volumes came from Muslim countries of the Near East, enemies of the Holy Roman Empire, and might therefore contain sedition. Rabbi Oppenheim must now have struggled with perhaps the hardest decision of his life. Instead of installing the library in Prague on his arrival in 1703, he resolved to send the entire collection to safety in Hanover, under the supervision of his father-in-law, the court Jew Leffman Behrens. Oppenheim's son and presumed heir, Joseph, became the principal curator and supervised access by readers. Oppenheim never ceased adding to the library, and he could still consult its resources for his duties in Prague, but the library was no longer in his daily custody. Loss and separation are recurrent themes in Jewish history, and it cannot have been easy.

Oppenheim's wife, Gnendel, died in 1712, at the relatively early age of fifty-four. He presented a curtain for the holy ark to the 'Old-New' Synagogue in her memory. Quite soon afterwards he married Shifra, daughter of Rabbi Benjamin Wolf Spira and widow of Isaac Bondy, both of Prague.

By now the collection consisted of approximately 780 manuscripts and some 6000 printed books. Shifra was perhaps glad not to have them in the house, but she may have regretted her husband's constant absences with her predecessor's family in Hanover, 250 miles away, unceasingly tending and arranging the library. At this time or earlier, the volumes were numbered on their spines, each with a letter in Hebrew and an Arabic number. Many of the manuscripts (but not all) had been fitted with engraved title-pages inserted at the front, with elaborate borders and apertures for titles to be added by hand. The designs resemble architectural gateways, with Moses and Aaron standing at the sides and King David singing the psalms from his harp at the top, flanked by angels holding palm leaves. David Oppenheim, 'Prince of the land of Israel', seems to have consciously adopted his royal biblical namesake, the scholar

דוד
מחזור וויטרי
תתקס״ח

king of Israel, as a model or spiritual patron. There is a manuscript of Nathan Spiro's notes on the *Tur Orah Hayyim* of Jacob ben Asher, written for Oppenheim by the scribe Samuel ben Moses in 1714. Its title-page includes drawings of the biblical patriarchs Jacob and Abraham on either side of David, but David is depicted here not as the king (as captioned) but as Rabbi Oppenheim himself, seated at a table with two manuscripts and an inkpot. His identification with the David of the Bible is echoed in one of the early catalogues of his library, where it was called the *Collectio Davidis*. Centuries later, Rabbi David Solomon Sassoon (1880–1942) did almost exactly the same, naming the catalogue of his own monumental collection of manuscripts *Ohel Dawid* (1932). *Ohel* is a tabernacle or monument, but it can also mean a tomb, like the sacred site of King David's grave on Mount Zion. *Collectio* in Latin can also represent a memory. Oppenheim's title-page added to his manuscripts resembles an eighteenth-century memorial tablet, like the finest in the Jewish cemetery, and he doubtless saw his library as an imperishable monument too. His divine mission in gathering together Hebrew manuscripts and books for all time had perhaps been as clear to him from the beginning as King David's destiny in building Jerusalem. Probably, like many owners of Hebrew manuscripts, he envisaged them as a legacy to his descendants for ever.

Rabbi David ben Abraham Oppenheim died at the age of seventy-two on 12 September 1736, and he was buried, as we know, beneath the symbol of King David in the cemetery in Prague. Contrary to plan, his son Joseph Oppenheim, the library's curator and inheritor, died only three years later in 1739.

From that moment, the whole edifice began to fall slowly apart. Two grandsons of Leffman Behrens lost their family's fortune and position as court Jews and had been obliged to leave Hanover in 1726. The collection passed in 1739 to Joseph's daughter Gnendel (named after her grandmother) and she and her husband transferred it for a time to Hildesheim. An inventory was compiled around 1740, listing locations of the books within the library. From these we learn that there were 106 shelves altogether, of which forty were filled with manuscripts. As Gnendel Oppenheim's debts

LEFT: A characteristic engraved title-page inserted by Oppenheim into many of his manuscripts, showing King David with Aaron and Moses around a handwritten description of the book.

mounted, the huge white elephant of her grandfather's books began to assume the character of a possible source of desperately needed income. As commonly happens, family legend exaggerated the sums supposedly spent on the collection and its likely value now. Gnendel made an unsuccessful attempt to sell some items in 1764. The whole library was eventually pawned by her to a cousin, who then made unseemly quick plans in 1782 for its disposal to the highest offer. A sale catalogue was published in Hamburg with titles in both German and Latin as well as Hebrew, so that it might appear also accessible to non-Jewish buyers. The listing of manuscripts occupied twenty-four pages. A valuation for the whole collection was given in 1784 at between 50,000 and 60,000 thalers. It is never easy to equate historical prices to modern money, but a thaler was valued at (and made of) three quarters of an ounce of silver: 50,000 thalers were therefore worth 4,166 lb of silver, or nearly 2 tons in weight.

In my own working life, there were not dissimilar visions of possible sales *en bloc* of the great Hebrew libraries of David Solomon Sassoon, already mentioned, Salman Schocken (1877–1959), and Valmadonna, the vast collection formed in London by Jack Lunzer (1924–2016). I had some part in all three, and in every case the initial financial aspiration was unmatched by reality. It was the same with the Oppenheim library. There were rumoured to have been inquiries from Catherine the Great. The duke of Württemberg was persuaded to spend one Saturday in 1786 inspecting the library accompanied by an advisor from the university of Tübingen, but his eventual offer was less than half of what the owners would accept. Possibly it was a mistake to hope for a conventional non-Jewish book collector, who might have succumbed in the late eighteenth century to illuminated Bibles and elegant Hebrew liturgy, which had not at all been the goal of Rabbi Oppenheim. The library's more esoteric shelves of Jewish mysticism and comprehensive Talmudic law in rabbinic cursive scripts, so distinctive of Oppenheim and dear to his heart, now appeared too alien for a wider market. There was also some uncertainty over actual title to the collection, disputed in an unhurried way between the heirs of Gnendel Oppenheim and those of her cousin, who had assumed possession of the library after lending her money secured against it. Nothing much happened; decades passed; descendants multiplied and died; hopes were raised and dissipated. Eventually, a full auction catalogue was prepared in 1826, in Latin and Hebrew, and a date was set for a sale in Hamburg on 11 June 1827, almost ninety years after the

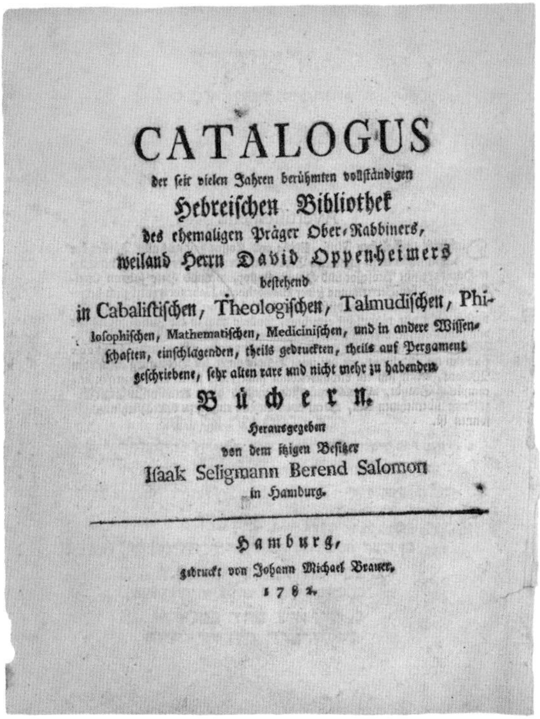
CATALOGUS
der seit vielen Jahren berühmten vollständigen
Hebreischen Bibliothek
des ehemaligen Präger Ober-Rabbiners,
weiland Herrn David Oppenheimers
bestehend
in Cabalistischen, Theologischen, Talmudischen, Philosophischen, Mathematischen, Medicinischen, und in andere Wissenschaften, einschlagenden, theils gedruckten, theils auf Pergament geschriebene, sehr alten rare und nicht mehr zu habenden
Büchern.
Herausgegeben
von dem itzigen Besitzer
Isaak Seligmann Berend Salomon
in Hamburg.

Hamburg,
gedruckt von Johann Michael Brauer,
1782.

Catalogue for the unsuccessful sale of the Oppenheim library, Hamburg, 1782.

rabbi's death. The title-page drew unsubtle attention to the great amount of money Oppenheim had spent on the collection.

There is a file of letters in the Bodleian Library tracing the progress of subsequent negotiations. Rumours of the imminent sale had come to the attention of Alexander Nicoll (1793–1828), Regius Professor of Hebrew in Oxford, who had written for information to J. J. C. Pappe, bookseller in Hamburg. Pappe's reply of 6 January 1827 opens the correspondence. He reported that someone in England was said to have offered £1850 for the collection, which had been rejected (possibly not true), and that the owners hoped for at least £2200, which would include settlement of any ongoing claims over title. Nicoll bravely proposed £2000 on behalf of Oxford University. This was a considerable sum in the 1820s but not a fortune. Pappe estimated it to be more than the collection would make at auction and he promised to do all he could. This is the kind of negotiation very familiar throughout the history of the art market. ("It is naught, it is naught, saith the buyer, but when he has gone his way, then he boasteth," Proverbs 20:14.) The proprietors of the Oppenheim library delayed and prevaricated. On 25 May, three weeks before the planned auction, they were still hoping for a higher offer, and Pappe asked Nicoll whether he might "add a few pounds" if that would tip the balance. It evidently did, and the public sale was cancelled. Nicoll went out to Hamburg himself to inspect the books and to ratify the deal on behalf of the University. He nearly despaired of the continuing complications. He was a Scotsman, from a background where commercial deals were expected to be fair but simple. The Bodleian's offer of £2080 was finally accepted by the family a whole year later on 2 May 1828. The sum was about 9000 *thalers*, around one seventh of that first optimistic valuation of 1784. Nicoll died of bronchitis in September and he never saw the transfer of the collection, which was packed into thirty-four crates and dispatched to England, at an additional cost for shipping of £42, on 22 May 1829.

Although no Jewish buyer had emerged in half a century of the Oppenheim collection being on the market, there was still a certain shock in some circles in seeing it pass into secular possession. The German Talmudic scholar Fürchtegott Lebrecht (1800–1876) declared ungraciously in 1844 that it would have been better for the Oppenheim library to have been carried off by Napoleon than to have been sold to Oxford. In 1930, Rabbi Charles Duschinsky (1878–1944) wrote quite seriously of his resentment at paying a train fare from London and the lack of a Jewish restaurant near the Bodleian when he arrived. However, Oxford University has many Jewish students and a faculty of Hebrew studies. The Regius Professorship of Hebrew was established as long ago as 1546. The Bodleian also owns the formidable Hebrew manuscript collections of Archbishop Laud (1573–1645), John Selden (1584–1654), Bishop Robert Huntington (1637–1701), Benjamin Kennicott (1718–83), Canonici, already mentioned, Isaac Samuel Reggio (1784–1855), Heimann Joseph Michael (1792–1846, with 860 manuscripts, no less) and many others. It is hard to think of a better, safer or more publicly friendly and accessible international library, and probably nowhere else on earth is closer to the scholarly and universal source of Judaic knowledge which would have been the ideal of Rabbi Oppenheim in Worms, Nikolsburg and Prague.

We will end with a fable. One would usually consult the former Oppenheim manuscripts in what is now called the Charles Wendell David Reading Room on the top floor of the Weston Library of the Bodleian.

It runs parallel to Broad Street, and one can see across the road to the Sheldonian Theatre and the Clarendon Building through the curtains of its lancet windows on the southern side. There are two rows of long tables and a purple carpet. It is the principal room for studying rare oriental books, which are taken to include items in Hebrew, as well as African and Commonwealth archives. Readers here are as diversely and obviously multi-ethnic as the boulevardiers on the bridge in Prague. I have asked to see MS Opp. 154, which I bring back to the table from the issue desk in a cardboard box, leaving my library card as security, and prop it up on the foam wedges provided. It is a collection of fables in Hebrew, called *Mashal ha-Qadmoni*, 'Fables from the Distant Past', composed by Isaac ben Solomon ibn Sahula (*c.*1244–*c.*1281 or later). It is a substantial book, about 10¾ by 6½ inches, in a deeply stamped sixteenth-century binding of leather over wooden boards, with marbled endleaves and blue speckled edges. It cannot have changed at all in appearance since it was acquired by David Oppenheim. It is written in black and red Hebrew script on quite thick and stiff parchment. The colophon records that it was copied by the scribe Samuel in the year 5210, which equates to AD 1450. The manuscript is well-known and admired now for its charming coloured drawings, which were dismissed by Neubauer as 'bad illuminations' and may have been of little interest to Oppenheim himself. The text opens with an extensive illustrated prologue, in which the author debates with a cynic over the value of telling fables. The first animal story has a picture of a fox accompanying a lion, which raises its paw towards a stag seated on the grass in front of him.

Even here there is an interesting point of crossing cultures between medieval Jews and the Christian world. Look at the stag. Notice its elaborate antlers and how its head is turned right back in profile over the body. See how its front legs are crossed and its back legs and tail are tucked in under the rump. This design is copied from an engraving by the Upper Rhenish artist known as the Master of the Playing Cards. He was working around 1435–40, probably in Alsace, and is named from what appear to be proof sheets (mostly now in the Kupferstich-Kabinett in Dresden) for a set of pictorial playing cards. One of the suits is stags, and the composition used in the *Mashal ha-Qadmoni* is taken from the lower animal in the 'three of stags' in the pack of cards, which cannot be coincidence. This not only helps localize the manuscript to somewhere like Strassburg, where there was a large Jewish population, but

ויאכל וישב לבו · ויתן לו תרופה ומעינים ; ויאמר הצבי לרוץ לפניהם יתחדש · ויצא
ושב כמראה הבזק ; וישתעשע האריה ויתן מחמד · אז יצא שחוק פיו ולשונו :
וזהו ענין האריה והשועל והצבי ריעיו התאומים · אהובים למלך ונאמנים · וכה
משפטם כל הימים ::

צורת האריה והצבי · לפניו השועל ומשרתו

ויהי בימים הרבים ההם ויאנחו הבהמות והחיות · ותעל שועתם אל
עליות ; ורוח לבשה את אריהם · וירעש בכל ארץ מגוריהם ; ויקבצו כל איש
אשר מעמי האריה שבע · כל הולך על גחון וכל הולך על ארבע ; ויבכו איש את
רעהו · ויאמרו רעו ; הבו לכם עצה · על דבר הרע המוצא ; הלא האריה בזדונו
החריבנו · אכלנו המנו · וכל רעך השיגנו והתמנו ; ושם נקרא שור לאחד
חכם וסבר · גם פרא לשור חבר ; ויספרו עליהם
בטוח חכמתם · ויקבלו עליהם לעשות כפי עצתם ; ויען השור ויעש והכין כלי
מלחמה · בכח ועצמה ; כולם מזוינים מנות טרפו · להיות מגן ביום חרון א
אפו ; ולסובב אותו כל בעלי קרנים בתריה · והרבות לו תאניה ואניה · מכות
חבורה ומכה טריה · להלחם בו בכל חזקה ובזרוע נטויה ; ולגור בו כל רב
ומעיר להכרו · ולהסיר מעלו כל פארו :

also shows that its artist was familiar with contemporary and secular art outside his ghetto.

In the stories here, the animals belong to a Jewish world. The fox, the lion and the stag would have been recognizable as common surnames, Fuchs, Lowe and Hirsch. The lion is the king of a distant land. His two counsellors are the wily fox and the gentle stag. The king uses them both to help him hunt for food. The fox would locate the grazing grounds of other animals and then the swift stag would outrun them and drive the prey back towards the king, who could kill them. As the years pass, the animals get together to decide what to do about this. There is a picture of two oxen in discussion. They resolve to migrate to another country. Under the leadership of the wild ass, they set off through the wilderness where the Israelites had once spent forty years. There is an illustration of the ass in the front, leading two goats, an ox and a bear. They reach a promised land, with fresh grass, milk, honey and fruit. The hungry king lion sends the fox to reason with them. In the meantime, he is tempted to eat the stag. The would-be victim, however, is also a kind of learned court Jew, who distracts the king lion by expounding knowledge of grammar, logic, mathematics, metaphysics, political science, astronomy and so on. The lion declares that his life is now transformed, and he names the stag 'ISRAEL' and garlands him with riches. Eventually the fox is eaten instead, and the lion and the stag go off together to live in peaceful harmony with all the other animals in the promised land. Much of the whole Jewish experience and hope is encapsulated in these few pages: persecution, exile, learning and a wish for peace at the end.

LEFT: Manuscript of the Hebrew fables of Isaac ben Solomon ibn Sahula, dated 1450, with the story of the king lion and his courtiers, the deer and the fox.

CHAPTER SEVEN

The Savant: Jean-Joseph Rive

For a priest, there was not much Christian generosity in the Abbé Jean-Joseph Rive (1730–91). *La Chasse aux bibliographes*, dated 1789, is the most bad-tempered book on manuscripts ever written. It pretends to be by an unnamed pupil of Rive, but it is hardly concealed that it is the unfettered work of the Abbé himself. The imprint states that it was published in London by a certain 'Aphobe', but the author cannot resist gleefully emphasizing that this is false (it was actually printed in Aix-en-Provence and 'Aphobe' means 'fearless'). The title, *La Chasse aux bibliographes et antiquaires mal-avisés*, echoes the wording of numerous aristocratic hunting manuals, which may be a veiled allusion to the Duc de La Vallière (1708–80), Rive's former employer in Paris, a passionate *chasseur* and *Grand fauconnier de France*, who shared many hunts with Louis XV. The year of publication was that of the outbreak of the French Revolution, which Rive endorsed with great enthusiasm, a moment when all the courtesies of eighteenth-century French manners and religion seemed to have been suddenly abolished, and the disaffected felt licensed to turn on their masters. This unexpected inversion of the order of things parallels the whimsical illuminations in the margins of many medieval manuscripts, in which the hare becomes the hunter, blows a horn, and chases the hounds.

Rive explains briefly that it is morally wrong that book collectors and the public are deceived by ignorant booksellers and so-called experts who make ill-founded attributions and spurious claims of rarity about early printed books and medieval manuscripts. From that reasonable premise, he then launches into more than 500 pages of tirade about the

RIGHT: The Abbé Jean-Joseph Rive (1730–91), pencil sketch from late in his life, which became the source for all subsequent portraits.

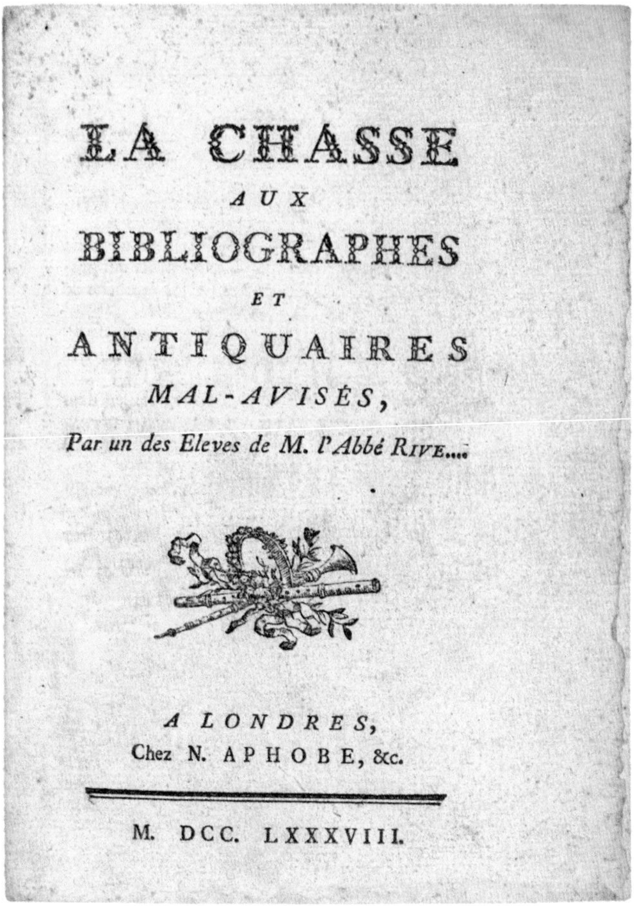

LA CHASSE

AUX

BIBLIOGRAPHES

ET

ANTIQUAIRES

MAL-AVISÉS,

Par un des Eleves de M. l'Abbé RIVE....

A LONDRES,

Chez N. APHOBE, &c.

M. DCC. LXXXVIII.

The *Chasse aux bibliographes,* Aix-en-Provence, 1789, falsely dated London, 1788, in which the Abbé Rive attacks all his fellow book historians and antiquaries.

unfairness he has endured through all his life and the wanton incompetence of seemingly everyone he has ever met or whose books he has read. He names them all, reserving special contempt for Jacques Le Long (1665–1721), Oratorian priest and antiquary, Barthélemy Mercier (1734–99), abbot of Saint-Léger and librarian of Sainte-Geneviève in Paris, and particularly for Guillaume De Bure *le jeune* (1734–1820), the best-known bookseller of his generation, and the young Joseph Van Praet (1754–1837), eventually one of the most eminent of all librarians of the new Bibliothèque nationale in Paris. There is always a certain diversion in reading insults about well-known people, but the Abbé Rive's diatribes are so relentless and his accusations so trivial that one sometimes longs for him only to be quiet, as doubtless they did too. Every page is padded with references to obscure reference books intended to demonstrate his own enormously wide reading and prodigious memory. We might now diagnose an element of autism.

Many of his criticisms represent tiny corrections to published texts. He was scandalized to find, for example, two very small errors in the vast works of Bernard de Montfaucon (1655–1741), French Benedictine and one of the founders of manuscript studies as an academic discipline. In 1739, Montfaucon had carelessly mentioned an early manuscript of Justinian in the royal library in Paris as having been made around the year 400, although the text was not written until 528, and he had listed a Spanish manuscript as "Libro de la Monteria, ou *maison rustique*", mistranslating *monteria*, which Rive says means 'hunting'. Strictly, it is 'riding' in Spanish, but we are back in the chase and Rive is in full gallop.

The Abbé would doubtless have read my present book if it had existed in his time, but I would dread to have had him as a reviewer. My chapters up to this point describe people he knew about. He had certainly read works of Saint Anselm, he mentions Robert Cotton and the fire of 1731, and he even knew of the library of Rabbi Oppenheim of Prague. In the *Chasse aux bibliographes* he writes about the Duc de Berry, practically the first time that now-famous collector was ever discussed in print. (The Duc's *Très Riches Heures* was unknown until 1855 and both the *Belles Heures* and the *Très Belles Heures* in Paris did not emerge until the 1880s.) Rive takes issue with Joseph Van Praet, who had catalogued one of the Duc de Berry's copies of the *Bible historiale* as dating from the fourteenth century. Rive quotes its ownership inscription in the Duc's hand, which includes his title as count of Boulogne, acquired on marrying the heiress Jeanne de Boulogne in 1389. He knew that the Duc died in 1416 and therefore proposes a reasonable middle date for the manuscript as being between these two fixed parameters, which would therefore be about 1403, by a small margin not in the fourteenth century. Actually, Van Praet was technically right. We now know, as above p. 76, that the Duc often bought his books second-hand, which had not occurred to Rive, and this *Bible historiale*, which is today in the Bibliothèque nationale de France, was in reality probably made in the 1380s but not inscribed by the Duc until some time later when it entered his possession.

The Duc de Berry's eldest brother, Charles V, had an even more spectacular *Bible historiale*, now in the Museum Meermanno in The Hague. This is the manuscript which the Duc had borrowed and had to be

The frontispiece of the *Bible historiale* of Charles V, painted in 1371 by 'Joannes de Brugis' (Jean Bondol), whom Rive was outraged to find identified with Jan Van Eyck.

claimed back by the royal library from his executors (above, p. 75). It has a famous frontispiece showing a kneeling figure of the royal servant Jean Vaudetar holding up the book for the king to admire, together with a poem in French describing how Vaudetar had been running backwards and forwards through the streets of Paris assembling the manuscript, even with the rain falling on his head. There is a contemporary inscription in gold letters saying that this frontispiece was made in 1371 by the painter 'Joannes de Brugis'. This was first published in 1723 in a book by Jacques Le Long and was quoted in the catalogue in 1769, when the manuscript came up in the sale of the library of Louis-Jean Gaignat, written by Guillaume De Bure, describing the artist as "le célèbre Jean de Bruges", implying (although not stating) that this was Jan Van Eyck. The Abbé Rive was incandescent with outrage. If either of them knew anything about art history, he wrote both in the margin of his own copy of the Gaignat sale catalogue and in the *Chasse aux bibliographes*, they would know that Van Eyck was between only two and four years old in 1371. Rive says that this false attribution would have elevated the price dishonestly had he not sat at the table before the auction, telling everyone who would listen that the inscription was a fake. The auctioneers must have hated him: we sometimes had interfering busybodies like that during public views at Sotheby's and they could destroy a sale. In the end, the manuscript was sold to Gerard Meerman for 399 *livres*, much less than it would have made without Rive's intervention, according to his own self-satisfied and righteous opinion.

Once again, Rive was wrong. The inscription is not a forgery, but it refers instead to the court artist Jean (or Hennequin) Bondol, documented 1368–81, who was indeed from Bruges. Despite being mistaken, however, Rive's remarks were revolutionary in the eighteenth century. He was looking at illuminated manuscripts as a book historian, attempting to date them by internal evidence and independent research, as we do now. That would have been inconceivable to Cotton or even Oppenheim. He cared who painted them, and he considered that date and attribution mattered and would affect the manuscripts' status and commercial value. He was even aware of the possibility of forgery. For the first time since the Middle Ages, he was seeing medieval manuscripts not just as texts or curios but as items of connoisseurship, with their place in the history of art and a value to collectors.

Jean-Joseph Rive was born in Apt, in Provence in the south of France, about forty miles east of Avignon, on 19 May 1730. He was baptized the same day in Apt Cathedral. His father was a goldsmith. Jean-Joseph trained as a priest in Avignon and in the 1750s he was teaching philosophy and physics at the *grand séminaire* of Saint-Charles d'Avignon. The chapel and cloister of the former seminary, built at just this time, survive on the southern side of the city centre, in what is still the Rue Saint-Charles. Rive himself dated his first interest in rare books to the age of fifteen; his nephew later said it was 'as early as his fourteenth year'. That is about normal for a life-long obsession. The sale catalogue of his considerable private library of bibliographical reference books, drawn up after Rive's death in 1791, said that it had been built up over forty years, which would take acquisitions back to 1751, when Rive was about twenty-one. He read his books with a very retentive memory. He shared his early enthusiasm with an exact contemporary, Joseph David (1730–84), member of a long-established bookselling and publishing family of Avignon. From 1765 until David's death they maintained a ceaseless correspondence, of which hundreds of letters still survive. It was one friendship which never turned sour; another was with his housekeeper, who stayed with him for twenty-four years and was heartbroken at his death (these facts are worth recording, because, despite his petulance in public, Rive was not unloved). There are several portraits of Rive from late in his life, versions of the same composition, showing a slight and thin man, holding an open book and looking back over his left shoulder. He has a large head, baleful eyes, a broad forehead, sunken cheeks and, by this time, receding hair still in curly tufts around his ears.

In 1764 he was appointed to his only job as an active priest in Mollégès, a small parish of a few hundred people about fifteen miles south-east of Avignon. Rive's church of Saint-Pierre-ès-Liens is still there. I cannot resist quoting from the English version of the village's tourist website today: "Everything is quiet and peaceful. Everybody knows each other, and the locals always have a smile on their faces . . . The women talk amongst themselves while a cat rubs against their legs. As for the men, they sit on a shady bench and watch the rare passersby." This does not sound a paradise for a quick-tongued and unsmiling young man longing for the bookshops and intellectual exhilaration of the eighteenth-century Enlightenment. Rive irritated his superiors with letters complaining about the clerical life. There is an unverifiable but early story of an affair with a married woman from Paris. Rive resigned in July 1766 and reported to Joseph David that he had taken refuge in the château de Mollégès, a house converted from the former abbey of Notre-Dame de Mollégès, almost adjacent to the church. He made a huge decision, helped by a sense of his own worth, and in the winter of 1766–7 he left southern

France for Paris, where he arrived, unemployed but with letters of introduction from David, on 4 January 1767. He was thirty-six years old.

Rive was welcomed initially into the bibliophilic fraternity of the Parisian booksellers and their clients. A passion for rare books is always a passport into like-minded company. He retained his clerical title of 'Abbé' throughout his life and used it to sign letters and on the title-pages of books he wrote. It probably seemed to convey a certain probity. Rive's first lodgings were in the quai des Augustins on the left bank, next door to the shop of the bookseller Jean-François De Bure, and by February he was in the Hôtel Saint-Louis in the Rue des Grands Augustins, which in the time of the Duc de Berry had already been the district of the university and the Parisian book trade, as it remains today. Rive was introduced to the royal library and elsewhere but failed to secure paid employment. The monk Barthélemy Mercier, whom he later castigated in the *Chasse*, appears to have been endlessly helpful to a fellow cleric, suggesting cataloguing work for the collector the Marquis de Paulmy (1722–87), which came to nothing.

Rive's first encounter with seriously important manuscripts took place on Saturday, 7 March 1767. He reported in a letter to David in Avignon that he had been brought by M. de Lenfant to see the abbey of Saint-Germain-des-Prés, where they were shown some of the treasures by Dom Pater. It is a rare glimpse of one of the outstanding monastic libraries of

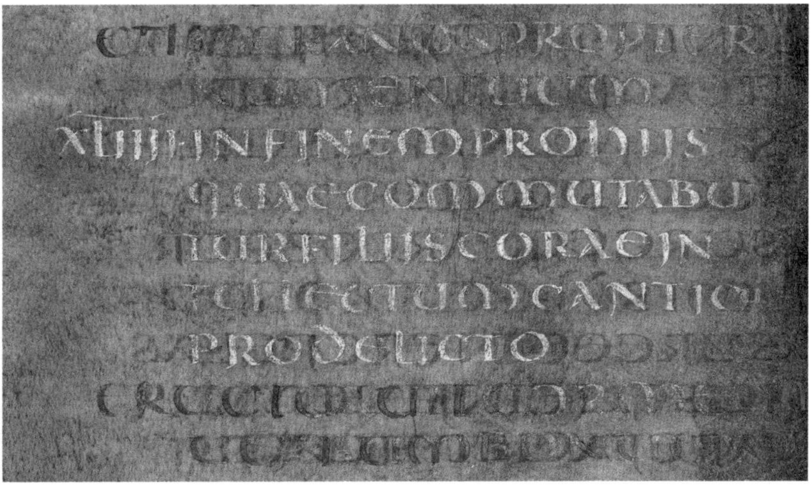

The 'Psalter of Saint Germain' written in silver and gold, sixth century, seen by Rive in 1767 when it belonged to the abbey of Saint-Germain-des-Prés.

France before its closure at the Revolution and the spiriting away of some of its best manuscripts to St Petersburg by Piotr Dubrowsky. They saw, according to Rive's breathless description, a Greek and Latin Psalter, written in uncials; another Psalter, on purple parchment, written in gold and silver ink, also in uncials, said to have been given to Saint Germain himself in Constantinople by the emperor Justinus; a Gospel of Saint Matthew, in gold on purple, like the second Psalter; and a manuscript written on papyrus containing the letters of Saint Augustine. Dom Pater told them that these all dated from the sixth century. This would make them consistent with Saint Germain himself, who died in 576. Rive immediately knew (so he said) that several of these manuscripts were mentioned by Burkhard Struve in chapter 3 of his *Introductio in notitiam rei litterariae* (1710), but that Struve, who did not question the dates, had not been able to examine them as closely as Rive proceeded to do. As a result, Rive could not resist informing his host that the letter 'h' in Latin manuscripts was not written in mid-word like other letters earlier than the ninth century but was written above the word, like a breathing mark in Greek script, and that accents were not used in writing Greek earlier than the seventh or eighth centuries. Dom Pater cried out, like an eagle (said Rive), declaring that he was overturning their most precious monuments of antiquity. 'I replied politely that this was following the rules of their own Montfaucon' – himself a Benedictine – 'and other modern diplomatists.' Undaunted, the curator produced a piece of writing from the time of Cicero which did indeed exhibit the use of accents on Greek words. Rive declared it to be from the tenth century, again citing the authority of Montfaucon. Poor Dom Pater conceded that he was sorry to learn this, but he remained courteous and said that he regretted the lack of scholarship among the monks. A less saintly man would have strangled his guest.

For over a year, Rive survived on small ventures in the buying and selling of books, some or all on behalf of Joseph David's business in Avignon. In June 1768 he was consulted on a bibliographical point by the Duc de La Vallière, and Rive resolved to do everything possible to secure permanent employment with this great prince of the book world. "La patience est ma resource," he wrote to David, the most untruthful self-diagnosis of his life. In July he was involved in acquisition of books from Provence for La Vallière, who (Rive later claimed) never reimbursed him. In October he was invited to dinner, and shortly before Christmas 1768 the Abbé Rive was finally taken on as the duke's full-time librarian. "Me

The Duc de La Vallière, drawn and engraved in 1757 by Charles-Nicolas Cochin.

voilà, cher ami, à la tête de la bibliothèque la plus curieuse de l'Europe", he wrote triumphantly to his friend.

Louis César de La Baume Le Blanc was the great-nephew of Louise de La Vallière, mistress of Louis XIV, and had succeeded to the dukedom of La Vallière in 1739. He was of immense wealth and courtly manners, "without ambition, with no great talents" (according to Richard Copley Christie), but clearly charming and likeable. He hunted with Louis XV, as we have seen, and had been a close friend of Madame de Pompadour (1721–64), royal favourite, and was director of her private theatre at Versailles, where he sometimes took parts himself. He too was a man of many romantic entanglements. He formed two huge libraries. The first, at the Château de Montrouge to the south of Paris (eventually demolished in 1875), was mostly sold in or before 1767. On moving his residence principally to the Hôtel de La Vallière in the Rue de Bac in central Paris, he began again, financing a new and far greater cabinet of bibliographical rarities, now entrusted to the care of the Abbé Rive.

It is easy to ridicule the Duc de La Vallière's enormous private collections of unread and mostly unreadable books (and many did), but the fact is that he revelled in the pure joy of bibliophily and chose his domestic settings among the finest monuments of literacy, with a particular passion for the company of old French poetry. The library brought him into agreeable and untaxing correspondence with Diderot, Voltaire, and other luminaries. Voltaire sent him the manuscript of *Candide*, chapter by chapter. La Vallière's books were usually made ready for placing on his shelves in bindings of beautiful deep red or green morocco, gilded on their spines, which must have glittered beneath the chandeliers: imagine them in a Louis XV interior with silk cushions and ormolu furniture, with guests in embroidered clothes and powdered wigs. A grand eighteenth-century private library involved at least four of the five senses, including the soft touch and intoxicating smell of new leather, the crackle of handmade paper and the riffle of parchment, and probably half the deadly sins – greed, envy and pride, bordering on lust (there were some books an *abbé* ought not to know about).

For the rest of his life, Rive always insisted that La Vallière's second library was entirely his own achievement. This was probably true. Without doubt, its sensational acquisitions in medieval manuscripts and the first printed books represented Rive's two great passions, which sometimes overlapped in books printed on vellum or illuminated by hand. Rive was given accommodation in the Hôtel de La Vallière, a step up from the curé's house in Mollégès. He was paid 900 *livres* a year, increased in 1775 to 1200 *livres*, still not enough in his opinion (often expressed). To judge from Rive's own allusions to conversations taking place over dinner one might believe him an intimate of the ducal household, although La Vallière seems to have regarded him as one of the domestic staff. Rive's quarrelsome and surly nature evidently amused his easy-going employer. A story, reported by Gabriel Peignot in 1804 and recounted by Thomas Dibdin in 1811, tells that when the Duc de La Vallière found himself struggling with argumentative guests, he would declare, "Gentlemen, I'll go and let loose my bull-dog", and his librarian would be summoned to do battle. Nonetheless, Rive was given all facilities and a freedom to make purchases at his own discretion. Almost 50,000 books were added during the twelve years of his employment, an average of about ten every day, year after year. Each volume had to be found and viewed before purchase, transacted and then brought back to the house, catalogued and often rebound, and then inserted into its appropriate place on the library shelves. Rive doubtless enjoyed himself enormously. He recounted attending a sale in 1779, for which La Vallière had lent him his coach; on the way home he had to call on a young nun in her convent and came in with an armful of rare books, not wishing to leave them unsupervised in the duke's coach outside.

It may be that the Duc de La Vallière had been motivated to take on Rive in December 1768 by the news of the imminent sales of the library of Louis-Jean Gaignat (1697–1767), which were scheduled to begin on 10 April 1769. Gaignat had been secretary to Louis XV and had formed a library almost the equal to that of the eventual collection of La Vallière himself, and indeed had acquired items from La Vallière's own earlier dispersals. His explicit wish was always that his library would be sold by auction after his death, so that others who shared his tastes could enjoy the excitement of acquisition. The Duc de La Vallière, on the Abbé Rive's advice, was by far the biggest buyer.

Rive went to inspect the books systematically beforehand in the Gaignat house in the Rue de Richelieu. His own copies of the four-volume sale catalogue survive, now in the Bibliothèque nationale in Paris (also in the Rue de Richelieu), and they include his handwritten notes. These are utterly fascinating. Over many decades, I have previewed countless auctions of manuscript and it is an experience I know well. You sit at the table in the viewing room and they bring you one volume after another. You pick up each book, weigh it in the hands, open it up and might scribble down a quick impression, whether it is lovely or disappointing (no sale catalogue can adequately convey this), and then you look more closely, turning pages, judging condition and comparing the auctioneers' description and making rapid judgements on their suggested attribution and date, and maybe comments on the manuscript's earlier history or anything relevant which might affect the price or indicate problems for a buyer, and you finally decide (if that is why you are there) whether it is a book to compete for, and to what price. Then you move to the next lot. Sometimes it takes only a few moments. This is raw connoisseurship at express speed, and every bookdealer lives by it.

Rive's annotations include aspects of all of this. He writes in ink, which implies the use of open inkwells at the table. Perhaps – not

XLI miniatures de la plus grande beauté, & parfaitement bien conservées. petit vol. in-4°. mar. rouge, avec dentelles.

Voy. *Bibliographie Instructive.* N°. 219.

195 L'Office de l'Eglise, ou Heures anciennes. MSS. *sur vélin en lettres gothiques, avec miniatures assez bien conservées. in-8°. mar. vert.*

196 Ancien Livre de Prieres, fait à l'usage de Louis I du nom, Duc d'Anjou, Roi de Hiérusalem & de Sicile. MSS. *sur vélin exécuté l'an 1390, & décoré de très belles miniatures. in-4°. mar. violet.*

Ce Manuscrit, que l'on peut regarder comme un des plus précieux que l'on connoisse en ce genre, renferme différens Traités particuliers dont nous allons donner le détail.

1°. Un Calendrier décoré de très jolies miniatures.

2°. Un Traité *intitulé*, l'Estimeur du Monde, qui enseigne & introduit tout homme de bien à honnêtement vivre selon Dieu.

3°. Li Enseignemens de Monseigneur Sainct Loys, jadis Roy de France, qu'il apprist et escript devant sa mort à son ainsné fils, & aussi comme pour testament lui laissa.

4°. Les Heures de Notre-Dame.

5°. Les Pseaumes de la Pénitence.

6°. Oraisons diverses de la Passion de J. C.

7°. Les Heures du Sainct Esperit.

8°. Les Heures de la Passion de J. C. avec Prieres, Oraisons, Litanies & Invocations.

9°. Les Lamentations de la Vierge.

10°. Oraisons particulieres pour être dites pendant la Messe.

necessarily – he was expected to report in advance to La Vallière. The duke had budgeted 30,000 *livres* for the Gaignat sales and ended up spending more than 86,000, nearly a hundred times the annual salary of his librarian. Rive attended to watch the sales, but the duke's bids were actually executed by Guillaume De Bure. Rive writes out his name in full each time he made a purchase with the epithet 'le jeune' (to distinguish him from his elder cousin Guillaume-François De Bure). Some routine items in every auction are tedious and slow-moving, and Rive doodled flowers in the margins of his catalogue, waiting for the big lots to come up. There he often recorded where the bidding began – "sur table" is the term he uses – and sometimes who else was in the running, and finally the eventual buyer when the hammer fell, and the price. If there is a moment when I can first share intimacy with the Abbé Rive, it is when holding his annotated copies of the Gaignat sale catalogues.

Like all his generation, Rive was not impressed by early manuscripts, regarding them as primitive; nor was Gaignat, who owned very few. Lot 93 in the first day's auction was the richly illustrated commentary of Beatus of Liébana on the Apocalypse from the abbey of Saint-Sever-sur-l'Adour in Gascony, now one of the most admired illuminated manuscripts of the eleventh century. Its brilliantly coloured and unearthly paintings were not compatible with the refinement of the 1760s. Even the auction catalogue was unable to say anything more favourable than that its painted figures were in the taste of those early centuries. Rive made notes on the book's script, observing the lack of abbreviations or dots over 'i's, but regarded the miniatures as "grossières", and the manuscript was not considered suitable for La Vallière. The auctioneer opened at 18 *livres*, and there were no further bids. Let modern collectors fantasize on that lost opportunity.

Another unimaginable bargain by our standards was lot 50, a large and flawless Psalter illuminated around 1170, perhaps for the royal family of Denmark, with thirteen full-page pictures and almost a hundred smaller miniatures. In this instance, Rive did not even bother to view the manuscript. It sold for 50 *livres*, bought by Dr William Hunter (1718–83), Scottish physician. It is now in Glasgow University Library, where it is known today as the Hunterian Psalter, probably the finest

LEFT: The Abbé Rive's copy of the Gaignat sale catalogue, 1769, with his notes, corrections and doodles.

medieval manuscript in Scotland. The very next lot in the sale was the printed Mainz Psalter of 1457, on poor-quality vellum, in the judgement of Rive, who examined it closely. It is one of ten extant copies of the earliest printed book with an exact date and was then a strong candidate for the oldest printed book of all. It made 1340 *livres*, more than twenty-five times the price a moment earlier of one of the greatest Romanesque manuscripts in existence. Rive later judged the Mainz Psalter of 1457 to be worth at least 4000 *livres*. Both books today, if they could ever come to the market, would achieve sums that would be front-page news across the world, but almost certainly the twelfth-century manuscript would now be the more expensive of the two. Money alone does not determine the intrinsic merit of a work of art (look at sums paid now for contemporary art), but a sale price is often the most quantifiable scale for measuring public appreciation and the changing of taste. Rive's assessments, and the prices achieved at the Gaignat sale, give us a strong impression of what was valued in Enlightenment France.

At any moment, a rare book or manuscript title has a certain status in the collectors' canon. Once there, the copy must then be graded by condition and level of desirability. (The Duc de Berry probably understood this second layer of refinement, but Cotton and Oppenheim perhaps did not.) Some manuscripts were dismissed by Rive in his copy of the Gaignat catalogue as being too damaged, such as a thirteenth-century volume of romances, or as having "miniatures très médiocres", as he wrote beside the entry for a volume of statutes dated 1352. He often made notes to himself on the script – cursive, gothic, round and so on – especially recording the use of abbreviations and whether the writing was well-formed or not. I am happy to recognize lot 1764, an early fifteenth-century *Roman de la Rose* with 101 miniatures in semi-grisaille, because I went to see the same manuscript in 1976 in a grand private house in Luzarches, north of Paris, and I recall telling its then owner that it seemed unexpected that a literary text was written in formal gothic script, like a Book of Hours. Rive noted exactly the same, "caractères gothiques", observing also that the book was very beautiful, as I too thought. The bidding opened at 120 *sur table* and rose to 192 *livres*. We were both inexperienced in those days. In my case, I excitedly promised the owner a minimum of £100,000 at auction. In its Sotheby's sale in 1977, there was no bid at 100, silence in a crowded room; "Ninety thousand?" inquired the auctioneer desperately; "Ninety-two", muttered the dealer

Book of Hours, France, 1524, a Renaissance manuscript which delighted Rive when it was lot 194 in the Gaignat sale.

H. P. Kraus half-heartedly. I was appalled to hear the hammer immediately fall and the manuscript announced triumphantly as sold, below the agreed reserve. I had an awkward telephone call to make, but the seller was happy, and the manuscript is now in the J. Paul Getty Museum. In a curious way, a work of art no longer has a financial value, or at least not a volatile one, once it is in public possession.

Very late manuscripts had the Abbé's approbation in the Gaignat sale, especially those of the French Renaissance. "Superbe mss – miniatures magnifiques", he recorded for a history of Troy dated 1495, more than four decades after the invention of printing. Bidding for that lot opened at 200 *livres* and it was rapidly acquired for La Vallière for 480. A French Book of Hours dated 1524 enraptured Rive: "miniatures exquisites d'un goût merveilleux", he wrote. It began at 300 *sur table*, and the manuscript went to La Vallière at 751 *livres*. Its subsequent owners included William Beckford (1760–1844), of Fonthill; the tenth duke of Hamilton (1767–1852); Robert Hoe III (1839–1909); Cortlandt Bishop (1870–1935); and Lessing Rosenwald (1891–1979). It is now in the Library of Congress. It is an extremely pretty manuscript in that late sugary style of the mannerist court of François I, but today worth a fraction of the value of Romanesque manuscripts so unappreciated in the eighteenth century.

Lot 188 was the second volume of a Franciscan breviary of the 1490s. We now know, although they did not, that it was made for René II, Duc de Lorraine. Rive wrote down that the script and the miniatures were very fine, which they are. It had an earlier saleroom history, he knew: it had been owned by the Comte d'Hoym (1694–1736) and sold for 103 *livres* in 1738; and then by Zacharie de Selle (1702–59), in whose sale in 1761 it had been bought by Gaignat for 252 *livres*. The previous lot in the de Selle sale was none other than the incomparable Sherborne Missal, probably the greatest of all English gothic illuminated manuscripts. It reached 800 *livres*. In 1998, I was responsible for its eventual private sale to the British Library for the highest price ever paid for any medieval book, even now, I believe. The surviving half of the Breviary of René de Lorraine, handsome though it is, would not be valued today at any significant fraction of the Sherborne Missal, and it could not possibly overtake it, as it did in 1769, when the Breviary was acquired for La Vallière at 840 *livres*.

There was one near disaster for Rive in the Gaignat sale. He had set his heart on buying lot 3004 for his employer, a manuscript of the chronicles of Enguerrand de Monstrelet written in Geneva in 1510 with delicate miniatures in *camaieu-gris*. The bidding opened at 500 *livres*. There was another participant to 750. However, it was lost at 870 *livres* to the bookseller Guillaume Saugrain, representing Gerard Meerman (1722–71), of Rotterdam and The Hague, buyer also of Charles V's *Bible historiale*. Rive later added a note in the lower margin of his catalogue explaining what happened next. When he got back to the house after the sale, the Duc de La Vallière saw him looking disconsolate and asked why. Rive admitted his misjudgement and disappointment, and the duke went out at once in his coach to see the Dutch envoy in Paris, had the sale cancelled, and secured the manuscript for his library after all. (It made 2700 *livres* when it was resold after the duke's death, fifteen years later.)

Not every manuscript acquired by the Abbé Rive for the Duc de La Vallière came from public auctions. Two of the most famous today were books which must have entered commerce following the suppression of

RIGHT: The Rohan Hours, perhaps Angers, *c.*1430–35, later owned by the Jesuits of Paris and acquired by Rive for the Duc de La Vallière after the suppression of the Jesuit Order in 1764.

Pour tes pechiez penitance feras. Au jour du jugement avecques moy seras.
In manus tuas domine commendo spiritum meum. Redemisti me domine deus veritatis.
Dilexi quoniam exaudiet dominus vocem orationis mee.

the Jesuit Order in France in 1764. The Abbé's clerical status and his early schooling with the Jesuits in Apt may have eased delicate negotiations. One was the Salisbury Breviary of John, duke of Bedford, brother of Henry V of England and regent of France 1422–9. The manuscript is one of several painted for him in Paris by the city's leading illuminator, now known for this reason as the Bedford Master. It had belonged to the Jesuits of Lyons. The other was the Rohan Hours, or *Grandes Heures de Rohan*, once owned by the vicomtes de Rohan and then by the Jesuits in Paris. It is one of the most hauntingly beautiful works of art from early fifteenth-century France, with miniatures as strange and ill-proportioned as anything by El Greco or Modigliani, by an artist known today from this supreme manuscript as the Rohan Master.

Some collections were secured for La Vallière *en bloc*. About 200 medieval manuscripts and books printed on vellum were bought as a group for 80,000 *livres* in 1776 from the library assembled by Claude d'Urfé (1501–58), French ambassador at the Council of Trent, which in turn included the medieval books of the family of Malet de Graville, brought in by his marriage in 1532. The d'Urfé library was extended by Honoré d'Urfé (1567–1625), who moved it to Paris in the 1620s. The last Marquise d'Urfé died in 1775. The manuscripts came not directly from her but through an intermediate collector, one M. le Bombarde. Many were still in their quaint sixteenth-century bindings of green velvet with copper fittings, some of which survived the campaigns of rebinding in the La Vallière library. The d'Urfé acquisition included a thirteenth-century illuminated *Chansonnier* of troubadour songs in *langue d'oc*. It was one of the oldest books Rive ever bought, but it touched his heart as a native Provençal and he planned a monograph on it, never completed. Among other books from the d'Urfé collection were the well-known and unusual Savoyard Book of Hours perhaps owned by Amadée de Saluces (1420–73), of Piedmont, now in the British Library; a spectacular late fifteenth-century manuscript of the *Forteresse de la foy*, made for Louis de Gruuthuse (1422–92), courtier of Philip the Good, whose great medieval house survives in Bruges; and a very large Book of Hours made in Rome in 1549 for Claude d'Urfé himself, now through many journeys in the Huntington Library in California.

RIGHT: The Saluces Hours, Savoy, mid-fifteenth century, acquired with the d'Urfé library and chosen by Rive for his projected essay on identifying manuscripts.

Secundum iohannem.
In illo tempore: Ap
prehendit pylatus
ihesum et flagella

We are so familiar in our time with manuscripts like these being in display cases and publications of the national and university libraries of Europe and America that it is hard to envisage an *ancien régime* when many of the cornerstones of medieval art were still out of captivity and unknown to anyone except their owners. It is far easier to see an illuminated manuscript today than it was in the eighteenth century, and it may even be easier to buy one. It is a truism so obvious that it is easily overlooked that collectors can only acquire what is available on the market. Sir Robert Cotton had gathered manuscripts mainly from the closure of the English monasteries at the Reformation. That supply was largely exhausted by the eighteenth century, despite the reappearance of the Sherborne Missal in 1761. However, the extraordinary diaspora of manuscripts during the Revolutionary and Napoleonic eras had not yet taken place. The tens of thousands of early monastic manuscripts from France, Germany and Italy, easily accessible to nineteenth-century collectors, were entirely unknown to a buyer such as the Abbé Rive for the Duc de La Vallière, however extensive their budget. Rive's most fertile sources for manuscripts were aristocratic families of France who had owned them since the Middle Ages or the Renaissance. Books tended to be late medieval, often in the vernacular, with particular emphasis on literature, chivalry, patriotic chronicles and domestic piety. In our time, such noble texts, which made up so much of eighteenth-century French libraries, have almost disappeared from the market.

Rive was familiar with relatively few Italian manuscripts. Despite the age's obsession with Roman civilization and architecture, classical texts of the kind supplied to Italian humanists by Vespasiano da Bisticci were not easily obtainable in France: they were in libraries in Italy, still untroubled by the edicts of Joseph II and the invasions of Napoleon. A small group of manuscripts was bought for La Vallière from George Jackson (1692–1763), an English merchant in Livorno. These included what was probably his best Italian Renaissance manuscript, the copy of Jerome on the Psalms written in Florence in 1488 by the scribe Antonio Sinibaldi, illuminated by Attavante for Matthias Corvinus, king of Hungary. It has a spectacular title-page in gold capitals on a disc of deep blue within an explosion of flowers, facing the opening of the text crowded with putti and royal emblems. In 1785, Rive published an account of an Italian manuscript of the *De excellentibus* of Galeotto Marzio, librarian to Matthias Corvinus, which had been given to Charles VIII in 1492–3. It was later in the collection of the chancellor, Henri-François d'Aguesseau (1668–1751). Both these royal manuscripts had survived outside Italy, and both are now in the Bibliothèque nationale de France.

There is an aspect of manuscript collecting which was new in the time of the Abbé Rive. We have often encountered the shared enjoyment of manuscripts as a common bond which crosses the social divides and the centuries: we now begin for the first time to see the manuscripts themselves as participants and even catalysts in creating that fraternity. At a simple level, the Duc de La Vallière used the presence of his library to suggest connoisseurship within his circle, and he showed rare books to visitors, as if in some way reaffirming his own cultural and even social status, as one might enjoy introducing famous guests to each other at dinner parties. The manuscripts' contacts and ability to bring people together also went backwards into the past. Rive was interested in provenance and writes with a real sense of kinship with previous owners of manuscripts he held in his hands every day – the Duc de Berry, Louis de Gruuthuse, Matthias Corvinus, Charles VIII and all the others. I doubt whether a seventeenth-century antiquary such as Cotton really identified with his manuscripts as part of the ancestry of his own taste, as Rive did. In dispersing collections, as Gaignat chose to do and La Vallière's family insisted on doing after his death, the line then went on to extend that fellowship infinitely into the future, like the thrill of having grandchildren. The descent can develop into pedigrees as strong as any in family genealogy. A published catalogue of the subsequent histories of all former La Vallière manuscripts would be compulsive reading for all book collectors.

The journeys of such manuscripts can sometimes be long. Rive viewed lot 2344 in the Gaignat sale. It was a history of Thebes and the fall of Troy in French, copied by the scribe Jacquotin de Lespluc in 1469, probably in Lille. The manuscript was not of use for any information its text could convey about the history of ancient kingdoms, as Oppenheim might have wanted a book for its contents; instead, it was desirable as a work of medieval art and literature. It had previously been owned by Louis de Gand (1678–1767), marshal of France. Rive rightly noted marginal damage to the first dozen leaves, now repaired, and he approved its purchase for La Vallière, when it cost 18 *livres* and 19 *sous*. (These very precise figures suggested a slow-moving sale; a brisk modern auction would rise in increments from 15 to 18, then 20, 22, 25, probably then

30, 35, 40, 50 and so on.) In the subsequent La Vallière sale in 1784, the history of Thebes sold for 28 *livres*, 1 *sou*, and passed apparently first to one William Harwood, whose bookplate it bears and who brought it to England, and then to John Towneley, of Chiswick, a member of the great Lancashire family of collectors, who died in 1813. When sold by his heirs in London in 1814, it achieved only £2. 21s. There were many manuscripts on the market at that moment, disgorged by the Revolution, and French texts were regarded as somewhat unpatriotic in England on the eve of Waterloo, a bit like German manuscripts in 1939. The new buyer was Edward Vernon Utterson, a founding member of the Roxburghe Club. When his library was sold in turn in 1852, the history of Thebes had gone up to £40, paid by Bertram, fourth earl of Ashburnham. His son, the fifth earl, resold it in 1897 with a large group of other manuscripts to Henry Yates Thompson, publishing magnate, who consigned this item to Sotheby's in 1899, where it was bought for £142 by the bookseller Leighton for his client Charles Fairfax Murray, the late Pre-Raphaelite, who sold it privately in 1906 to C. W. Dyson Perrins. (Many of these names will come back in Chapters 11–12.) At the Perrins sale after his death in 1958, the manuscript made £16,600 to the dealer H. P. Kraus, whom I knew well (I spoke at his memorial service in 1988), who catalogued it in New York in 1962 at $110,000, and sold it on to the Swiss banker Martin Bodmer, who left it in 1971 to the public foundation he established just outside Geneva, where I have looked at it. Every one of those names – de Gand, Gaignat, La Vallière, Towneley, Utterson, Ashburnham, Yates Thompson, Fairfax Murray, Dyson Perrins, Kraus and Bodmer – are brought together through their shared ownership of a single book, known intimately to the Abbé Rive.

A rather different example of a manuscript serving as a social catalyst is an even grander setting. The book is an early sixteenth-century illustrated French translation of the lives of Scipio and Pompey by Plutarch. It had been owned by Françoise-Louise de Bassompierre (1695–1758), *dame d'honneur* to the duchess of Lorraine. It was acquired after her death by Rive for the Duc de La Vallière. In his sale in 1784, the manuscript was sold to Jacob Joseph van den Bloeck, of Brussels, and was soon afterwards in the possession of an English collector with the most

RIGHT: Histories of Thebes and Troy, northern France 1469, here showing Jason setting out for the Golden Fleece; later owned by a long line of distinguished book collectors.

ennus les dieux vous en veullent delivrer sain et sauf

Comment Jazon entra en le petite nacelle pour aler au mouton

Quant il eubt congiet du Roy il se mist au chemin deuers vne petite ille en la quelle estoit la toison dor et entra en vne petitte nassellc Et mist ses armes et tous ses habillemens dedens puis passa oultre tout seul Et sy tost quil y fu arriue il sarma et se garny de toutes les choses que medee ly auoit bailliet Et

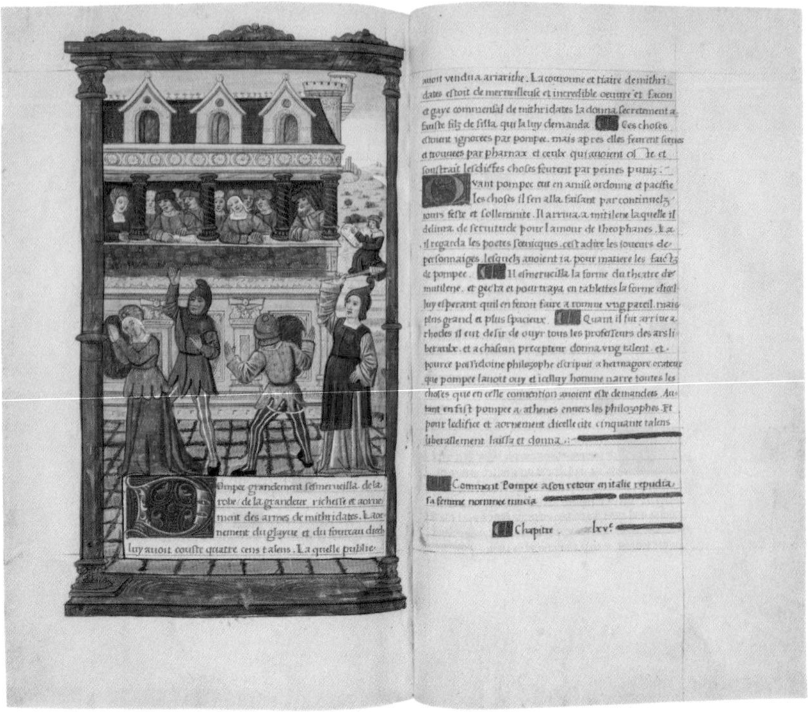

Plutarch's lives of Scipio and Pompey, in French, northern France, *c.*1508, owned by the Duc de La Vallière and later presented by Sir Thomas Phillipps to Queen Victoria, 1845.

perfect name for a bibliophile, Sir Gregory Page-Turner (1748–1805). At the dispersal of his library at Christie's in 1824 it was bought by Sir Thomas Phillipps. We will meet Phillipps properly in the next two chapters, a manuscripts obsessive without parallel but *nouveau* and socially insecure. By chance, he was a guest at Stowe, the famous house of the duke of Buckingham, when it was visited by Queen Victoria and Prince Albert in January 1845. There must have been some conversation about whether or how Sir Thomas himself might one day be appropriately presented to Her Majesty. Buckingham therefore arranged that Phillipps should attend a royal levée at St James's Palace in London on 23 April that year. This was an occasion which would have eclipsed even the salons of the Hôtel de La Vallière. Those in attendance included two royal dukes, two German reigning princes, thirteen ambassadors, five ordinary dukes, eleven marquesses, thirty-one earls and six bishops. Sir Thomas Phillipps was ushered forwards by the duke of Buckingham to make the presentation of the Duc de La Vallière's Plutarch to the queen, and the ultimate introduction in British society was facilitated by a medieval manuscript from the La Vallière library. It may not have been much appreciated by the recipient, but it is still safely at Windsor Castle.

It is through this shared familiarity with the same manuscripts that we can most easily envisage spending time with the Abbé Rive. I imagine that he would have had no small talk. Conversation would be about old books and nothing else. (I would not mind at all.) It would be very one-sided. He would tell me things, drawn from a huge range of reading and rapid recall, and he would talk about his work. As long as I was impressed and deferential, which I would probably have good reason to be, we would have a pleasant evening. If we went out for dinner, I expect I would have to pay.

In addition to acquisitions for the Duc de La Vallière, Rive prepared detailed descriptions of the manuscripts and major printed books, all in his neat and legible handwriting. He planned a series of publications on selected illuminated manuscripts in the ducal library. He had a weakness, not unknown among authors, for announcing intended books as if they were finished and published, and some of his boasted monographs seem to have existed only as dreams or as notes in draft. Two did appear in print in 1779, describing manuscripts in pairs under long titles, of which the first began *Notices historiques & critiques de deux manuscrits uniques & très précieux, de la bibliothèque de M. le Duc de La Vallière* . . . The manuscripts described were both seventeenth-century. If Rive was dismissive of anything earlier than about 1250 as crude and barbarian, he certainly considered that the art of illumination reached its highpoint of sophistication and refinement after the invention of printing. 'Good taste . . .', Voltaire wrote in a letter to the Duc de La Vallière in 1760, 'did not establish its reign until the century of Louis XIV.' The first manuscript presented in Rive's little monograph was the fabled *Guirlande de Julie*. This was a confection of romantic poetry commissioned by the Marquis de Montausier (1610–90) for presentation to the woman he loved, Julie d'Angennes (1606–71), daughter of the Marquis de Rambouillet, all of them intimates of the royal court. The texts were written out by the fashionable scribe Nicolas Jarry (*c.*1605/10–*c.*1674), whose delicate and minute calligraphy in roman script resembles the work of a fairy's typewriter. The manuscript is of exquisite courtly taste and frivolousness. Each poem is accompanied by an illuminated still-life painting of a different flower, executed by the botanical miniaturist

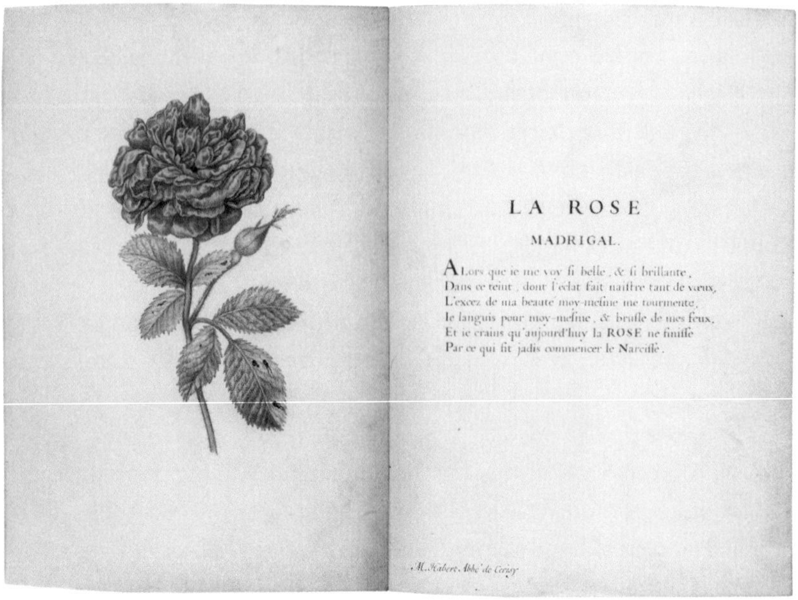

La Guirlande de Julie, by the scribe Nicolas Jarry and the artist Nicolas Robert, Paris, 1641, the most expensive manuscript in the world in the Duc de La Vallière's sale in 1783.

Nicolas Robert (1614–85), all making part of the garland of adoration for Julie herself. Her suitor left the manuscript beside her bed to find when she woke on 22 May 1641, the feast of Saint Julia of Corsica, her name-day festival. She finally agreed to marry him in 1645. She later became a friend of Louise de La Vallière, whose great-nephew may have had sentimental interest in securing the famous manuscript in the Gaignat sale in 1769. It was then given a six-line description, and nevertheless cost the duke 780 *livres*, more than almost any medieval book in the same sale. In the La Vallière auction in 1783, however, the catalogue entry now extended over three pages, citing the Abbé Rive's publication, and the *Guirlande de Julie* was sold this time for an astounding 14,510 *livres*, at that moment the most valuable manuscript in the world. Today, we would value it very differently, both financially and aesthetically.

For his second monograph, also 1779, Rive selected volumes of the romances of King Arthur and of the magic temptress Melusine. The first had been acquired with the d'Urfé library and the second from Gaignat. Rive's accounts are proprietorial, referring to "notre manuscrit", and they are careful but undeniably long-winded, the first steered off course by an unnecessary digression on the history of playing cards. The two descriptions together are swamped by 167 footnotes, all in a little book of only thirty-six pages. Rive was probably disappointed that his earnest efforts did not attract much public response. A third account by him, so little known that it was recently said to be one of those announced but never published, was printed as a separate appendix at the end of the fourth volume of Jean-Benjamin de La Borde's *Essai sur la musique ancienne et moderne*, 1780. It described La Vallière's two-volume manuscript of the poet and composer Guillaume de Machaut, bought from the Gaignat collection. Rive's text fills twelve pages and his footnotes fifteen. Other descriptions prepared but never sent to the printer included accounts of manuscripts in the La Vallière library with French versions of Quintus Curtius on the history of Alexander the Great and of Boethius in the translation of Jean de Meun, co-author of the *Roman de la Rose*.

In the late 1770s, while these were in preparation, Rive was working on his most important project, one which would ultimately transform the history of manuscript connoisseurship for ever. It was to be called *Essai sur l'art de vérifier l'âge des miniatures des manuscrits*, on how to date the illumination of medieval manuscripts. He planned to accompany the text with twenty-six life-sized colour reproductions, all taken from manuscripts owned by the Duc de La Vallière. He mentions the plan for these plates in a letter to Joseph David in August 1776. We are so familiar now with books about illuminated manuscripts being illustrated in colour that it is hard to imagine how unprecedented and technically difficult this was before photography or even lithographs (invented in 1796). Rive later claimed to have examined more than 12,000 medieval miniatures before making a final selection from nineteen different manuscripts, numbered in chronological order. Eight of these had been acquisitions from the Gaignat sale and five from the purchase of the d'Urfé library. They include what were doubtless the Abbé's favourite manuscripts, some of which we have already encountered – a chattering company of familiar friends, from the Rohan Hours, which Rive considered to be fourteenth-century, through to the seventeenth-century additions, attributed to Nicolas Jarry, scribe of the *Guirlande de Julie*, made to the Book of Hours of François I. The manuscripts include, in this sequence, the Breviary of the duke of Bedford (two plates); the *Forteresse de la foy* made for Louis de Gruuthuse (five plates); the translation of Quintus Curtius, on which he had been planning a monograph, never finished; the Breviary of René II de Lorraine, sold with the Sherborne Missal in the Gaignat sale; the Saluces Hours; the chronicle of Enguerrand de Monstrelet, which the duke had snatched from Meerman; that Book of Hours of 1524, now in the Library of Congress; and the Book of Hours commissioned in Rome in 1549 by Claude d'Urfé.

Rive explained afterwards that his choice of pictures was made to illustrate features which would be useful in the histories of architecture, religious and civil practices, costumes, fashion, furniture, utensils, and implements of warfare, and how these, in turn, might provide evidence for dating other manuscripts. The four illustrations from the *Forteresse de la foy*, for example, show the castle of Christianity being assaulted in turn by hordes of Saracens, heretics, Jews and demons, each precious for illustrating the different and distinctive costumes of the successive categories of assailant (maybe not so documentable for demons). His plate 16 is especially enchanting. It is from a French translation of the works of Julius Caesar, who is shown in the miniature dressed as a medieval emperor visiting a fifteenth-century bookshop, of which it is a marvellous and rare illustration. Perhaps it even appealed to the book-buying Duc de La Vallière, whose first names included César. The manuscript itself is now in the Bodleian Library.

Rive had all outlines of the chosen miniatures copied onto tracing paper placed directly over pages of the actual manuscripts. Some included details of minor decoration too, or samples of adjacent borders and initials and even occasional lines of script. These tracings, which still survive in the Département des Estampes in the Bibliothèque nationale, were then lightly engraved. For each sheet, a mastercopy was then painted by hand in exact facsimile made side by side with the original under Rive's constant supervision, using gold where needed, to serve as the artists' exemplars for hand-colouring the published sets. This process, Rive said, took three years and, in his opinion, nothing so luxurious had ever been attempted since the invention of printing.

As so often in the troubled life of the Abbé Rive, ambition ran ahead of reality. He never wrote the text. There were reasons for this, which we will come to in a moment. What we have instead is his eventual and privately published prospectus seeking subscriptions for the promised *Essai sur l'art de vérifier l'âge des miniatures des manuscrits*. Even the prospectus runs to seventy printed pages, of which two thirds are footnotes, and it gives a synopsis of what the whole book would have been. It was to contain a history of book illustration since Roman times, including accounts of famous early manuscripts such as the Cotton Genesis, which he knew by repute. Up to the tenth century, in Rive's judgement, some miniatures have a certain beauty, especially if Greek, but from the tenth to the mid-fourteenth centuries, however, "elles sont presque toutes affreuses," almost all dreadful. Then, slowly, classical taste begins to return, illuminations in manuscripts begin to detach themselves from initials and become art, reaching perfection by the high Renaissance, as the *Essai*'s illustrations would show.

The most important section of Rive's preview of his intended monograph on how to study manuscripts was a great fusillade of questions with which every manuscript should be interrogated. It reveals the author's intellectual energy and restlessness, and fills almost five pages as published:

> One must know about the works of an author, and to distinguish the merely attributed from those really from his own pen. Is a manuscript anonymous or pseudonymous? That determined, one must learn about its credence and literary reputation. Is the manuscript under investigation autograph, or a transcript? If a copy, of what century and country is it? Is any apparent date accurate or false? What material is the manuscript made of? Is it on parchment, vellum, human skin, papyrus, paper, tree bark, patra, palm leaves, or paper made from linen, cotton, bamboo, silk, or rag? With what implement were the letters written: a metal stylus, a brush, a reed or a quill? What colour are they and on what ground are they written? Who made them? Did the scribe leave his name in the manuscript? Is it his real name? When is he reputed to have lived? Did the scribe have a reputation? If so, was this more for his accuracy and wisdom than the beauty of his hand? Has the text been corrected? Who was the corrector? What was the corrector's name, his character and ability? Do we know of scholars or collectors who employed such a scribe or corrector? From what library or manuscript cabinet did the book emerge before passing into commerce? What arms, devices and symbols does it carry? Is it complete, or defective, or interpolated? Is it copied on a material reused from an earlier purpose? Are there notes and marginal corrections? Are they those of the author or another scholar? If by another, who was he? Is there any name? Is this name fictitious? Can it be checked against other signatures of the same writer? Has the manuscript been printed? If so, was it from an autograph copy or a later transcript? If autograph, was that from many centuries earlier than the date of printing? If it is

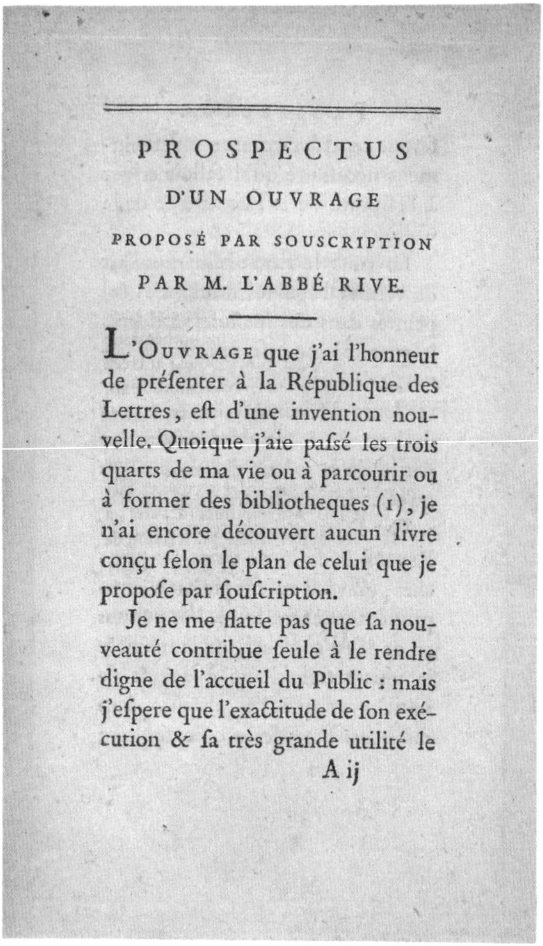

PROSPECTUS
D'UN OUVRAGE
PROPOSÉ PAR SOUSCRIPTION
PAR M. L'ABBÉ RIVE.

L'OUVRAGE que j'ai l'honneur de préſenter à la République des Lettres, eſt d'une invention nouvelle. Quoique j'aie paſsé les trois quarts de ma vie ou à parcourir ou à former des bibliotheques (1), je n'ai encore découvert aucun livre conçu ſelon le plan de celui que je propoſe par ſouſcription.

Je ne me flatte pas que ſa nouveauté contribue ſeule à le rendre digne de l'accueil du Public : mais j'eſpere que l'exactitude de ſon exécution & ſa très grande utilité le

A ij

The opening page of Rive's *Prospectus*, 1782, an announcement of a luxury publication never completed.

a copy, could it be later than the printed edition? If so, is it finely executed? What does the manuscript teach us? Is it ignorant or informed? If informed, is it exaggerated? Does it indicate foreign influence? What came before it and what followed, with regard to character, intellect and style of the author? If a manuscript is earlier than its printed edition, is it rare? If so, is this because of antiquity or paucity of copies? If it is later than the printed edition but magnificent, is it unique? What did it cost? What is contained in an unpublished manuscript? Is it interesting? Is it a text with order, intelligence, clarity, precision and erudition? Is it truly original? Is it copied from elsewhere? Is the author famous? Whether printed or not, is it in a living or an obsolete language? If a living language, is it

> an old one? If it seems recent, has it been updated? If that is so, is this found in other manuscripts of the same text, or only in printed editions? If its language is not updated, does it come from a period important in the evolution of that language? If so, what is its status? Are we looking at a Bible, a liturgical book, a work of a Church Father, a text of canon law? When were they written? Are there controversial passages? If so, have they been censored, interpolated or falsified either by Catholics or schismatics? Are foreign beliefs respected? What punctuation does the manuscript use? In what order are the books of the Bible? What chapter divisions do they use? Is the manuscript decorated with miniatures? Who was the artist, where was he from, and when did he live? Are the miniatures of the same date as the manuscript? Could they be later? What is their style? What is their distinctive characteristic? Are they monochrome or in multicolours? Are they heightened with gold? What do they tell of practices, fashions, and of other objects illustrated? What costumes are shown? Are these of the right period, and how do we know?

These are all fundamental questions we still ask in judging a medieval manuscript and assessing its importance. Every July for very many years I have spent a week as a guest of one of the great book collectors at his summer residence in Provence, and the Abbé Rive's inquisition might almost be word for word the conversations we have had countless times in discussion of manuscripts on the terrace late into the evenings, as the lights come on one by one across the darkening gulf of Saint-Tropez. Rive's prospectus circulated widely, and his methodology was picked up in England by Thomas Astle, *The Origins and Progress of Writing*, 1784, and in France by Jean-Baptiste Seroux d'Agincourt, *Histoire de l'art par les monumens*, IV, 1823. His sense of connoisseurship has become the basis of manuscript bibliophily ever since, especially in France, where condition and text are still pre-eminent, and his recording of evidence is part of the lore of manuscript scholarship. Rive's catechism of technical cross-examination is not so different from the listed 'Points to be Observed in the Description and Collation of Manuscripts' published by M. R. James in 1895 or the sixteen points which the manuscript cataloguer Neil Ker formulated in 1969. The process is now known in universities as the 'archaeology of the book'.

Plate 3 in the projected illustrations for Rive's *Essai* was to be a manuscript of Laurent de Premierfait's French translation of the *De casibus* of

Boccaccio dedicated to the Duc de Berry, discussed in Chapter 2, the text which portrays how at any moment of human ascendancy the wheel of fortune can suddenly turn and plunge the hero into devastating disaster. It happened to Rive. He was formulating his questions and preparing the pictures when, on 16 November 1780, the Duc de La Vallière died. His only child and sole heiress was his daughter, by then the Duchesse de Châtillon. She clearly loathed her father's librarian. That very night, Rive was dismissed from his post. In fury, he took with him all his working papers on the La Vallière books and manuscripts and left the house.

If I were writing a play, I would set an intermission at this point. When the audience is reseated and the curtains reopen, Rive would be seen living as a tenant of a medical doctor from Arles, César Coste, at 42 Rue du Cherche-Midi. The street is still there, running north-east from the boulevard du Montparnasse up to the Rue de Sèvres, and Rive's new lodgings, which he took on 1 December 1780, were on the left at the upper end of the street, opposite the turning into the Rue du Regard. On 22 December he wrote to his constant friend Joseph David in Avignon outlining his financial position. Instead of a pension for life, which the duke had originally promised him, he had been given a one-off bequest of 6000 *livres*, the equivalent of five years' salary (a generous legacy, in my opinion, but Rive felt thoroughly betrayed). What he perceived as an even worse insult was to follow. In early 1781 the Duchesse de Châtillon sent her father's vast library to auction, and she placed Guillaume De Bure *le jeune*, not the Abbé Rive, in charge of the cataloguing.

The sale catalogue for part I of the La Vallière library was in three volumes, with nearly 6000 lots, comprising almost all the best books. In a long and carefully worded introduction, De Bure graciously acknowledged the Abbé Rive's primacy in creating the collection and expressed regret in not having had access to the Abbé's descriptions and notes, which he said he understood to be outstanding. He began his work in May 1781 and the catalogue went to press in January 1782. The introduction and long lists of addenda were added in the course of that year. De Bure refers courteously to the prospectus for the *Essai sur l'art de vérifier l'âge des miniatures des manuscrits* and the high standards it set, and he realized that he was not competent to describe the manuscripts. For this, he therefore sub-contracted Joseph Van Praet. This ambitious young man, then aged twenty-six, was the son of a printer and bookseller in Bruges who in his teens had spent his pocket money buying the Gaignat sale catalogue and had come to Paris in 1779 to work with De Bure *l'aîné*. He was already passionate about medieval manuscripts and in 1780 had published an article on the Bruges collector Louis de Gruuthuse, patron of the *Forteresse de la foy* in the La Vallière collection. Between them, De Bure and Van Praet produced a first-class sale catalogue, almost certainly up to that point the best ever written, and it was greatly admired. Rive must have been furious, and it is no surprise that in the *Chasse aux bibliographes*, five years later, he reserved a special place in Hades for the two cataloguers with Judas Iscariot.

This first part of the Duc de La Vallière's library was dispersed between 12 January and 6 May 1784. The sales were very well attended, even attracting buyers from England. The total realized was 464,677 *livres* and 8 *sous*, with the top price of 14,510 *livres* for the *Guirlande de Julie*. The Bibliothèque royale in Paris bought 210 manuscripts, including the Rohan Hours (1850 *livres*) and the Bedford Breviary (5000 *livres*). The second portion of the duke's library, some 40,000 volumes but of lesser importance, was catalogued for sale by Jean-Luc Nyon in 1784 but was acquired instead in its entirety by the Marquis de Paulmy and resold in 1785 to the Comte d'Artois, brother of Louis XVI, from whom it was sequestered at the Revolution and is now in the Bibliothèque de l'Arsenal. The Duchesse de Châtillon survived the horrors and lived until 1812.

In the meantime, Rive was once again unemployed and almost wilfully antagonizing those who might have helped him. In July 1781 he was still trying to claim unpaid expenses from the estate of the Duc de La Vallière. By his calculation, he had already spent 26,000 *livres* on having the plates made for his promised *Essai sur l'art de vérifier l'âge des miniatures des manuscrits*. He finally issued the prospectus in June 1782. He offered eighty numbered and signed copies of the *Essai* at a special price for subscribers of 25 *louis d'or* each (600 *livres*). The address for inquiries was given as his lodgings in the Rue du Cherche-Midi, where he announced himself as available every morning until one o'clock. If all copies were sold, he would therefore have raised 48,000 *livres*. Orders trickled in from the king and other members of the court at Versailles, and from King Gustavus III of Sweden and collectors in Italy, Germany and England. With the self-destructive inevitability of classical tragedy, Rive then defaulted on delivering the book. Complaints were received on behalf of paid-up subscribers in 1787 and 1788. The Abbé prevaricated

Julius Caesar imagined in a late medieval bookshop, traced from the La Vallière manuscript of Jean Du Quesne's translation of Caesar, printed and hand-coloured for Rive's essay on identifying manuscripts, *c.*1782.

and pleaded ill-health, but he must have known that the La Vallière manuscripts were lost to him and that he had no heart to continue. Eventually he compromised and sets of the plates were issued on their own as bibliophilic luxuries at 400 *livres* each, supplemented by printed sheets of short descriptions. They are still valuable and collectable items. The most luxurious copy of all, printed on vellum, belonged to Marie Antoinette.

Throughout the 1780s, Rive became increasingly bitter and disillusioned, especially against fate and the untrustworthiness of aristocracy. In 1781 he printed his entry for a competition organized by the Académie

Française for a poem celebrating the royal abolition of serfdom in France in 1779, but his submitted verses are really a rant against tyranny and the kings of France; he did not win the prize. His one remaining friend, Joseph David, died in 1784. Rive suffered a stroke in August 1786 which left him paralysed on his right-hand side. This is doubtless why his late portrait shows him looking out obliquely over his left shoulder. In October that year he was fortunate to be invited by the archbishop of Aix, as administrator of Provence, to take charge of the vast library of the Marquis de Méjanes (1729–86), which had been bequeathed to the city of Aix-en-Provence. A contract was agreed in December and Rive gave notice on the apartment in the Rue du Cherche-Midi and began packing up his own reference library. On his way south, he inevitably visited the second-hand bookshops in Avignon, where he found for sale one of the books from the Méjanes library which he was due to be curating. Within months he was quarrelling with the municipality of Aix over his expenses and not being given sufficient authority and deference on arrival. He went to complain to the archbishop and was made to wait for an hour and a quarter. He tells all this (and much more) in the *Chasse aux bibliographes*.

In 1789 the Abbé Rive joined in the early stages of the French Revolution. He published intemperate pamphlets such as *Ode sur la liberté naturelle et politique* and another subtitled *Lettres . . . écrites contre les consuls d'Aix et procureurs du pays de Provence*, both in 1789. One of his reported harangues was against aristocratic hunting rights. He took part in a riot in Aix in 1790 which resulted in the death of a prominent lawyer; Rive himself was indirectly implicated in his murder and found it expedient to escape to Marseilles. Here he set up a local branch of the radical *Frères anti-politiques*, for whom he became principal spokesman, turning also against Christianity. However, shortly before the Revolution evolved into the Terror, Rive suffered a second stroke and died on 20 October 1791, far from home and on the run. His new politics did not prevent his burial in the cemetery of the church of Notre-Dame-des-Accoules in Marseilles.

The Abbé's immediate heir was his younger brother André-Simon Rive, who had continued their father's business as a goldsmith in Apt and had married a local woman. They had taken on her nephew Joseph-Elzéar Morénas (1776–1830) to learn the trade, but he had never settled and eventually became an orientalist and explorer. When André-Simon

Rive died soon afterwards in 1794, the late Abbé's papers passed to the young Morénas. There is an engaging account of him by the Reverend Thomas Frognall Dibdin (1776–1847), the nearest British equivalent to Rive in his limitless enthusiasm for rare books and his uninhibited prolixity in print, although he was an infinitely more clubbable man. Dibdin made a tour of France in 1818 and took the opportunity to call on Morénas, who had moved to Paris in 1797. He lived up two flights of stairs in the Rue du Vieux Colombier, near Saint-Sulpice, coincidentally only a street or two away from Rive's former lodgings in the Rue du Cherche-Midi. Morénas was preparing for another voyage to Senegal but welcomed Dibdin courteously. Above his fireplace was a pencil drawing of the Abbé, which Dibdin arranged to have copied and is now the basis of all subsequent portraits. Morénas, as Dibdin described his apartment,

> was surrounded by *trunks*, in which were deposited the literary remains of his uncle. In other words, these remains consisted of innumerable *cards*, closely packed, upon which the Abbé had written all his memoranda ... In one trunk, were about *six thousand* notices of MSS. of all ages; and of editions in the fifteenth century. In another trunk were wedged about *twelve thousand* descriptions of books in all languages, except those in French and Italian ... In a third trunk was a bundle of papers relating to the *History of the Troubadours*; in a fourth, was a collection of memoranda and literary sketches ... and pieces exclusively bibliographical ...

and much more. These were the papers removed in anger by Rive from the Hôtel de la Vallière in November 1780, and which were regrettably unavailable to De Bure and Van Praet when they were cataloguing the duke's library in 1781. They are likely to have been Rive's own trunks, packed up and moved on as the Abbé retreated first to Aix and then to Marseilles. Morénas had published a summary account of the archive probably in 1817, believing it to be very valuable. He offered it for 6000 francs to Dibdin, who replied tactfully that such a figure was beyond his resources. Eventually most of the papers passed in 1833 to the Bibliothèque royale (now nationale), including the tracings for the luxury plates, and the residue in 1837 to the municipal library in Carpentras.

The Abbé's huge and bulky reference collection was sold almost immediately after his death to the bookseller Denis Chauffard and the auctioneer Nicolas-Étienne Colomby, both of Marseilles. The Rive family were probably glad to get it cleared away, believing that the value lay in the Abbé's notes and file cards. A sale took place in Marseilles on 6 March 1793, comprising just over 1,500 lots. Although there were a few incunabula, it was primarily a scholarly library, not an antiquarian one. The oldest of several manuscripts owned by Rive was a copy of Justinus of 1527, and the most curious was a modern handmade facsimile on vellum of the blockbook *Speculum Humanae Salvationis* in the French royal library, said to have taken the copyist Lesclapart a year and a half to execute and to have been valued by Rive at 700–800 *livres*. The library covered all the subjects of the general knowledge which Rive had called on in his research and had cited in his endless footnotes. There were his working copies of familiar texts such as his volume of Le Long's *Bibliotheca Sacra*, castigated by him in the *Chasse aux bibliographes* for its supposedly misleading account of the *Bible historiale* of Charles V, and the catalogues of the Hoym and de Selle sales, for example, which Rive had used to trace back the provenance of the Breviary of René de Lorraine. A few contained additional information by Rive on the flyleaves, such as that a seventeenth-century book on church law had belonged to Gaignat himself, or that his copy of Godart de Beauchamps, *Recherches sur les théatres de France*, Paris, 1735, had been given to him as a birthday present by the Duc de La Vallière and was (he said) the only book he ever received from the duke. The really astonishing item was lot 4. It was described quite briefly as being an early printed two-volume Latin Bible of unknown date or place of publication, missing several leaves at the front. That book was a Gutenberg Bible. I do know, believe me, that this is not a manuscript, but it was the nearest imitation achievable when it was typeset by Johann Gutenberg and his assistants in Mainz in the early to mid-1450s. With the reader's indulgence, then, let this be our final example of a medieval book in the life of the Abbé Rive.

The exact status of a Gutenberg Bible was equivocal in the eighteenth century, but it was already one of several closely contested and iconic claimants to be the earliest book in printed type, and it had an undisputed value. A copy (not this one) had been sold in Lille in 1765 for 2025 *livres*. Gaignat had owned one too, which made 2100 *livres* in his sale in 1769, but Rive noted in the margin of his catalogue that Gaignat had paid 2600 *livres* for it plus at least 120 for its rebinding in red morocco.

It is a shock to find a giant of such stupendous significance almost unnoticed in the clearance of reference books of a supposedly threadbare bibliographer. It is not known where Rive had obtained it. It would be ungallant to suggest that a man of the Church might have stolen it, but this is a possibility. There was a rumour so widely whispered that Morénas was obliged to deny indignantly in 1817 that Rive had sometimes enriched his own collection with rare books actually bought for the Duc de La Vallière. Rive secured for the duke examples of most of the earliest monuments of printing from Mainz and elsewhere, and so it is odd that no Gutenberg Bible was found there when De Bure sorted and catalogued the collection in 1781. There might have been some reason (such as already owning one) why they were not competitors for the Gaignat copy, either in the auction of 1769 or when it was back on the market in Paris probably in 1776; nor was it a book unknown to the Duc de La Vallière, for he had been with Rive in 1770 to look at the most famous of all copies of the Gutenberg Bible in the Bibliothèque Mazarine.

One could imagine various possibilities. The Abbé Rive might have bought it privately for La Vallière and told him, as he would, never having sense to keep quiet, that it was missing four leaves at the front, in which case the duke might simply have rejected it, but perhaps it was already paid for and unreturnable. Maybe La Vallière graciously told Rive one day that he could choose any item he liked from the shelves after his death, if he should die first. That is possible, and this might well be a book Rive would have chosen. Situations like that do occur and are undocumented but never overlooked by the beneficiary. Conceivably, when Rive was peremptorily dismissed by the Duchesse de Châtillon in

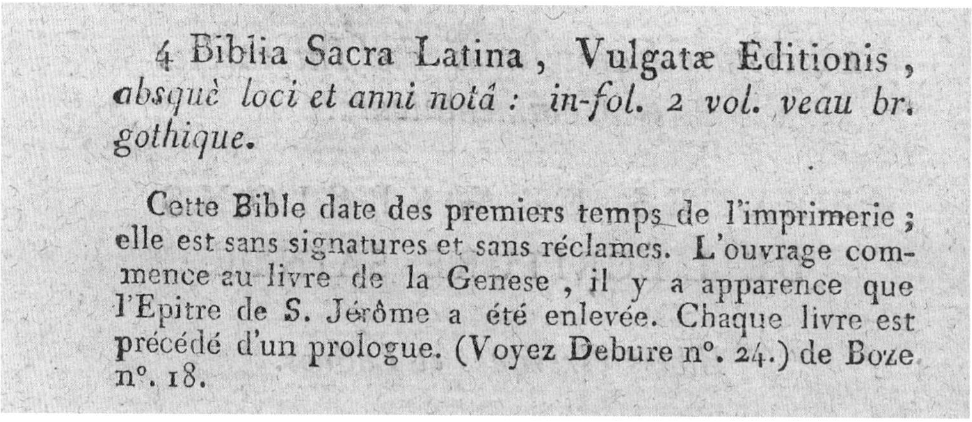
4 Biblia Sacra Latina, Vulgatæ Editionis, *absquè loci et anni notâ : in-fol. 2 vol. veau br. gothique.*

Cette Bible date des premiers temps de l'imprimerie ; elle est sans signatures et sans réclames. L'ouvrage commence au livre de la Genese, il y a apparence que l'Epitre de S. Jérôme a été enlevée. Chaque livre est précédé d'un prologue. (Voyez Debure n°. 24.) de Boze n°. 18.

The entry in Rive's posthumous sale, Marseilles, 1793, for an unrecognized copy of the Gutenberg Bible.

1780, he felt justified in squaring his offended sensibilities and outstanding expenses by a little creative conjuring. I regret that this is plausible too. It is curious that in his *Chasse aux bibliographes*, in 1789, Rive lists six copies of the Gutenberg Bible known to him but not the one in his own possession. It is almost inconceivable that it was bought by him after that date, and so it must have been a deliberate decision not to draw unnecessary attention in the *Chasse* to the copy he already owned.

As lot 4 in Rive's sale in 1793, his Gutenberg Bible sold for a mere 60 francs, fractionally over 60 *livres* in the pre-Revolutionary currency. This must rank among the missed investment opportunities of history, like the sale of Manhattan for a handful of beads in 1626 or the 10 per cent share in the Apple Computer Company cashed in by its co-founder for $800 in 1976. Today, a substantially complete Gutenberg Bible would probably be worth significantly more than the modern value of every one of the medieval manuscripts of the Duc de La Vallière's library put together. Rive's copy was bought at the auction by the bookselling family of David, the dynasty of his oldest friend. It passed eventually to the typographer Firmin-Didot (1764–1836), who had the missing leaves replaced in facsimile, a deception not noticed for a hundred years, and it was sent to London in 1816. By 1819 it was owned by George Hibbert (1757–1837), who sold it at auction in 1829 for £215 to John Wilks (*c.* 1765–1854), who in turn resold it at Sotheby's in 1847 for £500 to the American dealer George Palmer Putnam, on behalf of his client James Lenox (1800–1880), of New York. The underbidder at that auction was Sir Thomas Phillipps, manuscript collector, two years after his levée with Queen Victoria. Like me, Phillipps regarded a Gutenberg Bible as an honorary manuscript. In June 1847 the Bible was taken to America, the first copy to cross the Atlantic. Phillipps expressed a parting prayer that "it may not be swallowed up by the Deep Sea". It is now part of the magnificent Lenox bequest to the New York Public Library, a former friend and companion of the Abbé Rive in good company in the Land of Liberty.

CHAPTER EIGHT

The Librarian: Sir Frederic Madden

Loving your enemies is easy; it is your colleagues who are the problem. The history of the library of the British Museum is famous for the antagonism of two very different members of the staff, Antonio Panizzi (1797–1879), head of printed books, and Sir Frederic Madden (1801–73), keeper of manuscripts. They were both figures of strong personality and ambition. Madden continually denounced Panizzi as being peasant-born, foreign, scheming, untruthful, Roman Catholic, overweight, dishevelled, and a failed liberal activist who was said to have been at one time condemned to death in Italy for sedition. Panizzi considered Madden to be high-handed, dapper, Tory, xenophobic, snobbish, quick-tempered, easily offended and staggeringly uncooperative. All these statements were more or less true, exacerbated by Victorian prejudices of class and nationalism. Each of the two men, however, in his own way, was of exceptional and still-enduring importance in creating one of the outstanding public enterprises of the nineteenth century.

As we saw in Chapter 5, the Museum had been set up in 1753, coinciding with the urgent problem of the fire-ravaged Cotton manuscripts with opportunities to acquire on favourable terms the collection of books and artefacts assembled by Sir Hans Sloane and the Harleian manuscripts gathered by the earls of Oxford. The new British Museum originally occupied Montagu House, which was gradually demolished during the construction of the present building on the same site, completed in 1852. It was primarily a national library, with supplementary curiosities. There were initially only three departments, Manuscripts (which then included coins and drawings), Printed Books, and what was called Natural and

LEFT: Sir Frederic Madden (1801–73), portrait by William Drummond, 1837.

Artificial Productions, which encompassed stuffed animals, minerals and antiquities. The overall head of the institution, the person known today as the director, was called the Principal Librarian. He was responsible to a board of three main Trustees, comprising the Archbishop of Canterbury in the chair, the Lord Chancellor and the Speaker of the House of Commons, assisted by others including the Lord High Admiral, the Chancellor of the Exchequer, the Lord Chief Justice and a tableful of dukes, like figures from a comic opera. Through no great effort on the part of the Museum employees, the collections were augmented by the addition of the Old Royal Library (1757), the manuscripts of Lord Lansdowne (1805), the classical books of the Reverend Charles Burney (1818), and other purchases and bequests. Visitors were gently discouraged. It was a still tranquil resource for antiquarian gentlemen, schooled in Latin and Greek.

Some vision of this happy scholarly Arcadia impressed itself on the young Frederic Madden, who was born in Portsmouth on the English south coast on 16 February 1801. He came from a military family, originally of Irish ancestry. His father was a captain in the navy and his mother the daughter of a minor canon of Rochester Cathedral. Frederic was the eleventh of thirteen children, not all of whom survived to adulthood. In investigating his life, we have the most extraordinary resource. He kept an extremely detailed journal daily for fifty-four years, almost 18,000 pages, perhaps about 4,000,000 words in total, now in the Bodleian Library in Oxford. It is still unpublished, although it has been available for research since 1920 and is not unknown. Its scale is daunting, and the handwriting is not always easy. I cannot quite say that I have read every word, but I have looked at every page and I have listened in close detail to Madden's intimate thoughts and aspirations and opinions day by day from shortly before his eighteenth birthday until he became a shuffling retiree and grandfather. Often he wrote at great length and very personally, with startling lack of inhibition. It is like interviewing him every day throughout his career. He rants and he confides and he meticulously documents his antiquarian pursuits and adventures. His frequent outrage is expressed by underlinings and multiple exclamation marks, characteristic of the nineteenth century. I am now privy to things about Madden that probably even his wife did not know, or at least I hope not (we will touch on some of these). The journals also contain many thousands of references to identifiable medieval manuscripts and to all the manuscript scholars and collectors of his age, with the triumphs and frustrations of a life in the British Museum at its most formative and exhilarating period.

It is a strange experience to share the daily reflections of a man given to outpourings of self-doubt and self-pity and desperate worries about his own future, because at every moment of his distress I already know what will happen to him and he does not. He will take a temporary position at the British Museum in 1826, join the Department of Manuscripts in 1828 and become Keeper in 1837. I know which major manuscripts he will acquire for the British Museum and which he will fight for and lose. In 1829 he will marry Mary Hayton, his childhood sweetheart from Portsmouth, but she will die the following year. He will eventually remarry in 1837 and will have adored but unsatisfactory children, and he will finally retire in 1866 and his hated rival in the Museum will outlive him. Until it comes to pass, Madden knows none of this.

In 1872 he had several photographs made of his parents' old house at 31 St Thomas Street in Portsmouth. He had one framed and pasted another into his journal, "the House in which I was born, and where I passed the first twenty-three years of my life". St Thomas Street runs down towards the harbour in the old town, parallel to the High Street and within walking distance of the naval dockyards and (now) HMS *Victory* to the north. It was a grand eighteenth-century brick house with bow front and pillared portico opening onto the street, bought in 1800, just before Frederic Madden's birth. His bedroom was on the top floor, second window from the left, between the nursery and the breakfast room. The house had been owned by William Sloane, brother of Sir Hans, and if this was known to the Maddens, it is likely that allusion to the British Museum was part of family conversation.

Frederic was not sent to university, which his father considered unnecessary and expensive, and the journals open in 1819 during several years of autodidacticism at home, from which he longed to escape. He fancied himself as a would-be philosopher and intellectual. In that little bedroom he wrote pretentious and untutored essays into his journal on antiquarian or religious subjects, as teenagers do, and he practised Greek and Latin and taught himself Hebrew and Italian. In adulthood he wrote and read French fluently but seems not to have spoken it. He collected Roman coins and detached seals with as much passion as a schoolboy income allowed, deciphering their inscriptions and expanding the many

The house in Portsmouth where Madden spent his childhood, a photograph of 1872 annotated by him.

Latin abbreviations in accordance with likely meaning, a useful training for palaeography. On 6 March 1819 he was given two Hebrew manuscript phylacteries on parchment from a Jewish estate, probably that of Dr Samuel Eleazer Pyke, who died in Portsmouth in 1818. Madden transcribed them carefully and researched their use from the Old Testament. In April that year a visitor showed Madden his first medieval Latin manuscript: "a curious old original piece of music on parchment, written in the Gregorian manner & illuminated . . . It is part of an old monkish chant taken from one of their missals." He copied its fragmentary words of text into his journal.

Madden had a serious and like-minded young friend in Portsmouth, Lake Allen, with whom he visited old churches and read parish registers, role-playing lives as local antiquaries. They wrote several articles together in 1822, including one on the history of chess in the thirteenth century, and they had them published in the *New Monthly Magazine*, Madden's first appearances in print. Allen was articled to a local solicitor with an office in London, to which he was transferred, leaving his companion alone with his unsympathetic parents. "My father has treated me with great injustice in not sending me to College, or at least making some attempt to secure me a profession." In desperation, Madden consulted a family friend, who suggested the law, the Church, "or to be a *Land-Surveyor* or *Auctioneer*!!" (That does not seem too dreadful to me.) Allen's letters from London reported that he had also picked up part-time work doing transcriptions of medieval historical records for Henry Petrie, Keeper of Records in the Tower of London. "He tells me he has access to the MSS at the British Museum", Madden wrote, beside himself with envy; "How happy he will be, & how I hope he will take every advantage of it." Madden revelled in receiving extracts from medieval romances and other texts copied by Allen from manuscripts in the Cotton collection, although at first Madden failed to grasp the unusual use of emperors' names in their shelfmarks. On a visit back to Portsmouth, Allen lent him a fifteenth-century manuscript he had acquired in the metropolis, a defective and unimportant volume of the Statutes of England, which Madden collated patiently at home. Eventually, he could bear it no longer. He exclaimed on 13 June 1823: "Oh God! *when will my turn arrive?*"

In December that year his uncle invited him for a visit to London. It seems odd now that a young man of twenty-three had never travelled so far, a distance of some seventy miles, but it was a full day's journey on the 'Regulator' coach up from Portsmouth, arriving at 6.15 at the White Horse Cellar in Piccadilly, where he was met by his older brother, Henry. On the Monday morning he presented himself at the British Museum in Great Russell Street to apply for a reader's ticket, which took twenty-four hours and still survives, a thick card about 4¼ by 3 inches, admitting "Frederick Madden, Esq." to the Reading Room for six months from 8 December 1823. Between relentless sight-seeing and theatre attendance, eyes transfixed by the sight of semi-naked dancing girls, Madden sat breathlessly in the old reading-room of the Museum

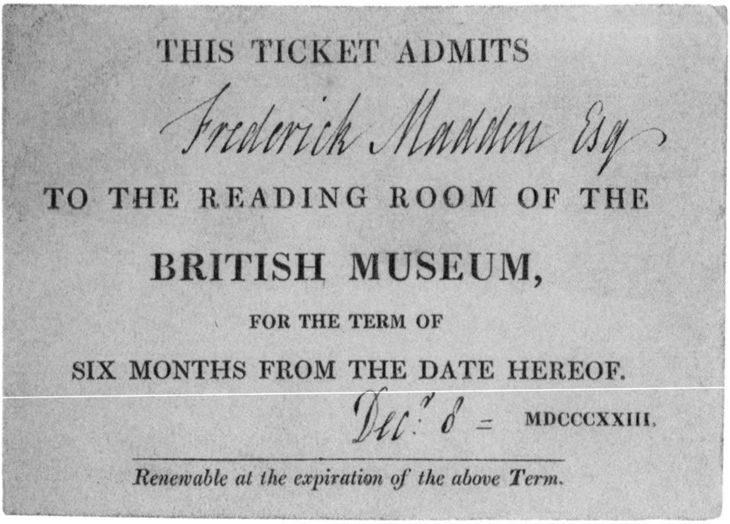
THIS TICKET ADMITS
Frederick Madden Esq
TO THE READING ROOM OF THE
BRITISH MUSEUM,
FOR THE TERM OF
SIX MONTHS FROM THE DATE HEREOF.
Decr. 8 = MDCCCXXIII.
Renewable at the expiration of the above Term.

Madden's first ticket for the British Museum reading room, 1823.

feasting on texts in Middle English and Latin from the Cotton and Harleian collections. From that moment he knew where he wanted to spend his life. Allen was unhelpful, fearing a trespass onto his own patch. However, Madden was sensibly urged by his brother to apply to Petrie too to copy manuscripts, which he then did without telling his friend. He delayed his departure from London to meet Petrie, who showed him a gothic manuscript in the Sloane Room at the Museum and asked him to read it, which Madden managed easily. He was told that there might be a vacancy in the New Year.

The formal interview took place in the British Museum on 12 March 1824. Madden made a sketch of the event, showing himself, just past his twenty-fourth birthday and wearing his best suit, approaching Henry Ellis, then Keeper of Manuscripts, and Petrie, standing legs astride and hands in pockets. Ellis (1777–1869) eventually became a major figure in Madden's professional career. He was stout and jovial, sometimes called 'Pickwickian' (he knew Dickens and might even have been the actual model), but Madden never really trusted him, for his loyalties blew this way and that. Petrie (1768–1842) was evidently ineffectual and likeable; he lived in Stockwell. He had the idea of publishing collections of original sources of British medieval history, resembling the then new *Monumenta Germaniae Historica* launched in Hanover in 1819. Petrie's enterprise produced only one volume (1848), and its mission was eventually taken

Madden's own sketch of his interview at the British Museum with Henry Ellis and Henry Petrie, 12 March 1824.

over by the better-organized 'Rolls Series'. Madden's job was to copy out texts chosen for the printer. He would be paid a few pence a page, depending on size, hardly enough to live on, but he sensibly took it.

Madden, as he appears in his drawing, was thin and of upright military bearing. His passport for a visit to Paris in 1846, attached in the journal for that year, describes him as having blue eyes and being 1 metre 79 cm in height, just under 5 foot 9 inches, not especially tall. He had curly black hair, and mutton-chop sideburns which became ever more opulent and whiter as he grew into his middle age and the hair of his head receded. Others described him as distinctly good-looking.

For several years Madden lived in lodgings, making little money but sitting daily among the manuscript researchers who peopled the reading-room of the British Museum. In time he secured some small work cataloguing in the printed-book department, while still transcribing Cotton manuscripts for Petrie. In conversations among colleagues it became clear to him that he lacked the qualifications others had, and he set about remedying this. First, he visited Oxford. Petrie introduced him to Philip Bliss (1787–1857), the most delightful of Oxford antiquaries and a book collector of boundless enthusiasm. He became a kind friend for many years. At their first meeting Bliss showed Madden his portfolios of medieval manuscript leaves extracted from reuse in strengthening early bookbindings and given to Bliss by Oxford binders in exchange for beer. His young visitor offered earnest identifications, not all of them accurate. With the help of Bliss, Madden enrolled as an undergraduate at Magdalen Hall in July 1825, naively expecting to accomplish a degree part-time from London. In 1831 he eventually abandoned this as unrealistic, declaring examinations a waste of time and no test of ability.

In the meantime, Madden agreed to take on a manuscript project which promised a serious publication with aristocratic endorsement, both of which might help advance his prospects. It is outlined in his journal in October 1825. There was – and still is – a magnificent private collection of almost 800 illuminated manuscripts at Holkham Hall near Wells-next-the-Sea in Norfolk, many of them collected in Italy by Thomas Coke (1697–1759). The wish of Coke's descendants to print a catalogue of them has been an ongoing enterprise since the eighteenth century and even now is not yet brought to conclusion. One volume was finally published in 2015 and many more are hoped for, although not necessarily expected in our lifetimes. The first in a very long line of cataloguers drowning in the immensity of the task was William Roscoe (1753–1831), who began in 1814 and by the 1820s had become overwhelmed. Roscoe's friend Francis Palgrave had met Madden in the Museum and suggested that this might be an ideal occupation for the industrious young man, offering an honorarium of several hundred pounds and his name on the title-page. Madden was delighted and plans were made. In March 1826 he travelled up to Holkham for the first time, getting up at 5 a.m. to catch the coach, which reached the Lion Inn in Fakenham late that same night. Finding there was no coach on to Wells for three days, Madden extravagantly took a chaise and arrived at Holkham in a style he came to appreciate. The Coke family treated him as a guest rather than as an employee. "Of the MSS themselves it is impossible to speak too highly. They are *superb*, & valuable beyond any estimate – equal to most of those at the Brit. Mus^{m}. or Oxford." He set to work expanding the dilettante work of Roscoe into a catalogue of immense detail.

When they were first brought to Holkham, the manuscripts had been stored out of sight in a series of attic rooms, but by the early nineteenth century books were becoming part of a fashionable interior, and the collection was moved in about 1816 down into what had been Thomas Coke's bedroom, now called the Manuscript Library, an anteroom to the earlier Long Library, still used as a family drawing room. The manuscripts today are exactly where they were when Madden began work in 1826, the only addition to the room being an aluminium ladder now brought out for reaching the highest shelves.

Madden was back at Holkham the following year. This time his fellow guest was Coke's nineteen-year-old granddaughter Jane Digby, by then the wife of Lord Ellenborough. Madden is not the only witness to describe her as the most beautiful woman in the world. His betrothed in Portsmouth and even the Holkham manuscripts were forgotten as they spent their days in enchanted idleness together. After cards one night, "Lady E. lingered behind the rest of the party, and at midnight I escorted her to her room – Fool that I was! I will not add what passed. Gracious God! was there ever such fortune!" Jane Digby's subsequent life was legendary. Following the most famous divorce of her generation (1830), she married or had long affairs (and often children) with a cousin, a German prince, an indulgent baron, the king of Bavaria, a Greek count, a brigand who became governor of Albania, and a Bedouin guide, by

Jane Digby, Lady Ellenborough, portrait miniature by William Charles Ross.

The Manuscript Library at Holkham Hall: the eight volumes of Madden's handwritten catalogue are visible on the middle shelf to the right of the door into the Long Library.

way of intimate flirtations with Honoré de Balzac, the king of Greece, and the emperor of Brazil, before finally marrying a nomadic sheikh half her age and dying in the desert in Damascus. In 1858, Madden confided to his journal a memory of that night, wondering whatever became of her. Gracious God again! He must have been the only person in Europe who did not know.

Madden's eventual and exhaustive Holkham catalogue in eight leather-bound handwritten volumes was accepted with grace by the Coke family, who deemed it unreadable and not quite what was intended, and it remains unpublished in the Manuscript Library at Holkham. It is now kept in case C, shelf 3, to the right of the door into the drawing room. Madden's disappointment was overtaken by the news that Henry Ellis had been elevated to Principal Librarian in the British Museum, allowing the promotion of his deputy, Josiah Forshall, to the Keepership of Manuscripts, which in turn created a vacancy for a new Assistant Keeper. With the important support now of Thomas Coke of Holkham, later to become earl of Leicester, Madden applied and was duly appointed on 2 February 1828. "How excellent a termination! My heart was as light as a feather", he wrote later that day, and he went off immediately to the auctioneer Evans to view manuscripts to be sold the following Tuesday. With the new prospect of an income, he even bought two himself, "very cheap". Lady Ellenborough notwithstanding, he finally married Mary Hayton in April 1829, and moved with the new Mrs Frederic Madden into the first of his staff apartments on the Museum premises, where he lived until retirement.

One aspect of working for a national museum was the easy intercourse with private collectors. They sought information and advice; the Museum hoped for eventual bequests. Names that are well-known to historians of manuscripts today, either as shelfmarks in libraries or as consignors of watershed auctions, became very real people in Madden's life, endeared to him by his evident manners and good accent and enthusiasm for manuscripts. Probably the most important of these over many years was Sir Thomas Phillipps (1792–1872), who appeared briefly in the previous chapter, presenting a manuscript to Queen Victoria; we will visit him at home in the next. Madden first encountered a reference to him only four days after his appointment in the Museum, writing it as "Philips". (The unusual spelling of the surname, with two pairs of double letters, can be used as a quick test when judging the merits of any book on manuscripts today: if an author misspells 'Phillipps' or 'minuscule' – also commonly wrong – the work is probably not professional; everyone is forgiven once, like Madden, but never again.) By the autumn, Phillipps was inviting Madden to dinner when in London and sharing possible plans for the future of his vast collection, hinting that the Museum might be the beneficiary. Phillipps was quite simply the most

INRI
Centurio
Ysaias

voracious and obsessive hoarder of manuscripts ever recorded, cramming Middle Hill, his house in Worcestershire, with many tens of thousands of manuscripts, still buying relentlessly and indiscriminately throughout the whole of the working life of Madden, who was both exhilarated and exasperated by the man. "We all say he must be *mad*", wrote Madden in November 1828, not untinged with a certain admiration. There is much more on Phillipps to come.

Another collector Madden met very early on was William Young Ottley (1771–1836). He had inherited £10,000 at the age of four, on the death of his father, who had sugar plantations in the West Indies, and (a bit like William Gray in the 1440s) he had meandered as a wealthy young man through Italy. He bought up Old Master pictures and illuminated initials cut from manuscripts, especially after the Napoleonic closure of Italian monasteries, judging them as separate works of art in their own right; he was one of the earliest connoisseurs of *quattrocento* art. Ottley lived in Devonshire Street, between Portland Place and Marylebone. Madden recalled him as a notable taker of snuff. His first visit to Ottley's house was in February 1829. "Amused myself all aftern. & evening by looking over his magnificent collection of Illuminations, taken chiefly from the Church Books of the Vatican, and other Italian Churches. As a whole it is certainly *unique*." For years afterwards, Madden could never forget a magnificent late thirteenth-century French Psalter he saw there. "I thought it the most beautiful book of the period I had ever seen", and he always regretted not having the courage to try to secure it at once for the Museum. Some time after Ottley's death, he recognized the manuscript again in the possession of Robert Holford, art collector and "stingy old curmudgeon", whose fortune had been made by supplying fresh water to London. Holford's descendants sold it in 1927 to J. Pierpont Morgan. It is now in New York, known as the Psalter-Hours of Yolande of Soissons.

In 1829, Madden did not yet have a sufficient eye for artistic quality, and he knew it. He was invited that year to see the famous Bedford Book of Hours, or 'Bedford Missal' as it was still called, then in the possession of John Milner. It was illuminated in the royal circle in Paris probably soon after the English conquest at Agincourt and upgraded around 1423

LEFT: The Psalter-Hours of Yolande of Soissons, Amiens, late thirteenth century, which so impressed Madden when he saw it in the collection of William Young Ottley.

for John, duke of Bedford, regent of France, whose wife later gave it to their nephew the young Henry VI. Madden took Ottley with him to tutor him gently on the book's illumination, which did not disappoint. The artist is now known as the Bedford Master, who also executed the duke's Salisbury Breviary in Paris (acquired by the Abbé Rive for the Duc de La Vallière and included in his *Essai*). "I covet this MS for the Museum exceedingly", wrote Madden. In 1833 he took Phillipps to look at it too, already dreaming of a possible national benefactor.

A third collector who was hospitable to Madden in the early days was Francis Douce (1757–1834; his name rhymes with 'mouse', not 'moose'). He had worked in the Museum, as indeed had Ottley for a while, but in 1823 had inherited £50,000 from the sculptor Joseph Nollekens, and for a decade indulged himself buying the very finest illuminated manuscripts on the market, which he preferred to working. Douce was a good gossip. He lived in Upper Gower Street and then Charlotte Street, both within easy walking distance from the Museum. Madden confided into his sympathetic ear his frustrations with Museum bureaucracy. Like many book collectors, Douce was secretive, showing his treasures to visitors only sparingly, one day bringing out a thirteenth-century Bestiary, and on another a manuscript of the miracles of the Virgin made for Philip of Burgundy, and on a third occasion two volumes of the *Grail* romance, formerly owned by the Duc de La Vallière. When he died, Madden was disappointed not to receive a personal legacy. He was even more shocked that Douce bequeathed his manuscripts to the Bodleian Library in Oxford. "I wish to God he had left his MSS to the Museum – for in leaving them to the Bodleian he consigns them to neglect and oblivion! Douce certainly has not behaved to me as I had reason to believe he would from our extreme literary intimacy, & his often repeated voluntary expressions of regard and respect. Fate is clearly against me!"

The cruelty of Fate becomes a theme which engulfs Madden's journal following the sudden death of his wife in childbirth in February 1830; their baby son survived for only a few days and died too. Madden's outpourings of grief and despair are long and unrestrained. The manuscripts fraternity rallied round. 22 April: "Rain. Sir T. Phillipps and Mr Douce called, & were very kind to me. But of what avail is kindness now?" Mary Madden was buried in St George's Church, Bloomsbury, two blocks south of the Museum. The inconsolable widower erected a touching marble monument, which is still there on the north wall of an alcove to the left of the altar, behind the pulpit. For a time, Madden sought out affairs and couplings with ladies of the night and others, described with a candour and a detail which most diarists would never commit to writing. He lived rather more expensively than his income allowed. One extravagance was a private horse and cab (65 and 60 guineas respectively), which he damaged within a week by driving it into a gate in Belgrave Square.

Within a year or so, Madden was beginning to weigh the options for remarriage, especially if it could also help him financially. He drew up ever-changing lists of possibly available candidates in numerical order, carefully noting their social connections and the likely size of their fortunes. He looked first among those who might inherit manuscripts. 10 February 1832: "Called on the Ottleys, and drank tea with them. Miss O is certainly a clever lively girl, but she has not a shilling . . . She would do excellently for a mistress, but not for *my* wife. Yet the O's are continually wanting me to propose to her. Of the two, I would decidedly choose Anna T." This referred to the daughter of Dawson Turner (1775–1858), Norfolk antiquary and major collector of autographs, who had been involved in the Holkham project, but Anna was then also eliminated for her tiresomely wholesome lifestyle and unreasonably early bedtimes. Sir Thomas Phillipps several times suggested the suitability of his own daughter Henrietta.

In 1831, Antonio Panizzi joined the Museum and was rapidly seen as an ascendant star. He was ambitious and was charming to those who mattered, soon anglicizing his first name to Anthony. Madden still had no paper qualifications (Panizzi had a doctorate in law) and he began to imagine the unassailable status among his colleagues and over Panizzi especially if he could acquire a knighthood. He calculated that a title would also further his hopes of an advantageous remarriage. "*If I should succeed*, it might enable me to choose a wife, who as plain Mrs M would not have me, or her papa would not, which is the same thing." He lobbied shamelessly among all his connections with a lack of subtlety that today seems extraordinary for a man of limited achievements in his early thirties. Philip Bliss, for instance, regretted that he could be of no help. There was a slightly back-door way in, used by Henry Ellis and Francis Palgrave, who had both become knights of the Royal Guelphic Order in 1831, as Madden would have known. This was an order of chivalry established

Anthony Panizzi, portrait by George Frederic Watts, *c.*1847.

in England in 1815 by the fact that George III was also still king of Hanover in Germany. A Guelphic knight in Britain would be entitled to the initials 'K. H.' after his name but would not actually be addressed as 'Sir'. Through the help of Lord Spencer, a Trustee of the Museum and one of the leading book collectors, Madden received his membership of the order in 1832. Even as he was being formally invested by William IV at St James's Palace in March 1833, Madden was not quite sure whether he could now call himself 'Sir Frederic', but, on rising to his feet, it was indicated to him by the king that he had at that moment also been made a Knight Bachelor. This was fortunate, as the Guelphic Order passed abroad in 1837, when under Salic Law Queen Victoria did not inherit the kingdom of Hanover, but with a simultaneous British knighthood he remained Sir Frederic Madden for the rest of his life.

At the Museum there was still practically no interest in medieval antiquities, and Madden was almost the only member of staff who knew anything of the period. In 1831 he was host to two visits by Sir Walter Scott, whose novels were then transforming fashion towards the Middle Ages and who was an enthusiastic collector of artefacts himself. On the second occasion, while Scott was there, a dealer from Edinburgh named Forrest brought in some "very curious and ancient chess-men", for which he asked 100 guineas, later reduced to 80, and Madden and Scott together were the first medievalists ever to unpack and examine the squat and solemn little figures in walrus ivory which are now among the most famous Romanesque works of art in Britain. Throughout his life Madden had been interested in the history of chess and he was a keen player himself. His inquiries led eventually to information from the Presbyterian minister in Uig that the twelfth-century chessmen had been excavated on the Isle of Lewis in the Outer Hebrides. He subsequently wrote an article about them for *Archaeologia*.

In 1836, Madden also first published what is now called the Moutier-Grandval Bible, a ninth-century giant among illustrated manuscripts of the Latin Vulgate. It was in the possession of a Swiss dealer giving his name as Henry de Speyer Passavant, who called on Madden at the Museum on 29 February (1836 was a leap year), inviting him to see it in his lodgings in Regent Street. It is a stupendous volume of almost a thousand huge pages illuminated in Tours in France with a series of marvellous and complex full-page illustrations. It has an inscription suggesting it was presented by Alcuin to Charlemagne himself, which Madden failed to notice was spuriously inserted later over an erasure, a great embarrassment to him when this was pointed out by Forshall, his head of department. The owner wanted £6500 for the manuscript, and he showed letters from European experts and collectors suggesting that it was saleable for far more. Forshall orchestrated a masterly but very risky strategy of calling his bluff, even allowing Passavant to put it into auction, where not a single bid was received, and then buying it afterwards for the Museum for £750. "It is certainly a very desirable acquisition", wrote Madden, somewhat grudgingly when he was told about this afterwards.

The following year, 1837, Forshall announced his intention to resign as Keeper, although he retained a presence as secretary of the Trustees. After pouring out many pages of nail-biting apprehension, Madden was appointed in his place, securing an increase in salary which he considered enabled him to marry his modestly wealthy choice for his second wife, Emily Robinson, daughter of a Scottish lawyer. At the same moment, Panizzi was elevated to the Keepership of Printed Books. By the chance of the archbishop of Canterbury being absent from Lambeth at a weekend, Panizzi's new appointment was actually signed three days earlier than Madden's, allowing a hair-splitting margin of seniority, a technicality Panizzi never forgot and Madden never forgave.

OVERLEAF: The Moutier-Grandval Bible, Tours, second quarter of the ninth century, bought by the British Museum in 1836.

INCIPIT LIBER EXODUS

HAEC SUNT NOMINA FILIORŪ ISRAHEL QUI INGRESSI SUNT IN AEGYPTŪ CUM IACOB SINGULI CUM DOMIBUS SUIS INTROIERUNT. Cap. I.

Ruben. Symeon. leui. Iuda. Issachar. zabulon
et beniamin. dan et nepthalim. gad et aser.
Erant igitur omnes animae eorum quae egres
sae sunt de femore iacob. septuaginta quinque.
Ioseph autem in aegypto erat. Quo mortuo et
uniuersis fratrib; eius omniq; cognatione sua.
filii isrl creuerunt. et quasi germinantes multi
plicati sunt. ac roborati nimis impleuer terrā.
Surrexit interea rex nouus super aegyptum
qui ignorabat ioseph. et ait ad populum suum.
Ecce populus filiorum isrl multus et fortior
nobis ē. uenite sapienter opprimamus eum. ne
forte multiplicetur. Et si ingruerit contra nos
bellum. addatur inimicis nris. Expugnatisq;
nobis. egrediatur e terra. Praeposuit itaq; eis
magistros operum ut affligerent eos oneribus.
III Aedificaueruntq; urbes tabernaculorum pha
raoni phiton et ramesses. Quantoq; opprime
bantur. tanto magis multiplicabantur et cres
cebant. Oderantq; filios isrl aegyptii et affli
gebant illudentes eis. atq; ad amaritudinem
perducebant uitam eorum. operib; duris luti et
lateris omniq; famulatu quo in terrae operib; p̄
mebantur. Dixit autem rex aegypti obstetrici
b; hebraeorum. quarum una uocabatur sephra
altera phua. praecipiens eis. quando obstetri
cabitis hebraeas et partus tempus aduenerit.
si masculus fuerit interficite illum. si femina
reseruate. Timuerunt autem obstetrices dm̄
et non fecerunt iuxta p̄ceptum regis aegypti sed
conseruabant mares. Quib; ad se accersitis rex
ait. Quidnam ē hoc quod facere uoluistis. ut
pueros seruaretis. Quae responderunt. Non
sunt hebraeae sicut aegyptiae mulieres. Ipsae eni
obstetricandi habent scientiam. Priusquam ue
niamus ad eas pariunt. Bene ergo fecit ds obste
tricib; et creuit populus. Confor
tatusq; ē nimis. Et quia timuerant obstetrices
dm̄. aedificauit illis domos. Praecepit ergo pha
rao omni populo suo dicens. Quicquid masculini
sexus natum fuerit. in flumine proicite. Quicquid
feminei. reseruate.
II Egressus ē post haec uir de domo leui. accepta uxo Cap: 2.
re stirpis suae. quae concepit et peperit filium.
Et uidens eum elegantem. abscondit trib; mensib;
Cumq; iam celare non posset. sumpsit fiscellā
scirpeam. et liniuit eam bitumine ac pice. posuitq;
intus infantulum et exposuit eum in carecto ripae
fluminis stante procul sorore eius. et considerante
euentum rei. Ecce autem descendebat filia pha
raonis. ut lauaretur in flumine. et puellae eius
gradiebantur per crepidinem aluei. Quae cum
uidisset fiscellam in papyrione. misit unam e fa
mulis suis. Et allatam aperiens. cernensq; in ea
paruulum uagientem. miserta eius. ait. De infan
tib; hebraeorum ē hic. Cui soror pueri. Uis in
quit ut uadam. et uocem tibi hebraeam mulierem
quae nutrire possit infantulum. Respondit.
Uade. Perrexit puella. et uocauit matrem eius.
Ad quam locuta filia pharaonis. Accipe ait pue
rum istum et nutri mihi. ego tibi dabo mercedē
tuam. Suscepit mulier. et nutriuit puerum.
Adultumq; tradidit filiae pharaonis. Quem
illa adoptauit in locum filii. Uocauitq; nomen
eius moyses dicens. quia de aqua tuli eum.
III In dieb; illis postquam creuerat moyses. egressus ad
fratres suos. uidit afflictionem eorum. et uirū
aegyptium percutientem quendam de hebraeis
fratrib; suis. Cumq; circumspexisset huc atq; il
luc et nullum adeē uidisset. percussum aegyp
tium abscondit sabulo. Et egressus die altero.
conspexit duos hebraeos rixantes. Dixitq; ei qui
faciebat iniuriam. Quare percutis proximum
tuum. Qui respondit. Quis constituit te principē
et iudicem super nos. Num occidere tu me uis. sicut
occidisti heri aegyptium. Timuit moyses et ait.
Quomodo palam factum ē uerbum istud. Audiuit
q; pharao sermonem hunc. et quaerebat occide
re moysen. Qui fugiens de conspectu eius. mora
tus ē in terra madian. et sedit iuxta puteum.
Erant sacerdoti madian septem filiae. quae ue
nerunt ad hauriendam aquam. Et impletis

The two new rival keepers sparred implacably over the allocation of space in the new Museum building, access by manuscript staff to printed books, and the unilateral seizure of a room in the Manuscript Department for the marvellous Grenville library of printed rarities secured by Panizzi in 1846. They were intelligent men but both behaved badly, like spoilt children, each maintaining that his own field was more important. Panizzi enforced the Copyright Act, modified in 1842 to make delivery of all British publications compulsory, and he used agents to buy up books across the world, as no library had ever done before. Madden argued passionately that manuscripts alone are what determine the greatness of a national collection, for every item is unique.

Both their professional lives were dedicated to the unique concept of the British Museum, a name which even now seems to represent probity and establishment not quite matched by any other museum in the world, but they viewed it differently. Madden, who was from a military family, would have laid emphasis on its Britishness and what this meant for the nation's reputation and glory (which is partly why he was scornful of Panizzi, at a time when expressing superiority over foreigners was acceptably patriotic). He was old enough to remember Waterloo and probably Trafalgar. Panizzi would have considered the Museum to be primarily a civic and public responsibility, not royal or national (although it included noble bequests), but universal, with a focus on education, comprehensive learning and perpetual access. For very different reasons, both put acquisition at the core of their duties.

It is easy now to look on the important medieval manuscript repositories of Europe and to imagine that their treasures have always been there, which of course they have not. Many of the largest collections of the world, such as those of Munich, Paris and the Vatican, or indeed the British Museum in its first generation, were made up mostly from locally formed libraries subsumed *en bloc* by the happenstance of revolutions or thrust upon often unwilling curators by governmental command, and they tend to be weighted towards books of their own countries. The British Library (as it is now) is different. It has tens of thousands of manuscripts acquired individually, each offered and sifted item by item and selected on merit, more as American rare-book libraries are obliged to do. The result is far more wide-ranging than any other national library of the world, aiming to represent all literate cultures and all languages, evidence of a truly international outlook in Victorian England which is neither exclusive nor chauvinistic. The different schools of manuscript illumination are quite evenly balanced across all of European and Near Eastern art, even occasionally from Central America. Like the British Empire, it reached its widest outreach in the middle third of the nineteenth century. Sir Frederic Madden as Keeper became probably the most important public acquisitor of manuscripts in any country or period of history. In late volumes of his journal, especially when he felt he had not received enough credit, Madden enjoyed calculating, like a miser huddled over his ledgers, that he had added more than 30,000 items to the collections of his department, more than doubling their size in three decades. Almost every manuscript was purchased. Apart from charters, of which he acquired over 16,000, and volumes bought from what is called the Egerton fund with their own numbering, the basic run of 'Additional Manuscripts' stood at 11,037 when he became Keeper and 27,300 on his retirement.

The Madden journals are filled with almost daily visits from booksellers and hopeful members of the public bearing manuscripts they wished to sell. Many owners, as today, had exaggerated ideas of the value of their possessions, and Madden became very practised in assigning realistic prices and in concluding deals. A perfectly presentable manuscript could be bought for £10 and a really good one usually for a few hundred. The number of medieval books still in private hands is extraordinary to witness, both in old family libraries in Britain and especially in Europe following the revolutions and Napoleonic upheavals; Madden was usually the first person to be shown items as they emerged for possible sale. He would often be out several times a week viewing manuscripts in auction houses, of which there were at least half a dozen in London with regular sales of rare books. He listed what he saw and made decisions. These all make fascinating reading. He viewed and attended the sales of the manuscripts of Richard Heber in 1836, buying, for example, lot 1488, a *Lancelot-Grail* romance of 1316 which had belonged to Charles VI of France and to the Duc de La Vallière, a "superb MS", but losing lot 1490 to Phillipps, the fourteenth-century Anglo-Norman romance of *Waldef*. Madden accompanied Philip Bliss to watch the sale on the premises at Strawberry Hill of Horace Walpole's manuscripts in 1842. He saw too and made notes on numerous manuscripts of the duke of Sussex before their auction in 1844, when they were still in Kensington Palace. Getting there involved a walk to Oxford Street, a cab to Piccadilly and then the

Kensington omnibus. He was present when the Abbé Rive's Gutenberg Bible was sold at Sotheby's for £500 in 1847.

Madden could afford to be very selective, judging items for quality, date, rarity and whether they would add to the range of the Museum's holdings. He was interested in both text and illumination. Manuscripts were commonly brought back as trophies from diplomatic or trade missions to exotic locations, and these too were shown to him for judgement. Today, non-European items in the British Library are handled by different departments, but in Madden's time all manuscripts were his responsibility, and his opinion was sought as often for items in Hebrew, Ge'ez, Arabic, Persian, Chinese or even Nahuatl. He had a certain discretionary budget, never enough in his opinion, and any purchase over £50 had to be approved in advance by the Trustees (a figure that remained unchanged until the 1950s). When competing at auctions, Madden would usually place the Museum's bids through a bookseller whose invoice would then be submitted afterwards for approval, the possibility of refusal being a risk taken by the bookseller in exchange for commission on lots accepted. Madden's most trusted dealer was Thomas Rodd, until his death in 1849; later he used William Boone. Meetings of the Trustees took place regularly on Saturdays, attended by Forshall as secretary. Sometimes they declined purchases on which Madden had expended much effort and trust. He despaired in 1841: "And this is the treatment I receive from these asses for all the trouble and pains I take to acquire MSS for the public!!! It really is too bad."

In Chapter 4, we encountered the beautiful genealogy of the Portuguese royal family illuminated by Simon Bening (pp. 133–5). The story of its acquisition and its earlier history is revealed in successive entries in Madden's journals. Eleven vast illuminated sheets were brought in to his department in a box on the morning of Saturday, 14 May 1842, by W. R. Hamilton (1777–1859), a Trustee whom Madden especially mistrusted, who had been secretary to Lord Elgin and had handled the shipping of the Parthenon Marbles and the Rosetta Stone. As anyone can see, the leaves of the genealogy are of truly astounding quality. "In regard to the art displayed in these paintings, it is the most exquisite & finished I ever beheld, and such was the opinion of all who looked at them, after myself . . .", wrote Madden that day; "Who was the artist? was the question immediately asked by all, and as Giulio Clovio is known to have worked for John III [of Portugal] . . . every probability seemed to point to his having also executed these drawings." The Croatian-born illuminator Clovio (1498–1578), artist in the papal court, was the darling of the age of Neoclassicism and the painter to whom any high-quality sixteenth-century manuscript was frequently attributed.

Hamilton explained that the leaves belonged to his friend Mr Newton Scott, who had been in the British Embassy in Madrid and had obtained them in Portugal. The price was £1000 but he reported that the owner would accept £600. With an urgency which Madden did not yet regard as suspicious, Hamilton offered to bring the purchase to the meeting of the Trustees that very day, if Madden would write in support, which he did at once. The Trustees were swayed by Hamilton, not usually a champion of manuscripts, and they agreed to the purchase and that the Treasury would be asked for a special grant of £600. The only doubt on the committee was voiced by the historian Henry Hallam ("a consummate ninny", Madden wrote), who questioned whether a library should be buying mere art at all.

Madden was overjoyed at this thunderbolt acquisition. "I confess I never had a greater treat." Before evening, he realized that the illumination could not possibly be by Clovio and must surely be either Portuguese or German, thinking perhaps of Cranach. By 28 May, only two weeks later, he had found the chronicle of Damião de Góis published in 1619 and had matched up the account of the royal genealogy being executed for Prince Fernando by one Simon of Bruges. On 14 June he realized the stylistic connection with the Grimani Breviary in Venice; on 8 July he identified from Vasari the full name of Simon Bening, illuminator, and the fact that his daughter came to England. This was a magnificent piece of historical detection, the first modern identification of any Bening manuscript, a full generation ahead of the archival researches of James Weale. For a few months, the leaves were brought out proudly for every distinguished visitor to the Museum, including the admiring king of Saxony, who "repeatedly called the attention of his suite to them". Madden was soon confronted by the dilemma familiar to so many scholar-curators of public collections, who privately hope to publish their discoveries. A casual inquirer at the Museum in 1843 announced an interest in writing something on the genealogy himself and asked Madden to tell him everything known about its possible artist. Madden gave a courteous but carefully reserved reply, but he never did write it up properly, except for his two-page entry rightly ascribing the illumination to Simon Bening in the *Catalogue of Additions to the Manuscripts of the British Museum*, 1851, for by then his heart had rather gone out of it.

Unsettling revelations began within a few days of the purchase. First of all, Mr Newton Scott's sister came in, a Mrs Barton, who told Madden that the leaves had belonged to the old family library of 'a Spanish gentleman' from whom her brother had bought them, and that they had been in England for a whole year and had been shown for sale elsewhere by Mr Scott's brother-in-law, Mr Judd. She revealed that they had been sent to Windsor Castle for inspection by Prince Albert, where the queen had remarked "that they were very pretty" but too expensive, and that they were sent back so carelessly that they were damaged. (There are indeed water stains on the final leaf.) Madden felt that "had all this been known before, I think the Trustees would have been justified in offering a less liberal price". Three months later, the Treasury declined to contribute to the cost, on the advice of the Prime Minister, Sir Robert Peel, and so the not negligible sum now had to come from the already small budget of the Department of Manuscripts. Madden began to suspect that he had been set up, and that Hamilton probably had a personal stake in a hurried sale at the Department's expense. Chancing to meet a friend of Newton Scott's at a dinner party in July 1843, Madden learned that only £20 had been paid for the leaves in Spain, and that the previous owner had actually been not a noble family at all but the bookbinder to the king of Portugal, from whose library Madden now supposed the leaves had probably been extracted. In 1849 he was told by the diplomat Lord Stuart de Rothesay, just back from the embassy in Madrid, that the £20 sale had been at an annual open-air street market, presumably allowing the law of *marché ouvert* to launder any incomplete line of provenance. Madden had a horror of sharp practice, especially if he felt he had been tricked. When Hamilton finally retired as a Trustee in 1858, Madden was beside himself with relief: "a more prejudiced person never existed, nor a greater *jobber* when it related to himself or his friends . . . I hope never again to see his ugly face."

Not everything offered could be transacted quickly enough to secure acquisition. In February 1841 the antiquary John Gage Rokewode informed Madden that a famous illustrated twelfth-century miscellany on the life and miracles of Saint Edmund of East Anglia was back on the market for the first time since 1816. The manuscript, which Madden went to see, is quite small, a little over 10½ by 7 inches, with thirty-two enchanting full-page English Romanesque miniatures of about 1130, filled with animated details showing ships and battles and all the ceremony of Anglo-Saxon kingship and martyrdom, like the Lewis chessmen come to life. It was to be sold in London by sealed bids. Madden wanted it desperately for the Museum but there was no meeting of the Trustees scheduled for six weeks, and "I dare not buy it on my own responsibility." Gage Rokewode himself agreed to put in an offer of £240, proposing to allow the Trustees first refusal at their meeting on 3 April, but his bid was topped by the booksellers Payne and Foss, who afterwards sold the manuscript for £300 to Robert Holford, that same buyer who had acquired Ottley's Psalter. Madden saw it in Holford's possession in December 1843, and was, I think, rather ungracious about Gage Rokewode's kind intervention: "This book *ought to* be in the Museum, as an Historical ornament, and *would have been*, had not the late Gage-Rokewode hesitated in offering so large a price for it as 250£ . . . Mr Holford has had the *bad*, the *execrable* taste, to strip off the ancient binding, and substitute a *smooth olive morocco*, tooled and lettered on the side in the style one would expect to find a Petrarch or an Aldine classic!!! It absolutely horrifies me to see such Gothicism . . ." (meaning barbarianism, not Pugin). The manuscript in its tidy binding is now in the Morgan Library in New York, probably the finest English twelfth-century book lost abroad in modern times.

A curious adventure with another Romanesque book was unfolding in the meantime. The historian J. G. Nichols happened to be in Winchester in January 1842, and in a very local sale there he noticed a large and undescribed twelfth-century cartulary of the cathedral priory, including the unique texts of many Anglo-Saxon charters, among books offered from the estate of the Reverend Thomas Watkins, precentor and minor canon of Winchester, who had died in 1839. Since Watkins had also been the cathedral librarian, it seemed that by some oversight the manuscript must have become confused with his own property. Nichols alerted relevant authorities and the book was withdrawn from sale. In June it was returned to Winchester Cathedral, where, in an unexpected development, the dean denied categorically that the manuscript had ever been in their possession. In 1844 it was lent to Madden, who was gratified to find it was in an "ancient binding of oak boards covered with white leather, curiously stamped". It was, as is now known, one of three blind-stamped bookbindings from twelfth-century Winchester, a type of

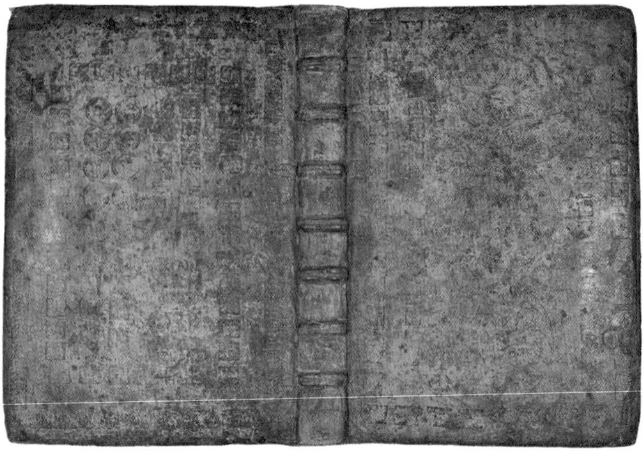

The twelfth-century stamped binding of the cartulary bought by Madden in 1844 from Winchester Cathedral.

decorated binding not made again in England until the fifteenth century. The flyleaves are formed from fragments of eighth-century uncial script. Again, Madden noted the cathedral's indifference to the manuscript. In October that year, he learned that William Vaux, a young recruit to the Department of Coins and Medals, was the son of a prebendary of Winchester. Madden saw his chance and wrote to Canon Vaux offering the dean and chapter £200 for the manuscript. Suddenly everything changed and at their chapter meeting on 25 November the canons quickly remembered that this book must indeed be theirs and that 200 *guineas* might be a better price. The deal was struck; the manuscript was sent back to London and on 24 December 1844, just in time for Christmas, Madden heard that the Museum Trustees had accepted the purchase: "This is good!" he declared happily. Two years later, William Alchin, librarian of the Guildhall and previously a solicitor in Winchester, told him a story about it. Madden had said that, in his opinion, it had probably not really been the cathedral's property at all. Alchin said it was, but that it was not in the library but the Singing School, where the smallest choristers used to sit on it, so that they could see over the pews.

Some time later, encouraged by this success, Madden made overtures to buy the most sensational possession of Winchester Cathedral. This was their supreme manuscript Bible, richly illuminated in the 1150s and 1160s by several of the most innovative and skilful artists in Europe, probably at the expense of the bishop of Winchester, Henry of Blois, brother of King Stephen. Madden was first told of it in 1849 by the priest and antiquary Dr Daniel Rock, who reported that the dean might be willing to part with it. Madden justified to himself the possible disposal of Church property: "The danger of having such volumes in libraries of cathedrals is proved by some of the miniatures having been recently cut out!" In October 1851, Madden went to see it with his wife, and they turned every page; Madden wrote of his earnest wish, as he called it, that the Winchester Bible could be transferred to the Museum, like the cartulary. In May 1852, Rock informed Madden that the dean was ready to sell. "I expressed myself much rejoiced at such a proposition", said Madden, "and authorized Dr Rock to name from 100 to 120 guineas as the equivalent for it." Nothing further seems to have happened.

It is a regret of all manuscript collectors that they are never the only buyers and that when one competitor fades there is always another in waiting with even more money to spend. Time after time, Madden prepared himself for possible purchases and spent nights of sleepless anxiety, only for the British Museum to be outbid by the voracious Sir Thomas Phillipps. There are numerous despairing outbursts of Madden's conviction that the national interest ought morally to come first. "By opposing the Museum, he prevents the public from having access to these works, merely to gratify a selfish and silly feeling, which manifests itself in carrying home cart-loads of MSS", which would then become unfindable in the confusion of Phillipps's house at Middle Hill. From the mid-1840s, Madden faced rivalry also from the imperious fourth earl of Ashburnham, whose ancestors had once occupied the house where the Cotton manuscripts were burned ("it's impossible for the Museum to compete with him"), and, when he ceased to be a threat, then from the charming French prince the Duc d'Aumale, who was exiled to England in 1848, and the tenth duke of Hamilton ("confound them both!"). In 1855 there were the earliest intimations of bidders from the United States ("if America begins to buy MSS of this class, *good bye* to any more acquisitions for the Museum"). The tensions in the journals as sales got nearer are palpable; one longs to reassure him. The reality of competition, however, was made clear at the Savile sale in 1861. There were two almost identical fourteenth-century manuscripts about Northamptonshire. Phillipps bought one, lot 40, for £82, underbid by the Museum, but he did not bid on the second, lot 52, which was then secured by Madden for £3. "Of what use are the masses of MSS at Middle Hill and Ashburnham

House?" asked Madden on another occasion; "One comfort is, that the Museum will continue to exist, when Lord A. and Sir T. P. are in their graves, and their collections dispersed." This proved to be true. A very desirable manuscript which Madden lost in 1847 was the Book of Hours of Bonaparte Ghislieri, a spectacular Bolognese volume of around 1500, which includes a signed miniature by Pietro Perugino, no less. It belonged to the Scottish antiquary James Dennistoun, who was discussing its bequest to the Museum when he received an irresistible offer of £700 from Lord Ashburnham. All was well in the long term, for it was eventually left to the British Museum anyway in 1928 by the will of Henry Yates Thompson, who had bought the remainder of Lord Ashburnham's library after his death.

The Maddens had six children. The birth announcements placed in the newspaper stated all as having been born in the British Museum, where the family now occupied the best staff apartments. Two died in infancy, to Madden's enormous distress. Sir Thomas Phillipps was made godfather to the second son, who was born in 1841 and duly named George Phillipps Madden, evidence that the cordial relationship of fellow manuscript enthusiasts could override saleroom rivalry. This was seriously tested when, instead of a sum of money or some useful piece of engraved silver, Phillipps sent as a christening present for the baby a spare set of unbound sheets of a Latin catalogue of manuscripts, with instructions to Madden to have it bound (which Phillipps had still not paid for in 1844).

Madden was an indulgent father, and the journals also contain accounts of treats and expeditions together, frequent trips to the zoo to see new animals as they arrived (the zoo, like the Museum, was an acquisitor), and family holidays usually in Kent or on the south coast. There was a succession of adored dogs, including Fido, whom Panizzi tried unsuccessfully to get banned from the Museum premises; Fido died in 1864 and was buried under a lilac bush in the Museum grounds. Madden was an accomplished dancer and frequently attended balls. He delighted in new inventions. He describes with joy his first rides on trains in 1835 and 1840. In 1849 he had his photograph taken by "the Talbotype artist in Regent St". In 1852 he pasted a pale photograph of a page of a medieval cartulary into his journal, remarking that the discovery might become a whole new way of transmitting unique manuscripts to other libraries. He visited the Great Exhibition numerous times. He used the London Underground trains, then pulled by steam engines, from 1863. He did not like the tiresome innovation of postage stamps in 1840, but on holiday in Brighton in 1868 he amused his youngest children by having novelty stamps made in imitation of Penny Reds, bearing his and their portraits instead of the queen's.

Despite all his public success and apparent social status, Madden is revealed in his journals as a man haunted by secret insecurity and worry in the black hours of the night. It is heartbreakingly easy to fall out with friends – oh! we all know – and once battle lines are drawn, recrossing them is difficult for an honourable man who has tried his best. Madden took offence easily, but he was unable to deal with it except by high-handedness, which usually made things worse. He felt that Fate was always against him. The stand-off with the ever-increasing circle of supporters around Panizzi caused Madden real distress, as did an eventual dissolution of his long friendship with Philip Bliss, which he could not understand. A more contented man might not have been such a restless acquisitor for the Museum or such a dedicated scholar.

Madden's published work runs to more than 150 titles. They included scrupulous editions of manuscripts of Middle English romances, such as *Havelok the Dane*, 1828, and *William and the Werwolf*, 1832. His huge four-volume edition of the Wycliffe Bible is still a definitive text, prepared with his colleague Josiah Forshall. They began in the late 1820s and finished in 1850, an enterprise involving the word-by-word collation of some 170 manuscripts, almost all done by Madden. His working out of the evolving versions of the medieval text occurs through many pages of the journal. On the birth of another son in 1850, the boy was christened James Arnold Wycliffe Madden, "to commemorate the completion of the *magnum opus* of twenty-two years". A copy of the edition was specially bound and inscribed for Prince Albert, and I am glad to report that it is still in the library at Windsor Castle, not far from the Duc de La Vallière's Plutarch.

In Chapter 5 we touched on the restoration of manuscripts recovered from the Cotton fire. This was entirely the initiative of Madden, who in 1837 gained the key to the old Charter Room upstairs in the Museum and found there many forgotten boxes of unsorted and charred fragments. Their painstaking identification and reassembly occupied many decades, work which was regarded by Madden later in life as among his greatest achievements. In 1831, Sir Thomas Phillipps had shown him a cartulary of the priory of St Nicholas in Exeter, which he had bought in Dublin and proved to be the long-lost Cotton Vitellius D. IX. In 1854, Phillipps finally agreed to sell it to the Museum for the cost price of £100, although he immediately insisted on borrowing it back and did not finally deliver it until six weeks after the Trustees had processed the purchase. Two other Cotton strays were pursued in vain. Madden learned in 1844 of the fragments from the Cotton Genesis which had wandered into the possession of the Baptist College in Bristol (see above, pp. 185–6), and during an autumn holiday in Bath the following year he made an expedition up to Bristol to see them. They were finally reacquired in 1962, nearly 120 years later. A greater loss and with no long-term success was the famous ninth-century Psalter in the university library of Utrecht. In 1856 the Keeper of the Signet Library in Edinburgh, David Laing, informed Madden that the Utrecht Psalter was none other than the missing Cotton Claudius C. VII (above, p. 175). Madden approached the British ambassador in The Hague about offering "a large sum" for it (perhaps £1000, he thought), but Laing, trying to be helpful, foolishly reported this in advance to the Utrecht librarian, F. B. Ader, allowing him to scupper a sale before the offer was formally received. Panizzi, as scheming as Madden believed him to be (but in this instance cleverly), suggested something much more subtle. The Dutch had been distressed to lose the great archive of Utrecht assembled by Petrus van Musschenbroek (1764–1823), bought in 1826 by Sir Thomas Phillipps. Panizzi therefore, backed by Lord Palmerston, the Prime Minister, proposed buying the archive from Phillipps and offering it in exchange, an idea well received in the Netherlands. Phillipps, however, also true to form, refused to cooperate, and the Psalter remains abroad.

One of the elusive manuscripts in private hands which had been haunting Madden for decades was the celebrated Bedford Book of Hours, which he had seen in 1829 and 1833 and desired dreadfully (above, pp. 307–8). On 10 January 1852 he was tipped off by the facsimilist Caleb Wing, who often copied illuminations in the reading-room, that it was being offered for sale to Lord Ashburnham by the Tobin family of Liverpool. Much astonished, Madden consulted the bookseller William Boone, who admitted that when he too had heard this same rumour

RIGHT: The Bedford Book of Hours, Paris, *c.*1410–30, the famous royal prayerbook seen by Madden in 1829 and 1833 and finally bought with the Tobin manuscripts in 1852.

Comme nre seigr crea adam et porta en paradis terrestre et fait eue de son coste et leur deffent le fruit he had pre-empted the earl and rushed to Liverpool himself, where he bought it immediately. It was not alone: it came with a group of six other manuscripts, all magnificent and in flawless condition. These included two large and spectacular Flemish manuscripts of the very late fifteenth century, one being the Book of Hours made for Joanna the Mad, wife of Philip the Fair of Burgundy, and the other the Breviary presented in 1497 to Isabella of Castile, patron of Columbus. Another was the Book of Hours of François I of France, which had been one of the manuscripts of the Duc de La Vallière that the Abbé Rive had selected for illustration in his *Essai sur l'art de vérifier l'âge des miniatures*. Boone's emotions on the train back to London can only be guessed at. The painters represented in these seven manuscripts included, in addition to the eponymous work of the Bedford Master, important illumination by artists now identified as Gerard David, who was also a panel painter, the Master of the David Scenes in the Grimani Breviary, the Master of François de Rohan, Étienne Colaud, the Master of the Cité des Dames (who had worked with Christine de Pizan) and an unnamed artist in the close circle of the court artist Jean Bourdichon. These painters are all among the giants of the illuminator's art in France and the southern Netherlands. Seldom can such a cascade of supreme manuscripts have emerged so fast and unexpectedly. Madden later learned that £1900 had been paid by Boone for the group of seven books, a huge sum in 1852. He never forgave the Tobin heirs for not offering the manuscripts directly to the Museum. However, he immediately rallied the Trustees, and he was given authority to negotiate up to £3000, a heady figure. "I felt a good deal excited when in Boone's shop, although I tried to appear cool." He offered £2500, or £2000 for the three best. Boone refused. "I could not get the affair out of my mind, and it kept me awake half the night." Two days later, on Monday, 2 February, he capitulated and agreed to £3000 for all seven, payable in instalments. It was the greatest single day of manuscript purchase in Madden's lifetime. Later, when examining the book in the Bourdichon style, Madden noticed two quite exquisite calendar miniatures by Simon Bening tucked in at the back, second in quality only to the Portuguese genealogy. They are now kept separately.

Another unexpected revelation followed. A few days after the purchase, Madden showed the Isabella Breviary to the bookseller Henry Foss, who told him that its formerly unfinished miniatures had been supplied relatively recently by the clever facsimilist John Harris (1791–1873). By

Calendar miniature for December illuminated by Simon Bening, found by Madden tucked into the back of one of the Books of Hours bought from the Tobin library in 1852.

chance, Harris was in the reading-room and so Madden summoned him. No, Harris explained, they were painted by his father (also John Harris, 1767–1832), but that he himself, the son, had supplied two miniatures in the famous Towneley Lectionary, mostly illuminated by Clovio. This is indeed news, if true. Madden had seen the Lectionary twice (1836 and 1848). It is now in the New York Public Library. Two of its large miniatures are attributed to an unidentifiable close follower of Clovio in sixteenth-century Rome. On this new evidence of Madden's journal for 20 February 1852, they may be nineteenth-century forgeries.

Two years later Madden had the experience of bidding at auction himself. This was the sale at Sotheby's in June 1855 of the library of the late Lord Stuart de Rothesay, the former ambassador who had told Madden about the street market in Madrid. Madden was captivated by lot 2353, a *Miroir historial* illuminated in Paris in 1459–63 for Jacques d'Armagnac, with 108 miniatures. It is a luxurious and highly commercial manuscript. Madden discussed it with Boone, who said knowingly that it would cost at least £500, and he refused to take a bid from the Museum because he already had a commission from another client (at that exact figure, it was hinted). Madden asked whether the would-be competitor might stand aside in the public interest, and two days later Boone told him that the client had refused. Therefore, very unusually, the Trustees authorized Madden himself to bid in the sale up to £525. He arrived early at 2.30 on 8 June. The room was full of booksellers. The *Miroir historial* finally came up around four o'clock, and it was placed on the table. The auctioneer, John Wilkinson, opened the bidding at £50, which was offered by Henry Bohn (the dealers Bohn and Boone were different people). Madden, knowing the price had to pass £500, said £100. Bohn responded with £120. Madden, standing up, called out £200. Bohn bid £210. Madden shouted "£300!" Let him now continue in his own words:

> The auctioneer seemed surprised, as did the spectators, and Mr H. B. waited a little, as he said, 'to fetch breath.' On he went, however, to £400, after which I followed him in bidding £10 at a time, till it rose to £480 on which, as my *dernier mot*, I bid 500 guineas. H. Bohn was silenced, and the whole room supposed that I was the purchaser, but I knew better, for close to Wilkinson's desk sat my opponent Mr Boone (and this vexes me the more, to be defeated by my own Agent), who, after the lapse of a minute, said distinctly *510 guineas*! I at once resumed my seat, as I had made up my mind previously to go no further, and after a fruitless appeal from the Auctioneer to me, the coveted volume was knocked down to Mr Boone. I left the room directly afterwards, feeling very cross about the transaction.

The buyer was actually the Duc d'Aumale, and the manuscript is now in the Musée Condé at Chantilly. It is a nice enough book, attributed to the Parisian illuminator Maître François. However, the sale was not all a disaster for the Museum. Having his authorized money unspent, Madden now gave a few bids to Boone, unencumbered by other clients, for later sessions of the sale, including a limit of £250 for a very pretty Italian

The Stuart de Rothesay Hours, probably Padua, *c.*1508, and Perugia, *c.*1535–8, bought by Madden in 1855, now known to have been written by Bartolomeo Sanvito and illuminated by Giulio Clovio.

Book of Hours, which was lot 2706. It was bought for only £115.10s. Not only was it written around 1508 by Bartolomeo Sanvito, the greatest Renaissance scribe, but it was illuminated in the 1530s for Cardinal Marino Grimani by the famous Giulio Clovio himself, with swaggering classical borders inspired by Michelangelo in the Sistine Chapel. It is mentioned by Vasari in his life of the artist. It is much more important than the *Miroir historial*. When the triumphant acquisition of the Stuart de Rothesay Hours (as it is now called) was brought to the Trustees for approval on 23 June, one of them, Sir David Dundas, former Solicitor General, asked in all seriousness whether the naked putti should be painted over before the manuscript was seen by the public.

Early in the following year, 1856, Sir Henry Ellis, Principal Librarian since 1827, was approaching eighty and in poor health and was discreetly encouraged into retirement. In a masterstroke of deft footwork,

Panizzi contrived to be appointed as his successor. Madden's pages of total despair are almost as moving to read as his distress at the deaths of his infant children. "And what has *he* ever done for the Museum & the Public that *I* have not done, ay, and ten times more?" Panizzi immediately set about regulating staff attendance hours, requiring signatures in what Madden called the 'Prison Book', inaugurating his new domed and circular reading-room (1857), which Madden refused to attend, and creating public exhibition spaces for books. It is interesting that display of rare books was a new and radical idea in the 1850s. Cotton or Rive would never have considered it. Even today, the department of Prints and Drawings in the British Museum has no permanent gallery space, on grounds of conservation. The modern British Library, however, has by far the finest permanent exhibition of treasures of any library in the world, a legacy of Panizzi. Madden consequently decided that to put manuscripts on public display was madness (he used the word often). He expressed horror at the thought of forcing precious and vulnerable illuminated manuscripts into cases, exposed, as he said, to gaslight and dust, and "more harm than good results from this display of art to the *mob*". One group of ignorant visitors brought round by Panizzi to see treasures of the Department of Manuscripts in 1860 even included foreigners and Americans: "I feel perfectly disgusted at the whole thing."

Let us suppose a visit to Madden in his office in the Museum at about this time. As it did within my own memory, the manuscript department occupied the south-eastern corner of the building at the right-hand side as you stand looking at the building from the main courtyard. It was not so easily reached during much of Madden's early tenure because construction work was ongoing for many decades, and until the entrance hall was finally opened in 1847 the public came into the Museum through what is now the rear of the building. To reach manuscripts you would walk through several rooms (past the old reading-room, which today has artefacts from Mexico) and right down the full length of the long King's Library, now called the Enlightenment Gallery. The completion of the front portico, however, reversed this access and Madden's department suddenly became the first encountered by visitors to the Museum, giving its location a new prominence which was quickly resented by Panizzi.

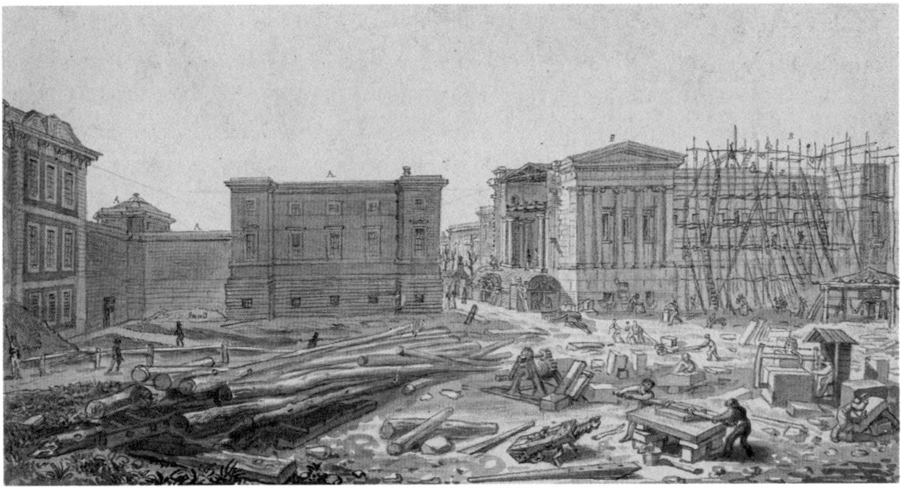

Construction of the British Museum, watercolour by George Scharf, 1828; Madden still occupied part of the seventeenth-century block on the far left.

An early visitor wrote:

> Entering the front yard of the Museum by the high, gilt-tipped gate, you pass along a paved walk and ascend the spacious flight of stone steps leading to the main entrance. You pull open the swinging door and find yourself in the high, grey somewhat gloomy vestibule, whence branch off to the right and the left the galleries crowded with the collected curiosities and wonders of the world.

Turn right in the lobby. The first room you enter today is the Museum shop. This had been the 'western saloon' at the furthest reaches of the Manuscript Department, used by Madden's staff for sorting and cataloguing manuscripts, but as soon as it became accessible from the new entrance, Panizzi shrewdly claimed it for housing and exhibiting the library of Thomas Grenville (1755–1846), civil servant and prime minister's son, which he had secured for the nation in January 1847. Madden's journals scream with helpless despair as Panizzi convinced the Trustees to endorse his unilateral occupation of what is still called the Grenville Room, which he fitted out with table cases on the left to display early printing, including Grenville's copy of the Gutenberg Bible on vellum.

Panizzi's new *Short Guide*, published to coincide with the Great Exhibition (1851), described the Grenville treasures, continuing briskly, "From this room visitors proceed to the Royal Library, passing through a *room containing manuscripts*." Madden copied this sentence into his journal, underlining the last three words and furiously adding triple exclamation marks, for this was an insult to the principal 'Manuscript Saloon' of the Museum. The *Illustrated London News* in the same year was hardly more complimentary than Panizzi: "From the Grenville Room we enter the MSS department, a large and heavy-looking room, whose dingy walls and blackened ceiling – strangers to whitewash for three-and-twenty years – give it a sort of solemn, grim, literary look."

This room, clean and brightly lit and now called 'Collecting the world', still opens on the left into a vista down the full length of the magnificent King's Library. On the right it leads into the gallery for the Waddesdon Bequest, which includes the Duc de Berry's reliquary of the Holy Thorn. There was originally also a second smaller room beyond the Waddesdon display: these two were the reading-rooms for manuscripts, with a new sorting room and other facilities on the far side. Straight ahead in the Manuscripts Saloon, furthest from the lobby, were formerly two offices. In the left-hand corner was a small windowless cubicle described in the Museum plan of 1857 as the "Assistant Keeper's Room". This would have been occupied by Madden's then deputy, Richard Holmes. Madden himself had the larger office opposite, to the right of the modern staff entrance into the department of Britain, Europe and Prehistory. Its site is now little more than a white-painted corridor, partly taken up by a lift, but the 1857 plan shows a substantial room here with windows looking out over the Museum gardens to the north-east. A note would be sent in (no telephones then) and then we would knock on one of its two doors off the Manuscripts Saloon. Rising from a desk strewn with paper, Madden would greet us cordially.

I tell him about progress on this book. He asks for more information on Rabbi Oppenheim, as he asked the Bodleian in reality in 1865. He knows more about Simon Bening than anyone in Europe and the Portuguese genealogy might be brought out. Madden is less impressed by the Duc de Berry: he had seen the *Grandes Heures* in Paris in 1846, commenting that it was "very barbarously ill-used"; he disdained one of the Duc's *Bibles historiales* quoted to him at £1,500 in 1853 ("I should think it *very dear* at £100"); and when told in 1856 that the Duc's *Cité de Dieu* could be inspected in London, he declared himself too busy to go. However, he is delighted at the inclusion of Cotton. He says (as he wrote in his journal in 1855):

> Anyone who had seen in 1837 the enormous mass of blackened fragments buried in dust, lying on the floor of the old Charter garret in the Old Building (now no more), would scarcely believe that every piece, to the smallest half an inch in length, has been examined, cleaned, flattened & inlaid; and by far the greater portion identified and bound in volumes.

Madden sighs, rolling his eyes towards Panizzi's new reading-room, and continues, "The Trustees and the Public owe me a debt of gratitude for my restoration of the Cottonian library, but I have never yet received even thanks for my trouble!!" We recognize now that salvaging the Cotton collection was an incomparable accomplishment in the history of libraries and, together with acquisition, the greatest achievement of any keeper of manuscripts.

By the last decade of Madden's career, the supply of major manuscripts for sale was already dwindling. Prices were rising and Madden found it hard to keep up. Often his purchases were autographs, fashionable in the nineteenth century, and even the occasional single miniature. The Museum had shown no interest when Ottley's collection of over 900 illuminated manuscript cuttings was dispersed by Sotheby's in 1838, but Madden began to feel that his territory was under threat in 1855 when Marlborough House (the ancestor of the Victoria and Albert Museum) began to buy miniatures cut from Italian choir books. He was even more vexed when the Keeper of Prints and Drawings at the British Museum itself announced his intention of bidding for illuminated miniatures at the Samuel Rogers sale in 1856. In desperation, Madden went to view the auction himself and made a point by buying for his Department an album of Italian cuttings from illuminated borders, formerly Ottley's, for £115.10s. However, he left only a modest bid of £12.12s. on the lovely miniature of the penitent David by Jean Fouquet from the dismembered Hours of Étienne Chevalier and lost it at £16.5s.6d. to the marquess of Breadalbane. In March 1861, Madden bought another album of cuttings from the sister-in-law of a baron in Austria for £180. This contained the separated leaves by Simon Bening from what is now called the 'Golf Book' (see above, p. 152). Madden made the connection with the artist of the calendar miniatures bound into the Bourdichon-style Book of Hours, as above, but not yet with Bening's Portuguese genealogy.

A month later, Madden arranged the highest bid he ever placed on a manuscript. This was for the famous Pontifical made *c.*1423–32 for John, duke of Bedford, and later completed for Jacques Jouvenel des Ursins, bishop of Poitiers 1449–57. It was illuminated by the Bedford Master once more, the artist both of Bedford's Salisbury Breviary in the Abbé Rive's *Essai* and of the celebrated Book of Hours bought by Madden nine years earlier. The Pontifical reappeared as lot 4 in the Soltykoff sale at the Hôtel Drouot in Paris in April 1861. It was examined by Madden's assistant, Richard Holmes, who reported back to London on its notable size, about 20 by 13 inches, and its close relationship to the Bedford Hours and its detailed picture of the interior of the Sainte-Chapelle in Paris. Madden secured approval in advance from the Trustees to an unprecedented level of £1000, a little over 20,000 francs, entrusted to William Boone, who crossed to Paris on the overnight ferry. Three days later Boone sent the disappointing result by telegram. The manuscript had sold for 34,250 francs, about £1,700, to the collector Ambroise Firmin-Didot. A few days afterwards he generously ceded it to the disappointed underbidder, the city of Paris. It was then totally destroyed in the burning of the Hôtel de Ville in Paris in May 1871 during the Franco-Prussian War.

As any museum curator knows, acquisitions are often brought about by long-term relationships. Madden's journals include first meetings with several remarkable manuscripts which would eventually find their way into the national collection but many generations later. Twelve of the manuscripts catalogued by Madden at Holkham in 1825–7 were bought by the British Museum in 1952, including the fourteenth-century 'Holkham Bible Picture Book'. In 1839 and again in 1862, Madden examined the East Anglian manuscript known as the Luttrell Psalter, then owned by the old Roman Catholic family of Weld, of Lulworth Castle in Dorset. "The art is not good, but the margins are filled with a prodigious number of the most grotesque and curious figures." The Psalter was placed on indefinite deposit at the Museum in 1896 and it was bought in 1929 for £33,000, at that time the highest price ever paid for a manuscript. In 1842 and 1858, Madden saw the enormous Sherborne Missal, mentioned in the previous chapter from its sale in France in 1761. It was owned by the duke of Northumberland. "I should judge it the most splendid specimen of English art of the 15th century in existence, and if sold now, could produce over £600." It has more than 1500 miniatures, including some of the earliest naturalistic paintings of birds in European art. The manuscript finally came to London on loan in 1983 and it was bought in 1998, mostly negotiated by me, for a price reported in the press as £15,000,000. In 1862, Madden inspected rather dubiously the tiny but magical late seventh- or early eighth-century Gospel of Saint John, found in the tomb of Saint Cuthbert in Durham in 1104. It survives in the oldest known European bookbinding. It was lent on deposit from 1979 and was at last acquired by the nation for approximately £9,000,000 in 2012. These are sums that would amaze Madden beyond measure.

Two astonishing and unexpected encounters took place with illuminated manuscripts no longer in Britain. The first is the Hours of Catherine of Cleves, richly illuminated for the duchess of Guelders around 1440 and the most important medieval Dutch manuscript of the Middle Ages. It is well known that it belonged in the mid-nineteenth century to a dealer in Paris, Jacques-Joseph Techener, who shuffled its leaves into two volumes, each cleverly constructed to appear complete, allowing one part to be sold to Baron Adolphe de Rothschild and the other eventually to Prince Charles d'Arenberg. By chance and different descents, both portions are now reunited side by side in the Morgan Library in New York. What does not seem to be known is that Techener sent one volume (the Arenberg half) to Sotheby's in London in 1858. Madden was keen to buy it ("I should like much to secure it") and he discussed it with Boone, who said that Techener had asked 20,000 francs but would settle for £600. Madden thought this too much. It was unsold at Sotheby's at £435 and was returned to Paris. Madden had examined it carefully and made drawings of the arms. Here is the surprise. He counted seventy miniatures. That volume now has sixty-four miniatures and gaps where six are missing. The probability is that they still exist somewhere.

The second encounter was on 16 February 1856, Madden's birthday, when the Duc and Duchesse d'Aumale called at the Museum with a manuscript which they had just bought in Genoa for 18,000 francs (less than Techener wanted for half of Catherine of Cleves). Madden had first met the Duc in 1849, remarking on his affability and good English. This time he was shown a volume bound in Italian armorial red morocco, which the Duc said he was going to have replaced with velvet. On lifting the cover, Madden gazed into the most extraordinary calendar. "It is a most beautiful and interesting volume, and I covet it exceedingly for the Museum . . . Some of the subjects are perfect *pictures*, for instance the cavalcade going *Maying*, to illustrate that month." He copied his

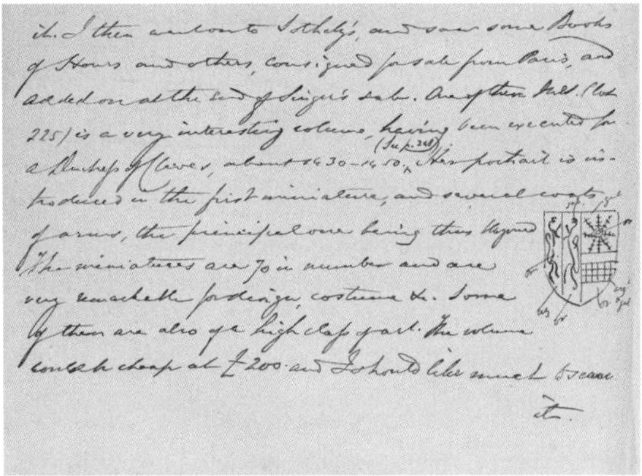

it. I then went on to Sotheby's, and saw some Books of Hours and others, consigned for sale from Paris, and added on at the end of Singer's sale. One of them (MS. Lot 225) is a very interesting volume, having been executed for a Duchess of Cleves, about 1430–1450. (See p. 248) Her portrait is introduced in the first miniature, and several coats of arms, the principal one being thus blazoned. The miniatures are 70 in number and are very remarkable for design, costume &c. Some of them are also of a high class of art. The volume would be cheap at £200 and I should like much to secure it.

The Hours of Catherine of Cleves, Utrecht, *c.*1425, and Madden's notes on it when it was shown to him in 1858.

observations that night into his journal, sketching out the family connections between the manuscript's apparent first owners. Those pages describe the earliest scholarly inspection of the *Très Riches Heures* of the Duc de Berry, now probably the most famous manuscript in the world.

In 1866, Panizzi retired. For a few moments, Madden considered applying for his post, but then decided to retire from the Museum himself. He had survived the tyranny to the very end, without capitulating or resigning; that was victory enough. He took the lease on a new house in St Stephen's Square, at the top end of what is now St Stephen's Road in Westbourne Park, W2. He entered his last entry in the Department's daily ledger, leaving for his successors "a deep curse on the unscrupulous, lying, scheming Italian villain, by whose enmity my official life has been embittered so many years, and my claims to promotion and liberal recompense frustrated and denied. F. Madden, 29th Sept. 1866". His final years were spent reading and in worrying about his disappointing children and grieving the slow death in 1865 of his beloved son George, aged twenty-four. The boy's godfather, Sir Thomas Phillipps, himself now old, never bothered to send condolence, which finally led to a falling out between these two nineteenth-century giants of manuscripts. For a time, Madden was tempted into spiritualism, then fashionable, until Panizzi failed to fulfil the ghostly prophecy of a planchette that he would die in 1872. "Daily, hourly, do I *curse him*!" Madden paid one last visit to his old Department in 1867 and was shown a recent acquisition, the Saluces Hours, another of the manuscripts gathered by the Abbé Rive for the Duc de La Vallière and used in the *Essai sur l'art de vérifier l'âge des miniatures*. He thought the price paid by the Museum of £928 plus 10 per cent commission was preposterous: £500, in his opinion, would have been quite enough. The final piece of manuscript news reported to him by Boone in 1869 was that the Museum had bought two further sheets from the jinxed Bening Portuguese genealogy. "I should very much like to know of whom these leaves were purchased and the sum given for them." The journal entries became shorter and shorter, ending in ill-health on 31 December 1872. Madden died at home on 8 April 1873, three weeks after the death of his wife. Their ashes are buried in Kensal Green cemetery in the catacomb of a chapel with a pillared portico, like a scaled-down model of the British Museum.

Madden's real monument today is the Manuscript Department of the British Library. His portrait, which used to hang in the old Students' Room for manuscript readers, is now in the Western Heritage meeting room of the Library's new building near Euston. In 1849, Madden had discussed the future of the Museum with Robert Lemon of the State Papers Office. They both agreed that one day, not yet but some day in the future, the library would get so big that it would break away to form a "*National Library*" (underlined), all on its own. They decided that there was only one building in London appropriate to accommodate it: Buckingham Palace. "*Nous verrons*", wrote Madden, 'We will see.'

CHAPTER NINE

The Forger: Constantine Simonides

In the summer of 1854, a purposeful and unusual-looking traveller arrived in Broadway in Worcestershire in west central England, with an overnight bag full of manuscripts. He was Constantine Simonides, a Greek who claimed to have lived among the monks of Mount Athos, and he certainly looked the part. There are descriptions and several early photographs, showing him as swarthy and with glossy black hair thrust to one side and usually a great unkempt dense beard like an Orthodox priest. He was quite short but with a large head and exceptionally high forehead, of the kind which in popular myth denotes intelligence. He had prominent dark eyebrows and deep-set clever and piercing eyes – "a face not easily forgotten", as was remarked. He was restless and voluble, as unceasing as the Ancient Mariner but usually in Greek. He looked as though he slept in his clothes, which were always black. In a rural Cotswold market town of the nineteenth century, as unlike the dusty and sun-baked landscape of Mount Athos as is possible to imagine, Simonides must have attracted some attention. He was here to see Sir Thomas Phillipps, baronet, of Middle Hill, Broadway, who had invited him to stay the night.

Phillipps had a part in Chapter 7 and stalked many times in and out of Chapter 8, like the wicked fairy, forever enthralling and provoking Sir Frederic Madden in London. Now it is time to visit him at home, which not so many of the manuscripts fraternity ever did. It is about three miles from the high street in Broadway out to Middle Hill. You turn south along Church Street, which quickly becomes Snowshill Road through

LEFT: Constantine Simonides (*c.*1824– *c.*1890), photograph probably of the 1850s, kept by Sir Thomas Phillipps.

the countryside, bringing you eventually to the medieval church of St Eadburgha, where Sir Thomas Phillipps himself is now buried. There is a place to leave the car. Immediately opposite, on the left (or east) side of the road, are the stone pillars and old iron gates of what was formerly the main entrance into the long drive up to Middle Hill, with a Victorian gatekeeper's lodge, whose current resident, pottering in his garden, kindly gave me directions and reminiscences of long ago. The way is now a public footpath called Coneygree Lane, rising steeply behind the lodge up through the woods eventually to the gothic folly of Broadway Tower at the very top of the hill. The track is rutted and muddy and it must have been a very steep ascent for visitors such as Simonides in a horse-drawn cab, or maybe he walked up on foot with his bag. After about ten minutes the path branches out diagonally across a field with spectacular views of the green valley below, and from here, instead of climbing further, the old drive once turned right, as the man below had explained, now leading through a gate and past a couple of new cottages, to Middle Hill itself.

It is a fine large and square eighteenth-century Cotswold stone house of two principal storeys with further attic windows above, added since

Middle Hill, Phillipps's house near Broadway, photograph, *c.*1860.

the time of Phillipps. The old main entrance is in front of you from that direction, under a stone porch with three arches. I have been inside only once, many years ago. Visitors today reach the house up a modern drive further along Snowshill Road, more suitable for cars, and Middle Hill is now so thoroughly and comfortably modernized that it is hard to envisage today what Simonides would have experienced in 1854, stepping through the porch from the summer sunshine into a dimly lit house which was a packed and airless mausoleum of medieval manuscripts.

Thomas Phillipps was the illegitimate and only son of a very successful calico manufacturer in Manchester. His father had purchased Middle Hill in 1794, and Thomas was brought up here, without knowing his mother. An isolated and friendless childhood may have been what started Robert Cotton on the companionship of manuscripts, and Phillipps too as a solitary teenager was already spending beyond his allowance on the acquisition of books and manuscripts about local history and topography. His father died in 1818, leaving him a considerable income but an entailed estate, one which could not be sold. The following year, Thomas married well, and his wife's obliging family was able to secure a convenient baronetcy for him. The new Sir Thomas then embarked on a lifetime of self-importance and unmerited hauteur. Like King Lear, he had three daughters, whom he bullied and taunted with ever-changing hints of eventual inheritances. All in all, Phillipps was not a very agreeable man, selfish, ill-tempered, grossly bigoted (notably towards Catholics), mean with money, litigious, and living forever in debt and on credit, as his dragon's hoard of manuscripts at Middle Hill grew from a merely vast private library into the absurd, with thousands upon thousands of volumes crammed into every room, including corridors, staircases and bedrooms, often in tottering piles leaving almost no floorspace for access between them or filling wooden boxes stacked to the ceilings. The quantities of manuscripts simply astounded anyone who saw inside the house. Of Phillipps's passion and obsession, there is no doubt. Madden frequently described it as bordering on insanity. For this reason, I expect I would have enjoyed an evening with Phillipps (as Madden often did), as long as I was neither Catholic nor a tradesman and did not stay too long.

His range of acquisition and interest was all-encompassing, extending with little discrimination from precious codices of late Antiquity right through to worthless manuscript papers of his own time. Many items were dirty and in poor condition, and Phillipps did not waste money

Sir Thomas Phillipps, photograph, 1860: the collector is holding a ninth-century Horace, now in the Houghton Library at Harvard, and on the table is a thirteenth-century Armenian Gospel Book, now in the Chester Beatty Library in Dublin.

on beautiful bindings or expensive repairs. The Abbé Rive would have been appalled. Like the British Museum, Phillipps was actively seeking out manuscripts of every nationality, and he benefited greatly from the dispersals following the French Revolution and the political turmoil of continental Europe in the nineteenth century. All foreign languages were included, although Phillipps himself read only Latin and Greek, neither especially well. Whenever possible, he bought in bulk. (He could have been a candidate for the Oppenheim manuscripts in Hebrew, even knowing he could never read them.) He kept a printing press on an upper floor of that neo-gothic tower at the top of Broadway Hill, part of the estate, where his harassed servants were made to print out numbered lists of the relentless purchases as they came in. A small oblong printed label with the number was then pasted to the spine of each book for identification. By the time of his death, Phillipps had perhaps as many as 60,000 manuscripts, documents as well as codices. Madden was right that they would one day all be scattered. There is hardly a rare-book library in the world today without at least one or two manuscripts that were formerly crammed into Middle Hill or into the even larger Thirlestaine House in Cheltenham, where Phillipps later moved. The collection took almost a hundred years to sift and disperse, beginning with a first auction in 1886, and I myself was initially employed by Sotheby's in 1975 for the principal purpose of cataloguing the very last instalments of manuscripts still being brought out in boxfuls from the Phillipps trove.

At the time of the visits by Constantine Simonides, Sir Thomas Phillipps was in his early sixties. His first wife died young and he had remarried. The childless and long-suffering second Lady Phillipps memorably claimed to have been "booked out of one wing and ratted out of the other." Photographs of Phillipps at this period show an upright unsmiling man with greying hair, soon to be white, slightly overlapping the tops of his ears. He had a straight nose and thick moustache. In pictures, at least, Phillipps appears carefully dressed in long dark jacket and white wing collar. Guests without business to transact testified to his courteous manners, but booksellers, competitors and most of his family despaired of his miserliness and single-minded obsession.

We are about to witness what was probably the third visit of Simonides to the baronet's house. On the first occasion, in 1853, the previous summer, Simonides had brought to Broadway a bundle of manuscript scrolls comprising short texts by the early Greek poet Hesiod, supposed to be of very ancient date, including the celebrated *Works and Days* on the origins of agriculture and labour, composed around 700 BC. There were ten narrow strips of seemingly old parchment, written on both sides in Greek, each about 10½ by 2 inches, attached together at the top onto a thin metal bar. Phillipps was sufficiently beguiled by the item to buy it. He had his printing press run off copies of a lithographed facsimile of its first lines of text, in a combination of large square Greek letters and a very strange-looking script resembling the spider-footprints of modern shorthand. When the manuscript eventually emerged from the Phillipps collection for resale at Sotheby's in 1972, it was obvious to twentieth-century eyes that the writing was an utter fabrication of no antiquity whatsoever. Phillipps had struggled to read it, not surprisingly, and, in a bizarre inversion of reality, Simonides then offered his skills as a palaeographer to transcribe the Hesiod neatly for Phillipps for an additional fee of £150 (Phillipps countered with £25 for a partial transcription). Simonides assured him that the manuscript included at least one unknown work of Hesiod. Phillipps had been to Rugby School and Oxford and this was exactly the bait to captivate a nineteenth-century Englishman drilled in the classics. All manuscript collectors are familiar with puzzled inquiries from unbookish neighbours as to what possible value there can be in gathering old books, and to have been able to announce the discovery of a lost classical text would have vindicated the entire library.

Later in 1853, Simonides had delivered five more scrolls of Greek texts to Middle Hill, comprising supposed works of Phocylides and Pythagoras and three Byzantine imperial documents. The receipt survives among Phillipps's papers now in the Bodleian. Again, Phillipps agreed in principle to buy the items if Simonides could make transcriptions for him. In May the following year, Phillipps proudly showed these startling acquisitions to Madden in the British Museum. He, in turn, recorded in his journal:

> I did not hesitate a moment to declare my opinion, that these were all by the same hand and gross forgeries; and I was *grieved*, but not *surprised* to hear Sir T. P. declare that in his opinion they were *genuine* (!) and probably relics of the Alexandrian library!!! Of course, although I did not express it to him, I feel the profoundest contempt for his opinion. In October last, when he wrote to me on the subject, I warned him against the purchase, but in vain. The vanity of possessing such *rarities* (supposing them to be genuine) has sufficed to counterbalance any doubts; and having paid a large price for these worthless specimens of modern knavery, of course Sir T. the more obstinately will defend their authenticity!

More was to come. Simonides had been hinting that he had a treasure greater than all these, nothing less than a classical manuscript of the *Iliad* of Homer. This was principally why Simonides was now returning to Middle Hill on 11 August 1854. By chance, we have a quite detailed record of the encounter because another visitor at that same time was the German map historian Johann Georg Kohl (1808–78), who was studying items in Phillipps's collection for his own researches and described the event in his volumes of reminiscences, published in Hanover in 1868. "Among the other guests . . .", Kohl recalled, "there was a Greek, whose name at that time was unfamiliar to me, but who had already made himself well enough known in the literary world. He . . . had brought with him various vellum rolls and pigskin volumes and like a pedlar had spread out his wares on the carpet, table and chairs."

The most important of these was the promised Homer. Kohl recalled it as "a small, thin, closely written, tightly wound, long roll of vellum which the Greek declared was the most valuable thing he had at the moment to offer." It comprised the whole of the first three books of the *Iliad* written in a script so microscopic that it all fitted onto both sides of a single scroll about 21½ inches long by about 2¼ wide, "so small", wrote Phillipps later, "as not to be read without a magnifying glass". Everything about it was eccentric, including the layout, which opened with a kind of pictographic design of a Greek temple formed of lines of tiny script. The left-hand edge of the whole scroll was written vertically with one letter below another, creating a cascade of letters right down the scroll and then all the way back up to the top again and then down to the bottom once more, and so on, in what is known as *boustrophedon*, meaning resemblance to the path of an ox plough, back and forth, or, in this case, up and down. It is a rare format known in archaic inscriptions on stone and pottery from the probable time of Homer himself, but then unprecedented in any surviving manuscript. It seemed a plausible indication of extreme antiquity. The text continued into the right-hand column in normal horizontal lines, as densely compacted as the grooves on a gramophone record. "Our conversation throughout the day turned on this remarkable object, and in the evening as well", wrote Kohl.

These discussions must have been complicated. Simonides knew some English, more than he pretended (as subsequent events showed), and Kohl and Phillipps had some classical Greek, which they were mostly obliged to write down to be comprehensible by the other. Where had Simonides found the Homer? "The Man is so mysterious about his acquisition of these MSS.", Phillipps wrote later in his printed catalogue; "a straight-forward honest person would state at once, with all candour, where he had obtained it, & how." In another memorandum to himself, kept with the Hesiod, Phillipps recorded, "He told me that that he was Cousin to one of the Abbots of a Monastery on Mount Athos; that the MSS he brought were either found in a Monastery on Mount Athos or in Egypt."

Several years later, Simonides modified this story to furnish further information. In 1859 a strange little book appeared by one Charles Stewart, *A Biographical Memoir of Constantine Simonides, Dr. ph., of Stageira, with a Brief Defence of the Authenticity of His Manuscripts*, published in London, printed in Brighton. The author is not clearly identifiable and the name was probably fictitious, but it may not be coincidence that it is a homonym of the Young Pretender and shares the initials

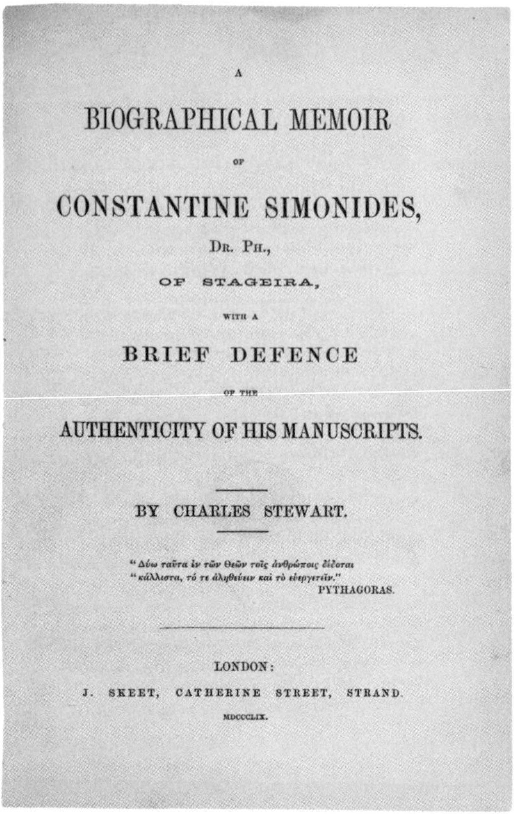

A

BIOGRAPHICAL MEMOIR

OF

CONSTANTINE SIMONIDES,

DR. PH.,

OF STAGEIRA,

WITH A

BRIEF DEFENCE

OF THE

AUTHENTICITY OF HIS MANUSCRIPTS.

BY CHARLES STEWART.

"Δύω ταῦτα ἐν τῶν Θεῶν τοῖς ἀνθρώποις δέδοται
"κάλλιστα, τό τε ἀληθεύειν καὶ τὸ εὐεργετεῖν."
PYTHAGORAS.

LONDON:
J. SKEET, CATHERINE STREET, STRAND.
MDCCCLIX.

The *Biographical Memoir* of Simonides, 1859, probably a fantasy by Simonides himself.

of Constantine Simonides. Phillipps, doubtless rightly, assumed that the book was really or mostly by Simonides himself, and certainly its careless orthography suggests material transmitted by dictation. In the *Memoir*, Simonides now seemed to remember that the abbot on Athos was his Uncle Benedict, that the manuscripts had been part of a library brought from Constantinople or Egypt by Saint Paul of Xeropotamou, son of the emperor Michael Kuropalatos (a real person, emperor 811–13), and that they had been hidden by the Orthodox monks beneath the ruins of a monastery on Mount Athos to save them from the Latinizers, or Roman Church, during the time of the Crusades. The *Memoir* recounts that Simonides had acquired the manuscripts from his uncle when he was living on Athos and removed them on a private ship to Syme on 29 August 1840, three months after Benedict's death. Detail was wanted: here it is, and the late Benedict could no longer confirm or refute it.

Hatred of the Roman Church, expressed fanatically by Phillipps, may oddly have been a common bond with Simonides, for even today the Greek Orthodox monks of Mount Athos are generally tolerant of almost any aberration of Christianity except Catholicism. Phillipps consulted George Bowen's recently published *Mount Athos* (1852) and learned there that some monks had fled to Athos at the time of the conquest of Egypt by the Saracens in the mid-seventh century, which seemed consistent with what he had suggested to Madden about manuscripts rescued from the Alexandrian Library, and he wondered whether "the Librarian might have put this roll, 2 inches broad, & half an inch thick, into his pocket, prior to the assault of the Caliph". Phillipps probably secretly imagined Middle Hill as a latter-day Library of Alexandria, the semi-mythical *el dorado* of all known manuscript texts, and the possession of one or two relics from the original *Mouseion* itself would to him be a dream and a link between collections beyond all others. Simonides apparently showed Phillipps supporting artefacts, including a small leaden jar, like an inkpot, in which he said the Hesiod had been found sealed up with bitumen. It all seemed almost credible.

The true identity of Constantine Simonides was puzzling too. This also came up in the conversations of 11 August 1854, as Kohl reported. Let Simonides himself reply. In a letter to the *Guardian* published on 21 January 1863 he said:

> Some ... state that I was born on Mount Athos, whereas at Athos no women are to be found, neither is a woman allowed, under any pretence, to visit Mount Athos, because this place was consecrated of old by the monks for retirement. Others say that I am Archbishop of the Island of Rhodes; some set me down as eighty-seven years of age, married, and the father of twenty-four children, four feet high, having hands of extraordinary length. Some again say that I am from Trebizond, Byzantium, Cappadocia, Odessa, Patara, Acanthus, Rhodes, and have a countenance very beautiful and like the fabulous Narcissus. Some write that I am a native of Abyssinia, because I have a very dark complexion. Each wrote and said what he pleased.

Simonides revelled in mystery. However, the *Biographical Memoir* asserts with unambiguous precision that he was born early on the morning of Thursday, 11 November 1824, on the island of Hydra, south of Athens, although his father was from Stageira. He also furnished Phillipps with a family tree, which Phillipps then had printed on his own press, as if doing so gave substance to something worryingly intangible. The *Memoir* tells that Simonides studied medieval manuscripts as a young man with his uncle on Mount Athos, and then moved around the eastern Mediterranean, obtained a doctorate (he said) in Moscow, and returned to Athos, Constantinople, Egypt and elsewhere, before arriving in England in February 1853.

While these matters were doubtless being spoken about in the drawing room at Middle Hill, Phillipps was still bewitched by the Homer, unable to leave it alone. Here is Kohl again:

> He took up this Homeric rarity, unrolled it, looked at the places where it had been damaged and the brown spots that were on it, examined the script alongside manuscripts he himself owned, held it in front of and behind the light, called in the aid of spectacles and a magnifying glass so as to inspect it in the greatest detail. The object obviously fascinated him; the vellum attracted and charmed him as a piece of jewellery would a woman . . .

There is no better description of a manuscripts obsessive, and the Duc de Berry and Robert Cotton and every real collector since the beginning of bibliophily have known and shared that exciting titillation of a potential acquisition, even when all common sense whispers caution. There is a willing suspension of disbelief, and a longing for possession which defies all rational logic.

Finally, Simonides went upstairs to bed. Phillipps, probably pouring more brandy, asked Kohl what he should do. The map historian pleaded that he was no expert on Greek manuscripts. Phillipps reluctantly admitted that there had been troubling rumours about the integrity of Simonides. He unlocked his desk and passed over "an issue of a German newspaper" which cast doubt on the man's reputation. Phillipps could read no German but Kohl could. It was doubtless the *Allgemeinische Zeitung* for 29 November 1853, the previous autumn, with an article afterwards conveniently reprinted in English in *The Athenaeum* in February 1856. The information there was credited to Andreas David Mordtmann (1811–79), *chargé d'affaires* of the Hanseatic League in Constantinople. It tells of Simonides in Athens trying to sell forged

RIGHT: The scroll of Homer, sold by Simonides to Phillipps in 1854, in full and with a detail of its opening.

manuscripts of classical texts which he claimed to have found on Mount Athos. "He was very mysterious and spoke always of his enemies and spies." This paranoia was a commonly reported characteristic of Simonides. The article recounted that when the manuscripts were denounced as fakes, Simonides, far from being discouraged, reappeared in Constantinople in 1851, declaring that he also owned a medieval treasure map recording the hiding places around the Bosphorus of manuscripts buried by the Comneni emperors (1081–1185), concealed to keep them from the hands of Latin crusaders, as the monks of Athos had done. The map indicated a site on the Prince Islands, where a manuscript of the lost acts of the first Apostolic Council of Antioch was apparently buried. Simonides was soliciting money to find it (or, no doubt, to supply it). The wise Arthimus IV, patriarch of Constantinople, refused to co-operate, declaring, "The acts of the Council of Antioch are superfluous; they would either confirm or would contradict the Canons of the Greek Church, and in either case it will be useless to dig."

Kohl was shocked. "After I had read the article, I had no difficulty in giving my host the advice he sought and my considered opinion. It was of course that it would be better for him to have nothing to do with the Homeric roll. And with that I withdrew to my manuscript-filled bedroom, while my bibliophile friend and host, with reading lamp, spectacles and magnifying glass at hand, continued for a long time to gaze thoughtfully at the ominous vellum, unrolling and re-rolling it", far into the night.

The following morning Kohl was down to breakfast late and was told that Simonides had already left. He congratulated Phillipps on escaping from a terrible misjudgement. The collector shuffled uncomfortably and brought out the roll of Homer, for which he had just paid £50, muttering that the possibility of its authenticity, however remote, had been too hard to pass up.

Nearly 170 years later, I went to see Phillipps's purchases from Simonides, many of which are now in the Beinecke Library at Yale University, in New Haven, Connecticut. This is one of the great buildings of America, designed by the architect Gordon Bunshaft in the early 1960s, a floating cube of translucent marble around a central tower of rare books. For the reading-room you descend into an elegant basement, lit by a sunken sculpture garden. There are long chrome and wooden tables. The first item I asked for was Beinecke MS 251, an entirely genuine (if routine) sixteenth- and seventeenth-century monastic manuscript in Greek comprising homilies and readings for saints' days between March and August. The front flyleaf has a flourished inscription in dark-blue ink in Greek, stating it to be a personal possession of "konstantinou simonidou"; it then became Phillipps MS 13864, bought from Simonides in 1854. One section is dated by a scribe, Cyrillus, in 1585 in the monastery of St Simon Petrus. This is indeed on Mount Athos, Simonopetra, 'Simon's Rock', founded on a high crag in the thirteenth century and still occupied. The nineteenth-century spine is lettered, no doubt for Phillipps, "LECTIONARY – GREEK MS. MOUNT ATHOS". It was Simonides' style to offer something modest but reassuringly authentic before producing his more exotic wares, and clearly Simonides really did have a source of manuscripts from Athos, as he said.

The next I saw was MS 581, given to the Beinecke by the dealer H. P. Kraus in 1976, as an acknowledged forgery. It is packaged in a special modern case, containing a compartment like a tiny sarcophagus, in which lies a nineteenth-century tubular wooden box for 'Congreve Matches' from the time of Phillipps. Shake it out and two tiny scrolls fall onto the table, each about the size of a single piece of macaroni, and as light and insubstantial as bubbles. The smallest puff of wind would blow them away. They unroll into strips up to 7 inches long. One comprises verses of Anacreon, the Greek lyric poet, in a script "so small as scarcely to be read with the magnifying glass", wrote Phillipps admiringly in his printed catalogue, "but as I have read some lines of it, I know it to be Anacreon". It is written at about 23 lines to the inch. The second scroll is the Pythagoras acquired by Phillipps from Simonides in 1853. "*Neither this, nor the* Anacreon, *do I believe to be forgeries*", Phillipps noted defiantly in italics. They are transparent fakes, in both senses, for their delicate parchment is as pellucid as cellophane. Phillipps, in a letter of 1856, suggested that such scrolls might have been written on skin made from the length of a boa constrictor. (Boa constrictors are in fact native only to the Americas.)

Then I fetched Beinecke MSS 582 and 583 from the issue desk and carried them back together to my table. The first of these contains verses of Phocylides and others, including the *Hymn to Virtue* of Aristotle. It is larger than the previous items, comprising seven pieces each about 13 by 4¼ inches. Although the *Biographical Memoir* of Simonides states that

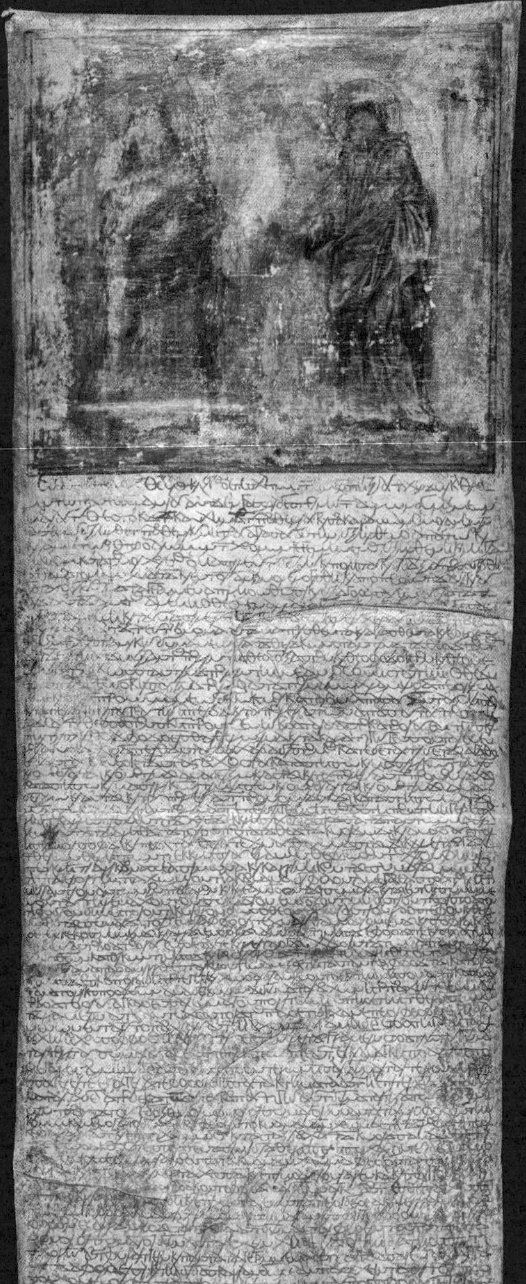

the manuscript was made in the fourth century and had been found on Mount Athos, Phillipps himself, inconsistently, was quite content in this instance to catalogue it as being "in the fine large hand of Simonides, & in his brown ink, which still smells strongly of the perfume in its composition". By dismissing some items as fakes, Phillipps probably felt that his judgement of others as authentic showed the thoughtful exercise of connoisseurship.

MS 583 is huge, formed of three unrolled sheets up to 28 inches long, now housed together by the Beinecke in a single box, as bulky as the first scrolls are microscopic. They are the three imperial charters bought by Phillipps with the Pythagoras and the Phocylides, supposedly from the chanceries of the emperors Theodosius II (AD 423), Michael (860) and Romanus (1031). Simonides did not conceal his connection to them, and even wrote his name on all three in small black script with the date 1852. The scrolls are mentioned in the *Biographical Memoir* also, claiming that the first two had been found by Simonides' Uncle Benedict on the island of Syme and the third on Mount Athos, and that the patriarch of Constantinople, Constantius (there were two of that name, 1830–35), had wept with joy when he was shown them. They are on thick nineteenth-century parchment, and are truly horrible. They open with dreadful illuminated illustrations of the emperors and various divine figures, now deliberately scrubbed away so that details of style are not clear. Here Phillipps again expressed uncertainty, rightly noting that all three had "a suspicious look of forgery".

Finally, I looked at the Homer. It has recently been transferred to the Beinecke Library from the celebrated manuscript collection of Professor Toshiyuki Takamiya, of Keio University in Tokyo, who had acquired it as a charming curiosity in the history of bibliophily, knowing it to be a notorious fake. I had lunch with him in New Haven later that same day, and he spoke of Simonides and Phillipps with tolerant amusement as his fellow fanatics. The Homer is a baffling and astonishing display of calligraphic virtuosity, not large, unrolled to about the length and width of a necktie. One cannot but admire the craftsmanship. Simonides is said to have darkened it with tobacco juice to create an effect of antiquity,

LEFT: A forged charter sold by Simonides to Phillipps in 1853, purporting to be an imperial chrysobull of Theodosius II (423), which Simonides said his late uncle Benedict had found on the island of Syme.

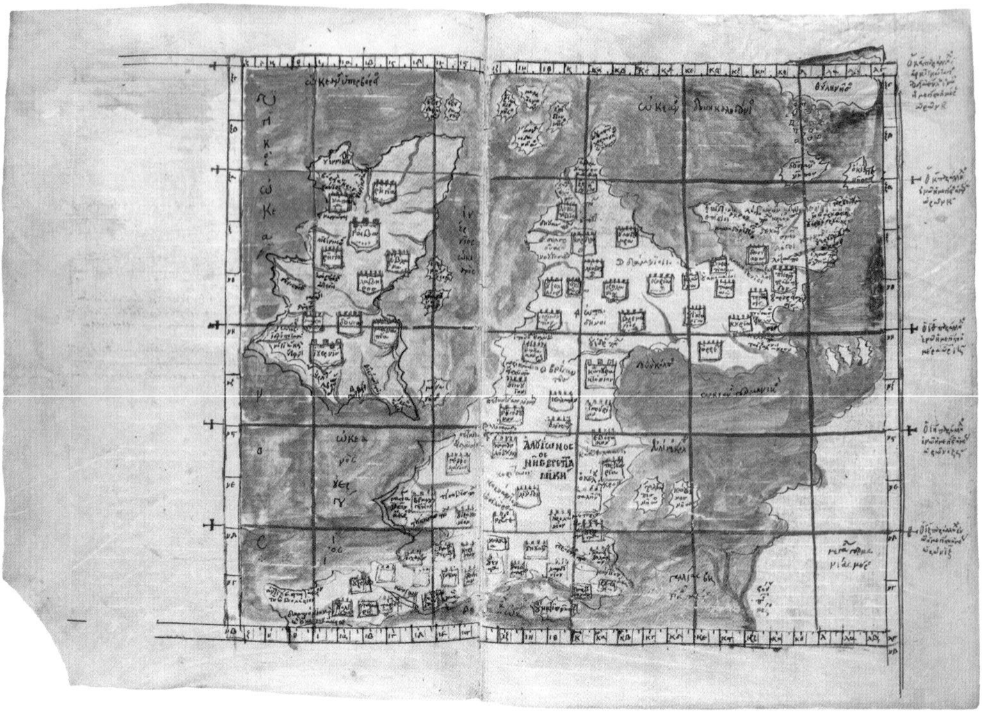

Map of the British Isles in a compendium of geographical texts in Greek, early fourteenth century, an authentic manuscript sold by Simonides to the British Museum in 1853.

the "brown spots" inspected by Phillipps, but even still it does not look to modern eyes to be older than the nineteenth century. Phillipps wilfully considered it probably the most precious of all his manuscripts.

During his negotiations with Middle Hill, Simonides was offering manuscripts to other libraries in England too. This was the great period not only of purchasing power in Britain but also of philhellenism across Europe, when Greek classical civilization and literature were especially admired. Keats and Byron were transported by Homer. The new building of the British Museum was itself modelled on the architecture of ancient Greece. On 22 February 1853, Simonides had presented himself there, in the company of W. B. Barker (1810–56), interpreter for the Foreign Office, and he showed his poetical scrolls to Sir Frederic Madden. "At first I was quite puzzled at their appearance," wrote Madden, "never having seen anything like them, but before I had completed my view of them, I unhesitatingly pronounced them to be recent forgeries, and declined having anything to do with them." Barker whispered to Madden in English that he believed Simonides to be a scoundrel. Nonetheless, they were both back at the Museum the next day with seven authentic Greek manuscripts of undoubted age, which Madden did agree to buy from Simonides, for a price probably of £35. The best of these, now Add. MS 19391, is a compendium of geographical texts of the early fourteenth century, including maps of Europe and of the British Isles. Once again, it demonstrably came from Mount Athos, and had belonged to the Vatopedi monastery on the north coast of the Athos peninsula. Today this would be a reason to decline a purchase, since no disposals by active monasteries are legal, and any national library would question not only the vendor's title but also legitimacy of export from Greece. In the nineteenth century, Mount Athos was a romantic provenance to be proudly trumpeted, like sculptures removed from the Parthenon.

Simonides came too to the Bodleian Library in Oxford, arriving on 10 November 1853 with a letter of introduction from Sir Thomas Phillipps. The Library staff had to take this seriously, since for decades Phillipps had been dangling his entire collection as a possible gift to his old university, under ever-changing and unacceptable conditions (such as that no Roman Catholic could ever be admitted to the University, a contentious issue at the time). Simonides met Henry Octavius Coxe (1811–81), then in charge of manuscripts and eventually becoming Bodley's Librarian. Coxe knew Greek well and was later part of a government mission to the monasteries of the Levant. There are two accounts of the interview, one from the perspective of the Library, first published in *The Athenaeum* in 1856, and the other related by Simonides to the writer of the *Biographical Memoir*. As usual, Simonides unpacked a mixture of genuine and spurious manuscripts. He showed the old items first and pretended not to know their age. This is good technique for a forger, since it does not actually require the telling of lies. Coxe informed him that the first pieces were twelfth-century. Their conversation is reported exactly.

"And these, Mr Coxe, belong to the tenth or eleventh century?", bringing out others.

"Yes, probably."

"And now, Mr Coxe," said Simonides, encouraged, "let me show you a very ancient and valuable manuscript I have for sale, and which I consider ought to be in your Library. To what century do you consider this belongs?"

"This, Mr Simonides, I have no doubt, belongs to the latter half of the nineteenth century." (The date of the conversation, we need hardly remind ourselves, was 1853.)

As Simonides recounted it, this icy response merely displayed the wanton ignorance of the Bodleian staff, since Sir Thomas Phillipps – "no mean judge of these affairs" – had accepted the manuscript's authenticity. Coxe then arranged to show his visitor some of the Library's own Greek manuscripts. One is described carefully enough in the *Memoir* to recognize it as MS Barocci 33, which Coxe told him was made in 1595, as indeed it was. In yet another strange reversal of reality, Simonides proclaimed it to be an obvious forgery.

It was not a happy meeting. The narrative in *The Athenaeum* concludes smugly, "Simonides gathered up his scrolls, and quitted Oxford by an early train." I have to say that this version of the encounter seems unnecessarily patronizing of a foreigner and "the products of his Eastern ingenuity". In fact, Simonides did not leave at once. By chance, the British Library copy of the *Biographical Memoir of Constantine Simonides*, which I asked to see simply for its text, belonged to the Oxford cleric William Tuckwell (1829–1919), who pasted into the front the original letter which Simonides wrote the following day to Coxe, who afterwards gave it to Tuckwell as a souvenir. It is dated from Dickeson's Hotel, Turl Street, Oxford, and is written in very old-fashioned and formal ecclesiastical Greek. Simonides realizes that the encounter had gone badly. The letter translates something like this:

> What wrong have I done you, honoured sir, that you showed me yesterday your worst disdain? I came to see you, without prejudgement, rather with courage as if you were my friend. However, if you consider yourself offended that I came, tell me and I will leave as I arrived. This, kind sir, I write with deepest sadness. Yesterday I understood nothing from the very beginning but LEAVE. Where did this come from? Only you know. Therefore, please explain my fault to me and I will apologise.

Simonides' clear inability to conceive how others saw him is the first evidence we have of his likely bipolarism.

Soon after parting with the Homer to Phillipps, Simonides was in Paris for several months in 1854–5. He came with a letter from the poet and critic Charles Sainte-Beuve (1804–69) dated 18 October 1854, introducing him to the Bibliothèque impériale (as the national collection was then called) and into literary society. The question has now been asked whether that letter was itself a clever forgery, in perfect French, saying of its subject, "mais il parle peu le français". Simonides made the acquaintance of the Comte de Marcellus (1795–1861/5), a Greek speaker, editor of Aeschylus and the man responsible for bringing the Venus de Milo to Paris. Marcellus was at that time working on an edition of the obscure Greek poet Nonnus of Panopolis, who apparently lived around the fourth or fifth century AD and converted to Christianity. He remarked to Simonides how almost nothing was known about the life of Nonnus. As Marcellus related afterwards, Simonides replied that he believed he owned exactly what was needed, among some manuscripts entrusted to him by an abbot in Greece. Fifteen days later he brought an old-looking Greek scroll with a detailed and very plausible biography of Nonnus, relating that the poet had been born in Heliopolis in the time of Constantine the Great but taught in Panopolis, where he eventually became a priest for thirty-seven years and died in the fourteenth year of the emperor Theodosius II (which would be AD 422), at the age of eighty-two. This was momentous information, if true. Marcellus transcribed it and then began to doubt its authenticity. If Nonnus was eighty-two in 422, his birth would have been in 340, three years after the death of Constantine. That is not necessarily evidence of falsification, for oral memory in Antiquity was often inexact on rulers' dates, a difficulty shared by the author of the nativity narrative in Luke's Gospel. Odder, however, is that Simonides' life of Nonnus was explicitly ascribed in the manuscript to Demetrius of Magnesia. This cannot be, if taken at face value, because Demetrius the famous biographer had lived in the time of Cicero, centuries earlier than Nonnus. Even here, there may be layers of deception and wordplay. The book of lives of authors by Demetrius, an attested but lost classical text, was called *Peri homonymon poieton kai suggrapheon*, literally 'On poets and writers with same-sounding names' – homonyms – and the conceit may be being carried forwards by the presumed invention of another later and also lost author of exactly the same name. It was all too unlikely for the Comte de Marcellus, who rejected the text as spurious. As he recounted, Simonides apparently showed neither emotion nor surprise on being told this, and Marcellus found the man's motives unfathomably mysterious.

In December 1855, shortly after his visit to Paris, Simonides appeared in Germany. Here he met the distinguished Leipzig classicist Karl Wilhelm

Dindorf (1802–83), showing him a twelfth-century Greek miscellany of religious texts. However, it appeared to be a palimpsest, prepared by erasing old parchment and rewriting on top of a much earlier chronicle in uncial script, identified by Simonides as the long-lost history of the kings of Egypt by Uranius, dedicated to one Deimachus. The dates of Uranius are as undocumented as those of Nonnus, but the assumption is of extreme antiquity. This manuscript is mentioned in the *Biographical Memoir*: "The importance of this work cannot be too highly appreciated, for it contains a treasure of historical matter hitherto unknown." Simonides had offered the palimpsest for sale to the Academy in Berlin for 3000 *thalers*. He assured Dindorf that he had many other potential buyers clamouring for it, but he allowed the professor time to piece out and transcribe the visible undertext of Uranius and to prepare a definitive edition of selected passages for Oxford University Press, *Uranii Alexandrini de Regibus Aegyptiorum libri tres*, Oxford, 1856. On the very day of publication, it was denounced by the German scholar Constantin von Tischendorf (1815–74) as a modern forgery. Simonides was arrested in Berlin but was released since the offence – if there had been one – had taken place in Leipzig under a different jurisdiction. On 4 February 1856, Dindorf wrote to the University Press in Oxford, "Under these circumstances I request you to stop the sale *immediately* and not to issue one single copy more . . . P. S. The question of Uranius will be also of peculiar interest for the British Museum and Sir Thomas Phillipps, who have purchased nearly 30 MSS from the same source." A handful of copies of Dindorf's edition had already been sold and are now rarities in the history of classical scholarship; the rest of the edition was pulped. The supposed original manuscript was evidently retained by Simonides.

By the late 1850s, Simonides was back in England. At the beginning of 1860, he moved to Liverpool, staying at first with the priest of the Greek Church there, one Nicolaides. He was introduced to Joseph Mayer (1803–86), immensely wealthy jeweller and collector of ancient art, who became the next important figure in the manuscript enterprises of Simonides. Their relationship ended several years later in a protracted legal dispute, the records of which were preserved by the Liverpool antiquary John Eliot Hodgkin (1829–1912), who was consistently sympathetic to Simonides. These include an extraordinarily detailed deposition by Simonides himself, and we may begin by listening to his side of the story.

Simonides attests that he had first met Mayer at his Egyptian Museum at 7 Colquitt Street in central Liverpool on 14 February 1860. The building has now gone, but early photographs show a gallery crammed with a treasury of ancient art and curiosities. Egyptology was fashionable in the nineteenth century, with its atmosphere of mystery and extreme antiquity. Mayer showed him a number of hieroglyphic inscriptions, which Simonides said he could easily translate for a fee. This he did, in a published pamphlet – "Price Half-a-crown" – dated 22 February 1860, scarcely a week later. In addition, "Mr Mayer then took from one of the glass cases a number of rolls of papyrus, which he stated had been purchased by him from Mr Stobart and asked me whether I could unroll, read, and interpret them. I replied that I could", Simonides affirmed, "but that it would require much time." In a different text, Simonides said of them that "These were, for the most part, so torn and damaged, lying pell-mell together, and offering neither connexion nor continuity . . . that at first I despaired at the formidable difficulties of my undertaking." Mayer, however, offered to pay Simonides handsomely for the work and an arrangement was made. Simonides emphasized in his deposition that he refused to take the scrolls home, since his host, Father Nicolaides, was uncomfortable with having valuable items in the house, and he attested that Mayer provided every facility for the unrolling to take place in the Museum.

So far, all this is entirely credible. The Reverend Henry Stobart (1824–95) had indeed bought a group of papyri in Thebes in Egypt in 1854 and had sold them unopened to Mayer in 1857; he confirmed this in a letter to *The Athenaeum* in 1861. Later, when the source of the papyri became controversial, Stobart pleaded that he could no longer be absolutely sure that they were the same items, and Simonides changed the provenance to remember that Mayer had probably acquired these particular scrolls from the dealer Joseph Sams (1784–1860), who had been in Egypt in 1822–3 and was now, like Uncle Benedict, conveniently dead.

The technique of opening the scrolls was to lay paste onto sheets of fine calico or paper attached to boards, and then to dampen the edges of the papyri gently with water and to roll them carefully over the adhesive surface, sticking and holding the pieces flat as each fragile section was loosened. By April 1860, Simonides was able to announce that astonishing discoveries were emerging. One of these was a partial text of the Gospel of Saint Matthew in Greek, ending with a startling colophon

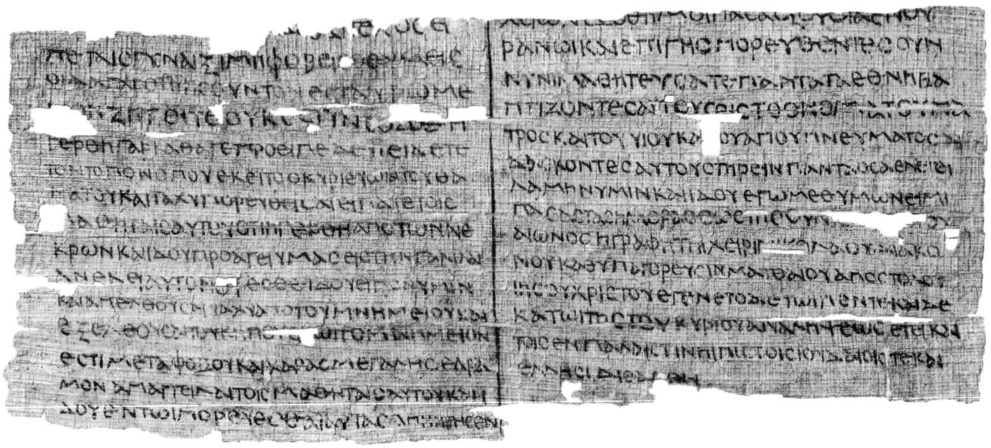

Papyrus of the Gospel of Saint Matthew, forged by Simonides in Liverpool in 1860.

stating that this scroll had been written by the hand of Nicolaus the deacon at the dictation of the apostle Matthew himself in the fifteenth year after the Ascension of our Lord and that it was circulated to believing Jews and Greeks in Palestine. This find was relayed to Mayer, who "was of course very much pleased", as Simonides recounted. Mayer announced it at a meeting of the local Historic Society on 1 May, and he was then already discussing plans for its publication. It was reported in the *Liverpool Mercury* on 2 May, "DISCOVERY OF ANCIENT BIBLICAL MANUSCRIPT AT MR MAYER'S MUSEUM", and the story was immediately picked up by the international press.

The date is significant. Charles Darwin's *Origin of Species* had been published a few months earlier in late November 1859. In the same year the discovery of the principal part of the fourth-century Codex Sinaiticus was announced to huge popular acclaim by Simonides' archnemesis and academic showman Constantin von Tischendorf: this was – and still is – the oldest substantially complete manuscript of the Bible in Greek, found in the monastery of St Catherine on Mount Sinai, in the wilderness between Egypt and Palestine. The drawing rooms of Europe were in uproar in 1860, suddenly divided between those who now felt sanctioned by Darwin to dismiss biblical testimony as a corrupted fiction and those overjoyed to have an accurate witness to the Scriptures from only 300 years after the life of Jesus. In a single stroke, however, Simonides appeared to have trounced Tischendorf with a Gospel manuscript datable to about AD 48, bearing the first-hand authority of the evangelist himself. This timely discovery, said Simonides, "will interest the whole Christian world ... as an evidence of the truth of Christianity." It gets better. One of the puzzling phrases of the New Testament is Jesus' statement that it is harder for a rich man to enter the kingdom of Heaven than for a camel to pass through the eye of a needle (Matthew 19:24). In the Mayer papyrus the word used is "κάλων", a rope, not "κάμηλον", a camel, now making logical sense. Stobart and Mayer were Anglicans. Hodgkin and Sams were Quakers. These were people to whom the Scriptures mattered very much. The news was sensational. Churches in Liverpool "heartily glorified God", as was reported, and evangelicals preached on the miracle manifested in their own age.

Simonides continued unrolling the Mayer papyri. Other biblical texts appeared, including seemingly contemporary manuscripts of the Epistles of James and Jude, and portions of Genesis with the Ten Commandments. It seemed that Simonides had the miraculous fortune throughout his career to disclose whatever people seemed to wish for most. Other happy finds in the papyri that year were part of an unknown work by Aristaeus, fragments of Zoroaster, and seven epistles of Hermippus. Liverpool was the busiest shipping port of Britain and people may have asked Simonides whether maritime texts ever occurred in manuscripts. Between 17 and 29 July 1860 he gradually uncovered the *Periplus* ('voyage') of King Hanno the Navigator, in ancient Greek script. This was indeed a rarity. In the fifth or sixth century BC, Hanno took an expedition by ship from Carthage out through the Pillars of Hercules and some considerable way down the west coast of Africa. His account of the journey was known to Pliny the Elder and other classical writers, who cite it. The narrative is famous for including a description of an island in a gulf named Notou Kera, inhabited by wild humans with hairy bodies. The Carthaginian sailors chased them and caught and killed three of the women, whom they skinned. These people, the *Periplus* tells us, were called "gorillas". When in 1836 the American naturalists Thomas Savage and Jeffries Wyman first recorded a new species of hairy African great ape, they knew their Pliny and so they called the animal a 'gorilla' after the ancient name used by Hanno: it is said to be the only Carthaginian word in common usage in modern English. The sole witness of Hanno's text to survive independently of Pliny is a Greek transcript of a long inscription reportedly set up by Hanno in the temple of Kronos in Carthage. This exists in two copies, both medieval. One is of the ninth century, now in Heidelberg.

The other is part of the fourteenth-century collection of geographical texts from Mount Athos, now British Library Add. MS 19391, described above, that very manuscript bought by Sir Frederic Madden in 1853 from none other than Constantine Simonides himself. He must have saved a transcript which later became his exemplar for the supposedly ancient papyrus of the same text.

Simonides was not modest about publishing his apparent discoveries with his name attached. He borrowed the New Testament papyri from Liverpool and took them to London, to see about having them traced by a lithographer. This is the only time when he is known to have had them in his unsupervised possession. In the event, he announced to Mayer that it would be cheaper and simpler to make the copies himself, as is imaginable knowing what we now know about him. The result is a large format book, about 15 by 11¾ inches, called *Fac-Similes of Certain Portions of The Gospel of St. Matthew, and of the Epistles of Ss. James & Jude, written on papyrus in the first century, and preserved in the Egyptian Museum of Joseph Mayer, Esq. Liverpool, with a Portrait of St. Matthew, from a fresco painting at Mount Athos ... by Constantine Simonides, Ph. D., Hon. Member of the Historic Society of Lancashire and Cheshire, &c. &c. &c.*, London, 1861. It is a religious-looking volume, like a

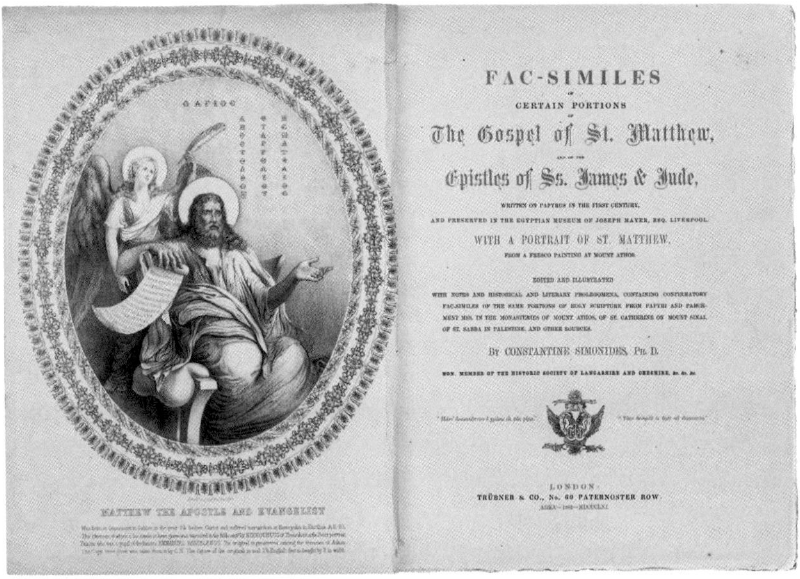

The book by Simonides on the New Testament manuscripts he claimed to have discovered in the Mayer Museum in Liverpool, 1861.

Victorian family Bible, with its title in red and black and the names of biblical texts in gothic type, and a thirty-six-page introduction in two columns. The frontispiece is a large drawing by 'C. S.' of a late mannerist fresco on Mount Athos showing Saint Matthew attended by an angel holding a pen aloft. It adds irrelevant Hellenic exoticism to a publication already steeped in saccharine religiosity. The *Periplus* too was published in more sober format with lithographs and a transcript by Simonides, *The Periplus of Hannon, King of the Karchedonians*, London, 1864, dedicated by its editor to the king of Greece. (Karchedon is the old name for Carthage.)

The papyri still exist and I have been to see them. The Mayer Collection is now part of what is called the World Museum in central Liverpool. The Matthew and the voyage of Hanno, both catalogued today as forgeries, are not on display. They survived a fire in May 1941, which destroyed many of the Museum's authentic papyri, and are kept in the Museum's off-site storage facility in the Liverpool district of Kirkdale. It is an area of scrap metal yards, builders' supplies and rental car parking. I wandered puzzled around the perimeter of the building described on my instructions, unable to find an entrance. Suddenly a wall seemed to spring open onto the street and a security guard asked if I was Christopher (I was). I was escorted by Chrissy Partheni, curator of Greek and Roman antiquities, up to a warehouse floor of metal shelves, filing cabinets and trolleys, all under strip lights, stacked with labelled stones and bones and pots and artefacts from across the globe. I sat at a huge table covered with a cloth of soft white foam. The pieces of papyri are either inset into apertures in conservation boxes tied with tapes or are sandwiched under glass in fitted grey card folders. All are still stretched out on the calico or paper which is itself then glued to larger card sheets. These are calligraphically inscribed in ink by Simonides in flamboyant Greek, which must have perplexed the public of Liverpool, identifying the texts and their discovery in the museum of the *kuriou Ioseppu Mauerou* by himself, 'Constantine Simonides, doctor of philosophy'. There was never to be any doubt where credit was due, strange since most forgers (one would have thought) might prefer to distance their names from their own productions. The best-preserved pieces of the Gospel papyrus are fortuitously the narrative of the Last Supper, which Saint Matthew witnessed and is of paramount importance in Christian liturgy, and the final columns of the text with the colophon naming the scribe, Nicolaus

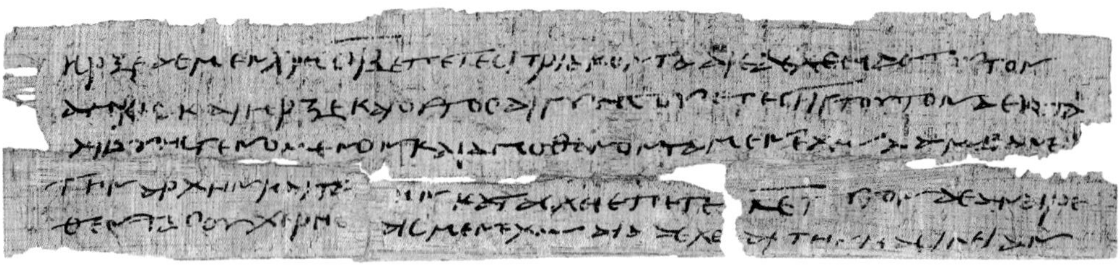

Part of the papyrus of the *Periplus* of King Hanno the Navigator, forged by Simonides in 1861.

the deacon, where the fragile papyrus has broken away precisely after the closing words. The *Periplus* opens with beautifully clear capitals "ΑΝΝΩΝ ΚΑΡΧΗΔΟΝΙΩΝ ΒΑCΙΛΕΥC . . .", unambiguously naming Hanno as king of the Karchedonians, dedicating the text to Kronos and to all the other gods worshipped in the same temple. The word 'gorillas' is easily readable in the second column of the second fragment. Oddly, several pieces of papyrus from the same apparent scrolls look different and are more hastily written. They are in inconsistent scripts and formats of very varying sizes and degrees of legibility, depending on the importance to modern readers of particular passages, a convenience uncharacteristic of ancient manuscripts.

Initially, these amazing finds gave very great satisfaction to Mayer, who sent Simonides a dozen bottles of wine on Christmas Eve 1860, with an invitation for the following day, which was declined. The local public response had been overwhelming. On 17 October 1860 the papyri were shown at a reception organized by the mayor of Liverpool in the Town Hall. On the 18th, Simonides presided over an exhibition at the opening of the new Free Library and Museum, including the biblical papyri and the *Periplus* of Hanno. In the exhilaration of being feted, he unwisely also included several Greek manuscripts in his own possession. Two, which caught the eye of the public, were described as "written on prepared human (female) skin, first century before Christ". Another was his palimpsest of the apparently long-lost text of Uranius of Alexandria on the ancient kings of Egypt. This was a great mistake. The supposed manuscripts on human skin ensured attention from the national press, and then the mention of Uranius stirred memories; old European newspaper cuttings were resurrected, and stories resurfaced.

One strange account emerged about how in 1847 Simonides had invented accusations against a blameless but clearly tedious and literal-minded American evangelical missionary in Athens, Jonas King

(1792–1869), charging him with holding Satanic orgies, which Simonides claimed to have witnessed. He regarded King as an enemy of the Greek Orthodox Church. The missionary had fled from Greece with his reputation destroyed, but it had escalated into a diplomatic incident in which eventually the king of Greece and the president of the United States themselves had both been obliged to intervene in 1854.

Most speculation concerned Simonides as a forger. The London press now became merciless, and journalists outdid themselves to find slurs on what they considered to be his irritating and self-congratulatory character. Stories from Constantinople, Middle Hill and Leipzig were now retold and syndicated. It was reported that in Germany Simonides had tried to sell a manuscript of forty-seven comedies by Menander, a playwright then known only in fragments, the complete plays of Sophocles and the library catalogue of Alexandria. *The Athenaeum* for 7 December 1861 opened an article, "Is there no limit to the public credulity?" Within a year, the excitement of the revelations in the Mayer Museum in Liverpool had escalated into international controversy. Both Mayer and Stobart began to distance themselves from the apparent discoveries. Madden found himself defending his own purchases of authentic manuscripts from Simonides in 1853, upset at suggestions that the British Museum had been duped. Phillipps, as one might expect, blustered indecisively, still hoping for vindication. Arguments flew back and forth over whether Simonides was a fantasist and forger, or an honest man much maligned for eccentricity and genius. There was an unpleasant whiff of xenophobia; the tiresome little man was indisputably not a gentleman. In the eyes of the popular press, he was already guilty before he had a chance to defend himself. In September 1862, Simonides' generous-minded supporter John Eliot Hodgkin wrote to his uncle, Dr Thomas Hodgkin, in the quaint diction of the Quakers and alluding to Matthew 25:35:

> A 'foreigner wanting help' has always a claim on thy kind attention. But this time it is not one in want of either money or health, but one who wants *fair play*. Simonides, whom the literary journals have been trying by wholesale vituperative, to tread out of notice, before his claims as a discoverer are heard, is well-known to me . . . All he wants is a friend or two.

In October, Simonides was persuaded to accompany several of the papyri to a meeting held at Christ's College in Cambridge, where the

Gospel fragments were inspected by invited scholars. Among those present was Thomas Wright, who reported to his fellow Quaker Hodgkin, "I am glad to say that, though they are all strongly prejudiced against Simonides, after an hour's careful examination, they came to the opinion that the MSS are genuine", subject to scientific analysis. Henry Bradshaw, who was there too, reported the consensus as less conclusive, remarking of Simonides, "He could speak and understand English pretty well."

One argument used against authenticity was that it was thought unlikely that any biblical papyri could survive at all from the ancient world, and in the 1860s none was known. A generation later, excavations in the Fayûm in Egypt and especially at Oxyrhynchus after 1896 furnished almost 150 authentic early Greek New Testament fragments on papyrus, and we now know that such items are by no means impossible. One is reminded of Moses Shapira (1830–84), a dealer from Jerusalem, who claimed to possess pieces of a 2000-year-old Hebrew scroll of Deuteronomy which he said had been found by Arabs in a cave in Jordan. In 1883 he offered it to the British Museum for a reputed million pounds (admittedly an absurd price) and he was widely ridiculed on the grounds that no item of such antiquity could possibly exist. Shapira shot himself in a hotel in Amsterdam and the scroll was said to have been sold for £25 to the Australian pioneer Sir Charles Nicholson (1808–1903), in whose office it was probably destroyed in a fire in 1899. Since the discovery of the Dead Sea Scrolls in 1947, some historians have wondered whether Shapira's manuscript might, in fact, have been genuine after all.

In January 1863 the Mayer papyri and the Uranius were finally brought to a scientific committee of the Royal Society of Literature, convened in London under the chairmanship of Sir Henry C. Rawlinson (1810–95), diplomat and Assyriologist. Those taking part included Sir Frederic Madden and Sir Charles Nicholson once more. Simonides was present with a Greek friend and was considered to be uncooperative and evasive. Neither on this occasion or any other did he offer an explanation. "The papyri lay on the table laid down within glazed frames, and the MS of Uranius was also there", wrote Madden in his journal. "It was, of course, impossible by candlelight to test the genuineness of these documents, and I therefore merely gazed at them, it being understood that they would remain for inspection a day or two after the meeting." Correspondence from Berlin was placed before the committee, with the incriminating evidence of the committee's own examination of the Uranius. The papyri were afterwards subjected to minute examination and comparison. The committee's report, published that year, leaves no ambiguity. The sheets of papyrus seemed to have been assembled by joining unconnected pieces, and they were deemed to have been deliberately discoloured before writing, to give an effect of age. The various scripts proved too similar to each other but inconsistent with the reputed range of dates. In places the writing was unnaturally strengthened as if retraced with excessive care, and it could be seen to have sometimes been steered crookedly around holes caused by later deterioration of the papyrus. Minute traces of modern blotting paper were said to have been found to be adhering to some letters. The committee was unanimous: "There are absolute grounds . . . for concluding that the papyrus examined . . . is a rank forgery, probably of very recent date."

This has been the universally accepted judgement ever since. The question remains of how Simonides did it. The unrolling of the scrolls was carried out in the museum under the supervision of the curator. Mayer or Hodgkin were sometimes also present, and both attest to this independently. The substitution of the texts was clearly some piece of clever conjuring, like the three-card trick, involving sleight of hand. This was the period of circus illusions and Simonides was a dextrous magician. I too have gazed at the pieces of papyrus. The material really does look ancient. This would be consistent with his falsification of those narrow rolls sold to Phillipps, which were quite possibly written on genuine strips of old parchment trimmed from the outer margins of real manuscripts. The Uranius too had at first deceived Dindorf by having been added to the pages of an obviously authentic medieval codex. In antiquity, writing on papyrus was usually on one side only, and the fact that the pieces in Mayer's museum were immediately pasted onto calico or paper which was then in turn stuck to cardboard before labelling means that the backs cannot be seen, even through bright light. Conceivably Simonides attached them face down, hiding original writing beneath, but I cannot detect any shadow of it, even when the papyrus is very thin. The discolouration noted in 1863 might have been caused by wiping away any original writing with a damp cloth. The film of brown wash skims the outer surface, with the result that the raised criss-cross fibres of the papyrus plant stand out unnaturally clearly, like the weft and warp of fabric. I myself have experimented with soaking modern papyrus in water: it becomes quite slimy and soft but does not disintegrate and it proves to be unexpectedly easy to scrape away a layer of writing. When it dries it is cockled and uneven, which would make pasting to card very sensible. The Mayer papyri are notably thin. In a nineteenth-century version, Simonides was making palimpsests of them. On the opening sheet of the *Periplus* I am fairly sure I can see faint traces of other letters in Greek still visible between lines 28 and 29 of the third column.

When first considering the problem, I had wondered whether the papyrus texts in Liverpool might eventually prove to have been originally genuine or partly so, and whether Simonides could have furtively substituted clever copies when he removed them for lithography, secretly keeping the actual manuscripts, rather as so-called restorers sometimes did with panels of stained glass or sculptures from gothic churches. However, the texts cannot have been ancient. We now know enough about the composition of the Gospel of Matthew to be certain that its text did not exist in the mid-first century; and the fact that Simonides himself had previously owned the only copy of the Periplus of Hanno to have been in private hands since the seventeenth century makes it overwhelmingly improbable that he should find another by coincidence alone.

Remember that when Coxe at the Bodleian told Simonides that his manuscripts were modern, he had responded by declaring that one of the Library's own treasures was itself a fake. Simonides evidently convinced himself that he was being persecuted by Tischendorf, who had denounced the Uranius and was now the darling of the press for finding the incomparable fourth-century Codex Sinaiticus. It was undoubtedly annoying for all patriotic citizens of Greece, newly independent, that the greatest Greek manuscript of all was associated with a strutting German. The discovery had occurred in stages. In 1844, Tischendorf had found a group of disbound fragments of the manuscript in the ancient monastery on Mount Sinai. He persuaded the monks to let him take forty-three leaves back to Leipzig. Here they became known as the Codex Friderico-Augustanus, named in honour of the king of Saxony, and they proved to be of quite exceptional value and the oldest witness to the biblical text. In 1859, shortly before Simonides was introduced to the Mayer Museum, Tischendorf returned to Sinai and was able to secure the rest of the manuscript, which he donated to the tsar of Russia and carried back in glory to St Petersburg in October 1862, just as the press were rounding on the forgeries of Liverpool. The response of Simonides was breathtaking. He

Constantin von Tischendorf, discoverer of the Codex Sinaiticus and archnemesis of Simonides.

declared that the Codex Sinaiticus was not only a modern forgery, but that he had made it himself.

According to Hodgkin, the first hint of this fantastic idea was made in a letter written by Simonides in January 1860, a few months after Tischendorf's initial announcement of the find. The *Literary Gazette* published gossip of this in 1861: "Should the rumour prove correct . . . the disclosures that will follow must be of the greatest interest to archaeology." Eventually, Simonides wrote to the *Guardian* in September 1862 with an extraordinary story. He remembered now that he had been on Mount Athos – not Mount Sinai – in November 1839, when his Uncle Benedict, abbot of the monastery of the holy martyr Panteleimon there, decided to send a new manuscript Bible as a diplomatic gift to Tsar Nicholas I, containing not only all the Scriptures in Greek but also texts of the seven apostolic fathers, copied in the traditional old style of the early Church. The monastery's resident scribe, Dionysius, declined the task, and young Simonides agreed to undertake it. He found a large bound manuscript "prepared many centuries ago" but hardly written and still with very many remaining leaves of blank parchment. He removed a short text at the front and copied the whole Bible and two other works quickly into the volume, stopping only when the supply of pages ran out. In the meantime, Uncle Benedict died (in the early summer of 1840, according to the *Biographical Memoir*) and the project was abandoned. Simonides carried his new Bible to Constantinople, where the former patriarch Constantius took possession of it in August 1841 to present instead to the monks of St Catherine on Mount Sinai. In 1846 he confirmed to Simonides that this had now been done. In 1852, Simonides himself went to Sinai and he saw it intact there, he said, except that his dedication to the tsar had been erased and the manuscript had been artificially aged to make it appear older.

Tischendorf and others rightly dismissed the claim as absurd. William Aldis Wright (1831–1914), then librarian of Trinity College, Cambridge, wrote to the *Guardian* in response that the Greek Bible consists of about 4,000,000 uncial letters and that it would be impossible to write and correct such a vast text in a little over nine months at most. He noted that Simonides was born – according to his own *Memoir* – in November 1824 and that therefore he was at the time only just (or hardly) fifteen. An official from the diocese of Salonika observed that it would have been illegal for a boy under twenty to stay on Athos. Others pointed out that the Leipzig leaves of the manuscript had already been abstracted from Sinai by Tischendorf in 1844, a fact Simonides evidently did not then know.

Reality never disconcerted Simonides, however. He simply saw these critics as enemies conspiring against him. After a short time, he too wrote back to the *Guardian* in January 1863 emending the published date of his birth, which he had previously given with such dogmatic precision, recalling now that he was actually born earlier, on 5 November 1820, bringing him more plausibly to nineteen when the Bible manuscript was supposedly made, and usefully producing a fresh-looking birth certificate to prove it. He revised his memory of seeing the manuscript at Sinai in 1852 and recalled now that the monks had damaged it and perhaps it was after all already missing some leaves by then. In the mid-1860s, the debate was still hurtling back and forth in the press, both in America and in England. Some journals, especially the *Literary Churchman*, were uncritically sympathetic to Simonides. Others checking anxiously with Mount Athos found no Abbot Benedict recorded. Simonides countered that a monk Kallinikos had been there at the time and would confirm the story, and when he proved unfindable on Athos, Simonides reported having just conveniently received two letters from Kallinikos the Hieromonk himself now in Alexandria and on his deathbed (effectively ending further correspondence), corroborating everything exactly as Simonides had claimed. When the monastery at Sinai denied receiving any visit from a Simonides in 1852, he explained that he had been travelling under another name. Finally, he insisted that he could prove that he wrote the manuscript since he had left personal inscriptions on several specified pages. When checked against the manuscript which was by then in St Petersburg, every one of these pages was missing or had been mysteriously mutilated. That, said Simonides, was further proof of conspiracy against him.

It is perhaps not generally known that the Leipzig portion of the Codex Sinaiticus was in London in 1865. It was brought over by Tischendorf to exhibit at a lecture he was to give in French at the Royal Society of Literature. On 3 February he took it to show to Sir Frederic Madden at the British Museum. Madden wrote, "Of course, we all looked at it with the greatest interest. For myself, I have never for a moment doubted its genuineness, in spite of the atrocious lies of Simonides, which will be a great satisfaction to English biblical scholars." In 1933 the principal part from St Petersburg (by then Leningrad) was sold by the cash-pressed Soviet government to the British Museum for a then unprecedented figure of £100,000. It is now Add. MS 43725 in the British Library.

The preposterous claim that Simonides created the Codex Sinaiticus has never quite died out. My mother's late cousin as a little girl put her sixpence in the collecting fund to help pay for it in 1933, but she told me sadly that she recalled that the manuscript was afterwards declared to be a fake. I actually decided to write this chapter after receiving an unsolicited email from an otherwise apparently rational American assuring me that Sinaiticus had been forged by Simonides and asking for my help in

ΚΑΙϹΥΒΗΘΛΕΕΜΓΗ
ΙΟΥΔΑΟΥΔΑΜΩϹΕ
ΛΑΧΙϹΤΗΕΙΕΝΤΟΙϹ
ΗΓΕΜΟϹΙΝΙΟΥΔΑΕΚ
ϹΟΥΕΞΕΛΕΥϹΕΤΑΙΗ
ΓΟΥΜΕΝΟϹΟϹΤΙϹ
ΠΟΙΜΑΝΕΙΤΟΝΛΑΟ
ΜΟΥΤΟΝΙΗΛ
ΤΟΤΕΗΡΩΔΗϹΛΑΘΡΑ
ΚΑΛΕϹΑϹΤΟΥϹΜΑΓΟΥϹ
ΗΚΡΙΒΩϹΕΝΠΑΡΑΥ
ΤΩΝΤΟΝΧΡΟΝΟΝ
ΤΟΥΦΑΙΝΟΜΕΝΟΥ
ΑϹΤΕΡΟϹΚΑΙΠΕΜ
ΨΑϹΑΥΤΟΥϹΕΙϹΒΗ
ΘΛΕΕΜΕΙΠΕΝΠΟ
ΡΕΥΘΕΝΤΕϹΕΞΕΤΑ
ϹΑΤΕΑΚΡΙΒΩϹΠΕ
ΡΙΤΟΥΠΑΙΔΙΟΥΕΠΑΝ
ΔΕΕΥΡΗΤΕΑΠΑΓΓΙ
ΛΑΤΕΜΟΙΟΠΩϹΚΑ
ΓΩΕΛΘΩΝΠΡΟϹ
ΚΥΝΗϹΩΑΥΤΩ
ΟΙΔΕΑΚΟΥϹΑΝΤΕϹ
ΤΟΥΒΑϹΙΛΕΩϹΕ
ΠΟΡΕΥΘΗϹΑΝΚΑΙ
ΙΔΟΥΟΑϹΤΗΡΟΝΕΙ
ΔΟΝΕΝΤΗΑΝΑΤΟ
ΛΗΠΡΟΗΓΕΝΑΥΤΟΥϹ
ΕΩϹΕΛΘΩΝΕϹΤΑ
ΘΗΕΠΑΝΩΟΥΗΝ
ΤΟΠΑΙΔΙΟΝ·ΙΔΟΝ
ΤΕϹΔΕΤΟΝΑϹΤΕΡΑ
ΕΧΑΡΗϹΑΝΧΑΡΑΝ
ΜΕΓΑΛΗΝϹΦΟΔΡΑ·
ΚΑΙΕΛΘΟΝΤΕϹΕΙϹ
ΤΗΝΟΙΚΙΑΝΙΔΟΝ
ΤΟΠΑΙΔΙΟΝΜΕΤΑ
ΜΑΡΙΑϹΤΗϹΜΗΤΡΟϹ
ΑΥΤΟΥΚΑΙΠΕϹΟΝ
ΤΕϹΠΡΟϹΕΚΥΝΗϹΑΝ
ΑΥΤΩΚΑΙΑΝΟΙΞΑΝ
ΤΕϹΤΟΥϹΘΗϹΑΥΡΟΥϹ
ΑΥΤΩΝΠΡΟϹΗΝΕΓ
ΚΑΝΑΥΤΩΔΩΡΑ
ΧΡΥϹΟΝΚΑΙΛΙΒΑΝ
ΚΑΙϹΜΥΡΝΑΝΚΑΙ
ΧΡΗΜΑΤΙϹΘΕΝΤΕϹ

ΚΑΤΟΝΑΡΜΗΑΝΑ
ΚΑΜΨΑΙΠΡΟϹΗΡΩ
ΔΗΝΔΙΑΛΛΗϹΟΔΟΥ
ΑΝΕΧΩΡΗϹΑΝΕΙϹ
ΤΗΝΕΑΥΤΩΝ·ΧΩ
ΡΑΝ
ΑΝΑΧΩΡΗϹΑΝΤΩ
ΔΕΑΥΤΩΝΙΔΟΥΑΓ
ΓΕΛΟϹΚΥΦΑΙΝΕ
ΤΑΙΚΑΤΟΝΑΡΤΩΙ
ΩϹΗΦΛΕΓΩΝΕΓΕΡ
ΘΕΙϹΠΑΡΑΛΑΒΕΤΟ
ΠΑΙΔΙΟΝΚΑΙΤΗΝ
ΜΗΤΕΡΑΑΥΤΟΥΚΑΙ
ΦΕΥΓΕΕΙϹΑΙΓΥΠΤΟΝ·
ΚΑΙΙϹΘΙΕΚΕΙΕΩϹ
ΑΝΕΙΠΩϹΟΙ·ΜΕΛ
ΛΕΙΓΑΡΗΡΩΔΗϹ
ΖΗΤΙΝΤΟΠΕΔΙΟΝ
ΤΟΥΑΠΟΛΕϹΕΑΥΤΟ·
ΟΔΕΕΓΕΡΘΕΙϹΠΑΡΑ
ΛΑΒΕΤΟΠΕΔΙΟΝ
ΚΑΙΤΗΝΜΗΤΕΡΑ
ΑΥΤΟΥΝΥΚΤΟϹΚΑΙ
ΑΝΕΧΩΡΗϹΕΝΕΙ
ϹΑΙΓΥΠΤΟΝ·ΚΑΙΗΝ
ΕΚΙΕΩϹΤΗϹΤΕΛΕΥ
ΤΗϹΗΡΩΔΟΥΙΝΑ
ΠΛΗΡΩΘΗΤΟΡΗΘΕΝ
ΥΠΟΚΥΔΙΑΤΟΥΠΡΟ
ΦΗΤΟΥΛΕΓΟΝΤΟϹ
ΕΞΑΙΓΥΠΤΟΥΕΚΑ
ΛΕϹΑΤΟΝΥΝΜΟΥ
ΤΟΤΕΗΡΩΔΗϹΙΔΩ
ΟΤΙΕΝΕΠΕΧΘΗΥ
ΠΟΤΩΝΜΑΓΩΝ
ΕΘΥΜΩΘΗΛΕΙΑΝ
ΚΑΙΑΠΟϹΤΙΛΑϹΑ
ΝΕΙΛΕΝΠΑΝΤΑϹ
ΤΟΥϹΠΑΙΔΑϹΤΟΥϹ
ΕΝΒΗΘΛΕΕΜ·ΚΑΙ
ΕΝΠΑϹΙΤΟΙϹΟΡΙΟΙϹ
ΑΥΤΗϹΑΠΟΔΙΕΤΟΥϹ
ΚΑΙΚΑΤΩΤΕΡΩΚΑ
ΤΑΤΟΝΧΡΟΝΟΝΟΝ
ΗΚΡΙΒΩϹΕΝΠΑ
ΡΑΤΩΝΜΑΓΩΝ·
ΤΟΤΕΕΠΛΗΡΩΘΗ

ΤΟΡΗΘΕΝΔΙΑΙΕΡΕ
ΜΙΟΥΤΟΥΠΡΟΦΗ
ΤΟΥΛΕΓΟΝΤΟϹ
ΦΩΝΗΕΝΡΑΜΑΗ
ΚΟΥϹΘΗ·ΚΛΑΥΘΜΟϹ
ΚΑΙΟΔΥΡΜΟϹΠΟΛΥϹ·
ΡΑΧΗΛΚΛΑΙΟΥϹΑΤΑ
ΤΕΚΝΑΑΥΤΗϹΚΑΙ
ΟΥΚΗΘΕΛΕΝΠΑΡΑ
ΚΛΗΘΗΝΑΙΟΤΙΟΥ
ΚΕΙϹΙΝ
ΤΕΛΕΥΤΗϹΑΝΤΟϹ
ΔΕΤΟΥΗΡΩΔΟΥΙ
ΔΟΥΑΓΓΕΛΟϹΚΥ
ΦΑΙΝΕΤΑΙΚΑΤΟΝΑΡ
ΤΩΙΩϹΗΦΕΝΑΙ
ΓΥΠΤΩΛΕΓΩΝΕ
ΓΕΡΘΕΙϹΠΑΡΑΛΑΒΕ
ΤΟΠΑΙΔΙΟΝΚΑΙΤΗΝ
ΜΡΑΑΥΤΟΥΚΑΙΠΟ
ΡΕΥΟΥΕΙϹΓΗΝΙΗΛ
ΤΕΘΝΗΚΑϹΙΝΓΑΡ
ΟΙΖΗΤΟΥΝΤΕϹΤΗΝ
ΨΥΧΗΝΤΟΥΠΕΔΙΟΥ·
ΟΔΕΕΓΕΡΘΙϹΠΑΡΕ
ΛΑΚΕΤΟΠΑΙΔΙΟΝ·
ΚΑΙΤΗΝΜΡΑΑΥΤΟΥ·
ΚΑΙΕΙϹΗΛΘΕΝΕΙϹ
ΓΗΝΙΗΛ
ΑΚΟΥϹΑϹΔΕΟΤΙΑΡ
ΧΕΛΑΟϹΒΑϹΙΛΕΥΕΙ
ΤΗϹΙΟΥΔΑΙΑϹΑΝΤΙ
ΤΟΥΠΡϹΑΥΤΟΥΗΡΩ
ΔΟΥΕΦΟΒΗΘΗΕΚΕΙ
ΑΠΕΛΘΕΙΝΧΡΗΜΑ
ΤΙϹΘΕΙϹΔΕΚΑΤΟΝΑΡ
ΑΝΕΧΩΡΗϹΕΝΕΙϹ
ΤΑΜΕΡΗΤΗϹΓΑΛΙ
ΛΑΙΑϹΚΑΙΕΛΘΩΝ
ΚΑΤΩΚΗϹΕΝΕΙϹ
ΠΟΛΙΝΛΕΓΟΜΕΝΗΝ
ΝΑΖΑΡΕΤΟΠΩϹ
ΠΛΗΡΩΘΗΤΟΡΗΘΕΝ
ΔΙΑΤΩΝΠΡΟΦΗΤΩΝ
ΟΤΙΝΑΖΩΡΑΙΟϹ
ΚΛΗΘΗϹΕΤΑΙ:
ΕΝΔΕΤΑΙϹΗΜΕΡΕϹ
ΕΚΕΙΝΑΙϹΠΑΡΑΓΕΙ

ΝΕΤΑΙΙΩΑΝΝΗϹΟ
ΒΑΠΤΙϹΤΗϹΚΗΡΥϹ
ϹΩΝΕΝΤΗΕΡΗΜΩ
ΤΗϹΙΟΥΔΕΑϹΛΕΓΩΝ·
ΜΕΤΑΝΟΕΙΤΕΗΓΓΙ
ΚΕΝΓΑΡΗΒΑϹΙΛΕΙΑ
ΤΩΝΟΥΝΩΝΟΥ
ΤΟϹΓΑΡΕϹΤΙΝΟΡΗ
ΘΙϹΔΙΑΗϹΑΙΟΥΤΟΥ
ΠΡΟΦΗΤΟΥΛΕΓΟΝ
ΤΟϹΦΩΝΗΒΟΩΝ
ΤΟϹΕΝΤΗΕΡΗΜΩ·
ΕΤΟΙΜΑϹΑΤΕΤΗΝ
ΟΔΟΝΚΥΕΥΘΙΑϹ
ΠΟΙΕΙΤΑΙΤΑϹΤΡΙ
ΒΟΥϹΑΥΤΟΥ
ΑΥΤΟϹΔΕΟΙΩΑΝ
ΝΗϹΕΙΧΕΝΤΟΕΝ
ΔΥΜΑΑΥΤΟΥΑΠΟ
ΤΡΙΧΩΝΚΑΜΗΛΟΥ·
ΚΑΙΖΩΝΗΝΔΕΡ
ΜΑΤΙΝΗΝΠΕΡΙ
ΤΗΝΟϹΦΥΝΑΥΤΟΥ·
ΗΔΕΤΡΟΦΗΗΝΑΥ
ΤΟΥΑΚΡΙΔΕϹΚΑΙΜΕ
ΛΙΑΓΡΙΟΝ
ΤΟΤΕΕΞΕΠΟΡΕΥΕ
ΤΟΠΡΟϹΑΥΤΟΝΙ
ΕΡΟϹΟΛΥΜΑΚΑΙ
ΠΑϹΑΗΙΟΥΔΕΑΚΑΙ
ΠΑϹΑΗΠΕΡΙΧΩ
ΡΟϹΤΟΥΙΟΡΔΑΝΟΥ
ΚΑΙΕΒΑΠΤΙΖΟΝΤΟ
ΕΝΤΩΙΟΡΔΑΝΗ
ΠΟΤΑΜΩΕΞΟΜΟ
ΛΟΓΟΥΜΕΝΟΙ
ΤΑϹΑΜΑΡΤΙΑϹΑΥ
ΤΩΝ·
ΙΔΩΝΔΕΠΟΛΛΟΥϹ
ΤΩΝΦΑΡΙϹΑΙΩΝ
ΚΑΙϹΑΔΔΟΥΚΑΙΩΝ
ΕΡΧΟΜΕΝΟΥϹΕ
ΠΙΤΟΒΑΠΤΙϹΜΑ
ΕΙΠΕΝΑΥΤΟΙϹΓΕΝ
ΝΗΜΑΤΑΕΧΙΔΝΩΝ
ΤΙϹΥΠΕΔΕΙΞΕΝΥ
ΜΙΝΦΥΓΙΝΑΠΟ
ΤΗϹΜΕΛΛΟΥϹΗϹ

proving it. I told him that such nonsense belonged with those credulous conspiracy theories such as that the moon landings of 1969 were faked, and he replied that indeed they were. He referred me to a book, which I have now read, *The Forging of Codex Sinaiticus. An Illustrated Consideration of the Anomalies and the Many Indicators of 19th-century Forgery Contained in the Manuscript* by Bill Cooper. The author is described as Adjunct Professor of Providential History and Apologetics at the Institute for Creation Research School of Biblical Apologetics. The gist is that Tischendorf was in a secret plot with the Vatican and the Jesuits to defraud evangelical Protestants of the received text of their English Bible and that Sinaiticus, together with the Codex Vaticanus and the Bodmer papyri and other great early biblical witnesses, are all fakes, and that Simonides had been unknowingly tricked into being an accomplice. I came down the stairs after reading this in the British Library shaking my head in despair at human nature, and I made for the Library's Treasures Gallery. There on permanent display is one volume of the Codex Sinaiticus in an area of the exhibition called 'Sacred Texts', appropriately open in the Gospel of Matthew. I gazed yet again at its huge pages, ancient undulating parchment and impeccably fourth-century script. The Codex Sinaiticus was not – let me repeat, was absolutely not – forged by Constantine Simonides.

What drove him? For a start, as suggested above, he probably suffered from what is now called bipolar disorder. Symptoms can include alternating episodes of euphoric fervour with rapid speech and a delusional sense of self-importance, followed by depression and a conviction of persecution. Both those fit accounts of Simonides. He was socially awkward and had little awareness of himself as he came across to other people. He was technically a very accomplished scribe, and he was fortunate that most European scholars, even those who knew Greek, were less familiar with the nuances of its script than they were with the Latin alphabet. Unlike many forgers, Simonides was not primarily motivated by money. The manuscripts of Demetrius of Magnesia and Uranius had no reward to him beyond the satisfaction of furnishing experts with the texts they longed to find, a rationale which the Comte de Marcellus found inexplicable. Although he fell out with Mayer in the end,

LEFT: The Codex Siniaticus, fourth century, the primary manuscript of the Greek Bible, found on Mount Sinai in 1859.

demanding payment for expenses which he reasonably claimed had been promised to him, he did not sell the Liverpool papyri and he never owned them or made money from them. He certainly enjoyed adulation as a manuscript scholar and discoverer. He revelled in glory. He was also a pathological liar. Like many such, he probably came to believe in his own fantasies and in the authenticity of his forgeries. This conviction made him very persuasive.

There may be a parallel with the making of Greek icons. There is a Byzantine tradition that an icon can be copied to replace an old one which is worn out, and that the new version somehow still continues to represent the sacred original. An icon which seems to a secular art historian to be patently of no great age may nonetheless still be claimed to be (for example) an actual portrait of the Mother of God painted by Saint Luke. Writing manuscripts in medieval Greek monasteries was rather like that. In Western Europe, a medieval scribe copying an early exemplar would usually preserve the original as well. In an Orthodox scriptorium the new manuscript took the place of the old one, which was often then discarded. Simonides was a product of that eastern Mediterranean religious world, so different from Worcestershire or Merseyside, and perhaps he too genuinely believed that his forgeries were in some way reborn originals, taking the legitimate place of manuscripts which had existed thousands of years earlier. His silent puzzlement, when accused of forgery, was possibly unfeigned.

It is said that every age makes forgeries of what its people care about most. In that sense, knowing what was being faked is essential to understanding any period of history. There would have been no place for a forger of manuscripts in the time of the Duc de Berry (relics perhaps, but not books), and probably not for Cotton or Oppenheim. The Abbé Rive was beginning to define and question authenticity in manuscripts. In the mid-nineteenth century, as Darwinism and science battled with religious revival, the popular need for ancient verities became paramount. Simonides provided exactly what people most wanted at that moment. The outrage expressed in the enormous press coverage of his forgeries would probably not happen today, when financial fraud is our major news instead.

In the end, we can be certain of very few absolute facts about the life of Constantine Simonides. He undoubtedly falsified his birth date and many aspects of his career. We do not even know for sure that Simonides was his real name. There was a poet Simonides of Ceos in the Greek islands in the fifth century BC, whose elusive identity might have seemed to him to be as re-creatable as a contemporaneous manuscript of Homer. As in the lost biographical homonyms of Demetrius of Magnesia, the name of a great poet or writer could reappear in another age. Simonides means son of Simon. He would have known too of Simon Magus, the magician described in the Acts of the Apostles. There is no better name for the conjurer of manuscripts than the magician's son. Even his death is perhaps a stage-managed illusion. Most historians, including Munby in his account of Phillipps, report that Simonides died of leprosy in Alexandria in September 1867, as was widely announced in the press. Leprosy seemed fittingly biblical and very final. Simonides had benefited previously from the death of witnesses as a way of terminating inquiries.

Then the stories began again. A British clergyman announced that he had encountered a man he believed to be Simonides in St Petersburg in the late 1860s. A correspondent of the Vienna *Tageblatt* recounted more credibly having met Simonides in Corfu in the 1880s, when the irrepressible sorcerer brought out what he claimed was a twelfth-century manuscript relating to the Crusades, which he was hoping to sell to the Academy of Sciences in Vienna. When told that everyone thought he was dead, Simonides said he had been, and had been buried, but that the sound of the gravel falling on his coffin had roused him just in time to be rescued from the grave. A second death of Constantine Simonides "the notorious Greek manuscript forger" in a little town in Albania was reported in *The Times* on 18 October 1890.

CHAPTER TEN

The Editor: Theodor Mommsen

There is a well-known mid-nineteenth-century painting by the Bavarian artist Carl Spitzweg (1808–85) called *Der Bücherwurm*, 'the book worm', caricaturing an obsessive researcher in a library. A myopic white-haired man is standing precariously on the very top of a high set of steps in the corner of a once-splendid baroque library, possibly monastic, its shelves filled almost to the ceiling with worn and ancient volumes bound in leather and parchment. The man's old-fashioned clothes are heedlessly dishevelled and a handkerchief dangles unnoticed from his back pocket. He is peering with utmost concentration into a big book held in his left hand; another open volume is in his right hand, a third is clamped under his arm and a fourth is clasped between his knees. He seems oblivious to the danger of his position and the risk to the books he holds.

The figure does not represent Theodor Mommsen (1817–1903) – it is too early, for one thing, and the hair is too short – but he may have known it, for it was widely reproduced, and more than anyone else Mommsen grew publicly into that role, revelling in an international reputation as a compulsive user of manuscripts and an unworldly and relentlessly hard-working Germanic intellectual. Practically every rare-book librarian of Europe would have met Mommsen at some time. There are good descriptions by his daughter Adelheid and others of his own vast library at home in his big house in Charlottenburg, now a western suburb of Berlin. The whole top floor was crammed with books, at least twelve shelves high, as well as in the corridors, attic and stairwell. These were reference books, not manuscripts or antiquarian material. Up against the bookcases, as in the Spitzweg painting, were wooden library ladders, which Mommsen would climb precariously in pursuit of

RIGHT: Theodor Mommsen (1817–1903), portrait by Ludwig Knaus, 1881.

Carl Spitzweg, *Der Bücherwurm*, *c.*1850, caricature of an obsessive bibliophile.

information, with his pen gripped in his mouth and his glasses propped up on his forehead, for like the man in the picture he was always very short-sighted. He too used many volumes at once. As described by his daughter, he would take a candle when working in his library late at night or before dawn, a habit with truly disastrous consequences for medieval manuscripts in 1880, as we will see.

Beyond his work at home, Mommsen was even in his lifetime a celebrity, lionized as a university professor had probably never been before, an acknowledged polymath, an outspoken liberal in politics, the world's leading Roman and legal historian, editor of classical texts, the author of more than 1500 publications, and the only manuscripts scholar ever to win a Nobel Prize. What amounts to a sacred shrine to his memory still exists in Garding, the town where he was born in Schleswig. At the time of his birth the region was an independent duchy within south-west Denmark, still administered by the Danish crown. His father, Jens

Mommsen, was the Lutheran pastor there and his name sounds Scandinavian, although their family was German. You can drive up there now from Hamburg, and as you finally leave the terrifying motorway complex over the Elbe river the landscape becomes pastoral and undulating, like most of Denmark. Garding is a small farming community on the Eiderstedt peninsula on the west coast, not far from the sea, about forty miles south of the current Danish border.

The heralded *Mommsen Geburtshaus* is a modest former parsonage in the cobbled *Markt* and is still a principal sight for visitors to the town, with its steep-gabled whitewashed frontage right on the edge of the road. Above the door is a plaque recording that Professor Theodor Mommsen was born in this house on 30 November 1817, a name so well-known when the plaque was erected in 1903 that it needed nothing further to explain who he was. There are three windows on the street level, two above, and a tiny attic window at the very top. The adjacent parish hall was adapted into a small museum about Mommsen in 1987, and there we can learn about his childhood and early life.

Although they commemorate him in Garding, the Mommsen family moved away in 1821 to a new parish in Bad Oldesloe, between Hamburg and Lübeck, where Theodor was actually brought up. He eventually had three brothers and two sisters. They belonged within that distinctively north European Protestant world which sets high value on education. The children were largely taught at home by their father, to save school fees, saturating them in languages and European literature. The second son, Tycho (born in 1819), became the notable German translator of Shakespeare. This was the great age of Northern Romanticism, represented in Weimar by Goethe (1749–1832), poet and genius and himself owner of several medieval manuscripts, and the painter Caspar David Friedrich (1774–1840) in Dresden, evoking immeasurably huge Baltic landscapes with gothic ruins and monks alone in the snow. Although Theodor Mommsen abandoned Christianity, he retained for ever the Lutheran ethics of industry and thrift and a northern feeling for the vastness of distance and time. He attended university in Kiel, then the least expensive option, graduating in philosophy and jurisprudence. He also wrote poetry, like Goethe, some of it published while he was still a student.

In 1843, aged twenty-six, Mommsen obtained a travel grant to France and Italy, and was away for four years. As a formative experience, it has parallels with Anselm's youthful meandering around France before settling on Bec, or William Gray's rambles through Europe buying books in the 1440s. Like both of those, Mommsen was already showing a precocious interest in manuscripts, especially texts of law and the Latin classics. He kept a diary of his travels, which includes the frustrations familiar to all of us when we begin to visit European research libraries. When he asked to see medieval manuscripts at the national library in Paris in October 1844, he was told to come back the next day; when he first went to the Biblioteca Riccardiana in Florence that December, it was shut. However, he managed with perseverance to gain access to manuscripts of Roman grammarians and historians in Paris, and what he described from no experience as their 'strange' copy of the Justinian law code. This was the same manuscript misdated by Montfaucon to *c.*400, as had so outraged the Abbé Rive (above, p. 257). In Florence, Mommsen examined manuscripts of Cicero, Lucretius, Varro, Pompeius Festus and Nonius, and letters from Niccolò Niccoli to Poggio Bracciolini. He was probably not sure what to be looking for. He confided to his diary some disappointment in not making important discoveries.

If manuscripts were initially discouraging for the young Mommsen, Roman monumental inscriptions were the great revelation of his journey into the Italian states. They were (and still are) to be found everywhere there, like classical ruins, hardly noticed at all by the local inhabitants. Together with Roman coins, lapidary inscriptions are a kind of manuscript, in the sense that they include texts in Latin of a period from which almost no conventional manuscripts survive, and they often reflect imperial or local administration undocumented elsewhere. This was the backdrop of Roman law, a subject which occupied Mommsen throughout his life. The humanist scholars of north-eastern Italy in the later fifteenth century had also regarded Roman inscriptions as legitimate classical texts. They copied them into sylloges, anthologies which were used both as historical sources and as models for letterforms in manuscripts and early printing. Robert Cotton too had collected Roman inscriptions as an inseparable part of his passion for the unpublished records of history.

On 17 January 1845, Mommsen wrote a letter from Rome respectfully introducing himself to the noted antiquary Bartolomeo Borghesi (1781–1860), numismatist and scholar of ancient inscriptions, who lived in San Marino in north-central Italy. He explained that he was considering making a collection of all Roman laws and decrees of the senate which survive written on either bronze or marble, saying that he had taken rubbings from originals in Genoa, Pisa, Florence and elsewhere and that he hoped that Borghesi might give him access to others, of which copies were known to be in his possession. Their fateful meeting took place in the summer. Mommsen's diary for 14 July 1845 describes Borghesi as 'an old magnificent man':

> He invited me to stay with him and I am living in his house. He impressed me as a scholar as no one else has so far. If I were to say what I think, I shall either have to put epigraphy aside or to attempt to become what he is.

Together they outlined a plan for Mommsen to record Roman monumental inscriptions of all kinds preserved in the kingdom of Naples, a vast undertaking finally published in 1852. A whimsical sketch made in 1846 by Julius Friedländer, one of his travelling companions, shows Mommsen on the back of a sleepy horse in the middle of a river in Abruzzo, balancing a ladder which he intends to climb up in order to reach a Roman inscription on the side of a bridge, cheered from the parapets by the astonished Italian bystanders.

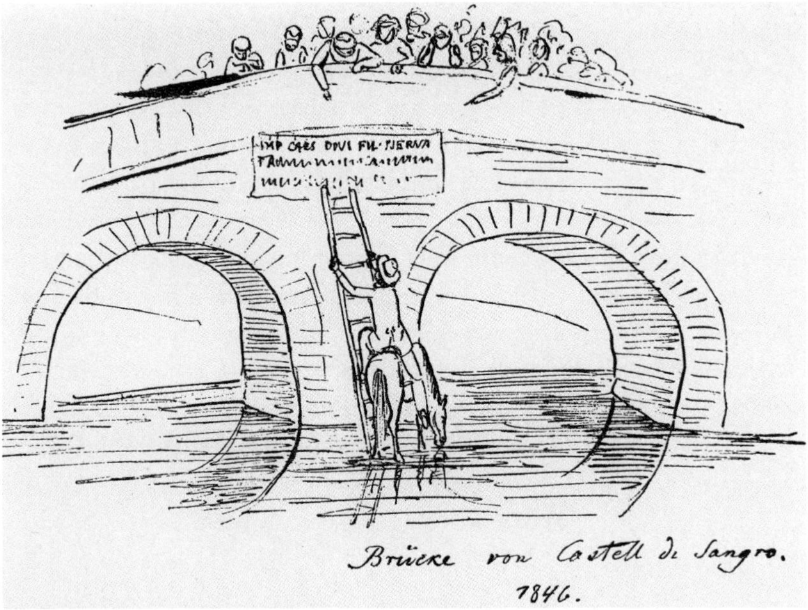

Mommsen climbing up to inspect a Roman inscription, sketch by his travelling-companion in Italy, Julius Friedländer, 1846.

Mommsen returned to northern Europe in 1847 and was appointed in due course to a lectureship in law at the University of Leipzig. Politics are never far below the surface in Germany. Like many intellectuals at the time, Mommsen supported the revolutions of 1848–9, seeking the radical reform of society, the abolition of local kingdoms and principalities, and the unification of Germany. He edited a liberal newspaper, the *Schleswig-Holstein Zeitung*, calling for the separation of his native region from Denmark. Following the failure of the uprising in Saxony in May 1849 and subsequent political indiscretions, Mommsen was dismissed from his post in Leipzig and moved to the University of Zurich. It was here that he wrote the first volumes of his majestic *Römische Geschichte*, or *History of Rome*, his most famous work, for which he was eventually awarded the Nobel Prize for Literature in 1902. He lodged with a bookbinder's family in Strehlgasse in what is now the Old Town of Zurich, between the river and the medieval Augustinerkirche. (The site is occupied today by a modern bedding shop and an upstairs beauty salon, but a plaque above the entrance records that this was where Mommsen had lived in 1852–4.) The popular success of the *Römische Geschichte* was in part because of its vivid parallels between ancient Rome and national events of the author's own time, comparing the consolidation of the Roman republic with contemporary movements for Italian unification. He wrote about historical figures as if he knew them personally and he reported events of long ago with the opinionated judgements of a political commentator. Mommsen greatly admired the statesmanship of Julius Caesar and scorned what he saw as the unprincipled opportunism of Cicero.

In 1854, Mommsen accepted a post at the University of Breslau, then in Prussia (now Wrocław in Poland). He married Marie Reimer, daughter of the publisher of his book in Leipzig. Mommsen was already forty-one. They went on to have sixteen children. Throughout this time, proposals he had first devised in Italy for an international project to publish Roman inscriptions were slowly unfolding and re-forming in Berlin. He was eventually appointed by the Berlin Academy to the directorship of the new *Corpus Inscriptionum Latinarum*, which still exists, and in 1858 to a full professorship of Roman history in Berlin, where he spent the rest of his life.

To many people at that time, the study of inscriptions as serious classical texts was absurd. Sir Frederic Madden's journal mentions a whimsical Latin pamphlet, *Inscriptio Antiqua*, Oxford, 1862 (I happen to own a copy), satirizing Mommsen as the futile expounder of the unreadable. It claims to have found an apparently ancient tablet beginning, "HEYDIDDLEDIDDLE THECATWITHTHEFIDDLE . . .", which it divides into arbitrary syllables and then painstakingly interprets as being written in a rare Etruscan dialect, half Greek, half Latin, with predictably comic effect, at least to readers who did not take this kind of scholarship as earnestly as the new German epigraphers.

Mommsen's return to medieval manuscripts took place gradually and grew out of his work on inscriptions and Roman history. An undertaking which fell somewhere between the two worlds was his edition of the *Res gestae divi Augusti*, published in Berlin in 1865. This is a classical text with an unusual history. Like the *Periplus* of Hanno the Carthaginian, copied by Simonides, the *Res gestae* began as a public monument. The emperor Augustus spent decades planning his own memorial in Rome. When he died in AD 14, his will stipulated that his personal account of his life's achievements should be inscribed on enormous bronze tablets in front of his mausoleum in the Field of Mars. No trace remains of the originals, doubtless melted for their metal at some time of crisis, but several copies of the text survived in Turkey, in what was then the Roman province of Galatia. The most complete of these is cut into the marble on either side of the atrium of the temple of Rome and Augustus, a substantial ruin in what is now the suburb of Altındağ in the city of Ankara, where a heading identifies it unambiguously as a copy of the original incised on bronze pillars in Rome. It is a long text for a public inscription, in thirty-five chapters, composed in Latin by Augustus in the first person. The words in the Ankara temple were originally coloured in red, and traces of pigment survived into the nineteenth century. At a very early date a Greek translation was added on the temple's outside wall, adapted slightly to make it more comprehensible to an audience unfamiliar with usages of Rome. The temple had a later history as a mosque and as supporting walls for peasant houses built in and around it, and the ancient inscriptions are pitted and not entirely complete. The Greek text is also found on the base of a monument in Apollonia (modern Uluborlu, about 180 miles south-west of Ankara). There are fragments too of the Latin text from a site in Antioch near Pisidia, but these were not known in Mommsen's time.

For Mommsen, as a historian writing about Rome at the beginning of its empire, this was a primary text and a first-hand source on the aims and ambitions of the first emperor. It also seemed to have a relevance to the European politics of Mommsen's own time. Italy had been reunified in 1861, re-creating the nation of ancient Rome, almost as encapsulated in Augustus' inscription. The text is a swaggering and bombastic record of achievement: 'The whole of Italy swore allegiance to my words willingly and demanded me as its leader for the war in which I was victorious at Actium; the provinces of Gaul, Hispania, Libya, Sicily and Sardinia swore allegiance to the same words.' (It is hardly a surprise that Mussolini had the bronze tablets replicated in the capital in 1938.) In 1862 the new king of Prussia, Wilhelm I, had appointed Bismarck as Minister President, with his own unfolding vision of a united German empire centred on Berlin, under a *Kaiser* (Caesar, family name of Augustus), achieved in 1871. Parallels with Roman aspiration at the same moment of its history were clear to all readers of Mommsen's *Römische Geschichte*, already in its fourth edition by 1864 and by then translated into English, Italian, French and Polish. In 1864 war was being fought over the sovereignty of Schleswig, eventually recovered for Germany. The *Res gestae* was exactly the kind of text to touch the imagination of political idealists such as Theodor Mommsen and his widespread academic audience. Its Chapter 26 extolls Augustus' expansion of his Roman empire to include Germania, explicitly stated as extending as far as the mouth of the river Elbe (near Hamburg, on the border of Schleswig-Holstein), a startlingly local reference directly from Antiquity.

Mommsen's edition of the *Res gestae* prints the text from Ankara as a virtual type facsimile in capitals on facing pages of Latin and Greek, with gaps where the originals are damaged, and then it repeats the text in normal type with critical apparatus, comparing variant readings exactly as in an edition using the authority of different manuscripts. The two languages, like a Rosetta Stone, allow some reciprocal reconstruction of lacunae. Mommsen never visited Turkey. His sources for the texts are the varying transcriptions by different European travellers, which he lists and classifies. They begin with the copy made in 1555 in the legation of Ogier Ghiselin de Busbecq (1522–92), ambassador of the Holy Roman emperor to Süleyman the Magnificent. Other versions were copied in Ankara shortly before 1689 and again in 1701, 1705 and so on, ending with drawings from the expedition of the young French archaeologist Georges Perrot (1832–1914), who had been sent out by Napoleon III in 1861, with the architect Edmond Guillaume. This must have been particularly galling for Mommsen, who was fifteen years older than Perrot. At this time there was acute rivalry between archaeological enterprises of France and Germany, like the American–Russian space race a century later, and Paris was still (but not for long) ahead of Berlin.

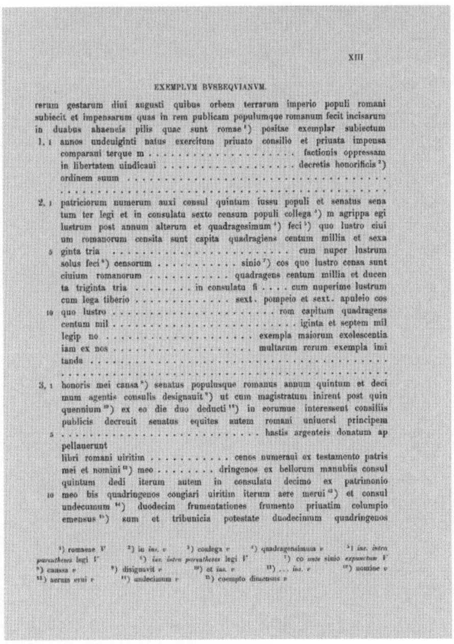

XIII

EXEMPLVM BVSBEQVIANVM.

rerum gestarum diui augusti quibus orbem terrarum imperio populi romani
subiecit et impensarum quas in rem publicam populumque romanum fecit incisarum
in duabus ahaeneis pilis quae sunt romae [1]) positae exemplar subiectum
1, annos undeuiginti natus exercitum priuato consilio et priuata impensa
comparaui terque m . . . . factionis oppressam
in libertatem uindicaui . . . . decretis honorificis [2])
ordinem suum . . . .
. . . .
2, patriciorum numerum auxi consul quintum iussu populi et senatus sena
tum ter legi et in consulatu sexto censum populi collega [3]) m agrippa egi
lustrum post annum alterum et quadragesimum [4]) feci [5]) quo lustro ciui
um romanorum censita sunt capita quadragiens centum millia et sexa
ginta tria . . . . cum nuper lustrum
solus feci [6]) censorum . . . . sinio [7]) cos quo lustro censa sunt
ciuium romanorum . . . . quadragens centum millia et ducen
ta triginta tria . . . . in consulatu fi . . . . cum nuperime lustrum
cum lega tiberio . . . . sext. pompeio et sext. apuleio cos
quo lustro . . . . rom capitum quadragens
centum mil . . . . iginta et septem mil
legip no . . . . exempla maiorum exolescentia
iam ex nos . . . . multarum rerum exempla imi
tanda . . . .
. . . .
3, honoris mei causa [8]) senatus populusque romanus annum quintum et deci
mum agentis consulis designauit [9]) ut cum magistratum inirent post quin
quennium [10]) ex eo die duo deducti [11]) in eorumue interessent consiliis
publicis decreuit senatus equites autem romani uniuersi principem
. . . . hastis argenteis donatum ap
pellauerunt
libri romani uiritim . . . . cenos numeraui ex testamento patris
mei et nomini [12]) meo . . . . dringenos ex bellorum manubiis consul
quintum dedi iterum autem in consulatu decimo ex patrimonio
meo bis quadringenos congiari uiritim iterum aere merui [13]) et consul
undecumum [14]) duodecim frumentationes frumento priuatim columpio
emensus [15]) sum et tribunicia potestate duodecimum quadringenos

[1]) romaeae V   [2]) in *ins. v*   [3]) coulega *v*   [4]) quadragensimum *v*   [5]) *ins. intra parentheses* legi V   [6]) *ins. intra parentheses* legi V   [7]) co *ante* sinio *expunctum* V
[8]) caussa *v*   [9]) disignavit *v*   [10]) et *ins. v*   [11]) ... *ins. v*   [12]) nomine *v*
[13]) aerum erui *v*   [14]) undeciumm *v*   [15]) coempto dimensus *v*

The *Res gestae* of Augustus, inscription in the ruins of the temple of Rome and Augustus in Ankara. Mommsen's transcription of it, Berlin, 1865 (left), and the plate of the same text reproduced by him in the second edition, Berlin, 1883 (right).

Each of these earlier transcriptions became, in effect, a separate and distinct manuscript source, assigned a *siglum* and to be compared and weighed word by word in reconstructing as pure a text as possible. Some had been printed but most were still unpublished. One manuscript was in the Vatican: Mommsen cannot resist saying that he had seen it, even though he does not use it. Others were in Vienna, the Herzog August Bibliothek in Wolfenbüttel and in the Universiteitsbibliotheek in Leiden. Here is the first revelation of what was to become a feature of Mommsen's manuscript research. He did not travel needlessly. Unlike temples, manuscripts are easily portable and generally robust. In a letter to the professor of Greek in Pisa in 1864, Mommsen mentions in passing that he has on his desk at that moment manuscripts lent to him by the libraries of Paris, Wolfenbüttel and Leiden. They were presumably his sources for the *Res gestae*, and he had contrived to have the originals at home.

Mommsen was a passionate advocate of what the Germans called *Altertumswissenschaft*, literally 'antiquity science', a new approach involving the all-embracing study of every aspect of ancient civilization, including the evidence of literature, linguistics, mythology, archaeology, epigraphy, numismatics and, of course, the witness transmitted through the medium of manuscripts. The nineteenth century was an exciting period for archaeological exploration. Mommsen was only a year or so older than Heinrich Schliemann, of Troy, and an exact contemporary of Austen Layard, of Nineveh, whose discoveries so captivated public imagination across the Western world. Manuscripts are different in that they have always been above ground and their texts at least knowable, but in one area they can be akin to an archaeological site, which is in the recovery of palimpsests. At certain early periods, parchment had sometimes been so expensive that it evidently seemed less trouble to a medieval scribe to erase writing from pages of an obsolete book and to reuse them for a new text deemed more useful. Revealing and reading the earlier text underneath resembles a miniature archaeological excavation and might be as thrilling as uncovering treasure from the ground. The pursuit of palimpsests caught the romantic imagination of the nineteenth century, as archaeology did. The forger Simonides had laid his bait skilfully by arranging for the German classicist Dindorf to 'discover' the lost history of Uranius in 1855 concealed as an apparent palimpsest. In reality, palimpsest manuscripts were never especially common, and most were rapidly found and exhausted by scholars of *Altertumswissenschaft*. The modern equivalent would be seeking out discarded fragments of early manuscripts reused as waste material in strengthening or lining early bookbindings, as fruitful a source of semi-archaeological discoveries of texts today as palimpsests were in the nineteenth century.

Mommsen mentioned palimpsests in a diary entry in 1844 when he heard rumours of seven leaves of an early law code discovered in Verona. His first detailed study of a manuscript, published in 1868, involved reading a palimpsest preserved in the capitular library in Verona. It included parts of an extremely early witness to the text of Livy's *Ab urbe condita*, the history of Rome from its foundation until the author's lifetime at the very beginning of the empire. This is generally regarded as the single most important text of national history from the classical world. Livy's work covers exactly the period of the *Römische Geschichte* of Mommsen, who may have imagined himself as a kind of Livy reborn. However, much of Livy's *Ab urbe condita* is lost and only thirty-five of the original 142 books are extant from Antiquity. What does survive has passed through a revision made in the late fourth or early fifth century, when a group of Roman aristocrats in the circle of Quintus Aurelius Symmachus, consul in AD 391, amused themselves in emending and enhancing the narrative. (I am reminded of a copy of the Second Folio of William Shakespeare, 1632, in the Royal Library at Windsor Castle in which Charles II has extensively improved the text in his own hand.) There is a reference to the revision of Livy in a letter written by Symmachus in 401. Several of the earliest manuscripts of the *Ab urbe condita* include subscriptions naming the correctors of the text, two of them members of the Nicomachus family. All surviving copies descend from this revised version, usually known as the Nicomachean recension.

A little book on Livy was published in Berlin in 1859 by August Wilhelm Zumpt (1815–77), giving sample readings from an early palimpsest in Verona and suggesting that these appeared to show a text which was earlier than the Nicomachean version and independent of it. If verifiable, this was sensational, for it would bring us closer to the author's uncontaminated original, and it was enough to capture the attention or even jealousy of Mommsen. In May 1866 he wrote to his friend the librarian in Verona, Carlo Giuliari (1810–92), saying that a proper study of the manuscript was necessary. Mommsen then spent most of April to June the following year in Verona. In outward appearance the manuscript

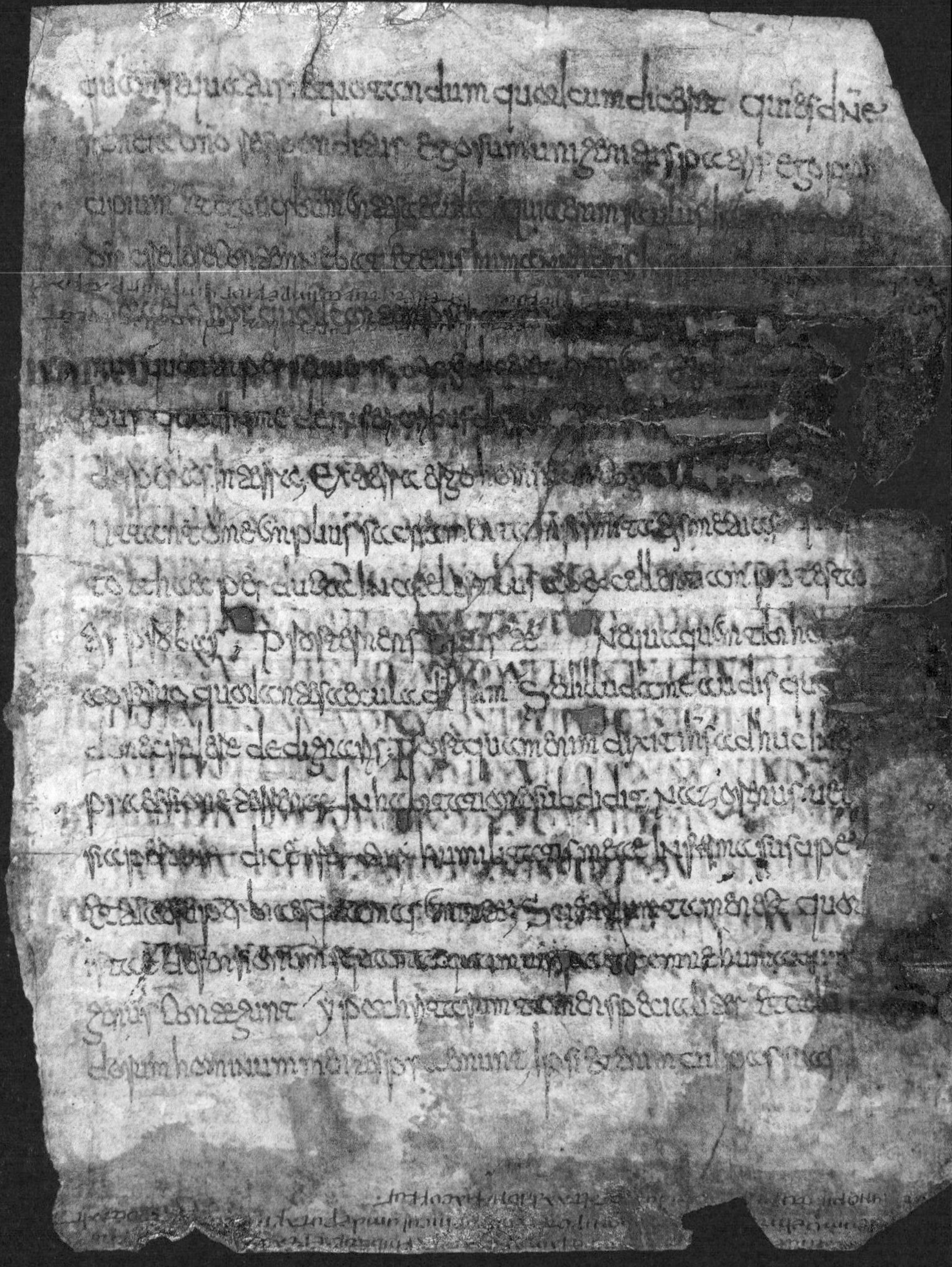

comprises the homilies of Gregory the Great, written in the first half of the eighth century apparently at Luxeuil Abbey, an early Irish foundation in Burgundy. However, the Merovingian scribe had erased and reused leaves from two much older manuscripts, both probably of the fifth century, one of them a copy of Virgil, and the other (most of the pages) with the portions of the tantalizing text of Livy.

Mommsen's daughter describes his method of reading palimpsests, with his fingers racing across pages where she could hardly see any words at all. When the undertext was not sufficiently legible, the standard practice in the nineteenth century was to wash the lines of handwriting with a chemical reagent. Mommsen's edition of the palimpsest Livy acknowledges this technique, saying that the mixture was kindly supplied by the helpful curator Carlo Giuliari in the library in Verona. Giuliari himself gave the formula in a book on the history of the collection published in 1888. They used prussiate of potash (potassium hexacyanoferrate), diluted with a light solution of ammonium, usually dabbed on with a sponge. Most medieval scribes wrote with iron-gall ink, made with ferrous sulphate. Even when it has been erased, traces of colourless iron residue survive imbedded in the parchment. These then react chemically with the liquid hexacyanoferrates and form the synthetic pigment known coincidentally as *Berliner Blau* or Prussian blue. It must have been thrilling to watch the long-vanished writing suddenly reappearing on the wet parchment in brilliant shining blue letters, in what Giuliari proudly called "una bellissima tintura". There are two disadvantages. One is that the chemicals, which are a form of cyanide, are extremely poisonous, as Mommsen acknowledged. The other, which no one then realized, is that they slowly destroy the manuscript. The blue writing fades as the solution dries, but with the passing of decades the whole area where the liquid was applied turns irreversibly to black, and the defaced manuscript gradually becomes illegible in both the undertext and the later writing on top. The modern non-invasive technique for reading erasures by ultra-violet light cannot now be used either, for the chemical solution prevents florescence, and nothing is ever readable again. The once-lovely ancient manuscript in Verona is heart-breaking to see today, striped with great disfiguring streaks of bluish black, like burns made with a hot poker, obliterating the pages.

LEFT: The palimpsest text of Livy, probably fifth century, overwritten at Luxeuil Abbey in the eighth century and severely damaged by Mommsen by use of a reagent in 1867.

There is no reason to doubt the meticulous accuracy of Mommsen's transcription of the pre-Nicomachean Livy, even if it can no longer be checked, but more recent scholarship accords the Verona manuscript rather less importance than Mommsen did. Where it supplies readings which are more likely to be authentic to Livy than the Nicomachean recension, these could mostly have been guessed anyway. Many other variants suggest that it was probably not a very good manuscript in the first place, carelessly and incorrectly copied by its original scribe.

By the late 1860s the march of publications by Mommsen seemed unstoppable, with forty-two titles in 1868 alone, for example, an average of almost one a week. Many were quite slight, brief signed notes in periodicals reporting finds of classical inscriptions or coins but also now commonly involving manuscripts as his principal subjects. He had also discovered late-medieval manuscripts as fertile sources for Roman inscriptions which no longer survive, writing accounts of sylloges in England (1871 and 1878), and an alphabetical glossary found in an Italian manuscript in the Vatican, which quotes from classical sources (1873). Other pieces in journals were announcements of classical texts he had encountered in libraries and sought to bring to public attention. In 1866, for example, Mommsen published separate notes on manuscripts of Pliny, Catullus, Livy, Vegetius, Sallust and Eutropius. Railways made research trips easy for his generation but travelling took time. Sometimes he relied on research assistants, such as Paul Krüger (1840–1926), his collaborator in their edition of Justinian, whom he acknowledges in an article in 1870 about a poem against pagans added at the end of a sixth-century manuscript of Prudentius in Paris.

In several instances we encounter again that extraordinary fact that Mommsen was able to convince libraries to lend him manuscripts to work on more conveniently at home in Berlin. The idea may have originated with Napoleon III, who had established the Second Empire in France in 1852 and perhaps coincidentally was a great admirer of the *Römische Geschichte*. On 10 May 1863 the French emperor wrote to Mommsen, saying that orders had been given to the Bibliothèque impériale in Paris to send to Germany any manuscripts he wanted to consult. In 1864, as we have seen, Mommsen already had a manuscript from Paris at home. In 1865 he published a note on the textual tradition of Pompeius Festus, using a manuscript owned by the university library in

Leiden, lent to him in Berlin through the kindness of the librarian Willem Pluygers. In 1872 he wrote about a manuscript in Oxford, a notebook by the Italian architect Pirro Ligorio (*c.*1512–83) with drawings of classical monuments, one of the manuscripts in the Canonici collection bought by the Bodleian Library in 1817. Mommsen did not visit England until 1885: instead, he acknowledged the generosity of the library staff in lending the manuscript to him for study in Berlin.

In 1870, Mommsen became interested in what are called the 'Arborea' manuscripts. This is a group of apparently very early medieval texts on parchment which had been acquired from a Franciscan friar in and after 1845 by the university library of Cagliari on the island of Sardinia. They included information that Saint Ignatius of Antioch, one of the earliest Christian writers, had been born in Nora in southern Sardinia, and they furnished historical records in a uniquely Sardinian language earlier than any Italianate vernacular, as well as poetry in a proto-Italian older than anything from the mainland. This provided apparent proof of the antiquity and importance of the kingdom of Sardinia, which was very timely as the islanders were struggling to assert cultural identity and independence, resenting absorption of Sardinia into a united Italy. The importance of the Arborea texts was much trumpeted by the Sardinian archaeologist, librarian and priest Giovanni Spano (1803–78). In March 1869, Mommsen was in Turin. Until Italian unification, Piedmont had been a political unity with Sardinia, and the two states remained closely connected, uneasy siblings. Mommsen persuaded the Accademia delle Scienze di Torino to arrange for the manuscripts from Arborea to be sent to him in Berlin, where he promptly denounced them as modern forgeries. He was no doubt correct, but the news was not welcomed in Sardinia. A cartoon in a local paper showed a joust in which Mommsen, preposterously dressed in a Prussian helmet and waving a sword called 'Critica archeologica', gallops into the lists, attacked by Spano and his furious colleagues throwing bottles and quill pens.

Mommsen was by this time very well known. He was chosen as rector of Berlin University in 1876. He had also entered politics, with the authority of history at his command. He was elected to the Prussian house of deputies in 1863–6 and again in 1873–9, and was later a member of the Reichstag. Many biographical accounts of Mommsen focus on his position in German politics and his subsequent disillusionment with Bismarck, not so relevant to his manuscript studies except that

Newspaper cartoon of Mommsen battling with Giovanni Spano over the authenticity of the 'Arborea' manuscripts in Sardinia, 1877.

it resulted in considerable public exposure. Like Charles Dickens and Abraham Lincoln, neither of them great beauties, Mommsen was conscious of the propaganda value of his own image and he benefited from mass photography. There are so many portraits and photographs of him that he must have tolerated if not encouraged the practice. When still in Zurich he presented friends with copies of a lithograph of himself made in 1854 by Carl Friedrich Irminger, showing a three-quarter-length figure with his right hand tucked into his waistcoat, like Napoleon. Although he remained clean-shaven, Mommsen's hair was always shoulder-length and untidy, turning grey and finally white, resembling a witch or a wizard, as his critics observed. Possibly through the fame of Mommsen, wild hair in old age became a recognizable badge of an eccentric professor or genius, cultivated later by Einstein and generations of academics ever since.

In other ways too, Mommsen seemed the very model of a modern academic. He was very thin and generally graceless in movement. He had a high forehead, a straight slightly aquiline nose and deep-set piercing eyes, beneath very dark eyebrows. His eyes were described both as pale blue and as almost black. He looked fearsomely clever; all people who met him agreed on this. He had great presence, and he was quick and dogmatic in giving opinions in a high-pitched voice. Throughout his adult life, he wore thick oval wire-rimmed glasses, which he pushed up onto the top of his head for close reading. He dressed formally, often in a bow tie, although his clothes were reported as being too big for him and looking slept in, like the *Bücherwurm* in that fictional painting by Spitzweg. Mommsen was immediately recognizable. Even the tram conductors in Berlin pointed him out with awe to visitors when he was seen in the street.

There are legends of eccentricities, doubtless exaggerated or even invented, like many student fables of their professors, such as that he put a baby in the wastepaper basket to stop it crying and that he did not remember his own children's names. A credible anecdote was told by his daughter. He always welcomed visitors at home in the ground-floor reception room in a formal tailcoat. One day in 1858 or 1859, he emerged to greet an important guest wearing the coat but having forgotten to change out of his yellow slippers. This became an often-repeated family joke for the rest of his life. If it does not seem especially funny to us now, it does tell us something of his Biedermeier world of middle-class respectability and convention, and how academia was the exception, forgiven or even admired for failing to conform.

In the later 1870s, Mommsen was working on his edition of the *Getica* of Jordanes, written in the mid-sixth century. It is a history of the Goths, *De origine actibusque Getarum* in its own title, recording their emergence from 'Scandza', a region somewhere at the top of Europe, and the adventurous deeds of these spirited northerners in the classical Mediterranean. What little is known of the author, who was a Goth himself, derives from what he tells us in the text, which is that he had been writing a chronicle of the Romans when he interrupted his own labours to assemble a parallel volume on the Goths, addressed to his friend Castalius. Mommsen, born on the border of Scandza, perhaps found sympathy with Jordanes, whose charming introduction begins:

> Though it had been my wish to glide in my little boat by the shore of a peaceful coast and, as a certain writer says, to gather little fishes from the pools of the ancients, you, brother Castalius, bid me set my sails towards the deep. You urge me to leave the little work I have in hand (that is, an abbreviation of the Chronicles) and to condense in my own style in this small book the twelve volumes of the Senator on the origin and deeds of

the Goths from olden times to the present day, descending through the generations of the kings . . .

The 'Senator' mentioned was Cassiodorus (*c.*485–*c.*585), whose own history of the Goths does not survive. Jordanes claims that he had borrowed Cassiodorus' twelve-volume text for three days and that he was able to abridge and reproduce it from memory, adding a few extra details from other authors, including Orosius. Although Jordanes himself is a relatively minor author and not a great stylist, who modestly calls himself "agrammaticus", 'scarcely literate', Cassiodorus is one of the giants of late-classical civilization. For Mommsen, here was a chance to present a Latin source on the role of a northern Germanic people in ancient Rome, and also to recover, by subtle textual archaeology, traces of a lost text of Cassiodorus himself. It was his belief that most of the apparent sources used in the *Getica* were lifted uncritically from the original of Cassiodorus. To Mommsen's mind, it was perfectly possible for Jordanes to borrow a manuscript and to read a long text in three days and reproduce it perfectly from memory months later, as he himself could have done, a claim dismissed as implausible by other and lesser classicists.

Jordanes is not widely known today but his work survives in numerous medieval manuscripts. Mommsen's introduction listed forty-one copies, which he classified into three main families. The principles of textual genetics were still relatively new, refined and formulated by the earlier Berlin philologist and editor of Lucretius, Karl Lachmann (1793–1851). The idea is that by plotting cumulative errors of transcription one can hypothesize the different ancestors of manuscripts and their moments of divergence, even if the prototypes themselves do not survive. (We saw something of this process with the manuscripts of Augustine's *De pastoribus* from Bec Abbey.) There is the complication with Jordanes that his own use of Latin was sometimes rustic and so a strange usage might be more authorially authentic than a later and more polished improvement by a well-educated scribe. Mommsen placed sixteen manuscripts in his first family, with half a dozen derivatives too corrupt to be useful; three in his second family, with another eight dismissible descendants; and eight in a third family, which he considered largely irrelevant. He had not inspected every manuscript. For some he relied on specimen readings supplied from descriptions by others, including Ludwig Bethmann (1812–67), who had seen the *Getica* manuscript in Bruges as long ago as 1839. Mommsen had examined and eliminated some manuscripts, including an eleventh-century copy in the Vatican, and there were others, such as that in the library of Salisbury Cathedral, which he said he had neither seen nor wished to. He could be quite harsh in declaring as useless any manuscripts he had not examined, including one in the Bodleian, which the curators this time were clearly not inclined to lend.

By far the most important and oldest of all the manuscripts of the *Getica* was that in the university library of Heidelberg, the primary text in Mommsen's first family. It was written in Anglo-Saxon script in the late eighth century in an Irish or English monastery in Germany, which Mommsen believed might have been Fulda. By the fifteenth century the manuscript belonged to the library of Mainz Cathedral. It was among the books gathered in the Rhineland by the Electors Palatine, possibly Ottheinrich (1502–59), prince of Neuburg, for the electors' court library in Heidelberg. In 1622 the armies of Maximilian of Bavaria overran Heidelberg in the Thirty Years' War and this volume was sent with a large number of looted manuscripts as a diplomatic gift to the pope in 1623. Thus the *Getica* entered the Vatican Library, which still owns many Palatine books. After the Napoleonic conquest of the Papal States in 1797, however, the *Getica* was one of about 500 selected manuscripts brought back as victors' spoils by Napoleon to Paris. Following the battle of Waterloo and the Treaty of Vienna in 1815, it was finally among the thirty-eight manuscripts restored in 1816 from Paris to Heidelberg, where it entered the Universitätsbibliothek. It is like a child in a disputed divorce, forever being assigned to different guardians among the quarrelling families. The extraordinary fact is that the university authorities in Heidelberg were somehow persuaded to lend it to Mommsen, and this immensely precious early codex was trustingly sent off to Berlin.

There were others. Mommsen had previously been an employee of the University of Breslau and doubtless knew the library staff well. They had a manuscript of the *Getica* of Jordanes written in the eleventh century and a good example of Mommsen's second family of the text. It came from the abbey of St Martin in Cologne and had been brought to Breslau by Thomas Rehdiger (1540–1576). It too was duly dispatched to Berlin.

Even more unexpectedly, Mommsen also convinced the library of Trinity College in Cambridge to lend him a manuscript. It was William Hepworth Thompson (1810–86), Master of Trinity, editor of Plato and a fellow classicist, who facilitated the gesture. The college's manuscript of the *Getica* with other texts was made around 1100 and had belonged to the cathedral priory of Christ Church, Canterbury. Saint Anselm might well have handled it. It was among the books given to Trinity in 1738 by Roger Gale (1672–1744). The loan is recorded in the minutes of the Conclusion Book of what was then called the 'Seniority' of the College, effectively its governing council, in a note signed by Thompson that permission was given to Professor Mommsen of the University of Berlin to borrow the manuscript for six months from 15 August 1879, "on giving the usual security", which normally meant a bond of £50. On 12 March 1880 the loan was extended for a further six months. The manuscript proved to be not especially important for Mommsen, who relegated it to his third family of the text. He may have thought it appropriate to collate it with another *Getica* from the same family in the Königliche Bibliothek in Berlin, twelfth-century, from the abbey of Liessies in Hainault.

Finally, a manuscript of Jordanes was lent by the Hofbibliothek in Vienna (now called the Nationalbibliothek). It was eleventh-century and came from the imperial abbey of Lorsch, near Worms. Mommsen assigned the manuscript's text to the lesser category within his second family and as the exemplar of a twelfth-century copy now in Munich. These are all the kind of relationships which make the study of texts so fascinating for the cultural history of the Middle Ages. This time there is a note in the library archives in Vienna signed by the curator, Joseph Haupt, recording that the manuscript was sent on loan on 23 September 1879 to the Königliche Bibliothek in Berlin for the use of Professor Mommsen, and that it was received in Berlin on 27 September and placed in the care of the chief librarian there, Dr Johann Schrader (1809–98).

Haupt's note suggests that the lenders in Vienna at least were expecting their manuscript to be consulted in the library, as the curators at Heidelberg, Breslau and Cambridge may have done too. His entry was subsequently endorsed, "Das Vertrauen wurde missbraucht" ('The trust was abused'). However, the name of the great professor was not to be gainsaid in Berlin, and Mommsen took all four manuscripts home to Charlottenburg, presumably on the tram, which was how he always travelled, together with the copy owned by the Königliche Bibliothek itself. The final collation of the sources and the preparation of the edition was almost entirely prepared in Mommsen's private study at home.

The five manuscripts were still in his house on the night of Sunday to Monday, 11–12 July 1880, even after the edition of the text had been sent to the printer. It was a stressful time for Mommsen. His daughter Kätchen, who was just sixteen, was dying, and his wife had taken her away for a few days to a sanitorium, in a last-resort and unsuccessful attempt to save her life. Perhaps with no one to summon him downstairs to bed and in need of distraction, Mommsen was still at work in the early hours of the morning of the 12th. He somehow upset a candle or a lamp and set his library on fire. The children on the floor beneath were woken by burning books falling past their window and they escaped to a neighbour. Mommsen spent the rest of the night attempting to move volumes to safety, burning his hands and his hair. In the morning it was found that all five borrowed manuscripts of the *Getica* of Jordanes had been destroyed.

The fire was international news. Stories were syndicated "by submarine telegraph", as one newspaper reported in Britain. Friedrich Nietzsche and countless others declared their shock and sympathy. The principal

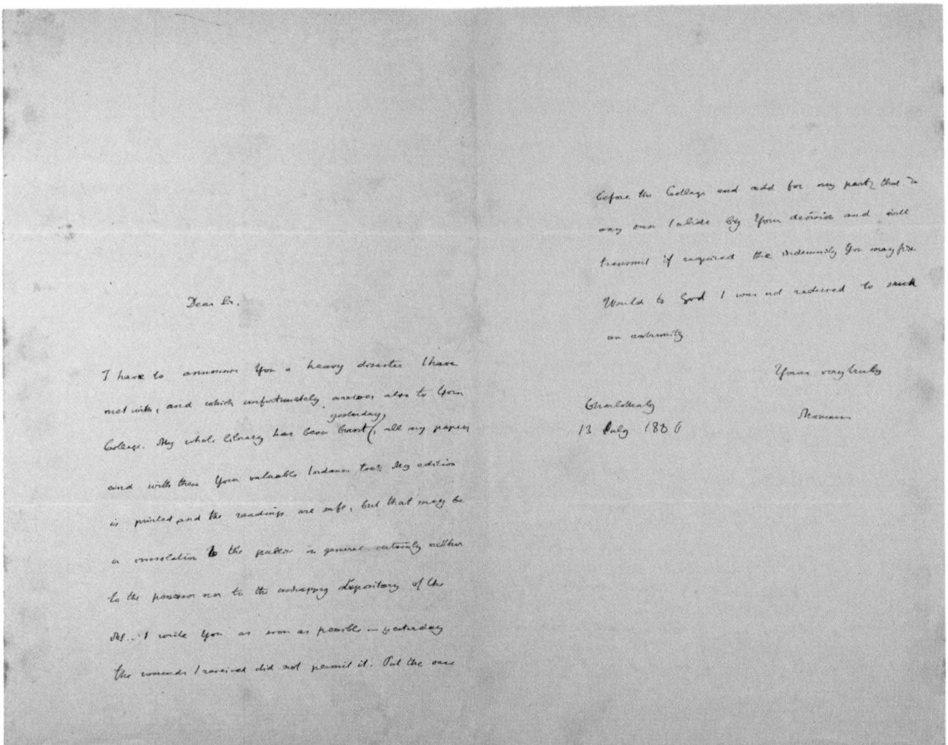

Dear Sir.

I have to announce you a heavy disaster I have met with, and which unfortunately answers also to Your College. My whole library has been burnt yesterday, all my papers and with them Your valuable Jordanes too. My edition is printed and the readings are safe, but that may be a consolation to the public in general certainly neither to the possessor nor to the unhappy depository of the MS. I write You as soon as possible — yesterday the wounds I received did not permit it. Put the case before the College and add for my part that I in any case abide by Your decision and will transmit if required the indemnity You may fix. Would to God I was not reduced to such an extremity.

Yours very truly

Mommsen

Charlottenburg
13 July 1886

The letter from Mommsen to Trinity College, Cambridge, reporting the destruction by fire of their manuscript of Jordanes, 13 July 1886.

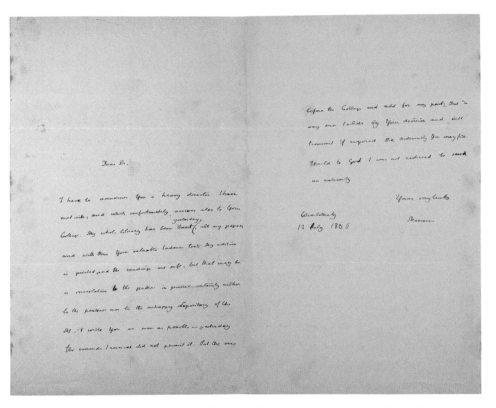

concern seemed to be that Mommsen's material for a final volume of his *Römische Geschichte* had been lost together with unpublished notes on inscriptions in Switzerland and southern Italy. The destruction of the medieval manuscripts took second place, even to Mommsen. He wrote, as indeed he should have done immediately, to Trinity College on Tuesday the 13th, in English:

> I have to announce You a heavy disaster I have met with, and which unfortunately arrives also to Your College. My whole library has been burnt yesterday, all my papers and with them Your valuable Iordanes too. My edition is printed and the readings are safe, but that may be a consolation to the public in general, certainly neither to the possessor nor to the unhappy depositary of the ms. I write You as soon as possible – yesterday the wound I received did not permit it.

The great Heidelberg codex was totally destroyed. (There is a certain irony that there was also a second manuscript of Jordanes sent from the Palatine library to Rome in 1623 but not deemed important enough for Napoleon to steal it back, and it is still safely in the Vatican, where Mommsen used it.) The Vienna manuscript was partially recovered in pieces, which were returned on 3 August. Mommsen eventually sent complimentary copies of his printed edition of Jordanes to each of the libraries. That at Trinity College, Cambridge, has an accompanying inscription from him:

> It is a very painful duty for me to forward You a copy of the new edition of Iordanes. I cannot restore to your library what is lost; but I shall never be able to forget that I have been the cause of it. But neither I will forget the generous way which You have treated this unhappy affair.

The librarian in acknowledging receipt of the edition said that the German embassy had informed the Foreign Office that scraps of their manuscript had also been recovered from the fire. He asked whether these might be returned to the College. Mommsen, who had been travelling in Italy, replied four months later, "Unfortunately the notice given to You by Your Foreign office is unfounded. It was the Vienna ms., of which some remains were found; of all the rest not a leave remained . . . the calamity was complete and total." However, this was not quite true. Thirty-one very burned fragments were returned to Breslau, where they were described in 1915, but they were lost in the cataclysm of the Second

World War. The Staatsbibliothek in Berlin also has a portfolio of 126 misshapen pieces, relics of their own unwisely lent manuscript.

The director of the library in Heidelberg, to give him all credit, was very philosophical about their loss. He announced on 23 August 1880 that their policy would remain unchanged, and that they would continue to lend manuscripts to other libraries and even to individuals for academic work and that they would hope for the same consideration in return. However, he added sadly, it had always been their requirement that if a manuscript was taken to a private house, it should be kept in a fireproof container when not in use.

There are aspects of the story of the fire which are hard to explain, including why Mommsen still had the manuscripts at home even when his edition was finished, and indeed whether it is possible to set a library alight at all so totally without noticing in time to extinguish the flames, for books do not burn quickly and tightly closed parchment is difficult to ignite except at high temperature. One newspaper muttered about insurance fraud, for which there is absolutely no evidence. It is conceivable that it was a suicide bid, in a time of great personal stress, envisaging a classical death in a pyre of his own books. It is most likely that Mommsen had left the room for some reason or had fallen asleep with a candle unsecured, although he did not admit to this. What is revealing about Mommsen is his general reassurance afterwards that the loss of the manuscripts was not as bad as it might be, because his edition was already in press and therefore the originals were no longer of such importance.

Stories of the fire included suggestions that manuscripts from the Bodleian, the Vatican, Halle, Brussels and elsewhere had also been destroyed, but, if true, which is improbable, they were not for the edition of Jordanes. Letters of condolence to Mommsen on the loss of his library were received from academic bodies in Paris and Oxford, with offers of money, which he refused, except for 106,000 marks collected by subscription from colleagues in Germany for the replacement of reference books. This he accepted on 30 November 1880, ostensibly to mark his sixty-fourth birthday.

One result of the fire was that manuscripts were no longer lent to him, and Mommsen's expeditions to libraries increased. Reduced duties in lecturing gave him more free time for research. He went to see manuscripts for critical editions of texts of the *Variae* – mostly letters – of Cassiodorus (1894), involving manuscripts as widespread as Naples,

Montpellier, Leiden, Brussels and the private library of Lord Ashburnham, and collected chronicles of the fourth to seventh centuries (1892–8), which included collation of six manuscripts in the Cotton collection in the British Museum, as well as volumes in Avranches, Chartres, St Gall, Einsiedeln Abbey and elsewhere. The introductions to the editions were always written in Latin. Mommsen was also working on an ever-complex project of gathering all traces of Roman law earlier than codes of Justinian in the sixth century, of which the principal source was a text known as the Codex Theodosianus (published in 1905). His journeys seem relentless. Mommsen was in Italy for the winter of 1882–3, for example, back in Berlin in February, and then between March and May 1883 he was in Rome, Naples, Florence, Bologna, Milan and Venice. Visits to libraries were intense, from the moment the doors opened until the reading-rooms closed each evening. The director of the Biblioteca Laurenziana in Florence described how Mommsen was there day after day, persuading them to allow him admission even on a Sunday, when the library was usually shut, from eight in the morning to five at night. His power of concentration was often remarked on. There was an occasion in May 1885 which caused some scandal. He was using a manuscript in the Vatican library when Pope Leo XIII happened to enter the room. As was customary, every reader stood up, except Mommsen, who failed to notice him. Diplomatic intervention was required to smooth over offended sensibilities.

Later that summer Mommsen made the first of his two visits to England. It is reported that in Oxford he was seen waiting outside the Bodleian Library at seven in the morning and was shocked to find it did not open until nine. He stayed at Exeter College, almost adjacent to the Bodleian, as the guest of Henry Pelham, ancient historian, and William Mitchell Ramsay, biblical archaeologist, both Fellows there. Ramsay had been Mommsen's guest in Berlin the previous year and was anxious to return the hospitality. He arranged for the colleges of All Souls, Magdalen and Merton to bring relevant manuscripts across to the Bodleian, for Mommsen's convenience. William Warde Fowler, a historian in his late thirties, bravely invited Mommsen to dinner at Lincoln College and found him less frightening than he expected:

> He talked, partly in English, partly in German, without the least constraint, and he enjoyed his dinner thoroughly. Now and then he flashed

> out with just a touch of that scornful opiniativeness which was one of his characteristics – perhaps one of his few weaknesses.

Mommsen went to Cambridge, staying at Trinity College (clearly feeling no awkwardness in doing so). He also managed to see the library of the late Sir Thomas Phillipps, then in Cheltenham in the custody of the collector's grandson, Thomas Fitzroy Fenwick. Such visits took effort to organize. Mommsen had asked for a letter of introduction from Edmund Maunde Thompson, a successor to Madden as Keeper of Manuscripts in the British Museum. Thompson wrote to Fenwick:

> You will find him a very pleasant man – and he speaks English very well. He is one of the most tremendous swells that they have in Germany – and at his name every German student shakes in his thick boots and knocks his shock head on the pavement in adoration. I believe he has never been known to make a mistake in his life, and he has the power of dictating ten books at a time to as many scribes. But as you are an Englishman you need not tremble – only be kind to him.

Mommsen's purpose in Cheltenham was to consult a tenth-century manuscript from Nonantola Abbey in northern Italy, needed for his edition of minor Latin chronicles, but in the process he discovered in the volume a copy of one of the earliest lists of the canonical books of the Bible, datable to the fourth century, which he published in 1886. It is still known as the 'Cheltenham List' or 'Mommsen Catalogue', an iconic document for biblical studies. The manuscript re-emerged in the Phillipps sale at Sotheby's in 1967 and is now in Rome. The contact with the collection provided an unanticipated bonus for Berlin, for when the Phillipps heirs were considering sales, Fitzroy Fenwick wrote to Mommsen in July 1886, asking whether the German government might be interested in purchasing the entire group of over 500 Latin manuscripts from the library of Gerard Meerman (1722–71), acquired by Phillipps in 1824. Mommsen made a recommendation to the Königliche Bibliothek, and the books were bought *en bloc* for Berlin. This success in turn gave confidence to Mommsen on his second visit to England in 1889, then looking at manuscripts of the *Variae* of Cassiodorus. There was one in the Phillipps collection. This time Mommsen virtually ordered Fitzroy Fenwick to bring it to London for him to examine. Mommsen was staying at the First Avenue Hotel in Holborn, convenient for the library of the British Museum, and he did not wish to miss a moment of research time. "Dear Sir", he demanded in a letter of 18 March, "I shall not leave my hôtel tomorrow morning before your arrival. If you could contrive to arrive earlier, I would be glad, as my work at the British Museum has to wait for it."

This determination not to waste time is a recurrent theme in the account of a journey to the libraries of Paris and northern Italy in 1898 in the company of his daughter Adelheid, who described it in her reminiscences. Mommsen was by then eighty-two. They travelled by train by way of Hamburg and Frankfurt, arriving in Paris in the evening. He had booked himself into the Hôtel Louvois in the Rue de Richelieu, near the Bibliothèque nationale, planning to send Adelheid off to a cheaper *pension* elsewhere. She objected and was eventually permitted an adjacent room at the Louvois. They had breakfast at seven o'clock precisely. Each day Mommsen was ready outside the manuscript department of the library half-way up the stairs for its opening at ten, and he worked there without pause on their sixth-century manuscript of the Codex Theodosianus until the room closed at three, when they met up for lunch. Occasionally Adelheid slipped silently into the reading-room to watch her father as he single-mindedly compared and copied the manuscript. (Madden had described the acquisition of the volume by the French national library in 1848, lamenting that he had not secured it for the British Museum.) In Turin the weather was immensely hot and Adelheid was envious of Mommsen in the cool of the library, studying the second principal surviving manuscript of the Codex Theodosianus while she looked round the city in the heat. A third manuscript of the text was in a monastery in Ivrea, where she was not allowed either, but their host, a brother of the poet Giuseppe Giacosa (presumably therefore the medical doctor Piero Giacosa, 1853–1928), told Mommsen of a new method of photographing every page of a manuscript, which sounds like an extremely early reference to microfilming. After inspecting results, Mommsen realized that he could now work at home in Charlottenburg and so he cancelled their planned week in Ivrea and they returned via Milan.

The memoir of Adelheid Mommsen is the best account too of their house in Berlin, especially as put back after the fire. It was at Marchstrasse

RIGHT: The sixth-century Codex Theodosianus, transcribed by Mommsen in Paris in 1898.

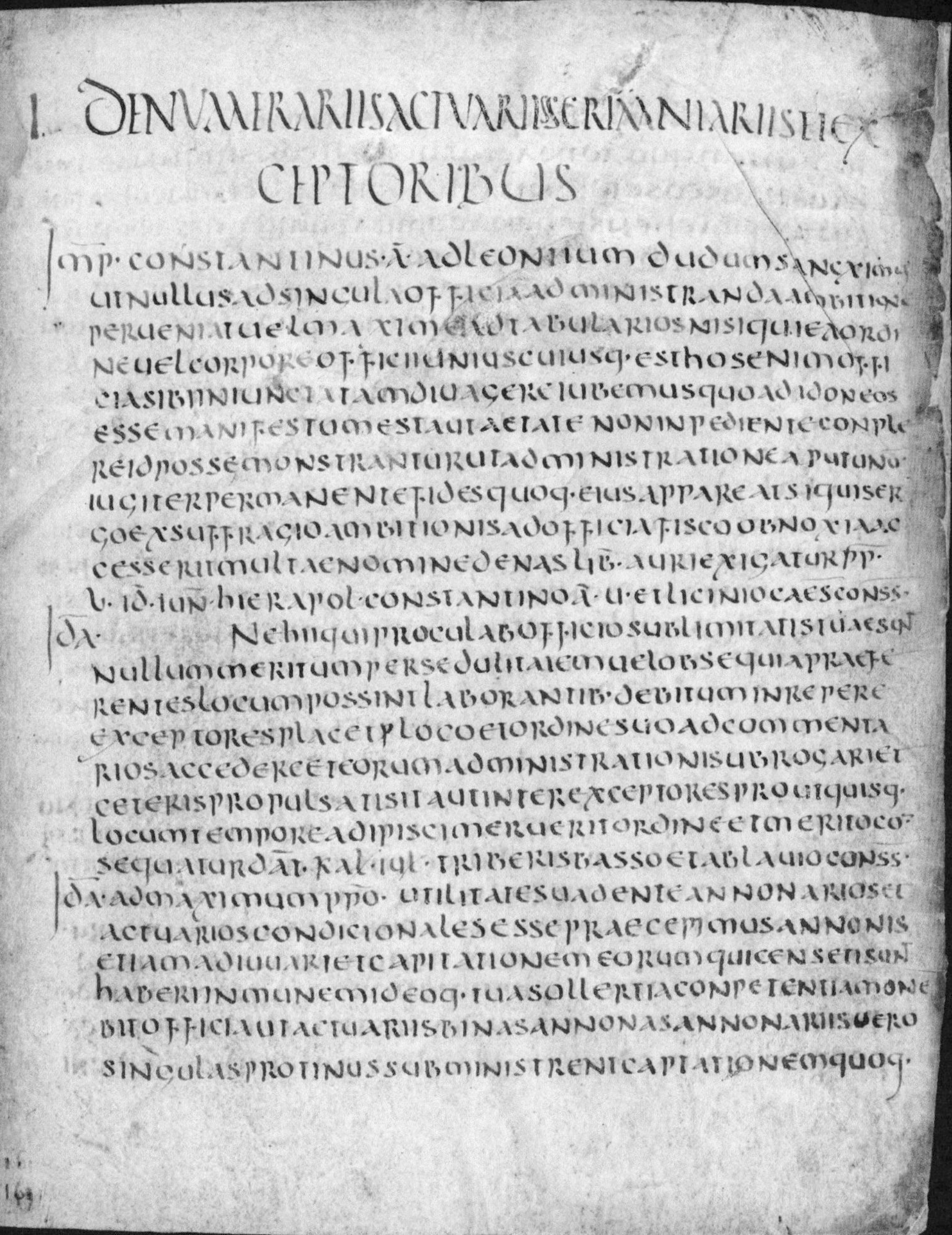

I. DE NUMERARIIS ACTUARIIS SCRINIARIIS ET EX
CEPTORIBUS

IMP. CONSTANTINUS A. AD LEONTIUM DUCUM SANE EX[illegible]
UT NULLUS AD SINGULA OFFICIA ADMINISTRANDA AMBITIONE
PERUENIAT UEL MAXIME AD TABULARIOS NISI QUI UEL ORDI
NE UEL CORPORE OFFICII EIUS CUIUSQ. EST HOS ENIM OFFI
CIA SIBI INIUNCTA TAMDIU AGERE IUBEMUS QUOAD IDONEOS
ESSE MANIFESTUM EST AUT AETATE NON INPEDIENTE CONPLE
RE ID POSSE MONSTRANTUR UT ADMINISTRATIONE APUT UNO
IUGITER PERMANENTE FIDES QUOQ. EIUS APPAREAT SI QUIS ER
GO EX SUFFRAGIO AMBITIONIS AD OFFICIA FISCO OBNOXIA AC
CESSERIT MULTAE NOMINE DENAS LIB. AURI EXIGATUR PP.
V. ID. IUN. HIERAPOL. CONSTANTINO A. V ET LICINIO CAES. CONSS.
IDA. NE HI QUI PROCUL AB OFFICIO SUBLIMITATIS TUAE SUNT
NULLUM MERITUM PER SEDULITATEM UEL OBSEQUIA PRAEFE
RENTES LOCUM POSSINT LABORANTIB. DEBITUM INREPERE
EXCEPTORES PLACET PRO LOCO ET ORDINE SUO AD COMMENTA
RIOS ACCEDERE ET EORUM ADMINISTRATIONI SUBROGARI ET
CETERIS PROPULSATIS UT INTER EXCEPTORES PRO UT QUISQ.
LOCUM TEMPORE ADIPISCI MERUERIT ORDINE ET MERITO CON
SEQUATUR DAT. KAL. IUL. TRIBERIS BASSO ET ABLAUIO CONSS.
IDA. AD MAXIMUM PPO. UTILITATE SUADENTE ANNONARIOS ET
ACTUARIOS CONDICIONALES ESSE PRAECEPIMUS ANNONIS
ETIAM ADIUUARI ET CAPITATIONEM EORUM QUI CENSENSUNT
HABERENT IMMUNEM IDEOQ. TUA SOLLERTIA CONPETENTIA MONE
BIT OFFICIA UT ACTUARIIS BINAS ANNONAS ANNONARIIS UERO
SINGULAS PROTINUS SUBMINISTRENT CAPITATIONEM QUOQ.

169

6, later renumbered 8, a wide street which crosses the Landwehr Canal in Charlottenburg. The house itself was destroyed in the bombing of the Second World War and the site is now part of the campus of the Technische Universität Berlin. A commemorative plaque, dedicated in 2017, records that Mommsen lived at the nearby address from 1874 until his death in 1903. It was a very large rectangular house almost on the street frontage with a classical triangular pediment at the centre front, set in a small but mature garden with ash and walnut trees and a lime tree that he had planted himself. There were wisteria and ivy on the walls. It was on a scale far beyond the little parsonage where he had been born in Garding and was no doubt made possible by royalties on his publications. Living and reception rooms were on the ground floor with family bedrooms above, while Mommsen's library and work rooms occupied the top floor. He was up there early every morning often by four or five o'clock, rarely later than six, with cold black coffee which he left out the night before. As before 1880, the space was entirely refilled with books, on the shelves around the walls and spilling over the floor and furniture. There were other lower bookcases back to back, one with reproductions of Roman busts on top, including a figure of Janus, who looks both into the past and the future. There were pot plants on the broad windowsills, tended by Adelheid's sister Lisbet. In the centre of the main room at the southern end of the floor was Mommsen's enormous work desk, piled with papers, letter-writing paraphernalia and an inkwell modelled on one of the pieces of Roman silver excavated in Hildesheim in 1868 (on which he had published a short article that year). Mommsen used a quill pen for most of his life. He was a tireless correspondent, although his letters are often rather dull, widely spaced, and focused on specific information, frequently signed only with his surname, like a duke. His rapid handwriting was notoriously difficult to read. On his desk too was a little box of treats for his dachshund, Lump, which would carry the morning's post up the stairs in its mouth and bark to be admitted. Others had to knock and wait for his "Herein!" Mommsen would be seated in his leather chair at the desk with his back to the door, writing.

Where Mommsen differs from other figures in this book is that he was a member of the faculty of a major university and benefited from the status which this brought as a professor, especially in Germany in the nineteenth century (and ever since). Often antiquaries of the past had been clerics, like the Abbé Rive, or gentleman amateurs. Sir Frederic

Madden was a government employee, ultimately serving the interested public. Mommsen, however, belonged to a new generation of professional scholars, with authority and a salary from a university position. This largely began in Germany. His nearest successors in Britain became M. R. James (1862–1936), inseparable from Eton and King's College, Cambridge, and the eventual professors of palaeography in the universities of Oxford and London. It represents a shift in the professionalization of scholarship which still endures.

In each chapter I have tried to imagine what it would be like to meet and talk to the person, and how this might come about. In some ways, Theodor Mommsen is the hardest to visualize. I still do not know how much joy he really experienced in manuscripts, or whether they were for him simply archaeological sites to be excavated for the knowledge they reveal and then discarded or built over. He was also extremely busy. I would probably need to catch his attention with a manuscript he would sell his soul to see, and I think I know what it is. It is the Codex Gregorianus and I own it.

This takes us back to the very early history of Roman law. The legal codes of Justinian I, emperor 527–65, are the foundation texts of all Western civil law, even today, probably second only to the Bible in their lasting influence on European civilization. The first volume, Justinian's *Codex*, was promulgated in 529. It is, however, a synthesis of even earlier texts. The opening paragraph of its preface states that it was based on three principal compilations, then known as the Codex Gregorianus (which contained laws from the emperors Hadrian in the second century to Diocletian around *c.*291), the Codex Hermogenianus (continuing from the year 293 onwards) and the Codex Theodosianus, which drew on both of them. Very little is extant from these ante-Justinian sources, as they are called. Mommsen spent many of the last years of his life preparing an edition of the Codex Theodosianus, as we have seen, finally published in 1905 shortly after his death, with the collaboration of Paul Meyer (1865–1935). It was the Hermogenian Code which Mommsen first heard of in 1844 as seven palimpsest fragments in Verona. No one had ever seen the Gregorian Code, the oldest of all. It was quoted by name five times in a legal text from the 390s which compares Jewish and Roman law codes, edited by Mommsen in 1890, but, as he acknowledged, the original text was wholly lost.

In November 2001, I bought from a London art dealer a limp plastic folder with seventeen very small parchment fragments of a very early Latin manuscript written on both sides in brown uncial script and red rustic capitals probably in the fifth century in the eastern empire, quite possibly in Constantinople. The pieces are doubtless salvage from inside an early bookbinding which reused waste parchment from an obsolete book, rather like a palimpsest. They are not items of great beauty. I must have dropped one in the car on the way home, for my wife picked it up from under the passenger seat several days later. I tried for years to identify the text, which seemed to be unknown, except that they were clearly legal pronouncements. The scraps have brown stains, suggesting that someone in the past has attempted to make the faded text clearer by use of a chemical reagent, presumably in vain.

Eventually, in 2009 I lent the fragments to Simon Corcoran and Benet Salway, then of the Projet Volterra, based at University College London, dedicated to recording legal texts from the Roman empire, a field infused with the name of Mommsen. On 26 January 2010 they announced their astonishing conclusion, based on multiple strands of converging reasoning, that these are fragments of the original Codex Gregorianus itself, lost since Antiquity. Their discovery was reported by the media across the world, from the London tabloid the *Evening Standard* to the *National*

Fragments of the lost Codex Gregorianus, late fifth century, discovered in 2010.

Geographic in America. Until this moment, I have never publicly confessed to being the unnamed owner.

If I could in reality, I might now write carefully to Professor Mommsen at Berlin University on the letterhead of my Cambridge college (he would respect that, *et in academia ego*), maybe mentioning that in addition I have a doctorate from Oxford and had a season at All Souls, offering to lend him these fragments. I know I would have received an invitation by return of post. Today I would travel out to Charlottenburg from my hotel in Berlin on the U-Bahn, nine stops on the U-2 line westwards from Stadtmitte to Ernst-Reuter-Platz, three minutes' walk from Marchstrasse. In Mommsen's time it might have been in the new horse-drawn tram, opened to Charlottenburg in 1865. As I arrived at the house, Mommsen would descend on my package with the velocity of an eagle, almost ripping the pieces from my hands. He would fix them with his famous gaze, thrusting his glasses further up his forehead, rapidly pronouncing, as I now know, that these include rulings from Caracella (emperor 211–17), Gordian III (238–44), Philip the Arab (244–9) and Philip II (247–9). He would inform me unhesitatingly that the script is a rather more archaic version of the eastern Latin uncial used in the sixth-century manuscript of Justinian's *Digest*, which he had worked on in the Biblioteca Laurenziana in Florence. I have been there too, and I would say so. Within minutes, we would be exchanging stories of libraries we had both used in Italy and elsewhere, tales of discoveries and disappointments, suspicious librarians and priests, opening hours and unpredictable Italian holidays, poor catalogues or none at all, train journeys, fleas, stifling heat and torrential rain leaking through library windows, and the thrill of a great manuscript finally brought out and opened up on a sun-bleached table.

I have decided that I like the man. He may not revel in the beauty of manuscripts or want to own them, but he reads them voraciously and with passion. He loves what they can do. He is able to equate events in Roman history with parallel politics and experiences of his own time and to understand the participants as fallible human beings rather than as romanticized heroes. Their world and his are not so far apart. Similarly, he employs manuscripts as the ancients used them, still as practical texts, reading, transcribing, reproducing, correcting (like Symmachus), summarizing (like Jordanes) and writing about them in Latin, for this purpose a language of genuine internationalism as it was then. In Mommsen and in the Berlin of his time one sees the final legacy of the Roman empire

Mommsen in old age in his study at home in Charlottenburg, photograph, *c.*1900.

still in operation. He has a dedication to texts and a strangely appealing vulnerability as people laugh at his oddities. He wants to be liked and admired. I might be asked to stay for supper. Adelheid Mommsen recorded that his favourite meals were smoked eel with lentils, memories of a childhood in Schleswig, and macaroni with cheese, discovered by him in Italy.

Mommsen's apotheosis was the award of the Nobel Prize for Literature in 1902, principally for the *Römische Geschichte*. Other nominees that year had included Leo Tolstoy, Henry James and Émile Zola. Mommsen was by then too old to travel to Stockholm, and the prize was accepted on his behalf by the German ambassador. The master of textual scholarship remained active among his books until shortly before his death, still working on the edition of the Codex Theodosianus. In his final illness he was moved into a room next to his library on the top floor in Charlottenburg. It was the first time in his life that he had ever spent a whole day in bed. As he lay dying, telegrams arrived daily from the Kaiser inquiring as to his health. He died at home on 1 November 1903, just short of his eighty-sixth birthday. His death was reported on the front page of *The New York Times*. Mommsen has never been forgotten. There are streets and schools named after him; his statue replaced one of Karl Marx in the former East Berlin in 1993; his portrait appeared on a set of German postage stamps for his bicentennial in 2017. His history of Rome remains in print, and his editions of classical texts and Roman laws are still to be reckoned with. The *Corpus Inscriptionum Latinarum* in Berlin is still publishing Roman monumental inscriptions, as dreamt up by Mommsen and Borghesi in the summer of 1845.

Let us end with a dinner rather different from the intimate family supper I imagined with the Mommsens at home. It was described by the American writer Mark Twain in a satirical article for the *Chicago Tribune* in 1892. He had been invited to a banquet in Berlin the previous October in honour of the seventieth birthdays of two well-known scientists. It was held in a huge hall with galleries above, attended by a thousand students in traditional festive costumes with swords and hats. Twain describes the thumping of beer mugs and the singing of patriotic songs, as distinguished academics continued to make their way into the hall to the sound of bugles:

> When apparently the last eminent guest had long ago taken his place, again those three bugle blasts rang out and once more the swords leapt from their scabbards. Who might this late comer be? Nobody was interested to inquire. Still, indolent eyes were turned toward the distant entrance; we saw the silken gleam and lifted swords of a guard of honor plowing through the remote crowds. Then we saw that end of the house rising to its feet; saw it rise abreast the advancing guard all along, like a wave. This supreme honor had been offered to no one before. There was an excited whisper at our table – "Mommsen!" – and the whole house rose. Rose and shouted and stamped and clapped, and banged the beer-mugs. Just simply a storm! Then the little man with his long hair and Emersonian face edged his way past us and took his seat. I could have touched him with my hand – Mommsen! – think of it!

CHAPTER ELEVEN

The Collector: Sir Sydney Cockerell

In the early summer of 1894, Sydney Carlyle Cockerell, newly appointed secretary of the Kelmscott Press, was revisiting northern France with his employer, the famous and deeply revered Pre-Raphaelite designer and craftsman William Morris. "On the first morning after we reached Beauvais, Morris rapped on my door soon after 7 o'clock and summoned me to 'come out and buy a manuscript!' . . .", Cockerell later recalled. "By an extraordinary stroke of luck, we found a thirteenth-century Justinian going for a song in an old curiosity shop and carried it back in triumph." The manuscript they bought, which cost the equivalent of £7, is now in the Lillian Goldman Law Library at Yale University. It has decorative initials descending in cascades of bright red and blue penwork, like the colours of the stained glass in Beauvais Cathedral, which Morris and Cockerell then visited before returning to their hotel for breakfast. Mommsen would have dismissed the manuscript as textually irrelevant for the transmission of Roman law, Madden as being of a most common type, and the Abbé Rive as damaged and unilluminated. For William Morris and his impressionable disciple, it was treasure indeed. It was a survival from an age when all books were handmade and when even utilitarian works usually included ornament. As a piece of book design, it is skilfully arranged with fifty lines to each column (the book you are reading, by contrast, has only thirty-eight), and the blocks of text are then encircled by marginal glosses and commentaries in a multitude of even smaller and perfectly formed scripts, admirably executed and legible. That all mattered to Morris, who was then designing his own books on medieval principles for the Kelmscott Press. Almost as important

LEFT: Sir Sydney Cockerell (1867–1962), photograph, 1933.

was that the manuscript was still in circulation, as if the Middle Ages were not quite over: it could be acquired, and the thrill of hunting and capture is a great part of the joy for any collector. The manuscript was afterwards inscribed by Morris, "Bought at Beauvais, May 1894", like a hunting trophy brought back from safari. It also has his printed book label of Kelmscott House on the Thames at Hammersmith, where Morris's library was kept, upriver from central London.

Cockerell (1867–1962) was then in his later twenties and becoming increasingly fascinated by medieval manuscripts. He had been born in Brighton on 16 July 1867 and was brought up by his widowed mother around south London and Kent. George Cockerell & Co. were long-established coal merchants. This was an essential business in Victorian Britain and the Cockerells were a prosperous and well-connected family (substitute 'oil' for a better sense of its equivalent social status in the twentieth century, or 'wool' in the fourteenth). The Carlyle of his middle name was in honour of one of his father's favourite authors. Even before discovering manuscripts, Carlie (as his parents' generation then called him) always understood the excitement of acquisition and classification. "I was a passionate collector from the cradle", he told his first biographer. "I collected mosses, butterflies and moths, all sorts of insects, shells, fossils, stamps – everything. I was very ardent, and very quick in determining what they were. The differences are often very small and it was a most useful training."

Cockerell won a scholarship to St Paul's, and after leaving school in 1884 was encouraged into the family firm, but his temperament was for art and the ideals of early Fabianism. Octavia Hill, social reformer, was a family friend. In 1886 he began keeping a diary, which he maintained daily for seventy-five years. It is very different indeed from the journals of Frederic Madden, which are sprawling and discursive and emotional. Cockerell's neat little pre-prepared pocket diaries in green cloth bindings allowed a small rectangle for every day, conscientiously filled each night in his precise and microscopic handwriting. I myself cannot read most entries without a magnifying glass, patiently provided by the staff of the British Library, where the diaries are kept. Cockerell was a meticulous observer, always curious about people. He documents with telegraphic

RIGHT: Manuscript of Justinian, Italy, thirteenth century, bought by William Morris and Cockerell in Beauvais in May 1894.

In nomine domini nostri Ihesu Christi de edictis et Falcidia constitutio prima. Si heres legata solvere noluerit. Constitutio imperatoris Iustiniani a. Iohi pp. ...

IMPERATOR

Occupatis nobis circa totius rei publice curis et nichil parvum eligentibus cogitare, sed quatenus Perse quidem conquiescant, Vandali vero cum Mauris obediant, et Carchedonii antiquam recipientes habeant libertatem, quam nisi nunc primum Romanorum facti rem publicam subiectos habeant, quod nondum ... nisi sub nostro imperio dedit Romanis deus. Incaminunt esse per sollicitudines annis subiectis septuaginta ... et quatuor singulis quidem dum competentem formam. Quecumque vero frequenti quidem perpetuum per partes auxilio possibilia tamen sunt scripta lege communem omnibus prestent in quibus opus habent utilitatem, hec oportere putamus et lege sancire et tradere subiectis per se vivaciter et non semper iussione imperatorum egentia. Sepe igitur nobis imperatum sunt. Alii quidem per legatis relictis non tamen pluribus adeuntes, alii vero pluribus ab ..., alii ob aliud quoddam quid transmittentes quidem heredes tamquam ... aut ficti constituerunt. Indevote autem et res adeunt et res perceperunt et quod est iussum non fecerunt, cum utique etiam a legis latoribus veteribus dictum sit competere defunctorum dispositiones quecumque non repugnant legibus omnibus modis impleri. Sed quoniam ita leges positas tam plurimque neglectas invenimus, separatim causam dicam ... et ... venientibus ... cautelam quam ... hinc ... liberare honorem. Primum itaque illud est cogitandum, quia testantibus aliis quidem necessitatem imponit lex distribuere quandam partem personis quibusdam tamquam hoc secundum naturam eis debeatur, quale est filiis et nepotibus et parentibus atque matribus. In aliis vero etiam fratribus et si quam huiusmodi personam aut in his que ex nobis sunt aut ex quibus sumus enumeraverunt leges. Aliis autem nulla consistit necessitas partem dare quibusdam proprie substantie, sed sua ei potestas largitur ad quoscumque testator voluerit proferendo. Omnes igitur a nobis precedentes sancimus eos qui ab aliquibus scripti sunt heredes aut meruerunt fideicommissa pro universitatem forsitan aut personam aut legitimum necessitatem habere, quecumque testator et honorantes eos disposuerit ex omnimodo complere, si quod precipitur legitimum sit aut si non illud aliqua lex vel si non fiat ab eo quibus honoratus est tamen eorum esse ... tam demonstret. Si quis autem non implens quod dispositum est, sed etiam competat ei qui honoratus est quod relictum est ex decreto iudicis admonitus annum totum preterierit non agens hoc quod preceptum est, siquidem aliquis est qui necessarie ex lege percipiunt, in plus autem quam lex ei dari vult scriptus est heres, tantum accipiat solum quantum lex ei dari vult, sed iure ab intestato partem concedit. Aliud vero totum auferri, et siquidem et alii quidam scripti sunt heredes accrescere illis secundum partem institutionis que unicuique distributa est. Si vero nullus alius sit heres aut sint quidem scripti quidem non autem adeant hereditatem, tunc quod aufertur aliis fieri admittatur, et licentia prebeatur et legatariis et fideicommissariis et servis libertate honoratis adire et hoc acquirere, ita ut omnibus modis quod preceptum est impleatur, cautione videlicet prius ab eis facta secundum quod ... vel rerum recipit modus, quatenus res accipientes agunt in eis que recte voluerunt testatores. Si vero nullus horum de quibus testamento memoria est facta voluerit adire, hoc est coheres aut legatarius aut fideicommissarius aut servus libertate honoratus, tunc ad alios quos lex ab intestato vocat post eum qui descriptus est et legitimam per hanc legem partem esse iussus deferri res, et ipsos similiter prebentes cautionem quia complent que testator commisit.

Hoc verum est intelligas si nullus fuerint substituti, vel si fuerint non vult hereditatem habere. Alioquin non accrescit coheredibus quia primo loco substituti ad ... ut subsequenti dicitur. xv.

Hinc ablatum ... facta suplex cautione vel coheredibus adiecta vel ceteris ex testamento.

[illegible]

precision where he went each day, the weather, the times of trains he caught, the names of everyone he met and wrote to, and the manuscripts he saw. Like the journals of Madden, Cockerell's diaries reveal the evolving life of a man for whom medieval manuscripts and their possession and study became the spark which animated his soul.

The two great formative heroes of Cockerell's early life were John Ruskin and William Morris. His diaries tell how he came into contact with each of them, in Ruskin's case initially by presenting him with part of his schoolboy collection of classified seashells. He was invited in 1887 (and later) to Brantwood, Ruskin's house in the Lake District, and then, by a fortuitous encounter in Abbeville in the summer of 1888, he travelled with him on a short tour of cathedrals in northern France. Ruskin wrote home to his niece that young Cockerell "carries my umbrella for me as if he were attending the Emperor of Japan".

John Ruskin owned medieval manuscripts, mostly kept in his 'Missal Cabinet' at Brantwood. He had already admitted to Madden in May 1853 that he was forming a collection. He bought his first manuscript in 1850 or 1852, a late thirteenth-century Book of Hours of the Use of Reims (now in the Victoria and Albert Museum). In his autobiography Ruskin described finding it by chance "at a bookseller's in a back

John Ruskin in his study at Brantwood, watercolour by William Collingwood, 1882.

alley", delighting like Morris in discovery and acquisition in an out-of-the-way place:

> The new worlds which every leaf of this book opened to me, and the joy I had, counting their letters, and unravelling their arabesques as if they had all been of beaten gold – as many of them indeed were – cannot be told . . .

Over the next thirty years, Ruskin acquired some ninety medieval manuscripts, especially Books of Hours and Psalters, most of which he called 'Missals' with defiant indifference to their contents. His watercolours by Turner and his manuscripts became his chief treasures. He wrote:

> I am sure I ought to take that text to heart, 'Covetousness which is idolatry', for I do idolize my Turners and missals, and I can't conceive anybody being ever tried with a heavier temptation than I am to save every farthing I can to collect a rich shelf of thirteenth-century manuscripts.

This was a revelation to Sydney Cockerell. He described sitting in the study at Brantwood turning the pages of Ruskin's glittering and undeniably royal 'Saint Louis Psalter', which had descended probably from the saint's sister, Isabelle of France, to Charles V, brother of the Duc de Berry. Even during that journey in France in 1888, Ruskin had several manuscripts in his pockets, a tiny thirteenth-century Bible, a Dutch Psalter and a Parisian Breviary, which he intended to give (but did not) to Beauvais Cathedral. Ruskin explained that he planned to show his manuscripts to the librarians of Laon, Reims and elsewhere, and by that means would strike a conversation and gain admission, a trick which I can report from experience almost never fails to work.

His diary for 1889, a year later, reveals Cockerell reading W. J. Loftie's *Lessons in the Art of Illuminating* (1885) and going on at least three occasions that year to the British Museum to look at medieval manuscripts in the display cases, including one visit on 16 July, his twenty-second birthday. Madden had agreed with Ruskin that showing manuscripts under glass was not the right way to appreciate them, but the public galleries of the Museum had an immense value to the education of Cockerell, who himself later maintained and promoted the same tradition of public exhibition of manuscripts when director of the Fitzwilliam Museum.

Cockerell's association with William Morris was even more important in directing his life into medieval manuscripts. He began attending events organized by Morris at the Art Workers' Guild and elsewhere, and by 1890 he had become a regular if silent and watchful member of the devotees who joined the great man afterwards for dinners at Gatti's in the Strand, near Charing Cross. While others were calling for carafes of wine during these convivial and often boisterous evenings, Cockerell sipped hot chocolate and remembered the conversations. Sometimes Morris's new manuscript acquisitions were passed round the table. Cockerell recorded in May 1892: "Morris had a beautiful illuminated MS which he bought with others yesterday at the Lawrence sale." It was a thirteenth-century French commentary on Aristotle, opening with a historiated initial showing a young man who raises his hand as a venerable bearded master holds out an open book, much as Morris did to Cockerell.

William Morris had first been enchanted by medieval illuminations as an undergraduate in Oxford with the future Pre-Raphaelite painter Edward Burne-Jones in the early 1850s, when they had looked at the thirteenth-century Apocalypse bequeathed by Francis Douce to the Bodleian Library. Manuscripts became models for Morris's own not very accomplished attempts at illumination and among the inspirations for his rebirth of medieval craftsmanship. It is no great leap from the border of a Book of Hours to a gothic tapestry or wallpaper of ivy leaves and birds. Morris was always a man of sudden and tremendous enthusiasms. At about the time Cockerell entered his circle, he was turning to the books of the Middle Ages with a new and frenzied passion. He founded the

William Morris in his study at Kelmscott House, Hammersmith, with part of his collection of rare books, photograph, 1890s.

Kelmscott Press in 1891, to re-create the artistry and design of medieval book production. He began rapidly buying manuscripts and in under a decade had gathered well over a hundred. There were two areas in his manuscript collecting. Like Ruskin, Morris revelled in early gothic illumination of the twelfth to fourteenth centuries, mostly religious, rich in northern European grotesquery and burnished gold. At the same time, he was fascinated by the graceful design and legibility of Italian Renaissance books, which had so entranced the humanists of *quattrocento* Florence. Among others, he owned two manuscripts copied by Ser Giovanni di Piero da Stia, a scribe employed by Vespasiano da Bisticci. Such books were unfashionable among most collectors of the nineteenth century and not expensive. Cockerell was well-placed to witness Morris's delight of rediscovery, not so different from the excitement documented by Vespasiano as the humanists around Niccolò Niccoli and Poggio Bracciolini found new joy in classical texts.

In the summer of 1892, Morris suggested that Cockerell might be the ideal cataloguer for his growing library of rare books in Hammersmith. Cockerell gratefully resigned from his clerkship in the family coal business and joined the court of William Morris, becoming in addition secretary of the Kelmscott Press two years later. He examined and collated the master's manuscripts and incunabula and wrote notes on their flyleaves in his elegant handwriting. He also witnessed and shared in acquisitions. A manuscript which tantalized Morris for years was the Huntingfield Psalter, named after the family who had owned it in the thirteenth century. It was being offered for sale by Bernard Quaritch (1819–99), the leading London bookseller, who optimistically attributed it to Mendham Priory in Suffolk around 1170, saying of it, "This grand volume is a treasury of early English art such as can no longer be found (with this single exception) out of the great public libraries." William Morris ordered it on approval. Cockerell's diary for 25 August 1892:

> looked at Psalters, including a splendid 12th c. (Huntingfield) Psalter, which WM has borrowed from Quaritch who asks £800 for it. The condition not quite perfect but the writing large and very beautiful. Thirty-four superb pictures at the beginning followed by a few less good ones. A great number of fish in the fillings of the lines.

Watch how the conversation must have gone with Morris, beginning first of all with the not inconsiderable price. Next, they inspected the condition (which is rather worse than Cockerell suggests, a fault that would have left Ruskin untroubled). Then they judge the book's grandeur and beauty, including the quality of script, and finally they carefully count the pictures, a new way of grading relative richness of manuscripts, rather like assessing a house by its number of bedrooms, and they notice details such as the fish. Although the full-page biblical scenes at the front of the Psalter are ill-proportioned and primitive, they include scenes of artisans earnestly building Noah's Ark and the Tower of Babel, activities which doubtless entranced the craftworkers of the Hammersmith household. Morris considered the manuscript indecisively for almost three years, before finally instructing Cockerell to write to Quaritch on 29 April 1895 definitively declining its purchase. However, manuscripts have a way of weakening resolve, like soulful puppies in dogs' homes. Only three days later, Cockerell's diary for 2 May records that Morris went to Quaritch's in Piccadilly and bought it after all. That month, Burne-Jones wrote of his oldest friend that he was enjoying the Psalter differently now as its happy new possessor:

> Well, about a fortnight ago he had a book sent to him . . . and he's given £800 for it and it's all his own and he's got it in his house, and now he can turn into an old gentleman and look at it every morning before he begins work and open the pages of it, and all the sunsets in the Mediterranean Sea are not equal to one of them – he possesses the entire Levant.

For several exhilarating years manuscripts arrived almost weekly in Hammersmith to be accessioned and foliated by Cockerell, especially Psalters and Bibles, but also, among others, a Florentine Cicero from the convent of San Marco, a *Roman de la Rose*, which Morris passed round at Gatti's in July 1895, and a twelfth-century Hegesippus from Winchester, in its original stamped binding comparable only to that bought by Madden for the British Museum for £200 in 1844. The Hegesippus had belonged to Sir Thomas Phillipps. Morris went with Cockerell to view it when the Phillipps heirs had consigned it to Sotheby's in 1896 and he left a bid with Quaritch for £100. After a probably sleepless night of worry, he increased his bid at the last moment to £150: there is the action of a true collector. In the sale, for such things can happen, it was bought for only £16, and Cockerell was delegated to fetch it.

The first time Cockerell bought a book for Morris at his own initiative, the response was muted. It was a thirteenth-century manuscript of Gregory's Decretals at Sotheby's in August 1894, not unlike the Justinian they had bought in Beauvais a few months earlier. "I daresay I shall be glad to keep the MS," Morris wrote in a note to Cockerell the next day when the result was reported to him. Gradually, however, Morris began to rely on Cockerell's ability to handle purchases and make deals. In April 1895 he used Cockerell to negotiate prices from Quaritch for a French Book of Hours and two German miniatures. In 1896 he sent him to try to get a thirteenth-century Gratian reduced from £180 to £160: "but don't lose the book", Morris cautioned him anxiously. Many years later, George Bernard Shaw recalled how Morris's scruffy appearance and manner had been off-putting to many booksellers. "When he went into a shop to buy a manuscript for hundreds of pounds they could not at first sight believe he was good for more than five shillings." Cockerell, however, was tidy and professional. His biggest adventure as Morris's representative was in April 1896. The dealer Jacques Rosenthal of Munich had acquired a marvellous twelfth-century English illustrated Bestiary which had been given in 1187 by a canon of Lincoln to Worksop Priory in Nottinghamshire, filled like Noah's Ark with all the animals of the medieval world and its credulous imagination. It was too valuable to send on approval. Cockerell was therefore dispatched to Germany, with money to spend and power to negotiate. The manuscript was by then in Stuttgart. Cockerell's diary for 30 April: "Saw Rosenthal & after much bargaining bought the Bestiary, which is very fine, for £900! & then started (at 12.39) for Heidelberg." On 4 May he carried the manuscript triumphantly to Morris at Kelmscott Manor near Oxford, stopping on the way at the Bodleian to compare it with their own Bestiaries. His reception that night was very gratifying: "the book voted by everyone a magnificent one. WM greatly pleased", wrote Cockerell. Burne-Jones again described the household's thrill at seeing the manuscript. "Morris took it, and in ten minutes his heart was aglow . . . a pea-green donkey . . . a most exceptional crocodile . . . an indigo bear." There is even a strutting bird like a crested cockerel in burnished gold. This must have been one of the proudest days of Cockerell's life, and it was one of Morris's last.

William Morris died in Hammersmith on 3 October 1896. Cockerell was in the house at the time, but across the corridor in the study at the moment of death. He was appointed as one of the two executors of Morris's estate, with the bookseller F. S. Ellis (1830–1901).

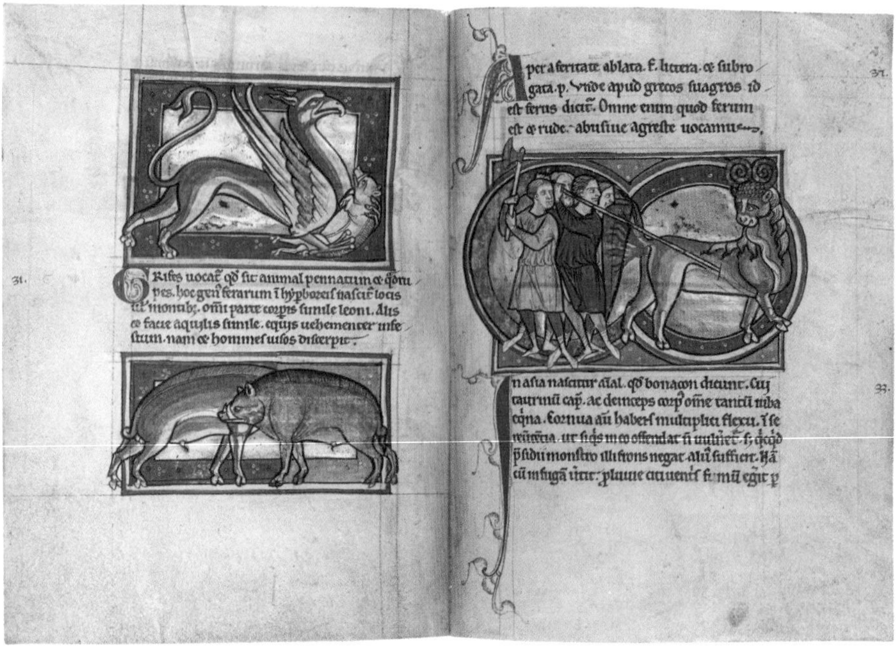

The Worksop Bestiary, Lincoln or York, *c.*1185, bought by Cockerell for Morris in Germany in 1896.

The valuing of Morris's books for probate was begun only four days after his funeral. The medieval manuscripts were assessed at £12,500, and everything was expected to be sold. Various would-be buyers and representatives of institutions came to see the collection, which also included some 800 volumes of early printing. Cockerell showed them round. Unexpectedly, the booksellers Pickering and Chatto presented themselves in early April 1897 with an offer of £18,000 for the entire library, which the executors accepted, with hindsight perhaps too hastily. Cockerell packed it up ("a dismal business", he wrote) and on 29 April he and the typographer Emery Walker took "a farewell look at the manuscripts". The anonymous buyer was rumoured to be either Mrs Rylands for the new John Rylands Library in Manchester, or the Princess Royal, dowager empress of Germany. It proved eventually to be a little-known investor in books and Chinese porcelain, Richard Bennett (1849–1911), a manufacturer of bleach from Lancashire. There was no space on Bennett's modern shelves for any books over 13 inches in height, which many were, for Morris had liked big books. (This would not have worried John Ruskin, who had been known to take a saw to any volume he deemed too tall.) Bennett quickly discarded everything beyond the maximum height to Sotheby's, 5 December 1898, *A Portion of the Valuable Collection of Manuscripts, Early Printed Books, &c., of the late William Morris of Kelmscott House, Hammersmith*, implying that this was an estate sale rather than the rejects of an opportunistic new owner. The auction attracted a great deal of public interest, even though most of the books had been on the market only recently. "It is not an every-day occurrence that a library dispersed at Sotheby's represents the tastes of a collector who was at once a distinguished poet, an artist, a socialist, a leading light in decorative production, and a reviver of ancient typography, illumination, and varied branches of book-lore", reported the London press.

The Justinian bought with Cockerell in Beauvais was lot 736 and now made £14.14s. to Henry Wellcome (1853–1936), pharmaceutical industrialist. The Aristotle passed round at Gatti's in 1892 was lot 134, £26 to Quaritch, sold on to Charles Fairfax Murray (1849–1919), the last of the Pre-Raphaelite artists. The Florentine Cicero from San Marco was lot 357, £27.10s., also to Quaritch, from whom it went to Laurence Hodson (1864–1933), a Kelmscott enthusiast for whose house near Wolverhampton Morris had designed a special wallpaper. The Hegesippus in the stamped binding from Winchester was lot 580, now fittingly increased to £180 to Henry Yates Thompson (1838–1928). All these three collectors would soon come to figure prominently in Cockerell's life, especially Yates Thompson. Cockerell attended the sale but was rather unenthusiastic: "The prices good but not extraordinary by any means." The circumstances made his position awkward and he was not a buyer personally, a regret he spent the rest of his life trying to put right. Bennett raised £11,000 by the sale and he soon profited from the residue. In 1902 he sold his entire library, including all Morris's books under 13 inches high, to J. Pierpont Morgan for a reputed but unconfirmed £140,000. Thus the Huntingfield Psalter (12½ inches), the twelfth-century Bestiary (8½ inches), most of the little Books of Hours and many others were destined for New York, and many were never seen by Cockerell again.

On 4 May 1899, Cockerell bought his own first medieval manuscript. That date became, in his own estimation, a turning-point in his life. The book cost £17 from Leighton & Co., London booksellers often used by Morris. It is a large copy of the Great Gloss by Peter Lombard on the Epistles of Saint Paul, written in France around 1230. It is one of those glossed manuscripts of complex page design, in which the biblical text is written in blocks of large script clinging to the left-hand edge of each column, surrounded on three sides by quotations from Saints Ambrose, Augustine and other commentators, flowing and ebbing around the words of the sacred Epistles, like seawater rushing and seething among rocks on the shore. By chance, Madden had been shown the manuscript by a dealer in 1866 and had rejected it as "badly written" and not worth £5. Apart from the intricate layout and red and blue penwork, resembling the Justinian bought with Morris in Beauvais, the particular appeal to Cockerell was because of a very old tradition that it had been owned in the fourteenth century by Petrarch, a link between French gothic and the dawn of the Italian Renaissance too tantalizing to pass up. The Petrarch provenance does not bear modern scrutiny (and Madden did not believe it), but to the end of his life Cockerell clung romantically and even stubbornly to the identification.

Cockerell was always fascinated by encounters with famous people. For a man of hardly thirty, it is remarkable what a galaxy of great authors and artists he had already brought into his personal circle, not only Ruskin and Morris with Burne-Jones and the Pre-Raphaelites, but also by then Bernard Shaw, with whom he went to Venice in 1891 and who remained a close friend until Shaw's death in 1950. He later became an intimate of very many of the greatest literary figures of twentieth-century Britain (and elsewhere, for he even travelled to Russia to meet Tolstoy in 1903), and their names are catalogued along the upper margins of the diaries. Cockerell sought out and cultivated these connections, almost as determinedly as he came to collect manuscripts. He eventually allowed the publication of two volumes of his correspondences with notable people. Relationships cannot be one-sided, however. Cockerell had good manners and a gift for friendship: people clearly liked him and enjoyed his company and receiving his letters, and he gave them intelligent attention, which was perhaps the key. In this he was very like Vespasiano da Bisticci. Intimacy, in Cockerell's mind, could also extend back into the past. Petrarch himself had used the metaphor of the books in his own library being among his friends: Cockerell knew the reference. In acquiring one of Petrarch's manuscripts, as he thought, the companionship of

RIGHT: Peter Lombard, Great Gloss on the Epistles of Saint Paul, France, *c.*1230, a part of the first manuscript bought by Cockerell in 1899 and later detached and given by him to the poet Siegfried Sassoon.

ut interpretetur.
care deberis: id est qui lo
quitur linguis et oret
dominum ut interpretetur. i. interpretandi gratiam det. vel sic orat
i. sic loquitur: ut et interpretetur. i. exponat. Nam si
aliter fecerit: non valet. Et hoc est quod subdit. Nam
si orem. i. loquar linguis
Nam si orem lin
sine interpretatione: spiritus meus.
gua: spiritus meus
i. spiritus sanctus a deo michi da
orat. mens autem
tus orat. i. facit me
mea: sine fructu est.
loqui. spiritus. i. vox. orat
i. facit me loqui quod
boni esse putatur. vel
spiritus hic vocatur vis
anime inferior mente. ubi corporalium rerum similitudines in
primuntur. ut ubi gratia spiritus prophetationis informatur
est: ut videret ymagines. et eius non ioseph illumi
nata est: ut intelligeret. Et est. spiritus meus orat. i. vis il
la inferior anime quam impresse sunt ymagines rerum facit
me loqui. mens autem mea. i. altera superior vis anime est
sine fructu. i. sine intelligentia eorum que dico. scio
enim non instruitur. Ita enim sit. si linguis incognita quis
loquitur. vel signa aliquarum rerum sine intellectu proferat:
sic solent latini homines greca cantare. oblec
tati sono verborum: nescientes tamen. quid dicatur.
Quid ergo est?
Quid ergo est utile: quid
ergo est faciendum? certe ora
Orabo spiritu: ora
bo. i. loquar spiritu. i. no
biliter. vel spiritu. i. lin
bo et mente.
gua a spiritu sancto data. Orabo et mente. i. intel
ligentia mentis. et orabo. s. orabo et mente. i. intel loqui
approbo: ut et signa rerum formentur in spiritu: et eorum in
tellectus refulgeat in mente. Sicut. Psallam spiritu
i. melodia cantus quod
Psallam spiritu:
minus est. et psallam
psallam et mente.
mente. i. spirituali intel
ligentia mentis quod
plus est. i. sic psallam
ut et consonantiam vo
Ceterum si bene
cis intelligam: et sibi
dixeris spiritu. quis
et concordiam in verbis
cernere esse debere. Ce
supplet locum
terum. q. ita est orandum. vel psallendum: ut dixi. Sed si
ydiote?
aliter feceris. s. si benedixeris. i. aliquid
bona dixeris spiritu. i. linguis per spiritum data. quis supplet
locum ydiote. i. illiterati et rudis. q. nullus. non
et sapiens: quia non intelligit. deinde apiens quis sit
locus ydiote: subdit.
Quomodo dicet
Quomodo dicet ali

amen super
quis amen. hic est locus ydio
tuam bene
te: et multis inveniuntur. super
dictionem:
mam benedictionem ut intelli
quoniam quid di
garetur: nullo modo. quoniam
cas nescit.
quid dicas nescit. Nota
quod hoc verbum amen non grecum est.
nec latinum est: sed hebreum.
et interpretatur verum. Quod quoniam
post dictum verum. vel fiat. amen.
non grece tamen non latine inter
pretes ausi sunt facere ne vilesceret nudatum: sed honorem
habet velamento secreti. Nam tu. q. ideo dico super
Nam tu quidem
tuam benedictionem. Nam tu.
bene gratias
et est vel una eminentia. q. hoc no
agis: sed alter
vo: quod ydiota non habet locum.
non edificatur.
Nam non hoc noto vel arguo
Gratias ago deo
quod agis: quia tu quidem gratias a bene
meo quod omni
gis in linguis: hic dicit. ne do
um vestrum lin
num spiritus sancti videretur repre
gua loquor.
hendere. agis gratias dico:
sed in ecclesia vo
sed alter non edificatur. et ne for
lo quinque ver
te qui eum per invidiam
ba meo sensu
dicere videretur: deprimens
loqui ut et ali
talibus quia ipse non haberet. ostendit
os instruam:
quia magis horum se loqui linguis.
quam decem milia
subdens. Gratias ago. hic
verborum in lin
proponit se exemplum. quod
gua. Fratres
non debent loqui linguis
mei nolite
non ad edificationem: sicut
pueri effici sen
ipse facit. quia omnibus linguis
sibus: sed malicia
novit. q. non in nobis vitu
po: quod ipse non habeo. quod
i. quia ego loquor linguis
omnium vestrum. i. quam loquitur ali
quis vestrum. et non gratias a
go deo meo. dico quod omnium
linguis loquor. Sed in ecclesia.
cui utilis esse debeo: nolo
magis loqui. vel. i. pauca
verba meo sensu. s. ut in
telligam. ut et alios de fide
et moribus instruam. quam x.
milia verborum. i. infinita ver
ba in linguis. Sic et nolo
Fratres mei a gentes. no
lite effici per impuritatem
pueri sensibus qui verba
explicant: quia non intelli
gunt. Nolite ergo esse
pueri sensibus ut non intel

another famous literary person was thus brought in 1899 into Cockerell's domestic world as the first of his medieval friends.

John Ruskin, Cockerell's second great hero, died at Brantwood on 20 January 1900, just over three years after Morris. The dispersal of Ruskin's manuscript collection was drawn out and complicated. Ruskin himself had casually disposed of many items in his lifetime, including manuscripts given to his secretary at Brantwood, Laurence Hilliard, who died still young in 1887 and whose family released them gradually onto the market in the twentieth century. Ruskin presented some manuscripts to the Guild of St George, now in Sheffield. He bequeathed Brantwood and its contents to his niece Joan Severn (known to Cockerell as Joanie) and her husband, Arthur, watercolourist, with the expectation that they would sell various books to pay for the ongoing upkeep of the house. Even in his letter of condolence to the Severns on 31 January 1900, Cockerell was already offering to act as their agent for sale of the illuminated manuscripts. As he did throughout the rest of his life, Cockerell invoked his experience as executor at Kelmscott House: "When Mr Morris died we were in some trouble about obtaining ready money to pay the heavy duties – and you may be in the same position."

In February 1901, Joan and Arthur Severn sent Cockerell the so-called 'Saint Louis Psalter', stating their minimum price to be £1000 but offering to split equally with Cockerell any sum he could achieve above that. The casualness with which precious manuscripts were sent by post seems astonishing today. Cockerell showed the Psalter to the Kelmscott circle, including Fairfax Murray, Hodson and May Morris, daughter of William. Within a month, he had sold it to Yates Thompson for £2000. Cockerell declined his commission but instead he took other manuscripts from Ruskin's collection on consignment and, more importantly, he was allowed to buy for himself a thirteenth-century Bible illuminated in York for the nominal price which Ruskin had paid for it some thirty years earlier. In April 1902, Cockerell was back at Brantwood. "After dinner Mrs S showed me where JR's manuscripts were, & handed over the study to me for the examination of them during the next few days." Several more were sold on the advice of Cockerell to Yates Thompson, including two

LEFT: John Ruskin's 'Saint Louis Psalter', Paris, *c.*1255, later identified by Cockerell as probably made for Isabelle of France, sister of Saint Louis.

Incipiunt
hore de beate
uirgine.
Domine la
bia mea a
peries: Et os
meum an
nuntiavit laudem tuam.
Deus in adiutorium meum
intende domine ad adiu
uandum me festina.
Gloria patri et filio et spiritui sancto.
Sicut erat in principio et nunc
et semper et in secula seculorum amen.

of the three volumes of the late thirteenth-century Beaupré Antiphoner (now in the Walters Art Museum in Baltimore) and a fascinating and strange monastic commentary on the Psalms from the period of Saint Anselm, which was sold to Laurence Hodson. From the success of this, Cockerell himself then bought from the Severns in February 1902 the manuscript now known as the 'Ruskin Hours'. This was a grand book, 10¼ inches high, made in north-eastern France in the early fourteenth century. Ruskin had included an engraving from it in his *Stones of Venice*. The manuscript has eleven large historiated initials and over a hundred smaller miniatures. "The style is that of several books written and decorated in the neighbourhood of Arras", wrote Cockerell, on examining it closely. It is now in the J. Paul Getty Museum in Los Angeles.

By the end of 1902, Cockerell was already an addicted buyer and owned more than twenty manuscripts. They included a Florentine humanistic miscellany of about 1480 and an eleventh-century Lectionary from the church of Santa Cecilia in Rome, both from Sotheby's (November 1900 and February 1901). One was soon extracted from his brother Douglas, who had found it in a small bookshop in South Molton Street, then a back alley but now a pedestrian walkway of fashionable shops behind Bond Street tube station. In June 1901 there was a notable sale at Sotheby's of manuscripts from the Barrois collection, acquired as a whole in 1849 by the fourth Earl of Ashburnham, a former nemesis (one of many) of Sir Frederic Madden. Cockerell bought four lots for himself, including, for a mere £7, a stately twelfth-century Cassiodorus which had been seen and used by Theodor Mommsen, and a very grand Florentine illuminated Polybius of about 1460, an extravagance (and he knew it) at £50. Later that same month he purchased two manuscripts from Jacques Rosenthal, the German dealer whom he had first met over the Bestiary purchase for Morris. One was a Florentine Cicero of 1421 and a prayer-book dated 1481 with the arms of Pope Sixtus IV. The social circle of his bookshelves was becoming as eminent as his connections in real life.

Such purchases were an achievement for a man who for much of that period hardly had a proper job and only an uncertain income. As co-executor of the Morris estate, he had been paid an honorarium for winding up and disposing of the assets of the Kelmscott Press. For a

LEFT: The 'Ruskin Hours', Picardy, early fourteenth century, bought by Cockerell from Ruskin's estate in 1902.

time, he secured a further £200 a year as part-time secretary to the great orientalist and rake Wilfrid Scawen Blunt. There was also a short-lived partnership with Emery Walker as processor engravers, which came to very little. Mostly, like Vespasiano long ago, he supported himself by acting as advisor and agent to other manuscript collectors of his time. This had already begun in 1898, when he had started buying printed books and Kelmscott material on behalf of Harold Peirce (1856–1932), of Philadelphia. Another client for a time was the Public Library in Boston, Massachusetts. His first approach had been a letter of May 1900: "After my training under Morris & my study of old books since his death, I think I can say without boasting that I know more about their intrinsic value than any bookseller in London." Boston allowed him $1000 to spend in the Ashburnham–Barrois sale in 1901, at which he secured twenty-one manuscripts for them in addition to the four he bought for himself. He had by then already negotiated the sale of several other manuscripts to the Boston Public Library, including two which had been owned by William Morris. One of these was a late thirteenth-century Bible which, Cockerell explained, with the reverence of a Gospel writer, Morris had "regarded with special affection on account of the extraordinary beauty of the penwork initials in it". It had been lot 169 in the Morris sale in 1898, bought by Pickering & Chatto for £47. "I have paid £72 for this, a considerable reduction on the price first asked, and I consider it a volume that for many reasons the Boston Public Library may be proud to possess." He also obtained a fifteenth-century Italian manuscript of Lactantius, which Yates Thompson had bought in the Morris sale for £19 and which he was persuaded by Cockerell to pass on to Boston for £20, a more modest profit than Pickering might have sought.

There was a new aspect of manuscript collecting in this period, which is that people were becoming very conscious of the prices, something which traditionally no gentleman would ever have deigned to discuss. The Abbé Rive, Sir Frederic Madden and Sir Thomas Phillipps had all known a great deal about the commercial values of manuscripts, because they would not want to pay too much, but once an item was secured its painful cost could be prudently blocked from memory. Cockerell's often-expressed opinion, however, was that the price of a manuscript was an essential part of its history and nothing to be ashamed of. He scrupulously recorded his own purchase costs in ink on the flyleaves or in accompanying notes of every manuscript he owned. Morris too knew exactly what he had paid for manuscripts and evidently introduced his Huntingfield Psalter to Burne-Jones as an £800 acquisition. Yates Thompson always wrote his purchase prices in a simple code on every bookplate. The important point, as Cockerell explained to the Boston Public Library in November 1900, was "that books with fine illuminations are very costly & that they are dearer each year owing to the increasing demand for them". To Harold Peirce he wrote in 1901, "The price of manuscripts advances every year so that now is the time to buy!" These simple exhortatory statements conceal a seismic shift from the old world, where works of art (including manuscripts) were bought because of their beauty or importance, into the new twentieth century when art became an asset and a recognized form of investment. Prices were seen to be rising faster than the value of money. That altered everything. It has been an almost universal feature of the art market and private collecting ever since.

Henry Yates Thompson was the first great English collector of manuscripts to whom their ever-increasing value was integral to his enjoyment of possession. Cockerell, not easily fazed by famous men, was slightly in awe of him. He was the son of a wealthy banker in Liverpool and through his mother the grandson of a manuscript collector. His wife, Elizabeth Smith, was a publishing heiress in her own right. In 1893 they had sold the *Pall Mall Gazette* to William Waldorf Astor for £50,000. In 1898 the Yates Thompsons invested £30,000 of this on buying the entire collection of something over 210 illuminated manuscripts assembled by the late Lord Ashburnham, known inelegantly as the 'Appendix', to distinguish it from other named collections bought *en bloc* by the earl (such as the Barrois manuscripts mentioned a few moments ago, dispersed through Sotheby's in 1901). The Appendix comprised the connoisseur's choice, items selected and bought one by one by Lord Ashburnham in the middle years of the nineteenth century. However, Yates Thompson had the idea that his own collection would be even more refined. He resolved that it should always comprise exactly one hundred manuscripts, never more, of the highest possible quality and value. Whenever the total went over a hundred, lesser items would be eliminated so that the fixed total was forever being improved and upgraded. Yates Thompson had first met Cockerell when inspecting the Morris manuscripts. In June 1898, six weeks after leaving the Kelmscott Press, Cockerell was retained by him to offer advice on which manuscripts from the Appendix should be kept and which discarded. It was exactly the kind of task Cockerell loved. He wrote in his diary that Yates Thompson "wishes me to go through the Ashburnham MSS with him, with a view to turning out all but the very best – a very interesting occupation". It was exercise of judgement infinitely more sophisticated than Richard Bennett's crass decisions with a tape measure, but in economic strategy not so different. Within a year, 177 of the Ashburnham Appendix manuscripts were eliminated and sent to Sotheby's, much as Bennett had consigned his Morris rejects.

Cockerell persuaded Yates Thompson to buy four manuscripts from the Morris sale, including the Winchester Hegesippus and the Lactantius discarded later to Boston and a Jean de Meun once owned by Joan of Navarre, queen of Henry IV. The Cockerell diaries around 1900 are filled with days spent among manuscripts in the Yates Thompsons' fine house in Portman Square, just north of Oxford Street in London. He wrote meticulous catalogue descriptions, extracting every possible clue to a book's origin and history. Manuscripts were constantly being offered for sale and it was an essential duty to be able to examine and grade their importance with some accuracy and speed, a training which Cockerell never forgot. Most decisions of what to keep or reject were made by Yates Thompson himself. In the drawing-room and around the dinner table in Portman Square he met many manuscript enthusiasts and others, for the Yates Thompsons moved in grand circles.

Cockerell accompanied his employer to Paris in 1902 and was introduced to Léopold Delisle, editor of the Duc de Berry's inventories, Comte Durrieu, art historian and collector, and Baron Edmond de Rothschild, possessor of the Duc's *Belles Heures*. It is inevitable that the Duc de Berry would be a principal subject of their conversation. Yates Thompson felt an especial kinship through manuscripts with his fellow Maecenas and autocrat of the Middle Ages, uninhibited by the 500 years which separated them. He came to possess several manuscripts once owned by the Duc and treasured them for that reason alone. He wrote of him in 1915 on familiar first-name terms that his predecessor had

> collected books and loved artists and authors, and it is pleasant to think of Jean . . . with his snub nose and genial smile, poring over one of these pretty manuscripts and discussing some literary or artistic point with Christine de Pisan or Pol de Limbourg, in one of his luxurious libraries at Paris or Bourges.

One manuscript the Duc must have enjoyed was the three-volume *Miroir historial* of Vincent of Beauvais, which he had given away to Jean de Montaigu and had then deftly reacquired when Montaigu was beheaded in 1409 (above, p. 78). Yates Thompson acquired the second volume of that set with the manuscripts of the Ashburnham Appendix in 1897. Quite unexpectedly the long-lost first volume then reappeared at Sotheby's in December 1906 and was recognized by Yates Thompson himself, who wrote to tell Cockerell of his discovery. It was bought for him by Quaritch for £1290 and "happily reunited in my library". The manuscript's third volume may have belonged to Sir Robert Cotton and survives now only as fragments of uncertain origin in the British Library.

As the Duc de Berry liked commissioning books as well as buying them, so too Yates Thompson delighted in sponsoring luxury publications about his own manuscripts and Cockerell was his ready scribe, bringing in Emery Walker as their illustrator. There may have been an unworthy thought that a manuscript with an enhanced public status might one day have a greater commercial value. Two of the manuscripts bought from Ruskin were published by the Chiswick Press in 1905, with descriptions by Cockerell and photogravures by Walker, the Hours of Yolande of Navarre (as *The Book of Hours of Yolande of Flanders*) and the Hours of Saint Louis (as *A Psalter and Hours Executed before 1270 for a Lady Connected with Saint Louis, Probably His Sister Isabelle of France*). Cockerell liked long book titles; even these are abbreviated. Cockerell wrote fluently, with great clarity and concise use of language. He also joined M. R. James in preparing entries for a series of *Descriptive Catalogues* of the Yates Thompson collection published by the Cambridge University Press, 1898–1912. They are supplemented by a series of *Illustrations* reproducing pages of manuscripts, seven volumes, 1907–1918. These are all complicated books to use, as each successive volume struggled with a numbering system of 1–100 which was ever changing with discards and accessions. Like many collectors, Yates Thompson was evangelical in his enthusiasm. Many of these publications were inscribed by him on the half-titles to friends and would-be manuscript admirers of his wide social circle. My copy of the first *Descriptive Catalogue* was presented by Yates Thompson to C. W. Dyson Perrins, who was just beginning his own collection.

As Yates Thompson's manuscript investments were being rounded off, Cockerell found himself consulted less often and he looked for other collectors who might benefit from his experience. Charles William Dyson Perrins (1864–1958) lived on the edge of Malvern in Worcestershire, about twenty miles from Phillipps's old house at Middle Hill. He was a small and modest man with owlish glasses, but very well-off. He was the Perrins of Lea & Perrins Worcestershire sauce, from which his family had made their fortune. He collected porcelain and early printed books with woodcuts. From about 1902 he had begun acquiring a few minor medieval manuscripts. As the story was told, he looked in at Sotheran's bookshop in London one day in July 1904 to buy a book to read on the train home and there he saw the Braybrooke (or Gorleston) Psalter, a large and richly illustrated early fourteenth-century East Anglian manuscript, on consignment from Lord Braybrooke of Audley End, south of Cambridge. The price of £5250 was heart-thumpingly high, even for a wealthy man. Yates Thompson had refused it. There is a classic Cockerell diary entry for 22 July: "Went down to Malvern on the 9.50 train to give advice to Mr Dyson Perrins as to the quality of the Braybrooke Psalter which had been offered to him . . . I saw his books and left at 5 for London." The Psalter was bought, and by the end of that year Cockerell knew its new owner well enough to offer him several other manuscripts, to escort him to the British Museum to examine the De Lisle Psalter and the Val-Dieu Apocalypse, and even to meet Perrins's mother. In no time, Cockerell was helping to weed and upgrade the collection. In 1904 Perrins bought a Statutes of England from the Morris library and in March 1905 the Mirandola Hours from that of Ruskin. Both must have been Cockerell's recommendations. In July 1905 they went together across to Douai, taking the Gorleston Psalter to compare with a related manuscript in the municipal library. (The story of Cockerell's life could be measured by trips to northern France with successive manuscript collectors.) The result of that visit was a book in large format, *The Gorleston Psalter. A Manuscript of the Beginning of the Fourteenth Century in the Library of C. W. Dyson Perrins, Described in Relation to Other East Anglian Books of the Period by Sydney C. Cockerell*, Chiswick Press, London, 1907. It is a very satisfying piece of research, never failing to invoke Morris, Ruskin and Yates Thompson.

Many of Dyson Perrins's best acquisitions of illuminated manuscripts

RIGHT: The Braybrooke (or Gorleston) Psalter, Suffolk, *c.*1310–24, bought by C. W. Dyson Perrins in 1904 and published by Cockerell in 1907.

non abiit in consilio impiorum
⁊ in via peccatorum non stetit: ⁊
in cathedra pestilencie non sedit.
Sed in lege dñi voluntas eius:
⁊ in lege eius meditabit᷑ die ac nocte.

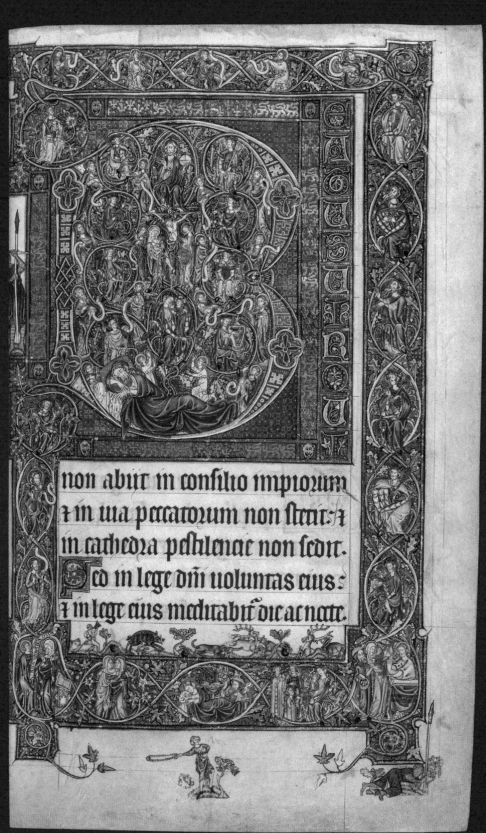

came from the collection of Charles Fairfax Murray, half genius, half Prince of Darkness, and undoubted bigamist from the Kelmscott days. Cockerell's relationship with Murray alternated between joyous memories of Morris and utter frustration. Murray lived partly in Florence and had an extraordinary ability to gather manuscripts of great quality which were forever potentially for resale at prices always just above their value, or usable as currency in amorous encounters. When in London, Murray lived at The Grange in West Kensington, the house previously occupied by Burne-Jones. Cockerell had taken Yates Thompson there to see the manuscripts in February 1900. In 1904 he tried to sell the whole collection on Murray's behalf to Mrs Rylands for Manchester, which came to nothing. In March 1905 he prepared a few possible purchases from Murray for Dyson Perrins, including a hauntingly beautiful English Apocalypse in not quite perfect condition. Two days later, after lunch at the Conservative Club, Perrins was brought round to the house in West Kensington and was convinced to buy seven manuscripts. It was a promising start. Cockerell wrote carefully afterwards to Fairfax Murray:

> I should like Perrins to have the Apocalypse to go beside his Braybrooke Psalter, & if ever you feel disposed to part with it . . . I will do my best to persuade him. At the price you named he did not seem at all tempted – & indeed I expect that for the present he feels that he has spent enough.

On his next visit, however, Dyson Perrins did indeed buy the Apocalypse, now in the J. Paul Getty Museum, and a great many more items. Cockerell took commission both in manuscripts and in money. In 1905, Murray gave him an illuminated florilegium from works of Saint Jerome signed and dated in northern Italy in 1449. Cockerell's notes for his own income tax declaration at the end of 1905 included £100 from Dyson Perrins, £160 from Fairfax Murray, and £31.5s. from Yates Thompson. An unmarried man, even a manuscript collector, could almost live on that.

Cockerell was of medium height, with a straight nose and by this time an already receding hairline. Looking back on his youth, he regarded his own appearance as having been presentable but never inconveniently handsome. In 1899 he grew an arched moustache, and during an adventure with W. S. Blunt in Egypt in 1900, which included a not very dangerous shipwreck, this evolved into a beard which in time was trimmed into a neat little Vandyke, maintained for the rest of his life. It was never a wild growth like those of Ruskin, Morris, Blunt, Shaw and Tolstoy. By middle life, Cockerell was already mostly bald and the tidy beard had become white, and he took to wearing rimless wire glasses. In old age he often wore a skullcap. He was a good conversationalist, well-informed and with quick recall, witty, but not comic. He spoke, as those who remember him tell me, with great precision and certainty, especially on the subject of manuscripts.

Cockerell took every opportunity to look at manuscripts, often comparing them in his mind with his own (as collectors do), and he especially enjoyed taking other people to see them. Every visit became a kind of tutorial. In May 1904, he went with Emery Walker and the bookbinder Katharine Adams to Balliol College in Oxford, as I have done, to see the Cicero of 1445 bought by William Gray from Vespasiano da Bisticci. In December 1905 he was at Holkham Hall, probably the first manuscript scholar there since Frederic Madden almost eighty years earlier. Cockerell wrote about his visit to M. R. James: "I started by glancing at every book on the shelves – which took two days – & then looked more carefully at the best things . . . I urged the librarian to foliate them, as he seems to have nothing to do." In the summer of 1906, he took Bernard Shaw to Chantilly, where together they turned the pages of the *Très Riches Heures* of the Duc de Berry. There was a curious consequence of that experience. In February 1924, Shaw sent Cockerell an advance copy of his new play, *Saint Joan*. Scene IV opens with what is perhaps the only description of a Book of Hours in any major work of English literature. "Now this is what I call workmanship", the earl of Warwick begins, riffling through the manuscript in France; "There is nothing on earth more exquisite than a bonny book, with well-placed columns of rich black writing in beautiful borders, and illuminated pictures cunningly inset." Notice the reference to columns. The *Très Riches Heures* is almost the only Book of Hours in two columns with miniatures inset, and it may easily have been the only one Shaw had ever held in his hands.

All collectors look back to lost opportunities of their past. Cockerell's great regret was not having started buying at the time of the Morris sale of 1898. He was prepared to sell or exchange manuscripts, if this allowed him to upgrade his own library or bring him closer to Morris and Ruskin. In August 1904 he bought a fine thirteenth-century Bible which had been presented around 1300 to Saint Augustine's Abbey in Canterbury by one Nicholas de Bello (Battle, a placename in East Sussex).

Terra autem erat inanis et
uacua: et tenebre erant super
faciem abyssi: et sp̄s dī fereba
tur sup aquas. Dixitque d̄s.
Fiat lux. Et facta est lux. Et
uidit d̄s lucem quod esset
bona: et diuisit lucem ac te
nebras. Appellauitque lucem
diem: et tenebras noctem. Fa
ctumque est uespe et mane: di
es unus. Dixit quoque d̄s. Fiat
firmamentum in medio a
quarum: et diuidat aquas
ab aquis. Et fecit d̄s firma
mentum: diuisitque aquas
que erant sub firmamento.
ab his que erant sup firma
mentum. Et factum est ita.
Vocauitque d̄s firmamentū
celum. Et factum est uespe et
mane: dies secundus. Dixit
uero d̄s. Congregentur aque
que sub celo sunt in locū unū:
et appareat arida. Factūque ē
ita. Et uocauit d̄s aridam
terram: congregationesque
aquarum appellauit maria.
Et uidit d̄s quod eēt bonū:
et ait. Germinet terra herbā
uirentem et facientē semen:

In November that year, Yates Thompson wrote asking whether he could ever be persuaded to part with it. Six months later, he finally agreed, ceding the Bible to Yates Thompson, together with the expensive Polybius he had bought in the Ashburnham sale in 1901. In return, Cockerell received £300 and another manuscript Bible once owned by Morris. An aspect of rising prices is that, if skilfully played, a collection could become self-financing. On the same day, in lieu of a debt of £31.13s. incurred in Paris, Yates Thompson also gave him the Jean de Meun which had belonged to Joan of Navarre and to Morris.

An opportunity to recapture opportunities from the Morris sale occurred in December 1906, when Laurence Hodson, "during a reversal of fortune" (as Cockerell expressed it), was obliged to sell a large part of his library, mostly at Sotheby's. Cockerell secured for himself a twelfth-century glossed Epistles of Saint Paul, once at Kelmscott House, and that same monastic commentary on the Psalms which he had earlier sold to Hodson from Ruskin's collection. A couple of days later, Cockerell made the most expensive purchase of his life. In the Hodson sale, Quaritch had spent £390 on three volumes of a huge late thirteenth-century Bible from Marquette Abbey, near Lille, with forty-six marvellous historiated initials like glittering stained-glass windows. It too had been owned by Morris. Cockerell then bought it from Quaritch on 6 December 1906 for £480, "all the money I have in the world". At that time, Cockerell was already discussing marriage to Florence Kingsford. His official biographer, with no understanding of collectors or the relative priorities of manuscripts and domesticity, comments dryly, "Though it was to prove a very shrewd investment, its purchase was hardly the act of a poor man contemplating immediate matrimony." "No more book buying for me!" Cockerell dutifully told the collector Harold Peirce in 1907 on announcing his engagement. This was, of course, completely untrue and they both knew it.

Florence Kingsford, known from her middle name as Kate, was a manuscript illuminator, trained at the Central School of Arts and Crafts and with the scribe Edward Johnston. She is first mentioned in Cockerell's diary in 1900. They were finally married in Iffley Church, near Oxford (his choice, not hers), on 4 November 1907. She was a superlative

LEFT: The Marquette Bible, northern France (probably Lille), *c.*1270, owned by Morris and bought by Cockerell in 1906 for "all the money I have in the world".

painter and gilder, as technically accomplished as any since Simon Bening or Nicolas Jarry, but she suffered from great shyness, and in 1916 she was diagnosed with multiple sclerosis. In time, they had three children, including the future inventor of the hovercraft. Kate Cockerell's social diffidence and later illness kept her generally at home, and her husband's public life continued usually alone, as was also the custom of those times.

With both marriage and his fortieth birthday, however, Cockerell suddenly found himself yearning for respected employment and a settled income. He realized that the glorious and exhilarating bachelor diet of manuscripts alone could not sustain a family for ever. There was always a lingering regret that he had no university experience, and like many outsiders he found himself looking enviously and naively at the apparent enchantments of Oxford and Cambridge. It was becoming the trend, as we saw with Mommsen, for palaeography and manuscript studies to benefit from academic endorsement. Early in 1907, Cockerell learned that M. R. James was likely to resign as director of the Fitzwilliam Museum, Cambridge University's art collection founded with many illuminated manuscripts in 1816. The long-expected vacancy was formally announced in April 1908. Cockerell's campaign to have himself appointed was calculated and unrelenting, leaving no contact unapproached and no conversation overlooked, and this was a man with many contacts. He had the essential qualification for the post, which was (and still is) pre-eminence in at least one major area represented in the holdings of the Museum. He now had a significant record of publication, including catalogues written for Yates Thompson jointly with the outgoing Fitzwilliam director. He was friends with collectors and potential donors of both art and money, and he would today be any university development office's dream candidate. He was personable and clever and energetic. Former intimacy with William Morris and the Pre-Raphaelites still carried great weight. His critical eye and connoisseurship of art were unquestionable. The only thing he lacked was experience in what is now called museology – the organization of exhibitions and displays, involving engagement of the public.

Cockerell's solution to this was to organize extremely rapidly what was to become the finest loan exhibition of illuminated manuscripts ever held in Britain, even today, at the Burlington Fine Arts Club in Savile Row, in the West End of London. Sepia photographs of the display cabinets show row after row of famous manuscripts, propped up vertically, every one of which is recognizable now with a magnifying glass. It was like the greatest red carpet of Hollywood celebrities across a thousand years of medieval art, with Cockerell as their master of ceremonies. There were 270 exhibits, lent by fifty-nine different owners. Items were borrowed from Windsor Castle, Lambeth Palace and the cathedrals of Winchester and Hereford, from Chatsworth and Belvoir Castle, and from Eton and several colleges of both Oxford and Cambridge, and many private collections across England and Scotland. George Holford obliged with his late father's life and miracles of Saint Edmund, lost by Madden in 1841, and the Psalter which Madden had so admired in the possession of Ottley in 1829. George Salting lent the self-portrait of Simon Bening now in the Victoria and Albert Museum, which opens Chapter 4 above. Many items, not unexpectedly, belonged to the collections of Yates Thompson, Dyson Perrins and, already among the paladins, Cockerell himself. Ten manuscripts in the exhibition had once been owned by Ruskin, including a thirteenth-century Bible not yet sold by the Severns; nineteen had been in the library of Morris, several of them lent by Pierpont Morgan, such as the Huntingfield Psalter and the Bestiary with the pea-green donkey, presumably both still in London at Morgan's house in Princes Gate.

A loan exhibition on such a scale today would take years of planning and negotiation. Cockerell had no such luxury. The first meeting of his

The case displaying manuscript Psalters in the Burlington Fine Arts Club exhibition in 1908.

organizing committee was held in December 1907 and included Yates Thompson and Perrins. Cockerell then recruited M. R. James to join them, strategically astute. Most loans were solicited in the New Year by Cockerell in person, very often coming away on the same day with the requested manuscripts on the train. He catalogued and photographed the exhibits as he was arranging them in the display cases. Kate Cockerell helped tie them open, and they often worked until ten or eleven at night. Proofs of his descriptions were being corrected and additions made even up to the last week. The first copy of Cockerell's 130-page catalogue was delivered to him on Saturday, 16 May 1908, the closing date for applications for the Fitzwilliam. The exhibition opened the following Monday. Even as the Cambridge electors were considering the candidates, more than 5000 people came to view the manuscripts displayed. Two weeks later, on 30 May, Cockerell was appointed director of the Fitzwilliam Museum.

It is very striking now to read through the catalogue of the Burlington Fine Arts Club exhibition and to realize how the field of medieval manuscripts was still dominated by private collections. This may be partly because such books were easier to borrow quickly than those in bureaucratic institutions. Almost 200 of the 270 exhibits were privately owned, including manuscripts now as famously public as the tenth-century Benedictional of Saint Æthelwold or the Hours of Jeanne de Navarre. These had been owned by individual people in the Middle Ages and many still remained so, in the possession of families and bookshops in back alleys. It was still possible for ordinary people to collect manuscripts in the early twentieth century. In 1908, before the waves of purchasing by mainly US libraries, the majority of medieval Books of Hours were not yet in institutional libraries. That is very different today and, although we must rejoice that manuscripts are safer than they have ever been, our world has lost something very ancient as, one by one, so many manuscripts in the wild have been hunted and captured. Cockerell was a woodsman and stalker long before he became a zookeeper in Cambridge, and that is what made him such a successful museum director.

Cockerell's fame at the Fitzwilliam is as its most skilful acquisitor. He treated his new employer exactly as he had when buying for any other collector, and he beguiled many items for the Museum out of the contacts he had formed since the 1890s. He persuaded the widow of Burne-Jones to present the manuscript of the Icelandic sagas written and illuminated by Morris, given in 1909, and W. S. Blunt in 1922 to donate the manuscript *Shahnameh* once owned by Morris. By gift or purchase he gathered in medieval manuscripts from owners he had met over loans to his Burlington Fine Arts Club exhibition, including Charles Brinsley Marlay (1831–1912), the Reverend Edward Samuel Dewick (1844–1917), which included five miniatures by Simon Bening, and Alfred Aaron de Pass (1861–1952). Cockerell hoped that Yates Thompson's manuscripts might be enticed into the Fitzwilliam, but when the collector announced in 1918 his bombshell decision to disperse them by auction, judging that his investment had reached maturity, Cockerell was at least able to secure Ruskin's 'Saint Louis Psalter' for the Museum for £4000, raised by last-minute donations. Cockerell also acquired great paintings for the Fitzwilliam by Titian, Pieter Bruegel the Younger, William Blake, Turner and many others, including Pre-Raphaelites. His mastery of fund-raising is still remembered in Cambridge with awe. "How you managed to squeeze £1000 out of a dinner table passes my understanding," wrote Thomas Hardy, who was convinced to present the manuscript of his *Jude the Obscure*. Cockerell's building projects included the Marlay Galleries (1922) and the Courtauld Wing (1931). He was elected a Fellow of Jesus College in 1910 and later of Downing College; he received an honorary doctorate in 1930, making up for not having a university degree, and a knighthood in 1934. All this is well known, and rightly acclaimed.

We are going to do something rather different: we will follow Cockerell home and look at what he was doing in the privacy of his own bookshelves, when he was by himself. The Cockerells, soon with growing children, lived at 3 Shaftesbury Road in Cambridge. It is about twenty minutes' walk from the Fitzwilliam, turning right from the front entrance of the Museum, up Trumpington Road to just beyond the botanical gardens, left along Brooklands Avenue and into the second street on the right. No. 3 is the first substantial house on the left, built around 1900 in pale brick. It has bow windows on either side of a central door, and a triangular gable rising above the three windows upstairs, not entirely unlike the former house of Theodor Mommsen in Charlottenburg. Visitors invited inside remarked on walls crammed with memorabilia rather than great art, but there were Morris curtains in the study and a Blake drawing in the dining-room. Above all, there were manuscripts. Cockerell owned about fifty medieval manuscripts by the time he moved to Cambridge. Seventeen were in the Burlington Fine Arts Club exhibition, including his self-indulgent Marquette Bible, "by several artists, one of whom employs a pattern of gold on burnished gold with extraordinary skill", as he wrote in the catalogue. Neither marriage nor joining the Fitzwilliam Museum curtailed his collecting. "I am like Morris", said Cockerell without shame; "It is no use my swearing never to buy another thing. The moment I am sufficiently tempted, I fall!" He could see manuscripts every day in the Fitzwilliam but, as when Morris gazed with new eyes after acquiring the Huntingfield Psalter, enjoyment becomes different with ownership.

In 1909, Cockerell was able to buy two more manuscripts privately from Laurence Hodson. One was a graceful Boethius from late Anglo-Saxon England, probably written in Canterbury, for which he paid £75. It was practically the last pre-Conquest manuscript still in private hands. A century later it was catalogued by me at Sotheby's when it made £680,000. Another was a twelfth-century Psalter from St Albans Abbey, previously owned by William Morris, with burnished gold initials for every psalm. Cockerell identified it with the 'precious Psalter illuminated throughout with gold' recorded in the possession of the abbot of St Albans who died in 1146. Morris had bought it from Quaritch in June 1896; a note by Cockerell at the front records that "it was, I believe, the last manuscript he handled and talked of a day or two before his death". This made it sacred to Cockerell, whose diary noted in triumph on 27 May 1909: "I bought the Golden Psalter which I have so long coveted for £150." He wrote on the flyleaf, "I bought it joyfully for that sum, which I consider far less than the value of a manuscript of such surpassing beauty and interest and one which Morris's love of it makes it doubly dear to me." (Cockerell's salary at the Fitzwilliam was £300 a year.)

By 1930, Cockerell owned about a hundred medieval manuscripts. Like Ruskin and Morris, he could not resist gothic books once owned by French cathedrals, deep with sentiment to him from many trips, and his purchases included both a Bible (1914) and a Missal (1922) from Notre-Dame in Paris, no less. His oldest manuscript was a ninth-century Saint Augustine, perhaps from Reims, bought from the booksellers Maggs in 1919. Cockerell had an English Bestiary, not a very good one but quite possibly from Fountains Abbey, acquired in 1920, a reminder of

RIGHT: The 'Golden Psalter' of St Albans Abbey, mid-twelfth century, owned by William Morris and finally bought by Cockerell from Laurence Hodson in 1909.

Superbo oculo, & insaciabili corde: cum
hoc non edebam.

Oculi mei ad fideles terre; ut sedeant
mecum: ambulans in uia immacu-
lata. hic michi ministrabat.

Non habitabit in medio domus mee; qui facit superbiam: qui loquitur iniqua non di-
rexit in conspectu oculorum meorum.

In matutino interficiebam omnes peccato-
res terre: ut disperderem de ciuitate domini
omnes operantes iniquitatem. V. Iubilate deo omnis terra

CI

M.20 DOMINE EXAUDI ORATIONEM
meam: & clamor meus
ad te ueniat.

Non auertas faciem
tuam a me: in quacumque
die tribulor: inclina ad me aurem tuam.

In quacumque die inuocauero te: uelo-

the greater and older manuscript he had secured for Morris to such acclaim in 1896. There were a few single miniatures of exceptional quality, including a missing leaf from the famous illustrated Shah Abbas Bible, made in France in the mid-thirteenth century perhaps for Saint Louis and later presented in 1604 by Cardinal Bernard Maciejowski to Abbas the Great, king of Persia 1587–1629. It was bought by Cockerell for £200 in 1910 from the Bond Street dealers Durlacher Bros. (There seems to have been no thought that it might be suitable for the Fitzwilliam; it went home to Shaftesbury Road.) Another was a set of eight superb pages of fifteenth-century illustrations from a chronicle on the heroes of Antiquity, derived ultimately from the wall paintings by Masolino in the Orsini Palace of Monte Giordano in Rome. They had been bought by Morris in 1894 and then exchanged with Fairfax Murray, from whose estate Cockerell finally secured them in 1919.

Like Morris, Cockerell was inspired to gather classical texts from Renaissance Italy, and he came to own manuscripts of Plato in Greek, Cicero, Virgil, Juvenal, Horace, Catullus (not common), Palladius (even rarer) and others, especially if they were either exceptionally well-written or signed by their scribes, or both. In 1920 he bought a Cicero finished in 1453 by Vespasiano's friend Gherardo del Ciriagio, who had been employed on the set of Cicero for William Gray. Cockerell himself had beautiful and calligraphic handwriting, derived from the scripts of the Italian Renaissance. The palaeographer E. A. Lowe described it as "very legible and full of a curious, almost feline, grace, the performance of one well versed in the secrets of calligraphy". He became greatly involved in the campaigns for the revival of italic script in twentieth-century England, a reform which still endures. Several of Cockerell's own Renaissance manuscripts are reproduced in the classic manual for practitioners by Edward Johnston, *Writing & Illuminating & Lettering* (1906 and frequently reprinted), including his prayerbook of Sixtus IV and the poems of Pietro Bembo, offering them as practical models for modern scribes. This was a new direction in the usefulness of manuscript collecting.

The good shepherd may know his sheep, but few collectors have ever known their manuscripts as intimately as Cockerell. Every one was inscribed and foliated and minutely examined and memorized. He was

RIGHT: Manuscript of the poems of Catullus, north-east Italy, late fifteenth century, bought by Cockerell in 1902.

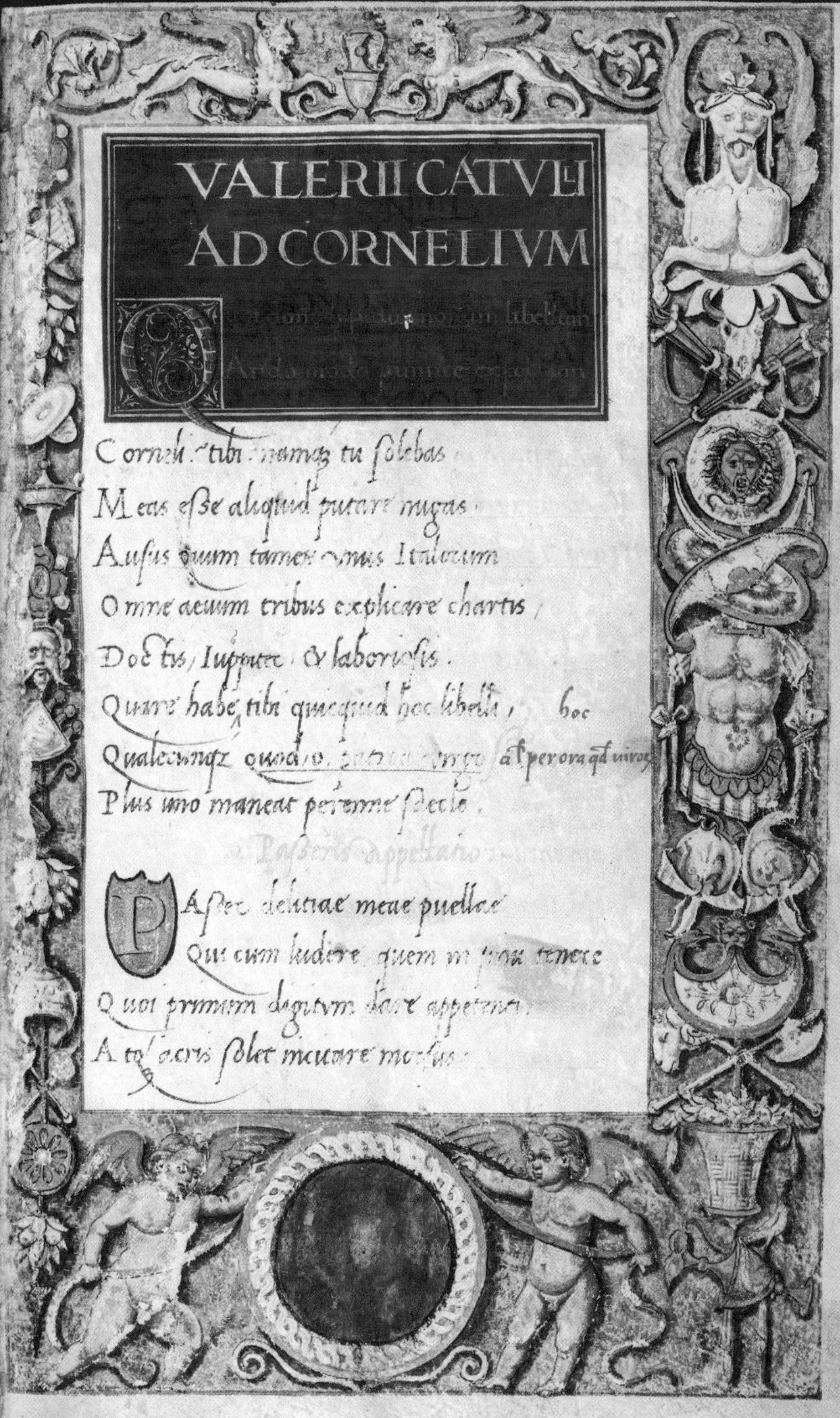

VALERII CATVLLI
AD CORNELIVM

QUoi dono lepidum nouum libellum
Arida modo pumice expolitum
Corneli: tibi: namq; tu solebas
Meas esse aliquid putare nugas.
Ausus quum tamen unus Italorum
Omne aeuum tribus explicare chartis,
Doctis, Iuppiter, & laboriosis.
Quare habe tibi quicquid hoc libelli, hoc
Qualecunq; quod o patrona virgo at per ora qd uiror
Plus uno maneat perenne saeclo.

Passeris appellatio

PAsser deliciae meae puellae
Qui cum ludere, quem in sinu tenere
Quoi primum digitum dare appetenti
Acris solet incitare morsus.

truly devoted to them. Each was accompanied by a large manilla envelope covered in his handwriting with collations and meticulous records of provenance traced through sale and exhibition catalogues and from inquiries forwarded to the consignors at auctions. The long chains of previous ownership were part of the unbroken fellowship of manuscript enthusiasts, what he called "provenancing". Cockerell identified with collectors of the past who shared his tastes, and he maintained an album of autographs of his forebears in bibliophily, including letters signed by Ferdinand of Aragon, Lord Harley, the Duc de La Vallière, Douce, Phillipps and Morris. The envelopes kept with each manuscript contained relevant cuttings, letters, photographs and comparisons, discoveries and observations made by all who saw them. These were not casual jottings, but represented innumerable hours of obsessive concentration and research, worked and reworked through the decades. Cockerell had many manuscripts rebound on acquisition, usually by his old friend the craft binder Katharine Adams (having them 'Katied', as he called it).

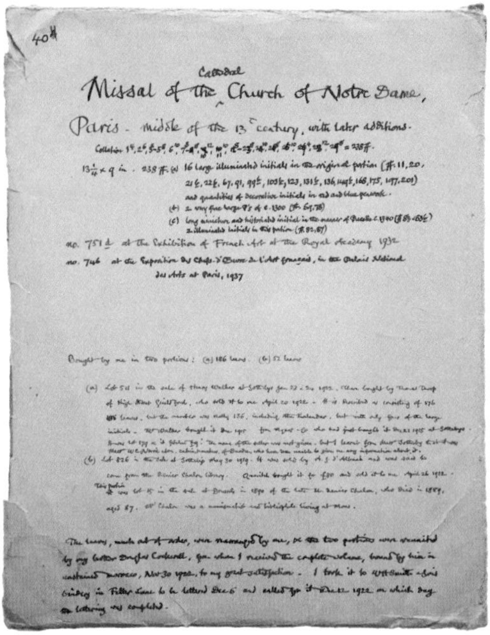

Cockerell's envelope of notes, accumulated over many years, about the Missal from Notre-Dame and the manuscript itself, Paris, mid-thirteenth century.

Most were kept in green cloth slipcases, lined with fleecy white cloth. He disliked full boxes, for the simple reason that he enjoyed seeing the spines on his shelves and could know at a glance that the manuscripts were safely there. I have no evidence, but I can almost guarantee that Cockerell gazed along the row of manuscripts every night before going to bed.

Visitors to Cambridge or promising undergraduates were sometimes invited home to tea on Sunday afternoons to see his collection. One guest recalled the treasures being brought out:

> He watched me as I turned the all-too sumptuous pages as a cat watches a bird. 'Be careful how you handle that book', he barked suddenly, 'Place it on top of that piece of tapestry.' I asked whether the massively mediaeval table I was sitting at was Morris' table. 'It was Webb's', he said. Fixing me with a piercing regard, he added, 'Like himself, it is solid through and through. Those men were giants!'

Not everyone gave the right responses. "I was rather unfavourably impressed by his way of looking at the books I showed him", wrote Cockerell in his diary about the monastic historian David Knowles, "which did not seem to indicate any appropriate enthusiasm." Others, judged by their reactions to the manuscripts, became immediate friends: Geoffrey Keynes, who brought Rupert Brooke, Belle da Costa Greene ("a very nice intelligent woman with a great enthusiasm for manuscripts"), Eric Millar, Wilfred Merton, Walter Oakeshott, Roger Mynors, the young A. N. L. Munby ("he is one of the few people who really understands manuscripts and looks at them with intelligence and enthusiasm"), and countless others for whom these visits were unforgettable. Siegfried Sassoon recalled, "On those Sunday nights in the quiet candlelit room, he seemed a sort of bearded and spectacled magician, conjuring up medieval illuminated missals and psalters." That miraculous and intoxicating experience of seeing manuscripts at home, as the late afternoon turned to dusk and the candles were brought out, has more in common with visiting the Duc de Berry at his castle of Mehun-sur-Yèvre than ever with requesting a book by its shelfmark in the strip-lit reading-room of a modern national library, and our lives are poorer if we have never done it.

To Cockerell, as to Petrarch, his manuscripts were his friends. He sometimes travelled with them, as he had to France with his living companions. He enjoyed introducing manuscripts to people, if he thought they had interests in common. At his first meeting with Sassoon, Cockerell brought out his manuscript of the poet Horace . He introduced his Pietro Bembo to Swinburne. He lent his prayerbook of Pope Sixtus IV to the Benedictine nuns of Stanbrook Abbey, in the hope that they might use it. Like Ruskin, he was even prepared to remove leaves from his own manuscripts to give to the right people, widening the circles of friendship. He detached a bifolium from his first manuscript, which had belonged to Petrarch (as he thought), and he gave it to Sassoon, a meeting of two poets. He gave to Madelyn Walker and Graily Hewitt, two of the best-known modern scribes and illuminators, leaves he had taken from his Cicero written by Gherardo del Ciriagio, their fellow master practitioner of five centuries earlier. On the other hand, he went to some trouble to recover and to restore leaves given away by Ruskin from the Saint Louis Psalter and the Beaupré Antiphoner, and when he identified a missing leaf from the Windmill Psalter, once owned by Morris, he gave it in 1916 to Pierpont Morgan, who then owned the manuscript itself. These too were ways of bringing manuscripts and people together.

All collectors are alike, but all justify and enjoy their addiction in their own way. Cockerell would entirely have understood the cravings of the

The Prayerbook of Sixtus IV, Rome or Naples, 1481, bought by Cockerell in 1901 and later lent by him to the nuns of Stanbrook Abbey.

Duc de Berry and Cotton and Phillipps, but he used his manuscripts differently. He was not at all interested in early printing, unlike Oppenheim, Rive and even Morris, although he maintained a good collection of Kelmscott material and memorabilia. For him, manuscripts had human interest, in the way that a printed book never quite did. They were handmade, by people not machines. Cockerell would have loved to have met Vespasiano. He would have had a thousand questions for Simon Bening. He rejoiced in manuscripts by identifiable scribes and artists, especially if signed. In 1904 he bought a thirteenth-century book naming its two scribes and even its illuminator. His was the first generation of manuscript scholars to benefit from widespread photography in making attributions. Even without that, he had a remarkable visual memory for detail and could match individual hands in his own manuscripts with others he encountered elsewhere. "Look at them properly – you aren't looking at them closely enough", he admonished one visitor. In 1906, Dyson Perrins acquired an early English Book of Hours with a tiny inscription in red, "w. de brail' q. me depeint", 'W. de Brailes who painted me', and Cockerell never forgot the artist's style. While arranging books for the Burlington Fine Arts Club exhibition two years later, he recognized twelve initials by the same artist in a large Psalter lent by New College in Oxford, and when he found one more in a manuscript at Sotheby's in 1909, he bought it for himself. "The point about W. de Brailes is essential, as he is one of a very few English illuminators of the 13th c. whose names are known", he wrote to Katharine Adams in 1910. The test of his credibility came in November 1920, when he was in New York with general permission to recommend purchases for the new collector of that decade, the mining magnate Alfred Chester Beatty (1875–1968). On a visit to the bookseller A. S. W. Rosenbach, Cockerell was shown a set of illuminated miniatures from a gothic Psalter priced at $6000. In an instant, as he wrote in his diary that night, "I recognised the hand of W. de Brailes", with such absolute certainty – "Cockerellsure" was a term people sometimes used – that he commanded Beatty to buy them. The next day, Cockerell took the purchases back to his hotel and examined them closely at leisure. In a corner of one page he noticed a little angel rescuing a small figure from Hell, holding an inscription in Latin this time, "W. de Brail' me fecit". The vindication of his eye, fourteen years after first seeing the only other signed example, gave him great satisfaction. We now know much more about the artist, almost certainly

William de Brailes, who lived with his wife, Celina, in a tenement in Catte Street in Oxford, *c.*1230–1252, on what is today approximately the site of All Souls College chapel, near the Bodleian.

Cockerell became the national arbiter of taste in the acquisition of illuminated manuscripts. Curators as well as private individuals sought his advice, and some received it whether they had asked for it or not. The generation of collectors following Yates Thompson and Perrins included Alfred Chester Beatty, just mentioned, C. H. St John Hornby (1867–1946), H. L. Bradfer-Lawrence (1887–1965), Eric Millar (1887–1966) and J. R. Abbey (1894–1969). They all put together libraries of illuminated manuscripts almost exclusively within the parameters of Cockerell's judgement and personal taste, including his delight in the Italian Renaissance. "I never felt that any acquisition was complete until he had seen and approved it", Millar recalled.

Conversation and correspondence about medieval manuscripts always formed a large part of Cockerell's social life. One of his especial friendships was with Dame Laurentia McLachlan, a Benedictine nun, prioress and then abbess of Stanbrook Abbey, near Malvern. Her knowledge and deep understanding of medieval liturgy and its books were second to none in Britain, and her extraordinary capacity for articulating the joy and beauty of her world is widely acknowledged. Cockerell was first taken to Stanbrook in 1907 by Dyson Perrins, who lived nearby, to discuss the thirteenth-century Oscott Psalter, which had been on loan to Dame Laurentia. For the next forty-six years the two maintained a correspondence and a relationship which became more devoted and probably closer than with any other woman in Cockerell's life. The unlikely intimacy between an enclosed nun and an atheist of the outside world was facilitated and brought to life by a shared devotion to the manuscripts of medieval Christendom. It was Dame Laurentia who identified the author of the commentary on the Psalms (formerly Ruskin's and Hodson's) as Odo of Asti, a little-known Benedictine possibly of Monte Cassino, who died around 1120. They shared many experiences of manuscripts. In 1924 they discovered that each was keeping the other's letters, and it was agreed that whoever survived longer would put the correspondence back together; their letters now fill eight bound volumes (and became the subject of a West End play in 1988, with Sir John Gielgud as Cockerell). As they grew into old age, they telephoned frequently, sometimes daily. Apart from two single and chaperoned dashes in 1923 to London,

Dame Laurentia McLachlan, abbess of Stanbrook, photograph.

Cambridge and Oxford, crammed with manuscripts and commemorated as red-letter anniversaries for the rest of their lives, they met only through the distance of the grill in the visitors' parlour in the abbey. There is no suggestion or possibility whatsoever of impropriety. Their affection was uncomplicated by any doubt about her spiritual vows or his faithfulness to a lonely marriage. The elusive definition of love is probably the oldest subject in literature, not to be resolved here, but if it is an intense sharing of minds and an enduring and reciprocal preoccupation with the thoughts and heartbeats of another person, then this was as close to love as any in human experience.

Cockerell retired from the Fitzwilliam without much regret in 1937 and moved to a house at 21 Kew Gardens Road in Richmond, west of London and not far from Hammersmith, where he had spent happy times with Morris. The house itself has been demolished. Cockerell bought a manuscript in Carcassonne in October 1937, on the holiday taken after leaving Cambridge. He continued adding to his collection, including a further Cicero written in Florence in 1442 by Domenico Cassio of Narni, who had also worked on Vespasiano's commission for William Gray (bought from Quaritch in 1945); a manuscript of Christine de Pizan, produced and corrected in Paris under the author's own supervision in *c.*1403–4 (bought at a further sale of the Phillipps manuscripts in 1946); and a pretty Italian Book of Hours, signed by the scribe Sigismondo de'

Sigismondi in 1498 (bought from a London bookshop in 1951, over fifty years after his first manuscript). Kate Cockerell died in 1949. Dame Laurentia died in 1953. Cockerell took to his bed in 1952 and remained there until his death a full decade later, on 1 May 1962, tended in the meantime by a succession of well-spoken women whom he called his 'angels'. He continued to receive visitors, who were shown manuscripts and were told about the golden days of Kelmscott.

The dilemma of what to do with a library of manuscripts occupies many collectors in old age. Although Cockerell was generous and he sometimes rewarded his angels and other helpers with gifts of manuscripts, there was never any consideration of bequeathing the collection to the Fitzwilliam Museum or of keeping it intact. He always planned that his captured manuscripts would be released back again into commerce, as Morris and Ruskin had done. The late Anthony Hobson told me that Cockerell was very aware that Dyson Perrins too was approaching extreme old age and had asked for Sotheby's to disperse his superb collection after his death. Cockerell was afraid that if Perrins died first, the value of his own manuscripts would suffer by comparison. Sir Walter Oakeshott, who knew Cockerell well, said that he simply could bear to wait no longer for the excitement and validation of watching people fighting for manuscripts which he had bought for modest sums so many years earlier.

In 1956, with the help of Brian Cron, a near neighbour and enthusiast, Cockerell decided on minimum prices for each book, as the Severns had done with Ruskin's manuscripts. Carefully selected booksellers were asked to the house and were invited to look along the shelves and to make choices. I was fortunate to have been just in time to have discussed these visits with nearly all the participants, and in detail with the late Brian Cron himself. One bookseller with a passion for manuscripts and for Morris was Alan Thomas:

> I went up from Bournemouth and was given dinner by Mrs Cron. Her small son, then passionately interested in railways, had commissioned her to enquire if I had travelled on 'The Bournemouth Belle'. Cron led me round to Sir Sydney's house. One might have expected that the man who had worked for William Morris in Kelmscott House (Hammersmith) and done so much to make the Fitzwilliam one of the most beautiful museums in England, would have created a beautiful setting for his own life – but there was dull Victorian furniture, and the only decoration one

> or two photographs of French medieval sculpture. At that time Cockerell, then in his nineties, was bedridden. He lived in a big double bed on the ground floor, his pulse rate said to be less than half the normal. I remember a bar, hung by a rope above his bed so that he could pull himself up. But, for all of that, his brain was still as active and sharp as could be ... Cockerell's manuscripts were kept upstairs, and Cron had a list with prices ... When we came downstairs I had quite a long conversation with Cockerell ... I was not overwhelmed with pride when I overheard Cockerell remark to Cron as I was leaving, 'That must be the most intelligent man in Bournemouth.'

Another account survives in the autobiography of H. P. Kraus, bookseller of New York. He arrived from America by aeroplane, a novel fact noted by Cockerell in his diary. He too tells of being taken upstairs to browse at will. "After having made your selections, you were ushered into the bedroom where Sir Sydney, supine and deathly pale, nearly paralyzed, negotiated the price." As described by Kraus, these discussions of manuscripts revitalized Cockerell and he records that the haggling over prices was long and hard. In reality, the prices paid by Kraus were neither more nor less than exactly those on the list prepared in advance by Cockerell and Cron.

Among other items, Kraus bought the leaf from the Shah Abbas Bible (£2000) and the Bestiary perhaps from Fountains Abbey (£1000, more than Cockerell had paid for the incomparably finer Bestiary for Morris in 1897). The firm of Quaritch spent £10,450: "a very satisfactory evening's work", wrote Cockerell in his diary that night. They bought mainly Bibles, including those from Marquette Abbey and Notre-Dame, hoping, probably wrongly, that Cockerell the atheist might have undervalued the Scriptures. In a visit of an hour and a half, a long one for him, Pierre Berès of Paris bought eleven manuscripts, especially French literary texts, including the *Roman de la Rose* (£600) and the Christine de Pizan (£700). Clifford Maggs, Heinrich Eisemann and Dawson's, represented by Helmut Feisenberger, also made purchases. Major J. R. Abbey, the only private collector invited in, bought well, including the prayerbook of Sixtus IV (£1000) and some very fine Italian humanistic manuscripts. Other items were sold and given to the Victoria and Albert Museum. By this round of sales, Cockerell realized just under £40,000. On 20 December 1956 he gave Cron his Golden Psalter from St Albans and

Miniature of the Last Judgement, attributed to the illuminator Maître François, Paris, *c.*1470, sold in Cockerell's sale in 1957 for £2100, then the highest price ever paid for a single miniature.

William Morris. "He was quite overcome with gratitude and delight," wrote Cockerell in his diary.

The remaining medieval manuscripts were collected by Sotheby's on 22 January 1957. A separate catalogue was issued for 3 April, *Nineteen Highly Distinguished Medieval and Renaissance Manuscripts, of the 10th to the 16th Century . . . The Property of Sir Sydney Cockerell, Litt.D.* It set a new standard of auction house description, introducing numbered sequences of the previous owners of each item, based on the accompanying notes. It is a seductive strategy because you watch the line of collectors and envisage your own name at the end of it. Since then, this practice has become commonplace in auction house and dealers' descriptions of manuscripts, an unheralded legacy of Cockerell's interest in provenance. The sale included the Peter Lombard, Cockerell's first manuscript, but as catalogued by Anthony Hobson the supposed connection with Petrarch's library was gently set aside (lot 6, £350 to Quaritch). Morris's Jean de Meun, acquired by Cockerell from Yates Thompson in 1905, was lot 9, £640, also to Quaritch. One framed miniature, attributed to the Parisian illuminator Maître François (lot 15), was bought by the Art Institute of Chicago for £2,100, then the highest price ever paid at auction for a single leaf. Spirited bids were received from Eisemann on behalf of the Swiss banker and passionate manuscripts collector Martin Bodmer (1899–1971). Among his purchases were the Anglo-Saxon Boethius, bought by Cockerell from Hodson (£6,600), the Catullus (£980), and, the great surprise of the day, Cockerell's Florentine manuscript of Plato in Greek (£5,800, compared with the £750 at which it had been priced by Cockerell for dealers' visits to his house). The sale made slightly over £27,000, about half as much again as Cockerell's own asking prices. A second but smaller sale of the residue followed in May 1958, *The Final Portion of the Celebrated Collection of Manuscripts and Miniatures*, adding a further £6000 or so to the total, including the Odo of Asti, from Ruskin and Hodson, identified by Dame Laurentia (£2600). As the last manuscripts finally left the house, Cockerell seemed strangely indifferent. "I can now", he told a friend, with a pause, "afford to have an egg with my tea."

Cockerell confined to his bed in old age, watercolour by Dorothy Hawksley, 1960.

CHAPTER TWELVE

The Curator: Belle da Costa Greene

"Tambales solmites famous gospels", began a Western Union cable dispatched in July 1899 from London by Junius Spencer Morgan II (1867–1932) to his uncle J. Pierpont Morgan (1837–1913) in New York, ". . . Cogote asked rebullir . . . parsees triturar." It employs the private code used for family telegraphs, at a time when the slightest hint of financial discussion in the affairs of Pierpont Morgan could send Wall Street crashing or the commodities market into frenzy. The message concerned the most valuable illuminated manuscript then still owned by the fifth Earl of Ashburnham, the supreme item held back when his late father's collection had been sold *en bloc* to Henry Yates Thompson in 1898. With the cipher words translated (rendered in italics here), the cable read, "*Can obtain for you* famous gospels ninth or tenth centuries gold and jewel binding of time treasure of great value *and interest* reported unequalled england or france ashburnhams *price* asked *£10,000* am told been offered *£8000 strongly recommended* mailing full description." It was followed up by a letter, explaining that there was nothing comparable to this jewelled manuscript in London or Paris and that only the treasury of Cologne Cathedral could match such an item. "The British Museum would like to buy it, but have not the money", wrote Junius Morgan.

Pierpont Morgan was at that time one of the richest men in the world with a personal income of well over a million dollars a year, almost unimaginable wealth in the late nineteenth century. He was the peerless colossus of American finance, with immense interests in banking, steel, shipping, electricity, mining, railroads and much else. He was also

RIGHT: Belle da Costa Greene (1879–1950), photograph by Clarence White, 1911.

a collector on a titanic scale. In 1899 he was not yet a focused connoisseur but a relentless acquisitor, buying up European art and history in quantity. He already had some trophy books, such as a Gutenberg Bible on vellum and a set of the four Shakespeare folios, bought as a collection in 1896. Mostly he was buying paintings, tapestries, sculpture and medieval metalwork. His nephew, however, was a book collector with a particular interest in classical texts (he would certainly have known of Mommsen), and he was anxious to rein in Morgan's limitless shopping, at least to the scale of items which could be stored on shelves in tidy order. In proposing the Gospel Book, he skilfully made comparisons with the museums of Europe, knowing that this would touch his uncle's American patriotism and competitiveness. There was also a financial incentive in buying manuscripts. By the United States Tariff Act of 1897, works of art became subject to a 20 per cent import tax, but books and libraries were exempt.

It took a couple of years before Lord Ashburnham's Gospel Book was finally gathered in, delayed by an unsuccessful public appeal to save it from export. The press in England deplored "that the authorities of the British Museum were not in a position to buy the costly manuscript", now usually known as the Lindau Gospels. It was made in the late ninth century almost certainly in the abbey of St Gall in Switzerland and was

LEFT: J. Pierpont Morgan, photograph, 1902.

RIGHT: The upper cover of the Lindau Gospels, St Gall Abbey, late ninth century, the first major manuscript bought by Morgan, acquired in 1901.

HIC EST
REX IV

afterwards owned by the nuns of the island convent of Lindau on Lake Constance, about thirty miles from St Gall. It has wonderful illumination in the interlaced Irish style, or as Irish as one might expect from a continental community founded 150 years earlier by Saint Columbanus and his fellow monks from south-east Ireland. Initially, however, Morgan would probably have cared more about the goldwork and jewels of the manuscript's sensational treasure binding. Like the Duc de Berry, he was already a major collector of rare gemstones. The lower cover of the Gospels, reused from an even earlier book, dates from the late eighth century, entwined with seething interlace like the Book of Kells wrought in shimmering gold and silver; the upper cover is contemporaneous with the manuscript and is heavily imbedded and studded with more than 300 pearls and gems, like a gilded Christmas cake of utmost richness. This was a banker's manuscript, both vulgar and fantastic.

In May 1903, Pierpont Morgan bought another iconic manuscript in a treasure binding. He was taking a cure at Aix-les-Bains in south-eastern France, when the dealers J. and S. Goldschmidt of Frankfurt showed him the Book of Hours written in 1546 for Cardinal Alessandro Farnese. It is the acknowledged masterpiece by the exalted illuminator Giulio Clovio, the Renaissance star to whom even the Bening Genealogy of Portugal was once preposterously ascribed. Here the attribution can be in no doubt: Clovio can be seen holding the Farnese Hours in his portrait by El Greco. It was described in detail by Vasari, who said that its production had been so complex 'that it would never be possible to pay for the work, regardless of the price'. Its illuminations resemble a ceiling of the Sistine Chapel conjured into miniature format, and the manuscript's elaborate pierced silver-gilt binding inset with ovals of the Annunciation was at one time attributed to the goldsmith Cellini. It had long been one of the most fabled but unseen manuscripts of Europe. Frederic Madden recorded in 1854 that it was then in the cabinet of the King of the Two Sicilies, kept in Naples under royal seal, which had to be broken if it was to be opened and then re-sealed afterwards by the king himself. He said in 1866 that it had been abandoned when the king had been forced to abdicate: "it ought to be looked after". The manuscript had been offered in 1898 to Baron Edmond de Rothschild for 500,000

RIGHT: The Farnese Book of Hours, illuminated by Giulio Clovio, Rome, 1546, bought by Morgan in 1903.

DEVS IN ADIVTORI
VM MEVM IN TENDE

francs (about $95,000), but it was rejected by him as too expensive. Pierpont Morgan bought it for $112,500, a bit over twice what he had paid for the Lindau Gospels.

These two manuscripts in their precious metal bindings are like the twin pillars of a hammock, supporting all the Middle Ages between them. Encouraged by Junius, Pierpont Morgan was already filling that space with single manuscripts as well as the wholesale acquisition of ready-made libraries of rare books. His purchases included the entire collection of Richard Bennett, bought in 1902, as we saw in the last chapter, with those of William Morris's books which were smaller than 13 inches high, as well as many other manuscripts bought elsewhere by Bennett. Morgan also secured the private library of Theodore Irwin (1827–1902), grain merchant and railroad investor in Oswego, at the extreme upper end of New York state on the edge of Lake Ontario. This was acquired in 1900 and brought Morgan a second Gutenberg Bible as well as the astonishing tenth-century Golden Gospels once owned by Henry VIII and a richly illustrated Apocalypse from the library of the Duc de Berry. These and other whole collections all carried many illuminated manuscripts with them on the incoming tide.

In the early years of the century, Junius Morgan was still acting as unofficial advisor and curator for his uncle's acquisitions. He was supervising catalogues and attempting to deal with the seeming torrent of acquisition. There are descriptions of tottering piles of rare books and manuscripts all over the furniture and floor of a basement room of the Morgan house in New York. On the advice of Junius, a special building for the escalating library was commissioned in New York in 1902 on the north side of East 36th Street, adjacent to Morgan's house, finally completed four years later at a total cost of about $1,200,000. Probably in 1903, Junius wrote to Quaritch in London that he had been "unpacking & arranging on shelves all Mr Morgan's large purchases . . . which have been in storage ever since".

In the long term, he was unable to devote sufficient time to organizing his uncle's rapidly expanding hoard. He travelled a great deal. He lived mainly in Princeton, more than fifty miles south-west of Manhattan, in a fine house called Constitution Hill, begun in 1897 and still standing, now divided into luxury apartments. He was a graduate of Princeton University and a notable benefactor of its library, where he had been given the honorary title of associate librarian, an office which carried

The newly designed Pierpont Morgan Library, watercolour by the architects, *c.*1906.

no responsibilities but presumably gave him a key to the building and access to the library staff. Among these was a junior assistant called Belle Greene, whose personality and aptitude evidently impressed him immensely. His own gifts to the library at Princeton had included Italian Renaissance manuscripts of Terence and Virgil, presented in 1896 and 1899 respectively, and a curious manuscript of around 1600 with the text of William Caxton's translation of the *Aeneid*, copied from the printed edition of 1490. It is more than likely that the impressionable young Belle Greene was introduced to these books by him and that her first exposure to Caxton, who became important in her later career, was actually a manuscript.

In late 1905, Junius Morgan brought Miss Greene to Pierpont Morgan in New York as a possible curator and organizer of the multiplying book collection. Fiction and myth have embroidered accounts of their first meeting, but no details of the interview are known. She was taken on in early 1906 at a starting salary of $75 a month. She was a woman people noticed. Morgan's biographer, Jean Strouse, says of her: "Small and slender, with dark hair and olive skin dramatically set off by light green eyes, Belle Greene had an extraordinary allure that appealed to both men and women, men in particular." The life by Heide Ardizzone adds, "By all accounts she was as beautiful as she was brilliant, although her beauty was usually qualified as exotic or unusual, with a cloud of dark hair and huge eyes, olive skin, and a proud carriage." She gave her full name as Belle da Costa Greene and her date of birth as 13 December 1883, which would make her a month over twenty-three when she began work for Pierpont Morgan in New York. Then or soon afterwards she would explain that 'da Costa' was the surname of her Portuguese grandmother, and that her mother was a widow, née Genevieve Van Vliet, from an old family in Virginia, fallen on hard times since the death of her husband.

These last two sentences include at least six deliberate lies, probably more.

The disentangling of the real identity of Belle da Costa Greene began with the sleuthing of Jean Strouse as recently as the 1990s. It transpired that Belle was actually born on 26 November 1879, which would mean that she was twenty-seven in 1906. She is not the first woman in history or the last to be creative over her date of birth (others include Anne Boleyn, Eva Perón and Doris Day). More importantly, the Portuguese connection and ancestral names were a fabrication. Both Belle Greene's parents were of African American descent, and her father was very much still alive.

He was Richard Theodore Greener (1844–1922), grandson of a former slave in Virginia, Jacob Greener, who had probably been born in Africa. Richard Greener was brought up mostly in Boston. He was clever and vocal. Even as a child he was taught French and Latin. He was sponsored first to Oberlin College and then in 1865 to Harvard, famously becoming the university's first Black graduate. He was appointed to a professorship in the University of South Carolina, where his statue stands outside the University Library, of which he was also librarian. He studied law and then moved to Washington as a Republican activist and campaigner for civil rights. In 1874 he married Genevieve Ida Fleet. Her own grandfather, Henry Fleet, had also been a slave, but they were by now an established and modestly professional Black family in Georgetown and Washington. Genevieve's father was a music teacher and her brothers (Belle's uncles) were named after composers, Mozart, Bellini and Mendelssohn. The first years of the life of Belle Marion Greener, as she was called, were spent in T Street NW in central Washington, between Le Droit Park and Eckington, in one of a row of small two-storey houses still there. Her birth certificate classified her as 'colored'. She had a brother and two sisters.

In 1885, when Belle was six, the family moved up to Manhattan when Richard Greener became secretary of the fundraising campaign to build a tomb and grand monument for the recently deceased Ulysses S. Grant,

Richard Theodore Greener,
Belle Greene's father,
photograph, *c.*1870.

the victorious Union general and later president, who had sought equal rights for all citizens. It stands by the Hudson River at 122nd Street. Greener resigned from the project in 1892 and continued working as an advocate and orator for African American causes. There was little money, and they lived at various addresses, latterly at 29 West 99th Street. By about 1897 the Greeners had separated. In an extraordinary turn of events, which seems scarcely imaginable outside the fiction of Jules Verne, Richard Greener joined the American delegation in Vladivostok, on the extreme eastern coast of Russia, where he moved in with a Japanese woman called Mishiyo Kawashima, with whom he had three more children (who later lived in China).

Genevieve Greener, Belle's mother, did not take kindly to this. She was probably the person who took the monumental decision which would distance her family for ever from her wayward and high-profile husband. She resolved to redefine them as being of exclusively European descent. The novelists Marie Benedict and Victoria Christopher Murray imagine her declaring, "In this country, as colored people, we have to use every advantage. Our pale complexion gives us a choice . . . I choose white for the children and myself." That is how she now identified herself (and them) in her New York census return of 1900. She first became Ida Green and then the more elite Genevieve Van Vliet Greene. The 'Vliet' was clearly adapted from her maiden name, Fleet. A Dutch or Dutch Portuguese connection would have seemed a plausible option for a new identity and ancestry. I originally supposed that Belle Greene's 'da Costa' might have been appropriated by her from the Da Costa Book of Hours, a manuscript illuminated by Simon Bening in the library of Pierpont Morgan. There would have been symmetry in the curator of Chapter 12 naming herself after a manuscript by the artist of Chapter 4, first recognized by the librarian of Chapter 8. However, Morgan did not buy the Book of Hours until 1910, and even then its sixteenth-century owner was not yet identified, whereas Belle's brother, Russell, had already been accorded the middle name of da Costa when his mother submitted their census information in 1900. If there was an actual family connection with any even slightly similar name, it is no longer knowable.

Invention of names and ancestry was not so unusual in 1900 as it might seem today. In the account of Simonides, p. 374, we learned that every age fabricates what it most desires. During the massive immigration into America in the late nineteenth century, countless east Europeans, Russians, Jews and many others were starting again with revised names and new family identities. (Even in Britain, surnames were commonly being upgraded: the nearly double-barrelled Yates Thompson and Dyson Perrins, for example, were a fashionable pretence, benignly accepted, and, when he came into money, Felix Hamel of Tamworth added a 'de' to his name in 1878 to suggest an ancestry which was almost certainly spurious.) The question of race was more complex. The United States remained a deeply segregated society, and the risk at that time of a person of Black ancestry posing as white allowed no margin of tolerance. It was a momentous secret that the 'Portuguese' Belle da Costa Greene could never for a second afford to reveal for the rest of her life.

In 1916, Belle Greene told the *New York Evening Sun*, "I knew definitely by the time I was twelve years old that I wanted to work with rare books. I loved them even then, the sight of them, the wonderful feel of them, the romance and the thrill of them." That a young girl from a modest background in America should have encountered such books at all may seem unexpected, but this was no normal family. It is unlikely that Madden's parents, or Cockerell's, or mine for that matter, had ever seen a medieval manuscript, but Richard Greener had. While at Harvard, he had been befriended by the Reverend Robert C. Waterston, who allowed him use of his private library, which included a thirteenth-century Decretals and two Flemish Books of Hours. More important was his close friendship with the senator and abolitionist Charles Sumner (1811–74), who had a very fine collection. In a tribute published after Sumner's death, Greener described being shown rare books at home: "With what tenderness he would bring forth his art and literary treasures, a missal, some book in law French or patois, a black lettered volume . . . *Cicero de Officiis* in MSS . . ." Sumner's Cicero survives in the Houghton Library at Harvard, written in Rome or possibly Florence in the 1450s, and now (by coincidence) including a note by Sydney Cockerell, who owned another by the same illuminator. This is not proof that Belle had heard of it, but if Greener's precocious daughter had ever asked about manuscripts, her father could have replied with first-hand experience.

Belle Greene had traced her falling in love with rare books to the age of twelve. As she was born at the end of 1879, this would have been in 1892, when the Greeners were living in New York. Illuminated manuscripts were not easy to encounter in America at that time. The Lenox and Astor Libraries, predecessors of the New York Public Library (1895), were for research only. An event which would fit the date exactly was the historic loan exhibition *Illuminated and Painted Manuscripts, Together with a Few Early Printed Books with Illuminations*, mounted at the Grolier Club, then in its old premises in East 32nd Street. This was probably the nearest America has held to the display of manuscripts organized by Cockerell in the Burlington Fine Arts Club in London in 1908. There is nothing quite comparable to the Grolier Club in Europe. It was founded in New York in 1884 and named after the great sixteenth-century French patron of beautiful book-bindings. It was (and still remains) an association of book collectors and it brings together enthusiasts who rejoice in acquisition and in showing and sharing their treasures. The exhibition of illuminated manuscripts opened to members of the Club on 5 May 1892 and to the public the following day. 1,851 tickets were issued, each admitting guests and unspecified numbers of friends, and it was so popular that the exhibition was extended from the planned closure on 20 May to the end of the month. Strictly, although not necessarily in practice, visitors were admitted only on the recommendation of members. It is not at all inconceivable that Richard Greener would have been invited. He had many connections with the book world and was secretary of the Grant Monument Association when the treasurer was Pierpont Morgan himself (although Morgan was not a member of the Grolier Club until 1897; his nephew Julius belonged from 1884). In 1892 the president of the Monument Association was Horace Porter, who was indeed a member of the Grolier Club, elected in 1889. It is easy to imagine Greener receiving a ticket and taking his daughter along.

There were 118 manuscripts and twenty-one early printed books on show, mostly from private collections, many of them owned by Robert Hoe (1839–1909), founder member and first president of the Club. Nearly all were fifteenth- or early sixteenth-century, especially Books of Hours, and there was nothing older than a thirteenth-century Bible. Nonetheless, it was a revelation to New Yorkers, who had never seen so many manuscripts and with opportunity for such close inspection. Exhibits also included a handmade facsimile of the *Guirlande de Julie*, the seventeenth-century manuscript once written up by the Abbé Rive. The published catalogue invokes the great patrons, including the Duc de Berry and the Medici in Florence, and it even mentions Sir Frederic Madden. The introduction concludes, "Art appeals to cultivated tastes in many other forms, but never with a greater charm than in these records of the past, the work of the scribe, the illuminator, and the miniaturist." If ever the twelve-year-old Belle Greener had an invitation to what she later remembered as her first sight, feel, romance and thrill of manuscripts, this was it.

By the time of the New York census of 1900, Belle's occupation was listed as librarian. In July to August that year, she attended a five-week summer school on librarianship at Amherst College in Massachusetts, about 130 miles north-east of Manhattan. Copies of the prospectus survive. The course was taught annually by the college librarian, William I. Fletcher, and comprised lectures in the mornings and practical sessions each afternoon, especially on cataloguing, including instruction in the Dewey Decimal classification, which was invented at Amherst. No previous knowledge of library work was required, but applicants were expected to have attended high school "and to show some special aptitude for work among books". The cost was $15, plus $2.50 for books and materials. At the end of their course on 14 August 1900, the class of that year put on an entertainment in Amherst Town Hall, at an admission price of 25 cents. The printed programme lists the opening number as 'Smoky Mokes' performed by six students, including "Miss Green". There was also a class photograph taken in 1900. The students and staff are sitting or standing outside the windows of the college library. Slightly apart on the steps at the far left is a girl with dark curly hair under an unusually flamboyant hat: I cannot quite decide whether this is Belle Greene, more than a decade earlier than any known photograph of her. She was then twenty-one. In a list at Amherst dated 1901 of the students in the previous year's summer school, with their then current addresses, she is recorded unambiguously, "Belle M. Greene – In Library of Princeton University, N. J.", which is where Junius Morgan found her four years later.

Once installed in Pierpont Morgan's employment, Belle Greene's first task was keeping track of the huge collection of books. Some were in New York in the new library building on 36th Street, completed that year; others were in Morgan's house in Princes Gate in London, or not yet sent by the dealers from whom they had been bought. Old invoices were checked and items were ticked off as Belle Greene identified them and recorded their locations. She assigned numbers to more than 200 illuminated manuscripts, preceded by the letter 'M', which stood for both 'Morgan' and 'manuscript'. The sequence must initially have been more or less as the manuscripts came to her attention. Printed books were mostly shelved in the galleried East Room; manuscripts were generally kept in the library's vault, opening off Morgan's office. The Ashburnham or Lindau Gospel Book in its treasure binding was designated 'M 1', perhaps for its quality or simply because it was the first she looked at, whereas 'M 3' was a Book of Hours newly bought only in 1906. The number 'M 69' was assigned to the Farnese Hours, probably deliberately, in the opinion of William Voelkle, in sly allusion to the sensuous naked figures of both sexes tumbling through the manuscript's borders, the first hint of the coquettish innuendo which reportedly characterized Belle Greene's dealings with her notoriously libidinous employer. (There is no reason to think it ever went further than banter.) In April 1907 she commissioned a special box for the safekeeping of the Farnese Hours in red morocco lined with velvet, ordered from the French bookbinder Léon Gruel. Rather than sending the precious original manuscript back across the Atlantic, she had a wooden replica made in the precise size, to ensure an exact fit.

In 1906, Morgan was in the process of buying one of his greatest illuminated manuscripts, acquired from the Parisian bookseller Ludovic Badin. It comprises the eight leaves from the end of a royal *Bible moralisée* with an iconic full-page dedication miniature showing the creation of the book under the direction of Queen Blanche of Castile (1188–1252) and her son Saint Louis (1214–70), king of France. The principal manuscript is in the cathedral library in Toledo in Spain. This final gathering of its third volume had apparently already been removed by about 1500 and was bound separately. It has fifty-six glittering miniatures in roundels illustrating the Apocalypse, the last book of the Bible, in the finest early gothic style, like the most marvellous stained-glass windows imaginable. The manuscript had been propelled rapidly around the book trade in Paris at rising prices, first at 15,000 francs in 1904 (about £600 or $2900), sold on at 35,000 francs to the next dealer, who ceded it for 60,000 to Badin, whose invoice to Morgan in July 1906 states that his acquisition cost was 100,000 francs to which a 10 per cent commission was then added, 110,000 francs altogether (about £4300 or $21,000). In fact, Morgan seems to have passed the purchasing on to one of his London booksellers, Pearson & Company, of 8 Pall Mall, in whose invoice it reappears on 11 August at £4000, which suggests that they had secured a small discount. The manuscript was dispatched to New York on the White Star steamer on 10 October 1906. Ships took about a week to cross the Atlantic. The arrival of the *Bible moralisée* must have been an eye-opener for Belle Greene in her first year. She gave it the number M 240. The flyleaf still contains a full page of slightly credulous notes in pencil in her handwriting, beginning, "A splendid example of the best French workmanship of the early French Renaissance, Executed in a monastery at or near Paris . . ."

There was a scare in September 1907 when Morgan seemed to have mislaid the *Bible moralisée*, and he asked his company in London to check whether Ludovic Badin still had it, which Badin denied. Morgan said that he "thought he had taken it to America himself", which we know he had not. They may have been looking for it because Sydney Cockerell had requested it for his Burlington Fine Arts Club exhibition of 1908, in which it was no. 133. It now became Belle Greene's duty to ensure that the location of every item was accounted for. Invoices from dealers were often the only record of purchases. Titles were often very brief and not necessarily in English or accurate, and matching them up was a big task. An example, among very many, was an invoice from Badin dated 30 April 1907, with medieval manuscripts including a late Romanesque Lectionary perhaps from Zeitz Abbey, near Halle, and part of the thirteenth-century English Ramsey Abbey Psalter. The list has been checked off twice, with ticks and crosses, and endorsed "O.K. and in Library 33 E. 36, Sept. 2 – 1907, Belle Greene", except for the final item, the wedding casket of Marie Antoinette, 1770, which she has marked "No" and subsequently added, "Given to Mrs Douglas by Mr Morgan, B. G.", referring to Adelaide Douglas, her employer's current mistress. The manuscripts were then assigned numbers, M 293, 295–7, 299–300 and 302, and they were put on the shelves.

She was also checking payments and shipments. There are several invoices from Quaritch in London, such as one dated 29 December 1906, endorsed by her in pencil "Not yet paid but OK. Jan. 9 – 07 BG", with "OK JSM" and "M" in other hands, doubtless authorization for payment from Julius Spencer Morgan and Pierpont Morgan himself. A month later, she seems to be approving payment herself, including £145 for a manuscript of Chaucer's *Canterbury Tales* from Quaritch, not expensive (M 249). A summary statement for the half-year was issued by Quaritch on 31 July 1907. It is marked up noting which items were delivered to Princes Gate and then shipped to New York on the *Cedric*, departing on 29 August, and which, such as the Chaucer, were delivered by Alfred Quaritch, the founder's son, who visited America regularly, all counted off on receipt in New York, "Articles checked are at The Library, Dec. 1907, Belle Greene".

The meticulous care of Belle Greene was evident in what is known as the Troussures affair. A Madame de Tonnay announced in 1907 that she represented the family of the Comte Marie-Louis le Caron de Troussures (1829–1914), who owned a large group of exceptionally early illuminated manuscripts, many of which had been acquired after the French Revolution from the ancient library of Beauvais Cathedral. Morgan agreed to buy the six most important for 50,000 francs immediate deposit (about $9500) followed by 100,000 francs in later payments. They included a Merovingian manuscript of Saint Augustine's homilies on the Gospel of Saint John dated 669, made at the Irish abbey of Luxeuil in Burgundy, and a Gospel Book illuminated for (and very probably

MVLTI
CONATI SVNT
ORDINARE
NARRATIONEM

by) Otbert, abbot of Saint-Bertin *c.*986–1007, with three spectacular full-page miniatures. The sale was handled by the count's son in partnership with Madame de Tonnay, who revealed that one item was now her own property. Belle Greene, feeling uneasy, as she said later, insisted on a contract and an affidavit signed by the count confirming authority to sell, and she had the manuscripts sent at once to New York. It then began to unravel that the elderly count had not understood that the sale was final and he pleaded eloquently through his lawyers in Paris for the manuscripts' return. Reading the letters, it is hard not to feel sorry for him. However, Pierpont Morgan did not become rich by sympathy. Belle Greene, on his behalf, refused, wielding her fortuitous and watertight documentation. The count's lawyers eventually capitulated in a cable to Belle Greene in May 1911 and reluctantly accepted the outstanding 100,000 francs.

Belle Greene had rapidly become irreplaceable in Morgan's daily life and confidence. She clearly took genuine delight in rare books and manuscripts, not to be underestimated, and she was extremely efficient. She was quick-witted and socially acute, often exploiting or exaggerating her girlishness, which was unusual, to say the least, in the very male world of bibliophily of the time. Booksellers, especially in Europe, had never encountered anyone quite like this before. Her business correspondence is often peppered with disarming informality, even jokey flirtatiousness. Those who met her commented on her stylish and flamboyant clothes, including a love of hats. Her often-cited "Just because I *am* a librarian doesn't mean I have to *dress* like one" is possibly apocryphal but entirely credible. (She was not always dressed at all: Matisse later drew her in the nude.) Through her intimacy in the Morgan household, she was easily swept up into the whirl of New York society anxious to get close to the great banker himself. Belle Greene was a centre of attention at exhibition openings and parties, and she used the Morgan box at the opera as if it were her own (*La Bohème* was her favourite), mingling with Astors and Vanderbilts and Guggenheims and Rockefellers. Because of manuscripts (and personality) she had crossed boundaries unimaginable to her mother and sisters, who now shared her apartment and her income.

LEFT: The Gospel Book of Otbert of Saint-Bertin, Saint-Omer, beginning of the eleventh century, one of the manuscripts bought from the comte de Troussures in 1907.

In December 1908, Belle Greene travelled to England for the first time, notionally chaperoned by her mother, mainly to collect books bought by Morgan. She went up to Cambridge to meet Sydney Cockerell, whom she utterly beguiled and who commented with delight on her enthusiasm for manuscripts (see above, p. 447). She in turn adored his Englishness and his knowledge. She later said that it was his guidance which led her to focus especially on books of the Middle Ages, and that she wished she could be his pupil.

In 1910, Belle Greene handled the acquisition of a Book of Hours illuminated by Simon Bening. It belonged to the estate of George C. Thomas (1839–1909), a banker and philanthropist in Philadelphia. He had bought it from Quaritch, who had published a special catalogue, *Description of a very Beautiful Book of Hours, Illuminated Probably by Hans Memling and Gérard David*, 1905 (reprinted by Thomas in 1908). The account begins, not inaccurately, by asserting that the manuscript was "of the very finest Flemish style, suggesting the workmanship of the greatest masters of the Bruges School", invoking the celebrated Grimani Breviary but not yet identifying Bening's name or the coat of arms at the front of the book. It actually dates from about 1515 and so the attribution to Memling (d. 1494) is not possible. Thomas's widow had sent several books up to New York for possible sale, including this, a Wycliffite New Testament and a Shakespeare quarto. Belle Greene acknowledged them to "My dear Mrs Thomas" on 18 January 1910. After courtesies, she continued:

> Mr Morgan would like to keep for his collection the Flemish manuscript, the New Testament manuscript, & The Merchant of Venice. In regard to the prices which were placed upon these, as Mr Morgan feels they are somewhat excessive, he presumes that they were made by your agent & may not be in accordance with your views.

and so Belle Greene, ever protective of Morgan's money (and yet exquisitely tactful to the vendor), offered $30,000 for the Book of Hours, $3,500 for the Wycliffe, and $2,000 for the Shakespeare. The following day, for post was quicker than it is now, Mrs Thomas accepted. She subsequently forwarded to New York related correspondence from her husband's files from Giulio Coggiola of the Biblioteca Marciana in Venice, comparing the Book of Hours further with their Grimani Breviary, including a letter of January 1908 identifying the arms as those of

The arms of the Portuguese family of da Costa, frontispiece added to the Da Costa Hours illuminated by Simon Bening, *c.*1515, bought by Belle Greene for Morgan in 1910.

the noble Portuguese family of da Costa. Belle Greene attached these letters into the manuscript itself.

Those words 'da Costa' must have leapt out at her. Her brother had been using this as a middle name for over a decade and she herself occasionally did so too, as in a letter to the library's architects, McKim, Mead and White, in March 1906, early in the job and before she knew of the Book of Hours. However, from 1910 onwards the Portuguese fiction became much more commonly part of her signature and public identity, perhaps because of the manuscript but also to give credence to her looks, which she now wished to justify to her new lover, the celebrity art historian Bernard Berenson (1865–1959). In general, people's romantic entanglements should be allowed to remain private, but Belle Greene's relationship with Berenson is too important to overlook.

"I would kiss you until you cried for mercy, and I would cuddle up in your arms and go to sleep with my mouth on yours and my heart on yours with your hands in my hair and with mine around your neck" (sentences like that do not occur in many books on medieval manuscripts: it is from a letter from Belle Greene to Berenson in May 1910). She had met him first at the very beginning of 1909, when he and his wife, Mary, were revisiting America from Florence, where they mostly now lived. Belle Greene's habitual flirtatiousness towards men (which Berenson commented on) soon took on a very new dimension. Mary Berenson tolerated and to some extent even encouraged the affair, and she was herself very taken with the unusual personality of this "most wild and woolly and EXTRAORDINARY young person", as she wrote in February 1909. Bernard Berenson was tantalized too by Belle's puzzling and inexplicable ancestry. He speculated that she might have been part Malay, but if he ever learned of Richard Greener it was discreetly overlooked. Make-believe might even have been a bond between them. Berenson himself was not quite the member of an old Bostonian Catholic family he let people believe, having been born as an Orthodox Jew, Bernhard Valvrojenski, in what is now Lithuania; he too knew what it was like to have secrets. After the Berensons returned to Italy in the spring of 1909, Belle Greene's letters to him became almost frantic with schemes to see him again.

This came about in August 1910. They met in London (no accompanying mother this time), where she was tasked with buying illuminated manuscripts. "The potentate", wrote Berenson to his wife on 25 August, referring to Morgan, "practically gives her carte blanche. Yesterday I showed her an MS in London for £8000. She cabled and today she has the answer to make her own judgement. I must say, she uses it well." The manuscript was evidently the marvellously illustrated Spanish manuscript of Beatus on the Apocalypse dated 1220, offered for sale by the dealer Lionel Harris. Before the deal was finalized, Belle Greene went on with Berenson to Paris, and from there by the Orient Express to Munich and then down into Italy, where they passed September visiting art galleries and libraries together, including seeing the manuscripts of Verona and the Vatican, where she was introduced to the prefect of the library, Franz Ehrle, later a cardinal. By the end of her blissful Italian summer with Berenson, Belle Greene was unwell and almost certainly pregnant. On 30 September she left Venice alone for London, where all evidence points to a discreet termination.

Her convalescence at Claridge's hotel did not inhibit her work for long. She dined with Henry Yates Thompson, who showed her some of his collection. On 12 October she had lunch at her hotel with Sydney Cockerell, who took her to see manuscripts at the Society of Antiquaries and the British Museum. That same day she concluded the deal with

Bernard Berenson in the gardens of his Villa I Tatti, near Florence, photograph, 1913.

Lionel Harris for the manuscript of Beatus on the Apocalypse, negotiating the price down to £6000. His premises were the Spanish Art Gallery in Conduit Street, easy walking distance from Claridge's, where he wrote to her as Miss Belle da Costa Greene, using the name she must have given him. The Beatus manuscript was shipped to America by the *St Louis* on the 15th, slightly ahead of her own departure on the *Oceanic*. She made friends on board with the actress Ellen Terry. While she charmed the customs officers on arrival with faux naivety into not noticing works of art hidden in her luggage, the manuscript was delayed by shipping brokers in Broadway in New York and was not disentangled and released until Belle Greene was back in her office.

The Beatus is a huge and spectacular book with forty-six full-page pictures and seventy-one smaller ones. It once belonged to the Spanish church of Las Huelgas de Burgos. In 1769 the Abbé Rive had scribbled notes on the primitive crudity and ugliness of a similar manuscript of Beatus. Today, the uninhibited style of the many Beatus manuscripts is greatly admired, as startlingly coloured as pictures by Matisse and as strange as many by Picasso. Archer M. Huntington, founder of the

OVERLEAF: The Beatus manuscript of Las Huelgas de Burgos, dated 1220, bought by Belle Greene in London in 1910.

scandala. aut dispationis lapsum incur
rant. Ut quem hic male dicit. si non
cognouerit. que sit: a recto tramite
deuiantes offendant. EXPLICIT.

Hispanic Society of America, wrote to Belle Greene on 9 December 1910, "Let me congratulate you once more for having found for Mr Morgan the Harris manuscript. It is a purchase you can never regret."

The following July, Lionel Harris in London forwarded another manuscript to Belle Greene in New York with a covering letter:

> In accordance with the wish of Mr Berenson, I am sending for your inspection, by this mail, an exceptionally fine small missal of the first quarter of the fourteenth century, which he says will be sure to interest you; – the lowest price of same is £2000 (Two thousand pounds). Should you not entertain the purchase of the book, would you kindly return it to me at your earliest convenience.

There is a subtext here. It was Berenson who had first told her of the Beatus and now he was recommending another manuscript (which was actually a Book of Hours). He was doubtless on a personal commission from Harris, a picture dealer, and Belle Greene must have known it. She wrote to Berenson that the manuscript had arrived, but that the asking price was not really justifiable. "Please don't think that I always want to beat people down but I hate to pay *more* than a liberal price for a thing." At that time, the £2000 figure was probably at least twice the manuscript's value. Harris reluctantly edged his price down to £1900, still not close enough to reality. However, Belle Greene managed to save Berenson's commission for him by unloading the book instead onto Harry Walters, as she calls him, a collector whose taste and knowledge she did not rate highly. It is now in the Walters Art Museum in Baltimore, a neat but rather soulless little manuscript, from the region of Saint-Omer in Artois, near Calais.

Bernard Berenson never really cared for manuscripts but built his career and fortune by exceptional connoisseurship of Italian medieval and Renaissance painting, weighing and judging the value of art by its aesthetic quality. That skill is what he taught Belle Greene during their summer of 1910 and in the many letters which followed. Illuminated manuscripts, unlike most printed books, require the exercise of artistic connoisseurship every time. Her experience with Berenson in the galleries of Europe undoubtedly shifted her focus, bringing her back over and over again to manuscripts as unique and painted works of art. She found she loved them. She told Berenson that one French gothic manuscript bought by Morgan in 1911 "made me *weep* actually it was so exquisite", and she confessed to him in 1914 how in private she kissed her favourite manuscripts when she took them from their shelves and kissed them when she put them back.

Berenson's concession to manuscripts was his own small collection of Persian and Indian illumination. He introduced Belle Greene to their unexpected beauty and quality, encouraging her to judge and admire their art even without prior knowledge of their history or any literacy in their languages. That can be a brave step to take. Together they had visited the comprehensive and formative loan exhibition *Meisterwerke Muhammedanischer Kunst* in Munich, which was as much of an eye-opener to Belle Greene as the Grolier Club exhibition of 1892 may have been. Her state of being in love doubtless heightened her experience. The section on oriental manuscripts and the book arts comprised almost 500 items, and she marked her copy of the catalogue with stars beside items she especially admired. One album of Persian and Mughal illumination of around 1600 had been lent to Munich personally by Charles Hercules Read, Keeper of British and Medieval Antiquities in the British Museum. It was Read who in 1910 had recommended Morgan to buy the superb twelfth-century Stavelot Triptych of gold and enamel. On this acquaintance, Belle Greene wrote to him in June 1911 about his oriental album, which she told him she considered to be among the finest things of the exhibition. She continued, "Mr Morgan himself is not particularly interested in Persian art; but it seems to me that, in a collection of manuscripts and drawings such as he has, it is very necessary for him to have a representation of this most important school, and I doubt if he would ever be able to find finer specimens than those which you are so lucky to own." She asked whether Read might ever be persuaded to sell it. The temptation of money is effective, and he was persuaded. The album became, entirely on Belle Greene's initiative and new-taught appreciation, one of the foundation items of Pierpont Morgan's small but increasingly impressive collection of oriental manuscripts.

Belle Greene's mysterious appearance lent itself to a usefully misleading smokescreen of orientalism, then fashionable, which, like the da Costa myth, she did nothing to dispel. She had a miniature portrait of herself painted in 1910 wrapped in apricot silk like an odalisque of the Middle East, explaining it to Berenson as showing "the Belle of one of my former incarnations – *Egyptienne*". Her new fascination with manuscripts from beyond the boundaries of Europe led to an unusual

Belle Greene, miniature portrait in oriental costume by Laura Coombs Hills, 1910.

acquisition in 1911. Peasants in Egypt digging the previous year for fertilizer in Hamuli in the oasis of Fayum, south-west of Cairo, had unearthed a group of fifty Coptic manuscripts of the ninth and tenth centuries, mostly in original bindings. The books seemed to be the entire library of an otherwise unknown Coptic monastery of Saint Michael, and they rapidly found their way at escalating prices into the antiquities trade in Paris. Belle Greene was begged by an academic in Washington to save this "rare and unique treasure" for America. She negotiated the price down by a third and bought them all, for a little under $200,000, although the astonished press reported the cost as up to a million dollars. The manuscripts reached New York in late December 1911. Their appearance proved to be dreadfully disappointing. They were falling apart and badly damaged by insects and water, and there must have been an awkward moment when her employer was first shown them. However, Belle Greene had been introduced by Berenson to Franz Ehrle in Rome, and in April 1912 she sent the collection for restoration in the conservation laboratories of the Vatican, reputed to be the best in the world. By American standards, the Vatican moves slowly. Ehrle retired as prefect of the Biblioteca Apostolica in 1914 and was succeeded by his deputy, Achille Ratti, with whom Belle Greene continued a spirited and playful correspondence. Many of the Hamuli manuscripts eventually came back to New York in 1922 and others followed in 1929. The catalogue, commissioned by Belle Greene, was not finally published until 2021 over a century later. In the meantime, Ratti had been elected as Pius XI in 1922 and, like Vespasiano in 1447, Belle Greene found herself on first-name terms with the Pope.

Within a few years of her employment, Belle Greene was intimately involved in all major purchases for Morgan's library, and many were on her own initiative. "J. P. is so well trained now that he *rarely* ever buys a book or manuscript without consulting me", she told Berenson in 1911. She was by then on a salary of $10,000 a year. At the sale in New York of Robert Hoe's books in April 1911, she bid in person, paying $42,800 for the only known complete copy of Malory's *Morte d'Arthur* printed by Caxton in 1485. Not unexpectedly, high-profile acquisitions like this caught the attention of the press. *The New York Times* wrote on 7 April 1912, "Miss Belle Green[e] can spend more money in an afternoon than any other young woman of 26 in New York City" (she was actually 32 but let the deception pass). "Is Miss Belle Greene the most clever woman in the country? J. Pierpont Morgan says she is", began an article in the *Chicago Tribune*, 11 August 1912: "She is chic, vivacious, and interesting, in fact a 'dandy wholesome American girl', says Mr Morgan. She wears her hair long and does not use glasses, runs to Europe on secret missions, and is the terror of continental collectors' agents." Seldom has any curator had such fun. "Her tremendously busy life has been a magnificent romp", said *Munsey's Magazine*, exhorting young people to train as librarians. "I really must be grudgingly admitted the most interesting person in New York, for it's all they talk about", she told Berenson in January 1912.

She was now constantly lifting the level of Morgan's library, exercising her own judgement. She returned some manuscripts shipped on approval by Ludovic Badin in 1911, explaining to him:

> You can understand that in a collection of over five hundred illuminated manuscripts are to be found already several of equally fine execution as those you sent us, and my policy in regard to the collection is not to buy anything which is not much finer than something we already have.

On the other hand, she welcomed an offer of a small group of books in July that year from Édouard Rahir, also of Paris: "I want to tell you that

I consider all these manuscripts of an exceptionally fine quality and that I am very pleased indeed to have you offer Mr Morgan manuscripts of this high order." The price was 50,000 francs (about $10,000) for eight items, including her second Book of Hours illuminated by Simon Bening. It has thirty-one full-page miniatures, and the script is signed and dated in 1531 by Bening's old colleague from the guild in Bruges, Antonius van Damme.

Two outstanding examples of English Romanesque illumination were added in 1912, both of them single leaves. Few libraries in Europe were then interested in separate miniatures, an area in which American museums seized the initiative. It may have been influenced by Belle Greene's new interest in oriental albums, in which single-sheet illuminations were always valued as works of art. The first leaf was a marvellous double-sided page of forty-eight rectangular scenes from the Gospels, once owned by Madden's friend William Young Ottley. It was offered by the dealer and bibliographer Joseph Martini, whose father had found it in Italy. It is now known to be from the prefatory cycle of the Canterbury, or Eadwine, Psalter in Cambridge, illuminated in the early 1160s, quite possibly under the patronage of Saint Thomas Becket. The price was £400, or $1500. The invoice is endorsed in pencil, "O.K. Belle Greene", paid on 12 January 1912. The second was even larger and finer, with dramatic illustrations from the life of King David. Morgan and his sister Mary had been shown it in Rome in April 1912 by the Florentine dealer Leo Olschki, and he passed the matter on to Belle Greene. Although no one yet realized, it is a missing leaf from the incomparable twelfth-century Winchester Bible, of which Madden reported in 1849 that several miniatures had been "recently cut out". The leaf was priced at 40,000 francs, and that invoice too is signed, "O.K. B. Greene". Olschki then applied to export it from Florence. However, as he wrote to Belle Greene, the authorities absolutely refused permission. Undaunted, Olschki simply took it to Rome and applied again under a different jurisdiction. It was duly sent to New York on the *König Friedrich der Grosse*, sailing from Genoa on 25 July.

*

RIGHT: Missing miniature from the Winchester Bible, Winchester, *c.*1160–70, bought by Belle Greene for Morgan in 1912.

1 De ionathe & dauid amore & de odiis saul in dauid · &
ubi in centu[m] p[re]putiis philistinor[um] accepit michol filia[m] sa
ul uxore[m] que patris dolu[m] p[ro]dens saluum fecit dauid ·
2 De fuga dauid ad samuelem · & quomodo q[ui] missi fuerant
ut eu[m] raperent p[ro]phetauerunt ubi & saul ipse ueniens pro
phetauit · & de pacto ac signo ionathe & dauid q[uo]d in in
icem p[er]cusserunt · Transit ad regem moab ·
3 De fuga dauid in nobee · & de his que abimelech sacerdote
facta esse referunt[ur] · & quomodo saul inmutauit uultu[m]
suu[m] cora[m] cora[m] achis rege geth & collabebat[ur] & cu[m] suis omnib[us];
4 De gad p[ro]ph[et]a ubi co[m]monuit dauid fugere in terram iuda in sal
tum fareth a facie dauid · & doech p[ro]dente occisus est abimelech
reliquis octoginta sacerdotib[us]: & quomodo dauid p[er]cussit phi
listiim & saluauit ceila ·
5 De saule quomodo uoluit dauid in ceila capere · qui con fugi
ens uenit in desertum ziph · ubi ionathan ad eum uenit · &
p[er]cussit uterq[ue] f[o]edus coram d[omi]no · & confortauit ionathas da
uid · & reuersus est in domum suam ·
6 De dauid in spelunca procidit coram clamidis saul silenter ·
& p[er]cussit cor suum dixitq[ue] ad uiros suos · propitius sit m[ihi] d[omi]n[u]s
ne mitta[m] manum mea[m] in d[omi]n[u]m meu[m] rege[m] · quia xp[istu]s d[omi]ni est
7 De samuhelis morte & sepulchro eius in ramatha & que de
nabal carmelo ac de abigail uxore eius gesta referuntur ·
8 De dauid ubi abigail & achinoem uxores accepit · & ubi sau
lis p[er]sequentis scyphum & hastam abstulit · et que sc[un]do pe
perit · Iterem co[n]i[ugi] fuluit · Occubuit ·
9 De transfugio dauid in geth ad achis regem philistiim &
que illic gesserit & de saule quomodo p[h]ythonissam mu
10 De philisteis aduersus saul congregatis ad monte[m] in bello
gelboe · & de dauid ubi p[er]cussit amalech omne[m] captiuitatem
& uxores suas reduxit in siceleg · dixeruntq[ue]: hec est preda dauid ·
11 De bello philistinor[um] in monte gelboe · in quo saul cum trib[us] filiis

The gilded age changed for ever at a few minutes past midday on Monday, 31 March 1913, when Pierpont Morgan died in a hotel in Rome. He was seventy-five. His body was brought back to New York, and his funeral took place on 14 April. Belle Greene was devastated. She wrote to Sydney Cockerell on 29 April. The letter is revealing about her relationship with Morgan, hinting at his substitution for her absconded father, and indeed on how her work had carried her across the barriers of social and financial inequality:

> I am sure you know how much I appreciate your note of sympathy to me in the loss of everything I loved and respected and revered. I don't look ahead very much for it seems so hopelessly dreary and desolate. I had come to rely so much upon telling him everything and talking over everything with him, – both cabbages and kings – and now there seems to be nowhere to turn or no-one to turn to . . . I feel as if Life had stopped for me and it is all I can do to go on without him. He was so much more than my 'boss'. He was almost a father to me – very often I felt like a *son* – and always the staunchest truest of friends, and his great confidence and trust in me bridged all the differences of age, wealth and position. So you can see I feel stranded and desolate.

She was not entirely abandoned. Morgan left her $50,000, the largest bequest to any individual outside his family, with a recommendation that she should be retained at least until decisions could be made about the future of the library. She bought herself a country cottage and a Mercedes motor car. Both Cockerell and Yates Thompson offered to help her find new employment, which she refused. Her position as librarian was eventually confirmed and her salary was again increased.

The new J. Pierpont Morgan, sharing his father's name but generally known as Jack, was at first only moderately interested in the art collections, and there was a real possibility that everything might be sold to pay the huge tax liability on the entire estate. Belle Greene was asked to draw up lists of what was most valuable or saleable. Not surprisingly, she omitted to include any illuminated manuscripts or early printed books, but very many works of art and pictures were duly disposed of. Very subtly, Belle Greene had now shifted the Morgan legacy from indiscriminate acquisition into a refinement of her own particular interest. Already by 1913 she had a secret dream, shared first with Berenson and eventually with the Morgan family, of a public collection in New York specializing in rare books and medieval manuscripts. In 1915 she told Quaritch that she would be allowed to continue buying when the war was over.

The decisive turning-point took place in 1916, when Belle Greene almost single-handedly acquired the greatest illuminated manuscript of her life. This was the thirteenth-century Shah Abbas Bible, sometimes called the Crusader Bible or Bible of Saint Louis, a biblical picture book of the highest quality and romance. It has already been mentioned, for a single lost leaf from the famous manuscript had been found by Sydney Cockerell in 1910 (above, p. 444). The whole volume, comprising forty-three leaves with 380 pictures, was in the residue of the collection of Sir Thomas Phillipps in Cheltenham.

As Madden had predicted, the Phillipps manuscripts were left in a legal labyrinth on the collector's death in 1872. Their custodian, Thomas Fitzroy Fenwick, Sir Thomas's grandson, was not the owner but a life tenant of the house and a trustee of the library, which was classified as an heirloom. Under the Settled Land Acts of 1882 and 1884, items were allowed to be sold for specific reasons, but sales had to be approved each time by the Court of Chancery. There had therefore been dispersals, including auctions at Sotheby's from which Morris and Cockerell had acquired items. In 1905–6, Quaritch had handled a sale to Morgan of five early manuscripts from the Phillipps collection, one of them late eighth-century, all gaudily embellished with pseudo-medieval jewelled bindings constructed for the notorious nineteenth-century manuscript thief Guglielmo Libri. In 1911, Morgan had bought the Gospels of Matilda of Tuscany, negotiated by Belle Greene through Quaritch again. It is a noble book with six full-page drawings heightened in gold, made at San Benedetto Po in the late eleventh century for Matilda of Canossa (*c.*1046–1115), countess and margravine of Tuscany. She was the woman to whom Saint Anselm had sent the luxury manuscript of his *Meditations*, probably in 1104 (above, p. 46). Fenwick had invited Quaritch to look for a buyer for this Gospel Book at £10,000. He had simultaneously instructed Sotheby's to offer it directly to Morgan for the same price and Belle Greene suspected, perhaps wrongly, that he was trying to play one off against the other. The reality is that there was only one customer in the world for such a book. Acting through Quaritch, she handled the sale herself, delaying until the price fell to £8000. The manuscript was finally delivered in London to Morgan, who brought it to New York at the end of December 1911. From the whole process, Belle Greene had

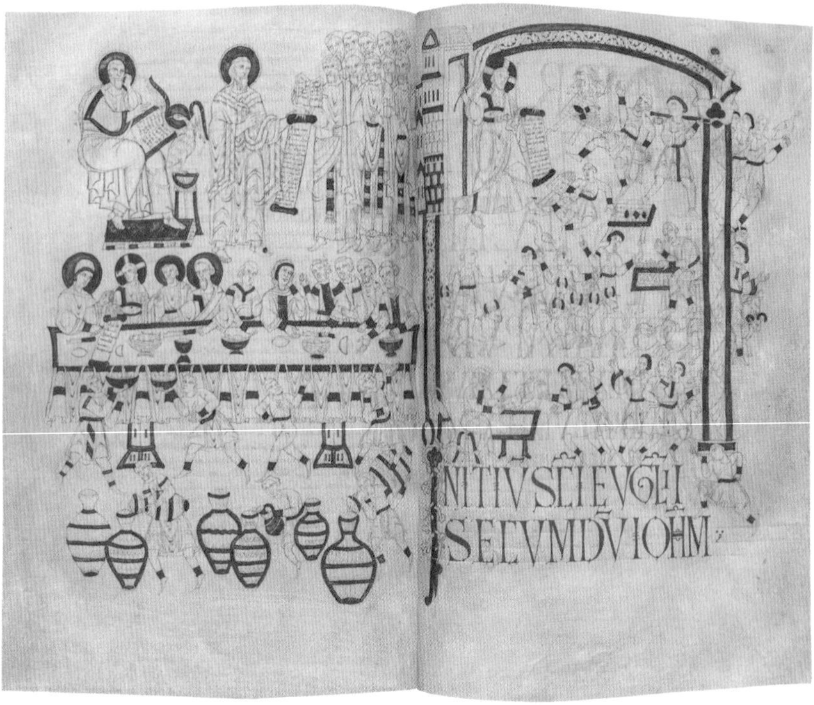

The Gospels of Matilda of Canossa, Lombardy (San Benedetto Po), last quarter of the eleventh century, bought from the Phillipps collection through Quaritch in 1911.

learned about the character of Fitzroy Fenwick and the practicalities of applying to the Judge in Chancery, both of which were important in her purchase five years later.

Belle Greene was in London in November 1916. America had not yet entered the Great War (that happened in April 1917) and she was shocked at the conditions in Britain and that Berenson was unable to join her from mainland Europe. On 7 November she had lunch at Claridge's with Sydney Cockerell and Henry Yates Thompson. They evidently discussed the Shah Abbas Bible. Cockerell had taken both Yates Thompson and Dyson Perrins to Cheltenham to see it in 1904 and 1908 respectively, but Fenwick had always refused to sell. However, the world looked different in the winter of 1916. This time, Belle Greene bypassed Quaritch and Sotheby's, for Fenwick was wary of the trade, and astutely enlisted Yates Thompson to help her. The next day, the 8th, he wrote to Fenwick asking whether he might bring her down to visit, knowing he would not be refused. On 16 November, Belle Greene spent a night in Cambridge, staying at the University Arms and being taken home by Cockerell for "supper & MSS", as he recorded in his diary. They doubtless looked at Cockerell's own leaf from the Shah Abbas Bible. She left Cambridge on the 11.15 train back to London the next day. On the 21st, she travelled to Cheltenham with Yates Thompson, where they were received graciously by Fenwick. Thirlestaine House, where the Phillipps collection had been moved in 1863–4, is a daunting neo-classical mansion entered off Bath Road to the south of the town centre, with a pillared portico, like the British Museum on a (slightly) smaller scale. Yates Thompson was then seventy-eight and Fenwick sixty, English gentlemen together, indulging (as Fenwick probably thought) some impressionable and unserious girl from America. Fenwick duly brought out the Shah Abbas manuscript for her and announced, to astonish his guest, that it would cost £10,000. As Belle Greene later told her friend Anne Haight, she replied in a flash, "I'll take it: you will receive a cheque." Fenwick, who had never anticipated this for a moment, was speechless, unable to go back on his word. Both Quaritch and Yates Thompson had already valued the book at upwards of £15,000.

Back in London, Belle Greene had both lunch and dinner with Cockerell again on 23 November and she recounted the purchase (this is in his diary too). He sent her a letter that night: "The manuscript you were clever enough to secure in Cheltenham is an incomparable treasure and would be cheap at any price. I have long regarded it as the most covetable manuscript of the 13th century in private hands." Belle Greene used this as well as their conversation when she wrote carefully to Jack Morgan on the 24th, only then finally confessing what she had done three days earlier. She told him that the manuscript was the finest example of French art of the period in private hands, and that there was one leaf in Cambridge: "For this single sheet they paid several years ago 300 pounds." Actually, 'they' was Cockerell himself, and it was £200, but 43 leaves x 300 is £12,900, which made the price seem better value. On the same day too, she wrote to the Court of Chancery. On 1 December, Fenwick informed her that consent had been granted. The manuscript was formally handed over on receipt of the money, a condition of the court, in late January 1917. Belle Greene wrote again to Cockerell from New York that Jack Morgan "quite thoroughly approves of my purchasing it,

OVERLEAF: The Shah Abbas Bible, picture book perhaps made for Saint Louis, France, mid-thirteenth century, bought by Belle Greene directly from the Phillipps collection in 1916.

Qualiter Samuel Saulem quem secreto unxerat. coram omni populo ungit in Regem. et cum summa leticia [...] ipse samuel quam populus sacrificant. ~

Qvalit' cu philistei innumeri exercitu ꝯgregassent ... pp'ls tristis effugisz et latitant' in speluncis. Saul aut' nõ nisi cum sexcentis uiris eet in campo. & sederet sub malo granato. Jonachas filius suus cũ unico armigo clam ignorãte patre p prerupta montiũ ac saxoꝝ ascẽdit ad hostiũ statioẽz. atq3 ex eis quos p'mo ꝯgressu repit miraclosam uictoriaz reportauit.

Qvaliter cum post uictoriam Jonache. mirabil' tumultus ortus eet i castris philistinoꝝ. ita ut gladius uniuscuiusq3 in suũ pximũ usus eet. Rex Saul cũ exercitus qui p metũ suorum p'mo quasi ad nichilum redactus erat / iam p superuenientẽ fiduciã reditegrari cepat clamans cũ archa domini ad pugnam procedit. precipiensq3 neqs suoꝝ comedat usq3 ad uespam et maledicens contra facientibus. Jonathas aut' filius / q preceptum patrium non audierat / inuento casuali fauo mell' uirgam quam manu gestabat extendit in eum et melle illitã iuit ad os suũ. et confortatus ẽ. Omis enim ualde defecerunt ppt' famẽ. et illo quem die magna de philisteis est quesita uictoria.

which is a good omen (for me) for the future". She was absolutely right. This is indeed a sensational manuscript filled with dramatic scenes of Old Testament narrative, captioned in Latin, Persian and Judaeo-Persian, added as successive generations of noble owners admired it on its journeys through Europe and the Middle East. It is still arguably the most important illuminated manuscript in America.

The omen was justified. With some view now to rounding out a library which might one day become public, purchases began again, consciously filling gaps. The first big challenge came with the thunderbolt announcement on 8 September 1918 when Yates Thompson wrote to Belle Greene to say that he intended to disperse his own collection of illuminated manuscripts in a series of three sales at Sotheby's. She reported that "an audible gasp went up in the library", for this was an opportunity from heaven. In England, however, the news was received with outrage and fierce opposition, as Cockerell and others had always hoped that the collection could be steered intact into some British institution. Yates Thompson's declared motive was that he was now over eighty and losing his eyesight, but his experience of Belle Greene's spending power in 1916 must have played its part. He moved the first sale from January to May 1919, to make it easier for her to attend from New York. She knew the collection well and immediately began cannonading Quaritch with questions and lists. She was suddenly the enemy of her manuscript friends in England. "I now hope to get to London early in May, as I want to look over all the manuscripts very carefully . . . I had quite made up my mind to bid on the Metz Pontifical and St-Omer Psalter, regardless of price, and so I am rather disappointed that they have gone", for they had been withdrawn and ceded as gifts to the Fitzwilliam and British Museum respectively to sooth the angry critics. She told Quaritch on 21 April 1919 that she was budgeting up to £15,000 in the first sale, and Edmund Dring, managing director, replied that this would not be enough.

Her shortlist eventually included lot 1, the eleventh-century Sacramentary of Mont Saint-Michel, not inconceivably known to Saint Anselm; lot 5, the fourteenth-century Book of Hours of Jeanne de Navarre, once owned by the Duc de Berry; lot 21, the tenth-century Beatus from San Salvador de Tábara, like the one she had bought from Harris in 1910 but earlier; lot 24, a ninth- to tenth-century Gospel Book perhaps from Liège; and lot 30, an Aristotle printed on vellum in 1483 with sensational illumination by Girolamo da Cremona, which had been published in the *Burlington Magazine* as perhaps "the most magnificent book in the world". All these had been part of Yates Thompson's purchase from Lord Ashburnham, selected by him and Cockerell as among the best. In the end, Belle did not get to London after all and Quaritch handled her bids. She secured seven lots altogether, five at the sale and two immediately afterwards from Quaritch, including the Mont Saint-Michel Sacramentary (£1000), the Beatus (£3000), the Gospel Book (£475) and the printed Aristotle (£2900), but she got nowhere close on the Jeanne de Navarre, bought by Edmond de Rothschild for £11,800. This last sum was a record price for any illuminated manuscript, and the manuscript fraternity was shocked. Belle Greene wrote to Dring, "I should have been heartily ashamed to have purchased it at that price, just as I should have been ashamed to buy the Aristotle at over £3000 – but Mr Morgan had set his heart on having the book and I pleaded with him, in vain, not to go over £3500." Fortunately, they did not have to.

At least Belle Greene now had Jack Morgan engaged in the collection, on the strength of her determination and enthusiasm alone, even if he was inclined to stray regrettably into printed books. Other purchases followed, including in the subsequent Yates Thompson sales (1920 and 1921) and two further Phillipps manuscripts bought from Fitzroy Fenwick in April 1920. One was a tenth-century herbal of Dioscorides in Greek, which had been bought by Phillipps in 1857 for £500 (the highest price he ever paid for a book), underbid at that time by Sir Frederic Madden, who had been heartbroken not to have acquired it for the British Museum. It now became M 652 in the Morgan collection.

Step by step, Belle Greene's vision of a public collection moved towards reality. She reported to Berenson in February 1924:

> We are *frightfully* busy reorganizing the Library to make it a permanent institution. I did (do) not want it *given* to the public who would only kill it, either with neglect, too much 'trampling over', or too much 'officialdom', & so we are arranging to make it an 'educational institution' somewhat along the lines of Harvard, Chantilly, etc. The papers have all been drawn up and I hope will go through this week or early next week – and *that* weight will be off my mind. I have been working ('on' Jack Morgan) to this end ever since his father died.

A month later, the Pierpont Morgan Library was formally incorporated as a public institution, with a board of trustees. *The New York Times* ran the story with a double headline, "J. P. Morgan Gives Library to the Public" and, in only slightly smaller type, "Belle da Costa Greene to Remain in Charge". She was appointed director of the Library. She was then forty-four but was thought to be younger, and in any case, as Jean Strouse remarks, she moved her birth date around as others move potted plants. Despite promises that she would remain in post for no more than five years ("*Pray* God I don't weaken !!! in 1929"), she stayed in office until her eventual retirement in 1948.

Acquisitions did not cease with the establishment of the Pierpont Morgan Library. Belle Greene wrote a review of her first five years as director, published in 1930. Her introduction devotes eighteen pages to the purchase of illuminated manuscripts during that time, eight to early printed books, and four to all acquisitions of prints and drawings. It is not hard to guess where her own preferences lay. All fourteen of her review's plates of acquisitions showed illuminated manuscripts, five of them from the Holford collection, being "of such importance as to demand special notice".

Robert Stayner Holford (1808–92) entered the life of Sir Frederic Madden as the infuriating buyer of the thirteenth-century Psalter-Hours, which Madden had seen with William Young Ottley and considered the most beautiful manuscript of the period he had ever encountered, and of the lustrous twelfth-century illustrated life and miracles of Saint Edmund, which he tried so hard to buy for the British Museum in 1841 (above, pp. 307 and 318–19). Holford's collection was inherited by his son, Sir George Holford (1860–1926), who sold most of the printed books to A. S. W. Rosenbach and commissioned his brother-in-law, Robert Benson, to catalogue the manuscripts (1924). In May 1927, Dring of Quaritch reported to Belle Greene rumours that the manuscripts might be sold, and he was mortified to learn from her reply that not only had Benson been to see her in New York to discuss this, but that she had also already looked at the library itself in London. "*Confidentially to you*", she wrote to Berenson on 22 April, underlining those words twice:

> all of the Holford MSS have been offered to us, but there are only 3 (and two single leaves) which we either want or need, and of these, the

RIGHT: Printed edition of Aristotle, Venice, 1483, with illumination by Girolamo da Cremona, bought on Jack Morgan's insistence at the Yates Thompson sale in 1919.

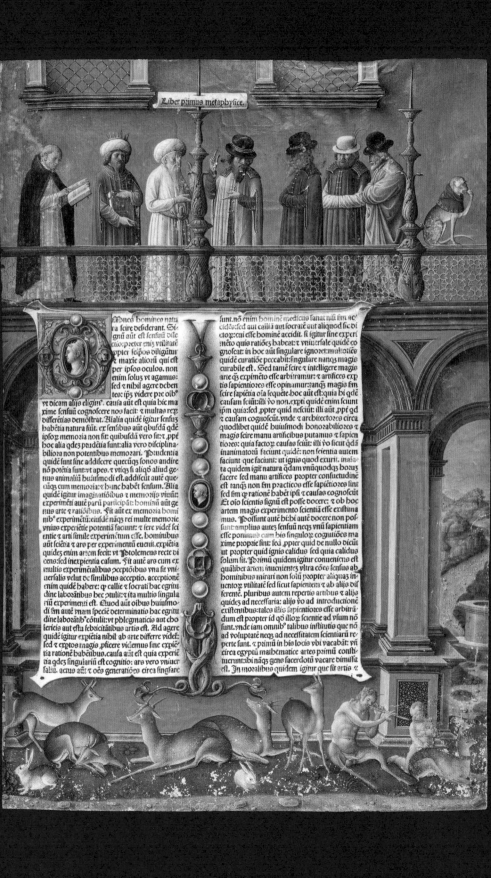

OMnes homines natu
ra scire desiderant. Si-
gnū aūt est sensuū dile
ctio: preter eniʒ vtilitatē
ꝓpter seipos diligūtur
ꝛ maxie aliorū qui est
per ipsos oculos. non
enim soluʒ vt agamus:
sed ꝛ nihil agere deben
tes: ipʒ videre pre oibꝰ
vt dicam alijs eligimꝰ. causa aūt est quia hic ma
xime sensuū cognoscere nos facit: ꝛ multas reꝝ
differētias demōstrat. Alalia quidē igitur sensuʒ
habētia natura fiūt. ex sensibus aūt qbusdā qdē
ipsoꝝ memoria non fit: quibusdā vero fit: ꝛ ꝓpt
hoc alia qdeʒ prudētia sunt: alia vero disciplina-
biliora non potentibus memorari. Prudentia
quidē sunt sine addiscere quecūqʒ sonos audire
nō potētia sunt: vt apes. ꝛ vtiqʒ si aliqd aliud ge-
nus animaliū huiusmodi est. addiscūt autē quecūqʒ cum memoria: ꝛ hunc habēt sensum. Alia
quidē igitur imaginatiōibus ꝛ memorijs viuūt:
experimēti autē parū participāt: hominū aūt ge
nus arte ꝛ ratiōibus. Fit aūt ex memoria homi
nibꝰ experimētū: eiusdē nāqʒ rei multe memorie
vnius experiētie potentiā faciunt: ꝛ fere videt̄ sci
entie ꝛ arti simile experimētum esse. hominibus
aūt sciētia ꝛ ars per experimentū euenit. expiētia
quideʒ enim artem fecit: vt Ptolemeus recte di
cens: sed inexpientia casum. Fit autē ars cum ex
multis experimētalibus ꝯceptōibus vna fit vni-
uersalis velut de similibus acceptio. acceptionē
enim quidē habere: ꝙ callie ꝛ socrati hac egritu
dine laborātibus hec ꝯtulit: ꝛ ita multis singula
riū experimenti est. Quod aūt oibus huiusmodi ſm autē vnam speciē determinatis hac egritu
dine laborātibꝰ cōtulit: vt phlegmaticis aut cho
lericis aut estu febricitātibus artis est. Ad agere
quidē igitur expiētia nihil ab arte differre videt̄:
sed ꝛ exptos magis ꝓficere videmus sine expiētia rationē habētibus. causa aūt est quia experiē
tia qdeʒ singulariū est cognitio: ars vero vniuer
saliū. actus aūt ꝛ oēs generatiōes circa singlare

sunt. nō enim hominē medicus sanat nisi ſm ac-
cidēs: sed aut calliā aut socratē aut aliquod sic di
ctoꝝ: cui esse hominē accidit. si igitur sine experi
mēto quis ratiōeʒ habeat: ꝛ vniuersale quidē co
gnoscat: in hoc aūt singulare ignoret: multotiēs
quidē curatiōe peccabit: singulare nanqʒ magis
curabile est. Sed tamē scire ꝛ intelligere magis
arte qʒ expimēto esse arbitramur: ꝛ artifices exp
tis sapientiores esse opinamur: tanqʒ magis ſm
scire sapiētia oīa sequēte. hoc aūt est: quia hi qdē
causam sciūt: illi vo non. expti quidē enim sciunt
ipm quia: sed ꝓpter quid nesciūt: illi aūt ꝓpt qd
ꝛ causam cognoscūt. vnde ꝛ architectores circa
quodlibet quidē huiusmodi honorabiliores ꝛ
magis scire manu artificibus putamus ꝛ sapien
tiores: quia factoꝝ causas sciūt: illi vo sicut q̄dā
inanimatorū faciunt quidē: non scientia autem
faciunt que faciunt: ut ignis quod exurit. inaia-
ta quidem igit̄ natura q̄dam vnūquodqʒ horuʒ
facere sed manu artifices propter consuetudinē
est tanqʒ non ſm practicos esse sapiētiores sint
sed ſm ꝙ rationē habēt ipsi ꝛ causas cognoscūt
Et oio scientis signū est posse docere: ꝛ ob hoc
artem magis experimento scientiā esse existima
mus. Possunt autē hi: hi autē docere non possunt: amplius autem sensuū neqʒ vnū sapientiam
esse ponimus cum his singuloꝝ cognitiōes ma
xime proprie sint: sed ꝓpter quid de nullo dicūt
ut propter quid ignis calidus sed quia calidus
solum sit. Primū quidem igitur conueniens est
quālibet artem inuenienteʒ vltra cōes sensus ab
hominibus mirari non solū propter aliquaʒ in-
uentoꝝ vtilitatē sed sicut sapientem ꝛ ab alijs dif
ferentē. pluribus autem repertis artibus ꝛ alijs
quideʒ ad necessaria: alijs vo ad introductionē
existentibus: tales illis sapientiores esse arbitrā-
dum est propter id qd illoꝝ scientie ad vsum nō
sunt. vnde iam omnibꝰ talibus institutis que nō
ad voluptatē neqʒ ad necessitatem scientiarū re-
perte sunt. ꝛ primū in his locis vbi vacabāt: vn̄
circa egyptū mathematice artes primū constituerunt: ibi nāqʒ gens sacerdotū vacare dimissa
est. In moralibus quidem igitur que sit artis ꝛ

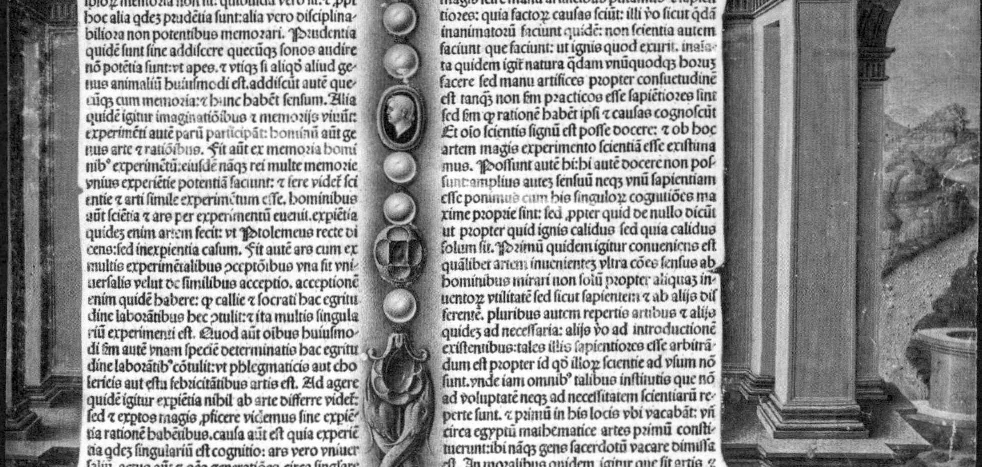

British Museum wants 1, and I am so stupidly fond of all the men there, that I shall probably refuse that (which I *most* want!) in order that they may get it at a low price.

The two single leaves which she coveted emerged first in a separate sale of Holford's illuminated miniatures at Sotheby's on 12 July 1927. Belle Greene left bids with Quaritch on both items. One was up to £400 on lot 29, an Italian cutting of around 1500 from the choir books of the Olivetan monastery at Lodi in Lombardy, showing the Adoration of the Magi. It is apparently signed with the tiny initials 'B. F.', and it is the key piece in a large group of miniatures by the now-called 'Master B. F.', close – sometimes inexplicably close – to compositions by Leonardo da Vinci. They secured it for £370. The other was lot 48. This was a second multiple miniature from that same twelfth-century Canterbury Psalter of which Belle Greene had bought one from Martini in 1910 for £400. This time she left a bid with Quaritch for £1500. "It is difficult for me

Single miniature by the Master B. F., Milan or Lodi, *c.*1500, bought by Belle Greene for the Morgan Library at the Holford sale in 1927.

to believe that this leaf will go to that *unholy* sum", she wrote to Dring, "and Mr Morgan and I realize perfectly well that you will use your discretion and get it for less if possible." Quaritch bought it for £1750 and she took it anyway.

Of the complete Holford manuscripts, the one which she most wanted was the unique twelfth-century life of Saint Edmund, an English national treasure by any definition. Belle Greene had told Benson that the Morgan Library would not consider it unless all reasonable opportunities had been exhausted for the British Museum to acquire it either as a gift or at a nominal price. After months of delay and no decision from the cash-strapped Museum, the Holford executors finally decided that, as they had already given one major picture to the nation and contributed largely to another, their patriotic obligations were fulfilled. They refused the Museum further time to raise a public appeal on the grounds that, if it failed, it would damage the subsequent value of the manuscript on the open market. They withdrew their offer to the Museum and sold six manuscripts directly to the Morgan, including the life of Saint Edmund. Among the other books were a superb illustrated ninth-century Gospel Book from Reims, in Belle Greene's opinion second only in quality to the jewelled Gospels from Lindau, and the enchanting Psalter-Hours which Madden loved.

This last manuscript was badly misbound, and it was not easy to put the leaves back into the right sequence of text of an immensely complex provincial liturgy. It was doubtless Sydney Cockerell who suggested that the man for the job was Eric Millar (1887–1966), curator and later Keeper of Manuscripts in the British Museum. Millar was brought to New York at the end of 1927, and under his guidance the manuscript was duly taken apart and reassembled by the Morgan's master binder, Marguerite Duprez Lahey. It is now known as the Psalter-Hours of Yolande of Soissons. Millar's visit was a huge success. It was he who noticed the connection between the leaf bought in Italy in 1912 and the Winchester Bible. He wrote afterwards that it was "one of the pleasantest and most inspiring two months" he had ever spent. The visit probably did a great deal to smooth any awkwardness over the life of Saint Edmund. Belle Greene urged him to return: "*we miss you!*" (underlined three times). She used to call him, not to his face, "our pet". I owe a story about the visit to Nicolas Barker. This was told by Millar to Barker and by Barker to me, and it comes with the caveats of any oral transmission. Millar

was looked after by Belle Greene and never saw Jack Morgan at all until one day he was eventually summoned. Morgan asked whether he would be willing to become director of the Library. Millar demurred, explaining that he was a civil servant with a good job in Britain, but here was a dilemma. Belle Greene was director. Did she know this offer was being made? Should he tell her? After some thought, he seized his appropriate moment and did so. "These Americans!" she exclaimed; "They are all like that: they think they can buy anything!"

The Morgans, *père* and *fils*, could indeed buy almost anything, as no manuscript collector since the Duc de Berry and Federico da Montefeltro could possibly have done, but, as Belle Greene said to Millar, they were not alone. The purchasing power of America in the late nineteenth and early twentieth centuries was phenomenal. In addition to extravagant American buyers of paintings, such as Henry Clay Frick (1849–1919) and Isabella Stewart Gardner (1840–1924), there were now many of their fellow countrymen collecting manuscripts and rare books, often with a focus and a connoisseurship unmatched in the Old World. That is different today, when the supremely wealthy tend to furnish their houses with contemporary art rather than antiquarian libraries. In Belle Greene's time, many newly rich Americans were buying into traditional European aristocratic taste, as if legitimizing their recent status by the visible reassurance of old culture, including books. Others were perhaps aspiring to the world of the Pierpont Morgans, whose ongoing commitment to manuscripts was promoted and orchestrated by Belle Greene. Tens of thousands of medieval manuscripts crossed the Atlantic in the first half of the twentieth century. The Morgan Library secured most of the absolute finest but not quite all. Among the trophies of Henry Huntington (1850–1927) in California was the Ellesmere Chaucer (bought in 1917), by far the best illuminated and one of the most textually important of all copies of the *Canterbury Tales*, and when Belle Greene finally saw the collection of Henry Walters (1848–1931), she was astonished at the quality of several of his manuscripts:

> I could hardly credit my own eyes. He has some splendid kufic writings, some excellent Carolingians, a 14th century Italian Bible of real

LEFT: Manuscript of the life and miracles of Saint Edmund, Bury St Edmunds, *c.*1130, bought by Belle Greene from the Holford collection, 1927.

significance in the history of Italian art . . . Then too he has the finest Armenian manuscript which I have ever beheld. It has about 20 full-page illuminations of a color-quality which I have only found in the very early enamels . . . I would have bought this manuscript in a second had it been offered to me.

The ready availability of American money caused some understandable resentment back in Europe as so many treasures seemed to be being lost abroad. This was already a refrain of the British press when Morgan was buying the Lindau Gospels from Lord Ashburnham, and it was no less when the British Museum was unable to afford the Holford manuscripts nearly thirty years later. It was self-perpetuating, because as ever higher sale prices were trumpeted in the news, so the public at home began to take artworks more seriously and deplore their loss. This was the theme of Henry James's novel *The Outcry* (1911), in which the millionaire collector Bender is a thinly disguised version of Morgan:

Hugh Crimble had a shudder of remembrance. 'Mr Bender?'

'The rich American who is going round.'

It gave him a sharper shock. 'The wretch who bagged Lady Lappidge's Longhi?'

Lady Grace showed surprise. 'Is he a wretch?'

Her visitor but asked to be extravagant. 'Rather – the scoundrel. He offered his infernal eight thousand down.'

'Oh, I thought you meant he had played a trick!'

'I wish he had – he could then have been collared.'

Belle Greene was unusually sensitive to the delicacy of export from England, and did not want either of the Morgans to be seen as scoundrels. In a long letter to Dring of Quaritch in 1919, she discussed the public spectre of Americans buying up everything: "I hate 'us' myself – It seems even to me, to be so *much* worse since the War. Our Fifth Avenue seems like the Highway of Sodom *and* Gomorrah." Presumably because of Belle Greene's friendship with both Cockerell and Millar, the younger Morgan went out of his way to help British institutions save manuscripts which he might have preferred for himself. He topped up the sum needed by the Fitzwilliam for the purchase of Ruskin's Saint Louis Psalter from Yates Thompson in 1919, and in 1929, a year after the incident of the life of Saint Edmund, he gave the British Museum interest-free loans for a year to enable it to buy both the Luttrell Psalter and the Bedford Psalter and Hours. One proposed kindness was in 1920. In the second Yates Thompson sale, the British Museum very much wanted lot 32, the late twelfth-century life of Saint Cuthbert, from Durham. Belle Greene had heard confidentially what the Museum's upper limit was to be. She instructed the firm of Quaritch (acting for the Museum) that if the bidding went above that figure, they were to continue, and then if successful to cede the manuscript graciously and as a surprise to the Museum, Morgan paying the difference between their highest bid and the final price. That was the idea. Unknown to Belle Greene, however, the national limit was greatly increased at the very last moment, and what she would have assumed was her own bid in the auction when the hammer fell was still that of the Museum itself, which bought the manuscript for £5000. It was paid with help from the National Art Collections Fund, but it would have been less costly for the nation if their first and lower figure had been left unchanged.

Belle Greene's habitual courtesy to the British would doubtless have made her a welcoming host if I could have visited her in New York, and so let us go together. From 1928 until 2003 you would enter the Pierpont Morgan Library (as I did countless times from the 1970s) through what was disingenuously called the Annex, up low steps at the Madison Avenue end of the north side of East 36th Street, leading into the very grand Marble Hall. There was an exhibition room on the left and the galleried reading-room on the right, presided over for twenty years by Belle Greene. You would have reached her office through a barrel-vaulted corridor known as the Vestibule at the far right-hand end of the Marble Hall, connecting the Annex to the original free-standing library building finished for Pierpont Morgan in 1906. Before 1928, however, the site of the Annex was still occupied by the brownstone house where the Morgans lived. You would therefore have come to see Belle Greene by the original high round-topped pillared entrance in the middle of the block between Madison and Park Avenue, through brass gates and up steps between two marble lions. It took you through a portico directly into the library's exquisite Rotunda, modelled on the Villa Madama in Rome, commissioned in 1518 by Cardinal Giulio de' Medici from Raphael. It has a beautiful inlaid marble floor copied from that of the Villa Pia in the gardens of the Vatican. On the left was Morgan's office, now

Belle Greene at her desk as director of the Morgan Library, photograph, 1940s.

called the Study or West Library. On the right was the tall East Room, one of the most spectacular library rooms in the world, with three soaring levels of rare books behind metal grilles and a stone fireplace on the far wall below a vast sixteenth-century Flemish tapestry of the Triumph of Avarice. Straight ahead off the Rotunda, however, in the centre of this trinity of rooms, was Belle Greene's own huge office. It is now sometimes called the North Room, used for exhibiting ancient art, including Asian seals and cuneiform tablets.

There is a photograph of Belle Greene late in life, seated small and slim and still expensively dressed behind a vast Renaissance desk, at right angles to the door. The setting suited her. Works of art decorated the room and the shelves of books behind her. There is a slightly critical account by one visitor in 1934, who described her then as fortyish (she was actually fifty-five) and recorded that she received her guests politely. She had, he said,

> brown hair and wears horn-rimmed spectacles. My first impression of her was that she looked bloated as if she had a touch of dropsy or perhaps drank too much, although she is not overly heavy . . . She was dressed

in a sort of classic garment of black velvet relieved here and there by bits of chartreuse lace. She has short, stubby fingers and chews her nails.

The biographers of the Philadelphia dealer A. S. W. Rosenbach comment admiringly on the 'whisky tenor' of her voice in later years (she drank her way uninhibitedly through Prohibition and could be noisy after a good lunch). "Of course I'm a Hussey (or is it Hussy?)", she wrote contentedly to Berenson in 1927, "but thanks be-to-Gawd, I've lived and am still Alive albeit decrepit." She would be hospitable to us too. She was always witty and quick, and she would be anxious for news of Cockerell and the other friends in England. She would fetch great manuscripts from the vault to impress us, a selection of what she called her "'Oh my!' stuff". The Da Costa Hours would come out, subtly reminding us of her middle name, and the Shah Abbas Bible, no doubt, with the *Bible moralisée* and surely the Farnese Hours in its little box. I would ask, as I did in reality on my very first visit, for the Winchester Bible leaf (and saw it). Belle Greene's own favourites, however, as she told Cockerell, were Carolingian manuscripts. These would be produced from the vault, one after another, the Lindau jewelled Gospels bought from Lord Ashburnham, the Golden Gospels of Henry VIII, the Gospel Book of Abbot Otbert from the Troussures collection, several Hamuli manuscripts (now restored), the Gospels of Matilda of Canossa, Yates Thompson's Missal of Mont Saint-Michel, the Dioscorides, and the marvellous Holford Gospels, more and more, until, like Berenson receiving kisses, we cry for mercy. It is still true that this is the finest library of illuminated manuscripts outside Europe.

Belle Greene also encouraged children and exhibitions, perhaps remembering a youthful visit to the Grolier Club in 1892. In 1934 she looked round the galleries of the British Museum thoughtfully and anonymously and wrote afterwards to congratulate Eric Millar on how manuscripts were displayed to "the '*peeple*'", as she fondly called the public. Belle Greene probably did as much as anyone in the United States to bring medieval manuscripts into popular consciousness in the second quarter of the twentieth century. Several of the great figures of manuscript studies in the next generation in America began as her assistants in the Morgan Library, including Dorothy Miner (hired in 1933), later curator of manuscripts in the Walters Art Gallery in Baltimore, and Philip Hofer (her assistant director in 1934), eventually a major manuscripts benefactor of Harvard. Clara Peck, an heiress of the Woolworth fortune, was so impressed with visiting Belle Greene that on her own death in 1983 she was unexpectedly found to have bequeathed to the Morgan Library her astonishing manuscript of the *Livre de chasse*, *c.*1406–7, made for Louis d'Orléans, nephew of the Duc de Berry.

The bright-eyed young organizer of Pierpont Morgan's early acquisitions had gradually evolved into a *grande dame* of America. She had her own apartment in Park Avenue. The da Costa Greene family fabricated by Genevieve Greener in 1900 had become, in effect, as aristocratic as they had pretended. Dorothy Miner later edited a posthumous volume of essays in Belle Greene's memory, including contributions from a duke, three knights, an earl and a cardinal. It sounds like Vespasiano's client list. Dorothy Miner described Belle Greene's wit and "breezy conversation over the years" but that she was also:

> as critical of human beings as of works of art. She could not tolerate mediocrity in either, for it bored her. For pretence and pompous fraud, whether in an object or a person, she had only swift scorn. These things would hardly be worth mentioning, were it not that they constituted in a very real sense part of Belle Greene's contribution to scholars and scholarship.

In this we can still see that brisk exercise of connoisseurship learned from Berenson, but Belle Greene's contempt of all falsity in people may seem at odds with the enormous deception of her own biography, which was never let up and never revealed. Maybe that is the explanation of her sensitivity to forgery elsewhere. She was as quick to denounce it in manuscripts as she was to overlook it in her family. It was Belle Greene who first recognized and named the Spanish Forger, a prolific fabricator of manuscript illumination operating probably in France in the late nineteenth and early twentieth centuries, whose work had deceived many museums. H. P. Kraus described how as a nervous young immigrant bookseller in the early 1940s he had brought a manuscript to her office: "her manner befitted her station, regal, aloof: I trembled". In one glance, she dismissed his proffered volume as a forgery, which, in fact, it was not.

Belle Greene made her last visit to Europe in 1936, when she attended the Music Festival in Salzburg and the Berlin Olympics. She may have watched the triumphs of the Black American sprinter Jesse Owens, which might have prompted reflexions long suppressed. Her mother died in 1941. By the 1940s her own health was declining. She suffered a fall and some loss of mobility. She retired in 1948 and died of cancer two years later in St Luke's Hospital in New York City. Her ashes are buried in Kensico Cemetery in Valhalla, a town north of Manhattan. There is a simple carved stone, her last manuscript, inscribed "Belle da Costa Greene, May 10, 1950 †", that one date being the only absolute fact of her extraordinary life then known.

We should end with a final purchase. In 1926 the younger Pierpont Morgan acquired four German manuscripts in jewelled bindings from Holkham Hall in Norfolk, glitzy banker's books, like his father's M 1. Thomas Coke had obtained them for only £100 in 1818, and they had been catalogued by Frederic Madden. Morgan was staying the night. Lord Leicester asked an inflexible £100,000 for the four books, a sum he happened to need for another reason. The figure, far beyond all sense and precedent, kept Morgan awake half the night. At breakfast the next morning he capitulated and bought the manuscripts, because, as he said afterwards, he was too frightened of Belle Greene to come home without them.

OVERLEAF: The Sacramentary of Berthold, abbot of Weingarten, Württemberg, 1215–17, one of four manuscripts bought by Jack Morgan from Holkham Hall in 1926.

ER·
OM
NIA·
SCLA·
SCLOR
AMEN
DOMIN'
UOBISCU·
ET·CU·SPU·TO
SURSU·CORDA
HABEM' AD DNM
GRACIAS·AGAM' DNO
DEO·NRO·DIGNU·& IUSTU·E

Epilogue: An Evening at the Morgan

All historical inquiry involves going back into the past and encountering people or events from long ago. We have shared twelve such expeditions. These cannot be real meetings, for research can go only as far as surviving evidence allows. There are things we can never discover, but we also have knowledge of outcomes which those same people in history could not possibly have imagined. Since 1720, Anselm, our host at Bec, has been venerated as a 'doctor of the Church', and his *Meditations* are still widely read nearly a thousand years after he arranged for the first copies to be made by scribes in his abbey scriptorium. Cotton's library did finally become a primary resource for history of the British nation, rendered even more international by the acquisitions made by Madden two centuries later and his work to restore the fire damage. Manuscripts commissioned by the Duc de Berry, or ordered through Vespasiano or illuminated by Bening, are once again sought after and are as expensive in relative terms as they were when they were newly made; and modern collectors and libraries judge their desirability according to criteria defined and enunciated by the Abbé Rive and Cockerell. We still use editions of texts established by Mommsen, and the tricks of Simonides are not all unmasked. The Jewish people are back in Israel and have a national library of their own in Jerusalem (which would have made Oppenheim very relieved), and racial diversity is now celebrated in our world, as Belle Greene's father always hoped. They knew none of these things in their lifetimes.

These dozen people were all caught up by medieval manuscripts for a wide range of reasons and in very different circumstances. That common passion running through all their lives is enough to convince me that I would have enjoyed spending time in the company of each one of them. Would this shared enthusiasm be the same if they could meet one another? Surely it would. We can imagine them being somehow conjured forwards into our own age, to attend the annual dinner of our fictional Manuscripts Club, together around a single circular dinner table, in the East Room of the Morgan Library perhaps. Try to envisage it. The walls are lined with books. Anselm is seated first, as befits a saint and the earliest person present. On his right is Belle Greene, director of this place and our host for the evening. Next to her, as she has insisted, is Cockerell. Beside him, and continuing around the table, are the Duc de Berry, Bening, Vespasiano, Mommsen, Simonides, Rive, Cotton, Oppenheim and Madden, bringing the circle back again to Anselm.

Belle Greene, friend of Pius XI, is thrilled to meet a saint. She puts her hand confidingly on his arm and tells him about the Library's purchase in 1911 of the Gospel Book of Matilda of Canossa, to whom Anselm sent a manuscript of his *Meditations* in about 1104. Several of his earliest patrons were women, he says, and this naturally pleases her. He remembers the Sacramentary of Mont Saint-Michel, which she bought in 1919, and is fascinated to learn of the Dioscorides in Greek, a text he knows of but has never seen. Anselm turns to his left. Madden is fluent in both Latin and Anglo-Norman, and within moments they are talking animatedly of the libraries of Normandy and Canterbury and their shared frustrations with the priests in Winchester. Belle Greene is now giggling with Cockerell over a story about Eric Millar. Cockerell, who admires dukes and speaks excellent French, is flattering the Duc de Berry and knows more about some of his Books of Hours than even the Duc does. He has anecdotes about Bernard Shaw and Yates Thompson and visits to Chantilly. The Duc is enchanted too to learn that his other neighbour, Bening, has also seen and admired the *Très Riches Heures* and that its calendar cycle was still transforming Flemish art far into the sixteenth century. In his time, Bening realizes, the Duc was intimate with many illuminators and evidently interacted with them on a level of mutual respect and equality unimaginable to most of the courtiers in his palaces of Bourges or Paris. Vespasiano wants to know exactly how Bening runs his business. Among other things, he is curious to learn how he collects payment from foreign clients. He elicits information and confidences that even the guild archives of Bruges can never reveal. Mommsen follows with passion the tales told by Vespasiano of Niccolò Niccoli and Poggio Bracciolini and the finding (and sometimes losing) of unknown classical texts. Turning to his right, Mommsen switches into Greek and within moments has given Simonides lists of the manuscript texts he most wishes he could see. The attentive Greek smiles knowingly and thinks he might be able to help. Rive on his other side informs him that his manuscripts are forgeries, and mysteriously Simonides does not deny it. Rive, however, is deeply respectful of Cotton, especially of his early Greek Genesis and his manuscripts of the Renaissance, and they share a deep sense of the injustices of fate and an uncaring public. Oppenheim leans forward and agrees, in a deep booming voice. He explains how he too sympathizes entirely with Cotton's dash against time to gather manuscript texts on the brink of oblivion. Madden beside him knows enough Hebrew to inquire about written sources of Jewish law and occult, before turning back to Anselm. The noise is extraordinary. They all talk at once, chattering and laughing, as if they have known each other for ever, as, in a sense, we all have.

At other tables in the room are Eadmer and Adelida, daughter of William the Conqueror. The Limbourg brothers have travelled from Bourges with Jacquemart de Hesdin and the Duc's cataloguer, Robinet d'Étampes. Christine de Pizan is there. So are William Gray and Antonio di Mario and Federico da Montefeltro. James Weale brings Antonius van Damme. Ben Jonson sits with William Camden. Prince Dietrichstein meets the Duc de La Vallière. Here too are Joseph Van Praet, Philip Bliss and Francis Douce, Sir Thomas Phillipps, Joseph Mayer, Ruskin and Morris, Yates Thompson, Junius Morgan, Robert Holford and many others. Panizzi has not been invited.

Each in his or her own way agrees that illuminated manuscripts are the most entrancing of artefacts, conveyors both of texts and of some of the most refined art ever painted. They know that manuscripts are windows into human aspirations, emotions and sense of beauty, and they all believe in manuscripts' enduring capacity to transmit knowledge. Many of them have held the same manuscripts in their hands, centuries apart. They are aware of the thrill of connection across time.

The Club is still open for membership. There is no subscription or obligation and all applicants are warmly admitted. It will continue as long as medieval manuscripts endure, which is likely to be measured in thousands of years. Most history books have an end, but this looks far into the future. We all hope to see one another there.

Bibliographies and Notes

Mrs Yates Thompson's remark on p. v is quoted in *Geoffrey Madan's Notebooks*, Oxford, 1981, p. 97. He dates it – no doubt in conversation with her – to 10 June 1932.

1. THE MONK: SAINT ANSELM

For my generation, scholarship on Saint Anselm revolved around the magisterial figure of Professor Sir Richard Southern (1912–2001). I went to some of his lectures in Oxford, when he was President of St John's College there. His principal relevant books are R. W. Southern, *Saint Anselm and his Biographer: A Study of Monastic Life and Thought, 1059–c.1130*, Cambridge, 1963, and *Saint Anselm: A Portrait in a Landscape*, Cambridge, 1990, used throughout this chapter, together with his edition and translation, *Eadmeri Vita sancti Anselmi: The Life of St Anselm, Archbishop of Canterbury, by Eadmer*, London, 1962. In discussing monastic life, I am not necessarily excluding nuns, but their lives tended to be less literate and not so well documented. I am grateful to both Michael Gullick and Rodney Thomson for reading drafts of this chapter. The British Library manuscript of Anselm's letters is Cotton MS Nero A. VII, fols. 41r–112v. It is discussed in Southern, *Portrait*, pp. 459–64, and in S. Niskanen, *The Letter Collections of Anselm of Canterbury*, Turnhout, 2011 (*Instrumenta Patristica et Mediaevalia: Research on the Inheritance of Early and Medieval Christianity*, 61), esp. pp. 74–86. The standard edition and numbering of the letters is F. S. Schmitt, *Anselmi Opera Omnia*, III, Edinburgh, 1946. For quotations I have generally used the translations of W. Fröhlich, *The Letters of Saint Anselm of Canterbury*, Kalamazoo, 1990 (*Cistercian Studies*, 96), hereafter Fröhlich: extracts cited here on pp. 13–16 are from nos. 23, 25 and 26 (Fröhlich, pp. 114, 118 and 119, corresponding to fols. 56r–v, 56v–57r and 74r of Cotton Nero A. VII), probably all of *c.*1072–3. The dates of Hernost's period at Saint-Étienne and his death in 1076 confirm that this whole exchange took place early in Anselm's priorate at Bec and not long after Lanfranc's appointment in Canterbury. The fact of William being the son of a bishop was not so unusual as it might have been later in the Middle Ages, since clerical celibacy, although always policy, was not enforced until the First Lateran Council in 1123. The tale of Lanfranc's request for a copy of the *Moralia* is also summarized by M. Gullick, 'How Fast Did Scribes Write?', pp. 39–58 in L. L. Brownrigg, ed., *Making the Medieval Book: Techniques of Production*, Los Altos Hills, 1995, p. 39. Gregory's *Moralia* exists in a number of late eleventh-century manuscripts from other Norman abbeys, such as Jumièges and Préaux, now Rouen, Médiathèque, mss 497–8 (I. 24 and A. 123: F. Avril, *Manuscrits normands, XI–XIIème siècles*, Rouen, 1975, pp. 37 and 60–61, nos. 25 and 58); another was among the manuscripts brought back from Normandy by Bishop William of Saint-Calais for the library of Durham, probably in 1091 (Durham Cathedral, MS B.III.10). They might all derive from this moment of propagation, but we cannot know since the Bec manuscript itself does not survive, and nor do those made for the abbot of Saint-Étienne in Caen or for Canterbury, which is listed in M. R. James, *The Ancient Libraries of Canterbury and Dover*, Cambridge, 1903, p. 32, nos. 142–3; the extant flyleaf from its second volume is bound into Cambridge, Trinity College, MS B.5.18 (M. R. James, *The Western Manuscripts* *in the Library of Trinity College, Cambridge*, I, Cambridge, 1900, p. 216, no. 164). There is also another second volume from a set of the *Moralia* from Canterbury from a generation later, written in England, probably at Canterbury and possibly copied from the manuscript sourced by Lanfranc (Trinity College, MS B.4.9, James, *Ancient Libraries*, pp. 146–7, no. 123). In the bookshop at Bec I bought and have used their illustrated guidebook *Abbaye Notre-Dame du Bec, Le Bec-Hellouin, Deux Monastères*, Moisenay, 1999. The composition of the icon's picture of Saint Anselm writing (p. 19) is derived from a twelfth-century image in a British Library manuscript showing Saint Dunstan, another archbishop of Canterbury, the frontispiece to Royal MS 10.A.XIII, fol. 2v, the Canterbury copy of the commentary on the Rule of Saint Benedict by Smaragdus; it is reproduced (among other places) on the title-page of my own *Scribes and Illuminators*, London, 1992, which may actually have been the icon painter's exemplar. For the identification of the wild flowers in the cloister at Bec and elsewhere in this book, I am indebted to Andrew Hollis. The quotation from the Rule of Saint Benedict on p. 20 is taken from the translation by L. Doyle, *The Rule of Saint Benedict*, Collegeville, Minn., 2001, p. 117, given to me by Eric Hollas, OSB. Eadmer's remark on Anselm as a conversationalist is in the *Vita Anselmi*, book II, cap. xi (Southern, ed., *Life of Anselm*, p. 78). The constructed 'conversation' with Anselm on pp. 20–21 is assembled as follows: "We were surprised . . ." (letter 24, Fröhlich, p. 116); 'Turn aside . . .' (*Proslogion*, cap. i, Schmitt, I, p. 97, translated by J. Hopkins and H. Richardson, *Complete Philosophical and Theological Treatises of Anselm of Canterbury*, Minneapolis, 2000, p. 90); and 'My life terrifies me . . .' (*Meditationes*, 1, cap. i, Schmitt, III, p. 76; B. Ward, *The Prayers and Meditations of St Anselm*, Harmondsworth, 1973, p. 221, cited here from its quotation by Durand, abbot of La Chasse-Dieu, translated in letter 70, Fröhlich, p. 193). Anselm's decision to become a monk and Lanfranc's remark 'Stay on this wood' are from Eadmer, *Life of Anselm*, pp. 8 and 11. Letter 121 ('I could tell you much . . .') is quoted from Fröhlich, p. 290. Anselm's prayer to Saint Benedict is from Ward, *Prayers and Meditations*, p. 199. For Anselm's life, I also looked at S. N. Vaughn, *Archbishop Anselm 1093–1109: Bec Missionary, Canterbury Primate, Patriarch of Another World*, Farnham and Burlington, Vt., 2012. The medieval library catalogues of Bec are in Avranches, Bibliothèque municipale Edouard Le Héricher, ms 159, fols. 1v–3r, and have been published several times, most recently by L. Cleaver, 'The Monastic Library at Le Bec', pp. 171–205 in B. Pohl and L. Gathagan, eds., *A Companion to the Abbey of Le Bec in the Central Middle Ages*, Leiden, 2017, pp. 190–95 and 195–205; I have used her numbering, which is not the same in all editions. A manuscript of Florus given to Bec by Philip of Harcourt (now Paris, BnF, ms lat. 5802) later belonged to Petrarch and the Visconti dukes of Milan, no less, a remarkable linking of manuscript collectors. The manuscript of Augustine, *De pastoribus*, etc., described on pp. 24–6, is Paris, BnF, ms lat. 12211. I am indebted to Laure Rioust for facilitating swift access. It is one of the manuscripts from provincial monastic libraries gathered in by the abbey of Saint-Germain-des-Prés in the seventeenth century, which passed from there at the Revolution to the national collection. Michael Gullick tells me of one other manuscript from this period which might be from the scriptorium and library of Bec, Bern, Burgerbibliothek, Cod. 160, Orosius bound with Justinus' epitome of Trogus Pompeius, of which there was indeed a copy at Bec (catalogue no. 99). Anselm's letter to Prior Ralph about lending manuscripts (p. 27) is letter 12 (Fröhlich, p. 96). The textual families of the *De pastoribus* were disentangled and classified by C. Lambot, 'Le sermon XLVI de saint Augustine *De pastoribus*', *Revue Bénédictine*, 63, 1953, pp. 165–210; Anne McLaughlin kindly conjured up a copy for me during the Corona lock-down. The manuscript from Bath Abbey is

British Library, Royal MS 5.B.II, partly digitized on-line. The copy from Mont-Saint-Michel is Avranches, Bibliothèque municipale Edouard Le Héricher, ms 94, classified by Lambot. Accounts of the library at Bec include G. Nortier, *Les Bibliothèques médiévales des abbayes bénédictines de Normandie*, Paris, 1971, pp. 34–60; J. Weston, 'Manuscripts and Book Production at Le Bec', pp. 171–205 in Pohl and Gathagan, eds., *Companion to the Abbey*, as above, with Laura Cleaver's article, as cited. The *De viris illustribus* at Bec was no. 64 in the catalogue, and Lanfranc's citation of it, mentioned here on p. 28, is taken from H. Clover and M. Gibson, eds., *The Letters of Lanfranc, Archbishop of Canterbury*, Oxford, 1979, p. 145. Anselm's letter about the Rule of Saint Dunstan is no. 42 (Fröhlich, p. 146; the text is usually called the *Regularis Concordia*); his letter to Folcard about the robbers is no. 55 (Fröhlich, p. 165). The accident on London Bridge is from the *Vita Anselmi*, book II, cap. lxxi (Southern, ed., *Life of Anselm*, p. 148). The letters to Maurice about the Hippocrates are nos. 43 and 60 (Fröhlich, pp. 148 and 173). The multiple copies at Canterbury are James, *Ancient Libraries*, pp. 56–7, nos. 446–9 and 454. Anselm's discussion with Eadmer on his first visit to England in 1079 is recalled in book I, cap. xxix, of the *Vita Anselmi* (Southern, ed., *Life of Anselm*, p. 50). For his knowledge of classical authors, see Southern, *Anselm and His Biographer*, p. 17. The Ovid is no. 157 in the Bec catalogue; the missing texts are the 'magnus' (presumably the *Metamorphoses*, his biggest extant work, unless it is an allusion to the lost *Medea*) and the *Fasti*. The letter urging the study of Virgil is no. 64, Fröhlich, p. 180, referring also to M. Gibson, *Lanfranc of Bec*, Oxford, 1978, pp. 44 and 181. Fulgentius is no. 107 in the Bec catalogue. The pope's speech of welcome in Rome, mentioned on p. 32, is described by Eadmer in the *Vita Anselmi*, book II, cap. xxix (Southern, ed., *Life of Anselm*, p. 105). Two composite manuscripts on the liberal arts in the Bec library catalogue are nos. 155–6. The first comprised Martianus Capella (early fifth century), *De nuptiis Mercurii et Philologiae et de vii artibus liberalibus*, and the commentary on it by Remigius of Auxerre (*c.*841–908); Priscian (fifth to sixth century), *De viii partibus et de constructionibus*, parts of his *Institutiones Grammaticae*; two texts on rhetoric, probably those of Priscian and Boethius (*c.*477–524), but possibly the *Rhetorica ad Herennium* then attributed to Cicero and known to Anselm; three books of dialectic, probably the first three books of the *De differentiis topicis* of Boethius; the commentaries of Boethius on the *Isagoge* of Porphyry (*c.*234–*c.* 305), and on Aristotle's *Categoriae* (or *Praedicamenta*) on logic and on the *Periermenias* (or *De interpretatione*) on the meaning of language; and the *Topica* of Cicero (see J. Archambault, 'The Teaching of the *Trivium* at Bec, and its Bearing upon the Anselmian Program of *fides quaerens intellectum*', in M. Healy-Varley *et al.*, eds., *Anselm of Canterbury: Communities, Contemporaries and Criticism*, Leiden, forthcoming but currently available on-line). The second volume comprised Boethius (presumably) on arithmetic and music; Macrobius on the *Somnium Scipionis*; more arithmetic; the *Geometria* of 'Gilbertus' (presumably actually Gerbert of Aurillac, the mathematician who became Pope Sylvester II and died in 1003); further unspecified texts by Boethius, Macrobius and Plato; and the commentary on Plato's *Timaeus* by Calcidius, the translator of Plato in the fourth century. There are at least eighteen texts in these two volumes, some of them very academic. The Bec copies of Anselm's own works are nos. 83–5. In the first volume were the *Monologion* ('Monologue', composed 1075–6) and the *Proslogion* ('Discourse', 1077–8), both applying Platonic reasoning to argue the existence of God, on the principle that God must be perfect and existence is an essential element of perfection; his prayers or *Meditations* (about 1070), probably Anselm's most widely used text among Christians today; the *De grammatico*, on logic (early 1080s), effectively a commentary on

Aristotle, an entirely secular text; and the *Epistola de incarnatione dei*, or 'Letter on the Incarnation of God' (1093), all five works bound up in one volume. In the second volume at Bec were his *De veritate*, 'On truth', and the *De libertate arbitrii*, 'On free will' (both 1080–85); the *De casu diaboli* 'On the fall of the Devil' (1085–90), on the nature of evil; the great *Cur deus homo*, 'Why God [became] man' (1098), on the necessity of atonement; the *De conceptu virginali* , 'On virginal conception' and original sin (1099–1100); and the *De processione spiritus sancti*, 'On the emanation of the Holy Spirit', which Anselm argued at the Council of Bari in 1098 proceeded from both the Father and the Son, in contradistinction to the Greek Church, for whom the Holy Spirit came only from the Father. The exchanges from the *De veritate* are taken, with small changes of wording, from the translation by J. Hopkins and H. Richardson, *Complete Philosophical and Theological Treatises of Anselm of Canterbury*, Minneapolis, 2000, p. 182; the quotation from the *Cur deus homo* is on p. 301. On the composition and dissemination of his books, see especially R. Sharpe, 'Anselm as Author: Publishing in the Late Eleventh Century', *The Journal of Medieval Latin*, 19, 2009, pp. 1–87 (and I record with sadness Richard Sharpe's early and sudden death during the drafting of this chapter). Eadmer's story of the wax tablets is in book I, cap. xix, of the *Vita Anselmi* (Southern, ed., *Life of Anselm*, pp. 30–32); see M. P. Brown, 'The Role of the Wax Tablet in Medieval Literacy: A Reconsideration in Light of a Recent Find from York', pp. 1–16 in *The British Library Journal*, 20, 1994, citing Eadmer on p. 10. The modern icon in the chapel at Bec showing Anselm composing should strictly have shown tablets, not a manuscript. The copy of the *Monologion* sent to Lanfranc is documented in letters 72, 74 and 77 (Fröhlich, pp. 197–8, 201–2 and 205–6); the copies sent to Abbot Rainold and Archbishop Hugh of Lyons are known from letters 83 and 100 (Fröhlich, pp. 217–18 and 250). I am indebted to Michael Gullick for the observation that the Canterbury copy of the early works of Anselm (James, *Ancient Libraries*, p. 23, no. 64) corresponds to the sequence of texts in the master copy at Bec, a combination which, he says, he does not recall noticing elsewhere. The Canterbury manuscript of Augustine's *De pastoribus* with the same accompanying texts as at Bec is James, *Ancient Libraries*, p. 15, no. 20, wrongly identified by James (p. 506) as Cambridge University Library, MS Ff. 4. 32 (see below). The Lanfranc and Anselm components of Cotton MS Nero A. VII are discussed especially in Clover and Gibson, *Lanfranc*. The manuscript is illustrated as their frontispiece and a possible connection with Rochester is hinted on p. 22; the British Library on-line manuscript catalogue states that the manuscript may have been made at Rochester. (There are now other entirely unrelated texts bound in, probably added by Cotton in the seventeenth century.) The item in the Rochester catalogue of 1122–3 lists the letters of Lanfranc 'with other texts' but more exactly in 1202 as "Epistole Lanfranci et Anselmi cum aliis in i volumine" (R. Sharpe, J. P. Carley, R. M. Thomson and A. G. Watson, eds., *English Benedictine Libraries: The Shorter Catalogues*, London, 1996 (*Corpus of British Medieval Library Catalogues*, 4), p. 489, no. 79, and p. 507, no. 84). The name Gundulf is generally assumed to be the source for that of Gandalf, invented by J. R. R. Tolkien, Anglo-Saxonist. Rochester also had its own copy of Augustine's *De pastoribus* with all its now familiar accompanying minor works, but it survives as Cambridge University Library, MS Ff. 4. 32, written by a well-known Rochester scribe who made at least a dozen books for the cathedral in the early twelfth century (N. R. Ker, *English Manuscripts in the Century after the Norman Conquest: The Lyell Lectures, 1952–3*, Oxford, 1960, p. 14, n. 3, and p. 31; P. Binski and P. Zutshi with S. Panayotova, *Western Illuminated Manuscripts: A Catalogue of the Collection in Cambridge University Library*, Cambridge, 2011, pp. 19–20, no. 18; it is too late for classification into the textual family by Dom Lambot, whose cut-off date was *c.*1100). In this case, the sequence of copying was probably Bec to Canterbury and then Canterbury to Rochester, whereas the Canterbury manuscript of the letters of Anselm, now Lambeth Palace, MS 59, dates probably from the late 1120s, far too late to have had any role in the parentage of the Rochester copy. Anselm's letters to Adelida and Gundulf, mentioned on p. 38, are nos. 10 and 28 (Fröhlich, pp. 92–3 and 121). The accounts of Anselm correcting books are in the *Vita Anselmi*, book I, caps. viii and xv (Southern, ed., *Life of Anselm*, pp. 14–15 and 24). The request for the *De temporibus* of Bede is letter 42 (Fröhlich, p. 146); the Bec copy was no. 77 in the Bec catalogue. Lanfranc also was known as a corrector of manuscripts: there is a twelfth-century obituary recording that books from his library were corrected in his own hand (Gibson, *Lanfranc of Bec*, p. 228) and there are manuscripts from Le Mans and Séez in Normandy with corrections described as being by 'Lanfranc', not necessarily the same man (Le Mans, Médiathèque Louis-Aragon, ms 15, and Alençon, Bibliothèque municipale, ms 36: Nortier, *Les Bibliothèques*, pp. 35–6). The copy of Bede's *De temporibus* was no. 78 in the Bec library catalogue. Anselm's letter sending Lanfranc's commentary on the Pauline Epistles to Canterbury is no. 66 (Fröhlich, p. 188); the three volumes are nos. 901–3 in the medieval catalogue at Canterbury (James, *Ancient Libraries*, p. 88), and for the complicated story of the text see A. Collins, *Teacher in Faith and Virtue: Lanfranc of Bec's Commentary on Saint Paul*, Leiden and Boston, 2007 (*Commentaria, Sacred Texts and Their Commentaries: Jewish, Christian and Islamic*, 1), esp. chap. 2 on the manuscripts. The copy of the decretals sent for Lanfranc from Bec to Canterbury is Trinity College, Cambridge, MS B.16.44 (James, *Western Manuscripts*, I, pp. 540–41, no. 405); see also M. Gullick, 'The English-Owned Manuscripts of the *Collectio Lanfranci*', pp. 99–117 in L. Dennison, ed., *The Legacy of M. R. James*, Donnington, 2001, pp. 99–102, and Gullick, 'Lanfranc and the Oldest Manuscript of the *Collectio Lanfranci*', pp. 79–89 in B. C. Brasington and K. G . Cushing, eds., *Bishops, Texts and the Use of Canon Law around 1100*, Aldershot, 2008, p. 79. For the first identification of the scribe of the Cambridge manuscript being the same as that of BnF, ms lat. 12211, see M. Gullick, 'Manuscrits et copistes normands en Angleterre (XIe–XIIe siècles)', pp. 83–93 in P. Bouet and M. Dosdat, eds., *Manuscrits et enluminures dans le monde normand (Xᵉ–XVᵉ siècles): Colloque de Cerisy-la-Salle (octobre 1995)*, Caen, 1999, p. 83. n. 4. Michael Gullick kindly confirms to me his renewed certainty that the scribe is the same in both books. This is important, because Philip of Harcourt also gave a manuscript of Augustine's *De pastoribus* to Bec (no. 12 in that catalogue, presumably yet another descendant in the orbit of Bec Abbey), but the identification of scribe places the Paris manuscript unambiguously into the scriptorium of Lanfranc and Anselm. Anselm's farewell (p. 41 here) is from letter 133 in Fröhlich, p. 310. With a slight stretch, the list of English archbishops from Bec could even be supplemented by the name of the London merchant Gilbert Becket, father of Thomas Becket, whose family had been local and whose surname probably derives from the abbey. On the change from an oral to a literate culture following the Norman Conquest, see M. T. Clanchy, *From Memory to Written Record: England 1066–1307*, 3rd edn, Malden, Mass., and Oxford, 2013. The moment coincides too with a new move for the uniformity of Western Christendom, promoted by Gregory VII, pope 1073–85, who had been trained as a Benedictine monk. He began tightening papal control and introducing consistency of liturgy and religious practice across all of Europe. Gregory hoped that the conquest of England would be part of that campaign of standardization (Clanchy, *Memory*, p. 17). On Eadmer and the story of the witticism by the pope, told here on p. 44, see M. Gibson, 'Normans and Angevins, 1070–1220', pp. 38–68 in P. Collinson, N. Ramsay and M. Sparks, eds., *A History of Canterbury Cathedral*, Oxford, 1995, p. 47; it derives from William of Malmesbury, *Gesta Pontificum Anglorum*, 1. 65. 3. Anselm's letter to Bec, probably in 1099, is no. 209, cited here from Sharpe, 'Anselm as Author', p. 48. The library and script of Canterbury in the eleventh to twelfth century is now well studied: see C. R. Dodwell, *The Canterbury School of Illumination*, Cambridge, 1954, esp. pp. 6–20; Ker, *Century after the Norman Conquest*, as above, pp. 25–9; T. Webber, 'Script and Manuscript Production at Christ Church, Canterbury, after the Norman Conquest', pp. 145–58 in R. Eales and R. Sharpe, eds., *Canterbury and the Norman Conquest: Churches, Saints and Scholars, 1066–1109*, London and Rio Grande, 1995; M. Gullick, 'The Scribal Work of Eadmer of Canterbury to 1109', *Archaeologia Cantiana*, 118, 1998, pp. 173–89; T. Webber, 'Les Manuscrits de Christ Church (Cantorbéry) et de Salisbury à la fin du XIe siècle', pp. 95–105 in *Manuscrits et enluminures*, cited above, 1999, with the Gullick article in the same volume; and M. B. Parkes, *Their Hands Before Our Eyes: A Closer Look at Scribes, The Lyell Lectures Delivered in the University of Oxford, 1999*, Aldershot and Burlington, Vt, 2008, pp. 94–6. The manuscripts destined for Malchus, Walram, Paschal II and Matilda of Canossa are all cited in Sharpe, 'Anselm as Author', pp. 44, 52–3, 56 and 56–7 respectively. The manuscript probably sent to the bishop of Arras is Arras, Bibliothèque municipale, ms 484, written in a Canterbury hand of the early twelfth century (R. Sharpe and T. Webber, 'Four Early Booklets of Anselm's Works from Salisbury Cathedral, MS Cambridge, Trinity College, B.1.37', pp. 58–72 in *Scriptorium*, 63, 2009, p. 59, in an article on a manuscript of Anselm either sent from Canterbury to Saint Osmund, bishop of Salisbury, or copied from a manuscript which was). On the likelihood that Matilda's manuscript was illustrated and that copies of these pictures are found in Admont, Stiftsbibliothek, MS 289, and its descendants, see O. Pächt, 'The Illustrations of Anselm's Prayers and Meditations', *Journal of the Warburg and Courtauld Institutes*, 19, 1966, pp. 68–83; the presentation scene showing a jewelled binding is pl. 16a there (and is also reproduced on the front cover of Fröhlich); see also C. M. Kauffmann, 'New Images for Anselm's Table Talk: An Illustrated Manuscript of the *Liber de Similitudinis*', *Journal of the Warburg and Courtauld Institutes*, 74, 2011, pp. 87–119. My own little scrap of the *Meditations* was Sotheby's, 21 June 1993, part of lot 4. Michael Gullick suggests that it was part of no. 64 in the Canterbury catalogue but no. 69 may be more likely, since that was a separate text (James, *Ancient Libraries*, pp. 23–4). I now also own other fragments from manuscripts of Anselm's *Monologion*, the *Cur deus homo* and *De conceptu virginali* and of the posthumous *Similitudines*. The translation on p. 48 here is that of Sister Benedicta Ward, *Prayers and Meditations*, pp. 223–4. The account of Anselm's wish to destroy the biography and Eadmer's preservation of a copy is told in *Vita Anselmi*, book II, cap. lxxii (Southern, ed., *Life of Anselm*, pp. 150–51).

2. THE PRINCE: THE DUC DE BERRY

There are several modern biographies of the Duc de Berry, including F. Lehoux, *Jean de France, duc de Berri: Sa vie, son action politique (1340–1416)*, Paris, 1967; P. Duhamel, *Jean de Berry: Le frère du roi*, Paris, 1996; and F. Autrand, *Jean de Berry: L'art et le pouvoir*, Paris, 2000, all of which I looked at, but for his life among manuscripts the first resource will always be M. Meiss, *French Painting in the Time of Jean de Berry: The Late Fourteenth Century and the Patronage of the Duc*, London and New York, 1967 (*National Gallery of Art, Kress Foundation Studies in the History of European Art*, 2), esp. pp. 30–97, and subsequent volumes including his *The Limbourgs and Their Contemporaries*, 1974, supplemented now by the less intense and much more readable T. B. Husband, *The Art of Illumination: The Limbourg Brothers and the Belles Heures of Jean de France, Duc de Berry*, New York, New Haven and London, 2008, esp. pp. 10–31. The *Très Riches Heures* is Chantilly, Musée Condé, ms 65. There are luxury facsimiles, including those with commentaries by R. Cazelles and J. Rathofer (Luzern and Munich, 1984) and by P. Stirnemann and I. Villela-Petit (Modena, 2011). I have used the more modest Thames & Hudson version, *Les Très Riches Heures du Duc de Berry, Musée Condé, Chantilly*, with commentaries by J. Longnon and R. Cazelles, London and New York, 1969. My copy, bought on publication, is more worn than the original manuscript. For the palace in Bourges and the Duc's Sainte-Chapelle I am especially indebted to the exhibition catalogue, *La Sainte-Chapelle de Bourges: Une fondation disparue de Jean de France, duc de Berry*, Paris and Bourges, 2004, with contributions by F. Autrand, C. Raynaud and others, including C. Rabel on the manuscripts, pp. 168–71. The papal bull authorizing the foundation is illustrated on p. 180 there, no. 2. There are simply astounding on-line digital re-creations of the ducal palace in the Middle Ages, *Une nouvelle collection de vues 3D sur Bourges au XVème siècle*, part of an evolving website, *Jean de Berry, Homme d'Etat et Prince des Arts*. The pictures of construction in Jerusalem in the *Très Riches Heures* are on fols. 35v and 49v, and it is not certain whether the king directing operations is David or Solomon. The Seneca and Virgil given to the Sainte-Chapelle are now Paris, BnF, ms lat. 8717 (and lat. 8055, pp. 179–456), and Turin, Biblioteca Nazionale Universitaria, I.IV.16 (ms lat. 611): *Fondation disparu*, pp. 168 and 170. The four-volume Lectionary, described here on pp. 57–9, is Bourges, Bibliothèque patrimoniale, mss 33-6 (C. Rabel in *Fondation disparue*, p. 209, no. 56); the miniature of the Duc is in ms 35, folio 17v. If the Duc's emblems do indeed date from his imprisonment, the captive bear could be a good-natured pun on 'Berry', for *bere* in the Middle English of his gaolers has two syllables. It has been suggested to me that the Duc's little dogs may have been French whippets. All the volumes of the Lectionary end with inscriptions of ownership by the Sainte-Chapelle in Bourges. They correspond closely to an entry in a contemporary list of books delivered by the Duc de Berry in the very early 1400s to Arnoul Belin, first treasurer of the Sainte-Chapelle in Bourges, "Un Lectionnaire escript de lettre de forme, ouquel sont les leçons qui se disent tout au long de l'année, tant du temps comme des festes des saints" (J. Guiffrey, ed., *Inventaires de Jean duc de Berry (1401–1416)*, II, Paris, 1894, p. 317, no. 44); the uncertainty is that stylistically the manuscripts look sightly later, perhaps around 1410. The inventories are the primary text for this chapter, two volumes of all the Duc's possessions edited by Jules Guiffrey (1840–1918), both 1894, and extracts for the manuscripts rearranged and numbered in subject order by the librarian Léopold Delisle (1826–1910), L. Delisle, *Recherches sur la librairie de Charles V, roi de France, 1337–1380*, II, Paris, 1907, pp. 219*–334*. For convenience here, since there are so many citations, the Guiffrey edition will be abbreviated to JG and that of Delisle as LD (by number only, without page references). The *Sallière du pavillon* shown on the table at the January feast is JG, I, p. 171, no. 649. The Hours of Jeanne de Navarre once owned by Bonne of Luxembourg, is BnF, ms n. a. lat. 3145 (C. de Hamel, *Meetings with Remarkable Manuscripts*, London, 2016, chapter 9, pp. 376–425, reproducing the entry in the Duc's inventory on p. 414); the Book of Hours given to the Duc's nursemaid, "sa mère de lait" (p. 60 here), is cited in JG, II, p. 337; the book from which Jean II had learned to read is JG, I, p. 257, no. 968 (LD 96). The *Bible Historiale* of Jean II, captured at the Battle of Poitiers, is BL, Royal MS 19.D.II. The inventories of the Duc de Berry in the order listed here are Paris, BnF, ms fr.

11496, dated 1401–2 (JG, II, pp. 1–166); Paris, Archives nationales, KK 258, dated 1413–16 (JG, I, pp. 7–336; see M. Meiss and S. Off, 'The Bookkeeping of Robinet d'Estampes and the Chronology of Jean de Berry's Manuscripts', *The Art Bulletin*, 53, 1971, pp. 225–35); BnF, mss n. a. fr. 1363 and lat. 17173, gifts for the Sainte-Chapelle (JG, II, pp. 171–86 and 306–16); and Paris, Bibliothèque Sainte-Geneviève, ms 841, posthumous inventory, with much duplication but describing tapestries, for example, which had not been included before (JG, II, pp. 206–91). There are also some archival accounts of expenditure on art, and there are surviving manuscripts with inscriptions or arms of the Duc not identifiable in any inventory. The items of little value mentioned on p. 61 are JG, I, pp. 152–4, nos. 558, 570 and 571 (suggesting that the giant's tooth may have been a molar from an elephant or hippopotamus). The ring with his father's image is JG, I, p. 144, no. 485. The chronicle in bad French is JG, I, p. 232, no. 888 (LD 251). The ancient history is JG, I, p. 227, no. 861 (LD 232), now BnF, ms fr. 246, signed by the scribe Mathieu de Rivau, which could have been acquired later but was "presumably written for Jean duc de Berry, its first known owner" (R. H. Rouse and M. A. Rouse, *Manuscripts and Their Makers: Commercial Book Producers in Medieval Paris, 1200–1500*, II, Turnhout, 2000, p. 95). The *Grain d'orge* and the *Ruby de la fossete* (p. 62) are JG, I, pp. 102–3, nos. 349 and 348; other rubies with names included the '*Cuer de France*' bequeathed to the Duc by his nephew the duke of Orléans in 1407, and a gem called the '*Dyament de Chartres*', given to him by the cathedral chapter there and reclaimed after his death (JG, I, pp. 131–2, nos. 435 and 441). The story by Thomas de Saluces (1356–1416) is told in his *Chevalier errant* (Meiss, *Late Fourteenth Century*, p. 70). For the mystical significance of gemstones, see J. Evans, *Magical Jewels of the Middle Ages and Renaissance*, Oxford, 1922, and their religious importance to the Duc, Autrand, *Jean de Berry*, pp. 477–8. Boucicaut's magic gem, doubtless actually a gallstone, is JG, I, p. 159, no. 594. Assassination by poison was a real danger in the Middle Ages. The reference in Bartholomaeus Anglicus, *De proprietatibus rerum*, is book XV, cap. 86. Gemstones in the Scriptures include those on the breastplate of Aaron in Exodus 28 (ruby, topaz, emerald, turquoise, sapphire, diamond and many others), the foundation stones of the New Jerusalem in Revelation 21 (including jasper, sapphire, chalcedony and emerald), and on the throne of God itself, set with emerald (Exodus 24:10; Revelation 25:31), 'like the essence of a clear blue sky'. The Duc's relics include pieces from nine of the twelve apostles, and from three of the four evangelists (lacking Saint Luke); pieces of Saints John the Baptist, Stephen the protomartyr, George, Christopher, Margaret, Lucy and so on; and relics of the national saints of France, Denis, Hilary, Radegund, Charlemagne and very many more. The Virgin's ring, the bread-shaped stone and the Holy Innocent (cited on p. 63) are JG, I, p. 161, no. 600, II, p. 17 no. 54, and I, p. 56, no. 138. The pieces of the True Cross bought by Saint Louis around 1238 were plausibly assumed to be part of what had been found by Saint Helen, mother of the emperor Constantine; the classic argument for their authenticity is Evelyn Waugh's introduction to his *Helena*, 1950. The gift of the Holy Nails is mentioned by the chronicler Jean Jouvenal des Ursins (Meiss, *Late Fourteenth Century*, p. 39); the relics of the 11,000 Virgins are JG, II, pp. 181, and 61, nos. 204 (given by Katherine de Liskerke) and 438, and the unidentifiable package is *ibid.*, p. 78, no. 647. The martyrdom of the 11,000 Virgins becomes a miniature in the *Belles Heures* (fol. 178v). The great ruby bought in 1408 (p. 64 here) is JG, I, pp. 61–2, no. 162; the sapphire from the duchess's coronet is *ibid.*, p. 121, no. 396. The crown including Holy Thorns in the inventory of 1402 is JG, II, p. 6, no. 10. The reliquary in the British Museum is WB 67: see J. Cherry, *The Holy Thorn Reliquary*, London,

2010; N. MacGregor, *A History of the World in 100 Objects*, London, 2010, no. 66; and D. Thornton, *A Rothschild Renaissance: Treasures from the Waddesdon Bequest*, London, 2015, pp. 74–87. John Cherry doubts the identification with the 1402 entry on the main grounds that the Duc's arms were altered in 1397 (pp. 46–7); however, exactly the same bordered arms of *France ancienne* were still being used unchanged by the Duc in the Lectionary in Bourges, the *Grandes Heures*, the *Belles Heures* and in other manuscripts well after 1402. The castle at Mehun-sur-Yèvre (pp. 65–7) is shown on fol. 161v of the *Très Riches Heures*. The books being read on sloping shelves are on fol. 45r. The Belleville Breviary is JG, I, pp. 254–5, no. 963 (LD, no. 55); it is now BnF, mss lat. 10483–4. The *Grandes Heures* is JG, I, pp. 253–4, no. 961 (LD 99); now BnF, ms lat. 919 (facsimile, comm. by M. Thomas, Paris, 1971). The *Très Belles Heures* in Brussels also attributed in the inventories to Jacquemart (pp. 68–9 here) is JG, II, pp. 132–3, no. 1050 (LD 98), now Brussels, Bibliothèque royale, ms 719. The Psalter by André Beauneveu is JG, I, p. 235, no. 906 (LD 30), now BnF, ms fr. 13091. For other work by him, see H. Bober, 'André Beauneveu and Mehun-sur-Yèvre', *Speculum*, 28, 1953, pp. 741–53. The Hours of Jeanne d'Évreux is JG, I, p. 223, no. 850 (LD 108), now New York, Metropolitan Museum of Art, 54.1.2 (facsimile, comm. by B. Drake Boehm, A. Quandt and W. D. Wixom, Luzern, 2000). The miniature Gospel of John the size of *un blanc* is JG, I, pp. 74–5, no. 208 (LD 35). I am indebted to James Morton for finding me an original *blanc* of Charles VI, datable to between 1399 and 1401. There was a tradition which goes back to early Christianity of using all or part of Saint John's Gospel in miniature talismanic amulets; an example, which the Duc might have known, is BnF, ms lat. 10439 in Latin uncials, Italy, fifth to sixth century, about 2¾ by 2¼ inches, formerly in a reliquary in Chartres Cathedral (the Duc cannot have requisitioned it, for it is more than twice the size of a *blanc*). For the documents on Pucelle, see Rouse and Rouse, *Manuscripts and Their Makers*, I, p. 264, and II, pp. 82–3. The *Très Riches Heures* is JG, II, p. 280, no. 1164 (LD 101); the *Belles Heures* is JG, I, p. 253, no. 960 (LD 100), and the manuscript itself is New York, Metropolitan Museum of Art, 54.1.1 (facsimile, comm. E. König, Luzern, 2002–3, and Husband, *Art of Illumination*). For the Limbourgs, see R. Dückers and P. Roelofs, eds., *The Limbourg Brothers: Nijmegen Masters at the French Court, 1400–1416*, Nijmegen, 2005. The gifts they received from the Duc are JG, I, pp. 125–6 and 265, nos. 415 and 994. The additions made to manuscripts remind us of an overlooked truth, "that illuminated manuscripts in the Middle Ages were often multimedia objects, incorporating a range of techniques and materials including metalwork, ivories, textiles, relics and precious gems" (J. F. Hamburger and J. O'Driscoll, *Imperial Splendor: The Art of the Book in the Holy Roman Empire, 800–1500*, New York and Lewes, 2021, p. 23). The bags of lapis, mentioned on p. 73, are JG, II, p. 35, no. 210. My statistics on the *libraires* in Paris are from Rouse and Rouse. The king's dedication copy of the French translation of Aristotle by Nicole (or Nicolas) Oresme is now The Hague, Museum Meermanno, MS 10.D.1; the Duc de Berry's copy made from it was orchestrated by Bureau de Dampmartin, a financial broker in Paris who was the intermediary in a number of transactions on behalf of the Duc, including purchases of books and jewels (JG, I, p. 250, no. 953, and LD 150; for Dampmartin, see Rouse and Rouse, II, p. 21, perhaps related to the Duc's architect Guy de Dampmartin). On the copying of the royal Livy translated by Pierre Bersuire, see Autrand, *Jean de Berry*, p. 468. Charles V's *Bible Historiale* of Jean de Vaudetar is Museum Meermanno, MS 10.B.23, and will reappear in Chapter 7 below; LD, pp. 6–7*, no. 21. The borrowed *Grandes Chroniques* is JG, I, pp. 335–6, no. 1249 (LD 238). On the text and its value in the identity of

France, see A. D. Hedeman, *The Royal Image: Illustrations of the Grandes Chroniques de France, 1274–1422*, Berkeley, 1991. One copy in French with the Duc's arms re-emerged at Sotheby's in my time, 8 December 1981, lot 94, and is now BnF, ms n. a. fr. 28876. The pun between *paris* and *paradis*, or *Parisius* and *paradisus*, is used by Jean de Jandun, *Éloge de la cité de Paris*, 1323, and doubtless elsewhere (M. Camille, *Master of Death*, New Haven and London, 1996, p. 26, with references). In ordering manuscripts from commercial workshops, the Duc or his agents would also have to give instructions for illumination. That Lectionary we saw in Bourges was doubtless commissioned from a professional workshop in Paris, but patterns must have been supplied for its personalized borders including the Duc's bear and swan. An order for a manuscript would also have specified the number of miniatures. If the Duc wanted more pictures than were in the exemplar or standard repertoires of illustration, these would either be discussed in advance or left to the artist's imagination and a careful reading of the text. The Duc must sometimes have requested certain trusted professional illuminators by name but, if so, his inventories tell us nothing. The Duc's Anglo-Saxon Psalter, described on pp. 76–7, is BnF, ms lat. 8824 (JG, II, p. 131, no. 1027 (LD 18); the exhibition catalogue, C. Breay and J. Story, eds., *Anglo-Saxon Kingdoms: Art, Word, War*, London, 2018, pp. 240–41, no. 91, does not even mention the Duc de Berry, even though his arms were just visible as the book was displayed. The exceptionally large Peter Lombard, also mentioned on p. 76, is Bourges, Bibliothèque Patrimoniale, ms 124 (C. Rabel in *Fondation disparue*, p. 210, no. 58). The Psalter said to have been Becket's is JG, I, p. 231, no. 882 (LD 19; C. de Hamel, *The Book in the Cathedral: The Last Relic of Thomas Becket*, London, 2020, p. 51). It might have come from the cathedral of Sens, which owned a number of reputed possessions of Becket and whose bishop gave the Duc a Missal in 1410 (JG, I, pp. 264–5, no. 992; LD 77). The Bible of Saint Louis is JG, I, p. 333, no. 1242 (LD 5), now BnF, ms lat. 10426; the former ownership by Saint Louis is attested by Flamel on the flyleaf, not in the inventory. The book on the Crusades was the *Livre Godefroi de Billon*, bought from Bureau de Dampmartin: JG, I, p. 242, no. 929 (LD 255). The Bible of Philippe le Bel is BnF, ms lat. 248, not in the inventories but inscribed by Flamel (LD 6); that of Clement VII is JG, II, p. 122, no. 951 (LD 3); and that of Robert of Anjou is JG, I, pp. 255–6, no. 965 (LD 1). The *Miroir historial* cited on p. 78 is JG, I, pp. 258–9, no. 972 (LD 201), now BnF, mss n. a, fr. 15939–44; Jean de Montaigu's Psalter is JG, I, pp. 259–60, no. 975 (LD 31), which refers to Fremin de Revelle, for whom see Rouse and Rouse, II, p. 30; the Breviary is JG, I, pp. 331–2, no. 1237, identified with Montaigu's copy in LD 50; the source of the jewels for the *Grandes Heures* is in the entry for that manuscript, JG, I, p. 254. The Montaigu heirs claimed not only the Breviary but also (unsuccessfully) the Bible of Robert of Anjou: L. Delisle, *Le cabinet des manuscrits de la Bibliothèque nationale*, III, Paris, 1881, p. 174, and JG, II, p. 140, n. 3, citing Delisle. The Duc's son Jean, comte de Montpensier, died in 1397 (Meiss, *Late Fourteenth Century*, p. 349); some on-line sources give the date as 1397 or 1401. For Renaut de Montet (pp. 79–81 here), see Rouse and Rouse, II, pp. 123–5. The inventories spell his first name as Regnault. The purchases from him listed on pp. 79–80 are, in sequence: sayings of the philosophers, JG, I, p. 238, no. 917 (LD 168); Thebes, etc., JG, I, p. 239, no. 919 (LD 146); *Lancelot*, JG, I, p. 239, no. 920 (LD 270, now BnF, mss frs. 117–20); *Livre de l'Information*, JG, I, p. 263, no. 989 (LD 167, now BnF, ms fr. 1210); Church fathers, JG, I, pp. 263–4, no. 990 (LD 212 *bis*); marvels, JG, I, p. 268, no. 1000 (LD 198); Missal, JG, I, p. 268, no. 1001 (LD 76); Hours, JG, I, p. 269, no. 1002 (LD 107); *Dialogues*, JG, I, p. 329, no. 1229 (LD 121); *Cy nous dit*, JG, I, pp. 328–9, no. 1228 (LD 42); Corbechon, etc., JG, I, p. 331, nos. 1234–6 (LD 144, 204 and 279). The chronicle bought in 1407, described on pp. 80–81, is BL, Royal MS 19.E.VI, *Les Croniques de Burgues* by Gonzales d'Hinojosa, bishop of Burgos 1313–27, in the French translation of Jean Goulin (d. 1403); it is JG, I, p. 251, no. 955 (LD 254); the miniature of Charlemagne is on fol. 325v; another curious miniature is on fol. 176r showing Titus sieging Jerusalem in AD 70, using a mortar (first known at the Battle of Crécy, 1346). The Duc owned an apparently unillustrated copy of the same text which he had bought from the bookseller Hennequin de Virelay at his shop in the Rue Neuve Notre-Dame in 1402 for 200 gold shillings (JG, I, p. 237, no. 913, LD 253). The Duc's piece of the Chartres relic of the True Cross is LG, I, p. 36, no. 69. Citations of different scripts in the inventories are too numerous to list, but the "lettre gascoigne" is JG, I, p. 234, no. 902 (LD 296, spelled "gascongne"). The copies of Anselm, mentioned on pp. 83–4, are JG, I, p. 260, no. 976, and II, p. 119, no. 944 (LD 125 and 132). The Seneca sent from Milan is JG, II, p. 175, no. 171 (LD 156); and two copies of Marco Polo are JG, I, pp. 262 and 270, nos. 982 and 1005 (LD 197 and 196; they are now BnF, mss fr. 5631 and 2810). The coconuts are JG, I, pp. 46–7, no. 101): coconuts are native to the Pacific but by the Middle Ages had reached India and were said to neutralize poison (O. Rackham, *Treasures of Silver at Corpus Christi College, Cambridge*, Cambridge, 2002, pp. 50–51). On the recently discovered ownership by the Duc of a Machaut manuscript, still in private hands, see L. Earp in *The Ferrell-Vogüé Machaut Manuscript*, Oxford, 2014, pp. 35–44; when the Duc gave it away, he retained a transcript, now BnF, ms fr. 1585. I owe Christine de Pizan's description of the Duc, quoted on p. 85, to A. D. Hedeman, *Translating the Past: Laurent de Premierfait and Boccaccio's De Casibus*, Los Angeles, 2008, p. 3; it is from Christine's *Livre des fais et bonnes meurs du sage roy Charles*, book II, cap. xii, written in 1404. The Duc's four copies of the *Livre du gouvernement* (pp. 85 and 87 here), which may well include those used by his parents in his own education, are JG, I, p. 230, no. 878, p. 233, nos. 893–4, and II, pp. 277–8, no. 1135 (LD, nos. 161–3 and 166). The dedication copy of Laurent de Premierfait's translation of Boccaccio's *De casibus*, mentioned on pp. 87–8, is JG, I, p. 265, no. 993 (LD 208) and is now Geneva, Bibliothèque publique et universitaire, ms fr. 190; the dissemination of its text is the principal subject of Hedeman, *Translating the Past*, as above. The Duc de Berry's relationship with Christine de Pizan is interesting and elusive, in a world where neither had close friendships. In 1403 the gift of her *Chemin de long estude* was inventoried as "compilé par une femme appellée Cristine" (that was the oddity), but by 1405 she had become the "demoiselle Christine de Pizan" and was soon on the Duc's New Year present list (Autrand, *Jean de Berry*, p. 472). In order of citation, the books by her mentioned here are from JG, I, pp. 249, 243–4, 250, 332 and 252–3, nos. 949, 932, 952, 1239 and 959 (LD 290, 286, 287, 288 and 291). For the story of the duke of Guyenne, see K. Green, C. J. Mews and J. Pinder, eds., *The Book of Peace by Christine de Pizan*, University Park, Pa., 2008, p. 62. The Missal which the Duc gave to the Sainte-Chapelle in 1404 and later took back (p. 88 here) is JG, II, p. 123, no. 957 (LD 71, with note), now Munich, Bayerische Staatsbibliothek, clm 10072, with signed illumination by Niccolò da Bologna, 1374. The Duc also took back gold and silver to pay troops defending Bourges in the siege of 1412. On *étrennes* in general, see B. Buettner, 'Past Presents: New Year's Gifts at the Valois Courts, ca. 1400', *The Art Bulletin*, 83, 2001, pp. 598–625, and J. Hirschbiegel, *Étrennes: Untersuchungen zum höfischen Geschenkverkehr im spätmittelalterlichen Frankreich der Zeit König Karls VI (1380–1422)*, Munich, 2003. The list of gifts to the Duc on New Year's Day 1413 appear as '1412', since the numbering of the medieval year did not advance until 25 March, on the principle that the Incarnation began nine months before the Nativity, printed as '1413' (new style) by Delisle. In order, they are: diamond in a gold ring, JG, I, p. 135, no. 454; gold goblet, JG, I, pp. 215–16, no. 831; Marco Polo, JG, I, p. 270, no. 1005 (LD 196; the manuscript is now BnF, ms fr. 2810); great ruby, JG, I, pp. 104–5, no. 356; gold ewer, JG, I, p. 216, no. 832 (Guiffrey's footnote suggests that the bishop had appropriated it from the treasury of his own cathedral); gold cup, JG, I, p. 216, no. 833; gold reliquary, JG, I, pp. 40–41, no. 80; enamel pax, JG, I, p. 47, no. 103; carbuncle ruby, JG, I, p. 105, no. 357; gold ring with cameo, JG, I, p. 163, no. 611; gold ring with bear, JG, I, p. 163, no. 612; agate salt cellar, JG, I, p. 183, no. 694; salt cellar on wheels, JG, I, pp. 183–4, no. 695; salt cellar like a little dog, JG, I, p. 184, no. 696; goblet with three bears, JG, I, p. 216, no. 834 (given by Bureau de Dampmartin, the Duc's sometimes agent); medical manuscript, JG, I, p. 269, no. 1003 (LD 185); and Christine de Pizan, JG, I, p. 270, no. 1004 (LD 289).

3. THE BOOKSELLER: VESPASIANO DA BISTICCI

This chapter owes almost everything to the research and passion of Albinia de la Mare (1932–2001), 'Tilly' to her many friends, as committed a manuscript obsessive as anyone in this book. I knew her well for more than thirty years, in the Bodleian Library, where her tottering nest of papers and joyous laughter astounded readers at the hushed desks of Selden End, later in London, where she became reluctant Professor of Palaeography, and at her book-filled home in Cumnor. When she died at only sixty-nine, I wrote her obituary for *The Times*. She had an unparalleled ability to recognize the hands of individual Italian scribes. Her excited discoveries, thousands of them, tumbled out so fast that Tilly herself could never keep up, which meant that most promised books were unfinished and those that publishers wrenched from her were at once embellished with addenda and further finds often added in her handwriting. Her doctoral thesis on Vespasiano remains unpublished. Much of it and more was poured into A. C. de la Mare, 'New Research on Humanistic Scribes in Florence', pp. 395–600 of A. Garzelli, ed., *Miniatura Fiorentina del Rinascimento, 1440–1525: Un primo Censimento*, Florence, 1985, including pp. 401–6 on Vespasiano. It is a difficult book to use, for there is no index (not the author's responsibility) and facts spill out of pages as ceaselessly and unexpectedly as they did from Tilly's conversations and lectures; a new edition is promised, edited by Xavier van Binnebeke. I have endeavoured to key in all principal references in the notes which follow, but please assume that 'New Research' is the default source for many facts used here. There is also very much in A. C. de la Mare, 'Vespasiano da Bisticci as Producer of Classical Manuscripts in Fifteenth-Century Florence', pp. 166–207 in C. A. Chavannes-Mazel and M. M. Smith, eds., *Medieval Manuscripts of the Latin Classics: Production and Use. Proceedings of the Seminar in the History of the Book to 1500, Leiden, 1993*, Los Altos Hills and London, 1996 (reprinted in J. Roberts and P. Robinson, eds., *The History of the Book in the West, 400 AD–1455*, I, Farnham and Burlington, Vt., 2010, pp. 439–80). For Tilly's own meeting with Vespasiano, see A. C. de la Mare, 'A Palaeographer's Odyssey', pp. 87–107 in J. Onians, ed., *Sight and Insight: Essays on Art and Culture in Honour of E. H. Gombrich at 85*, London, 1994; and R. Black, J. Kraye and L. Nuvoloni, eds., *Palaeography, Manuscript Illumination and Humanism in Renaissance Italy: Studies in Memory of A. C. de la Mare*, London, 2016 (*Warburg Institute Colloquia*, 28), esp. V. Fera, 'L'umanesimo di Albinia C. de la Mare', pp. 1–12, and C. Bianca, 'Albinia C. de la Mare (biblioteche senza inventario)', pp. 13–19. In addition to all this, I must recount every author's nightmare. After this chapter and its notes were entirely finished, a publisher wrote to ask whether I would care to read and perhaps endorse an exciting new book by Ross King, whom I confess I had not heard of, *The Bookseller of Florence: Vespasiano da Bisticci and the Manuscripts that Illuminated the Renaissance*, London, 2021. I envisaged my entire chapter as superseded and to be abandoned. I seized the book with nail-biting anxiety. Extraordinarily, we hardly overlap. His is a wide-ranging survey of the cultural Renaissance, culled in part from Vespasiano's biographical memoirs. There is very little on manuscript production as such (more on early printing) and much of that is non-specific, and nothing changed my text. I greet Mr King genially as a fellow tourist in the Via dei Librai but our shopping bags are different. My own text has been read with exemplary care by both Nicolas Barker, to whom I am indebted for kindnesses over many decades, and David Rundle. For Vespasiano's own biographies, I used W. G. Waters and E. Waters, transl., *The Vespasiano Memoirs: Lives of Illustrious Men of the XVth Century*, London, 1926, and the translations I quote are all theirs except where I have occasionally reworded them slightly by comparing the originals from P. d'Ancona and E. Aeschlimann, eds., Vespasiano da Bisticci, *Vite di uomini illustri del secolo XV*, Milan, 1951. For William Gray and his manuscripts, see R. A. B. Mynors, *Catalogue of the Manuscripts of Balliol College, Oxford*, Oxford, 1963, esp. pp. xxiv–xlv, and A. C. de la Mare, 'Vespasiano da Bisticci and Gray', *The Journal of the Warburg and Courtauld Institutes*, 20, 1957, pp. 174–6. Gray's *Wanderjahre* (p.93) lasted through most of the 1440s. For the business of a *cartolaio*, see A. C. de la Mare, 'The Shop of a Florentine *Cartolaio* in 1426', pp. 237–48 in B. M. Biagiarelli and D. E. Rhodes, eds., *Studi offerti a Roberto Ridolfi, direttore de 'La Bibliofilia'*, Florence, 1973 (*Biblioteca di bibliografia italiana*, 71). The location of Vespasiano's shop in the Via dei Librai was discussed by David Rundle, 'Where's Vespasiano Now?' in his occasional on-line blog *Bonae Litterae*, 1 June 2010, updated in June 2011, "Where's Vespasiano a Year On?" Vespasiano's description of the arrival of János Pannonius (pp. 94–5 here) is *Vespasiano Memoirs*, p. 192. Pannonius (1434–74) was later bishop of Pécs. Vespasiano's account of Gray is *ibid.*, pp. 184–6 (the extract here is from p. 185). Gray's father appears in Shakespeare's *Henry V*, act II, scene 2. Vespasiano's remarks on the book collecting of Niccoli and Poggio are *Vespasiano Memoirs*, pp. 396 and 351. The sentiment on the necessity to collect without regard to cost has been echoed by booksellers at all periods, including Lou Weinstein of the Heritage Book Shop in Los Angeles: "There are no restrictions on budget, which is the only way to do something like this" (N. A. Basbanes, *A Gentle Madness: Bibliophiles, Bibliomanes, and the Eternal Passion for Books*, New York, 1995, p. 414). It suited the early humanists to claim that all libraries where they extracted manuscripts were dusty and neglected, not always necessarily true. The first illuminated initials with white-vine ornament were imitated from eleventh- and twelfth-century Tuscan manuscripts, which the early humanists may have thought were older than they actually were. Books made for Gray presumably in Cologne dated 1444 are Oxford, Balliol College MS 67A and 69 (Franciscus de Mayronis), MS 181 (Johannes de Hesdinio) and MS 224b (Bartoldus de Mosburch); for others attributable to the same period, see Mynors, pp. xxix–xxx. The new humanistic style was not as unknown to Gray as Vespasiano might have thought, and it was beginning to be known even in Oxford. Vespasiano's accounts of Pannonius reading Plotinus and Gray ordering books (pp. 97–8) are *Vespasiano Memoirs*, pp. 195 and 185. The five manuscripts of Cicero bought by Gray from Vespasiano are all Balliol College MS 248, but sub-numbered A–E. The first volume proved to be too heavy for the capacity of my scales, and I owe measurement of its weight to the Assistant Librarian, Nigel Buckley. Volume V, dated 1445, comprises the *Opera rhetorica*

(MS 248E: Mynors, pp. 272–3; fifty manuscripts copied by Ser Antonio di Mario are listed by de la Mare, 'New Research', pp. 482–4); volume II, dated 1447, contains the Philippic and Verrine orations (MS 248B: Mynors, p. 271; forty-five manuscripts copied by Gherardo del Ciriagio are listed by de la Mare, 'New Research', pp. 496–7); and volume III has the *Epistolae ad familiares* (MS 248C: Mynors, pp. 271–2; twenty-seven manuscripts copied by Domenico Cassio are listed by de la Mare, 'New Research', pp. 491–2, including Auckland Public Libraries, Med. MS G. 147, Josephus, *De bello Judaico* in the Latin translation of Rufinus). For the recovery of texts of Cicero, see R. H. Rouse, M. D. Reeve, M. Winterbottom, J. G. F. Powell and L. D. Reynolds in L. D. Reynolds, ed., *Texts and Transmission: A Survey of the Latin Classics*, Oxford, 1983, pp. 54–142. Cicero became the first classical author in print (1465). There was no question of serious humanists reading Cicero in any language but the original Latin; if the Duc de Berry had owned a copy, which he did not, he would probably have commissioned it in French, and Vespasiano's client John Tiptoft, earl of Worcester, translated Cicero into English for his less civilized compatriots. The *De oratore* and *Brutus* are in volume V of Gray's set; Vespasiano's account of Niccoli finding these texts is *Vespasiano Memoirs*, p. 397. The *Pro Murena* is in volume I (MS 248A, Mynors, pp. 270–71); the marginal note referred to on p. 101 is "In codice antiquissimo nil aliud erat nisi partes iste que sunt addite", fol. 141v, referring to nine words in slightly darker script, which are all that survive from the missing passage of text. Other marginal notes include "In vetustissimo exemplari deest una carta" (fol. 263r) and "Nil deficiebat in exemplari" (fol. 57r). Vespasiano's letter to Jouffroy, see M. A. Ganz, 'A Florentine Friendship: Donato Acciaiuoli and Vespasiano da Bisticci', pp. 372–83 in *Renaissance Quarterly*, 43, 1990, p. 378, and G. M. Cagni, ed., *Vespasiano da Bisticci e il suo epistolario*, Rome, 1969 (*Temi e testi*, 15), pp. 142–3, no. 19; many of Vespasiano's letters are now on-line, *Vespasiano da Bisticci, Lettere*, from the Dipartimento di Filologia e Italianista, University of Bologna. The abbot in Arezzo in 1446 was Girolamo Aliotti, abbot of SS. Fiore e Lucilla (de la Mare, 'New Research', p. 401, and 'Classical Manuscripts', p. 182); a manuscript ordered by Aliotti in 1460 from Vespasiano for presentation to Pius II was Forum Auctions, London, 9 June 2020, lot 202. The friend in Rome in 1454 seeking exemplars was Giannozzo Manetti (Cagni, *Epistolario,* pp. 131–3, no. 11). For the Greek words added to Gray's copy of Cicero's epistles, Balliol MS 248C (p. 102 here), see de la Mare, 'New Research', p. 492, no. 15; for her "fortunate discovery" of Vespasiano's own hand in Gray's copy of Cicero's speeches, see de la Mare, 'Classical Manuscripts', p. 179 and fig. 11, reproducing a detail from Balliol MS 248A, fol. 223r. Guide letters for the illuminator survive in MS 248A, fols. 160v and 172v. On Filippo Torelli, see *ibid.*, p. 180, and D. Galizzi in M. Bollati, ed., *Dizionario biografico dei miniatori italiani*, Milan, 2004, pp. 956–8. The letters to Piero de' Medici in 1458 are Cagni, *Epistolario,* pp. 139–41, nos. 16–17. The wanton mutilation of so many manuscripts at Balliol and in other colleges for their illumination, probably in the seventeenth or eighteenth century, is also part of the history of (misguided) manuscript enthusiasm and would merit study in its own right; there might be scrapbooks somewhere with all the missing Balliol pieces, but none has yet been found. There is a paradox here. Because the manuscripts were chained up for safety in the library at Balliol until the late eighteenth century, the thief could not take the whole book. If he or she had, it would probably still survive intact, although now elsewhere. Six manuscripts from Balliol were taken to Antwerp by Catholic refugees in the sixteenth century, including three once owned by Gray (Antwerp, Museum Plantin-Moretus, MSS 8, 17 and 61). The putti blowing wind instruments (one looks more like an oboe) are in Balliol MS

248E, fol. 2r; the epigram on battle trumpets is on fol. 45r. Gray's other manuscripts mentioned on p. 104 are Sallust (given to Balliol but now London, Lambeth Palace, MS 759, another that got away), Quintilian (Balliol MS 138), Virgil (Balliol MS 140) and Pliny (Balliol MS 249). For Piero Strozzi, see A. C. de la Mare, 'Messer Piero Strozzi, A Florentine Priest and Scribe', pp. 55–68 in A. S. Osley, ed., *Calligraphy and Palaeography: Essays Presented to Alfred Fairbank on His 70th Birthday*, London, 1965, supplemented by her list of sixty-six manuscripts by him in 'New Research', pp. 530–32; Vespasiano mentions Piero in the *Vita di Benedetto Strozzi*, cited in *ibid.*, p. 431, but that biography circulated separately and is not in *Vespasiano Memoirs*. The other manuscripts copied by Antonio di Mario for Gray, with the friendly colophons, are Balliol MS 78B (John Climacus and John Chrysostom, dated 1448) and Balliol MS 154 (John Chrysostom, dated 1447, plus the final text now in MS 78B which was listed as an original component in MS 154). Vespasiano's quotation of Aquinas on Chrysostom is *Vespasiano Memoirs*, pp. 51 and 406. For the letters written by Acciaiuoli on behalf of Vespasiano, pp. 104–5, see de la Mare, 'Bisticci and Gray'; Cagni, *Epistolario,* pp. 120–21, no. 5; and Ganz, 'Florentine Friendship'. The family affairs of Vespasiano are recounted in Cagni, *Epistolario,* pp. 11–45, supplemented by de la Mare, 'New Research', esp. pp. 401–3. His consideration of the priesthood is *Vespasiano Memoirs*, p. 128. The presumed portrait is London, BL, Add. MS 9770, fol. 6r. The discussion on the priority of Moses or Homer is in Ganz, p. 376, and Cagni, *Epistolario,* pp. 124–5, part of no. 6. Vespasiano's life of Cosimo de' Medici is *Vespasiano Memoirs*, pp. 213–34. His letter to Lorenzo the Magnificent in 1476, quoted on p. 108, is Cagni, *Epistolario,* pp. 159–61, no. 31. The citation of Niccoli's wish to make his manuscripts publicly available in San Marco is *Vespasiano Memoirs*, pp. 401–2. The magisterial account of equipping San Marco with manuscripts is B. L. Ullman and P. A. Stadter, *The Public Library of Renaissance Florence: Niccolò Niccoli, Cosimo de' Medici and the Library of San Marco*, Padua, 1972, including the book-buying trips to Siena and Lucca on pp. 16–19. For Vespasiano's work for Piero and Giovanni de' Medici, see F. Ames-Lewis, *The Library and Manuscripts of Piero di Cosimo de' Medici*, London, 1984; de la Mare, 'New Research', pp. 427–8; the letters of 1458 are Cagni, *Epistolario,* pp. 139–42, nos. 16–18. A substantial but somewhat disappointing study of the creation of the Badia library (pp. 108–13 here), with the library catalogue of 1465, is A. Dressen, *The Library of the Badia Fiesolana: Intellectual History and Education under the Medici (1462–1494)*, Florence, 2013 (*Repertorio di inventari e cataloghi di biblioteche medievali dal secolo VI al 1520*, 1). Vespasiano's conversation with Cosimo, quoted at length on p. 109, is from *Vespasiano Memoirs*, pp. 221–2. His life of Tommaso Parentucelli (Pope Nicholas V) is *ibid.*, pp. 31–58, mentioning the meetings in Vespasiano's shop on p. 35; see also A. Manfredi, 'Per la biblioteca di Tommaso Parentucelli negli anni del Consilio fiorentino', pp. 649–712 in P. Viti, ed., *Firenze e il Concilio del 1439*, Florence, 1994, and C. Vasoli, 'La biblioteca progettata da un Papa: Niccolò V e il "suo canone"', *Babel*, 6, 2002, pp. 219–39. The manuscript bought "per manum Vespasiani" by Parentucelli is Vatican, cod. Vat. lat. 833, Aegidius Romanus and Albertus Magnus, formerly owned by Coluccio Salutati. The library catalogue of 1465 (pp. 111–12 here) is Florence, Biblioteca Medicea Laurenziana, MS Fiesolano 227 (Dressen, pls. 1–3). Extant books from the Badia and their sources are appendix II, 'Manuscripts identifiable from the accounts for the library of the Badia of Fiesole' in de la Mare, 'New Research', pp. 555–64, naming the scribes, and on Fra Girolamo da Matelica, *ibid.*, pp. 434, 444 and 498, no. 26. My quotation from Angelo Decembrio (p. 114 here) was taken from A. Grafton, *Commerce with the Classics: Ancient Books and Renaissance Readers*, Ann Arbor,

1997, p. 40; the letter from Germany in 1469 is from Prospero Schiaffini da Camogli, then in Krainburg (Kranj), printed in de la Mare, 'Classical Manuscripts', pp. 200–201, n. 105. Vespasiano's recollections of Nicholas V, Archbishop Vitéz, Cardinal Cesarini, Cardinal Branda and Alfonso the Magnanimous are from *Vespasiano Memoirs*, pp. 37, 189, 125, 120 and 80. The wish of Nicholas V to buy books and build houses was also expressed in the 1890s by William Morris: "if I were asked to say what is . . . the thing most longed for, I should answer a beautiful house, and if I were further asked . . . a beautiful book" (William Morris, *The Ideal Book*, ed. W. S. Peterson, Berkeley and Los Angeles, 1982, p. 1). David Rundle tells me that Poggio may also have met the Duc de Berry in Paris. Vespasiano's account of Poggio copying Quintilian is *ibid.*, p. 352. The Pliny copied in 1465 (p. 115) is Naples, Biblioteca nazionale, V.I.3 (de la Mare, 'New Research', p. 421, n. 218). Perotti's letter of 1454 is Cagni, *Epistolario*, pp. 130–31, no. 10. Tiptoft's visit to Florence is *Vespasiano Memoirs*, p. 336; Andrew Holes's shipment is *ibid.*, pp. 207–8. The letter to Jouffroy in 1461 is Cagni, *Epistolario,* pp. 142–3, no. 19, and de la Mare, 'Classical Manuscripts', pp. 189–90. Manuscripts inscribed as made for Vespasiano are listed in de la Mare, 'New Research', pp. 565–7 (with one more, 'Classical Manuscripts', p. 201). The sample inscription given on p. 116 is from Vatican, cod. Vat. lat. 1712, Cicero, front flyleaf in the hand of Gherardo del Ciriagio, bought by Jean Jouffroy. The distinction between books bought ready-made and those commissioned may be reflected in Vespasiano's account of Alessandro Sforza, who wrote from Milan 'ordering the purchase of all the books which were available, and that others should be transcribed' (*Vespasiano Memoirs*, p. 114). The manuscript in Brescia is Biblioteca Queriniana, B.VII.33, Pseudo-Phalaris; that in Valencia is Biblioteca Universitaria cod. 595 (437), Matteo Palmieri. On the possible trade with printers' bookshops, see L. Böninger, 'Da Vespasiano da Bisticci a Franz Renner e Bartolomeo Lupoto: Appunti sul commercio librario tra Venezia, la Toscana e Genova (ca. 1459–1487)', pp. 623–48 in C. Dondi, ed., *Printing (R)evolution and Society, 1450–1500: Fifty Years That Changed Europe*, Venice, 2020 (*Studi di storia*, 13). The consignment to Naples in 1457 is mentioned in de la Mare, 'New Research', p. 404, n. 63. The map of Florence with Vespasiano's house is in Paris, BnF, ms lat. 4802, fol. 132v; it was discovered by de la Mare and reproduced in her thesis and in 'A Palaeographer's Odyssey', pl. 73; see also 'New Research', p. 567, n. 22. Vespasiano's recollection of Cosimo de' Medici gardening is *Vespasiano Memoirs*, p. 224; Gray's garden is mentioned in H. Maynard Smith, *Pre-Reformation England*, II, London, 1938, p. 434. Vespasiano's dismissal of Guzmán's library as lightweight (here p. 120) is *Vespasiano Memoirs*, p. 434. His famous claim about the Montefeltro library is *ibid.*, p. 104, and often quoted elsewhere. A poem in praise of the library by Giovanni Battista Valentini in the 1490s says that it does not include transitory printed letters but works painted with a skilful hand (H. Hofmann, 'Literary Culture at the Court of Urbino during the Reign of Federico da Montefeltro', pp. 5–59 in *Humanistica Lovaniensia*, 57, 2008, p. 8). Montefeltro's printed copy of Origen, *Contra Celsum*, Rome, 1481, was lent by Bryn Mawr to the exhibition *Federico da Montefeltro and His Library* at the Morgan Library, New York, 2007, no. 11, "one of the three extant incunables bearing Federico da Montefeltro's arms". King, *Bookseller of Florence*, pp. 285–6, makes the interesting point that they might have been acquired as exemplars for making manuscripts, although they would surely not then have been illuminated for the owner with his arms. Vespasiano's account of Montefeltro's library, quoted at length here on pp. 120–21, is from *Vespasiano Memoirs*, p. 102. For the formation of the library in Urbino, see de la Mare, 'New Research', esp. pp. 448–51; A. C. de la Mare, 'Vespasiano da Bisticci e i copisti fiorentini di Federico', pp. 81–96 in G. Cerboni Baiardi, G. Chittolini and P. Floriani, eds., *Federico da Montefeltro: Lo stato, le arti, la cultura*, III, Rome, 1986; and M. Peruzzi, *Cultura, potere, imagine: La biblioteca di Federico di Montefeltro*, Urbino, 2004 (*Collana di Studi e Testi*, 20). The trilingual Psalter, presumably although not explicitly commissioned through Vespasiano, is cited in *Vespasiano Memoirs*, p. 104, and is Vatican, cod. Urb. lat. 9 (M. Beit-Arié in B. Richler, ed., *Hebrew Manuscripts in the Vatican Library*, Vatican City, 2008, p. 638; the part of a Vatican shelfmark with the abbreviation "Urb." shows a book to be from the library of Urbino bought in 1657). Montefeltro had also looted a thirteenth-century Hebrew Bible at the sack of Volterra in 1472 (cod. Urb. ebr. 1). The manuscript of Plato's *Dialogues*, mentioned on p. 121, is Vatican, cod. Urb. lat. 1314 (de la Mare, 'New Research', p. 567, no. 17, and her 'Classical Manuscripts', pp. 199–200 and fig. 26). Vespasiano's remarks on bringing library catalogues to Urbino and on Duns Scotus are from *Vespasiano Memoirs*, pp. 105 and 100. Montefeltro's incomparable Bible is cod. Vat. Urb. lat, 1, 2: see A. Garzelli, *La Bibbia di Federico da Montefeltro: Un' officina libraria fiorentina, 1476–1478*, Rome, 1977; I. F. Walther and N. Wolf, *Codices Illustres: The World's Most Famous Illuminated Manuscripts, 400 to 1600*, Cologne, 2001, pp. 374–9. Vespasiano's account of it, as quoted here (p. 124), is *Vespasiano Memoirs*, pp. 103 and 104. For Francesco di Antonio del Chierico, see M. Bollati in *Dizionario . . . miniatori italiani*, pp. 228–32, and for Ugo de Comminelli, de la Mare, 'New Research', pp. 461–2 and 505–6. The scribe's date on the first volume is 25 February '1476' (fol. 240r) in a calendar where a year ended in March and so this is 1477 as we number it now. The letters between Montefeltro and Lorenzo the Magnificent are quoted by Garzelli, *Bibbia*, p. 22. The volumes of the Bible have title-pages: these are rare in manuscripts and develop probably from the mid-1470s, when they first occur in printed books, and it may be that Montefeltro's greatest manuscript owes more to printing than he knew. My counting of printed Latin Bibles earlier than Montefeltro's manuscript (pp. 124 and 126) was based on W. A. Copinger, *Incunabula Biblica, or, the First Half Century of the Latin Bible*, London, 1892. On the first printers in Florence, see now L. Böninger, *Niccolò di Lorenzo della Magna and the Social World of Florentine Printing, ca. 1470–1493*, Cambridge, Mass., 2021, and on their competition for Vespasiano, de la Mare, 'New Research', pp. 412–14; Machiavelli's father's Livy is mentioned in C. Olschki, ed., *Bernardo Machiavelli: Libro di ricordi*, Florence, 1954, p. 10. The quotation from Landucci (p. 127) was taken from M. J. Unger, *Magnifico: The Brilliant Life and Violent Times of Lorenzo de' Medici*, London, 2008, p. 338; the source is A. de R. Jervis, transl., I. del Badia, ed., *Luca Landucci: A Florentine Diary from 1450 to 1516*, London, 1927. The manuscripts given by Vespasiano to San Marco on the closure of the shop are described in de la Mare, 'New Research', pp. 573–4. Vespasiano's invitation to Pandolfini on pp. 127–8 is from Cagni, *Epistolario*, pp. 178–80, no. 41, esp. p. 179; I am greatly indebted to Laura Nuvoloni for many things, including help with this translation. Vespasiano's reflections on the fates of the libraries of Nicholas V, Mateu Malfrit, Nuño de Guzmán, John Tiptoft and William Gray are in *Vespasiano Memoirs*, pp. 186–7, 333, 434, 337–8 and 186. On Tiptoft's death and his manuscripts, see D. Rundle, *The Renaissance Reform of the Book and Britain: The English Quattrocento*, Cambridge, 2019, chapter 5, pp. 174–227. A presentation manuscript of Vespasiano's *Vita di messer Gianozzo Manetti* is London, BL, Add. MS 9770 (with the presumed portrait of the author in old age); another with his *Vita della Alessandra di Bardo de' Bardi* emerged at Christie's, 3 December 1997, lot 227. Cardinal Mai's edition of the *Vite* from Vatican, cod. Vat. lat. 3224, is *Virorum illustrium CIII qui saeculo XV extiterunt Vitae, auctore coaevo Vespasiano Florentino*, Rome, 1839–[43] (*Spicilegium Romanum*,

I). There is a certain symmetry about Vespasiano being in the church of Santa Croce in Florence and Gray's library in the church of St Cross in Oxford (and Simon Bening of Chapter 4 was probably buried in the church of Sint-Kruis in Bruges). On the use of Vespasiano's *Vite* by Burckhardt, see H. Wieruszowski, 'Jacob Burckhardt (1818–1897) and Vespasiano da Bisticci (1422–1498)', pp. 387–405 in E. Mahoney, ed., *Philosophy and Humanism: Renaissance Essays in Honor of Paul Oskar Kristeller*, New York, 1976: although she downplays Vespasiano as Burckhardt's sole inspiration, she quotes him as saying it was.

4. THE ILLUMINATOR: SIMON BENING

Like Shakespeare, Simon Bening has left a corpus of outstanding work but very little personal documentation, and much of that is quite slight. There are no letters from him and no reported conversations in his own words. We rely on precious inclusions of the name Bening, Benig, Bieninc or Binnink in administrative archives. Despite his importance as an artist, however, Simon Bening still lacks any dedicated published monograph, except as introductions to modern facsimile editions of manuscripts he painted. Thomas Kren, James Marrow and especially Judith Testa have written extensively about individual works by Bening, as will appear below, and I am grateful to all of them for conversations over many years, perhaps not remembered as well as they should have been, as I am to Sandra Hindman, Rowan Watson, Gregory Clark, Evelien Hauwaerts, Bodo Brinkmann and the late Georges Dogaer. The most accessible introduction to Bening is probably that of Dr Kren in the exhibition catalogue T. Kren and S. McKendrick, eds., *Illuminating the Renaissance: The Triumph of Flemish Manuscript Painting in Europe*, Los Angeles, 2003, pp. 447–87, and I was glad to have the clear summary of published material in C. Hourihane, ed., *Grove Encyclopedia of Medieval Art and Architecture*, II, New York, 2012, pp. 306–9. Through the kindness of Elizabeth Morrison and, through her, the author, I was privileged to see the still unpublished doctoral thesis of J. C. Heyder, 'Simon Bening und die Kunst der Wiederholung – Zur Langlebigkeit der Motive in der Gent-Brügger Buchmalerei', 2 vols., Freie Universität Berlin, 2017, especially useful to me for its transcripts of all surviving documents mentioning Bening. I am greatly indebted to Lieve De Kesel, historian of Flemish illumination, who has constantly guided me through the deceptive pitfalls of the Flemish language, and to libraries and other places in both Ghent and Bruges. Bening's self-portrait in the Victoria and Albert Museum is inv. P 159-1910 (*Illuminating the Renaissance*, pp. 485–6, no. 161; R. Gameson in S. Panayotova, ed., *Colour: The Art & Science of Illuminated Manuscripts*, London and Turnhout, 2016, pp. 86–7, no. 18). The fact that Bening shows himself painting the Virgin and Child is to equate him with Saint Luke, who did the same. The now-destroyed Diksmuide Missal of 1530–31 was reproduced in *Exposition des Primitifs flamands: Section des manuscrits, miniatures, archives, sceaux, méreaux, monnaies et médailles. Catalogue*, Bruges (exhibition at the Hôtel Gruuthuuse), 1902, no. 59, and from there in B. Brinkmann and E. König, *Das Blumen-Stundenbuch, Clm 23637, Bayerische Staatsbibliothek München: Kommentarband*, Luzern, 1991, pp. 22–7. The genealogy of the Portuguese royal family (pp. 133–5 and 316–18 here) is London, BL, Add. MS 12531 (A. de Aguiar, *A Genealogia Iluminada do Infante Dom Fernando, por António de Holanda e Simão Bening*, Lisbon, 1962, and *Illuminating the Renaissance*, pp. 460–63, no. 147, and the picture on the catalogue's front cover). Damião de Góis appears in M. Pye, *Antwerp: The Glory Years*, London, 2021, pp. 95–7. The manuscript by Holanda for the counts of Pereira was Sotheby's, 5 December

1989, lot 103 (now Lisbon, Arquivo Nacional da Torre do Tombo, PT/TT/GMS/106). The quotation about Bening from Francesco de Holanda is "e que melhor lavrou as árvores e os longes" (J. de Vasconcellos, ed., *Francisco de Holanda: De pintura antigua*, 2nd edn, Porto, 1930, p. 286). The five dated manuscripts by Bening listed on p. 136 are: (a) prayerbook of 1511 (privately owned; Sotheby's, 21 June 1988, lot 107, written by me, and Christie's, Arcana sale, 6 July 2011, lot 26; *Illuminating the Renaissance*, pp. 448–9, no. 139); (b) miniatures of 1521 (New York, Brooklyn Museum, 11.502–5: J. Marrow, 'Simon Bening in 1521: A Group of Dated Miniatures', pp. 537–59 in F. Vanwijngaerden *et al.*, eds., *Liber Amicorum Herman Liebaers*, Brussels, 1984); (c) contributions to the Holford Hours, including a date 1526 (Lisbon, Museu Calouste Gulbenkian, inv. LA210: L. De Kesel (there misprinted de Kessel) in F. Avril and A. Dillon Bussi, eds., *European Illuminated Manuscripts in the Calouste Gulbenkian Collection*, Lisbon, 2020, pp. 264–75; (d) Book of Hours of 1531 (New York, Morgan Library, M 451: *Illuminating the Renaissance*, pp. 464–5, no. 148); and (e) Rosarium of 1545 (privately owned; E. König, *Leuchtendes Mittelalters*, III, Antiquariat Heribert Tenschert cat. XXVII, Rotthalmünster, 1991, pp. 530–45, no. 34, and Sotheby's, 6 July 2000, lot 57). The question of collaboration within single pictures (hinted at here) is complicated and may be more common than we think. The figures in the Diksmuide Crucifixion look to me hardly good enough for Bening but the landscape does. The Prayerbook of Joanna de Ghistelles is BL, Egerton MS 2125 (*Illuminating the Renaissance*, p. 452, no. 141). Ludwig Bloc's panel stamp includes an oblong scene of dancing rustics playing musical instruments which so resembles the dancing shepherds painted by Bening for the Nativity (fol. 180v) that it is possible that Bening designed his pictorial stamps for him, an artistic crossover not unimaginable among colleagues. Bloc's spelling "XPRISTI" is technically incorrect, since the 'P' is a Greek 'r'. The same stamp occurs on the binding of Bening's Benedictional of Robert de Clercq (Cambridge University Library, Nn.4.1; P. Binski and P. Zutshi, *Western Illuminated Manuscripts: A Catalogue of the Collection in Cambridge University Library*, Cambridge, 2011, pp. 362–3, no. 388). For Weale (1832–1917), see H. P. Mitchell, 'The Late Mr W. H. James Weale', *The Burlington Magazine*, 30, 1917, pp. 241–3; M. W. Brockwell, 'W. H. James Weale, the Pioneer', *The Library*, 5 ser., 6, 1951, pp. 200–211; and L. van Biervliet, *Leven en werk van W. H. James Weale, een Engels kunsthistoricus in Vlaanderen in de 19de eeuw*, Brussels, 1991. I am grateful to Ludo Vandamme of the Openbare Bibliotheek, the city library, for advice on the different collections in Bruges with sources for the life of Bening. Weale's notebooks in the Openbare Bibliotheek are ms 599, itself made up of 230 items. The document mentioning Agnes Zegaerts is in ms 599:6, p. 125; in the same volume Weale transcribes eighteen archival references to the binder Ludwig Bloc. The unpublished document on Bening in April 1551 is ms 599:12, p. 55. These many notebooks were the sources for W. H. J. Weale, 'Les enlumineurs de Bruges', *Le Beffroi*, 2, 1864–5, pp. 298–319 (esp. pp. 306–19 on Bening), and 'Documents inédits sur les enlumineurs de Bruges', *Le Beffroi*, 4, 1872–3, pp. 111–19 (esp. pp. 118–19 on the Diksmuide Missal) and 238–337. His first publication of the Prayerbook of Joanna de Ghistelles is 'Manuscrit enluminé de l'abbaye de Messines, *c.* 1530', *ibid.*, pp. 195–7. Weale's account of the Portuguese genealogy is a review of the reproductions by L. J. K. Kämmerer and H. G. Ströhl, *Ahnenreihen aus dem Stammbaum des portugiesischen Königshauses*, Stuttgart, 1903, in *The Burlington Magazine*, 3, 1903, pp. 321–4; his specialized article on Bening is 'Simon Binnink, Miniaturist', *The Burlington Magazine*, 8, 1905–6, pp. 355–7. In the latter, p. 355, Weale says that Bening was born in Ghent, whereas the article in *Le Beffroi*, 2, p. 307, had suggested that he was a native of Antwerp. The first Prayerbook of Maximilian, *c.*1486, which gives the name to the artist who was very probably Alexander Bening, father of Simon (pp. 138–9 here), is Vienna, Österreichische Nationalbibliothek, Cod. 1907. The manuscript (and consequently its illuminator) is sometimes referred to as the 'older Prayerbook of Maximilian': it is the same thing. The artist had a part in the Spinola Hours in the J. Paul Getty Museum, MS Ludwig IX.18, and so he appears in my *Meetings with Remarkable Manuscripts*, esp. p. 544. For background on late-medieval Bruges, I looked at G. D. Painter, *William Caxton: A Quincentenary Biography of England's First Printer*, London, 1976, pp. 22–4; A. Brown, *Civic Ceremony and Religion in Medieval Bruges, c. 1300–1520*, Cambridge, 2011; and A. Brown and J. Dumolyn, eds., *Medieval Bruges, c. 850–1550*, Cambridge, 2018. The term 'Ghent–Bruges' illumination was invented by Paul Durrieu (1855–1925). The trading connections between Bruges and England go back to at least the thirteenth century: K. Carlvant, *Manuscript Painting in Thirteenth-Century Flanders: Bruges, Ghent and the Circle of the Counts*, London and Turnhout, 2012, esp. pp. 10–12. The Book of Hours for English use made in Bruges in 1409 (mentioned on p. 141) is Durham University Library, Ushaw College MS 10 (R. Gameson, 'Exporting Private Prayer', pp. 58–61 in J. E. Kelly, ed., *Treasures of Ushaw College, Durham's Hidden Gem*, London and Durham, 2015); the manuscript is dated as having been completed on 21 January '1408' (fol. 132v) but the year ended on 25 March and so this is what we would now call 1409. The Hennessy Hours is Brussels, Bibliothèque royale de Belgique, ms II.158 (*Illuminating the Renaissance*, pp. 467–70, no. 150). There is a miniature by Bening in the Museum voor Schone Kunsten in Ghent, 1924-D, bought in 1922; Lieve De Kesel took me to see it. Other manuscripts in Belgium at one time attributed to Bening, probably both wrongly, are an Armorial of the Golden Fleece (Brussels, Bibliothèque royale, ms IV.84, bought from H. P. Kraus, cat. 88, 1958, no. 39) and the notable Breviary in the Museum Mayer van den Bergh in Antwerp, inv. 946, bought at Christie's in London in 1898. My visit to the Stadsarchief in Bruges was facilitated by Jan D'hondt. The medieval crane, demonstrated by the wooden model mentioned on p. 143, was a real piece of machinery in Bruges, and is illustrated in the Grimani Breviary of *c.*1515 in the construction of the Tower of Babel (Venice, Biblioteca Nazionale Marciana, ms lat. I 99, fol. 206r). The two manuscripts first described here in the Stadsarchief are both part of the records of the painters' guild of Saint Luke, Oud Archief 314 (A. Vandewalle, *Beknopte Inventaris van het Stadsarchief van Brugge*, I, *Oud Archief*, Bruges, 1979, p. 129). The first is the "Memorielijst" of the guild, called an *obituarium* by Vandewalle. It is also described in C. Vanden Haute, *La Corporation des Peintres de Bruges, Registres d'admission, A, 1453–1587, B, 1618–1781, Obituaire, XV*e *s.–1801*, Bruges and Courtrai, 1913, pp. 194–210, dating the manuscript to 1487–*c.*1490. The names I noted are Petrus Christus (p. 15), Jan le Tavernier (p. 16) and Gerard David (p. 27). The second volume is the register of admissions to the painters' guild, 1445–1801. The introduction to the registration of illuminators in 1501 begins on fol. 112v and the twelve names with their distinctive marks are on fol. 113r. The record is actually dated 21 March '1500', but as the year then ended on 25 March, this is what we call 1501. The second page is reproduced in Vanden Haute, pl. I, opp. p. 88, and the text is printed and translated into French by Weale, *Belfroi*, 2, pp. 298–300, with copies of the marks beside each of his subsequent accounts of the individual illuminators. We do not know where an artist might be expected to place a registered mark. Many routine miniatures from Bruges were painted on single leaves for subsequent binding into books, and the marks (if actually used at all) might have been on the stubs or extreme edges or even on the outside of packets of miniatures. The occurrence of tiny printed stamps in margins beside miniatures used in some Bruges manuscripts in the second quarter of the fifteenth century, as described here on p. 146, was first revealed by J. D. Farquhar, 'Identity in an Anonymous Age: Bruges Manuscript Illuminators and Their Signs', *Viator*, 11, 1980, pp. 371–84, one of the most revelatory and transformative publications on manuscript production ever made (another was Destrez, *La Pecia*, in 1935); see now S. van Bergen, 'The Use of Stamps in Bruges Book Production', pp. 323–37 in S. Hindman and J . H. Marrow, eds., *Books of Hours Reconsidered*, London and Turnhout, 2013. Bening's Prayerbook of Albrecht of Brandenburg is Los Angeles, J. Paul Getty Museum, MS Ludwig IX.19 (J. M. Plotzek, *Die Handschriften der Sammlung Ludwig*, II, Cologne, 1982, pp. 286–313; the possible 'SB' monogram is on fol. 336r, fig. 542). The final manuscript I saw in the town archive in Bruges, described on pp. 146–7 here, was the ledger for the book trade confraternity of Saint John the Evangelist, Oud Archief 384, item 76. It is one of two volumes, the first (this one) for 1454–1523, and the second (which we will come to in a moment) for 1524–55, now in the state archive: see A. Schouteet, 'Inventaris van het archief van het voormaligegild van de librariers en van de vereniging van schoolmeesters te Brugge', pp. 228–69 in *Handelingen van het Genootschap voor Geschiedenis 'Société d'Emulation' te Brugge*, 100, 1963, nos. 76 (pp. 252–5) and 77 (pp. 255–7). Names leap out of the pages. These are the principal sources from which Weale compiled most of his biographical data. Entries mentioning the Bening family are very usefully transcribed from both volumes, not always precisely as I read them (although with no variants affecting the sense), in Heyder, 'Simon Bening', pp. 242–52. There is Alexander Bening paying his dues in volume 1, fols. 123v, 126r and so on, through to fol. 144r. Simon first appears on fol. 156v and was absent in 1508 (fol. 160v). The Imhof Prayerbook made by him in Antwerp in 1511, mentioned here, has already been referred to above (Sotheby's, 21 June 1988, lot 107, etc.). Any erroneous doubt that Antwerp was then some provincial backwater is redressed by Pye, *Antwerp*, as above. Simon is back in the Bruges ledger, called "de verlichter", the illuminator, for the first time in 1512 (fol. 170v). His signature as dean of the confraternity in 1524 is on fol. 199r, "symon bynninnk". Volume II of the ledger is in the state archives, as distinct from those of the city, but it continues without interruption from 1524 onwards (C. Vanden Haute, *Inventaire sommaire des archives des corporations de la ville de Bruges, conservés aux Archives de l'État*, Brussels, 1909, p. 14, no. 207). It is even richer in its references to Bening and others of his family and circle. The name 'Master of the Garish Features' (as on p. 149 here), who collaborated with Bening in the Brandenburg Hours and other manuscripts, was named by A. M. W. As-Vijvers, *Re-Making the Margin: The Master of the David Scenes and Flemish Manuscript Painting around 1500*, Turnhout, 2013, pp. 306–15; there is a second collaborator she calls 'Simon Bening's Principal Associate'. The enduring Catholicism of Bruges, appreciated by Weale over three centuries later, seems to have been entrenched even before the Reformation: Bruges never had a house of the brothers of the Common Life, a widespread precursor to reform in many parts of the Netherlands. The cutting by Bening showing the people lining up outside a church, described here on p. 150, is J. Paul Getty Museum, MS 50 (*Illuminating the Renaissance*, p. 485, no. 160, two miniatures, of which the other is illustrated there; both are reproduced in T. Kren, *Illuminated Manuscripts from Belgium and the Netherlands in the J. Paul Getty Museum*, Los Angeles, 2010, p. 121); a very similar church from exactly the same perspective is in the February miniature of Bening's 'Golf' Book of Hours, BL, Add. MS 24098, fol. 18v. The pictures by Bening of a funeral procession and service in a Book of Hours in the Victoria and Albert Museum is MSL/1981/39, fols. 21v–22r (R. Watson, *Victoria and Albert Museum: Western Illuminated Manuscripts*, II, London, 2011, pp. 734–41, no. 139). The cost of the funeral of Simon's father is on fol. 185v of the first volume of the ledger, the fourth entry in the first column; the funeral Masses for Simon's successive wives are in the second volume, fols. 73v ("de husvrauwe van mester syemoen benyn") and 121v ("m. symoen wyf"). Documents for the fraternity's altarpiece commission by Vrelant were published by Weale, recording payment to 'Master Hans', universally accepted as Hans Memling, Vrelant's near neighbour in the Sint-Jorisstraat in Bruges. No suggested identifications with extant altarpieces are credible (J. D. Farquhar, 'The Vrelant Enigma: Is the Style the Man?', pp. 100–108 in *Quaerendo*, 4, 1974, pp. 102–3; B. Bousmanne, *'Item a Guillaume Wyelant aussi enlumineur', Willem Vrelant: Un aspect de l'enluminure dans les Pays-Bas méridionaux sous le mécenat des ducs de Bourgogne, Philippe le Bon et Charles le Téměraire*, Turnhout, 1997, pp. 52–3). The detail of the new Missal for the confraternity's use in Eekhout Abbey in 1522, printed by Weale, *Beffroi*, 2, p. 311, is from the first volume of the ledger, fol. 198r; a later reader, not me, had added the word "Nota" in the margin beside this entry. References to meetings in the "*colve*" occur in volume 1, fol. 186v, 198r and doubtless elsewhere. I owe to Lieve De Kesel the reference to the sale of no. 9 Hoogstraat in 1618 as being "nu één met het volgende huis De Colve", as recorded on the website of Erfgoed Brugge (their ref. JAN/0243). The 'Golf Book', an album of leaves from a Book of Hours by Simon Bening, is B.L., Add. MS 24098; the putative golf players are on fol. 27r. For the manuscript, see *Illuminating the Renaissance*, pp. 477–8, no. 155, and now C. Miranda García-Tejedor, *Golf Book*, Barcelona, 2021, kindly sent to me by Marina Martin and the publisher Manuel Moleiro; it discusses the golf scene on pp. 131 and 134. The word '*colve*' can also mean a mallet or stick with which a ball could be hit, probably a more likely derivation of the word. Bening's Da Costa Hours is New York, Morgan Library, M 399 (*Illuminating the Renaissance*, pp. 450–51, no. 140, and also the facsimile, *Das Costa-Stundenbuch*, with commentary volume by Gregory T. Clark, Graz, 2010); the winter scene of serving dinner is on fol. 2v. The dinner of 1518 in the Colve is recorded on fol. 184v of the account book; Bening's signature in 1524 is on fol. 199r. The presence of the *Très Riches Heures* in Flanders (p. 156 here) is discussed in my *Meetings with Remarkable Manuscripts*, pp. 553 and 558–60. Some of its miniatures were directly copied into the Grimani Breviary, to which Bening and probably his father contributed. The influence of its calendar first on Horenbout and then on Bening is discussed by Thomas Kren in his section 'Calendar Cycles by Simon Bening', pp. 235–62 of the commentary volume of the facsimile, *Simon Bening: Flämischer Kalendar – Flemish calendar – Calendrier flamand*, Luzern, 1988, which reproduces Munich, Staatsbibliothek, clm. 23638. Leaves from the fragmentary Rosary Psalter are in the Boston Public Library, MS pb Med. 35 (L. Ransom in J. F. Hamburger, W. Stoneman, *et al.*, eds., *Beyond Words: Illuminated Manuscripts in Boston Collections*, Boston, 2016, pp. 151–2, no. 117), Cambridge, Fitzwilliam Museum, MS 257a–b (*Illuminating the Renaissance*, pp. 455–6, no. 144; N. Morgan and S. Panayotova, eds., *A Catalogue of Western Book Illumination in the Fitzwilliam Museum and the Cambridge Colleges*, I, ii, London and Turnhout, 2009, p. 239, no. 446), and elsewhere. The two-volume Hours of Albrecht of Brandenburg, in private hands, was Sotheby's, 21 June 1988, lot 65, and 19 June 2001, lot 36, both catalogued by me; for its detached miniatures, see esp. S. Hindman in *The Robert Lehman Collection*, IV, *Illuminations*, New York and Princeton, 1997, pp. 99–112, no. 13, and also A. M. W. As-Vijvers in A. M. W. As-Vijvers and A. S. Korteweg, eds., *Splendour of the Burgundian Netherlands*, Utrecht, Zwolle and

The Hague, 2018, pp. 282–3, no. 76. The Brandenburg Prayerbook has already been cited (Getty, MS Ludwig IX.19); the miniatures mentioned on p. 156 are on fols. 102v, 107v, 113v, 123v, 311v and 78r. The classic statement of the co-existence of manuscripts and early printing is C. Bühler, *The Fifteenth-Century Book*, Philadelphia, 1960. For manuscripts copied from printed texts for Mercatellis, see esp. A. Derolez, *The Library of Raphael de Marcatellis*, Ghent, 1979, and Derolez, 'Early Humanism in Flanders', pp. 37–57 in R. de Smet, ed., *Les humanistes et leur bibliothèque*, Louvain, 2002. For the printed exemplars of the Da Costa Hours and the Brandenburg Prayerbook (p. 157 here), see Clark, *Costa-Stundenbuch*, pp. 20–21 (it was a discovery first made by Belle Greene) and Plotzek, *Sammlung Ludwig*, II, pp. 291–2. There is a reflexion of the sense that an archaic manuscript format is more dignified for prayer in the figure of Saint John the Baptist praising God in the Van Eycks' Ghent Altarpiece: the manuscript he holds is unambiguously late twelfth-century, then 250 years old. The accolade by Vasari is in G. Milanese, ed., *Le vite de' più eccellenti pittori, scultori ed architettori scritte da Giorgio Vasari*, VII, Florence, 1881, p. 587, or in translation, G. Vasari, *The Lives of the Painters, Sculptors and Architects*, London, IV, 1927, p. 254. The Book of Hours of Isabella of Portugal, cited here on p. 158, is San Marino, Huntington Library, HM 1162 (*Illuminating the Renaissance*, pp. 470–71, no. 151); it has fifteen miniatures by Bening from the life of Virgin carefully pasted in and surrounded by borders by a local Spanish artist. The Beatty Rosarium is Dublin, Chester Beatty Library, MS W. 99 (J. A. Testa, *The Beatty Rosarium: A Manuscript with Paintings by Simon Bening*, Dornspijk, 1986; *Illuminating the Renaissance*, pp. 478–80, no. 156). The folding boards of miniatures in Baltimore, sometimes called the Stein Quadriptych, are Walters Art Museum, W 442 (*Illuminating the Renaissance*, pp. 458–60, no. 146). The triptych visible in the Prayerbook of Joanna de Ghistelles is BL, Egerton MS 2125, fol. 142v. The Last Supper, cited here on p. 160, was Christie's, Collection of Nico and Nanni Israel, 11 December 2019, lot 3; the Virgin and Child at Sotheby's, for which I seriously considered selling everything I own, was 1 December 2020, lot 74, £1,467,000 inclusive. Free-standing miniatures attributed to Bening and probably always mounted as separate devotional panels include a privately owned triptych (*Illuminating the Renaissance*, pp. 480–81, no. 157) and Victoria and Albert Museum, E. 635-1998 (*ibid.*, pp. 481–2, no. 158). A bigger question is asked in M. W. Ainsworth, 'Was Simon Bening a Panel Painter?', pp. 1–25 in B. Cardon, ed., *'Als Ich Can', Liber Amicorum in Memory of Professor Dr. Maurits Smeyers*, Louvain, 2002. Portrait miniatures attributed to Bening include Paris, Musée du Louvre, RF. 3.925 (*Illuminating the Renaissance*, pp. 472–3, no. 153; T. Kren in F. Avril, N. Reynaud and D. Cordellier, eds., *Les Enluminures du Louvre, Moyen Âge et Renaissance*, Paris, 2011, pp. 328–9, no. 168). Calendar scenes which were possibly never part of books include the set divided between London, BL, Add. MS 18855, fols. 108–9, and Victoria and Albert Museum, Salting MSS 2538 and 2600 (E. 4575-1910 and 4576-1910; *Illuminating the Renaissance*, pp. 483–4, no. 159). The Rosarium of 1545 is mentioned above (Sotheby's, 6 July 2000, lot 57, etc.). The signatures of Bening in 1535 and 1545 in the ledger in the Rijksarchief, cited on p. 160, are on fols. 49v and 83r; the entry naming scribes, illuminators and printers is on fol. 91v. Brody Neuenschwander can be found on Wikipedia and elsewhere, including J. Middendorp *et al.*, *Textasy: The Work of Brody Neuenschwander*, Ghent, 2006 (Brody is from Texas); as well as being a full-time scribe and illuminator, he also has a PhD from the Courtauld in art history. I owe the idea of Bening's dog entirely to Elizabeth Morrison, who sent me her on-line article, 'An Artist's Pet Dog Photobombs the Middle Ages', *The Iris: Behind the Scenes at the Getty*, 3 August

2016. The examples I give on pp. 161–2 on the dog in Bening miniatures, all from her, are Brandenburg Prayerbook, Getty, MS Ludwig IX.19, fol. 147v; Hennessy Hours, Brussels, BR, ms II. 158, fol. 3v; Book of the Deeds of Jacques de Lalaing, Getty, MS 114, fol. 10r; and Golf Hours, BL, Add. MS 24098, fol. 27v. The most recent account of the dispersed Enriquez de Ribera Prayerbook is a sale catalogue for three new miniatures, including the one I borrowed for pigment analysis, S. Hindman with L. Light and M. J. Westerby, *Simon Bening and the Enríques de Ribera Prayerbook*, Paris, New York and Chicago, 2021, citing earlier literature, including Sandra Hindman's initial catalogue for Hazlitt, Gooden and Fox, in association with Bruce Ferrini and Sam Fogg, *Four Miniatures by Simon Bening*, London, 1989, and J. A. Testa, 'Fragments of a Spanish Prayerbook with Miniatures by Simon Bening', *Oud Holland*, 105, 1991, pp. 89–115 (and 'Addendum', *ibid.*, 106, 1992, p. 32). Other miniatures from the manuscript include Philadelphia Free Library, Lewis M6:1–2; Cleveland Museum of Art, 2002.52; Morgan Library, M. 1151; St Louis Museum of Art, 66.1952; and the Louvre, Cabinet des dessins, RFML, AG 2020.5.1–2. The leaf I borrowed has four compartments showing Joseph of Arimathea making arrangements for taking down Christ's body from the Cross (Hindman, Light and Westerby, pp. 50–55 and p. 79, no. 8). I must emphasize again my gratitude to Sandra Hindman and Keegan Goepfert for facilitating the loan and to Andrew Beeby and Richard Gameson, with the staff of the conservation department in the Bodleian Library, for timely analysis of the pigments. There is now a further study of Bening's pigments (with consistent results) by S. Panayotova, P. Ricciardi and N. Turner in S. Panayotova, ed., *The Art & Science of Illuminated Manuscripts: A Handbook*, London and Turnhout, 2020, pp. 454–61, no. 54. On Bening's technique, see L. M. J. Delaissé, J. Marrow and J. de Wit, *The James A. de Rothschild Collection at Waddeson Manor: Illuminated Manuscripts*, Fribourg, 1977, p. 577, and N. K. Turner, 'The Suggestive Brush: Painting Techniques in Flemish Manuscripts from the Collections of the J. Paul Getty Museum and the Huntington Library', pp. 57–74 in E. Morrison and T. Kren, eds., *Flemish Manuscript Painting in Context: Recent Research*, Los Angeles, 2006, esp. pp. 68–71. The references to the death and funeral of Bening's wife are in the second volume of the register, fols. 117v and 121v. For Levina (pp. 167–8), Simon Bening's eldest daughter, see S. Bergmans, 'The Miniatures of Levina Teerling', *The Burlington Magazine*, 64, 1934, pp. 232–6, and the exhibition catalogue, R. Strong, *Artists of the Tudor Court: The Portrait Miniature Rediscovered, 1520–1620*, London, 1983, pp. 52–7. There are puzzles about some of the late miniatures attributed to Simon Bening, such as the two Calendar scenes in the Getty, MS 50. The overall style is certainly Simon's with the fine winter landscapes, but the figures of the families lining up for church are decidedly inferior. I have wondered whether this might be the work of Levina learning at her father's desk, before her marriage in 1545. Vasari's reference to Levina (p. 168 here) is on the same page as that for Simon Bening, as above. Giucciardini's sentence about Simon Bening is in *Descrittione di M. Lodovico Guicciardini Patricio Fiorentino: Di tutti i Paesi Bassi, Altrimenti detti Germania Inferiore*, Antwerp, 1567, p. 98, also mentioning Levina on p. 100. The suggestion about the Bening pattern sheets, Goltzius and Bruegel is from T.-H. Borchert, 'Pieter Bruegel the Elder and Flemish Book Illumination', pp. 96–109 in A. Hoppe-Harnoncourt *et al.*, eds., *Bruegel: The Hand of the Master. Essays in Context*, Vienna, 2018 (a reference I owe to Sandra Hindman). Goltzius's wife's sister was Pieter Bruegel's mother-in-law. The twin of Bening's self-portrait in the Metropolitan Museum is 1975.1.2487, admirably discussed in Hindman, *Lehman Collection*, pp. 112–19, no. 14. It is conceivable that the version in New York went to Bening's daughter Alexandrine (for whom her grandfather's name of Alexander would be relevant), a dealer in art: a generation later it can be recognized propped up among other collectible artworks in the painting by Frans Francken the younger, *Een Kunstkamer*, 1619, now not far away in the Koninklijk Museum voor Schone Kunsten in Antwerp (Inv. 816; Hindman, Lehman, p. 114, fig. 14. 2); and so possibly then the London version was given to Levina, who died in England, where it was first found in the nineteenth century.

5. THE ANTIQUARY: SIR ROBERT COTTON

Knowledge of the library of Sir Robert Cotton owes an enormous amount to the long obsession – and I use the word as a compliment – of Colin Tite (1933–2017), a relentless enthusiast with just enough money to indulge himself in marvellous research, a "tall thin chap with close-cut hair, wearing a T-shirt, jeans and boots, and with a tattoo on his upper arm" (J. Carley in *The Book Collector*, 66, 2017, p. 636). His principal publications are C. G. C. Tite, ed., *Catalogue of the Manuscripts in the Cottonian Library, 1696 (Catalogus librorum manuscriptorum bibliothecae Cottoniae), Thomas Smith, Reprinted from Sir Robert Harley's copy, annotated by Humfrey Wanley, together with documents relating to the fire of 1731*, Cambridge, 1984; Tite, *The Manuscript Library of Sir Robert Cotton*, London, 1994 (The Panizzi Lectures, 1993); and Tite, *The Early Records of Sir Robert Cotton's Library: Formation, Cataloguing, Use*, London, 2003. Articles by Tite are cited below, including the two in the very useful C. J. Wright, ed., *Sir Robert Cotton as a Collector: Essays on an Early Stuart Courtier and His Legacy*, London, 1997. I have also used or depended on H. Mirrlees, *A Fly in Amber, being an Extravagant Biography of the Romantic Antiquary Sir Robert Bruce Cotton*, London, 1962; K. Sharpe, *Sir Robert Cotton 1586–1631: History and Politics in Early Modern England*, Oxford, 1979; G. Parry, *The Trophies of Time: English Antiquarians of the Seventeenth Century*, Oxford, 1995, esp. pp. 70–94; and the entry on Cotton by Stuart Handley in the online *Oxford Dictionary of National Biography*. Many Cotton manuscripts are in C. Breay and J. Story, eds., *Anglo-Saxon Kingdoms: Art, Word, War*, London, 2018, and I benefited from that exhibition while writing the chapter. I am indebted to Elizabeth Hallam-Smith, former librarian of the House of Lords, who read this chapter in an early draft and made valuable suggestions. It was she, for example, who told me that the library room had been the chapel of Saint Laurence, into which Henry III could look through a window from his great bed in the adjoining Painted Chamber: P. Binski, *The Painted Chamber at Westminster*, London, 1986 (*Society of Antiquaries of London, Occasional Paper*, n.s., IX), p. 13. The layout of the room in Cotton's time, pp. 171–2 here, is from the description and envisioned drawings in Tite, *Manuscript Library*, esp. pp. 89–99. The manuscripts cited here from the Nero cupboard are BL Cotton MSS Nero A. VII (letters of Anselm) and A. I (laws of Alfred), A. IV (Bestiary), A. X (*Pearl* and *Gawain*), A. XIV (*Ancrene Riwle*), A. XII (Beaulieu cartulary), A. XVI (Ely chronicle), B.I–XI (state papers), C. IV (Winchester Psalter), C. X (Edward VI's diary), D. I (Matthew Paris), D. IV (Lindisfarne Gospels), E. IV (cosmography), E. VII (Walsingham cartulary) and E. II (*Grandes Chroniques*). The Cotton Genesis is Otho B. VI; the five Anglo-Saxon Chronicles are Tiberius A. VI, Tiberius B. I, Tiberius B. IV, Domitian A. VIII, and (destroyed in 1731) Otho B. XI; Asser's life of Alfred and the *Battle of Maldon* were in Otho A. XII, destroyed in 1731 (H. L. Rogers, '*The Battle of Maldon*: David Casley's Transcript', *Notes and Queries*, n. s., 32, 1985, pp. 147–55); the Gospels of Æthelstan, or 'Coronation Gospels', are Tiberius A. II; the copies of Magna Carta are Augustus II. 106 and Cotton Charter XIII. 31A; and *Beowulf* is Vitellius A. XV. The Utrecht Psalter was formerly Claudius C. VII and is now Utrecht, Universiteitsbibliotheek, MS 32 (see, especially, K. van der Horst, W. Noel and W. C. M. Wüstefeld, eds., *The Utrecht Psalter in Medieval Art: Picturing the Psalms of David*, 't Goy, 1996, and *Anglo-Saxon Kingdoms*, pp. 342–4, no. 137). Other escapees from the Cotton collection are described in C. G. C. Tite, '"Lost or Stolen or Strayed", A Survey of Manuscripts formerly in the Cotton Library', *British Library Journal,* 18, 1992, pp. 107–47, reprinted in *Cotton as Collector*, pp. 262–306, and Tite, 'Sir Robert Cotton, Sir Thomas Tempest and an Anglo-Saxon Gospel Book: A Cottonian Paper in the Harleian Library', pp. 429–39 in J. P. Carley and C. G. C. Tite, eds., *Books and Collectors, 1200–1700: Essays Presented to Andrew Watson*, London, 1997. The poem cited here on p. 175, "See what a glorious Trophy . . ." is from T. Wintour, ed., *Poems on Several Occasions, by the late Reverend Thomas Fitzgerald*, Oxford, 1781, p. 71, 'Upon the burning of the Cottonian Manuscripts at Ashburnham House, MDCCXXXI'. Sir Christopher Wren was unimpressed by the Cotton collection in 1703, considering that it needed weeding of "much uselesse trash" (E. Miller, *That Noble Cabinet: A History of the British Museum*, London, 1973, p. 32). In addition to the general sources cited above, my account of the library between 1702 and 1731 draws on S. Keynes, 'Reconstruction of a Burnt Cottonian Manuscript: The Case of Cotton Ms Otho A. I', *British Library Journal*, 22, 1996, pp. 113–60. On the name 'Ashburnham', Koert van der Horst wryly remarks, "*nomen est omen*" (Van der Horst *et al*., eds., *Utrecht Psalter*, p. 34). My debt to Elizabeth Wells is acknowledged in the text. She told me of the blog by Benedict Randall Shaw and Iskander Mathews for the Westminster School Archive, on the probably exaggerated heroism of Dr Bentley, and that Professor Matthew Fisher of UCLA has also been researching the Cotton fire. There is a magisterial article by E. Smith, 'Westminster School Buildings, 1630–1730', pp. 372–415 in W. Rodwell and T. Tatton-Brown, eds., *Westminster: The Art, Architecture and Archaeology of the Royal Abbey and Palace*, Leeds, 2015 (British Archaeological Association, Conference Transactions, 39, i). Another account of visiting the site is now in M. Wellesley, *Hidden Hands: The Lives of Manuscripts and Their Makers*, London, 2021 pp. 60–67. On the remedial work following the fire, see especially A. Prescott, '"Their Present Miserable State of Cremation": The Restoration of the Cotton Library', pp. 391–454 in Wright, ed., *Cotton as a Collector*, a very fine article. The question of what happened to the busts of the emperors, if ever at Ashburnham House at all, seems to be unresolved, and it is probably only coincidence that a similar set now presides between the bookcases in the Münzkabinett at Schloss Friedenstein in Gotha, built for Friedrich II (1676–1736), duke of Saxe-Gotha-Altenburg, whose daughter married Frederick, Prince of Wales, in 1736. The ruined Magna Carta is Cotton Charter XIII 31A, and the charred relics of the bull of 1521 are Vitellius B. IV/1. It may be that much damage to the Magna Carta was caused more by misguided restoration rather than by the fire itself, since a still-legible engraving was made in 1733 (C. Breay and J. Harrison, eds., *Magna Carta: Law, Liberty, Legacy*, London, 2015, pp. 216–17). The dreadful contrast between the two parts of the 'London–Cambridge' Gospels, MS Otho C. V and Corpus Christi College MS 197b, are graphically apparent in *Anglo-Saxon Kingdoms*, pp. 114–15, nos. 27–8. The scraps from Æthelstan's Gospel Book are Otho B. IX. Not everyone considered manuscripts were worth saving at all (see, for example, C. B. Lake, *Artifacts: How We Think and Write about Found Objects*, Baltimore, 2020, pp. 111–18). For the foundation of the British Museum and its library I returned, as so often, to that most perfect of books, A. Hobson, *Great Libraries*, London, 1970, pp. 242–7, from which I learned of the open fireplaces in the original reading room. Even in Sir Robert Smirke's British Museum there were still coal fires in the manuscript curators' offices until within living memory (see the obituary of Michael Borrie by Ann Payne and Christopher Wright in *The Book Collector*, 64, 2015, p. 640). In addition to those given earlier, pressmarks of manuscripts cited on p. 182 are Vitellius A. VI (Gildas), Otho C. I/1 (Gospels from Malmesbury), Otho A. VI (Boethius), and Vitellius C. III (herbal). For the transcripts made from the charred *Beowulf* manuscript in the 1780s and later by the Icelandic–Danish scholar Grímur Jónsson Thorkelin (1752–1829), see K. S. Kiernan, *Beowulf and the Beowulf Manuscript*, New Brunswick, 1981, and Kiernan, *The Thorkelin Transcripts of Beowulf*, Copenhagen, 1986. The *Pastoral Care* largely destroyed in 1865 was Tiberius B. XI. The famous portrait of Cotton in 1626 with his hand on the Genesis, often engraved and reproduced, is by Cornelius Johnson and belongs to Lord Clinton. On my most recent visit to the manuscripts reading-room, Hillary Mantel had disappeared from the wall; I hope she returns. The principal monograph on the Cotton Genesis is K. Weitzmann and H. L. Kessler, *The Cotton Genesis: British Library Codex Cotton Otho B. VI*, Princeton, 1986, with further observations in M. Giannoulis, 'The Book of Genesis', chapter 2, pp. 197–206, in V. Tsamakda, ed., *A Companion to Byzantine Illustrated Manuscripts*, Leiden and Boston, 2017, esp. pp. 198–203, and several articles by John Lowden, including 'Concerning the Cotton Genesis and Other Illustrated Manuscripts of Genesis', *Gesta*, 31, 1992, pp. 40–53, 'The Beginnings of Biblical Illustration', pp. 9–59 in J. Williams, ed., *Imaging the Early Medieval Bible*, University Park, Pa., 1999 (reprinted in E. R. Hoffman, ed., *Late Antique and Medieval Art of the Mediterranean World*, Oxford, 2007, pp. 117–33), and his entry in S. McKendrick, J. Lowden and K. Doyle, eds., *Royal Manuscripts, The Genius of Illumination*, London, 2011, pp. 190–91, no. 46. The quotation from Wanley (1672–1726) on p. 183 is from P. L. Heyworth, ed., *Letters of Humfrey Wanley, Palaeographer, Anglo-Saxonist, Librarian, 1672–1726*, Oxford, 1989, p. 15; the Codex Alexandrinus, now BL, Royal MS 1.D.V–VIII, is probably slightly earlier, although not illustrated. On the arrival of the Genesis in England, see J. Carley, 'Thomas Wakefield, Robert Wakefield and the Cotton Genesis', *Transactions of the Cambridge Bibliographical Society*, 12, 2002, pp. 246–65. The engravings of Vertue's copies of miniatures from the Genesis, mentioned on p. 185, were published in *Vetusta Monumenta: quae ad rerum Britannicarum memoriam conservandam Societatis Antiquariorum Londini sumptu suo edenda curavit*, I, London, 1747, plates LXVII–VIII (the on-line reprint is dated 1767). Cotton's bust by Roubiliac in the British Library is high up, but the one halfway down on the left in the Wren Library of Trinity College is the same height as me and I can examine him nose to nose; there is another in terracotta in the old King's Library (Enlightenment Gallery) in the British Museum, 1924, 0412.1. For Cotton and the Elizabethan and Stuart antiquaries (from p. 187), I am especially indebted to Parry, *Trophies of Time*, esp. pp. 22–48 on William Camden, and K. Sharpe, 'Introduction: Rewriting Sir Robert Cotton', pp. 1–39 in Wright, ed., *Cotton as Collector*. Cotton's early acquisitions listed here on pp. 187–8 are now Vespasian D. XV, fols. 68–83 (Penitential Manual), Nero D. VIII, fols. 176–344 (*Polychronicon*) and Oxford, Bodleian Library, MS Bodley 181 (Giles of Rome; the picture of making gunpowder is on folio 97v). On Agarde's acknowledgement of Cotton in 1599, see Sharpe, 'Rewriting', p. 19; Agarde gave the Ely cartulary to Cotton (Tiberius A. VI, inscription on fol. 36r) and his own papers are in Vitellius E. XIV. The examples of Cosimo de' Medici and Baron James de Rothschild using wealth to obtain congenial membership of circles of antiquaries (compared here on p. 189) are recounted in my own books, *A History of Illuminated Manuscripts*, 2nd edn, London, 1994, p. 240, and *The Rothschilds and Their*

Collections of Illuminated Manuscripts, London, 2005, pp. 61–2. Cotton's Roman inscriptions obtained in northern England are described in D. McKitterick, 'From Camden to Cambridge: Sir Robert Cotton's Roman Inscriptions, and Their Subsequent Treatment', pp. 105–28 in Wright, ed., *Cotton as Collector*, and G. Davies, 'Sir Robert Cotton's Collection of Roman Stones: A Catalogue with Commentary', pp. 129–67 in *ibid*. The altar to Fortune found at Bowes is now Cambridge University Museum of Archaeology and Anthropology, inv. D. 1970.3. The parliamentary 'rotten borough' of Old Sarum, unpopulated since the fourteenth century, was abolished in 1832. There is much literature now on the early antiquaries from Leland to Parker, but especially useful are the introduction in J. P. Carley, *John Leland. De viris illustribus: On Famous Men*, Toronto and Oxford, 2020; R. I. Page, *Matthew Parker and His Books: Sandars Lectures in Bibliography Delivered on 14, 16 and 18 May 1990 at the University of Cambridge*, Kalamazoo, 1993; and T. Graham and A. G. Watson, *The Recovery of the Past in Early Elizabethan England*, Cambridge, 1998 (Cambridge Bibliographical Society Monograph 13). I hope that I do not need to say that the quotation on p. 192 about "bare ruin'd choirs" is from Shakespeare's Sonnet 73 or that "This royal throne" (p. 193) is from his *Richard II*, act 2. The petition to Elizabeth is Faustina E. V, fol. 896. Monastic cartularies owned by Cotton are listed throughout G. R. C. Davis, *Medieval Cartularies of Great Britain and Ireland*, revised by C. Breay, J. Harrison and D. M. Smith, London, 2010, and manuscripts from English monasteries in N. R. Ker, *Medieval Libraries of Great Britain: A List of Surviving Books*, London, 2nd edn, 1964 (Royal Historical Society Guides and Handbooks, 3), esp. the index on pp. 355–9. Three of Cotton's cartularies were destroyed in the fire. The account of loans from the Cotton library on pp. 195, 197–9 and 201 offers only a tiny sample from the thousands of entries which make up the text of Tite, *Early Records*, which is based on seven extant manuscripts and notebooks, of which the most comprehensive is BL, Harley MS 6018, fols. 147r–191v. The borrowers in the examples here are: Henry Howard (Caligula C. I–II and IX); James I (Vespasian A. VIII); Clement Edmunds (Cleopatra F. IV–V); Francis Bacon (either Julius C. II or Nero A. I and Julius E. II or Vespasian A. XIII); Daniel Dunn and Samuel Pepys (Vespasian B. XXII); Fulke Greville (Cleopatra A. XVI); and Henry Montagu (Otho E. X). Ben Jonson's letter about Campana is Cotton Julius C. III, fol. 222r; its date and relevance to Sejanus are discussed in M. Bland, 'Jonson, "*Biathanatos*" and the Interpretation of Manuscript Evidence', pp. 154–82 in *Studies in Bibliography*, 51, 1998, esp. pp, 163–7. Jonson borrowed Claudius E. III, with the life of Henry V, and Julius A. II; references to Anglo-Saxon usage are in Jonson's *The English Grammar*, [London,] 1640, pp. 47, 50, 51, etc.). Inigo Jones borrowed Vespasian B. II and Titus A. XVII). The letter of John Donne to Cotton in 1602 is Julius C. III, fols. 153–4 (E. Gosse, *The Life and Letters of John Donne, Dean of St Paul's, etc.*, I, London, 1899, p. 109, with plate facing p. 108). Donne borrowed Cleopatra F. VII, with a printed text by Don Diego Valdés, and his letter returning it is now fol. 293 in the manuscript (Gosse, *Life and Letters*, I, pp. 123–5; H. Adlington, 'More Books from the Library of John Donne', pp. 55–64 in *The Book Collector*, 61, 2012, pp. 61–2, no. L289). My account of Donne's image of the woman's hair is derived from P. D. Carleton, 'John Donne's "Bracelet of Bright Hair about the Bone"', *Modern Language Notes*, 56, 1941, pp. 366–8, identifying the likely source as either Giraldus Cambrensis, *Speculum ecclesiae*, "tricam muliebrem flavam et formosam, miroque artificio consertam" (Tiberius B. XIII: Carleton expands the second word as *muliebram*), or his *De principiis instructione*, "trica comae muliebris flava cum integritate pristina et colore reperta fuit" (Julius B. XIII). Both these manuscripts are unique and were unpublished until the nineteenth century (by which time Tiberius B. XIII had been badly burnt). Camden had seen them, for he cites Giraldus by name in his description of Arthur's grave in his *Britannia* (without reference to the hair), and the detail might have been passed to Donne by conversation rather than inspection. The image was used in Donne's poem 'The Funeral' as well as in 'The Relic'. Camden's letter asking to borrow anything at all (p. 199 here) is Julius C. III, fol. 61r (printed in H. Ellis, *Original Letters of Eminent Literary Men of the Sixteenth, Seventeenth, and Eighteenth Centuries*, London, 1843, p. 124). The Matthew Paris manuscript, Claudius D. VI, was borrowed in 1608 by Richard Bancroft, in or by 1611 by Patrick Young, royal librarian, by John Selden, by John Speed in 1621–2 and by Symonds D'Ewes in 1626. The Hexateuch, Claudius B. IV, was borrowed in 1611 by Francis Tate, an original member of the Society of Antiquaries, in 1621 by William L'Isle, Anglo-Saxonist, in that year or later by John Selden, in 1641 by William Le Neve and in 1653 by William Dugdale. The acknowledgement by Speed is taken from Parry, *Trophies of Time*, p. 75. Although Cotton wrote his apparent and credible acquisition date of 1599 in the Vespasian Psalter (Vespasian A. I), he may have done so later, since it includes Bruce as his middle name, not usually adopted until about 1603. Other manuscripts cited here are the Coronation Book of Charles V (Tiberius B. VIII) and the books from John Dee's library (Vespasian B. X, fols. 31–124, and Vitellius E. XVIII). For the collections of Lord Lumley, see S. Jayne and F. R. Johnson, *The Lumley Library: The Catalogue of 1609*, London, 1956, and M. Evans, ed., *Art Collecting and Lineage in the Elizabethan Age: The Lumley Inventory and Pedigree*, London, 2010, which I owe to James Stourton. Cotton's list of 'Books I want' is in Harley MS 1879, fol. 10v; cf. Tite, *Early Records*, pp. 74–5. Manuscripts extracted from the Royal Library or Lumley's bequest to Prince Henry, cited here, are Gower (Tiberius A. IV), Asser (Otho A. XII), the Æthelstan Psalter (Galba A. XVIII) and the Coronation Gospels (Tiberius A. II). The manuscript of Anselm's letters in Chapter 1 probably came from Lumley. The books given to Sir Thomas Bodley cited here are MSS Bodley 422 (Origen) and 181 (with the gunpowder drawings); in 1614 he also gave a thirteenth-century Flemish Psalter to Dr William Butler, now Bodleian MS Auct. D.4.2. Acquisitions by Cotton cited here are from the collections of Robert Cecil (Tite, *Early Records*, pp. 100–101), Robert Bowyer (Tiberius B. I and Nero D. IV), Francis Bacon (Nero D. VII, note that Bacon was Viscount St Albans and lived in the city), Humphrey Wyems (Augustus II, 106) and Edward Dering (Cotton Charter XIII. 31A; Dering's letter is in Julius C. III, reproduced on the British Library *Magna Carta* website). On Cotton's habit of breaking up and reassembling manuscripts, see J. P. Carley and C. G. C. Tite, 'Sir Robert Cotton as Collector of Manuscripts and the Question of Dismemberment: British Library, MSS Royal 13 D. I and Cotton Otho D. VIII', *The Library*, 6 ser., 14, 1992, pp. 94–9, and especially M. P. Brown, 'Sir Robert Cotton, Collector and Connoisseur?', pp. 281–98 in M. P. Brown and S. McKendrick, eds., *Illuminating the Book: Makers and Interpreters. Essays in Honour of Janet Backhouse*, London and Toronto, 1998. The instruction to "Bind this Book as strong as you can . . ." (p. 206) occurs in Titus E. VII (Tite, *Manuscript Library*, p. 47, fig. 16a); similar notes are preserved in Tiberius B. VIII, Domitian A. VII and elsewhere. The leaves which Cotton removed from his Coronation Gospels (Tiberius A. II) were bound into Claudius A. III, fols. 2–7 and 9*, and Faustina B. VI, fols. 98–100. The leaf cut from the Utrecht Psalter is Augustus II.2; for the leaves added to the Psalter, see Van der Horst *et al.*, eds., *Utrecht Psalter*, pp. 30–32. The leaf added to the Vespasian Psalter is no. 46 in N. Morgan, *Early Gothic Manuscripts*, I, *1190–1250*, Oxford and New York, 1982, pp. 93–4; it is about the right size to have been the missing Beatus page of a northern English Psalter which was Sotheby's, 23 June 1993, lot 45, and Maggs, cat. 1262 (1998), no. 7. The Breviary of Margaret of York quarried by Cotton is now Cambridge, St John's College, MS H. 13 (N. Morgan and S. Panayotova, *A Catalogue of Western Book Illumination in the Fitzwilliam Museum and the Cambridge Colleges*, I, ii, London and Turnhout, 2009, pp. 166–9, no. 210). The Codex Purpureus leaves are Titus C. XV; for the added papyrus, see E. A. Lowe, *Codices Latini Antiquiores*, II, Oxford, 1935, p. 21, no. 192, and R. G. Babcock, 'A Papyrus Codex of Gregory the Great's *Forty Homilies on the Gospels* (London, Cotton-titus [*sic*] C.XV)', *Scriptorium*, 54, 2000, pp. 280–89. There is a letter from the Earl of Arundel to Cotton, written from prison in the Tower of London in May 1621, asking to borrow "some one or more of yr bokes to reade" (Cotton Julius C. III, fol. 208r). The story about Cotton waiting in vain with his Coronation Gospels in 1626 is from a letter of Sir Symonds D'Ewes to Martin Stutville, now BL, Harley MS 383, fol. 24, and in J. O. Halliwell, ed., *The Autobiography and Correspondence of Sir Simonds D'Ewes, Bart., During the Reigns of James I and Charles I*, London, 1845, pp. 291–2, a reference I owe to Elizabeth Hallam-Smith. She tells me that sovereigns would normally have disembarked at King's Bridge, or Westminster Stairs, near New Palace Yard, but that the royal barge now had to deposit the king in the wet mud at Queen's Bridge, behind Parliament. She informs me too of another later twist of fate: Charles I did indeed land at Cotton's stairs in January 1649 on the way to his trial, and that he was imprisoned in Cotton House, in a bedroom near the library. Cotton's *Short View of the Long Life* was reprinted in London, 1820; the quotation here is from p. 5. In 2018 the Cotton collection in the British Library was added to the UNESCO Memory of the World UK Register.

6. THE RABBI: DAVID OPPENHEIM

I owe the idea for this chapter and help on every page to Brian Deutsch. If I could dedicate one chapter, this would be to him. He has inspired and followed every part of it. My second debt is almost as great, to a writer I have not met. I had already visited the Czech Republic and progressed some way into writing the chapter when I learned of J. Teplitsky, *Prince of the Press: How One Collector Built History's Most Enduring and Remarkable Jewish Library*, New Haven and London, 2019. His book changed everything for me. I now cannot imagine this chapter without the good fortune of using it. Professor Teplitsky is principally concerned with printing and Oppenheim's use of the press, hardly with manuscripts, but nearly everything I have learned about our subject's life is taken or guided from him. I follow Teplitsky in using 'Oppenheim' rather than 'Oppenheimer'; Oppenheim's first names are expressed as either David Abraham or David ben Abraham ('son of'), as used in the *Jewish Encyclopedia*. I am grateful too to Rabbi Jeremy Lawrence of the Finchley United Synagogue for kindly reading a draft of the chapter and similarly to César Merchán-Hamann of the Bodleian Library. Other accounts I looked at included A. Marx, 'The History of David Oppenheimer's Library', chapter XIV, pp. 238–55, in his *Studies in Jewish History and Booklore*, New York, 1944, reprinted from pp. 451–60 in *Mélanges offerts à M. Israel Lévi par ses élèves et ses amis à l'occasion de son 70e anniversaire*, Paris, 1926 (*Revue des études juives*, 82); C. Duschinsky, 'Rabbi David Oppenheimer: Glimpses of his Life and Activity, Derived from His Manuscripts in the Bodleian Library', *The Jewish Quarterly Review*, 20, 1930, pp. 217–47; and M. Keil, 'Oppenheimer, David', *Neue Deutsche Biographie*, 19, Berlin, 1999, pp. 570–71. I read and re-read A. D. Neubauer, *Catalogue of the Hebrew Manuscripts in the Bodleian Library and in the College Libraries of Oxford*, Oxford, 1886, facsimile reprint, Oxford, 1994, photocopying countless pages where I needed to consult Brian Deutsch. Further identifications and dates, often ignored by Neubauer, are in R. A. May, ed., *Supplement of Addenda and Corrigenda to Vol. I, Compiled under the Direction of Malachi Beit-Arié*, Oxford, 1994. I bought several guidebooks in the Pinkas Synagogue shop, three mainly by A. Pařík, *Jewish Prague*, Prague, 2002, *Prague Jewish Cemeteries*, Prague, 2003, and *Prague Synagogues*, Prague, 2011, as well as A. Putík and O. Sixtová, *History of the Jews in Bohemia and Moravia, from the First Settlements until Emancipation*, Prague, 2006 (exhibition catalogue, The Jewish Museum in Prague). The portrait of Oppenheim is from a drawing by Johann Kleinhard (1742–94), engraved by Jan Jiří Baltzer (1738–99), *Effigies virorum eruditorum atque artificum Bohemiae et Moraviae, una cum brevi vitae operumque ipsorum enarratione*, I, Prague, 1773, pp. 570–71. Oppenheim's early manuscript acquisition, later used for his first catalogue (p. 219 here), is Bodleian, MS Opp. 699 (Neubauer, col. 709, no. 2075; Teplitsky, pp. 34–8); from here on, all cited "Opp." shelfmarks are items in the Bodleian Library (any beginning "Opp. Add." are later additions to the sequence and did not belong to Oppenheim himself). The commentary on the midrash on Genesis by Loans is MS Opp. 199 (Neubauer, col. 24, no. 149); it now has the rather sour smell of manuscripts written on cheap paper in very acidic ink. The story of the Rashbam from the *genizah* of Worms is discussed in Marx, 'David Oppenheimer's Library', suggesting the identification of the dealer (p. 239, n. 6), and in Teplitsky, pp. 135–9. Rashbam (*c.*1085–1158) was the maternal grandson of Rashi (1040–1105). I am glad to mention Professor Chimen Abramsky (1916–2010), p. 222, who enchanted and exasperated us at Sotheby's; I contributed a piece on him to his *Chimen: A 90th Birthday Celebration*, London, 2007. The Mahzor Vitry is MS Opp. 59 (Neubauer, cols. 306–10, no. 1100); among other sources, see J. Isserles, '*Mahzor Vitry*: A Study of Liturgical-Halakhic Compendia from Medieval Franco-Germany', pp. 1–29 in *Jewish History*, 35, 2021. The note about fleeing from branch to branch (p. 223) is from Teplitsky, p. 33, citing the printed book, Opp. 8°. 1137. The Pentateuch from Worms with charred edges is MS Opp. 186 (Neubauer, col. 8, no. 37). Manuscripts from the Dietrichstein castle library, pp. 225–6 here, are described in B. Dudik, 'Handschriften der Fürstlich Dietrichstein'schen Bibliothek zu Nikosburg in Mähren', *Archiv für Österreichische Geschichte*, 39, 1868, pp. 417–534, and U.-D. Oppitz, 'Die deutschsprachigen Handschriften der Fürsten Dietrichstein aus Nikolsburg/Mähren', pp. 187–214 in R. Bentzinger and U.-D. Oppitz, eds., *Fata Libellorum, Festschrift für Franzjosef Pensel zum 70. Geburtstag*, Göppingen, 1999 (*Göppinger Arbeiten zur Germanistik*, 648). The sale was *Bibliothek Alexander Fürst Dietrichstein, Schloss Nikolsburg*, Luzern, Gilhofer and Ranschburg, 21–22 November 1933; the manuscripts were section XVI; the Judaica was section XVIII, lots 473–502. The *Weltchronik* mentioned here was lot 396 and is now Munich, Bayerische Staatsbibliothek, cgm 7364. The Hebrew manuscripts are listed in Dudik, p. 429, and esp. in A. Z. Schwarz, 'Nikolsburger hebräische Handschriften', *Studies in Jewish Bibliography and Related Subjects, in Memory of Abraham Solomon Freidus*, New York, 1929, pp. 170–81; most are now in the Solomon M. Hyams Collection of Hebraic Medical Literature in the Boston Medical Library at the Center for the History of Medicine, Boston; one is New York, Jewish Theological Seminary, MS Mic. 2977, and one in the Bodleian, MS Lyell empt. 62 (B. Richler, *Guide to Hebrew Manuscript Collections*, Jerusalem, 1994, pp. 135–6; A. de la Mare, *Catalogue of the Collection of Medieval Manuscripts Bequeathed to the Bodleian Library by James P. R. Lyell*, Oxford, 1971, p. 321, not mentioning Dietrichstein). The Talmud given to Oppenheim in Nikolsburg (p. 227) is MS Opp. 765 (Neubauer, col. 81, no. 374.1). The letter from Rabbi Meir Katzenellenbogen about buying manuscripts is bound into Bodleian, MS Mich. 479, p. 38, letters addressed to Oppenheim (Neubauer, col. 768, no. 2226), cited by Duschinsky, 'Glimpses', pp. 240–41. Acquisitions by Eleazer ha-Levi are mentioned by Teplitsky, p. 88; the manuscript sent from Jerusalem in 1703 is MS Opp. 197 (Neubauer, cols. 36–7, no. 212). The Jewish Byzantine manuscripts on p. 228 are MSS Opp. 219, 218 and especially 26 (Neubauer, col. 41, no. 227, cols. 48–9, no. 251, and cols. 57–8, no. 290). On the Karaites, see M. Polliack, ed., *Karaite Judaism: A Guide to Its History and Literary Sources*, Leiden and Boston, 2003 (*Handbuch der Orientalistik*, ser. i, *Der Nahe und der Mittlere Osten*, 73). Another important fifteenth-century Byzantine manuscript in the collection is MS Opp. 688 (Neubauer, cols. 726–7, no. 2123), with medical texts in Byzantine, Sephardi and Ashkenazi scripts, as well as pieces in Spanish and French in Hebrew letters (H. R. Jacobus, *Zodiac Calendars in the Dead Sea Scrolls and Their Reception: Ancient Astronomy and Astrology in Early Judaism*, Leiden, 2014, chapter 6, 'A Late Medieval Astrological Hebrew Text', pp. 426–50). The Salzburg manuscript Missal at Nikolsburg (p. 231) was lot 374 in the sale of November 1933. In recounting the inspection of manuscripts with Brian Deutsch, I must acknowledge the kindness and infinite patience of Stephen Hebron of the Bodleian Library, who on two occasions allowed us to look at trolleys of manuscripts in his office, where we could converse without disturbing other readers. The three biblical manuscripts described here are: (a) Pentateuch dated 1302, MS Opp. 13 (Neubauer, col. 5, no. 23), (b) Pentateuch dated 1340, MS Opp. 14 (Neubauer, col. 4, no. 20), and (c) Pentateuch of *c.*1400 with notes on copying Torah scrolls, MS Opp. 186 (Neubauer, col. 8, no. 37), mentioned above because of its charred edges. A very rare text on the fringes of the biblical canon is the book of Enoch in MS Opp. 556 (Neubauer, col. 578, no. 1656), published from this manuscript by H. Odeberg, *3 Enoch, or, The Hebrew Book of Enoch, Edited and Translated for the First Time*, Cambridge, 1928, reprinted with an introduction by J. C. Greenfield, New York, 1973. The commentary on the Song of Songs, mentioned on p. 232, is part of MS Opp. 625 (Neubauer, cols. 518–19, no. 1465); S. Japhet and B. D. Walfish, *The Way of Lovers: The Oxford Anonymous Commentary on the Song of Songs (Bodleian Library MS Opp. 625). An Edition of the Hebrew Text, with English Translation and Introduction*, Leiden and Boston, 2017 (*Commentaria: Sacred Texts and Their Commentaries*, 8), and C. Aslanov, 'The Old French Glosses of an Anonymous *Peshat* Commentary on the Song of Songs', *Jewish Quarterly Review*, 109, 2019, pp. 38–53. On Oppenheim's interest in Yiddish, see S. Berger, 'The Oppenheim Collection and Early Modern Yiddish Books: Prague Yiddish, 1550–1750', *Bodleian Library Record*, 25, 2012, pp. 37–51. The Pentateuch translated into Judaeo-German in 1544 is MS Opp. 19 (Neubauer, col. 28, no. 170); the manuscript also includes a unique translation of Esther, published in L. Landau, 'A Hebrew-German (Judaeo-German) Paraphrase of the Book of Esther of the Fifteenth Century', *Journal of English and Germanic Philology*, 18, 1919, pp. 497–555. The copy of Rashi dated 1408 (p. 235 here) is MS Opp. 35 (Neubauer, col. 32, no. 188); the title-page added by Oppenheim says that it is dated 1399, but 1408 is right (5169 in the Jewish era). The Latin Bible manuscripts in the Dietrichstein library were lots 422–4 in the sale of November 1933; the illustrated Bible lectionary in German was lot 385 (Oppitz, 1999, p. 199; on-line Marburg Repertorium, Handschriftenbeschreibung 8436). The library also contained printed Bibles in Hebrew, mostly from the Hoffman purchase, which Oppenheim would certainly have respected, including the Complutensian and Plantin

Polyglots, 1514–17 and 1569–72, and the Hebrew Bibles of Antwerp, 1580–82, and Hamburg, 1603. The Rashi mentioned on p. 236 is MS Opp. 34 (Neubauer, col. 31, no. 186). The principal exception to the prohibition of illustrating the Hebrew scriptures occurred in decorated Megillah scrolls, which contain the book of Esther as read twice on the feast of Purim, often at home: eighteenth-century copies were often richly illustrated, commonly in Venice or the Netherlands. The illuminated *Siddur* (pp. 236–7) is MS Opp. 776 (Neubauer, col. 326, no. 1126, misdated as 1271); S. Wijsman, 'The Oppenheimer Siddur: Artist and Scribe in a Fifteenth-Century Hebrew Prayer Book', pp. 69–84 in P. van Boxel and S. Arndt, eds., *Crossing Borders: Hebrew Manuscripts as Meeting-Places of Cultures*, Oxford, 2009. The lawsuit of 1717–18 against Oppenheim's use of the title 'prince', arguably treasonable in a class-conscious monarchy, was brought by the owner of the first coffee shop in Prague and by a Jewish convert to Catholicism (Teplitsky, pp. 180–86). The story of the *hazzan* and *shohet* in Kolín, told on pp. 242–3, is from Duschinsky, 'Glimpses', pp. 235–6. The dilemma of the chicken's heart and the cat is from Teplitsky, pp. 112–15; the manuscript Oppenheim consulted to resolve it is now Jerusalem, National Library of Israel, MS Heb. 4° 966 (fol. 264r). The Megillah copied by Oppenheim's daughter is cited by Teplitsky, p. 54, commenting on the rarity of such a task being undertaken by a woman. For Oppenheim's practice of having manuscripts transcribed from Sephardi into Ashkenazi scripts, p. 244, see Teplitsky, p. 51. The Sephardi manuscript of Asher ben Jehiel made in 1506 and its Ashkenazi transcription of 1701 are MSS Opp. 383–4 (Neubauer, col. 89, nos. 815–16); other examples are MSS. Opp. 331 and 330 (Neubauer, col. 164, nos. 815–16), *Responsa* in Spanish rabbinic cursive transcribed into Ashkenazi script for Oppenheim. The autobiographical reflexions of the scribe in 1716 are in MS Opp. 289 (Neubauer, col. 135, no. 686; Teplitsky, pp. 49–50). The quotation, "I am in Vienna . . ." (p. 244) is from Duschinsky, 'Glimpses', p. 241. The suggestion that books from Turkey might contain sedition is in *ibid.*, p. 240; see also, M. L. Miller, 'Rabbi David Oppenheim on Trial: Turks, Titles, and Tribute in Counter-Reformation Prague', *Jewish Quarterly Review*, 106, 2016, pp. 42–75. Examples of Oppenheim's numbering on the spines and his engraved title-pages are Teplitsky, figs. 3.2 and 2.1, 3.3 and 4.1. The manuscript written in 1714 with Oppenheim as King David (p. 247) is Opp. 258 (Neubauer, col, 144, no. 727; Teplitsky, p. 58 and fig, 2.2). The Sassoon catalogue is D. S. Sassoon, *Ohel Dawid: Descriptive Catalogue of the Hebrew and Samaritan Manuscripts in the Sassoon Library, London*, Oxford, 1932. In addition to the epilogue in Teplitsky, pp. 188–204, the history of the Oppenheim library between the collector's death and its acquisition by the Bodleian is the especial subject of Marx, 'David Oppenheimer's Library', and F. Lebrecht, 'Die Oppenheimer'sche Bibliothek', *Literaturblatt des Orients: Berichte, Studien und Kritiken für jüdische Geschichte und Literatur*, 5, 1844, cols. 247–50 and 273–8, and H. Meyer, 'Materialen zur Geschichte der Bibliothek David Oppenheims', *Soncino-Blätter, Beiträge zur Kunde des Jüdischen Buches*, 2, 1927, pp. 59–80, all of which I have used. The catalogue compiled in Hildesheim *c.*1740 is MS Opp. Add. 4° 135 (Neubauer, col. 850, no. 2418); the first printed sale catalogue was *Catalogus der seit vielen Jahren berühmten vollständigen Hebreischen Bibliothek des ehemaligen Präger Ober-Rabbiners weiland Herrn David Oppenheimers*, Hamburg, 1782. I am glad to remember with affection Jack Lunzer, mentioned here, creator of the extraordinary Valmadonna Library of Hebrew books, whom I knew for many decades; I spoke at the memorial service held on the anniversary of his death. The Latin title of the Oppenheim sale catalogue of 1826 (I am unable to transcribe the Hebrew) is *Collectio Davidis, i.e. Catalogus celeberrimae illius Bibliothecae hebraeae,* *quam indefesso studio magnaque pecuniae impensa collegit R. Davides Oppenheimerus*, Hamburg, 1826. The Bodleian file, which I have read, is MS Add. C. 166 there. The ungracious comment by Lebrecht about the collection passing out of Jewish possession (p. 250 here) is in his 'Oppenheimer'sche Bibliothek', as above, cols. 472–3; that of Duschinsky in his 'Glimpses', p. 221; even Teplitsky, citing other Jewish regrets at the sale, characterizes it as "an act of cultural plunder" (p. 201). For the manuscript of fables, MS Opp. 154 (Neubauer, col. 503, no. 1405), see O. Pächt and J. J. G. Alexander, *Illuminated Manuscripts in the Bodleian Library, Oxford*, I, *German, Dutch, Flemish, French and Spanish Schools*, Oxford, 1966, p. 12, no. 162; C. Merchán-Hamann, 'Fables from East to West', pp. 35–43 in Boxel and Arndt, eds., *Crossing Borders*, as above, esp. pp. 40–43; and S. Offenberg, 'On a Pious Man, Adulterous Wife, and the Pleasure of Preaching to Others in Yitshaq Ibn Sahula's *Meshal ha-Qadmoni*', *Hispania Judaica Bulletin*, 12, 2016, pp. 103–25. The text is published in R. Loewe, ed. and transl., *Meshal Haqadmoni: Fables from the Distant Past. A Parallel Hebrew–English Text*, Oxford and Portland, Ore., 2004. Further examples of the engravings of the deer paralleled in manuscript decoration are discussed in H. Lehmann-Haupt, *Gutenberg and the Master of the Playing Cards*, New Haven and London, 1966, and M. Wolff, 'Some Manuscript Sources for the Playing-Card Master's Number Cards', *The Art Bulletin*, 64, 1982, pp. 587–600 (reproducing the Three of Stags on p. 594, fig. 15). There is another derivation from the Master of the Playing Cards in the slightly later Oppenheim Siddur of 1471 (MS Opp. 776, as above), where the illuminated panel on fol. 45v includes a hunched baby bear facing to the left with its right paw emerging from behind its snout, almost identical to the bear at the top right of the Nine of Wild Animals. The lion, the deer and the wolf in the fables were also symbols for tribes of Israel, as we saw carved in the tombstones of Prague.

7. THE SAVANT: JEAN-JOSEPH RIVE

The only modern monograph on the Abbé Rive focuses specifically on the design and making of the illustrations for his intended book on dating medieval manuscripts, but it also includes an introduction to his life: A. Delle Foglie and F. Manzari, *Riscoperta e riproduzione della miniatura in Francia nel Settecento: L'abbé Rive e l'Essai sur l'art de vérifier l'âge des miniatures des manuscrits*, Rome, 2016. As with so much on the history of the bibliophily of illuminated manuscripts, I first learned of Rive from A. N. L. Munby, *Connoisseurs and Medieval Miniatures, 1750–1850*, Oxford, 1972, which I bought on publication, esp. pp. 14–18. Rive has a small but notable part in M. Camille, S. Hindman and R. Watson, '"Curiosities", Appreciation of Manuscript Illumination in the Eighteenth Century', pp. 5–45 in S. Hindman and N. Rowe, eds., *Manuscript Illumination in the Modern Age: Recovery and Reconstruction*, Evanston, Ill., 2001, esp. pp. 13–16. I gratefully used A. Worm, 'Reproducing the Middle Ages: Abbé Jean-Joseph Rive (1730–91) and the Study of Manuscript Illumination at the Turn of the Early Modern Period', pp. 347–89 in A. C. Montoya, S. van Romburgh and W. van Anrooij, eds., *Early Modern Medievalisms: The Interplay between Scholarly Reflection and Artistic Production*, Leiden, 2010, although her promised article for the Cambridge Bibliographical Society seems not to have appeared. I benefited from F. Moureau, 'L'abbé Rive ou l' homme-bibliothèque: une "physiologie"', *Babel*, 6, 2002, pp. 105–25, and I fell back when needed on the long entry on Rive in C.-F.-H. Barjavel, *Dictionnaire historique, biographique et bibliographique du Département de Vaucluse*, II, Carpentras, 1841, pp. 332–41. There is a first-class on-line blog by J.-P. Fontaine ("dit le Bibliophile Rhemus"), 'L'abbé Rive

(1730–1791), bibliognoste orgueilleux et patriote malfaisant', dated 6 July 2018. He is especially interested, as I am, in places where Rive lived. Eighteenth-century French bibliographical books and sale catalogues are extremely well digitized on-line, not least by the Gallica website of the Bibliothèque nationale de France, and I have read every publication cited here, including Rive's *Chasse aux Bibliographes*. For the *Chasse*, see A. Serrai, '*La Chasse aux Bibliographes*, perizia e paranoia nell' Abbé Rive', pp. 463–72 in *Libri, tipografi, biblioteche: Ricerche storiche dedicate a Luigi Balsamo*, II, Florence, 1997 (*Biblioteca di bibliografia italiana*, 148). Rive's corrections to Montfaucon (*Chasse*, pp. 163–4) refer to B. de Montfaucon, *Bibliotheca Bibliothecarum Manuscriptorum nova*, II, Paris, 1739, pp. 796 and 794. The name "De Bure", which I first use on p. 261, is sometimes written as "de Bure" or "Debure" and I do not know which is preferable; I have adopted the orthography as Rive wrote it. Similarly, "de La Vallière" is sometimes also written as "de la Vallière", even by Rive, but I believe a capital 'L' is correct. Rive mentions Cotton in his *Prospectus*, 1782, which we will come to later, pp. 33–4, n. 11, and Oppenheim in the *Chasse*, p. 512. His criticism of Van Praet on the Duc de Berry's manuscript (*Chasse*, pp. 272–3) relates his entry in the La Vallière sale catalogue, part 1, 1784, lot 113; the manuscript is now Paris, BnF, ms fr. 20090, digitized in full. His comments on Charles V's *Bible Historiale* (*Chasse*, pp. 158–62) refer to J. Le Long, *Bibliotheca Sacra*, I, Paris, 1723, p. 316 (although the text had also appeared in the Leipzig edition of 1709, II, pp. 11–13) and then to De Bure in the Gaignat sale catalogue, 1769, lot 58; the manuscript is now The Hague, Museum Meermanno, MS 10. B. 23 (it is also mentioned in my chapter 2 above, p. 75); Rive was wrong too in saying Van Eyck was a child in 1371, as he probably was not born until the 1380s. Rive himself dated his own passion for old books to the age of fifteen (*Lettres purpuracées, ou, Lettres consulaires et provinciales, écrites contre les consuls d'Aix et procureurs du pays de Provence*, Aix, 1789, p. 113); his nephew-in-law said "as early as his fourteenth year" (T. F. Dibdin, *Bibliographical, Antiquarian and Picturesque Tour in France and Germany*, II, London, 1821, p. 385). Rive's letters to Joseph David, introduced on p. 260, are Paris, Bibliothèque de l'Arsenal, mss 6392–3, part of the Éméric-David archive (G. Éboli, *Livres et lecteurs en Provence au XVIIIe siècle: Autour de David, imprimeurs-libraires à Aix*, Méolans-Revel, 2008, esp. pp. 182–5 and 296). The rumour of an affair with an unnamed woman from Paris is gleefully told by E. G. Peignot, *Dictionnaire raisonné de bibliologie*, Paris, 1804, p. 277, n. 1. I do not know whether there is any connection between that story and Rive's flight from the curé's house to the château de Mollégès and the 22,000 francs lent to him by a Mlle. de Mollégès ([J.-E. Morénas], *Notice des Ouvrages imprimés et manuscrits de l'Abbé Rive*, Paris, *c.*1817, pp. 2–3; the digitized version on Google Books gives the date as 1795, which must be wrong). The letter recounting of the visit to Saint-Germain-des-Prés is printed in H. Martin [i.e. Martin-Dairvault], 'L'odyssée d'un bibliognoste (Lettres inédites de l'Abbé Rive)', pp. 337–64 in *Bulletin du bibliophile et du bibliothécaire*, 1892, pp. 345–7. On Dubrowsky, see my *Meetings with Remarkable Manuscripts*, pp. 471–2. The manuscripts they saw were (a) a Greek and Latin Psalter in uncials, now BnF ms Coislin 186, formerly bound with ms lat. 10592, seventh century, acquired by Saint-Germain-des-Prés with the manuscripts of Henri de Coislin, bishop of Metz 1697–1732 (E. A. Lowe, *Codices Latini Antiquiores*, V, Oxford, 1950, p. 2, no. 520); (b) the Psalter of Saint Germain, in gold and silver on purple parchment, now BnF, ms lat. 11947, sixth century (*ibid.*, pp. 28–9, no. 616, commenting that its use by Saint Germain himself is at least "palaeographically possible"); (c) Saint Matthew's Gospel Book in gold on purple parchment, perhaps the ninth-century Gospel in gold on purple parchment which belonged to Piotr Dubrowsky, who acquired very many manuscripts from Saint-Germain-des-Prés, and is now St Petersburg, Hermitage 5.2.1 (T. Voronova and A. Sterligov, *Western European Illuminated Manuscripts of the 8th to the 16th Centuries in the National Library of Russia, St Petersburg*, Bournemouth and St Petersburg, 1996, pp. 44–5); and (d) papyrus with letters of Augustine, now BnF, ms lat. 11641, together with a stray leaf which also belonged to Dubrowsky and is now St Petersburg, National Library, Lat. F. pap. I. 1 (Lowe, *Codices Latini Antiquiores*, V, p. 28, no. 614, and XI, 1966, p. 4; fifty-three leaves separated by at least 1530 are now Geneva, Bibliothèque de Genève, ms lat. 16 (*ibid.*, VII, 1956, p. 15). Rive's reference to Struve is to his *Introductio in notitiam rei litterariae et usum blibiothecarum*, Jena, 1710, p. 91. Rive was quite wrong about the use of the letter 'h' in Latin script. The quotation "La patience . . ." (p. 262 here) is from Martin, 'L'odyssée d'un bibliognoste', p. 350; that "Me voilà . . ." is widely quoted, including by Worm, 'Reproducing the Middle Ages', p. 350. The reference to acquiring books for the Duc de La Vallière in Provence in July 1768 is in a letter from Rive still claiming the expenses from the duke's estate in 1781, bound into a copy of Rive's *Éclaircissements historiques et critiques sur l'invention des cartes à jouer*, Paris, 1780, from the Monckton Milnes library, now owned by Richard Linenthal, to whom I am grateful for this and much other help. For the Duc de La Vallière, see D. Coq, 'Le paragon du bibliophile français: le duc de la Vallière et sa collection', pp. 316–31 in C. Jolly, ed., *Histoire des bibliothèques françaises*, II, *Les bibliothèques sous l'Ancien Régime, 1580–1789*, Paris, 1988. The quotation from Christie (p. 263), originally published in the *Library Chronicle*, 2, 1885, is from W. A. Shaw, ed., *Selected Essays and Papers of Richard Copley Christie*, London, 1902, p. 280. The manuscript of Voltaire's *Candide* is now Paris, Bibliothèque de l'Arsenal, ms 3160. We all know the seductive smell of a shop selling fresh leather goods: when an eighteenth-century library was newly rebound, as the Duc de La Vallière's was almost entirely in high-quality goatskin, the smell must have been wonderful, a sensual experience lost and unconsidered when examining the same bindings three centuries later. It is unusual for a ducal collector that La Vallière did not generally have his arms stamped on his bindings and sometimes his books are only recognizable now from the eventual sale's lot numbers added on the endleaves. One manuscript in the La Vallière library with a certain erotic frisson was the seventeenth-century Book of Hours of Roger de Rabutin, comte de Bussy, now New York, Morgan Library, M 370, in which supposed miniatures of saints are portraits of cuckolds and adulteresses of the French court. The duke's Château de Montrouge was adjacent to the site of what is now the Montrouge station at the southern end of the Paris Métro line 4. Rive's assertions that he was solely responsible for the second La Vallière library occur, among other places, in his *Lettre vraiment philosophique à Monseigneur l'évêque de Clermont*, 'Nomopolis' [variously stated to be Aix, Nîmes or Paris], 1790, pp. 169 and 293; a reference to his discussions with the duke over dinner is *Chasse*, pp. 73–4. The story of the bull-dog, *dogue* in French, p. 264 here, is Peignat, *Dictionnaire*, 1804, p. 279, n. 1, and T. F. Dibdin, *Bibliomania, or Book Madness: A Bibliographical Romance, in Six Parts*, London, 1811, p. 79. The account of visiting the nun in 1779 is told by Rive in the *Lettre vraiment philosophique*, p. 369. The Gaignat sale catalogues have the unusual title *Supplément à la Bibliographie Instructive, ou Catalogue des livres du cabinet de feu M. Louis Jean Gaignat*, because they were actually issued as volume 8–9 (each in two parts) of the ongoing bibliography of rare books by Guillaume-François De Bure, *Bibliographie instructive, ou traité de la connoissance des livres rares et singuliers*, 10 vols., Paris, 1763–82 (see M. North and E. Holzenberg, eds., *Printed Catalogues of French Book Auctions and Sales by Private Treaty 1643–1830 in the Library of the Grolier Club*, New York, 2004, p. 115, no.

193). The volumes of Rive's own set of the Gaignat catalogue are BnF, Réserve des Imprimés, Q. 538-41, digitized on Gallica. The Gaignat manuscripts viewed by Rive and mentioned here on pp. 267–70 are: lot 93, the Saint-Sever Beatus, eleventh century (now BnF, ms lat. 8878); lot 50, the Hunterian Psalter, *c.*1170 (now Glasgow University Library, MS Hunter 229, discussed also in chapter 7 of my *Meetings with Remarkable Manuscripts*, illustration on p. 320); lot 1751, romances, late thirteenth century (now BnF ms fr. 24405); lot 5192, statutes dated 1352 ("miniatures très médiocres"); lot 1764, *Roman de la Rose*, *c.*1405 (Sotheby's, 13 July 1977, lot 48, now Los Angeles, J. Paul Getty Museum, MS Ludwig XV. 7); lot 2339, Lefèvre, *Recueil des histoires troyennes*, 1495 (now BnF ms fr. 22552); lot 194, Book of Hours, 1524 (now Washington, Library of Congress, MS 52); lot 188, Breviary of René II de Lorraine, lot 278 in the Hoym sale and lot 82 in the de Selle sale (now Paris, Petit Palais, ms Dutuit 42); and lot 3004, chronicles of Enguerrand de Monstrelet, 1510 (now BnF, ms fr. 20360). The Sherborne Missal (now BL, Add. MS 74236) may have remained unsold at the 800 *livres* given as its stated hammer price as lot 81 in the de Selle sale: see J. Backhouse, *The Sherborne Missal*, London, 1999, p. 56. The Salisbury Breviary of the Duke of Bedford is now BnF, ms lat. 17294; the Rohan Hours is BnF, ms lat. 9471. The manuscripts from the d'Urfé purchase mentioned here (p. 272) are the Provençal *Chansonnier* (now BnF, ms fr. 22543); the Saluces Hours (now BL, Add. MS 27697); Pierre Richart, *La Forteresse de la foy* (now BnF, mss fr. 20067–9); and the Hours of Claude d'Urfé (now Huntington, HM 1102); see also A. Vernet, 'Les manuscrits de Claude d'Urfé (1501–1558) au château de La Bastie', pp. 81–97 in *Comptes rendus des séances de l'Académie des Inscriptions et Belles-Lettres*, 120–21, 1976. The library of George Jackson (here p. 274) was the subject of an on-line blog by Peter Kidd, Medieval Manuscripts Provenance, 18 February 2017. The Jerome on the Psalms is now BnF, ms lat. 16839, not 13686 as cited by Kidd. Rive's publication is *Galeotti Martii Narniensis Liber excellentium sive de Excellentibus*, pp. 3–16 as the *première* (and only) *notice* in *Diverses notices calligraphiques et typographiques par M. l'Abbé Rive*, Paris, 1785; the manuscript, which was not part of the La Vallière library and later belonged to Lord Ashburnham, is now BnF, ms n. a. lat. 731. Marzio appears in chapter 13 of Walter Scott's *Quentin Durward* (1823) as "the celebrated astrologer, poet, and philosopher". The *Histoire de Thèbes* with *Histoire de la destruction de Troye*, followed on pp. 275–6, is now Cologny–Geneva, Fondation Martin Bodmer, Cod. Bodmer 160 (F. Vielliard, *Manuscrits français du Moyen Âge*, Cologny–Genève, 1975, pp. 79–85, with bibliography). Phillipps's visit to Stowe (p. 278 here) is mentioned in A. N. L. Munby, *The Formation of the Phillipps Library between 1841 and 1872*, Cambridge, 1956 (*Phillipps Studies*, IV), p. 24, but, oddly, his attendance at the royal levée is not described by Munby. My sources were the newspaper accounts in the *Evening Standard*, 24 April 1845, and the *Worcestershire Chronicle*, 30 April 1845. The Duke of Buckingham was then on the brink of bankruptcy and facing the the imminent likelihood of having to sell his manuscript library, which may be why be went to the trouble to humour the biggest buyer of manuscripts in Britain. Phillipps recounted the event to Sir Frederic Madden, explaining that the manuscript was merely one of two very similar volumes in his possession (Madden's journal, 1 May 1845, Bodleian, MS Eng. hist. c.158, p. 121); it was reported by the Royal Librarian as missing in 1856 (*ibid.*, 24 May and 6 June, MS Eng. hist. c.169, pp. 196 and 208–9), but it was seen by Madden in the Royal Library at Windsor Castle ten years later (*ibid.*, 9 August 1866, MS Eng. hist. c.179, p. 219). It is still there, now RCIN 1047552; there are good images on the Royal Collection Trust website. A list of Rive's writings, actual and projected, is in [Morénas], *Ouvrages imprimés et manuscrits*, and in Barjavel, *Dictionnaire*, II, pp. 335–41. The full title of his first monograph on manuscripts was *Notices historiques & critiques de deux manuscrits, uniques & très précieux, de la bibliothèque de M. le Duc de La Vallière, dont l'un a pour titre: La Guirlande de Julie, & l'autre, Recueil de fleurs & insectes, peints par Daniel Rabel en 1624*, Paris, 1779. Voltaire wrote to the Duc de La Vallière in 1761, "Le bon goût en tout genre n'établit son empire que dans le siècle de Louis XIV": *Oeuvres complètes de Voltaire*, 41 (Correspondences, ix), Paris, 1881, p. 277. The once-famous productions of Nicolas Jarry have passed so far out of fashion that there has still been no serious study or census of his many manuscripts since R. Portalis, 'Nicolas Jarry et la calligraphie au XVIIe siècle', *Bulletin du bibliophile*, 1896, but see R. Watson, *Victoria and Albert Museum, Western Illuminated Manuscripts*, III, London, 2011, pp. 934–5, no. 186, and R. H. Rouse and M. A. Rouse, *Renaissance Illuminators in Paris: Artists & Artisans, 1500–1717*, London and Turnhout, 2019, pp. 205–6. The *Guirlande de Julie* was lot 1867 in the Gaignat sale and lot 3247 in that of the Duc de La Vallière; it later belonged to Martine de Béhague and her heirs the comtes de Ganay, and it passed relatively recently to the BnF (ms n. a. fr. 19735; I. Frain, *La Guirlande de Julie*, Paris, 1991; it is digitized on Gallica; a second unillustrated copy from 1641 retained by the donor also belonged to Gaignat and La Vallière and is now in the Rothschild collection at Waddesdon Manor: G. Barber *et al.*, *Printed Books and Bookbindings*, Waddesdon, 2013, pp. 949–53, no. 506). Rive's second manuscript monograph (here pp. 280–81) was *Notices historiques & critiques de deux manuscrits de la bibliothèque de M. le Duc de La Vallière, dont l'un a pour titre: Le roman d'Artus comte de Bretaigne, & l'autre, le Rommant de Pertenay ou de Lusignen*, Paris, 1779. Rive's essay on the two-volume manuscript of Guillaume de Machaut, now BnF, mss fr. 22545–6, is sometimes said to remain unpublished as Carpentras, Bibliothèque municipale, ms 1259 (e. g., L. Earp, *Guillaume de Machaut: A Guide to Research*, New York and London, 1995, p. 104); in fact, it appeared as *Notice d'un Manuscrit de la Bibliothèque de M. le Duc de La Vallière, contenant les Poésies de Guillaume de Machau, accompagnée de Recherches historiques & critiques, pour servir à la vie de ce Poëte* as a separately paginated addition following p. 476 of J.-B. de La Borde's *Essai sur la musique ancienne et moderne*, IV, Paris, 1780. Rive's project for an *Essai sur l'art de vérifier l'âge des miniatures des manuscrits*, which forms pp. 282–8 here, is the subject of Delle Foglie and Manzari, *Riscoperta e riproduzione*. Rive eventually described and summarized it in his *Prospectus d'un ouvrage proposé par souscription*, Paris, 1782, which was by then already promising a text unlikely to appear. The twenty-six plates selected from the La Vallière library with current locations are: (1) the Rohan Hours, BnF, ms lat. 9471, fol. 19r; (2) Jean de Courcy, *La Bouquechardière*, BnF, ms fr. 20124, fol. 331r; (3) Laurent de Premierfait translating Boccaccio, *De cas des nobles hommes et femmes*, Cologny-Geneva, Fondation Martin Bodmer, Cod. Bodmer 174, fol. 230r; (4)–(5) the Salisbury Breviary of the Duke of Bedford, BnF, ms lat. 17294, fols. 106r and 518r; (6) Pierre Salmon, *Dialogues*, BnF, ms fr. 23279, fol. 53r; (7) Jean de Wavrin, *Histoire de Gérard de Nevers*, BnF, ms fr. 24378, fol. 1r; (8) René of Anjou, *Le livre du Coeur d'amour épris*, BnF, ms fr. 24399, fol. 76r; (9)–(13) Pierre Richart translating Alfonso de Spina, *La Forteresse de la foy*, BnF, ms fr. 20069, fols. 272r, 78r, 125r, 397r and 1r; (14)–(15) Vasco de Lucena translating Quintus Curtius, *Faits et gestes d'Alexandre*, BnF ms fr. 22547, fols. 1r and 112r; (16) Jean Du Quesne translating Julius Caesar, *Commentaires*, Oxford, Bodleian Library, MS Douce 208, fol. 4r; (17) Guillaume Le Menand translating Ludolf of Saxony, *Vie du Christ*, BnF, ms fr. 20096, fol. 4r; (18) the Breviary of René II de Lorraine, Paris, Petit Palais, ms Dutuit 42, fol. 20r; (19)–(20), Raoul Lefèvre, *Recueil des histoires de Troie*, BnF, ms fr. 22552, fols. 1r and 6r; (21), the

Saluces Hours, London, BL, Add. MS 27697, fol. 194r; (22) *Chronique d'Enguerrand de Monstrelet*, BnF, ms fr. 20360, fol. 145r; (23) Petrarch, *Triomphes* in French, BnF, ms fr. 22541, fol. 77v; (24) Book of Hours, Washington, Library of Congress, MS 52, fols. 53r and 104r; (25) the Hours of Claude d'Urfé, San Marino, Huntington Library, HM 1102, fol. 47v; and (26) the Hours of François I, London, BL, Add. MS 18853, fol. 5v. The lovely picture of Caesar in a bookshop is a surprise to me: I thought I had discovered it myself, when I reproduced it in my *Making Medieval Manuscripts*, Oxford, 2018, pl. on p. 16: here it is, already chosen by the Abbé Rive 240 years earlier. The original tracings for the reproductions are in the BnF, Estampes, SNR-3, pls. XXVII–LI in Delle Foglie and Manzari, *Riscoperta e riproduzione*. Rive's judgement "presque toutes affreuses" is from the *Prospectus*, p. 12. Rive's long litany of questions, translated fairly freely by me here on pp. 83–5, is also cited or abridged in Camille, Hindman and Watson, 'Curiosities, pp. 14–15; Worm, 'Reproducing the Middle Ages', pp. 365–6; and Delle Foglie and Manzari, *Riscoperta e riproduzione*, pp. 43–4. The points listed by M. R. James are in his *Descriptive Catalogue of the Manuscripts in the Fitzwilliam Museum*, Cambridge, 1895, pp. xix–xli, and those of N. R. Ker in *Medieval Manuscripts in British Libraries*, I, *London*, Oxford, 1969, pp. vii–xiii. Rive's report on his financial position after the duke's death is printed by Martin, 'L'odyssée d'un bibliognoste', pp. 354–60. The *Catalogue des livres de la bibliothèque de feu M. le duc de La Vallière*, 1783, is no. 312 in North and Holzenberg, *French Book Auctions*, pp. 159–61. De Bure's remarks on Rive are in the preliminary *Avertissement*, pp. iii–viii. Rive, instead of being mollified by De Bure's generous tributes, initiated legal action (P. H. Maty in *A New Review, with Literary Curiosities and Literary Intelligence*, III, 1783, p. 351). On Joseph Van Praet, see P.-C.-F. Daunou, *Notice historique sur la vie et les ouvrages de M. Van Praet*, Paris, 1839. On early subscribers in response to Rive's *Prospectus* (here pp. 287–8), see Delle Foglie and Manzari, *Riscoperta e riproduzione*, pp. 52–6. I myself own a receipt for a copy signed by Rive on 17 January 1783 for 600 *livres* from the agent for the duke of Saxe-Gotha. On the very reasonable complaints for non-delivery of the promised book, see the letters from the secretaries of Marie-Antoinette, 29 March 1787, and Cardinal de Brienne, December 1788 (Delle Foglie and Manzari, *Riscoperta e riproduzione*, pp. 63–5). Marie-Antoinette's copy on vellum of the plates alone is now BnF, Réserve des Imprimés, Vélins 30. Another copy on vellum, sold in London in 1791 for £56.14s. Rive's entry for the prize poem (pp. 288–9 here) was *Ode sur l'abolition récente de l'esclavage en France, suivie de notes critiques*, 'Londres' (perhaps Brussels), 1781: it includes verses such as "Ce ne sont pas des Turcs, des Scythes, des Tartares, / Que la raison appelle à ses premiers Lois: / Ce sont des Rois Chrétiens, qui cent fois plus barbares, / De leurs oracles saints méconnoissent la voix" (p. 10). Rive's complaints about his treatment over the Méjanes library fill pp. ix–l of the 'Preface', which follows the main text of the *Chasse aux Bibliographes*. Dibdin's visit to Morénas is recounted in his *Bibliographical . . . Tour in France and Germany*, pp. 381–5. The account of the archive by Morénas is the *Ouvrages imprimés et manuscrits*, also cited; its eventual fate is recalled in R. Reboul, *L'abbé Rive et ses manuscrits*, Paris, 1872. The sale catalogue of Rive's reference library is *Catalogue de la bibliothèque des livres de feu l'abbé Rive, acquise par les Citoyens Chauffard et Colomby, Mis en ordre par C. F. Achard, M. D. M.*, Marseille, 1793 (North and Holzenberg, *French Book Auctions*, p. 180, no. 359). Lots mentioned here are Justinus (1527), *Speculum* facsimile (16), Le Long (1974*), Hoym (2096), de Selle (2103), Gaignat's copy of *La Sausse-Robert justifiée*, 1679 (398) and Godart de Beauchamps (1149). The *Speculum* facsimile emerged in the library of Cornelius J. Hauck, Christie's, New York, 28 June 2006, lot 472, and at Bichoche et Giquello,

Paris, 19 November 2021, lot 85. The entry for the Gutenberg Bible, lot 4, is reproduced in R. Folter, 'The Gutenberg Bible in the Antiquarian Book Trade', pp. 271–351 in M. Davies, ed., *Incunabula: Studies in Fifteenth-Century Printed Books Presented to Lotte Hellinga*, London, 1999, p. 282, no. 10. The subsequent fate of this copy is recounted, with much interesting detail, in E. M. White, *Editio Princeps: A History of the Gutenberg Bible*, London and Turnhout, 2017, pp. 148–51. For the sale in 1765, not Rive's copy since its opening leaves were explicitly present, see Folter, 'Gutenberg Bible', p. 278, no. 7, and White, *Editio Princeps*, pp. 109–11; Gaignat's copy on vellum is Folter, 'Gutenberg Bible', p. 279, no. 8, and White, *Editio Princeps*, pp. 111–14, "we do not know where Gaignat acquired it". Rive learned a little more, since he annotated his copy of the Gaignat catalogue, lot 16, "elle avait couté à mr. gaignat 2600 *ll.* & aux moins 120 *ll.* de relier, je le tiens de De Bure le jeune". Productions of the earliest Mainz press in the La Vallière library included Durandus, 1459 (lot 214, now in the Library of Congress), Clement V, 1460 (lot 1054), Bible, 1462, on vellum (lot 28, now in the Bodleian), and the Bulla of Pius II, 1463 (lot 4525), as well as two original wooden printing blocks for a Donatus (lot 2179). He did not own the Psalter of 1457, although Rive wrote about the Gaignat copy in his *Prospectus*, p. 28, valuing it at 4,000 *livres*, when it belonged to Count MacCarthy-Reagh. The participation of Phillipps in the sale of 1847 is told by Munby, *Phillipps Studies*, IV, pp. 22–4 (the quotation about the "Deep Sea" on p. 24).

8. THE LIBRARIAN: SIR FREDERIC MADDEN

The nearest to a biography of Madden is an engaging little book reproduced from a typescript, R. W. Ackerman and G. P. Ackerman, *Sir Frederic Madden: A Biographical Sketch and Bibliography*, New York and London, 1979, a masterly survey of the journals and available sources, although hardly touching on specific medieval manuscripts. I owe much to the succinct and crisp entry by the late Michael Borrie on Madden in the *Oxford Dictionary of National Biography*, 2004. For Panizzi, I read E. J. Miller, *Prince of Librarians: The Life and Times of Antonio Panizzi of the British Museum*, London, 1967, and for the Museum especially E. Miller, *That Noble Cabinet: A History of the British Museum*, London, 1973, and D. M. Wilson, *The British Museum: A History*, London, 2002, supplemented, as so often, by A. Hobson, *Great Libraries*, London, 1970, pp. 242–7 on the British Museum. My chapter has been read by Marjorie Caygill, who has generously added many suggestions and ideas from her lifetime's experience in the Museum. I am grateful too to Mirjam Foot, who saw an early draft. Madden's journals are Oxford, Bodleian Library, MSS Eng. hist. c.140–82, bequeathed by Madden to Oxford but not to be opened until 1920. They were photographed for World Microfilms, 1973. Various attempts have been begun to transcribe them with a view to publication, especially under the initiatives of Michael Borrie and Robin Alston with the Madden Society, but no real progress is reported. A preliminary foretaste from a single year is A. Bell, 'The Journal of Sir Frederic Madden, 1852', *The Library*, 5 ser., 29, 1974, pp. 405–21. Four million words is nearly a million more than the Bible. To save endlessly repeating "MS Eng. hist.", my references here abbreviate the journals' shelfmarks to 'c.' and the number of the volume. For actual quotations, identified here by their opening words, I will give the page number; all other references are to date only. Where an event or remark is ascribed in my text or notes to an exact date, that may be taken as being from the journal, unless otherwise credited. Early in his life, Madden was sometimes inconsistent in spelling his first name with or without a final 'k', but 'Frederic' became his preference.

The photograph of 31 St Thomas Street, pp. 297–8 here, is in the journal for 22 April 1868; "the House . . ." is c.180, p. 323. A brief history of the house, with an earlier picture, occurs in the web page 'Memorials and Monuments in Portsmouth' about tablets in the Royal Garrison Church, where Madden's parents were buried. All remaining old houses in the street were finally obliterated in bombing during the Second World War. Marjorie Caygill tells me of a booklet, J. Webb, *Sir Frederic Madden and Portsmouth*, Portsmouth, 1987 (*The Portsmouth Papers*, 47), which I have not seen. Madden says the Hebrew phylacteries (p. 298) were "the property of a Jew named Pyke, at whose decease they were found" (c.140, p. 13); I owe my probable identification to the website of Henry Roche, 'Portsmouth Synagogue Early Membership List, 1765–1843'. The piece of a Latin manuscript is described on 22 April 1819; "a curious old . . ." is c.140, p. 38. The article by Lake Allen with the help of Madden was 'On the Game of Chess in Europe during the Thirteenth Century', *New Monthly Magazine*, 4, 1822, pp. 316–20 (not in the Ackermans' bibliography of Madden's publications). "My father . . ." is c.144, p. 55, 18 March 1823. The family friend was James Rice, his father's business agent in London, 2 November 1823; "or to be . . ." is c.144, p. 219. The letter from Allen, quoted here on p. 299, was received on 3 August 1820; "He tells me . . ." is c.141, p. 219. The first Cotton manuscript mentioned, without knowing that 'Cleopatra' was part of the shelfmark, is on 21 May 1821. Madden borrowed Allen's manuscript of Statutes on 20 March 1821 and again 20 July 1823. "Oh God . . ." is c.144, p. 119. The visit to London began on 5 December 1823. Madden's reader's ticket is attached in BL, Egerton MS 2837, folio 3, together with printed rules for the use of the reading-room and the envelope in which they were sent to Madden, which, presumably still being in his pocket, he used the following week for making a sketch of the White Horse of Uffington (folio 5). The increasingly strained relationship with Lake Allen was in part because of Allen's extreme ill-health, ending with his death on 18 April 1824. Petrie's letter inviting Madden to apply for the imminent vacancy was dated 14 February 1824 and is BL, Egerton MS 2837, fol. 9. Madden's drawing of his interview on 12 March 1824 is c.145, p. 203a. The suggestion that Ellis may have been the model for Dickens's Pickwick is made by Wilson, *British Museum*, pp. 82–3. Madden's passport for his trip to Paris to see the Libri manuscripts in May 1846 is inserted into c.159, between pp. 156 and 157. Extracts from Madden's account of visiting Oxford from 3 May to 9 July 1825 (p. 302) are printed in C. K. F. Brown, 'Sir Frederic Madden at Oxford', *Oxoniensia*, 35, 1970, pp. 34–52. On Bliss and his portfolios of fragments, see S. Gibson and C. J. Hindle, 'Philip Bliss (1787–1857), Editor and Bibliographer', pp. 173–260 in *Proceedings and Papers, Oxford Bibliographical Society*, III, Oxford, 1933, esp. p. 188, and C. de Hamel, 'Philip Bliss, the Lilly, and Me', pp. 49–61 in R. Ring, ed., *A Bibliophilic Tribute to Joel Silver*, Providence, 2021. Some of the fragments seen by Madden on 15 May 1845 were given to the Bodleian Library in 1964 and are MS Lat. misc. b.18, and most of the rest were dispersed by the booksellers Quaritch in their catalogues 1036 (1984) and 1056 (1985). Madden matriculated at Magdalen Hall on 9 July 1825 and withdrew on 6 January 1831. His first description of the Holkham proposal is on 22 October 1825. The one volume so far published is S. Reynolds, *A Catalogue of the Manuscripts in the Library at Holkham Hall*, I, i, Turnhout, 2015. I am grateful to Lord Leicester and to Laura Nuvoloni, current cataloguer in a long line from Madden, for allowing me time in the Manuscript Library at Holkham. Not all the manuscripts in Madden's time are still there, and there are groups now transferred to the British Library, the Bodleian and elsewhere (current locations are in Reynolds, pp. xv–xxiv). The best overall survey is still W. O. Hassall, ed., *The Holkham Library: Illuminations and Illustrations in the Manuscript Library of the Earl of Leicester*, Oxford, 1970. Palgrave (1788–1861, father of the *Golden Treasury* editor) was son-in-law of the Norfolk antiquary Dawson Turner (1775–1858), who had been helping Roscoe with the catalogue. A good account of the project is J. E. Graham, 'The Cataloguing of the Holkham Manuscripts', *Transactions of the Cambridge Bibliographical Society*, 4, 1965, pp. 128–54; for Madden's involvement, see also D. P. Mortlock, *Holkham Library: A History and Description*, Roxburghe Club, 2006, pp. 106–8, and Reynolds, pp. 19–20. Madden's first visit to Holkham was 1–24 March 1826. "Of the MSS . . ." (quoted here on p. 302) is c.146, p. 385. The second visit was 10 March to 21 April 1827. "Lady E. lingered . . ." is c.147, fol. 15v (that volume is unpaginated). On Jane Digby (1807–81), then Lady Ellenborough, see M. S. Lovell, *A Scandalous Life: The Biography of Jane Digby*, London and New York, 1996, her involvement with Madden being on pp. 30–34. Madden's later recollection followed a nostalgic conversation on 13 April 1858 with Admiral Greville, who had also been there then. Madden's catalogue is now Holkham MS 770. His jubilation on appointment to the Museum, "How excellent . . ." is c.147, fol. 56r. The two manuscripts acquired by Madden personally were (a) a late thirteenth-century two-volume Bible bought for £1.15s., taken by him to Puttick's for sale on 26 June 1865 but unsold at £9.15s., sold at Sotheby's, 29 June 1867, lot 317, £11, and now Leicester University Library MSS 9–10; and (b) *Agrimensores Romanorum* and other classical texts, early twelfth century, bought for £1.8s. ("This I consider very cheap", c.147, also fol. 56r), given on 20 November 1831 to Sir Thomas Phillipps, his MS 7017, his sale at Sotheby's, 30 November 1976, lot 857, described by me, later Tenschert, *Leuchtendes Mittelalters*, II, cat. XXV, 1990, no. 2. Madden's first marriage was on 18 April 1829, not 18 March as reported by the Ackermans and from there erroneously into the *Dictionary of National Biography*. Madden occupied three successive houses on the Museum premises. The first two were in a late seventeenth-century three-storey block which was on the left as you entered the Museum courtyard from Great Russell Street, entirely demolished in 1847. A detailed architectural plan by Augustus Pugin is in W. H. Leeds, *Illustrations of the Public Buildings of London, with Historical and Descriptive Accounts of each Edifice by Pugin and Britton*, II, London, 1838, pl. opp. p. 177, and its five occupants are named in several watercolours by John Wykeham Archer (1808–64), including British Museum 1939,0310.1; from 1829, Madden lived immediately to the right of the principal entrance, and in 1837, on becoming keeper, he moved into the apartment on the left of the entrance, adjacent to Panizzi's at the south-western end. In 1847 he was transferred across to the new east wing built for curators' residences, still there on the far right-hand side of the Museum forecourt and now used for administrative offices, parallel to Montague Street and almost reaching to the edge of Great Russell Street: the Maddens occupied the apartment at the extreme outer end of the wing nearest the street, furthest from the larger house of Panizzi, which adjoined the Museum building. It is now reconfigured inside but the Maddens' front door at the end of the wing is still used, as is the original staircase to the left as you come in; until recently at least, Marjorie Caygill tells me, Madden's built-in bookcases survived in what had been his study. The house was afterwards occupied by Sidney Colvin (1845–1927), whose friend Robert Louis Stevenson recalled staying there in his poem 'Apemama to S.C.' in his *Songs of Travel and Other Verses* (1896):

> In the upper room I lay, and heard far off
> The unsleeping city murmur like a shell;

The muffled tramp of the Museum guard
Once more went by me; I beheld again
Lamps vainly brighten the dispeopled street . . .

For Phillipps (pp. 305 and 307), the principal resource is and always will be A. N. L. Munby, *Phillipps Studies*, I–V, Cambridge, 1951–60. Madden first mentioned Phillipps on 7 February 1828. "We all say . . ." is c.147, fol. 99r. For Ottley, see A. N. L. Munby, *Connoisseurs and Medieval Miniatures, 1750–1850*, Oxford, 1972, pp. 62–8, and my 'Italian Choirbooks and the First Collectors of Miniatures', pp. 19–33 in S. Hindman and F. Toniolo, eds., *The Burke Collection of Italian Manuscript Paintings*, London, 2021, esp. pp. 26–9. Madden's recollection of snuff was on 15 July 1849. His "Amused myself . . ." (p. 307 here) is from 11 February 1829, c.147, fol. 110r. Ottley's collection of illuminations was sold at Sotheby's, 11 May 1838. The Psalter was lot 244 but Madden noticed that a group of single miniatures in lot 127 had been cut out of it by Ottley and these were reunited in time for the sale, when it made £37.10s. Madden had been told it was bought by the Duke of Lucca and so was surprised to see it with Holford on 4 November 1843: "I thought it . . ." is c.156, p. 356; "a stingy old . . ." is c.167, p. 131, on 30 March 1854. The manuscript is now New York, Morgan Library, M 729. Madden's visits to see the Bedford Hours were on 8 June 1829 and 20 May 1833; "I covet . . ." is c.147, fol. 119v. For Douce, see Munby, *Connoisseurs*, chapter 3, pp. 35–56, and S. G. Gillam, ed. (but mostly by A. C. de la Mare), *The Douce Legacy: An Exhibition to Commemorate the 150th Anniversary of the Bequest of Francis Douce (1757–1834)*, Oxford, 1984. He appears many times in R. Hill, *Time's Witness: History in the Age of Romanticism*, London, 2021. The manuscripts Douce showed to Madden were 9 November 1832, Bestiary (probably now Bodleian, MS Douce 167); 7 July 1833, miracles of the Virgin (now MS Douce 374); and 30 November 1833, *Graal* (now MS Douce 215, formerly La Vallière sale, 1783, lot 4006). "I wish to God . . ." is 2 April 1834, c.149, p. 114. Madden's wife, Mary, died of puerperal fever on 26 February 1830. For six weeks he wrote nothing and then inscribed great ghostly capitals across the page: "SHE IS DEAD! I can write no more . . ." (c.147, fol. 146r); the baby, quickly baptized 'Frederick', died on 3 March. "Rain. Sir T. Phillipps . . ." is c.147, fol. 161v; Bliss too was supportive. "The long-drawn agony of grief makes this part of the journal almost too painful to read, even after the lapse of more than a century" (Munby, *Phillipps Studies*, III, 1954, p. 110). The monument is still in Saint George's Church, but it was partly replaced in 1862 when Madden had the expressions of excessive inconsolability toned down. One paramour threatened blackmail (30 January 1834); another claimed to have been made pregnant (16 November 1834). "Damn all women, one pays too dear for them!" (c.149, p. 221). The expensive damage to his cab was on 24 May 1834. Lists of possibilities for a new wife occur on 5 January 1833, 11 March 1835, etc. "Called on the Ottleys . . ." is c.148, p. 93. On Anna Turner, see 13 and 17 January 1832. Phillipps suggested his eldest daughter, Henrietta, then only twelve, on 13 October 1831 and 20 June 1834, and then on 25 March 1835 he flatly denied ever saying so. Running through the story of the knighthood (pp. 509–10 here) is the delicate matter of social class and entitlement, crucial in understanding British society in the nineteenth century and not dissipated even today, although sometimes now operating in reverse. Madden would have spoken and behaved with the accent of a naval officer's family, which Panizzi decidedly did not, and his uncle, George Madden, already had a knighthood. Madden's "If I should succeed . . ." is c.148, p. 101, 11 March 1832. I am grateful to Sir Thomas Woodcock, then Garter King of Arms, for explaining the Royal Guelphic Order to me. Madden also became a Gentleman of the Privy Chamber to William IV and then Queen Victoria, until the office was abolished, and there are numerous accounts of royal levées and functions. He was in Westminster Abbey for the coronation of Victoria. The visits from Sir Walter Scott were on 7 and 17 October 1831 ("very curious ..." is c.148, p. 61); Scott is a key figure throughout Hill, *Time's Witness*, esp. pp. 197–202, but probably did not collect manuscripts (the fifteenth-century 'Haye Manuscript' at Abbotsford was recorded there only after Scott's death). Madden received a letter from the Rev. Mr McLeod of Uig on Lewis on 19 November 1832. Madden's article was 'Historical Remarks on the Introduction of the Game of Chess into Europe, and on Ancient Chessmen Discovered in the Isle of Lewis', *Archaeologia*, 34, 1831–2, pp. 203–91. A principal guidebook to the pieces is now N. Stratford, *The Lewis Chessmen and the Enigma of the Hoard*, London, 1997; more controversial (and longer) is N. M. Brown, *Ivory Vikings: The Mystery of the Most Famous Chessmen in the World and the Woman Who Made Them*, New York, 2015, crediting Madden, pp. 6–7. The acquisition of the Moutier-Grandval Bible, then called the 'Alcuin Bible', p. 311, is told at much greater length in Munby, *Connoisseurs*, pp. 150–55. "It is certainly ..." is c.151, p. 164, 15 June 1836. The manuscript is Add. MS 10546. Madden's article is 'Alchuine's Bible in the British Museum', *The Gentleman's Magazine*, n. s., 6, 1836, pp. 358–63, 468–77 and 580–87. For the rivalry of the two new Keepers, see M. A. F. Borrie, 'Panizzi and Madden', *British Library Journal*, 5, 1979, pp. 18–36. Madden's only real competitor as great public acquisitor of manuscripts would be Léopold Delisle (1826–1910), who became *conservateur* (keeper) of manuscripts in the Bibliothèque nationale in Paris in 1871, already a generation too late to match the opportunities Madden had. The last of many calculations by Madden of manuscripts added to the Museum during his keepership was on 11 October 1862. The *Lancelot-Grail* bought at the Heber sale (p. 315) is Add. MS 10292; the *Waldef* lost is now Cologny–Geneva, Fondation Martin Bodmer, Cod. Bodmer 168. Viewing the Sussex manuscripts at Kensington Palace was on 25 April 1844; by July, he was sleepless with worry about the auction. "And this is the treatment ..." (cited here on p. 316) is c.154, p. 287, 12 October 1841 ('asses' here is the English for donkeys, not the American for something different). William Richard Hamilton (1777–1859), a Trustee 1838–58, had also been Under-Secretary for Foreign Affairs and British Minister in Naples. Sources here are "In regard to the art ..." (c.155, p. 110) and "Who was the artist? ..." (*ibid.*, p. 111). It is curious that Clovio was then as much the default name for sixteenth-century illumination (Munby, *Connoisseurs*, pp. 25–6) as Bening has now become in our own time (see above, p. 136). The Portuguese genealogy is Add. MS 12531. Quotations "a consummate ninny" are c.155, p. 112, "I confess ..." (*ibid.*, p. 113), and "repeatedly called ..." (c.157, fol. 95r, 11 June 1844). A Mr Wright inquired on 14 February 1843 about publishing whatever Madden could tell him; Gustav Waagen revisited the British Museum in 1850 and, although he acknowledged the hospitality of Madden (who had a low opinion of him), he was not told anything about the artist of the genealogy, which he still attributed vaguely to the circle of Jan Mostaert (Waagen, *Treasures of Art in Great Britain, being an Account of the Chief Collections of Paintings, Drawings, Sculptures, Illuminated MSS, &c. &c.*, London, 1854, I, pp. 133–5). Subsequent revelations about its provenance included Mrs Barton's visit, 24 May; the Queen's observation that the leaves were "very pretty", told by Hamilton on 31 May (c.155, p. 132); "had all this been known ..." (*ibid.*, p. 124); the Treasury's refusal on 20 August; and information from Newton Scott's friend Mr Mansel on 20 July 1843 and from Stuart de Rothesay on 3 May 1849. On 15 December 1842, Madden was told by another friend of Scott's that the Escorial library had tried to stop the export from Spain. Even if the leaves were indeed in the royal library of Portugal, it is possible that they were given or even sold legitimately to a faithful employee. A. de Aguiar, *A Genealogia iluminada do Infante Dom Fernando por António de Holanda e Simão Bening, Estudo histórico e critic*, Lisbon, 1962, pp. 53 and 205, suggests that the leaves were stolen from the Spanish royal library, inconsistent with Madden's evidence, and F. F. de la Figanière, *Catalogo dos manuscriptos portuguezes existentes no Museu Britanico*, Lisbon, 1853, p. 270, says that they were bought in Lisbon for £40 by a "Mr Newton Smith", which is simply wrong (but still sometimes repeated in the literature). Madden's "a more prejudiced . . ." is c.171, p. 50, 11 February 1858. John Gage (1786–1842), pp. 318–19 here, added the surname Rokewode in 1838. His visits were 16 and 22 February 1841. "I dare not . . ." is c.154, p. 133. "This book ought . . ." is c.156, p. 281, 3 December 1843. The life of Saint Edmund is Morgan Library, M 736. John Gough Nichols (1806–73), p. 319, was a printer and antiquary. Madden reported the visit to Winchester on 15 January 1842, and Nichols reaffirmed details on 26 November 1844. The return of the manuscript to Winchester Cathedral was noted on 9 June 1842. It was lent to Madden on 12 April 1844: "ancient binding . . ." is c.157, fol. 51r. Madden calls it 'white': it was once pink, and traces of colour remain on the turn-ins. William Vaux (1818–85) was later Keeper of Coins and Medals (1861). Madden wrote to Canon Vaux (d. 1844) on 16 November. The letters from the Cathedral are in Egerton MS 2843, fols. 373, 375 and 377. "This is good" is c.157, fol. 206r. The conversation with William Turner Alchin (1790–1865) was on 5 January 1846. The cartulary is BL, Add. MS 15350, known as the Codex Wintoniensis (Davis, *Medieval Cartularies*, no. 1042). The stamped binding was removed by the Museum custodians in 1961, as regrettable a decision as Holford's rebinding of his life of St Edmund, although at least it was preserved (now Add. MS 15350/1). The flirtations with buying the Winchester Bible are recorded on 9 May 1849 (c.162, p. 153), 2 October 1851 (c.164, p. 330–31) and 6 May 1852 (c.165, p. 156). The manuscript is probably the finest work of art in the possession of the Church of England, Winchester Cathedral MS 17, now in its own shrine in the south transept. The literature on it is extensive, including C. Donovan, *The Winchester Bible*, London and Winchester, 1993. There was also an incident with the Mappa Mundi from Hereford Cathedral, which Madden longed to acquire. It was brought to him in London in 1855 and taken by the British Museum bindery from its medieval wooden frame to be cleaned and flattened. Unfortunately, they also removed the original decorated border from the map itself: "I am angry at such folly, but the deed is done, and no one but myself will ever notice the deficiency" (27 August 1855, c.168. p. 272); it seems that no one ever did. In 1988 the Mappa Mundi was in my own custody at Sotheby's in London when the Cathedral really did get close to selling it. "By opposing the Museum . . ." (p. 321) is c.151, p. 86, on 19 February 1836; "it's impossible . . ." is c.161, p. 111, on 27 April 1848; and "confound them both!" is c.168, p. 147, on 6 June 1855. "If America . . ." is c.168, p. 202, on 14 July 1855 (Madden actually wrote good "buy" for "bye"), occasioned by the sale of a Wycliffite New Testament for £129 for which the American bookseller Henry Stevens held a bid of £200 (now New York Public Library, MA 65); a very similar remark was made by Madden on 1 July 1853 when Stevens bought an early ninth-century Gospel Lectionary for £51 against the Museum's bid of £40 (now Williams College, Mass., Chapin Library, MS 7). The account of the Savile sale is on 6 February 1861. The manuscript bought is BL, Add. MS 24063. "Of what use . . ." and "One comfort . . ." are c.161, p. 229, on 11 August 1848. Madden is referring to Ashburnham Place, near Battle in Sussex, not the Ashburnham House in Westminster. The discussions and then loss of the

Ghislieri Hours were on 7 May and 6 and 19 July 1847. Madden suspected his assistant, John Holmes, of double-crossing the Museum, which seems probable. I have written about Dennistoun (1803–55) in *The Medieval World at Our Fingertips*, London and Turnhout, 2018, pp. 66–72. The manuscript is now BL, Yates Thompson MS 29. There is also a huge amount in the Madden journals on negotiations over the manuscript collections of Guglielmo Libri (1802–69), Italian confidence trickster and evident thief, bracketed easily by Madden with Panizzi, who introduced him to the Museum in 1846. His manuscripts were sold too, perhaps with more connivance of Holmes than was proper, to Ashburnham. I have not included Libri here from lack of space and the fact that the story is told in A. N. L. Munby, *Essays and Papers*, London, 1978, pp. 175–205, and P. A. Maccioni, 'Guglielmo Libri and the British Museum, A Case of Scandal Averted', *British Library Journal*, 17, 1991, pp. 36–60. Libri appears in my *Meetings with Remarkable Manuscripts*, pp. 195–8, as the seller of the Morgan Beatus to Ashburnham, but I did not then know that the manuscript was already on approval to Madden at a price of £60, before Libri bought it (15 April, 21 and 30 June, and 1 and 31 August 1855). Sir Thomas Phillipps agreed to be godfather to the Maddens' second son on 11 July 1841, p. 322 here; his unusual christening present arrived on the 27th. Fido was a Blenheim spaniel; he was preceded by Dash (d. 1864) and followed by Lady Fan. The Maddens also kept cats, including Mouton (d. 1859), acquired in Paris and given to Madden on Christmas Day 1854 by William Boone. On 28 June 1855, Mouton went missing. On the 29th, Madden reported the loss to the police and had notices printed offering 20 shillings reward for the cat's recovery. On the 30th, Mouton was found, locked in Panizzi's cellar. Madden's first ride on a train was on the Dublin and Kingston Railway, the earliest in Ireland, on 11 April 1835, less than a year after it opened; he first took a train from Paddington in 1840: "This is indeed travelling in ease and comfort" (c.153, p. 111). The "Talbotype artist" (c.162, p. 166) was presumably Richard Beard (1801–85), who opened in Regent Street in 1841. The photograph of a cartulary, p. 322, was pasted in on 6 November 1852. In 1856, Madden commissioned Roger Fenton (1819–69), just returned as photographer in the Crimean War, to take images from the Codex Alexandrinus, for what became the earliest published copy by photography of any medieval manuscript, *Photographic Facsimiles of the Remains of the Epistles of Clement of Rome*, published by the Museum, 1856, with a preface by Madden. The novelty postage stamp imitations, made by one Dixey, of Ship Street, Brighton, are pasted in on 11 September 1868 and 9 January 1869; I am indebted to my late cousin Timothy Maclaren, who included a note on them in *Cinderella Philatelist*, April 2021, p. 74, eliciting a response from a collector with another example by the same maker, but the Madden versions appear to be unrecorded. A list of Madden's publications is in Ackerman and Ackerman, pp. 45–70; see also R. W. Ackerman, 'Sir Frederic Madden and Medieval Scholarship', *Neuphilologische Mitteilungen*, 73, 1972, pp. 1–14. On the Wycliffite Bible, see A. Hudson, 'The Making of a Monumental Edition: *The Holy Bible ... The Earliest English Versions Made from the Latin Vulgate by John Wyclif and His Followers*', pp. 127–50 in S. M. Rowley, ed., *Writers, Editors and Exemplars in Medieval English Texts*, Basingstoke, 2021. Forshall and Madden's volumes are partly superseded by the editions of individual texts by C. Lindberg, 1959–2004. Madden's "to commemorate ..." is c.163, p. 351, on 21 October 1850. The copy for Prince Albert was sent for binding on 4 December 1850 and conveyed to Windsor on 13 January 1851. Madden was shown it in the Royal Library on 8 October 1852, "I ... trust it will remain there as long as the Castle itself endures" (c.165, p. 262). I am grateful to Stella Panayotova, Royal Librarian, for confirming that it is still there, inscribed by Madden as "most respectfully presented by ... the Originator and joint-Editor of the Work". In 1866, Madden published a variant he had noticed in several Museum copies of Valerius Maximus. He had written to the Burgerbibliothek in Bern, to check the reading in the oldest manuscript of the text, Cod. 366 there, ninth century, but the librarian, unable to read it, cut out the relevant half-page and sent it by post to Madden in London: "I feel quite *flabberghasted* [*sic*] at such an act of Vandal politeness!" (c.177, p. 30, 4 February 1864; Madden posted it back on 12 February and it is now resewn into the manuscript). On the restoration of the Cotton manuscripts (p. 323), see Andrew Prescott's article of 1997 cited in the notes to Chapter 5; pp. 409–31 are on Madden in particular. The Bishop of Durham offered to pay for a new binding for the Lindisfarne Gospels, Cotton Nero D. IV, and Madden was shocked at its vulgarity ("the result to myself, I confess, is very mortifying", c.166, p. 157, 6 May 1853; looking at J. Backhouse, *The Lindisfarne Gospels*, Oxford, 1981, pl. 63, it is hard to disagree). Phillipps's former Cotton cartulary from Exeter (Davis, *Medieval Cartularies*, no. 392) is discussed on 8 April 1831, 14 February 1851, 2, 5, 12 and 13 May and 28 June 1854, and the Cotton Genesis fragments in Bristol on 17 August 1844, 28 October 1845 and 13 March 1856 ("It is a scandalous shame that they should not be restored", c.169, p. 90). Attempts to retrieve the Utrecht Psalter are recounted on 1, 16 and 29 December 1856, and 7 and 21–22 January and 19 March 1857; see also D. Grosheide, A. D. A. Monna and P. N. G. Pesch, eds., *Vier eeuwen Universiteitsbibliotheek Utrecht*, I, *De eerste drie eeuwen*, Utrecht, 1986, pp. 236–8); the Musschenbroek archive was acquired by Utrecht anyway for £2000 in 1888 (Munby, *Phillipps Studies*, V, pp. 26–8). The glittering path of the Bedford Hours through numerous collections (p. 324 here) is recounted by Munby, *Connoisseurs*, pp. 2–13. The indiscreet Caleb Wing (1801–75) was restorer to the jeweller and dealer John Boykett Jarman (1782–1864), whose planned visit to Liverpool is what precipitated Boone's quick trip (for Wing and Jarman, see my *Fingertips*, pp. 135–42). "I felt a good deal . . ." is c.165, p. 42; "could not get . . ." is *ibid.*, p. 43. The seven manuscripts are (1) the Bedford Hours (Add. MS 18850); (2) the Breviary of Isabella of Castile, illuminated by Gerard David, the Dresden Master, and others (Add. MS 18851, which Madden had first seen on 30 March 1832); (3) the Hours of Joanna the Mad, illuminated by the Master of the David Scenes in the Grimani Breviary (Add. MS 18852); (4) the Hours of François I, illuminated by the Master of François de Rohan (Add. MS 18853, pl. 26 in Rive's *Essai sur l'art*); (5) the Hours of François de Dinteville, illuminated by Étienne Colaud (Add. MS 18854); (6) a Book of Hours from the workshop of Jean Bourdichon, with two separate miniatures by Simon Bening (Add. MS 18855); and (7) Guyart des Moulins, two-volume *Bible historiale*, illuminated by the Master of the Cité des Dames and the Bedford Master again (Add. MS 18856-57). The miniatures in the Breviary which are nineteenth century (as is now well-known) are those on fols. 363v, 344r, 367r, 368r and 385v. The Towneley Lectionary is New York Public Library, MA 91. Its miniatures on fols. 11v and 20v are presumed to be only slightly later (J. J. G. Alexander, *The Towneley Lectionary, Illuminated for Cardinal Alessandro Farnese by Giulio Clovio*, Roxburghe Club, 1997, pp. 17–19, and Alexander in J. J. G. Alexander, J. H. Marrow and L. F. Sandler, eds., *The Splendor of the Word*, New York, London and Turnhout, 2006, pp. 159–60). The sale of the extensive library of Lord Stuart de Rothesay (1779–1845), pp. 328–9 here, began at Sotheby's on 31 May 1855 and lasted fifteen days. Madden's conversations about lot 2353 were reported on 8, 10, 26 and 30 May, and on 6 and 8 June. "The auctioneer seemed . . ." is c.168, p. 149. The *Miroir historial* is Chantilly, Musée Condé, ms 722. The Stuart de Rothesay Hours is BL, Add. MS 20927. It is no. 120 in A. C. de la Mare and L. Nuvoloni, *Bartolomeo Sanvito: The Life & Work of a Renaissance*

Scribe, Paris, 2006, pp. 366–7, with details on the artist and patronage, although Sanvito was not known in Madden's time. Madden's "And what has *he* done . . ." on Panizzi's appointment (p. 330) is c.169, p. 74, 1 March 1856. The "madness" of exhibiting manuscripts is 17 January 1862 (c.175, p. 74). His fear of gaslight and dust was actually directed at displays of manuscripts in the museum in South Kensington (2 May 1861); "more harm than good . . ." was a comment agreeing with the opinion of John Ruskin, who had referred mischievously to "those tumultuous and congested national *toy-displays*" (*ibid.*, p. 94, 31 March 1862). "I feel perfectly disgusted" is c.173, p. 236, 20 July 1860. I owe my visit to the sites of the old Manuscripts department to Francesca Hillier, the Museum's archivist, and Marjorie Caygill, who guided us both with her great knowledge and with her book written with Christopher Date, *Building the British Museum*, London, 1999. "Entering the front yard . . ." (pp. 330–31) is from 'The British Museum and its Reading Room', pp. 198–209 in *Harper's New Monthly Magazine*, 46, no. 272, January 1873, p. 2. "From this room . . ." is A. Panizzi, *A Short Guide to that Portion of the Library of Printed Books now open to the Public*, London, 1851, p. 5, describing the displays laid out in the Museum to coincide with the Great Exhibition, to which Madden reluctantly contributed. His outage at Panizzi's dismissal of the Manuscripts Saloon was on 19 May 1851, adding, "Dirty blackguard! This room containing MSS is of ten times more value and interest than the libraries of Grenville and George III put together!" (c.164, p. 143, 19 May 1851). The *Illustrated London News* for 1851, "From the Grenville Room . . .", is p. 505 there, noted by Madden in his journal for 7 June. The detailed plan I used was *British Museum: Plan of the Ground Floor*, drawn 1857, "N°. 379, Ordered by the House of Commons to be printed", 1858, shown to me by Marjorie Caygill. The layout was discussed in A. Prescott, 'What's in a Number? The Physical Organization of the Collections in the British Library', pp. 471–526 in A. N. Doane and K. Wolf, eds., *Beatus Vir: Studies in Early English and Norse Manuscripts in Memory of Phillip Pulsiano*, Tempe, Ariz., 2006. Richard Holmes (1835–1911) was the son of John Holmes, Madden's previous assistant, and was later Royal Librarian at Windsor. The space occupied by his office in the Museum was later known as the 'Old Sanskrit Library', and that occupied by Madden as the 'Bible' or 'Crawford' Room, both redundant when the British Library left the building. Madden's question about the Oppenheim manuscripts was addressed to Henry Coxe at the Bodleian (journal, 2 June 1865). He saw the Duc de Berry's *Grandes Heures* on 26 May 1846 ("very barbarously . . .", c.159, p. 235, but "still forms one of the great monuments of the library", p. 236); he looked at the *Bible historiale* (now Baltimore Walters Art Museum, MS W. 125) on 22 April 1853, having been told on the 20th that the Duke of Sussex had offered £1500 for it ("*incredible sum*!", c.166, p. 132, and "I should think . . .", p. 139); the *Cité de Dieu* (now Harvard, Houghton Library, MS Typ. 201, with a further volume) belonged to N. W. Thompson of Lincoln's Inn (10 July 1856). The long quotation, "Anyone who had seen . . ." is 18 December 1855 (c.168, p. 395, with adjusted punctuation); he later described the Cotton collection as "doubtless the most valuable present ever bestowed on the Nation" (12 July 1866, c.179, p. 176). Autographs (p. 333) were sought after in the nineteenth century and what the public asked for, which is probably less true now. Marlborough House (later the Museum of Ornamental Art, later still the South Kensington Museum, finally the Victoria and Albert Museum) bought its first single miniature in James Dennistoun's sale, Christie's, 14 June 1855, lot 47 (now V. & A., 7019-1855), and others in 1856 and 1858, "forming a rival Museum", said Madden (c.171, p. 102, 23 March 1858), and later that such items "ought properly to be in my Department" (c.174, p. 98). The Keeper of Prints and Drawings threatening to buy miniatures at the Rogers sale was W. H. Carpenter (1792–1866): 22 April and 5 and 8 May 1856. Madden then bought lot 1006 at the sale for £115.10s., an album to which he added other Italian cuttings bought as lots 1002, 1005 and 1008–9, all becoming Add. MS 21412, separated into its component parts again in 1989. The Étienne Chevalier miniature was finally bought in 1886, now Add. MS 37421. The Bening miniatures known as the 'Golf Book' are Add. MS 24098, brought to Madden on 9 March 1861 and agreed by the Trustees on 13 April 1861. A note in Madden's hand on the flyleaf reports that the illuminator might be Gerard Horenbout. For the sale of the Pontifical in Paris (pp. 333–4), see C. Reynolds and J. Stratford, 'Le manuscrit dit "Le Pontifical de Poitiers"', *Revue de l'Art*, 84, 1989, pp. 61–80, and A. Jammes with F. Courbage, *Les Didot*, Paris, 1998, pp. 96–7, no. 247, as well as journal entries from 10–30 April 1861. On 12 August 1871, Madden learned of the Pontifical's destruction: "This is too shocking!" (c.182, p. 266). The Holkham Bible Picture Book is Add. MS 47682. The Luttrell Psalter is Add. MS 42130, and "the art is . . ." is c.152, p. 271, 20 January 1839. The Sherborne Missal is Add. MS 74236, and "I should judge . . ." is c.155, pp. 129–30, 30 May 1842. The Saint Cuthbert (or 'Stonyhurst') Gospel is Add. MS 89000, seen on 5 May 1862 by Madden, who was not prepared to guess at the age of its binding. The two parts of the Hours of Catherine of Cleves (p. 335) are New York, Morgan Library, M 917 (formerly Rothschild) and M 945 (formerly Arenberg). The most useful introduction, probably the first book on manuscripts I ever bought, is J. Plummer, *The Hours of Catherine of Cleves: Introduction and Commentaries*, New York and London, 1966, and the most comprehensive is R. Dückers and R. Priem, eds., *The Hours of Catherine of Cleves: Devotion, Demons and Daily Life in the Fifteenth Century*, New York, 2009. The not-yet-Arenberg volume was lot 225 added to the end of the sale of the library of S. W. Singer, Sotheby's, 3 August 1858. "I should like . . ." is c.171, p. 242, 22 July 1858; the conversation with Boone was on the 30th. That volume now has 15 full-page miniatures, 48 half-page miniatures and one historiated initial (fol. 47v), a total of 64. The 'Codicological Diagram' by Dückers in *Devotion, Demons*, pp. 88–99 (corrected in his later commentary to the facsimile, 2009–10, pp. 107–21), is missing miniatures after fols. 10, 89, 108, 123, 130 and 150, which would bring the total to Madden's seventy. The volume's next absolute date is 1896, the death of Prince Charles d'Arenberg, who had bought it for his wife, who in that year passed it on to her nephew. Madden's first meeting with the Duc d'Aumale was 3 August 1849. "It is a most . . ." is c.169, p. 49. For the *Très Riches Heures* (Musée Condé, ms 65), see Chapter 2, and references. It is fortunately still in its red morocco binding. On its purchase in January 1856, see my *Meetings with Remarkable Manuscripts*, pp. 560–62. Panizzi later arranged for the manuscript to be shown to Queen Victoria at Windsor. Madden's "a deep curse . . ." (p. 337) is c.179, p. 272. The children who lived to adulthood were Frederic William (1839–1904), known as Fritz, who married so far beneath his father's expectations that they hardly spoke again, carelessly lost several early jobs and ended up as chief librarian of Brighton Public Library; George Ernest Phillipps (1841–65), whose early death at twenty-four was attributed to syphilis; Emily Mary (1848–1923), known as Mary, who in 1870 married Lieutenant-Colonel William Tedlie (1828–77) and went out to India, and as his widow later married Windham Hunt Holley (1835–98); and James Arnold Wycliffe (1850–84), known as Arnold, who died as a tea planter in Ceylon aged thirty-four. The planchette, a writing machine used by spiritualists, was consulted on 18 March 1869; Madden's disappointment was expressed on 31 December 1872, showing it to be "a *lie*, a *deception and a sham*" (c.182, p. 427). "Daily, hourly . . ." is *ibid.*, p. 389 (1 September 1872). He saw the Saluces Hours on 20 June 1867; it had been pl. 21 in Rive's *Essai* and is now Add. MS 27697. The Portuguese genealogy leaves were added to Add. MS 12531, fols. 5* and 9*. "I should like . . ." is c.181, p. 172, 21 May 1869 (the price, which he so wanted to know, was £40, according to Aguiar, *Genealogia iluminada*, p. 48). Kathleen Doyle located the portrait for me. The burial records of Kensal Green list him as being in vault 188 of Catacomb B, part of the Anglican chapel in the centre of the cemetery, but when I pushed inside I could see no inscriptions or tablets. Madden's conversation with Lemon was on 12 October 1849; "*nous verrons*" is c.162, p. 318.

9. THE FORGER: CONSTANTINE SIMONIDES

"Facts about Simonides are not easy to come by", wrote A. N. L. Munby, *Phillipps Studies*, IV, 1956, p. 114, in which his chapter VI, pp. 114–31, is my principal source for the visit of Simonides to Middle Hill. Munby, in turn, drew from J. A. Farrer, *Literary Forgeries*, London, 1907, chapter III, 'Greek Forgery: Constantine Simonides', pp. 39–66. There is still no modern narrative dedicated to the career of Simonides; a biography was at one time announced from Bruce Whiteman, whose papers for the project now appear to be in the Thomas Fisher Rare Book Library in Toronto. There is a volume of essays of mixed value, some good, A. E. Müller, L. Diamantopoulou, C. Gastgeber and A. Katsiakiori-Rankl, eds., *Die getäuschte Wissenschaft: Ein Genie betrügt Europa – Konstantinos Simonides*, Vienna, 2017, and a slight little book, R. Schaper, *Die Odyssee des Fälschers: Die abenteuerliche Geschichte des Konstantin Simonides, der Europa zum Narren hielt und nebenbei die Antike erfand*, Munich, 2011. There are brief pieces on Simonides in E. Richardson, *Classical Victorians: Scholars, Scoundrels and Generals in Pursuit of Antiquity*, Cambridge, 2013, esp. pp. 142–8 on 'The Curious Mr Simonides', and C. P. Jones, 'A Syntax of Forgery', *Proceedings of the American Philosophical Society*, 160, 2016, pp. 26–36. The quotation about the face of Simonides being not easily forgotten is from a letter from Charles Stewart, supposed author of the *Biographical Memoir*, 1859 (mentioned on p. 345), quoted by Farrer, *Literary Forgeries*, p. 58, and Munby, *Phillipps Studies*, IV, p. 115. Broadway Tower, which belonged to Phillipps, was later rented by William Morris, who used to stay here with Dante Gabriel Rosetti, Burne-Jones and others. It is open to the public. The often-cited quotation from Lady Phillipps in a letter to a friend about being 'booked out of one wing . . . ', p. 343 here, is originally from Munby, *Phillipps Studies*, II, 1952, p. 91. Phillipps's lithograph of the Hesiod is no. 347 in E. Holzenberg, *The Middle Hill Press: A Checklist of the Horblit Collection . . . Now in the Library of the Grolier Club*, New York, 1997, p. 95. The quotation from Madden's journal on p. 344 is for 5 May 1854 (Bodleian, MS Eng. hist. c.167, pp. 148–9), printed with an unimportant variant in Munby, *Phillipps Studies*, II, pp. 122–3, and that from Kohl is extracted from *ibid.*, pp. 124–6, where it was translated from J. G. Kohl, *Vom Markt und aus der Zelle: Populäre Vorträge und vermischte kleine Schriften*, II, Hanover, 1868, pp. 55–9 (reproduced also in G. A. E. Bogeng, *Die grossen Bibliophilen*, I, Leipzig, 1922, pp. 481–90). My quotations from Phillipps describing Simonides and his manuscripts are all taken either from his own printed *Catalogus Librorum Manuscriptorum in Bibliotheca D. Thomæ Phillipps, Bart.*, Middle Hill, 1837–71, pp. 254–5, or from notes enclosed with the purchases, cited in the Sotheby's sale catalogue of 1972. The opening of the Homer scroll with lines of micrography forming outlines of a picture reflects a tradition found in medieval Hebrew manuscripts, as above, p. 236, in texts where illustration was forbidden but excused if it was merely script; figurative art was also prohibited during the iconoclastic period of Byzantium in the eighth to ninth centuries, but micrographic alternatives were not a Greek tradition. The account of Simonides' Uncle Benedict on Mount Athos is found in the *Biographical Memoir*, pp. 3–4. The antipathy of the monks of Athos to Catholicism is recounted in W. Dalrymple, *From the Holy Mountain*, London, 1988, pp. 9–10. Phillipps's reference to 'Mr Bowen' in his printed catalogue comes from G. F. Bowen, *Mount Athos, Thessaly, and Epirus: A Diary of a Journey from Constantinople to Corfu*, London, 1852, p. 72. The fantasy of any manuscript obsessive to own a relic from the library of Alexandria, p. 347, is conjured by the modern collector Martin Schøyen, who is also proud to name Phillipps among his heroes and role models, 'The Saga of Christianity's Oldest Liturgical Book', pp. 405–11 in J. H. Marrow, R. A. Linenthal and W. Noel, eds., *The Medieval Book: Glosses from Friends & Colleagues of Christopher de Hamel*, 't Goy-Houten, 2010. The letter of Simonides to the *Guardian* in 1863, quoted here on p. 347, is from L. Diamantopoulou, 'Konstantinos Simonides: Leben und Werk. Ein tabellarischer Überblick', pp. 305–25 in Müller *et al.*, eds., *Die getäuschte Wissenschaft*, as above, p. 305. The denunciation of Simonides in the *Allgemeinische Zeitung* of November 1853 appeared in English in *The Athenaeum*, no. 1478, 23 February 1856, p. 233, which I have read in British Library 1700.b.4, a volume of newspaper cuttings relating to Simonides; it was also published in French in *L'Athenaeum Française*, December 1853, pp. 1185–6. The remark of Patriarch Arthimus IV echoes the sentiment of the Caliph Omar on the destruction of the library of Alexandria in the mid-seventh century: 'If these writings of the Greeks agree with the book of God, they are useless and need not be preserved; if they disagree, they are pernicious and ought to be destroyed' (R. Ovenden, *Burning the Books*, Cambridge, Mass., 2020, p. 32). Simonides may nonetheless have staged a show excavation in Constantinople. "He declared that at a certain spot an Arabic MS in Syriac characters would be discovered by digging. Workmen were accordingly employed, Simonides himself not being allowed to descend. By-and-bye a pause was made for luncheon, and not long afterwards Simonides called out, 'There it is, bring it up.' The soil about it, however, was quite different from that of the ground. The workmen . . . when interrogated confessed that during luncheon the Greek came out for a short time and jumped into the pit, and began to burrow" (*London Evening Standard*, 1 October 1867, and other newspapers, including *The New York Times*, 20 October 1867). Phillipps's habit of staying up late (p. 350 here) is confirmed by Madden on a visit to Middle Hill: "Sir Thos. always keeps me up, and shows me MSS till my eyes ache" (journal, 31 August 1846; Bodleian, MS Eng. hist. c.159, p. 362; elsewhere Madden says that Phillipps often did not go to bed at all but stayed downstairs fully dressed on the sofa). The various different forgeries (and probable forgeries) bought from Simonides by Phillipps at different times are listed in his catalogue under the following titles, (1) "Panselinos twn Zographwn, *or* Manual of Painters" (MS 13871; Sotheby's, 4 July 1972, lot 1730; now St John's University, Collegeville, Minnesota, Kacmarcik MS 21, Arca Artium Collection); (2) "Meletius's History of Byzantine Painting" (MS 13872; Sotheby's, 1972, as above, lot 1731; A. Freeman, *Bibliotheca Fictiva: A Collection of Books & Manuscripts Relating to Literary Forgery, 400 BC–AD 2000*, London, 2014, pp. 376–7, no. 1504, with plate; now the Sheridan Libraries, Johns Hopkins University, Baltimore); (3)–(5) "A MS. in Arrowhead Character on Vellum", "Euleri Ethnica" and "Neocomi Historia Byzantina" (MSS 13873–5; together, Sotheby's, 1972, lot 1732); (6) "Homeri Ilias" (MS 13877; Sotheby's, 1972, lot 1724; now Yale University, Beinecke Library, Osborn d543, bought from Professor Takamiya on the James Marshall and Marie-Louise Osborn Collection Fund, 2019); (7) "Hesiodi Opera" (MS

13878; Sotheby's, 1972, lot 1725); (8)–(9) "Anacreontis Carmina" and "Pythagoræ Aurea Carmina" (MSS 13879–80; together, Sotheby's, 1972, part of lot 1726; now Beinecke MS 581); (10) "Tyrtæi Odæ" (MS 13881; Sotheby's, 1972, lot 1727; now Beinecke MS 580; C. E. Lutz, 'A Forged Manuscript in Boustrophedon', *Yale University Library Gazette*, 53, 1978, pp. 28–44); (11) "Phocylidis Carmina, &c." (MS 13882; Sotheby's, 1972, lot 1728; now Beinecke MS 582); and (12)–(13) "A Charter . . .", "Another similar Charter . . .", "A third Charter more suspicious than the others" (MSS 13883-85; together, Sotheby's, 1972, lot 1729; now Beinecke MS 583). Beinecke MS 251, which is genuine, is listed in B. M. W. Knox *et al.*, 'The Ziskind Collection of Greek Manuscripts', pp. 39–56 in *The Yale University Library Gazette*, 32, 1957, p. 51. Phillipps's suggestion that the scrolls might be made from boa constrictor skin occurs in his letter to S. L. Sotheby, who printed it in his *Principia Typographica*, II, London, 1858, p. 136e. I am grateful to Professor Takamiya for advice on the Homer and for allowing me to see it. The visits of Simonides to the British Museum, pp. 354–5, are recounted in Madden's journal for 22–23 February 1853. The quotation "At first . . ." is Bodleian, MS Eng. hist. c.166, p. 65. Madden also wrote a recollection of the same visit in his journal on 23 April 1856, quoted by Munby, *Phillipps Studies*, IV again, pp. 116–18. That is the source for the discreet aside by Barker, traveller and orientalist (and member of a family of shipping agents in Alexandria), who died of cholera in the Crimean War. Madden's purchases of authentic manuscripts from Simonides are now BL, Add. MSS 19386–93 (*Catalogue of Additions to the Manuscripts in the British Museum in the Years MDCCCXLVIII–MDCCCLIII*, London, 1868, pp. 228–9); on 1 March 1853 he recorded the agreed price as £35 but in the later account remembered it as £42. On 3 March 1853, the dealer William Boone showed Madden several Greek manuscripts which he too had evidently bought from Simonides. The two versions of Simonides' visit to the Bodleian Library occur in *The Athenaeum*, no. 1479, 4 March 1856, included in the volume of newspaper cuttings cited above, and in the *Biographical Memoir*, pp. 26–9. The encounter is also described in W. D. Macray, *Annals of the Bodleian Library, Oxford, A.D. 1598–A.D. 1867*, [London], 1868, pp. 280–81, and H. H. E. Craster, *History of the Bodleian Library, 1845–1945*, Oxford, 1952, p. 88. Bodleian, MS Barocci 33 is a collection of texts by Matthaeus Blastares, Gemistus Pletho and others, in its original blind-stamped binding. I owe the translation of the letter to Coxe, cited here on p. 356, entirely to the kindness of Dr Mae A. Goldgraben and her mother, Dr Giannoula I. Mihailidou. The story of Simonides in Paris is from *L'Athenaeum Française*, V, 23 February 1856, pp. 156–7, supplemented by Farrer, *Literary Forgeries*, p. 156; O. Masson, 'Le faussaire grec C. Simonides à Paris en 1854, avec deux lettres inconnues de Sainte-Beuve et un récit du comte de Marcellus', pp. 367–79 in *Journal des Savants*, 1994, including but dismissing the theory that Simonides had faked the letter from Sainte-Beuve (p. 372); and D. Hernández de la Fuente, 'The Poet and the Forger: On Nonnius' False Biography by Constantine Simonides', pp. 59–71 in J. Martínez, ed., *Fakes and Forgeries of Classical Literature*, Leiden and Boston, 2014. The date of the death of Marcellus is sometimes given as 1861, but 1865 appears to be the consensus. The price of the supposed Uranius palimpsest to Berlin (p. 358 here) was sometimes reported as 5000 Thalers, of which 2000 had been paid as a deposit (e. g. *St James's Chronicle*, 14 February 1856). Dindorf's embarrassing edition of Uranius is *Uranii Alexandrini De regibus Aegyptiorum libri tres, Operis ex codice palimpsesto edendi specimina proposuit Gulielmus Dindorfius*, Oxford, 1856. Six copies are known to survive: see P. M. Pinto, 'Simonides in England: A Forger's Progress', pp. 109–26 in Müller *et al.*, eds., *Die getäuschte Wissenschaft*, pp. 114–15. The adjective 'Uranian' was not used with sexual connotations until the 1860s. The letter from Dindorf to the University Press is bound into BL, Add. MS 81080, A–O, fol. 51. For Mayer (from pp. 358 onwards here), see M. Gibson and S. M. Wright, eds., *Joseph Mayer of Liverpool, 1803–1886*, London, 1988 (*Society of Antiquaries, Occasional Papers*, n. s., XI), esp. A. F. Shore, 'The Egyptian Collection', pp. 45–70. For his dealings with Simonides I used two volumes of papers in the British Library, Add. MSS 42502 A–B (some of it in Greek, which I have not read), assembled by the antiquary John Eliot Hodgkin. His family were Quakers and looked for the good in all people; the twentieth-century artist Howard Hodgkin was a direct descendant. The first volume includes the deposition of Simonides (in English), fols. 359–85, which gave me several quotations here in the voice of Simonides. His report of the Mayer hieroglyphics (p. 359) was published as Επιστολιμαια *περι ίερογλυφικων γραμματων διατριβη* (*A Brief Dissertation on Hieroglyphic Letters*), London and Liverpool, 1860, in the form of an epistolary essay addressed to Mayer "as a small mark of personal attachment"; citing Egyptian sources, including his own Uranius, Simonides stubbornly explains hieroglyphs as purely symbolic, not alphabetical or phonetic, as in the interpretations of Champollion (1822) and Lepsius (1837). Stobart's confirmation that he had acquired papyrus scrolls in Egypt and sold them to Mayer is in *The Athenaeum*, no. 1781, 14 December 1861, p. 807, and Mayer in turn confirmed that the scrolls had come from both Stobart and Sams, categorically not from Simonides (*The Athenaeum*, no. 1783, 28 December 1861). Stobart had previously offered his papyri to the British Museum (Madden's journal, 19 September 1856; Bodleian, MS Eng. hist. c.169, p. 307); Madden had a low opinion of Sams, "a sad rogue, I believe" (journal, 7 December 1850, MS Eng. hist. c.163, p. 389). Tischendorf had found a fragment of the Codex Sinaiticus in 1844, but the principal part in 1859, almost simultaneous with Darwin's *Origin of Species*. Another forgery of the same momentous year attempted to debunk Christianity from a supposed manuscript source: the *Wichtige historische Enthüllungen über die wirkliche Todesart Jesu*, Leipzig, 1859, went through at least six editions, claiming to publish an ancient manuscript found in a cave in Alexandria showing that the Resurrection was a hoax perpetrated by the Essenes; it was later shown to derive from a novel published in 1800 (Freeman, *Bibliotheca Fictiva*, pp. 354–5, nos. 1387–9). Simonides' huge book *Fac-Similes of Certain Portions of the Gospel of Matthew*, 1861, as described on p. 362, recounts the stages of the unrolling and revelation, including the headline from the *Liverpool Mercury* and reports of the public glorifying God (p. 7). The variant reading of 'cable' for 'camel' is the plate between pp. 44 and 45. There is a long and useful article by F. H. A. Scrivener, 'Constantine Simonides and His Biblical Studies', in the guise of a review of *Fac-Similes* and of Tischendorf's publication of the Sinaiticus New Testament in *The Christian Remembrancer*, 46, July 1863, pp. 175–208, again rehearsing and refining the stages of the discoveries and critically assessing the accompanying claims. Simonides' edition of *The Periplus of Hannon, King of the Karchedonians*, London, 1864, includes attestations by Mayer that the scrolls were in his possession long before Simonides made his finds (p. 2) and that they were unrolled in the museum in the presence of the curator (p. 4). On the reuse of the word 'gorilla', see T. S. Savage and J. Wyman, 'Notice of the External Characters and Habits of *Troglodytes gorilla*', *Boston Journal of Natural History*, 5, 1847, pp. 417–42, and M. Mund-Dopchie, 'Les humanistes face aux Gorilles d'Hannon', pp. 331–42 in *Proses et Prosateurs de la Renaissance: Mélanges offerts à M. le Professeur Robert Aulotte*, Paris, 1988. The two known manuscripts of the *Periplus* of Hanno are Heidelberg, Universitätsbibliothek, Cod. Pal. G. 398, fols. 55r–56r, and BL, Add. MS 19391, folio 12r–v. I am indebted to Ashley Cooper and Chrissy Partheni for advice on the papyri in Liverpool and for facilitating my visit.

The exhibits in Liverpool at the opening of the Free Library were reported in the *Northern Daily Times*, 20 October 1860. The accusations of Simonides against Jonas King (pp. 364–5) are recounted in 'Letter from Mr King, August 27, 1847', *The Missionary Herald, containing the Proceedings of the American Board of Commissioners for Foreign Missions, with a View of Other Benevolent Operations*, 43, 1847, pp. 366–72; *Message from the President of the United States, Communicating, in Compliance with a Resolution of the Senate, Copies of the Communications from Mr Marsh, the American Minister at Constantinople, Relative to the Case of the Reverend Mr King*, Washington, 1854, pp. 66 and 119–22; F. E. H. H[aynes], *Jonas King, Missionary to Syria and Greece*, New York, 1879, pp. 308–9; and L. Bossina, 'Konstantinos Simonides, die Vereinigten Staaten und der 'griechische Luther'', pp. 143–86 in Müller *et al.*, eds., *Die getäuschte Wissenschaft*. The article in *The Athenaeum*, "Is there no limit . . .", quoted on p. 365 is in no. 1780, 7 December 1861, pp. 755–86, ostensibly a review of Simonides' *Fac-Similies* but largely a reminder of his earlier life, drawing on previous pieces in *The Athenaeum*, including the translation of the article from the *Allgemeinische Zeitung*, cited above, and the opinions of Madden (no. 1480, 8 March 1856, pp. 298–9) and Phillipps (no. 1536, 4 April 1857, p. 438). The letter of Hodgkin to his uncle, p. 365, is in BL, Add. MS 42502A, fol. 146, and that of Thomas Wright (1810–77) to Hodgkin is fol. 153. Bradshaw's account of the meeting in Cambridge is told in a letter to the *Guardian*, 28 January 1863, reprinted in G. W. Prothero, *Memoir of Henry Bradshaw, Fellow of King's College, Cambridge, and University Librarian*, London, 1888, pp. 95–6. On the scroll of Deuteronomy reputedly found in a cave in Jordan (p. 366 here), see J. M. Allegro, *The Shapira Affair*, London, 1965, and B. S. Hill, 'Ephraim Deinard on the Shapira Affair', in R. Linenthal, ed., *The Book Collector: Special Number for the 150th Anniversary of Bernard Quaritch*, London, 1997, pp. 167–79. Arguments in favour of the authenticity of the Shapira fragments are in I. Dershowitz, *Valediction of Moses: A Proto-Biblical Book*, Tübingen, 2021 (*Forschungen zum Alten Testament*, 145), severely challenged in an on-line review, C. Rollston, 'Déjà Vu All Over Again: The Antiquities Market, the Shapira Strips, Menahem Mansoor, and Idan Dershowitz', March 2021. Madden's account of the meeting of the scientific committee, cited here on p. 366, is in his journal entry for 7 January 1863 (Bodleian, MS Eng. hist. c.176. p. 5). The papyri were put out for public inspection in the rooms of the Royal Society from 11a.m. to 3 p.m. each day on 9–10 January (*Saint James's Chronicle*, 10 January 1863). Madden declined Hodgkin's offer to place the Uranius in the custody of the British Museum, even if only for examination, fearing that this might be misconstrued as endorsement (BL, Add. MS 42502, fol. 166, Madden to Hodgkin, 10 January 1863). The committee's findings were published as the *Report of the Council of the Royal Society of Literature, on some of the Mayer Papyri, and the palimpsest MS of Uranius belonging to M. Simonides, with Letters from MM. Pertz, Ehrenberg, and Dindorf*, London, 1863; the conclusion quoted here is on p. 7. Belief that the Mayer biblical papyri are nevertheless genuine survived into Farrer, *Literary Forgeries*, p. 56, and even Freeman, *Bibliotheca Fictiva*, p. 378. There is another fragment, nothing to do with Simonides, known popularly as the 'Jesus wife papyrus', which came to light in 2012. It is unquestionably a crude modern fake (I have held it in my hands) but it still attracts myriads of credulous adherents. There is immense literature on the Codex Sinaiticus (BL Add. MS 43725) but a very good introduction is D. C. Parker, *Codex Sinaiticus: The Story of the World's Oldest Bible*, London, 2010 (dismissing involvement of Simonides as "ridiculous", p. 152). A sound rebuttal of Simonides' pretence, and indeed a coherent summary of his career, is J. K. Elliott, *Codex Sinaiticus and the Simonides Affair: An Examination of the*

Nineteenth-Century Claim That Codex Sinaiticus was Not an Ancient Manuscript, Thessalonikē, 1982 (*Analekta Vlatadōn*, 33). The letter of Simonides in January 1860 first hinting at having made Sinaiticus is addressed to 'Charles Stewart', reputed author of the *Biographical Memoir*, cited by Elliott, *Codex Sinaiticus*, pp. 26–30. The issue of the *Literary Gazette* was no. 161, 27 July 1861. Simonides' long letter to the *Guardian* was published on 3 September 1862, and reprinted often, as in *The Journal of Sacred Literature and Biblical Record*, n. s., II, 1863, pp. 248–50. Wright's letter to the *Guardian* about the impossibility of such a task appeared on 27 October 1862, and reappears in Scrivener's review, 'Constantine Simonides and his Biblical Studies', as above, p. 202. The letter about no children being allowed on Mount Athos was from S. Nicolaides, archdeacon of the Metropolis of Salonica, published in *The Pantheon*, no. 44, 28 February 1863, adding also that he knew Athos well and had never heard of a Benedict living there (this, like many of my newspaper references, is in that British Library album of press cuttings). Further exchanges in the press, including those of Simonides himself and his summoning of corroboration from the monk Kallinikos, are conveniently reprinted in sequence in B. Harris Cowper, ed., *The Journal of Sacred Literature and Biblical Record*, n. s., II, 1863, pp. 248–53 and 488–91, and III, 1863, pp. 210–34 and 478–98, available on-line. The 'originals' of the letters from Kallinikos are among the Hodgson papers, BL, Add. MSS 42502B, fols. 132, 155 and 172, and were printed in English in *The Literary Churchman*, 16 January 1863. Madden's account of seeing the Leipzig leaves of Sinaiticus in London is in his journal for that day, Bodleian, MS Eng. hist. c.178, pp. 22–3. Tischendorf's lecture was published as *Mémoire sur la découverte et l'antiquité du Codex Sinaiticus (Lu à la séance du 15 février 1865)*, London, 1865, not mentioning the presence of the original leaves, although this was recorded by a witness in *The Journal of Sacred Literature*, 7, 1865, p. 108. Cooper's strange book *The Forging of Codex Sinaiticus*, cited on p. 373, was published in Portsmouth, 2016. The Codex Vaticanus (Vatican, cod. Vat. gr. 1209) has been known and documented since the fifteenth century, and the Bodmer papyri (Cologny–Geneva, Bibliotheca Bodmeriana, pap. I–XLIV) were first excavated in Egypt in or not long before 1952. A few moments' idle trawling through the internet will bring up numerous conspiracy theories crediting Simonides not only with Sinaiticus, against all rational and chronological evidence, but also with the Artemidorus papyrus, owned by a bank in Turin, in which he had no part either. The death of Simonides in Alexandria in September 1867 was reported in the *Daily News*, 4 October 1867, p. 3; *Notes & Queries*, 3 ser., XII, 22 October 1867, p. 339; *The London Review*, 2 November 1867, p. 503; and to Phillipps by letter (Munby, *Phillipps Studies*, IV, p. 130). Madden noted the death from leprosy in his journal with an exclamation mark and "I wonder what has become of his MS of Uranius" (26 October 1867; Bodleian, MS Eng. hist. c.180, p. 220). The posthumous sighting of Simonides in St Petersburg was mentioned by S. P. Tregelles, 'Codex Mayerianus and Simonides', *Notes and Queries*, 4 ser., III, 24 April 1869, p. 389, and in F. H. Scrivener, *Six Lectures on the Text of the New Testament*, Cambridge, 1875, p. 40. On the report in the *Tageblatt* in Vienna and a second death in October 1890, see Pinto, 'Simonides in England', pp. 123–4.

10. THE EDITOR: THEODOR MOMMSEN

Theodor Mommsen was a man of such wide interests that there are many specialist biographies and studies, especially on his role in intellectual history and in German politics at the time of Unification, although I know of nothing specifically on Mommsen and his use of medieval manuscripts. An early biography is L. M. Hartmann, *Theodor Mommsen: Eine biographische Skizze*, Gotha, 1908, and the most extensive is L. Wickert, *Theodor Mommsen: Eine Biographie*, Frankfurt am Main, 1959–80, more than 2,000 pages spread over four volumes, better on his early life than the last part: I, *Lehrjahre, 1817–1844*; II, *Wanderjahre, Frankreich und Italien*; III, *Wanderjahre: Leipzig–Zürich–Breslau–Berlin*; and IV, *Grösse und Grenzen*. I have especially used S. Rebenich, *Theodor Mommsen: Eine Biographie*, Munich, 2002, and the enchanting reminiscences of his daughter Adelheid: A. Mommsen, *Theodor Mommsen im Kreise der Seinen: Erinnerungen seiner Töchter*, Berlin, 1936, reprinted as *Mein Vater: Erinnerungen an Theodor Mommsen*, Munich, 1992. The painting of the *Bücherwurm* by Spitzweg is in the Museum Georg Schäfer in Schweinfurt and there is a later version in the Grohmann Museum in Milwaukee. (Georg Schäfer's brother Otto, whom I knew, had a library like this and some good medieval manuscripts.) Mommsen's travel diary, mentioned on p. 380, is G. Walser and B. Walser, eds., *Theodor Mommsen: Tagebuch der französisch-italienischen Reise, 1844/1845*, Bern and Frankfurt, 1976, describing seeing manuscripts in Paris on pp. 34–5 and in Florence, pp. 103–4 and 112; his disappointment is on p. 35. Mommsen's letter to Borghesi in January 1845 is M. Buonocore, ed., *Lettere di Theodor Mommsen agli Italiani*, Vatican City, 2017 (*Studi e Testi*, 519–20), I, pp. 291–2, no. 1. His diary entry on arrival with Borghesi is in Walser and Walser, eds., *Tagebuch*, p. 185, translated on p. 73 of H. W. Benario, 'Theodor Mommsen: In Commemoration of the Ninetieth Anniversary of His Death', *The Classical Outlook*, 71, 1994, pp. 73–8. The sketch by Friedländer is reproduced in Walser and Walser, eds., *Tagebuch*, pl. III, Rebenich, *Mommsen*, p. 59, and elsewhere. There is a detailed account of Mommsen in Switzerland on the website of the University of Zurich (*www.nobelpreis.uzh.ch*), crediting M. Wyder, *Einstein und Co. – Nobelpreisträger in Zürich*, Zurich, 2015. I am grateful to Edwin de Hamel for visiting Strehlgasse for me. A succinct survey of Mommsen as a historian is in A. Grafton, 'Roman Monument', *History Today*, 56, 2006, pp. 48–50. The mock-Latin pamphlet is described in Madden's journal, 7 March 1862 (Bodleian, MS Eng. hist. c.175, pp. 70–71); the title begins *Inscriptio Antiqua, in agro Bruttio nuper reperta: edidit et interpretatus est Johannes Brownius, A. M.*, and Madden names the author as the classicist and politician Sir G. C. Lewis (1806–63). It reminds me of an inscription on a bench by the Cherwell in Oxford, "Ore stabit fortis arare placet ore stat", which makes better sense if the words are separated differently. For the *Res gestae*, described here on pp. 383–6, I used A. E. Cooley, *Res Gestae Divi Augusti: Text, Translation and Commentary*, Cambridge, 2009, and also read A. E. Gordon, 'Notes on the *Res Gestae* of Augustus', *California Studies in Classical Antiquity*, I, 1968, pp. 125–38, and S. Güven, 'Displaying the *Res Gestae* of Augustus: A Monument of Imperial Image for All', *Journal of the Society of Architectural Historians*, 57, 1998, pp. 30–45, as well as Mommsen's two editions, *Res Gestae Divi Augusti, ex Monumentis Ancyrano et Apolloniensi*, Berlin, 1865, and the revision of 1883. The quotation on p. 384 'The whole of Italy . . .' is from cap. xxv, as translated by Cooley, p. 89. Mommsen himself called the *Res gestae* the 'queen of inscriptions', as unique and unclassifiable as Dante's *Divina Commedia* or Goethe's *Faust* ('Der Rechenschaftsbereicht des Augustus', *Historische Zeitschrift*, 57, 1887, pp. 385–97). The letter (p. 386) mentioning having manuscripts from Wolfenbüttel, Leiden and Paris at home is Buonocore, *Lettere*, pp. 470–73, no. 123; Buonocore identifies all these as manuscripts of Solinus (Wolfenbüttel, Cod. Guelf 163 Gud. lat. Leiden, Voss. Lat. Q. 87, and Paris, BnF, ms lat. 6810) but, given the date, the *Res gestae* is overwhelmingly more probable. Much later, in 1882 and at Mommsen's suggestion, the Berlin Academy commissioned the railway engineer and archaeologist Carl Humann (1839–96) to make plaster casts of the temple inscriptions in Ankara, which involved getting local permission to demolish constructions built up against the originals. The casts were shipped back in sections and many are now in the Berlin Pergamon Museum. In 1883, Mommsen then published a revised *Res gestae divi Augusti* with heliogravure reproductions of the plaster replicas. On the concept of *Altertumswissenschaft*, see R. Pfeiffer, *History of Classical Scholarship from 1300 to 1850*, Oxford, 1976, pp. 183–90. For the textual families of Livy's *Ab urbe condita*, see L. D. Reynolds in Reynolds, ed., *Texts and Transmission: A Survey of the Latin Classics*, Oxford, 1983, reprinted 2005, pp. 205–14, and J. E. G. Zetzel, 'The Subscriptions in the Manuscripts of Livy and Fronto and the Meaning of Emendatio', *Classical Philology*, 75, 1980, pp. 38–59. The book by Zumpt, mentioned here on p. 387, is A. W. Zumpt, *De Livianorum Librorum Inscriptione et Codice Antiquissimo Veronensi Commentatio*, Berlin, 1859; the significance of the palimpsest was also noted by S. D. F. Detlefsen, 'Nota', *Philologus*, 14, 1859, pp. 158–60. The manuscript in Verona is Biblioteca Capitolare, cod. XL (38): E. A. Lowe, *Codices Latini Antiquiores*, IV, *Italy: Perugia – Verona*, Oxford, 1947, pp. 27–8, nos. 497–501. Mommsen's correspondence with the librarian is published in V. La Monaca, 'Lettere inedite di Theodor Mommsen a Giovan Battista Carlo Giuliari', pp. 309–35 in A. Buonopane, M. Buora and A. Marcone, eds., *La ricerca epigrafica e antiquaria nelle Venezie dall'età napoleonica all'Unità*, Udine, 2006, recounting Mommsen's visit to study the Livy on pp. 314 and 316–17. His edition is *T. Livii Ab urbe condita lib. III–VI quae supersunt in codice rescripto Veronensi*, Berlin, 1868, describing the use of a poisonous reagent on p. 157. The formula is given in G. B. C. Giuliari, *La Capitolare Biblioteca di Verona*, Verona, 1888, p. 250. In 1839, Sir Frederic Madden deplored the use of reagents which turn pages blue and destroy manuscripts (journal, 28 October; Bodleian, MS Eng. hist. c. 152, pp. 144–5). On reagents, see R. Fuchs, 'The History of Chemical Reinforcement in Texts of Manuscripts: What shall we do now?', *Care and Conservation of Manuscripts*, 7, 2003, pp. 159–70, and O. Bock, 'C. Maier's Use of a Reagent in the Vercelli Book', *The Library*, ser. vii, 16, 2015, pp. 249–81. Later reflections on the manuscript are in C. M. Knight, 'The Importance of the Veronese Palimpsest in the First Decade of Livy', *The Classical Quarterly*, 8, 1914, pp. 166–80. For Mommsen's publications, I made constant use of K. Zangemeister, *Theodor Mommsen als Schriftsteller: Verzeichniss seiner bis jetzt erschienenen Bücher und Abhandlungen, zum 70. Geburtstag am 30. November 1887 überreicht*, Heidelberg, 1887. In 1876 he described an early ninth-century manuscript of Eutropius from Murbach Abbey acquired in 1795 by the ducal library at Gotha, about 170 miles south-west of Berlin, where he collated its text for the first time, simply for his own interest, he said ('Die Gothaer Handschrift des Eutropius', *Jahrbücher für Philologie und Pädagogik*, CXIII, 1876, p. 648 (Zangemeister no. 585). On the poem in BnF, ms lat. 8084, see 'Carmen codicis Parisini 8084', *Hermes*, 4, 1870, pp. 350–63 (Zangemeister no. 458). The letter from Napoleon III, "J'ai donné l'ordre de vous faire parvenir les manuscrits en Allemagne si vous le désirez", is printed in P. Orth, M. Mersiowsky, *et al.*, eds., *Théodore Mommsen et le Moyen Âge: Catalogue de l'exposition préparée par les Monumenta Germaniae Historica à l'occasion du centième anniversaire de la mort de Théodore Mommsen*, Paris, 2004, p. 12. The manuscript lent from Leiden was Voss. Lat. oct. 9, communicated by Mommsen to the Königliche Akademie on 9 June 1864 and published by him, 'Festi codicis quaternionem decimum sextum', *Philologische und historische Abhandlungen der Königlichen Akademie der Wissenschaften zu Berlin*, 1865, pp. 57–86; it is possible that it was this manuscript from Leiden, rather than their transcript of the *Res gestae*, which Mommsen mentioned in his letter to the professor in Pisa as being in his custody in 1864. It is described in K. A. de Meyier, *Codices Vossiani Latini*, III, *Codices in Octavo*, Leiden, 1977, pp. 20–21. The manuscript lent by Oxford is Ligorio's *Libri dell'antichità*, MS Canon. ital. 138: see Mommsen, 'Über die in Oxford aufbewahrte Handschrift des Pirro Ligorio', *Archäeologische Zeitung*, n. s., 4, 1872, p. 45. On the Arborea manuscripts (p. 391 here), see Mommsen and M. Haupt, 'Bericht über die Handschriften von Arborea', *Monatsberichte der Königlich Preussischen Akademie der Wissenschaften zu Berlin*, 1870, pp. 64–74 and 100–104; the article also appeared in Italian, 'Relazione sui manoscritti d'Arborea', *Archivio storico italiano*, 3 ser., 12, 1870, pp. 243–80. Modern references include L. Marrocu, *Theodor Mommsen nell'isola dei falsari: Storici e critica storica in Sardegna tra Ottocento e Novecento*, Cagliari, 2009; B. Wagner, 'Die Carte d'Arborea: Eine sardische Geschichtsfälschung aus dem 19. Jahrhundert und ihre literarischen Folgen', pp. 281–9 in Müller *et al.*, eds., *Die getäuschte Wissenschaft* (Chapter 9); and S. Giorcelli Bersani and F. Carlà-Uhink, *'Monsieur le Professeur . . . '. Correspondences italiennes 1853–1888: Theodor Mommsen, Carlo, Domenico, Vincenzo Promis*, Paris, 2018 (*Mémoires de l'Académie des Inscriptions et Belles-Lettres*, 53), pp. 102–17. The symbolism of medieval manuscripts as definers of national identity was a new development of nineteenth-century European politics, even if for the Sardinians it was a false hope. Manuscripts were acquiring a status unimaginable in earlier generations. An example invoked by the new German empire was the Manasse Codex, the most extensive and beautiful medieval manuscript of Minnesinger poetry, regarded as symbolic of the nation's knightly ancestry and literature, made in the opening years of the fourteenth century. Since 1657 it had belonged to the French royal library in Paris, subsequently the Bibliothèque nationale, and would today be inalienable. In 1888, Wilhelm I and Bismarck headed a campaign to purchase it for Germany, and Mommsen was consulted on its status and financial value. It is now Heidelberg, Universitätsbibliothek, Cod. Pal. Germ. 848; for Mommsen's involvement, see A.-K. Ziesak with H.-R. Cram, K.-G. Cram and A. Terwey, *Der Verlag Walter de Gruyter, 1749–1999*, Berlin and New York, 1999, pp. 180–81. More sinister were the manic attempts by the Nazis, especially Himmler, to locate and secure the elusive Codex Aesinas, regarded as the primary manuscript of the *Germania* of Tacitus and the foundation stone of German identity (it is now Rome, Biblioteca Nazionale Centrale, cod. Vitt. Em. 1631; C. Krebs, *A Most Dangerous Book: Tacitus' Germania from the Roman Empire to the Third Reich*, New York and London, 1911). The description of Mommsen as resembling a witch or wizard (p. 392) and, a few sentences later, of his clothes looking too big for him, is from 'A Reminiscence of Mommsen', sent from Paris, *Truth* newspaper, 12 November 1903. The composer Franz Liszt (1811–86) also wore his white hair long in old age, as many musicians with aspiration to genius have done since. On the colour of Mommsen's eyes, compare "his eyes, though light blue, are piercing" (R. Keeps, 'Ernst Curtius, Müller and Mommsen', *International Revue*, 2, 1875, p. 759), and "the most piercingly brilliant black eyes that I have ever seen in a human being" (W. Ward Fowler, 'Theodor Mommsen, His Life and Work', pp. 250–68 in his *Roman Essays and Interpretations*, Oxford, 1920, p. 251). The tales of the wastepaper basket and not knowing the children's names was reported in the obituary in the *Daily News*, 2 November 1903, and elsewhere. The yellow slippers incident is recounted as "eine lustige Geschichte" (a funny story) in Adelheid Mommsen's *Mein Vater*, pp. 20–21. Tolerance and even esteem for academic eccentricity has survived in America today, perhaps through nineteenth-century mid-European immigration, but not generally in Britain, unless the professor has a Germanic or east European accent. For Jordanes, pp. 393–4 here, see C. C. Mierow, *The Gothic History of Jordanes, in English version, with an Introduction and Commentary*, Princeton, 1915, based on Mommsen's text, *Iordanis Romana et Getica*, Berlin, 1882 (*Monumenta Germaniae Historica, Auctorum antiquissimorum tomi*, V, i); P. J. Heather, 'The Historical Value of Jordanes' Getica', chapter 2 in his *Goths and Romans, 332–489*, Oxford, 1991, pp. 34–67; D. R. Bradley, 'Manuscript Evidence for the Text of the "Getica" of Jordanes', *Hermes*, 123, 1995, pp. 346–62 and 490–503; A. S. Christiansen, *Cassiodorus, Jordanes and the History of the Goths: Studies in a Migration Myth*, Copenhagen, 2002, suggesting controversially that the sources were fabricated; and A.-L. Morand, 'Édition critique, traduction et commentaire des *Romana* de Jordanès', dissertation, University of Louvain, 2019, available on-line. The quotation from the opening paragraph, "Though it had been my wish . . .", is mostly from Mierow, *Gothic History of Jordanes*, p. 51. The Bruges manuscript of Jordanes is mentioned by L. K. Bethmann, *Reise durch die Niederlande, Belgien und Frankreich*, Hanover, 1842, p. 78; Mommsen relied too on Bethmann's collations of manuscripts in Cesena, Avranches, Stockholm and elsewhere. The Salisbury Cathedral copy, which he rejected, is MS 80 there. The Heidelberg manuscript, described on p. 395, was Cod. Pal. Lat. 921: Lowe, *Codices Latini Antiquiores*, VIII, *Germany, Altenburg – Leipzig*, Oxford, 1959, p. 56, no. 1224, and B. Bischoff, *Katalog der festländischen Handschriften des 9. Jahrhunderts*, Wiesbaden, 1998, p. 317, no. 1516. The Breslau manuscript, MS R. 84 there, had been listed in A. Wachler, *Thomas Rehdiger und seine Büchersammlung in Breslau*, Breslau, 1828, p. 29; Mommsen calls it Rehdig 106 (in error for 116, its previous number). The copy from Trinity College, Cambridge, was O.4.36 (M. R. James, *The Western Manuscripts in the Library of Trinity College, Cambridge, A Descriptive Catalogue*, III, Cambridge, 1902, pp. 284–5, no. 1266), containing also the Antonine Itinerary and the *Cosmographica* of Aethicus Ister, an eighth-century fiction masquerading as a classical text. It was previously bound with Trinity College O.4.34, Orosius, and both parts had belonged as one volume to the cathedral priory of Christ Church, Canterbury (M. R. James, *The Ancient Libraries of Canterbury and Dover*, Cambridge, 1903, p. 41, no. 221; N. R. Ker, *Medieval Libraries of Great Britain: A List of Surviving Books*, 2nd edn, London, 1964, p. 34 and n. 8). A comparison with the Berlin manuscript (MS Lat. Fol. 359) from Liessies Abbey might determine a common exemplar, since both also contained Aethicus Ister and Orosius, and an illuminator from Liessies was employed probably in Canterbury after 1148, working on the Lambeth Bible. The Vienna manuscript was Österreichische Nationalbibliothek Cod. 203. It is described on the website *Bibliotheca Laureshamensis digital* on the manuscripts from Lorsch Abbey, with a facsimile of the note by Joseph Haupt, and a full bibliography. The exact date of the fire in Mommsen's house varies with different accounts (Haupt's note, for example, says 15–16 July) but the date as I give it on p. 396 is confirmed by Mommsen's letters that week. Even Rebenich is misleading in calling it the 'night of the 12th' (*Mommsen*, p. 204), only technically correct since the fire was after midnight. The event is described by his daughter, who was there (A[delheid]. Mommsen, *Mein Vater*, pp. 82–4). All accounts of the fire acknowledge O. Diliberto, *La biblioteca stregata: Tracce dei libri di Theodor Mommsen in Italia*, Rome, 1999, a trite and disappointing little book, although it is the source of my reference to Nietzsche. Much the best is G. Mandatori, "But the calamity was complete and total', Mommsen, Giordane et i dotti inglesi', *Quaderni di storia*, 86, 2017, pp. 117–202, including the letter of 19 July 1882, which I quote on p. 398, beginning "Unfortunately the notice . . .", which the author found in a bookshop in East Sussex in 2016. I acknowledge my immense debt to Nicolas Bell, Fellow Librarian of Trinity College, Cambridge, who patiently answered questions and scoured the College's archives for the references I use here. The thirty-one fragments returned to Breslau were described in K. Ziegler, *Catalogus codicum Latinorum classicorum qui in Bibliotheca Urbica Wratislaviensi adservantur*, Breslau, 1915, pp. 52–5; Dr Michał Broda of the Biblioteka Uniwersytecka in Wrocław kindly tells me that nothing of them now survives. The charred pieces in Berlin are described and illustrated in A. Fingernagel, *Die illuminierten lateinischen Handschriften süd-, west- und nordeuropäischer Provenienz der Staatsbibliothek Preussischer Kulturbesitz Berlin, 8.–12. Jahrhundert*, Wiesbaden, 1999, pp. 89–90 and pls. 242–4. The good-natured director of the library in Heidelberg was Karl Zangemeister (1837–1902), who later compiled the bibliography *Mommsen als Schriftsteller*, cited above. His letter is published by M. Mersiowsky, *Phönix aus der Asche: Theodor Mommsen und die Monumenta Germaniae Historica*, exhib. cat., Munich and Berlin, 2005, pp. 20–21, and also in French in *Théodore Mommsen et le Moyen Âge*, as above, pp. 50–51. There is a possibility, not very likely, that a fragment now in Lausanne (Bibliothèque centrale et universitaire, ms 398) is a stray from the destroyed Heidelberg manuscript: S. Bertelli, 'Sul frammento dei *Getica* di Giordano conservato a Losanna', pp. 1–8 in F. T. Coulson and A. A. Grotans, eds., *Classica et Beneventana: Essays Presented to Virginia Brown on the Occasion of her 65th Birthday*, Turnhout, 2008 (*Textes et Études du Moyen-Âge*, 36). The hint of insurance fraud (p. 399 here) was made in the Berlin paper *Kladderadatsch* (Rebenich, *Mommsen*, p. 205). Mommsen had evidently been suffering from depression in the 1870s (R. T. Ridley, 'Scholarly Exchanges in Mommsen's Italy', pp. lxiv–lxviii in *Histos*, 12, 2018, p. lxvii). There was another occasion in January 1903 when Mommsen was climbing a ladder in his library with a candle when he set fire to his hair; he called for help and was able to smother the flames with a coat. Some accounts suggested that the fire of 1880 destroyed manuscripts lent by Brussels and Halle (Adelheid in *Mein Vater*, p. 82), the Vatican (a correspondent in the *Bristol Mercury*, 27 July 1880) and the Bodleian (W. W. Jackson, *Ingram Bywater: The Memoir of an Oxford Scholar, 1840–1914*, Oxford, 1917, p. 53). The 106,000 marks is as reported in the *London Daily News*, 21 December 1880. The Bodleian specifically refused requests from Mommsen to borrow manuscripts in 1883 and 1898 and a Miss Parkes was employed to make notes in Oxford on his behalf (B. Croke, 'Mommsen in Oxford', pp. 50–57 in the *Liverpool Classical Monthly*, 16, 1991, p. 55). H. W. Chandler, *Remarks on the Practice and Policy of Lending Bodleian Printed Books and Manuscripts*, Oxford, 1887, p. 59, refers to the Mommsen fire as a reason never to lend to individuals. Mommsen's after-hours work in the Laurenziana (p. 400 here) was recalled by the director, Guido Biagi (1855–1925), in P. Vian, 'Leone XIII e Theodor Mommsen: Un incontro mancato in Biblioteca Vaticana', pp. 765–79 in *Strenna dei Romanisti*, 66, 2005, pp. 777–8, principally concerned with the incident when Mommsen failed to stand up for the pope, discussed further in M. Buonocore, 'Per una edizione delle lettere di Theodor Mommsen agli Italiani', pp. 11–38 in *Mediterraneo Antico*, 16, 2013, esp. pp. 21–2. The visits to England are recounted in Croke, as above, and Fowler, 'Mommsen', 1920: his dinner at Lincoln College is p. 251 there. The likelihood of the (credible) story of waiting outside the Bodleian at 7 a.m. is weighed in R. L. Fowler, 'Blood for the Ghosts: Wilamowitz in Oxford', pp. 171–213 in *Syllecta Classica*, 20, 2009, pp. 171–2, n. 1. The letter from Maunde Thompson is quoted in Munby, *Phillipps Studies*, V, pp. 19–20. The manuscript in the Phillipps collection (p. 401) was MS 12266, described by Mommsen, 'Zur lateinischen Stichometrie', *Hermes*, 21, 1886, pp. 142–56. It is often stated to be untraced or in Berlin: in fact, it was Sotheby's, 28 November 1967, lot 85, and is now Rome,

Biblioteca Nazionale Centrale Vittorio Emanuele II, cod. Vitt. Em. 1325. Fitzroy Fenwick's letter to Mommsen about the Meerman manuscripts is Munby, *Phillipps Studies*, V, pp. 22–3. Mommsen's letter to Fitzroy Fenwick in 1889 is in S. Rebenich, 'Theodor Mommsen und das Verhältnis von Alter Geschichte und Patristik', pp. 131–54 in R. Herzog, J. Fontaine and K. Pollmann, eds., *Patristique et Antiquité tardive en France et en Allemagne de 1870 à 1930: Influence et échanges. Actes du Colloque franco-allemand de Chantilly (25–27 octobre 1991)*, Paris, 1993, pp. 32–3, and the same author's *Theodor Mommsen und Adolf Harnack: Wissenschaft und Politik im Berlin des ausgehenden 19. Jahrhunderts*, Berlin and New York, 1997, p. 90. Adelheid's account of their trip to Paris and Italy is *Mein Vater*, pp. 100–126. Madden's record of the purchase of the Codex Theodosianus for the equivalent of £225 is in his journal for 29 February 1848 (a leap year): Bodleian, MS Eng. hist. c.161, p. 52. For Adelheid's description of the Mommsen house, see *Mein Vater*, especially pp. 18–26; the 1992 edition includes a photograph on the front cover of Mommsen with Lump. The pet dogs of manuscript enthusiasts provide an unexpected subplot, and Mommsen's Lump joins the company of the Duc de Berry's Lion, Bening's Kooikerhondje, and Madden's Fido. On the self-righteousness of universities in antiquarian inquiry since the nineteenth century (p. 405), cf. "One of the greatest universities in the world informed me, in writing, that research apart from a university could not be regarded as research" (L. G. Pine, *The Genealogist's Encyclopedia*, Newton Abbot and New York, 1969, p. 10). Mommsen's principal editions of ante-Justinian law codes are *Fragmenta Vaticana: Mosaicarum et Romanarum Legum Collatio*, pp. 107–98 in P. Krüger, T. Mommsen and W. Studemund, eds., *Collectio Librorum Iuris Anteiustiniani in usum scholarum*, III, Berlin, 1890, mentioning the Codex Gregorianus by name on pp. 134, n. 1 (as lost), 139, 140, 1548, 172 and 187; and with P. M. Meyer, *Theodosiani libri XVI cum Constitutionibus Sirmondianis et Leges Novellae ad Theodosianum pertinentes*, Berlin, 1905, mentioning the Codex Gregorianus on p. xxviii. My summary of the three sources for the Justinian Code is a slight simplification, to keep the narrative moving. The first accounts of the identification of the fragments were S. Corcoran and B. Salway, 'A lost law-code rediscovered? The Fragmenta Londiniensia Anteiustiniana', *Zeitschrift der Savigny-Stiftung für Rechtsgeschichte*, 127, 2010, pp. 677–8; S. Corcoran and B. Salway, 'Fragmenta Londiniensia Anteiustiniana: Preliminary Observations', *Roman Legal Tradition*, 8, 2012, pp. 63–83; and S. Corcoran, 'The Gregorianus and Hermogenianus Assembled and Shattered', *Mélanges de l'École française de Rome – Antiquité*, 125, 2013, pp. 1–32. The essay by Twain is 'The German Chicago', pp. 244–62 in *The Writings of Mark Twain*, XXII, *Literary Essays*, New York, 1923, here from pp. 261–2

11. THE COLLECTOR : SIR SYDNEY COCKERELL

The standard biography of Cockerell, published shortly after his death and including results of many conversations with him, is W. Blunt, *Cockerell: Sydney Carlyle Cockerell, Friend of Ruskin and William Morris and Director of the Fitzwilliam Museum, Cambridge*, London, 1964; I have avoided citing the author by name in the text above, to avoid confusion with his distant kinsman, W. S. Blunt, who employed Cockerell soon after the death of Morris, but here in the notes 'Blunt' refers to the biographer. I have been interested in Cockerell for a very long time, and I have benefited over the decades from much information from people who knew him well, and I am grateful for continued kindnesses and help from his granddaughter and literary executor Frances Cockerell (Mrs F. K. Airy). In this chapter I have reused and sometimes lifted phrases from my own publications: 'Medieval and Renaissance Manuscripts from the Library of Sir Sydney Cockerell (1867–1962)', *The British Library Journal*, 13, 1987, pp. 186–210; *Sydney Carlyle Cockerell: The Robert Nykirk Lecture 2000*, New York, 2001; my three Sandars Lectures, University of Cambridge, March 2004, printed as 'Cockerell as Entrepreneur', 'Cockerell as Museum Director' and 'Cockerell as Collector', *The Book Collector*, 55, 2006, pp. 49–72, 201–23 and 339–66; and 'Sydney Cockerell and Medieval Manuscripts in the Twentieth Century', pp. 339–43 in S. Panayotova, ed., *Art, Academia and the Trade: Sir Sydney Cockerell (1867–1962)*, Cambridge, 2010 (*Transactions of the Cambridge Bibliographical Society*, 13, 2007). Especially valuable to me among recent publications was S. Panayotova, *'I Turned It into a Palace': Sydney Cockerell and the Fitzwilliam Museum*, Cambridge, 2008.

The recollection of Morris rapping on his door in Beauvais is from Blunt, *Cockerell*, p. 59. The purchase is also described in Cockerell's diary, BL, Add. MS 52631, 13 May 1894. The manuscript is New Haven, Lillian Goldman Law Library, Rare Flat 11-0030: M. Braesel, *William Morris und die Buchmalerei*, Vienna, Cologne and Weimar, 2019 (which includes an invaluable catalogue of all Morris's medieval manuscripts), p. 590, no. IX.7; there is also an illustrated website by Sylvia Holton Peterson and William Peterson, 'The Library of William Morris: A Catalogue'. "I was a passionate collector . . .", p. 412, is from Blunt, *Cockerell*, p. 13. Cockerell's first publication was on shells, 'A List of Land and Freshwater Shells occurring near London', *Hardwick's Science-Gossip*, 19, 1883, p. 9. Cockerell's diaries are BL, Add. MSS 52623-50702, one a year sequentially from 1886 to 1962, with two each for 1926 and 1945–6. In quoting entries, I give the manuscript number and the date, but not the folio. Ruskin's "carries my umbrella . . ." (p. 414) is from a letter to Joan Severn (Blunt, *Cockerell*, p. 43); the "Emperor of Japan" echoes *The Mikado* (1885). Ruskin's first manuscript is now London, Victoria and Albert Museum, Reid 83 (MSL/1903/2074): R. Watson, *Western Illuminated Manuscripts: A Catalogue of Works in the National Art Library*, London, 2011, I, pp. 114–21, no. 18, and J. S. Dearden, *The Library of John Ruskin*, Oxford, 2012, pp. 168–9, no. 1330. Ruskin's account of it is in his *Praeterita* (E. T. Cook and A. Wedderburn, eds., *The Works of John Ruskin*, XXXV, London, 1908, pp. 490–91), cited by Dearden, *Library*. Ruskin's "I am sure . . .", p. 415 here, is from a letter to his father in 1853 (Cook and Wedderburn, eds., *Works*, XII, pp. lxviii–ix, and Dearden, *Library*, p. xx); it was later quoted approvingly by both Yates Thompson and Eric Millar (E. G. Millar, *The Parisian Miniaturist Honoré*, London, 1959, p. 5, dedicated to Cockerell). Cockerell's examination of the Saint Louis Psalter at Brantwood is in his diary for 7 November 1899 (Add. MS 52636; Blunt, *Cockerell*, p. 45). The manuscripts Ruskin took to France in 1888 were requested in a letter to Joan Severn from Beauvais on 11 and 17 July (Dearden, *Library*, p. xxxi); Cockerell left Beauvais on 13 July. The three manuscripts are now New York, Morgan Library, M 112 and M 113, and Cambridge, Fitzwilliam Museum, MS CFM 4. Scott Schwartz and I once gained admission to the library of Montserrat Abbey in Spain because he had a Book of Hours in his pocket. Cockerell's reading of Loftie and his visits to the British Museum are in the diary for 1889 (Add. MS 52626), 16 August, and 30 April, 16 July and 20 August. Cockerell with his hot chocolate at Gatti's (p. 416) is described in F. MacCarthy, *William Morris: A Life for Our Time*, London, 1995, p. 601. The Aristotle is mentioned in the diary, Add. MS 52629, 12 May 1892; it is now Fitzwilliam Museum, MS CFM 14 (Braesel, *William Morris*, p. 585, no. IX.2). For Morris's library, see also P. Needham, ed. and principal contributor, *William Morris and the Art of the Book*, New York and

Oxford, 1976. The scribe Ser Giovanni di Piero da Stia (*c.*1406–74) copied London, Wellcome Library, MS 591, Palmieri, and Oxford, Bodleian, MS Buchanan d. 4, Poggio, both owned by Morris (de la Mare, 'New Research', as above, p. 524, pp. 426 and 500, nos. 20 and 23). The Huntingfield Psalter is New York, Morgan Library, M 43, attributed now to *c.* 1215, perhaps from Oxford. The Quaritch description is cited from his *A Catalogue of Medieval Literature, especially Romances of Chivalry*, London, 1890, p. 21, no. 82, priced at £800, which was never negotiated; Morris's purchase is Braesel, *William Morris*, pp. 510–13, no. II.2, including the quotations here from Cockerell and Burne-Jones. The Cicero from San Marco is New Haven, Beinecke Library, MS 93 (*ibid.*, pp. 594–5, no. X.4); the *Roman de la Rose* is Morgan Library, M 132 (*ibid.*, pp. 588–9, no. IX.5); and the Hegesippus is Winchester Cathedral MS 20 (*ibid.*, pp. 576–7, no, VIII.5), given by C. W. Dyson Perrins in 1947, complicating the not absolute certainty that it was ever originally at Winchester at all; Richard Linenthal first told me of Morris's last-minute increase in his bid, marked in the Quaritch copy of the catalogue. The Decretals of Gregory is Liverpool University, Sydney Jones Library, MS F. 4. 20 (*ibid.*, pp. 568–9, no. VII.9, citing the response of Morris); Morris's coolness was perhaps because he had no pleasure in the chase. The other examples here of Morris using Cockerell in 1895–6 are from *ibid.*, pp. 556, 604 and 575. Shaw's recollection, quoted on p. 419, is from V. Meynell, ed., *The Best of Friends: Further Letters to Sydney Carlyle Cockerell*, London, 1956, p. 192, postcard dated 3 August 1949. The Worksop Bestiary is Morgan Library, M 81 (Needham, *Art of the Book*, p. 103, no. 24; Braesel, *William Morris*, pp. 570–73, no. VIII.1; Cockerell's diary for 1896, Add. MS 52633, esp. 22 April, 27 April, 30 April and 4 May). It had been in the Hamilton Palace library, sold to the government in Berlin in 1882 and then deaccessioned through Sotheby's, 23 May 1889, lot 2, £205 to Quaritch; Nicolas Bell tells me that the underbidder was evidently M. R. James for the Fitzwilliam Museum, which would have brought the manuscript eventually into Cockerell's custody anyway. The golden bird on fol. 52v is not actually a cockerel, although clearly modelled on one, but the fictitious ercinee bird, which glows in the dark. For the valuing and sale of the Morris library, see Needham, *Art of the Book*, pp. 45–6, and Cockerell's diary for 1897, Add. MS 52634, 26–29 April. Richard Bennett, who bought Thornby Hall, Northamptonshire, was notoriously private; he also owned a collection of Chinese porcelain which he tried to sell for a reputed £300,000 in 1911 and then sued the would-be buyer for revealing his identity (B. Lewis, *'So Clean': Lord Leverhulme, Soap and Civilization*, Manchester, 2008, p. 41; he was also a victim of forged cheques). A few books under his size limit did get into the sale in 1898. The press report, "It is not an every-day . . ." is from the *London Daily News*, 6 December 1898, p. 3. "The prices good . . ." is from Add. MS 56235, Cockerell's diary for 5 December 1898. The price paid by Morgan for Bennett's library is an unconfirmed £140,000 in Needham, *Art of the Book*, p. 46, but an assured $700,000 (the same thing) is J. Strouse, *Morgan, American Financier*, New York, 2014, p. 490. Cockerell's first manuscript (pp. 421–2) is mostly now Morgan Library, M 940, but forty-nine leaves sold by Cockerell in 1913 are now in the Netherlands: A. S. Korteweg, *Catalogue of Medieval Manuscripts and Incunabula at Huis Bergh Castle in 's-Heerenberg*, 's-Heerenberg, 2013, p. 109, no. 59. Madden had been offered it on 16 April 1866 (Bodleian, MS Eng. hist. c.179, p. 90, no. 4). It was among the manuscripts from the Carthusian abbey of Garegnano, Milan, later believed without evidence to have been given by Petrarch, who had stayed there in 1353 (G. F. Tomasini, *Petrarca Redivivus*, Padua, 1650, p. 281, no. VIII; see now G. Cantoni Alzati, 'La presunta biblioteca del Petrarca a Linterno: codici e falsificazioni' in R. Avesani, ed., *Vestigia: Studi in onore di Giuseppe Billanovich*, Rome, 1984 (*Raccolta di studi e testi*, 162–3), pp. 131–58, and S. Donghi, 'Un nuovo codice della presunta biblioteca di Petrarca a Literno', *Italia Medioevale e Umanistica*, 47, 2006, pp. 293–8). Cockerell came to know A. C. Swinburne, Rudyard Kipling, J. M. Barrie, Bernard Shaw, Tolstoy, Hilaire Belloc, John Galsworthy, W. B. Yeats, Laurence Housman, Max Beerbohm, T. E. Lawrence ('of Arabia'), Thomas Hardy, Siegfried Sassoon, Walter de la Mare, T. H. White, Ezra Pound, Alec Guinness, and many others; he met Robert Browning (whom he once introduced to Ruskin), Henry James, Albert Einstein and very many more. The volumes of correspondences with famous people were *Friends of a Lifetime: Letters to Sydney Carlyle Cockerell*, London, 1940, and *The Best of Friends*, as above, both edited by Viola Meynell. The term 'hidden friends' was applied by Petrarch to his books in his *Epistolae metricae*, 6, line 181, and 'Comites Latentes' was the name of the manuscript library of my own friend Sion Segre Amar (1910–2003). When a piece appeared in *The Times* in 1927 quoting Petrarch's phrase, Cockerell cut it out and kept it (now in the envelope accompanying his 'Petrarch' manuscript in New York). On the dispersal of Ruskin's library (pp. 425–7), see Dearden, *Library*, pp. lxviii–xciii, including his important gifts to the Guild of St George (now in the Millennium Gallery of the Museum of Sheffield). Cockerell's letter of condolence is *ibid*., p. lxxxii. His "After dinner . . ." is from his diary for 4–11 April (written as one narrative) 1902, Add. MS 52639. For the Saint Louis Psalter, eventually acquired by the Fitzwilliam Museum, MS 300, see S. Panayotova, 'A Ruskinian Project with a Cockerellian flavour', *The Book Collector*, 54, 2005, pp. 357–74, including the recovery of leaves removed by Ruskin. The Beaupré Antiphoner is Baltimore, Walters Art Museum, W 759–62, with stray leaves elsewhere; the commentary on the Psalms, now known to be by Odo of Asti, is Morgan Library, G 51; the 'Ruskin Hours' is Los Angeles, J. Paul Getty Museum, MS Ludwig IX. 3 (the quotation from Cockerell here is from his Burlington Fine Arts Club catalogue, *Exhibition of Illuminated Manuscripts*, London, 1908, p. 67, which we will come back to in a few moments); the humanistic miscellany is Victoria and Albert Museum, L. 1348-1957; the Lectionary from Santa Cecilia is New Haven, Beinecke Library, MS 1000; the Cassiodorus used by Mommsen is still, at the time of writing, in private hands (last published in Quaritch, *From Carolingian to Gothic: Four Centuries of Medieval Manuscripts from an English Private Collection*, 2005, no. [9]; the Cicero of 1421 is Beinecke Library, Marston MS 184; and the prayerbook of Sixtus IV is Rome, Biblioteca nazionale centrale Vittorio Emanuele II, cod. Vitt. Em, 1430. I am indebted to Peter Kidd for the prices from the Ashburnham sale. For Peirce, p. 428 here, see A. L. Schwarz, *Dear Mr Cockerell, Dear Mr Peirce: An Annotated Description of the Correspondence of Sydney C. Cockerell and Harold Peirce in the Grolier Club Archive*, High Wycombe, 2006. I have enjoyed many conversations with Arthur Schwarz. For this period, especially on Cockerell's work for Boston, see W. P. Stoneman, 'Variously Employed: The Pre-Fitzwilliam Career of Sydney Carlyle Cockerell', pp. 345–62 in Panayotova, *Art, Academia and the Trade*, as above; the quotation about Morris regarding the Bible with affection is on p. 355. The Bible is Boston Public Library MS f Med. 1 (formerly G. 401.11) and the Lactantius is MS f Med. 14 (formerly G. 401.10). Cockerell's dictum that the price is part of a manuscript's history was often quoted to me by Brian Cron, who knew him well. In several publications, including early printings of *Meetings with Remarkable Manuscripts*, p. 202, I gave Yates Thompson's purchase code as "bryanstone" (b=1, r=2, and so on), but Peter Kidd corrected this as "bryanstole", which avoids repeating 'n'; cf., esp., 'Exhumation' [I. Jackson] with P. Kidd, *Chamberpot & Motherfuck*, 2nd edn, Narberth, Pa., 2017, pp.

16–17. Cockerell's statement "that books . . ." (p. 429) is from Stoneman, 'Variously Employed', p. 353; his "The price of manuscripts . . ." is from Schwarz, *Dear Mr Cockerell*, p. 72, letter of 3 September 1901. For Yates Thompson and his constant awareness of commercial value, see my own 'Was Yates Thompson a Gentleman?', pp. 77–89 in R. Myers and M. Harris, eds., *Property of a Gentleman: The Formation, Organisation and Dispersal of the Private Library, 1620–1920*, Winchester, 1991, and the tactful follow-up, W. P. Stoneman, 'Henry Yates Thompson, Gentleman', pp. 344–54 in J. H. Marrow, R. A. Linenthal and W. Noel, eds., *The Medieval Book: Glosses from Friends & Colleagues of Christopher de Hamel*, 't Goy-Houten, 2010, my festschrift; Yates Thompson also walks into my *Meetings* twice, pp. 199–202 and 420–22. Cockerell's "wishes me to go through . . ." is from his diary, 14 June 1898, Add. MS 52635. One marvellous manuscript brought to Yates Thompson during Cockerell's employment was the Dante of King Alfonso of Aragon (now BL, Yates Thompson MS 36); Cockerell considered its miniatures "rather ugly" but they are now ascribed to the Sienese panel painter Giovanni di Paolo (diary, 20 May 1901, Add. MS 52638: J. Pope-Hennessy, *Paradiso: The Illuminations to Dante's Divine Comedy by Giovanni di Paolo*, London, 1993). Yates Thompson's account of the Duc de Berry is in his *Illustrations from One Hundred Manuscripts in the Library of Henry Yates Thompson*, [V], London, 1915, pp. iii–iv. The Vincent of Beauvais is now BnF, mss n. a. fr. 15939–44. Yates Thompson's letter to Cockerell about its first volume was 30 November 1906, BL, Add. MS 52755, fol. 171; his "happily reunited" is in his *Illustrations*, p. [xxi]; the forty-eight miniatures from volume III were found by Francis Douce uncatalogued in the British Museum in the early nineteenth century, now BL, Add. MS 6416, but it was never clear whether they had been Cotton fragments. Yates Thompson also owned the Duc's *Bible historiale*, now Walters Art Museum, W. MSS 125-6, and his Augustine, *La cité de Dieu*, now Harvard, Houghton Library, MS Typ. 201; both manuscripts are mentioned on p. 332. Apart from what I learned in decades spent at Sotheby's, when Dyson Perrins was still a living memory to many people, I am indebted recently to L. Cleaver, 'Charles William Dyson Perrins as a Collector of Medieval and Renaissance Manuscripts, *c.* 1900–1920', *Perspectives Médiévales*, 41, 2020, on-line, unpaginated, from which I took my reference to the visit to Sotheran's and the quotation, "I should like Perrins . . ." (p. 434). Cockerell's diary for 22 July 1904 is Add. MS 52641. The Braybrooke (or Gorleston) Psalter is now BL, Add. MS 49622; the Statutes from Morris's library was last at Sotheby's, 9 December 1958, lot 23; the Mirandola Hours is BL, Add. MS 50002 (its bibliography includes C. de Hamel and U. Bauer-Eberhardt, *Das Mirandola Stundenbuch*, Lachen, 1995). Like Cockerell, Fairfax Murray (p. 434) had been inspired to collect medieval manuscripts by William Morris (D. B. Elliott, *Fairfax Murray, The Unknown Pre-Raphaelite*, Lewes and New Castle, Del., 2000, pp. 164–5). Altogether, Perrins bought at least thirty-five manuscripts from him, his largest single source, including the Apocalypse, now Los Angeles, J. Paul Getty Museum, MS Ludwig III.1. The florilegium from Jerome, given by Murray to Cockerell, is Brussels, Bibliothèque Royale, ms IV. 83. Cockerell's assessment of his own appearance as a young man is Blunt, *Cockerell*, p. 118. His visit to Balliol (p. 435) is in the diary, 14 May 1904 (Add. MS 52641); to Holkham, 15–19 December 1905 (Add. MS 52642; his letter to M. R. James is Cambridge University Library, MS Add. 7482, c.99, 21 December 1905); the visit to Chantilly with Shaw is in the diary, 11 August 1906 (Add. MS 52643). The enigmatic Nicholas de Bello is discussed in B. C. Barker-Benfield, *St Augustine's Abbey*, London, 2008 (*Corpus of British Medieval Library Catalogues*, 13), I, pp. 580–81; his Bible is Morgan Library, M 970. The Jean de

Meun which Cockerell received in part exchange is Harvard, Houghton Library, MS Typ. 749. The £300 in the deal seems to have represented a misjudgement, "My object being to buy the wonderful little MS for which Rosenthal asks £350 (but priced at £475 in his cat.)" (diary, 4 May 1905, Add. MS 52642). In my Sandars Lectures, 'Cockerell as Collector', p. 347, I suggested that the book he hoped and failed to buy might have been the Bentivoglio Hours (Jacques Rosenthal, cat. 36, 1905, no. 226, now Morgan Library, M 53), but Heribert Tenschert kindly tells me that it must have been no. 230, a Book of Hours from Ferrara, priced at 9500 marks, then indeed approximately £475, apparently bought instead by Paul Durrieu (1855–1925). The traded Polybius is now Cologny–Geneva, Fondation Martin Bodmer, Cod. 139. Cockerell's "during a reversal" is from memories of Hodson in the annual summary of deaths in his diary for 1933, Add. MS 52671. Morris's glossed Epistles from Hodson is untraced (Braesel, *William Morris*, pp. 507–8, no. I. 21); the Psalm commentary, as said above, is Morgan Library G 51; the Marquette Bible is J. Paul Getty Museum, MS Ludwig I. 8. "All the money . . ." is the diary for 6 December 1906 (Add. MS 52643); "Though it was to prove . . ." is Blunt, *Cockerell*, p. 123; "No more . . ." is Schwarz, *Dear Mr Cockerell*, p. 111, 22 August 1907. The Burlington Fine Arts Club catalogue (pp. 438–40 here) was referred to above; see also J. Backhouse, 'Manuscripts on Display: Some Landmarks in the Exhibition and Popular Publication of Illuminated Books', pp. 37–52 in L. Dennison, ed., *The Legacy of M. R. James: Papers from the 1995 Cambridge Symposium*, Donnington, 2001, esp. pp. 47–50, and an on-line current location list by Peter Kidd of the manuscripts exhibited, 2004. For Cockerell in the Fitzwilliam, in addition to the sources above, especially Panayotova, *'I Turned it into a Palace'*, see S. Panayotova, 'Cockerell and Riches', pp. 377–86 in *The Medieval Book*, my festschrift, as above. "How you managed . . ." (p. 441) is Blunt, *Cockerell*, p. 142. His "by several artists . . ." is *Exhibition*, p. 52, no. 111; his "I am like Morris . . ." is Blunt, *Cockerell*, p. 131. The early eleventh-century Anglo-Saxon Boethius reappeared as Sotheby's, 5 July 2005, lot 80, back in private hands after nearly fifty years in the Bodmer Foundation. The 'Golden Psalter' of St Albans is now BL, Add. MS 81084; Cockerell's acquisition, as cited, is in the diary for 1909, Add. MS 52646. Cockerell's Bible and Missal from Notre-Dame are respectively Fitzwilliam Museum, MSS 1060-1975 and 84-1972. The ninth-century Augustine is Fondation Bodmer, Cod. 173. The Bestiary probably from Fountains is Morgan Library, M 890; Alan Robiette has been working on its history and it is to be hoped he will publish his findings. Cockerell's leaf of the Shah Abbas Bible is J. Paul Getty Museum, MS Ludwig I. 6 (the whole manuscript was written up by Cockerell as *A Book of Old Testament Illustrations*, Roxburghe Club, 1927, reprinted as *Old Testament Miniatures*, London, 1969); the Getty's curator, Thomas Kren, called it quite simply "one of the greatest of all medieval manuscripts", serious praise (*French Illuminated Manuscripts*, Los Angeles, 2007, p. xii). The illustrations of heroes of antiquity were dispersed in 1958; they were once thought to be Italian but are now attributed to Barthélemy d'Eyck: see, for example, N. Reynaud in F. Avril and N. Reynaud, eds., *Les manuscrits à peintures en France, 1440–1520*, Paris, 1993, pp. 225–6, no. 121 (Amsterdam, Rijksprentenkabinett, RP-T-1959-16), and P. Kayser in B. Stocks and N. Morgan, eds., *The Medieval Imagination*, Melbourne, 2008, pp. 238–9 no. 83 (Melbourne, National Gallery of Victoria, MS Felton 1663–5). The Cicero of 1453 is now in the library of Nicolas Barker, who has kindly allowed me to see it. The quotation from Lowe, "very legible . . ." (p. 444) is from F. Corrigan, *The Nun, the Infidel & the Superman: The Remarkable Friendships of Dame Laurentia McLachlan with Sydney Cockerell, Bernard Shaw, and Others*, London, 1985, pp.

41–2; Belle Greene wrote to Cockerell about his exquisite handwriting on 10 March 1914: "In the first place you must have (in a previous life) given Sigismondus de Sigismondis points on writing, for I have *never*, in any manuscripts, seen script to equal yours (after the kufic and Carolingian!)" (BL, Add. MS 52727, fol. 6). A piece by Cockerell on 'Good Handwriting' appeared in A. S. Osley, ed., *Calligraphy and Palaeography: Essays Presented to Alfred Fairbank on His 70th Birthday*, London, 1965, Fairbank festschrift, pp. 257–8. The account of being shown manuscripts by Cockerell ("He watched me . . .", p. 447) was actually in Kew, after Cockerell's retirement, but the experience is consistent: P. Henderson, 'Visiting Sir Sydney', pp. 12–14 in *The Journal of the William Morris Society*, 1, ii, Winter 1962, p. 13. Webb was the architect Philip Webb (1831–1915). I cited "I was rather unfavourably . . ." in my *Sydney Carlyle Cockerell*, 2001, p. 15, from the diary, but I failed to note the date; "a very nice intelligent woman . . ." is 7 December 1908 (Add. MS 52645); "he is one of the few . . ." is 10 August 1948 (Add. MS 52688). "On those Sunday nights . . ." is S. Sassoon, *Siegfried's Journey, 1916–1920*, London, 1945, pp. 148–9, cited by Blunt, *Cockerell*, p. 164. The relic given to Sassoon from the supposed Petrarch manuscript belongs to me. The Ciriagio leaves given to Walker and Hewitt were subsequently presented to Alfred Fairbank (who showed it to me once) and to the Society of Scribes & Illuminators (and I am indebted to Donna Foster for advice on what might have happened to it); a third leaf from the manuscript given away by Cockerell is BL, Add. MS 52444 (A. G. Watson, *Catalogue of Dated and Datable Manuscripts, c. 700–1600*, London, 1979, p. 87, no. 425, pl. 534). The leaf from the Windmill Psalter had been part of an album of fragments which is now Columbia, University of Missouri, Fragmenta Manuscripta; the recovered leaf is now reattached to the end of the Psalter itself, Morgan Library, M 102. The signed book bought in 1904 (p. 449) was Prosper of Aquitaine, *Epigrammata*, etc., inscribed by the scribes Johannes dictus Campions and Arnulphus de Camphaing and the illuminator Gossuins de Lecaucie, now BL, Add. MS 78830. Cockerell later wrote a series of articles, 'Signed Manuscripts in My Collection', *The Book Handbook*, 1, 1948–50, pp. 321–38, 402–4, 429–49, and II, 1951, pp. 13–26, and *The Book Collector*, 1, 1952, pp. 77–91. Cockerell's "Look at them properly . . ." was addressed to Bernard Breslauer, cited in M. Laird, 'Bernd (Bernard) Hartmut Breslauer (1918–2004): A Personal Memoir', part II, pp. 57–68 in *Gazette of the Grolier Club*, n. s., 71, 2021, p. 60. Dyson Perrins's Book of Hours signed by W. de Brailes is now BL, Add. MS 49999; the Psalter at New College is MS 322; the manuscript bought in 1909, also a Psalter, is now Stockholm, Nationalmuseum, B.2010; the leaves found in 1920 are now Fitzwilliam Museum, MS 330. Cockerell's "The point about W. de Brailes . . ." is a letter to Adams, 17 April 1910 (Meynell, ed., *Best of Friends*, p. 16); his "I recognised the hand . . ." (p. 449) is his diary for 10 November 1920 (Add. MS 52657). He wrote the manuscripts up for a Roxburghe Club book, S. C. Cockerell, *The Work of W. de Brailes: An English Illuminator of the Thirteenth Century*, Cambridge, 1930. The tentative identification with the resident of Oxford, overwhelmingly probable but just short of proof, was first made by Graham Pollard; see also C. Donovan, *The de Brailes Hours*, London, 1991. Cockerell's involvement with the Chester Beatty collection was especially significant, comparable to that with Yates Thompson and Dyson Perrins; part of the story is told in my 'Cockerell as Museum Director', pp. 214–18, and in L. Cleaver, 'The Western Manuscript Collection of Alfred Chester Beatty (ca. 1915–1930)', *Manuscript Studies*, 2, 2018, on-line. "I never felt . . ." is from Blunt, *Cockerell*, p. 313, citing Millar's appreciation of Cockerell in *The Book Collector*, 11, 1962, p. 286. The principal narrative on Cockerell and Dame Laurentia (pp. 450–51) is by her fellow nun, Felicitas Corrigan, *The Nun, the Infidel & the Superman*, as above, esp. pp. 41–82; see also Blunt, *Cockerell*, chapter 9, pp. 224–32. The 'Dame' is a religious title, like Dom for a monk, not a civil honour. The relationship was dramatized by Hugh Whitemore as *The Best of Friends*, which I have seen twice, once with Gielgud as Cockerell (1988) and once with Patricia Routledge as Dame Laurentia (2006); there is a film version, 1991, directed by Alvin Rakoff. The rapid visits to London, Cambridge and Oxford at the beginning and end of a fortnight's dispensation to train a monastic choir in Suffolk are described by Blunt, *Cockerell*, pp. 229–30. The manuscript bought in Carcasonne concerns a chapel at Ocaña and is now Harvard, Houghton Library, MS Typ. 279. The Cicero of 1442 has reappeared several times in recent decades: Christie's, 11 July 2000, lot 79; Sotheby's, 18 June 2002, lot 40; Sam Fogg, *Medieval Manuscripts, Art and Ownership*, 2014, no. 11; and Christie's online sale ending 30 July 2020. The Christine de Pizan is still in private hands. The Book of Hours of 1498 is Boston Public Library, MS q Med. 200. My sources for Cockerell's dilemma on his library (p. 452) include conversations I had with Anthony Hobson (1921–2014) and Sir Walter Oakeshott (1903–87); Perrins did indeed die before Cockerell and, after certain bequests to the British Museum, including the Gorleston Psalter, his manuscripts were sold at Sotheby's in 1958–60. I was able to talk about Cockerell's sales with many of the participants, including the late Edmund Dring (1906–90, of Quaritch), Pierre Berès (1913–2008), Anthony Hobson, who represented Sotheby's, Alan G. Thomas (1911–92, also mentioned in Chapter 1) and above all with Brian Cron (1913–2002), who all supplied me with much information. The recollection by Alan Thomas, "I went up from Bournemouth . . ." (pp. 452–3) was typed up for me by him. Frances Cockerell, who remembers her grandfather from that time, tells me that it was a single not a double bed. Cron as Cockerell's honorary assistant during all sales was rewarded by gifts of several manuscripts and opportunities to purchase others, then and later: see R. A. Linenthal, 'Medieval and Renaissance Manuscripts: A Handlist of the Collection of B. S. Cron', *The Book Collector*, 54, 2005, pp. 553–63. Cron's lists of prices are preserved in BL, Add. MS 52773, fols. 264–70. The account by H. P. Kraus is his autobiography, *A Rare Book Saga*, London, 1978, chapter 27, pp. 201–4, the quotation "After having . . ." being from p. 202. Kraus says (p. 201) that Sir Frederic Madden had been a personal friend of Cockerell, which I wish had been true, but Madden died in 1873, when Cockerell was 5: he may have been thinking of Falconer Madan (1851–1935). Cockerell's "a very satisfactory . . ." (p. 453) is in the diary for 18 January 1957 (Add. MS 52697). "He was quite overcome . . ." is from the diary on the date given (Add. MS 52696): the full entry is, "I gave Brian Cron, who has been invaluable to me, especially lately, my greatly prized Golden Psalter. He was quite overcome with gratitude and delight. I should have been grieved to see it pass into the hands of an unworthy owner." Cron wrote a little book about it, *The Recent Owners of the Golden Psalter*, London, 1963, and also printed a checklist, which he claimed he regretted, *A Handlist of Western Manuscripts from the Library of B. S. Cron*, Kew, 1965, in which the Psalter is p. 8, no. 5. On his death, the manuscript was accepted by the British Library in lieu of tax. The "egg with my tea" is Blunt, *Cockerell*, p. 344.

12. THE CURATOR: BELLE DA COSTA GREENE

Before all else, I must acknowledge two people who made this chapter possible. One is William Voelkle, former Curator of Manuscripts at the Morgan, who worked under every director of the Library except Belle Greene and whose knowledge and experience have helped me in almost every major publication I have ever written, including this. The second is Emily Quint-Hoover, who found and sent me photographs from countless files in the Morgan Library, when the international travel restrictions of Covid suddenly prevented my return to New York. This narrative could not have been attempted on schedule without her. Belle Greene destroyed her personal letters. The principal source in New York is the Library's comprehensive Morgan Collection Correspondence, ARC 1310, divided into folders alphabetically by the names of the vendors, often retaining carbon copies of Belle Greene's halves of the exchanges. I also received guidance from Christine Nelson and Philip Palmer. Belle Greene's many letters to Bernard Berenson, 1909–44 (mostly 1909–16), are in his archive at the Villa I Tatti, the Harvard University Center for Italian Renaissance Studies, near Florence, and I am indebted to Ilaria Della Monica for allowing me access to the originals, and to Thomas Gruber for his hospitality on my visit there; copies of the letters are now in the Morgan Library and are being prepared for public access. I am very grateful too to Alex Day, of Bernard Quaritch Ltd, for unrestricted use of that firm's extensive and unpublished correspondences with Morgan and Belle Greene, either in files or bound up in sale catalogues. Richard Linenthal, Laura Cleaver, Nicolas Barker, Mary Belmont and Davina Honess have all given useful advice. For most of its history, the principal collection in this chapter has been called the Pierpont Morgan Library; it has now changed its name, to seem to be more inclusive and less cerebral, to the Morgan Library and Museum. The primary biography of Belle Greene is H. Ardizzone, *An Illuminated Life: Belle da Costa Greene's Journey from Prejudice to Privilege*, New York and London, 2007, earnest and absolutely essential on matters of feminism and race, but with little feeling for rare books. I also relied on J. Strouse, *Morgan, American Financier*, New York, 1999, using the paperback edition of 2014, the very readable and important biography of the elder Pierpont Morgan which first exposed Belle Greene's actual family and background, especially Chapter 25, 'Singular Woman', pp. 509–31. I ordered two books, believing them to be new biographies, M. Benedict and V. Christopher Murray, *The Personal Librarian*, New York, 2021, and A. Lapierre, *Belle Greene*, Paris, 2020, and both proved on arrival to be novels; the former is delightful and credible, and the latter, which is in French, has the best published bibliography of the sources of Belle Greene's life. The traditional facts are told by her friends D. Miner and A. Haight in their entry for Belle da Costa Greene in E. T. James, J. W. James and P. S. Boyer, eds., *Notable American Women, 1607–1951: A Biographical Dictionary*, II, Cambridge, Mass., 1971, pp. 83–5.

The cable of Junius Morgan in 1899 (p. 456 here) is cited in Strouse, *Morgan*, p. 379, and reproduced by her, 'Mr. Morgan and His Library', pp. 11–27 in *The Morgan Library: An American Masterpiece*, New York and London, 2000, p. 19; the letter of Junius Morgan is in P. Needham, *Twelve Centuries of Bookbinding, 400–1600*, New York and London, 1979, p. 26, n. 1. The price was staggeringly expensive for the time. The press story was syndicated around Britain, and my source was the *Reading Mercury*, 2 February 1901. The Lindau Gospel Book is Morgan Library, M 1 (cf., e. g., Needham, *Art of the Book*, pp. 24–9, and J. F. Hamburger and J. O'Driscoll, *Imperial Splendor: The Art of the Book in the Holy Roman Empire, 800–1500*, New York, 2021, esp. pp. 51–4). All Morgan Library medieval manuscripts are catalogued with updated bibliographies and generally excellent photographs on their Corsair website, which has been a constant and invaluable source. Morgan's gemstone collection was mostly given to the American Museum of Natural History in New York, including the 'Star of India' sapphire. The failure of an appeal to save the Lindau Gospels for Britain was printed in *The Times*, 9 February 1901, reprinted also in *The New York Times*. The Farnese Hours, Morgan M 69, is reproduced in facsimile with commentary by

W. M. Voelkle and I. Golub, Graz, 2001, and partially in W. Smith, *The Farnese Hours*, New York, *c.* 1976; it is described by Voelkle in J. J. G. Alexander, ed., *The Painted Page*, London and Munich, 1994, pp. 246–8, no. 132, from which I take the quotation from G. Vasari, *The Lives of the Painters, Sculptors and Architects*, London, IV, 1927, p. 246. Madden's remarks are in his journal, 4 August 1854 (Bodleian, MS Eng. hist. c. 167) and 6 May 1866 (*ibid.*, c. 179, p. 108). Its rejection by Edmond de Rothschild is in my *The Rothschilds and Their Collections of Illuminated Manuscripts*, London, 2005, p. 30. The Golden Gospels of Henry VIII and the Duc de Berry's Apocalypse, both cited on p. 462, are M 23 and M 133 (here and in further citations below, 'M' numbers all refer to manuscripts in the Morgan Library). Other significant individual early purchases by Morgan include the so-called Hours of Cardinal Pierre de Foix, illuminated by Simon Marmion (M 6, bought in 1900), the Breviary of Eleanor of Portugal, illuminated by the Master of the First Prayerbook of Maximilian (the presumed Alexander Bening, M 52, bought in 1905), and the Bentivoglio Hours, made in Bologna in 1497 (M 53, also bought in 1905). A four-volume catalogue of all early acquisitions was overseen by Junius Morgan, *Catalogue of Manuscripts and Early Printed Books from the Libraries of William Morris, Richard Bennett, Bertram Fourth Earl of Ashburnham, and Other Sources, Now Forming Portion of the Library of J. Pierpont Morgan*, London, 1906–7, effectively all acquisitions from before Belle Greene's time, including volume I, M. R. James, *Manuscripts*, 1906; because of this, many of the manuscripts had been retained in England so that James could work on them. A. Hobson, *Great Libraries*, London, 1970, p. 291, cites the piles of books in the Morgan basement, in a recollection of Morgan's son-in-law Herbert Satterlee. The letter from Junius Morgan about his uncle's purchases is in the Quaritch archive. It is dated Tuesday, 6 January (no year): that was a Tuesday in 1903 and not again until 1908, and since it also refers to progress on the Bennett catalogue, presumably the former year is meant, although that seems early for unpacking. On Junius Morgan and Princeton, see D. C. Skemer, *Medieval & Renaissance Manuscripts in the Princeton University Library*, I, Princeton, 2013, p. xiii; his manuscripts are Terence, Princeton MS 28, Virgil, MS 38, and Caxton, MS 128. The quotations on p. 463 "Small and slender . . ." and "By all accounts . . ." are from Strouse, *Morgan*, p. 509, and Ardizzone, *Illuminated Life*, p. 3, both with slightly emended punctuation by me. Many contemporary descriptions of Belle Greene include phrases such as "dark, slender, and vivacious, with flashing black eyes" (*Metropolitan Magazine*, July 1911, although I took this from its reprinting in the *Birmingham Age-Herald*, 16 July 1911, p. 15). For Greener, I used M. R. Mounter, 'Richard Theodore Greener: The Idealist, Statesman, Scholar and South Carolinian', PhD diss., University of South Carolina, 2002, in a digitized copy kindly forwarded to me by Scott Gwara; and K. R. Chaddock, *Uncompromising Activist: Richard Greener, First Black Graduate of Harvard College*, Baltimore, 2017. The fictional "In this country . . ." (p. 466) is Benedict and Murray, *Personal Librarian*, Chapter 2 (p. 19 in the edition I have). In their notes, they refer to A. V. Hobbs, *A Chosen Exile: A History of Racial Passing in American Life*, Cambridge, Mass., 2014. Other almost double-barrelled surnames in the manuscripts world of this time include Fairfax Murray, Fitzroy Fenwick, Chester Beatty and even Pierpont Morgan. Belle Greene's "I knew definitely . . ." is cited by Strouse, *Morgan*, p. 509, and by Ardizzone, *Illuminated Life*, p. 71. On Greener and the Rev. Robert Cassie Waterston (1812–93), see Mounter, 'Richard Theodore Greener', p. 59: his manuscripts in the Massachusetts Historical Society, Boston, are listed in S. de Ricci with W. J. Wilson, *Census of Medieval and Renaissance Manuscripts in the United States and Canada*, New York, 1935, pp. 940–41, including the three mentioned here, J.III.1 (Decretals) and D.V.1 and D.V.3 (both Books of Hours). My quotation "With what tenderness . . ." is from R. T. Greener, *Charles Sumner, The Idealist, Statesman and Scholar*, Columbia, SC, 1874, p. 30. The Cicero is Harvard, Houghton Library, MS Lat. 77. For Sumner, see too R. Dennis, 'The World of Madness and the World of Dreams: Charles Sumner and Philip Hofer as Collectors of Early Manuscripts', *Gazette of the Grolier Club*, n. s., 42, 1990, pp. 17–37. Scott Gwara first suggested to me the significance of the Grolier Club exhibition of 1892. Scott Schwartz gave me a copy of the catalogue in 2006. I owe information on the exhibition to Meghan Constantinou, Librarian of the Club, who checked the Council Minutes from that year. The quotation, "Art appeals . . ." is from the catalogue, p. xxxiii. The printed programmes and records of the summer school on librarianship (pp. 468–9) are at Amherst College, Archives & Special Collections, Amherst Summer School Collection (identifier MA 00058), and I am immensely grateful to Margaret Dakin for sending me scans of the entire file in Box 1. The comic song 'Smoky Mokes', written by Abe Holzmann, had been described as "the cakewalk hit of the season" in 1899. The Morgan *Bible moralisée* is M 240, extracted long ago from the end of Toledo, Tesoro del Catedral, *Biblia de San Luis* (J. Lowden, *The Making of the Bibles Moralisées*, I, *The Manuscripts*, University Park, Pa., 2000, chapter 4, pp. 95–137). The sale prices cited are from H.-W. Stork, commentary volume to *Die Bibel Ludwigs des Heiligen*, facsimile, Graz, 1995, p. 45. The Badin letters and invoices are in the Morgan ARC 1310 file under his name; the involvement of Pearson, not hitherto suspected, is in the corresponding file under 'P', made unambiguous by Pearson forwarding on 12 October 1906 the report they had commissioned on the 'Apocalypse' (as they call it) from J. W. Bradley (1830–1916). The Zeitz Abbey Lectionary and the Ramsey Abbey Psalter, both cited on p. 471 (still from the ARC file for Badin), are M 299 and M 302. The Quaritch invoices and the account of the Troussures affair are similarly from ARC 1310 files under Quaritch (1900–1910) and T-Misc. The manuscript of Augustine dated 669 is M 334 (E. A. Lowe, *Codices Latini Antiquiores*, XI, Oxford, 1966, p. 23, no. 1659, sharing its Luxeuil provenance with the pre-Nicomachean Livy palimpsest in Verona, read by Mommsen); the Gospel Book of Otbert of Saint-Bertin is M 333 (the suggestion that it was painted by Otbert himself is J. J. G. Alexander, *Medieval Illuminators and Their Methods of Work*, New Haven and London, 1992, pp. 9–10). The manuscript which Madame de Tonnay claimed was now her own property and asked an additional $2000 for is M 338, a Psalter, *c.*1200, with the French gloss of Simon of Tournai, which I first went to see in New York almost fifty years ago, for it has a stamped binding, like those from twelfth-century Winchester (Needham, *Twelve Centuries*, pp. 61–4, no. 15). "Just because I *am* a librarian . . ." (p. 473) is dismissed by Ardizzone as perhaps fictitious (*Illuminated Life*, p. 4), but a source is given by W. Voelkle, 'The Crusader Bible: Introduction and Provenance. A Curatorial Perspective', pp. 297–315 in *La Biblia de los Cruzados*, commentary volume to the facsimile of M 638, Valencia, 2015, p. 304. The Matisse drawing of a nude, 1912, assumed to show Belle Greene herself, was bequeathed by her to the Morgan, 1950.14 (cf. Ardizzone, *Illuminated Life*, p. 274). Belle Greene's wish to be Cockerell's pupil is in her letter to him, 29 April 1913, BL, Add. MS 52717, fol. 5. The correspondence on the purchase of the Da Costa Hours from Mrs Thomas is in the ARC 1310 file for T-Misc; see also G. T. Clark, commentary volume to the facsimile, *Das Da Costa-Stundenbuch*, Graz, 2010, esp. pp. 17–18. The story of the manuscript's purchase in Benedict and Murray, *Personal Librarian* pp. 184–7, is fictitious and impossible. The quotation from the Quaritch *Description* is from p. 1; Memling died in 1494 and there is no possibility of his participation in the illumination. The Da Costa Hours is M 399; the Wycliffite New Testament is M 400. Copies of the correspondence by Coggiola, marked by Belle Greene in 1910 as having been laid into the manuscript, are in the internal files for MS M 399, Medieval and Renaissance Manuscripts Department. Christine Nelson kindly told me of the letter in the Library files signed as Belle da Costa Greene on 8 March 1906. For Berenson and Belle Greene, see E. Samuels with J. Newcomer Samuels, *Bernard Berenson: The Making of a Legend*, Cambridge, Mass., and London, 1987, esp. chapter XII, 'Idyll with Belle da Costa Greene', pp. 109–18, and R. Cohen, *Bernard Berenson: A Life in the Picture Trade*, New Haven and London, 2013, esp. pp. 171–84. Berenson's comments on her habitual flirtatiousness are in Ardizzone, *Illuminated Life*, pp. 234–35. Her "I would kiss you . . ." (p. 475 here) is from Samuels, p. 109. The quotations "most wild and woolly" are from Ardizzone, *Illuminated Life*, p. 123, and "the potentate" from F. Gennari-Santori, '"This Feminine Scholar": Belle da Costa Greene and the Shaping of J. P. Morgan's Legacy', pp. 182–97 in *Visual Resources*, 33, 2017, p. 188. The correspondence with Lionel Harris is in the ARC 1310 file, H-Misc, as is the letter from Archer Huntington. The Beatus is M 429; its picture of a scriptorium is illustrated in my *Meetings with Remarkable Manuscripts*, p. 227. Belle Greene's letter to Berenson about the value of the offered Book of Hours is dated 11 August 1911 (folder 60.19, fols. 796–7, at the Biblioteca Berenson, I Tatti – The Harvard University Center for Italian Renaissance Studies: this and six further quotations from the archive listed below are acknowledged as courtesy of the President and Fellows of Harvard College). Belle Greene's opinion on the taste of Henry Walters (1848–1931), p. 480 here, is expressed in a letter to Cockerell, 10 March 1914, BL, Add. MS 52717, fols. 6–9, "It seemed to me that all the trash of the world had been swept up and *dumped* into that poor building" in Baltimore. She told Berenson in 1924 that she would try to persuade Walters to cede his best manuscripts to the Morgan Library (I Tatti, folder 63.16, fol. 336). The Book of Hours bought from Harris is now Baltimore, Walters Art Museum, W 90 (L. M. C. Randall, *Medieval and Renaissance Manuscripts in the Walters Art Gallery*, I, *France, 875–1420*, Baltimore and London, 1989, pp. 138–42, no. 54). The admission to weeping at the beauty of illumination is in the same letter of 11 August 1911, cited above, at I Tatti; from the context, the manuscript was probably M 456, a little manuscript with 140 miniatures, apparently commissioned in 1347–50 by Jean II of France for the education of his sons, including Jean, Duc de Berry. Belle Greene's confession to kissing manuscripts is Ardizzone, *Illuminated Life*, p. 309, 4 January 1914. The best account of Belle Greene's conversion to Middle Eastern manuscripts is W. M. Voelkle, 'History of the Collection', pp. 1–5 in B. Schmitz *et al.*, *Islamic and Indian Manuscripts and Paintings in the Pierpont Morgan Library*, New York, 1997, esp. pp. 1–2. Charles Hercules Read (1857–1929) was later knighted; his album was numbered M 386, but subsequently the Persian and Indian components were separated, some becoming M 458. Belle Greene's own collection of oriental manuscripts and miniatures, not all of the highest quality, was bequeathed by her to the Morgan in 1950, where they are now M 835-44 and 846-49. The portrait of Belle Greene in oriental guise is by Laura Coombs Hills (1859–1952), who had originally proposed that she should be shown sitting on a leopard skin; it too was bequeathed by Belle Greene to the Morgan, AZ 164; "*Egyptienne*" (my italics, p. 481 here) is from Ardizzone, *Illuminated Life*, p. 170. There is an on-line blog from the Institute of English Studies, University of London, 'Belle da Costa Greene in Love with Islamic Book Art', summarizing a conference paper by Karen Winslow in 2018. On the Coptic manuscripts of Hamuli (sometimes Hamouli), see Ardizzone, *Illuminated Life*, pp.

275–8 and 394–5, citing on p. 276 the plea of Father Thomas Shahan to save them for America, 11 September 1911, and now F. H. Trujillo in Trujillo, ed., T. C. Petersen, *Coptic Bookbindings in the Pierpont Morgan Library*, Ann Arbor, 2021, esp. pp. i–vii, and the catalogue undertaken by Father Petersen in 1928. "J. P. is so well trained . . ." (p. 483) is from Strouse, *Morgan*, p. 656. The Caxton Malory of 31 July 1486 (now PML 17560) was lot 2110 in the Hoe sale on 24 April 1911; the only other copy known is in the John Rylands University Library in Manchester, lacking ten leaves. The *New York Times* article is called 'Spending J. P. Morgan's Money for Rare Books', p. M8; that of *The Chicago Tribune*, p. G2, is reproduced in Ardizzone, *Illuminated Life*, opp. p. 213; the story from *Munsey's Magazine* was syndicated, and I took it from the *Dundee Evening Telegraph*, 7 May 1914; "I really must be . . ." is cited from Ardizzone, *Illuminated Life*, p. 1. The letters to Badin and Rahir are from the respective files in ARC 1310. The little Bening Book of Hours of 1531 is M 451. The exchanges with Martini and Olschki too are from their files in ARC 1310. The pictures from the Gospels are M 521. The leaf had been in the Ottley sale, Sotheby's, 12 May 1838, lot 133. Other leaves from the same series are BL, Add. MS 37472, and Victoria & Albert Museum, 816–1894; they are from the lost prefatory cycle of the Eadwine Psalter, Cambridge, Trinity College, MS R.17.1. The leaf bought from Olschki is now M 619. The artist is now known eponymously as the Master of the Morgan Leaf. That it was once part of MS 17 in Winchester Cathedral was finally proven by C. Donovan, *The Winchester Bible*, London and Winchester, 1993, p. 33. Belle Greene's letter to Cockerell, "I am sure you know . . .", p. 486, is BL, Add. MS 52717, fol. 5. Belle Greene's dream to establish a research library "for scholars in certain fields, to make our material available to them, and to make them welcome here", was in a letter to Berenson, 9 May 1913, cited in Gennari-Santori, 'This Feminine Scholar'. The letter to Quaritch in 1915 is taken from William Voelkle's commonly delivered 'Great Legacy' lecture on the Morgan Library, which he has kindly allowed me to cite. For the Phillipps manuscripts after 1872, see especially A. N. L. Munby, *Phillipps Studies*, V, 1960, on the sales to Morgan, p. 53, and to Belle Greene, pp. 68–71. The manuscripts in pastiche jewelled bindings were Phillipps MSS 16387–88, 16396, 16400 and 16411, now respectively M 564, M 565, M 561, M 563 and M 562. Despite their bindings, they are nevertheless fine manuscripts. In the Quaritch files is a receipt of 10 April 1906, when they were handed over to Junius Morgan. The protracted negotiations for the Gospels of Matilda of Canossa, Phillipps MS 3500, are very fully documented in the ARC 1310 file for Quaritch, 1910. The manuscript is M 492. A study of it was commissioned from George Warner (in 1912, Belle Greene had hoped that Cockerell would do it) and was presented to the Roxburghe Club, 1917, *Gospels of Matilda, Countess of Tuscany, 1055–1115*, "in fulfilment of the intention of John Pierpont Morgan (died March 31, 1923) by his son". Belle Greene's acquisition of the Shah Abbas Bible, here on pp. 488–92, is recounted at length in Voelkle, 'The Crusader Bible', pp. 297–315, which I have supplemented from Munby and from Cockerell's diary, BL, Add. MS 56283. The quotations, "I'll take it", "The manuscript you were clever enough . . .", "For this single sheet . . ." and "quite thoroughly approves" are all from Voelkle, 'The Crusader Bible', pp. 306–7; Belle Greene's letter to Cockerell on 12 December 1916 includes "Every day I regret more strongly that you are such thousands of miles away – and more that I did not carry you off with me as I did the Fenwick leaves." He did get to New York in 1921. It is sometimes hinted that perhaps Belle Greene had an affair with Cockerell, which I emphatically do not believe. The Shah Abbas Bible is M 638. One recent study is W. Noel and D. Weiss, eds., *The Book of*

Kings: Art, War and the Morgan Library's Medieval Picture Bible, Baltimore and Lingfield (Surrey), 2002. The shocked reaction to Yates Thompson's announcement in late 1918 (p. 492) is a story I have told elsewhere, including 'Was Henry Yates Thompson a Gentleman?', pp. 77–89 in R. Myers and M. Harris, eds., *Property of a Gentleman*, Winchester, 1991, esp. p. 87; 'Cockerell as Museum Director', pp. 201–23 in *The Book Collector*, 56, 2006, esp. pp. 208–14; and *Meetings with Remarkable Manuscripts*, pp. 199–200. The postponement of the first sale for Belle Greene is Ardizzone, *Illuminated Life*, p. 367. The letters "I now hope . . .", 19 February 1919, on budgeting £15,000, and with evolving shortlists are all from the files at Quaritch. The Metz Pontifical is Fitzwilliam Museum MS 298; the Saint-Omer Psalter is BL, Yates Thompson MS 14 (formerly Add. MS 39810, renumbered after the bequest from Yates Thompson's widow in 1941). Purchases for Morgan cited here are M 641, Sacramentary; M 644, Beatus; M 640, Gospels; and PML 21194-95, Aristotle. The Beatus, which they bought, and the Jeanne de Navarre, which they lost, are both subjects of full chapters in my *Meetings*, Chapters 5, pp. 188–231, and 9, pp. 376–425. Belle Greene's letter to Dring, "I should have been . . ." was 17 June 1919 (in the Quaritch file); another similar letter from her, written before the sale, is quoted by Hobson, *Great Libraries*, p. 294: "I am, personally, *quite* opposed to buying the Aristotle at any such ridiculous price as £6000, but I shall put it up to Mr Morgan . . . I should *very* much like a copy of the *book* itself on vellum, but do not particularly care for this 'Most Beautiful Copy In The World'." Madden's account of bidding for the Dioscorides in 1857 is printed in Munby, *Phillipps Studies*, IV, 1956, pp. 78–80 and pl. V. Belle Greene paid Fenwick £10,500 for the Dioscorides (M 652) and an eleventh-century Gospel Book from Cologne in a composite but mostly later treasure binding (M 651). Belle Greene's letter to Berenson, "We are *frightfully* busy . . ." (p. 493) was 12 February 1924 (I Tatti, folder 63.16, fols. 334–5, including the "*Pray* God I don't weaken!!!"). The *New York Times* headlines are cited by Ardizzone, *Illuminated Life*, p. 532, n. 106; Strouse comparing potted plants is on her p. 517. The report by Belle Greene is *The Pierpont Morgan Library: A Review of the Growth, Development and Activities of the Library during the Period between Its Establishment as an Educational Institution in February 1924 and the Close of the Year 1929*, New York, 1930; the manuscript acquisitions are surveyed on pp. 12–29 and listed on pp. 47–70 (the "of such importance" is from p. 16). Her lack of interest in purchasing prints was expressed in a letter to Berenson, 22 April 1927, "I can imagine *nothing* more – *nullifying* (the only word I can think of at the moment that expresses it) than the study and collecting of *Prints – just Prints*" (I Tatti, folder 63.24, fol. 468). In her *Review*, p. 14, she said that manuscripts contained the "fullest, most authentic, and most convenient source for the comparative study of painting and the allied arts during the Middle Ages". It is, in my opinion, a development which Belle Greene would have regretted that no director of the Library since her time has been especially interested in the medieval manuscripts or incunabula (and none since Frederick Adams in 1948–69 has been primarily a bookman at all), and the main focus seems now to be contemporary museology and popular art, for which the Morgan is not even the best collection in Manhattan, whereas the illuminated manuscripts are truly among the very finest in the world. I would reassure her and Sydney Cockerell too that the best-attended public exhibition ever held by the Fitzwilliam Museum was medieval manuscripts, *The Cambridge Illuminations*, in 2005. The Holford catalogue was *The Holford Collection Illustrated with One Hundred and One Plates, Selected from Twelve Illuminated Manuscripts at Dorchester House and One Hundred and Seven Pictures at Westonbirt in Gloucestershire*, Oxford, 1924. Benson (1850–1929) had married Evelyn, daughter of Robert Holford. Sir George Holford had no children and Benson, as executor, was responsible for the division of the estate. The letter from Dring, 3 May 1927, is in the Belle Greene correspondence at Quaritch. Her letter to Berenson, "*Confidentially to you* . . ." (pp. 494 and 496) is I Tatti, folder 63.24, fol. 466, and that to Dring, "It is difficult . . .", is at Quaritch. Recent discussion of the Master B. F. includes my *The Medieval World at Our Fingertips: Manuscript Illuminations from the Collection of Sandra Hindman*, London and Turnhout, 2018, pp. 212–21, and A.-M. Eze in S. Hindman and F. Toniolo, eds., *The Burke Collection of Italian Manuscript Painting*, London, 2021, pp. 354–63. The miniatures are M 725, by the Master B. F., and M 724, from the Eadwine Psalter. The story of the British Museum and the life of Saint Edmund is told by Sir Frederick Kenyon, director at the time, 'A Tribute from the British Museum', pp. 4–5 in D. Miner, ed., *Studies in Art and Literature for Belle da Costa Greene*, Princeton, 1954, p. 5. The six manuscripts bought from the Holford estate are: (1) M 728, ninth-century Gospel Book, illuminated in Reims for the abbey of Saint-Remy (compared by Belle Greene with M 1 in her *Review*, 1930, pp. 16–17); (2) M 729, the Psalter-Hours of Yolande of Soissons; (3) M 730, the Psalter-Hours of Guilluys de Boisleux; (4) M 731, a poem on governance made for Eleanor of Aragon, *c.*1478–9; (5) M 732, the Hours of Cardinal Cristoforo Madruzzo, illuminated by Jean Bourdichon; and (6) M 736, the life of Saint Edmund. Others were sold elsewhere, including the now-called 'Holford Hours', which went to Chester Beatty (now Lisbon, Museu Calouste Gulbenkian, Inv. LA210). Millar's "one of the pleasantest . . ." (p. 497) is Ardizzone, *Illuminated Life*, p. 419; Belle Greene's "*we miss you*" is BL, Add. MS 54323 (Millar papers), fol. 123. The reference to Millar as "our Pet" is in an undated letter to F. S. Ferguson at Quaritch, apparently late March 1932, which I owe to photographs sent to me by Laura Cleaver. In fairness to Morgan, his sounding out of Millar as a possible director may have been in response to Belle Greene's threats to resign in 1929, which Millar would not have known. The Ellesmere Chaucer is San Marino, Henry E. Huntington library, MS El. 26.C.9. The "I could hardly credit . . ." is from Belle Greene's letter to Cockerell, 10 March 1914, cited above from BL Add MS 52717; the letter is a later transcript for Cockerell by a helper not always able to read Belle Greene's handwriting, and puts "keefic" for "kufic" and "American" for "Armenian", but the original meaning is unambiguous. The Italian Bible was probably the Conradin Bible (now Walters Art Museum W. 152, bought in 1905) and the Armenian manuscript probably the Gospels illuminated in Cilicia in 1193 (W. 538, bought some time after 1903). The quotation from James's *The Outcry* is from Book I, Chapter 4. The gradual imposition of European art export laws is a huge and ongoing subject, culminating in Britain with the establishment in 1952 of the Reviewing Committee on the Export of Works of Art, to which manuscripts and other artworks sold to overseas buyers are still submitted today, with options which can prevent their departure. The United States, by contrast, still has no art export laws of its own, even for items of American heritage. Belle Greene's "I hate 'us' . . ." (p. 500) is from the Quaritch files, 18 March 1919. The Luttrell Psalter and the Bedford Hours and Psalter, both known to Madden, were to be sold at Sotheby's in 1929 but were withdrawn to allow the national collection to raise money; Morgan's deal was that if his loan was not repaid, the manuscripts would become his. They are now respectively BL, Add. MSS 42130 and 42131. The bidding on the life of Saint Cuthbert is recounted by Kenyon, 'A Tribute', p. 4; it became Add. MS 39943, later renumbered Yates Thompson MS 26. In describing the buildings in E 36th Street, I took advantage of the blog on the Library's website, 'Visiting the Morgan in 1928' by Jennifer Tonkovich, January 2020.

The visitor in 1934 was Ernest Maun, describing her in a letter to Morris Parrish, cited in Ardizzone, *Illuminated Life*, pp. 442–3 and in a blog 'A Look at Belle da Costa Greene' on the website of the Rare Book Collection at Princeton University Library, August 2010. The allusion to Belle Greene's "whisky tenor" is E. Wolf and J. F. Fleming, *Rosenbach: A Biography*, Cleveland and New York, 1960, p. 241; she also smoked uninhibitedly. Her "Of course I'm a Hussey . . ." (p. 503) is from her letter to Berenson, 22 April 1927, cited above (I Tatti, folder 63.24, fol. 469). Her visit to the galleries of the British Museum is told in a letter to Millar, 29 October 1934, in BL, Add. MS 54323, fol. 121; Seymour de Ricci happened to be there that day, and bored her; her engagement with "the '*peeple*" was found also in the late Janet Backhouse of the British Library, who often spoke of 'Joe Public' as her primary audience. The note about Clara Peck (1896–1983) is from W. Voelkle, 'Le Livre de chasse: Making and provenance of the manuscript', pp. 11–27 in the commentary volume to the facsimile, *Gaston Phoebus: Le Livre de Chasse. Das Buch der Jagd*, Luzern, 2006, pp. 24–5; the manuscript is now M 1044. Dorothy Miner's remark on Belle Greene and falsity is from her foreword to *Studies in Art and Literature*, as above, pp. xi–xii; she also says that Belle Greene "refused to cooperate with efforts to record her life, scorning such personal history as unimportant and of no concern to anyone", p. xi, understandable with the hindsight we now have. D. Rosen, 'The Restoration of a Botticellesque Tondo in the Morgan Library', pp. 129–31 in *Studies in Art and Literature*, says of Belle Greene too, "Pretence or evasion of any kind she found intolerable" (p. 129). Belle Greene's naming of the Spanish Forger, not Spanish at all, is in W. Voelkle with R. S. Wieck, *The Spanish Forger*, New York, 1978, p. 9. The visit of H. P. Kraus is in his *A Rare Book Saga*, New York and London, 1979, pp. 87–8; the manuscript itself, now in the collection of the late Sir Paul Getty, was exhibited at the Morgan Library in 1999: H. G. Fletcher, ed., *The Wormsley Library*, London and New York, 1999, pp. 36–9, no. 13. The purchase from Holkham is recounted by Kenyon, pp. 4–5, and by William Voelkle in accompanying commentaries to two facsimiles, *Das Berthold Sakramentar*, Graz, 1995 (*Codices Selecti*, C), pp. 91–2, and *Das Hainricus-Missale*, Graz, 2005 (*Codices Selecti*, CX), pp. 41–2. Madden in his catalogue at Holkham had described them as "one of the principal ornaments of the library" (vol. I, p, 35); we now know, which Madden did not, that they were all from the Benedictine abbey of Weingarten in Baden-Württemberg. Much later, Madden speculated in his journal that they could by then even be worth as much as a thousand pounds (11 July 1841, Bodleian, MS Eng. hist. c.154, p. 203). The four manuscripts are now (1)–(2) M 708–9, two Gospel Books made *c.*1065 probably for Judith of Flanders, wife of Tostwig Godwinson, Earl of Northumbria; (3) M 710, the Berthold Sacramentary, *c.* 1215–17; and (4) M 711, the Gradual and Sacramentary of Hainricus, sacristan of Weingarten. Belle Greene's secret strategy in not wanting to lose the four manuscripts, explained in a letter to Berenson, 20 January 1927 ("*This point must be shut in your heart* and no-one else know it"), was that, once those were acquired, she would then be allowed to buy whatever else she wanted from Holkham, fortunately for Britain a fantasy unfulfilled (I Tatti, folder 63.24, fols. 445–6).

List of Illustrations

Every effort has been made to contact all rights holders. The publishers will be pleased to amend in future editions any errors or omissions brought to their attention.

p. 378. Carl Spitzweg, *Der Bücherworm*. Schweinfurt, Museum Georg Schäfer *(Heritage Image Partnership / Alamy*
p. 381. Julius Friedländer, *Mommsen at the Ponte della Maddalena, Castel di Sangro*, 1846
p. 385. *(Above)* John Henry Haynes, photograph of the north pronoas wall of the Temple of Rome and Augustus, Ankara. Philadelphia, Penn Museum, image no. 195181 *(Courtesy of the Penn Museum)*; *(bottom left)* Theodor Mommsen, *Res Gestae Divi Augusti, ex Monumentis Ancyrano et Apolloniensi iterum*, 1st edition, Berlin, 1865, page XIII; *(bottom right)* Theodor Mommsen, *Res Gestae Divi Augusti, ex Monumentis Ancyrano et Apolloniensi iterum*, 2nd edition, Berlin, 1883, plate I *(Courtesy of the University of St Andrews Libraries and Museums, classmark rfPA6220.A85R4)*
p. 388. Verona, Biblioteca Capitolare, Cod. XL (38), folio 256r *(Courtesy Fondazione Biblioteca Capitolare di Verona)*
p. 392. *Alla ricossa! Spano, De Castro, canonici*, cartoon from an Italian journal, 1877
p. 397. Cambridge, Trinity College, Add. MS a.73-50 *(Reproduced by permission of the Master and Fellows of Trinity College, Cambridge)*
p. 403. Paris, Bibliothèque nationale de France, Département des manuscrits, ms lat. 9643, folio 82r *(© BnF)*
p. 406. Private collection
p. 408. Mommsen in his study *(ullstein bild / Getty Images)*
p. 410. Lafayette, photograph of Sir Sydney Cockerell *(© National Portrait Gallery, London)*
p. 413. New Haven, Rare Book Collection, Lillian Goldman Law Library, Yale Law School, MssJ C817 no.1 flat
p. 414. William Collingwood, John Ruskin in his Study at Brantwood. Coniston, Ruskin Museum *(Bridgeman Images)*
p. 416. Henry Halliday Sparling, photograph of William Morris *(© National Portrait Gallery, London)*
p. 420. New York, Morgan Library and Museum, M 81, folios 36v-37r *(© 2022. Photo The Morgan Library & Museum / Art Resource, NY / Scala, Florence)*
p. 423. Private collection
p. 424. Cambridge, Fitzwilliam Museum, MS 300, folio Vv *(Fitzwilliam Museum / Bridgeman Images)*
p. 426. Los Angeles, J. Paul Getty Museum, MS Ludwig IX 3 (83.ML.99), folio 37v
p. 433. London, British Library, Add. MS 49622, folio 8r *(© British Library Board. All Rights Reserved / Bridgeman Images)*
p. 436. Los Angeles, J. Paul Getty Museum, MS Ludwig I 8, v1 (83.MA.57.1), folio 10v
p. 439. *Illustrated catalogue of Illuminated Manuscripts*, Burlington Fine Arts Club, 1908, Volume 2, Plate 2 *(Harvard University, Houghton Library)*
p. 443. London, British Library, Add. MS 81084, folio 111r *(© British Library Board. All Rights Reserved / Bridgeman Images)*
p. 445. Cologny (Geneva), Fondation Martin Bodmer, Codex Bodmer 47, folio 1r
p. 446. *(Left)* private collection; *(right)* Cambridge, Fitzwilliam Museum, MS 84-1972, folio 83r *(© Fitzwilliam Museum / Bridgeman Images)*
p. 448. Rome, Biblioteca nazionale centrale Vittorio Emanuele II, Cod. Vitt.Em.1430, folio 2r
p. 451. Anon., photograph of Dame Laurentia McLachlan *(TopFoto)*
p. 454. Chicago, Art Institute, Ada Turnbull Hertle Fund, 1957.162
p. 455. Dorothy Hawksley, portrait of Sir Sydney Cockerell *(© National Portrait Gallery, London)*
p. 457. Clarence White, photograph of Belle da Costa Greene *(Biblioteca Berenson, I Tatti-The Harvard University Center for Italian Renaissance Studies, courtesy of the President and Fellows of Harvard College)*

p. 458. J. Pierpont Morgan *(Granger / Alamy)*
p. 459. New York, Morgan Library and Museum, M.1, upper cover *(© 2022. Photo The Morgan Library & Museum / Art Resource, NY / Scala, Florence)*
p. 461. New York, Morgan Library and Museum, M 69, folio 30v *(© 2022. The Morgan Library & Museum / Art Resource, NY / Scala, Florence. Photographer: Joseph Zehavi)*
p. 463. Hughson Frederick Hawley, *Perspective of the Proposed Library of J. Pierpont Morgan by the architects McKim, Mead & White*, 1902. New York, Morgan Library and Museum. Morgan Family Collection, 1958.24 *(© 2022. Photo The Morgan Library & Museum / Art Resource, NY / Scala, Florence)*
p. 465. Richard Theodore Greener *(Harvard University Archives, call no. HUP Greener, R.T. (2a))*
p. 472. New York, Morgan Library and Museum, M 333, folio 51r *(© 2022. Photo The Morgan Library & Museum / Art Resource, NY / Scala, Florence)*
p. 475. New York, Morgan Library and Museum, M 399, vol. I, folio 1v, detail *(Digital image courtesy of Faksimile Verlag Luzern © 2022. Photo The Morgan Library & Museum / Art Resource, NY / Scala, Florence)*
p. 477. Bernard Berenson in the gardens of I Tatti (*Biblioteca Berenson, I Tatti-The Harvard University Center for Italian Renaissance Studies, courtesy of the President and Fellows of Harvard College)*
pp. 478–9. New York, Morgan Library and Museum, M 429, folios 146v-147r. Purchased by J. Pierpont Morgan in 1910 *(© 2022. Photo The Morgan Library & Museum / Art Resource, NY / Scala, Florence)*
p. 482. Laura Coombs Hills, *Belle da Costa Greene in Egyptian Costume*. New York, Morgan Library and Museum, Bequest of Belle da Costa Greene, 1950, AZ 164 *(© 2022. Photo The Morgan Library & Museum / Art Resource, NY / Scala, Florence)*
p. 485. New York, Morgan Library and Museum, M 619, recto *(© 2022. Photo The Morgan Library & Museum / Art Resource, NY / Scala, Florence)*
p. 488. New York, Morgan Library and Museum, M 492, folios 83v-84r *(© 2022. Photo The Morgan Library & Museum / Art Resource, NY / Scala, Florence)*
pp. 490–91. New York, Morgan Library and Museum, M 638, folios 23v-24r *(© 2022. Photo The Morgan Library & Museum / Art Resource, NY / Scala, Florence)*
p. 495. New York, Morgan Library and Museum, PML 21194-95, Vol II, frontispiece *(© 2022. Photo The Morgan Library & Museum / Art Resource, NY / Scala, Florence)*
p. 496. New York, Morgan Library and Museum, M 725 *(© 2022. Photo The Morgan Library & Museum / Art Resource, NY / Scala, Florence)*
p. 498. New York, Morgan Library and Museum, M 736, folio 9v *(© 2022. Photo The Morgan Library & Museum / Art Resource, NY / Scala, Florence)*
p. 502. Peter A. Juley & Son, photograph of Belle da Costa Greene *(Biblioteca Berenson, I Tatti-The Harvard University Center for Italian Renaissance Studies, courtesy of the President and Fellows of Harvard College)*
p. 506. New York, Morgan Library and Museum, M 710, folio 8v *(© 2022. Photo The Morgan Library & Museum / Art Resource, NY/Scala, Florence)*

Index of Manuscripts

Index of People